POLITICS AND VISION

Continuity and Innovation in Western Political Thought

POLITICS AND VISION

ఆక్ Continuity and Innovation in Western Political Thought ౭ఌ

SHELDON S. WOLIN

University of California, Berkeley

Little, Brown and Company

Boston

This book is dedicated to Emily and Rose

Fourth Printing

Published simultaneously in Canada
by Little, Brown & Company (Canada) Limited

PRINTED IN THE UNITED STATES OF AMERICA

✑ PREFACE ☙

In this book I have attempted to describe and to analyze some of the continuing and changing concerns of political philosophy. In many intellectual circles today there exists a marked hostility towards, and even contempt for, political philosophy in its traditional form. My hope is that this volume, if it does not give pause to those who are eager to jettison what remains of the tradition of political philosophy, may at least succeed in making clear what it is we shall have discarded.

Although the approach adopted in this work is historical, it has not been my intention to offer a comprehensive and detailed history of political thought. On the whole, the selection of an historical approach has been dictated by a belief that it represents the best method for understanding the preoccupations of political philosophy and its character as an intellectual enterprise. It is also my conviction that an historical perspective is more effective than any other in exposing the nature of our present predicaments; if it is not the source of political wisdom, it is at least the precondition. The reader will quickly discover that a great many topics and writers usually included in the standard histories have been omitted and that in other matters I have departed considerably from prevailing interpretations. Where significant omissions occur, as is the case with the great part of mediaeval political thought, they should not be construed as evidence of an adverse judgment on my part, but only as the inevitable accompaniment to a work that is primarily interpretive.

My intellectual debts are many, and it is a pleasure to acknowledge them. To Professors John D. Lewis and Frederick B. Artz of Oberlin College more is owed than can ever be repaid. Beginning in my undergraduate days and continuing to the present, they have combined the roles of teacher, scholar, and friend and provided the encouragement for undertaking a work of this kind. I should also like to extend my appreciation to Professors Thomas Jenkin of the University of California at Los Angeles and Louis Hartz of Harvard University for reading the entire manuscript and offering suggestions for its improvement; to my colleague, Professor Norman Jacobson, with whom I have discussed some of the problems of the book and who has been an unfailing source of intellectual stimulation; to Mr. Robert J. Pranger who not only spared me the tedious task of tracking down numerous references but also criticized the early formulation of some of the ideas in the last chapter; and, above all, to another of my colleagues, Professor John Schaar, whose discriminating taste and intelligence have contributed greatly to whatever merit this work way have.

I am also grateful to several typists for their skill, cooperation, and patience: Jean Gilpin, Sylvia Diegnau, Sue K. Young, and, especially, Francine Barban. I should like to express my appreciation to the Editor of the *American Political Science Review* for permission to reproduce in somewhat altered form the two articles which are the basis of Chapters V and VI. The major part of this study was made possible by the Rockefeller Foundation whose generous financial support enabled me to gain some respite from the normal teaching duties.

S. S. W.

Berkeley, 1960

✑ CONTENTS ☙

POLITICS AND VISION

Continuity and Innovation in Western Political Thought

ଏଣ୍ଡ ONE ଟ୍ଟ

Political Philosophy
and Philosophy

*. . . To express various meanings on complex things with a scanty vo-
cabulary of fastened senses.*

WALTER BAGEHOT

Political philosophy as a form of inquiry. This is a book about a special
tradition of discourse — political philosophy. In it I shall attempt to discuss the general character of that tradition, the varying concerns of those who
have helped to build it, and the vicissitudes that have marked the main lines
of its development. At the same time, I shall also try to say something about
the enterprise of political philosophy itself. This statement of intentions
naturally induces the expectation that the discussion will begin with a definition of political philosophy. To attempt to satisfy this expectation, however,
would be fruitless, not merely because a few sentences cannot accomplish
what an entire book intends, but also because political philosophy is not an
essence with an eternal nature. It is, instead, a complex activity which is

best understood by analyzing the many ways that the acknowledged masters have practiced it. No single philosopher and no one historical age can be said to have defined it conclusively, any more than any one painter or school of painting has practiced all that we mean by painting.

If there is more to political philosophy than any great philosopher has expressed, there is some justification for believing that political philosophy constitutes an activity whose characteristics are most clearly revealed over time. Stated somewhat differently, political philosophy is to be understood in the same way that we go about understanding a varied and complex tradition.

Although it may not be possible to reduce political philosophy to a brief definition, it is possible to elucidate the characteristics that distinguish it from, as well as connect it with, other forms of inquiry. I shall discuss these considerations under the following headings: political philosophy's relations with philosophy, the charactertistics of political philosophy as an activity, its subject-matter and language, the problem of perspectives or angle of vision, and the manner in which a tradition operates.

Ever since Plato first perceived that the inquiry into the nature of the good life of the individual was necessarily associated with a converging (and not parallel) inquiry into the nature of the good community, a close and continuing association has persisted between political philosophy and philosophy in general. Not only have most of the eminent philosophers contributed generously to the main stock of our political ideas, but they have given the political theorist many of his methods of analysis and criteria of judgment. Historically, the main difference between philosophy and political philosophy has been a matter of specialization rather than one of method or temper. By virtue of this alliance, political theorists accepted as their own the basic quest of the philosopher for systematic knowledge.

There is a still another fundamental sense in which political theory is linked to philosophy. Philosophy can be distinguished from other methods of eliciting truths, such as the mystic vision, the secret rite, truths of conscience or of private feelings. Philosophy claims to deal with truths publicly arrived at and publicly demonstrable.[1] At the same time, one of the essential qualities of what is political, and one that has powerfully shaped the view of political theorists about their subject-matter, is its relationship to what is "public." Cicero had this in mind when he called the commonwealth a *res publica,* a "public thing" or the "property of a people." Of all the authoritative institutions in society, the political arrangement has been singled out as uniquely concerned with what is "common" to the whole community. Certain functions, such as national defense, internal order, the dispensing of justice, and economic regulation, have been declared the primary responsibility of political institutions, largely on the grounds that the interests and ends served by these functions were beneficial to all of the members of the community. The only institution that ever rivaled the authority of the political order was the mediaeval Church; yet this was made possible only because the Church, in assuming the characteristics of a political regime, had become something other than a religious body. The intimate connection existing between political institutions and public concerns has been taken over in the practices of philosophers; political philosophy has been taken to mean reflection on matters that concern the community as a whole.

It is fitting, therefore, that the inquiry into public matters should be conducted according to the canons of a public type of knowledge. To take the other alternative, to ally political knowledge with private modes of cognition, would be incongruous and self-defeating. The dramatic symbol of the right alliance was the demand of the Roman plebs that the status of the Twelve Tables of the law be transformed from a priestly mystery cognizable only by the few to a public form of knowledge accessible to all.

II **Form and substance.** Turning next to the subject-matter of political philosophy, even the most cursory examination of the masterpieces of political literature discloses the continual reappearance of certain problem-topics. Many examples could be listed, but here we need mention only a few, such as the power relationships between ruler and ruled, the nature of authority, the problems posed by social conflict, the status of certain goals or purposes as objectives of political action, and the character of political knowledge. No political philosopher has been interested in all of these problems to the same degree, yet there has been a sufficiently widespread consensus about the identity of the problems to warrant the belief that a continuity of preoccupations has existed. Nor does the fact that philosophers have often violently disagreed about solutions cast doubt upon the existence of a common subject-matter. What is important is the continuity of preoccupations, not the unanimity of response.

Agreement about subject-matter presupposes in turn that those who are interested in extending knowledge of a particular field share in a common understanding about what is relevant to their subject and what ought to be excluded. In reference to political philosophy, this means that the philosopher should be clear about what is political and what is not. Aristotle, for example, argued in the opening pages of the *Politics* that the role of the statesman (*politikos*) ought not to be confused with that of the slave-owner or head of a household; the first was properly political, the latter were not. The point that Aristotle was making is still of vital importance, and the difficulties of preserving a clear notion of what is political forms the basic theme of this book. Aristotle was alluding to the troubles that the political philosopher experiences in trying to isolate a subject-matter which, in reality, cannot be isolated. There are two main reasons for the difficulty. In the first place, a political institution, for example, is exposed to impinging influences of a non-political kind so that it becomes a perplexing problem of explanation as to where the political begins and the non-political leaves off. Secondly, there is the widespread tendency to utilize the same words and notions in describing non-political phenomena that we do in talking about political matters. In contrast to the restricted technical usages of mathematics and the natural sciences, phrases like "the authority of the father," the "authority of the church," or "the authority of Parliament" are evidence of the parallel usages prevailing in social and political discussions.

This poses one of the basic problems confronting the political philosopher when he tries to assert the distinctiveness of his subject-matter: what is political? what is it that distinguishes, say, political authority from other forms of authority, or membership in a political society from membership in other types of associations? In attempting an answer to these questions, centuries of philosophers have contributed to a conception of political philosophy as a continuing form of discourse concerning what is political and to a picture of the political philosopher as one who philosophizes about the political. How have they gone about doing this? How have they come to single out certain human actions and interactions, institutions and values, and to designate them "political"? What is the distinctive common feature of certain types of situations or activities, such as voting and legislating, that allows us to call them political? Or what conditions must a given action or situation satisfy in order to be called political?

In one sense, the process of defining the area of what is political has not been markedly different from that which has taken place in other fields of inquiry. No one would seriously contend, for example, that the fields of physics or chemistry have always existed in a self-evident, determinate form waiting only to be discovered by Galileo or Lavoisier. If we grant that a field of inquiry is, to an important degree, a product of definition, the political field can be viewed as an area whose boundaries have been marked out by centuries of political discussion. Just as other fields have changed their outlines, so the boundaries of what is political have been shifting ones, sometimes including more, sometimes less of human life and thought. The present age of totalitarianism produces the lament that "this is a political age. War, fascism, concentration camps, rubber truncheons, atomic bombs, etc., are what we think about." In other and more serene times the political is less ubiquitous. Aquinas could write that "man is not formed for political fellowship in his entirety, or in all that he has . . ." [2] What I should like to insist upon, however, is that the field of politics is and has been, in a significant and radical sense, a created one. The designation of certain activities and arrangements as political, the characteristic way that we think about them, and the concepts we employ to communicate our observations and reactions — none of these are written into the nature of things but are the legacy accruing from the historical activity of political philosophers.

I do not mean to suggest by these remarks that the political philosopher has been at liberty to call "political" whatever he chose, or that, like the poet of Lord Kames, he has been busy "fabricating images without any foundation in reality." Nor do I mean to imply that the phenomena we designate political are, in a literal sense, "created" by the theorist. It is readily admitted that established practices and institutional arrangements have furnished political writers with their basic data, and I shall discuss this point shortly. It is true, too, that many of the subjects treated by a theorist owe their inclusion to the simple fact that in existing linguistic conventions such subjects are referred to as political. It is also true, on the other hand, that the ideas and categories that we use in political analysis are not of the same order as institutional "facts," nor are they "contained," so to speak, in the facts. They represent, instead, an added element, something created by the political theorist. Concepts like "power," "authority," "consent," and so forth are not real "things," although they are intended to point to some significant aspect about political things. Their function is to render political facts significant, either for purposes of analysis, criticism, or justification, or a combination of all three. When political concepts are put into the form of an assertion, such as, "It is not the rights and privileges which he enjoys which makes a man a citizen, but the mutual obligation between subject and sovereign," the validity of the statement is not to be settled by referring to the facts of political life. This would be a circular procedure, since the form of the statement would inevitably govern the interpretation of the facts. Stated somewhat differently, political theory is not so much interested in political practices, or how they operate, but rather in their meaning. Thus, in the statement just quoted from Bodin, the fact that by law or practice the member of society owed certain obligations to his sovereign, and vice versa, was not as important as that these duties could be understood in a way suggestive of something important about membership and, in the later phases of Bodin's argument, about sovereign authority and its conditions. In other words, the concept of membership permitted Bodin to draw out the implications and interconnections between certain practices or institutions that were not self-evident on the basis of the facts themselves. When such concepts become more or less stable in their meaning, they serve as pointers that "cue" us to look for certain things or to keep certain considerations in mind when we try to understand a political situation or make a judgment about it. In this way, the concepts and categories that make up our political understanding help us to draw connections between political phenomena; they impart some order to what might otherwise appear to be a hopeless chaos of activities; they mediate between us and the political world we seek to render intelligible; they create an area of determinate awareness and thus help to separate the relevant phenomena from the irrelevant.

III **Political thought and political institutions.** The philosopher's attempt to give meaning to political phenomena is both assisted and delimited by the fact that societies possess some measure of order, some degree of arrangement which exists whether philosophers philosophize or not. In other words, the boundaries and substance of the subject-matter of political philosophy are determined to a large extent by the practices of existing societies. By practices is meant the institutionalized processes and settled procedures regularly used for handling public matters. What is important for political theory is that these institutionalized practices play a fundamental role in ordering and directing human behavior and in determining the character of events. The organizing role of institutions and customary practices creates a "nature" or field of phenomena that is roughtly analogous to the nature confronted by the natural scientist. Perhaps I can clarify the meaning of "political nature" by describing something of the function of institutions.

The system of political institutions in a given society represents an arrangement of power and authority. At some point within the system, certain institutions are recognized as having the authority to make decisions applicable to the whole community. The exercise of this function naturally attracts the attention of groups and individuals who feel that their interests and purposes will be affected by the decisions taken. When this awareness takes the form of action directed towards political institutions, the activities become "political" and a part of political nature. The initiative may originate with the institutions themselves, or rather with the men who operate them. A public decision, such as one controlling the manufacturing of woolens or one prohibiting the propagation of certain doctrines, has the effect of connecting these activities to the political order and making them, at least in part, political phenomena. Although one could multiply the ways in which human activities become "political," the main point lies in the "relating" function performed by political institutions. Through the decisions taken and enforced by public officials, scattered activities are brought together, endowed with a new coherence, and their future course shaped according to "public" considerations. In this way political institutions give additional dimensions to political nature. They serve to define, so to speak, "political space" or the locus wherein the tensional forces of society are related, as in a courtroom, a legislature, an administrative hearing, or the convention of a political party. They serve also to define "political time" or the temporal period within which decision, resolution, or compromise occur. Thus political arrangements provide a setting wherein the activities of individuals and groups are connected spatially and temporally. Consider, for example, the workings of a national system of social security. A tax official collects revenue from a corporation's earnings of the preceding year; the revenue, in turn, might be used to establish a social security or pension system that would benefit workers otherwise unconnected with the corporation. But the benefits in question may not actually be received by the worker until a quarter of a century later. Here, in the form of a revenue agent, is a political institution whose operation integrates a series of otherwise unconnected activities and imparts to them a significance extended over time.[3]

A contemporary philosopher has said that, by means of the concepts and symbols used in our thinking, we try to make a "temporal order of words" stand for "a relational order of things."[4] If we apply this to political matters, we can say that political institutions provide the internal relationships between the "things" or phenomena of political nature and that political philosophy seeks to make meaningful assertions about these "things." In other words, institutions establish a previous coherence among political phenomena; hence, when the political philosopher reflects upon society, he is not confronted by a whirl of disconnected events or activities hurtling through a Democritean void but by phenomena already endowed with coherence and interrelationships.

IV Political philosophy and the political. At the same time, however, most of the great statements of political philosophy have been put forward in times of crisis; that is, when political phenomena are less effectively integrated by institutional forms. Institutional breakdown releases phenomena, so to speak, causing political behavior and events to take on something of a random quality, and destroying the customary meanings that had been part of the old political world. From the time that Greek thought first became fascinated by the instabilities that afflicted political life, Western political philosophers have been troubled by the wasteland that comes when the web of political relationships has dissolved and the ties of loyalty have snapped. Evidence of this preoccupation is to be found in the endless discussions of Greek and Roman writers concerning the rhythmic cycles which governmental forms were destined to follow; in the fine distinctions that Machiavelli drew between the political contingencies that man could master and those that left him helpless; in the seventeenth-century notion of a "state of nature" as a condition lacking the settled relationships and institutional forms characteristic of a functioning political system; and in the mighty effort of Hobbes to found a political science that would enable men, once and for all, to create an abiding commonwealth that could weather the vicissitudes of politics. Although the task of political philosophy is greatly complicated in a period of disintegration, the theories of Plato, Machiavelli, and Hobbes, for example, are evidence of a "challenge and response" relationship between the disorder of the actual world and the role of the political philosopher as the encompasser of disorder. The range of possibilities appears infinite, for now the political philosopher is not confined to criticism and interpretation; he must reconstruct a shattered world of meanings and their accompanying institutional expressions; he must, in short, fashion a political cosmos out of political chaos.

Although conditions of extreme political disorganization lend an added urgency to the quest for order, the political theorist writing for less heroic times has also ranked order as a fundamental problem of his subject-matter. No political theorist has ever advocated a disordered society, and no political theorist has ever proposed permanent revolution as a way of life. In its most elemental meaning, order has signified a condition of peace and security that makes civilized life possible. Saint Augustine's overriding concern for man's transcendent destiny did not blind him to the fact that the preparations for salvation presupposed an earthly setting wherein the basic requirements of peace and security were being met by the political order, and it was this recognition that drew from him the admission that even a pagan polity was of some value. The preoccupation with order has left its mark on the vocabulary of the political theorist. Words like "peace," "stability," "harmony," and "balance" are encountered in the writings of every major theorist. Similarly, every political inquiry is, in some degree, directed at the factors conducive to, or militating against, the maintenance of order. The political philosopher has asked: what is the function of power and authority in sustaining the basis of social life? what does the preservation of order demand of the members in the way of a code of civility? what kind of knowledge is needed by both ruler and ruled alike if peace and stability are to be maintained? what are the sources of disorder, and how can they be controlled?

At the same time, and with important exceptions, most political writers have accepted in some form the Aristotelian dictum that men living a life of association desire not only life but the attainment of the good life; that is, that men have aspirations beyond the satisfaction of certain elemental, almost biologic needs, such as domestic peace, defense against external enemies, and the protection of life and possessions. Order, as Augustine defined it, contained a hierarchy of goods, rising from the protection of life to the promotion of the highest type of life. Throughout the history of political philosophy, there have been varying notions about what was to be included under order, and these have ranged from the Greek idea of individual self-fulfillment, through the Christian conception of the political order as a kind of *praeparatio evangelica,* to the modern liberal view that the political order has little to do with either psyches or souls. Irrespectively of the particular emphasis, the preoccupation with order has drawn the political theorist into considering the kinds of goals and purposes proper to a political society. This brings us to the second broad aspect of the subject-matter: what kinds of things are proper to a *political* society and why?

In our earlier discussion of political philosophy and its relation to philosophy, we touched very briefly on the notion that political philosophy dealt with *public* matters. Here I should like to point out that the words "public," "common," and "general" have a long tradition of usage which has made them synonyms for what is political. For this reason they serve as important clues to the subject-matter of political philosophy. From its very beginnings in Greece, the Western political tradition has looked upon the political order as a common order created to deal with those concerns in which all of the members of society have some interest. The concept of an order that was at once political and common was stated most eloquently in Plato's dialogue

Protagoras. There it was related that the gods gave men the arts and talents necessary for their physical survival, yet when men formed cities, conflict and violence continually erupted and threatened to return mankind to a brutal and savage condition. Protagoras then described how the gods, fearful that men would destroy each other, decided to provide justice and virtue:

> Zeus feared that the entire race would be exterminated, and so he sent Hermes to them, bearing reverence and justice to be the ordering principles of cities and the bonds of friendship and conciliation. Hermes asked Zeus how he should impart justice and reverence among men: — Should he distribute them as the arts are distributed; that is to say, to a favored few only [or] . . . to all? "To all," said Zeus; "I should like them all to have a share; for cities cannot exist, if a few share only in the virtues, as in the arts . . ."[5]

The "commonness" of the political order has been reflected both in the range of topics selected by political theorists as proper to their subject and in the way that these topics have been treated in political theory. It is seen in the basic belief of theorists that political rule is concerned with those general interests shared by all the members of the community; that political authority is distinguished from other forms of authority in that it speaks in the name of a society considered in its common quality; that membership in a political society is a token of a life of common involvements; and that the order that political authority presides over is one that should extend throughout the length and breadth of society as a whole. The broad problem that is posed by these and similar topics comes from the fact that the objects and activities that they treat are not isolated. The member of society may share some interests with his fellows, but there are other interests that may be peculiar to him or to some group to which he belongs; similarly, political authority is not only one of several authorities in society, but finds itself competing with them on certain matters.

That the political inheres in a situation of intersecting considerations suggests that the task of defining what is political is a continual one. This becomes more evident if we now turn to consider another aspect of the subject-matter; namely, political activity or politics. For the purposes of this study I shall take "politics" to include the following: (a) a form of activity centering around the quest for competitive advantage between groups, individuals, or societies; (b) a form of activity conditioned by the fact that it occurs within a situation of change and relative scarcity; (c) a form of activity in which the pursuit of advantage produces consequences of such a magnitude that they affect in a significant way the whole society or a substantial portion of it. Throughout most of the last twenty-five hundred years, Western communities have been compelled to undergo drastic readjustments to changes induced both from within and without. Politics as one reflection of this phenomenon has come to be an activity expressive of society's need for constant readjustment. The effects of change are not only to disturb the relative positions of social groups but also to modify the objectives for which individuals and groups are contending. Thus the territorial expansion of a society may open new sources of wealth and power which will disturb the competitive positions of various domestic groups; changes in the modes of economic production may result in the redistribution of wealth and influence in such a way as to provoke protest and agitation on the part of those whose status has been adversely affected by the new order; vast increases in population and the injection of new racial elements, as took place at Rome, may bring demands for the extension of political privileges and by that demand offer an inviting element for political manipulation; or a religious prophet may come proclaiming a new faith and calling for the extirpation of the old rites and beliefs which time and habit had woven into the existing fabric of expectations. Looked at in one way, political activities are a response to fundamental changes taking place in society. From another point of view, these activities provoke conflict because they represent intersecting lines of action whereby individuals and groups seek to stabilize a situation in a way congenial to their aspirations and needs. Thus politics is both a source of conflict and a mode of activity that seeks to resolve conflicts and promote readjustment.

We can summarize this discussion by saying that the subject-matter of political philosophy has consisted in large measure of the attempt to render politics compatible with the requirements of order. The history of political philosophy has been a dialogue on this theme; sometimes the vision of the philosopher has been of an order purged of politics, and he has produced a political philosophy from which politics, and a good deal of what has been meant by political, have been expunged; other times, he has permitted such a wide scope to politics that the case for order appears to have been neglected.

V   **The vocabulary of political philosophy.** One important characteristic of a body of knowledge is that it is conveyed through a rather specialized language, by which we mean that words are used in certain special senses and that certain concepts and categories are treated as fundamental to an understanding of the subject. This aspect of a body of knowledge is its language or vocabulary. To a large extent, any specialized language represents an artificial creation because it is self-consciously constructed to express meanings and definitions as precisely as possible. For example, mathematicians have developed a highly complex system of signs and symbols, as well as a recognized set of conventions governing their manipulation; physicists, too, employ a number of special definitions to facilitate explanation and prediction. The language of the political theorist has its own peculiarities. Some of these have been pointed out by critics who have complained of the vagueness of traditional political concepts as contrasted with the precision characteristic of scientific discourse, or they have drawn equally unfavorable parallels between the low predictive quality of political theories and the great success of scientific theories in this respect.

Without wishing to add one more contribution to the dreary controversy over whether political science is, or can be, a true science, some misconceptions may be avoided by stating briefly what political theorists have tried to express through their specialized vocabulary. We might begin by quoting a few characteristic statements selected from some political philosophers:

Security for man is impossible unless it be conjoined with power. (Machiavelli)

There can be no true Allegiance and there must remain perpetual seeds of Resistance against a power that is built upon such an unnatural Foundation, as that of fear and terrour. (Halifax)

As soon as man enters into a state of society he loses the sense of his weakness; equality ceases, and then commences the state of war. (Montesquieu)

Admittedly the language and concepts contained in the above statements are so vague as to defy the rigorous testing prescribed by scientific experiments. In the strict sense, concepts like "the state of nature" or "civil society" are not even subject to observation. Yet it would be wrong to conclude that these and other concepts of political theory are deliberately employed to avoid describing the world of political experience. The sentence quoted from Machiavelli alludes to the fact that life and possessions tend to become insecure when the governors of society lack the power to enforce law and order. "Security," on the other hand, is a kind of shorthand expression for the fact that most men prefer a condition of assured expectations for their lives and property. Taken as a whole, the sentence from Machiavelli states a generalization consisting of two key concepts, power and security, both of which "contain," so to speak, a common sense understanding of their practical implications. Thus security implies certain activities; namely, that the members of the society can use and enjoy their possessions with the full knowledge that these will not be taken away forcibly. Similarly, the exercise of effective power will be accompanied by certain familiar actions, such as declaring laws, punishments, and so forth. What is not so apparent to common sense, however, is the connection between power and security, and it is this the political theorist seeks to establish. The use of concepts and a special language enable him to bring together a variety of common experiences and practices, such as those connected with the enjoyment of security and the exercise of power, and to show their interconnections.

Although these generalizations may state important things, they do not permit exact predictions in the way that a law of physics will. The concepts are far too general for this, and the evidence would be too flimsy to support any of the assertions quoted earlier. This is not to say that it is impossible to formulate rigorous propositions concerning politics which could be subjected to empirical testing. It is only suggested that these are not the sort of statements that have traditionally occupied the attention of political theorists. Therefore, instead of assigning low marks to the theorists for a badly executed enterprise which they never entertained, it would be more useful to inquire whether the political theorist was attempting something similar to prediction but less rigorous. Instead of predictions, I would suggest first that theorists have been intent on posting warnings. Machiavelli cautions that in the absence of an effective ruling authority there will be insecurity; Halifax, that an authority that places excessive reliance on fear will eventually provoke resistance. Although each of these admonitions bears some similarity to a prediction, it differs in two important respects. In the first place, a warning implies an unpleasant or undesirable consequence, while a scientific prediction is neutral. Secondly, a warning is usually made by a person who feels some involvement with the party or person being warned; a warning, in short, tokens a commitment that is lacking in predictions. In keeping with this function of posting warnings, the language of political theory contains many concepts designed to express warning signals: disorder, revolution, conflict, and instability are some of them.

Political theory, however, has involved more than the prognostication of disaster. It deals also in possibilities; it tries to state the necessary or sufficient conditions for attaining ends which, for one reason or another, are deemed good or desirable. Thus Machiavelli's statement contained both a warning and a possibility: power was the condition of achieving security, but ineffective power would open the way for insecurity.

One obvious objection to the line of argument above is that it places the political theorist in a position of being able to advance propositions and to employ concepts that cannot be adjudged true or false by a rigorous empirical standard. This objection is readily admitted insofar as it pertains to a large number of the statements and concepts contained in most political theories. It is not, however, a conclusive objection, because it assumes that an empirical test affords the only method for determining whether or not a statement is meaningful. Rather than dwell on the scientific shortcomings of political theories, it might be more fruitful to consider political theory as belonging to a different form of discourse. Following this suggestion we can adopt for our purposes a proposal advanced by Carnap.[6] He has suggested the term "explication" to cover certain expressions used both in everyday speech and scientific discussion. Explication employs meanings that are less precise than those ideally suited for rigorous discussion, yet they are handy and, when redefined and rendered more precise, can perform extremely useful service in a theory. Examples of such words would be "law," "cause," and "truth." Inasmuch as these words are advanced as proposals, they cannot be qualified as true or false. The language of political theory abounds with concepts that are used to explicate certain problems. Frequently they are words that are similar to those in ordinary usage, but they have been redefined and touched up to make them more serviceable. The word that the theorist uses may be guided by common usage, but it is not necessarily restricted by the common meaning. For example, Aristotle's definition of a good citizen as one who had both the knowledge and the capacity for ruling and being ruled contained much that was familiar to Athenians. At the same time, the issues that Aristotle was seeking to clarify required that he refashion or reconstruct the accepted meanings. This same procedure has been followed in the formation of other key concepts in the language of political theory; concepts like "authority," "obligation," and "justice" retain some contact with common meanings and experience, yet they have been refashioned to meet the requirements of systematic discourse.

This point has been emphasized at some length in order to bring out the connections between the concepts of political theory and political experience. This connection suggests that a political theory is not an arbitrary construction, because its concepts are linked at several points with experience. A systematic theory, such as the one formulated by Hobbes, consists of a network of interrelated and (ideally) consistent concepts; none of the concepts is identical with experience, yet none are wholly severed from it. Perhaps the whole procedure may be better understood if a genetic explanation is introduced. Political theory forms no exception to the general principle that most specialized vocabularies in the early stages of their development rely on the vocabulary of everyday language to express their meanings. The concepts of early Greek political thought, for example, could be understood in reference to ordinary usage and hardly went beyond. With the systematization of political thinking, as exemplified by Plato and Aristotle, the language of political theory became more specialized and abstract. The language of everyday conversation was modified and redefined so that the theorist might state his ideas with a precision, consistency, and scope that ordinary usage would not allow. Yet a connecting thread persisted between the polished concept and the old usages. It has often been pointed out that the concept of justice (*diké*) underwent a long evolution before it became a political concept. In Homeric times, it had carried several meanings, such as to "show," "point out," or to indicate "the way things normally happen." In Hesiod's *Works and Days,* it is appropriated for political use. Hesiod warned against the prince who rendered "crooked" *diké,* and he reminded men that they were different from the animals who were ignorant of the rules of *diké.*[7] In the philosophies of Plato and Aristotle, the concept of justice was formulated in more abstract fashion and could hardly be said to be identical with common meanings. Yet it is worth noting that in Plato's *Republic* the discussion of justice was initiated by having several speakers advance common notions of justice. Although some of these were discarded, others were treated as insufficient, which is to say that they were incorporated in modified form into the more comprehensive and abstract definition of justice which we associate with the dialogue. In this way, Plato constructed a concept of justice that was linked at many points with a tradition of common usage.

Although the vocabulary of the political theorist carries the traces of everyday language and experience, it is largely the product of the theorist's creative efforts. The concepts that constitute his vocabulary are shaped to fit the over-all structure of meanings of his theory. This structure of meanings not only contains political concepts, such as law, authority, and order, but also a subtle blend of philosophical and political ideas, a concealed or latent metaphysic. Every political theory that has aimed at a measure of comprehensiveness has adopted some implicit or explicit propositions about "time," "space," "reality," or "energy." Although most of these are the traditional categories of metaphysicians, the political theorist does not state his propositions or formulate his concepts in the same manner as the metaphysician. The concern of the theorist has not been with space and time as categories referring to the world of natural phenomena, but to the world of political phenomena; that is, to the world of political nature. If he cared to be precise and explicit in these matters, he would write of "political" space, "political" time, and so forth. Admittedly, few if any writers have employed this form of terminology. Rather, the political theorist has used synonyms; instead of political space he may have written about the city, the state, or the nation; instead of time, he may have referred to history or tradition; instead of energy, he may have spoken about power. The complex of these categories we can call a political metaphysic.[8]

The metaphysical categories resident in political theory can be illustrated by the notion of political space. One might begin by pointing out how this had its origin in the ancient world in the evolution of national consciousness. The Hebraic idea of a separate people, the Greek distinction between Hellene and barbarian, the Roman pride in *Romanitas,* the mediaeval notion of Christendom, all contributed to sharpen the sense of distinctive identity which then became associated with a determinate geographic area and a particular culture.

But the concept of political space turned on more than a distinction between the "inside" of a specific and differentiated context of actions and events and an "outside" that was largely unknown and undifferentiated. It involved also the crucial question of the arrangements for settling the problems arising out of the fact that a large number of human beings, possessing a common cultural identity, occupied the same determinate area. If for the moment we were to suspend our sophisticated notions of a political society, with its impressive hierarchies of power, its rationalized institutional arrangements, and its established grooves through which behavior smoothly runs, and think of these as constituting a determinate area, a "political space," where the plans, ambitions, and actions of individuals and groups incessantly jar against each other — colliding, blocking, coalescing, separating — we could better appreciate the ingenious role of these arrangements in reducing frictions. By a variety of means, a society seeks to structure its space: by systems of rights and duties, class and social distinctions, legal and extra-legal restraints and inhibitions, favors and punishments, permissions and tabus. These arrangements serve to mark out paths along which human motions can proceed harmlessly or beneficially. We can find this sense of structured space reflected in most political theories. It was strikingly illustrated by Hobbes:

> For whatsoever is so tyed, or environed, as it cannot move, but within a certain space, which space is determined by the opposition of some externall body, we say it hath not liberty to go further . . . The Liberty of a Subject

lyeth therefore only in those things, which in regulating their actions, the Soveraign hath praetermitted: such is the Liberty to buy, and sell, and otherwise contract with one another . . .[9]

In a similar vein Locke defended the utility of legal restraints: "that ill deserves the name of confinement which hedges us in only from bogs and precipices." [10]

As we have inferred above, political space becomes a problem when human energies cannot be controlled by existing arrangements. During the Reformation and its aftermath, it was the vitalities of religion that threatened the structural principles fashioned by mediaeval political societies. In the eighteenth century, it was the ambitions of the entrepreneur that were cramped by the elaborate network of mercantilism. "We have no need of favour — we require only a secure and open path." [11] The theories of the Physiocrats, Adam Smith, and Bentham responded by drawing new avenues and redefining the spatial dimension. If one wished to continue this analysis, it could be shown how Malthus called into question the spatial theory of the liberal economists by warning of the rising pressures stemming from the growth in population. It might also be possible to interpret the great revolutionary movements of the nineteenth century, such as Marxism, as articulate challenges to, as well as a demand for the reorganization of, the space-structure created by bourgeois industrial society. Or a novel, like Thomas Mann's *Dr. Faustus,* might be taken as representative of the viewpoint of the generation at the turn of the present century and its frustrating sense of suffocation at the restraints imposed by national and international arrangements:

> A new break-through seemed due . . . We were bursting with the consciousness that this was Germany's century . . . it was our turn to put our stamp on the world and be its leader; . . . that now, at the end of the bourgeois epoch begun some hundred and twenty years before, the world was to renew itself in our sign . . .[12]

VI Vision and political imagination. Our discussion of political space provides a clue to another aspect of political philosophy. The varied conceptions of space indicate that each theorist has viewed the problem from a different perspective, a particular angle of vision. This suggests that political philosophy constitutes a form of "seeing" political phenomena and that the way in which the phenomena will be visualized depends in large measure on where the viewer "stands." There are two distinct but related senses of "vision" that I wish to discuss; both of them have played an important part in political theory. Vision is commonly used to mean an act of perception. Thus we say that we see the speaker addressing a political rally. In this sense, "vision" is a descriptive report about an object or an event. But "vision" is also used in another sense, as when one talks about an aesthetic vision or a religious vision. In this second meaning, it is the imaginative, not the descriptive, element that is uppermost.

Ever since the scientific revolution of the sixteenth and seventeenth centuries, this first type of "objective" vision, devoted to dispassionate reportage, has been commonly associated with scientific observation. It is rather widely acknowledged now that this conception of science errs by underestimating the role that imagination plays in the construction of scientific theories. Nevertheless, there remains a persistent belief that the scientist is akin to a highly skilled reporter in that he strives to provide a verbatim report of "reality." This notion has been repeatedly translated into a criticism of political theorists. Spinoza, for example, accused political theorists of being satirists. They assume, he wrote, that "theory is supposed to be at variance with practice . . . They conceive of men, not as they are, but as they themselves would like them to be." Although Spinoza may have overlooked the point that many political theorists have seriously tried to look at political facts as they "really" are, he was quite right in saying that the picture of society given by most political theorists is not a "real" or literal one. But the question is, are these pictures in the nature of satires? Why is it that most political writers, even avowedly scientific ones like Comte, have felt constrained to envision a right pattern for the political order? What did they hope to gain in the way of theoretical insight by adding an imaginative dimension to their representation? What, in short, did they conceive the function of political theory to be?

We can easily dispose of the possibility that political theorists were unaware that they were injecting imagination or fancy into their theories. There are too many testimonials to their self-awareness on this score.[13] Rather, they believed that fancy, exaggeration, even extravagance, sometimes permit us to see things that are not otherwise apparent. The imaginative element has played a role in political philosophy similar to that Coleridge assigned to imagination in poetry, an "esemplastic" power that "forms all into one graceful intelligent whole." [14] When Hobbes, for example, depicted a multitude of men self-consciously agreeing to form a political society, he knew quite well that such an act had never "really" occurred. But by means of this fanciful picture, he hoped to assist his readers in seeing some of the basic presuppositions on which a political order rests. Hobbes was aware, as most political philosophers have been, that fanciful statements are not of the same status as propositions that seek to prove or disprove. Fancy neither proves nor disproves; it seeks, instead, to illuminate, to help us become wiser about political things.

At the same time, most political thinkers have believed imagination to be a necessary element in theorizing because they have recognized that, in order to render political phenomena intellectually manageable, they must be presented in what we can call "a corrected fullness." Theorists have given us pictures of political life in miniature, pictures in which what is extraneous to the theorist's purpose has been deleted. The necessity for doing this lies in the fact that political theorists, like the rest of mankind, are prevented from "seeing" all political things at first hand. The impossibility of direct observation compels the theorist to epitomize a society by abstracting certain phenomena and providing interconnections where none can be seen. Imagination is the theorist's means for understanding a world he can never "know" in an intimate way.

If the imaginative element in political thought were merely a methodological convenience which enabled the theorist to handle his materials more effectively, it would hardly warrant the extended attention we have given it. Imagination has involved far more than the construction of models. It has been the medium for expressing the fundamental values of the theorist; it has been the means by which the political theorist has sought to transcend history. The imaginative vision to which I am referring here was displayed at its artistic best by Plato. In his picture of the political community, guided by the divine art of the statesman, reaching out towards the idea of the Good, Plato exhibited a form of vision essentially architectonic. An architectonic vision is one wherein the political imagination attempts to mould the totality of political phenomena to accord with some vision of the Good that lies outside the political order. The impulse towards the total ordering of political phenomena has taken many forms in the course of Western political thought. In the case of Plato, the architectonic impulse assumed an essentially aesthetic cast: ". . . the true lawgiver, like an archer, aims only at that on which some eternal beauty is always attending . . ."[15] Something of the same quality reappeared in the finely chiseled system of Aquinas where the political order was allotted a precise niche in the soaring cathedral that was all of creation. At other times, the ordering vision has been an aggressively religious one, as occurred in seventeenth-century England when the millenarian sects dreamed of a resplendent New Jerusalem to replace the hopelessly corrupt order then existing. Or, again, the vision may take its origin in a view of history like that of Hegel, where the phenomena of politics acquire a temporal depth, an historical dimension, as they are swept up into an overriding purpose that shapes them towards an ultimate end. In more recent times, fittingly enough, the outside vision has frequently been colored by economic considerations. Under this view, political phenomena are to be harnessed to the demands of economic productivity, and the political order becomes the instrument of technological advance:

> . . . The sole aim of our thoughts and our exertions must be the kind of organization most favorable to industry . . . The kind of organization favorable to industry consists in a government in which the political power has no more force or activity than is necessary to see that useful work is not hindered.[16]

Whatever the form manifested by the architectonic impulse, its result has been to lend differing dimensions to the perspectives of political philosophy: dimensions of aesthetic beauty, religious truth, historical time, scientific exactitude, and economic advance. All of these dimensions possess a futurist quality, a projection of the political order into a time that is yet to be. This has been true not only of political theories that have been avowedly reformist or even revolutionary, but of conservative theories as well. The conservatism of Burke, for example, consisted in the attempt to project a continuous past into the future, and even a confessed reactionary, like de Maistre, sought to recapture a "lost past" in the hope that it could be restored in the future.

For most theorists, the imaginative reordering of political life that takes place in theorizing is not confined to helping us to understand politics. Contrary to what Spinoza argued, most political thinkers have believed that precisely because political philosophy was "political," it was committed to lessening the gap between the possibilities grasped through political imagination and the actualities of political existence. Plato recognized that political action was highly purposive in character, that it was largely conscious and deliberate; to "take counsel" before acting was seen to be a distinguishing requirement of political activity, as characteristic of Homeric kings as of Athenian statesmen. But to act intelligently and nobly demanded a perspective wider than the immediate situation for which the action was intended; intelligence and nobility were not *ad hoc* qualities, but aspects of a more comprehensive vision of things. This more comprehensive vision was provided by thinking about the political society in its corrected fullness, not as it is but as it might be. Precisely because political theory pictured society in an exaggerated, "unreal" way, it was a necessary complement to action. Precisely because action involved intervention into existing affairs, it sorely needed a perspective of tantalizing possibilities.

This transcending form of vision has not been shared by the scientist until modern times.[17] When the early scientific theorists described with poetic overtones the harmony of the spheres, their vision lacked the essential element present in political philosophy: the ideal of an order subject to human control and one that could be transfigured through a combination of thought and action.

VII

Political concepts and political phenomena. The exercise of imagination in political theory has ruled out the portrayal of the political order in terms of a representational likeness, but it has not released theorizing from the limitations inherent in the categories employed by the theorist. Every political philosophy, no matter how sophisticated or varied its categories, represents a necessarily limited perspective from which it views the phenomena of political nature. The statements and propositions that it produces are, in Cassirer's phrase, "abbreviations of reality" which do not exhaust the vast range of political experience. The concepts and categories of a political philosophy may be likened to a net that is cast out to capture political phenomena, which are then drawn in and sorted in a way that seems meaningful and relevant to the particular thinker. But in the whole procedure, he has selected a particular net and he has cast it in a chosen place.

We can observe this process at work by turning to an historical illustration. To a philosopher like Thomas Hobbes, who lived during the political turmoil of seventeenth-century England, the urgent task of political philosophy was to define the conditions making for a stable political order. In this respect, he was not unique among his contemporaries, but being a rigorously systematic thinker, he far surpassed them in the thoroughness with which he explored the conditions for peace. Consequently, this category of "peace" or "order" became in his philosophy a magnetic center which drew into its orbit only those phenomena that Hobbes felt had some relevancy to the problem of order. There was much that he missed or barely noted: the influence of social classes, problems of foreign relations, matters of governmental administration (in the narrow sense).

Thus the use of certain political categories brings into play a principle of "speculative exclusiveness" whereby some aspects of political phenomena and some political concepts are advanced for consideration, while others are allowed to languish. As Whitehead has said, "Each mode of consideration is a sort of searchlight elucidating some of the facts and retreating the remainder into an omitted brackground."[18] Selectivity, however, is not solely a matter of choice or of the idiosyncrasies of a particular philosopher. A philosopher's thought is influenced to a great extent by the problems agitating his society. If he wishes to gain the attention of his contemporaries, he must address himself to their problems and accept the terms of debate imposed by those concerns.

VIII A tradition of discourse. Of all the restraints upon the political philosopher's freedom to speculate, none has been so powerful as the tradition of political philosophy itself. In the act of philosophizing, the theorist enters into a debate the terms of which have largely been set beforehand. Many preceding philosophers have been at work collecting and systematizing the words and concepts of political discourse. In the course of time, this collection has been further refined and transmitted as a cultural legacy; these concepts have been taught and discussed; they have been pondered and frequently altered. They have become, in brief, an inherited body of knowledge. When they are handed down from one age to another, they act as conservatizing agencies within the theory of a particular philosopher, preserving the insights, experience, and refinements of the past, and compelling those who would participate in the Western political dialogue to abide by certain rules and usages.[19] The tenacity of the tradition has been such that even the highly individualistic rebels, like Hobbes, Bentham, and Marx, came to accept so much of the tradition that they succeeded neither in destroying it nor putting it on an entirely new basis. Instead, they only broadened it. One of the most remarkable testimonials to the tenacity of traditions was supplied by a writer who is often taken as one of its arch enemies, Niccolò Machiavelli. Writing during his enforced retirement from public life, he gives a vivid picture of what it means to participate in the perennial dialogue:

> In the evening, I return to my house, and go into my study. At the door I take off the clothes I have worn all day, mud spotted and dirty, and put on regal and courtly garments. Thus appropriately clothed, I enter into the ancient courts of ancient men, where, being lovingly received, I feed on that food which alone is mine, and which I was born for; I am not ashamed to speak with them and to ask the reasons for their actions, and they courteously answer me. For four hours I feel no boredom and forget every worry; I do not fear poverty, and death does not terrify me. I give myself completely

over to the ancients. And because Dante says that there is no knowledge unless one retains what one has read, I have written down the profit I have gained from their conversation, and composed a little book *De Principatibus,* in which I go as deep as I can into reflections on this subject, debating what a principate is, what the species are, how they are gained, how they are kept, and why they are lost.[20]

A continuous tradition of political thought presents many advantages to both the political thinker and to the political actor. It gives them the sense of traveling in a familiar world where the landscape has already been explored; and where it has not, there still exists a wide variety of suggestions concerning alternative routes. It allows, too, for communication between contemporaries on the basis of a common language even when translated into different tongues. The concepts and categories of politics serve as a convenient "shorthand" or symbolic language which enables one user to understand what another is saying when he refers to "civil rights," "arbitrary power," or "sovereignty." In this way, too, social experience can be shared and social cohesion enhanced. A tradition of political philosophy also contributes to the endless task of accommodating new political experience to the existing scheme of things. A whole book might be written showing the success that political reformers have achieved when they have been able to convince men that proposed changes were really continuities perfectly in accord with existing ideas and practices. Finally, it should be mentioned that a tradition of political thought provides a connecting link between past and present; the facts that succeeding political thinkers have generally adhered to a common political vocabulary and have accepted a core of problems as being properly the subject of political inquiry have served to make the political thought of earlier centuries comprehensible, as well as exciting. By contrast, the discontinuities evident in scientific fields make it quite unlikely that a modern scientist would repair to mediaeval science, for example, either for support or inspiration. This, of course, has no bearing on the alleged superiority of scientific over philosophical inquiry. It is mentioned merely to point out that the tradition of political thought is not so much a tradition of discovery as one of meanings extended over time.

IX **Tradition and innovation.** In emphasizing the speculative horizon that bounds each political thinker, it is essential not to ignore the highly original and creative responses that have occurred. By viewing common political experience from a slightly different angle than the prevailing one, by framing an old question in a novel way, by rebelling against the conservative tendencies of thought and language, particular thinkers have helped to unfasten established ways of thought and to thrust on their contemporaries and posterity the necessity of rethinking political experience. Thus when Plato asked, "What is justice and what is its relationship to the political community?" a fresh series of problems was created and new lines of political speculation were opened. The same was true of the opening sentence of the *Social Contract* and the closing sentences of the *Communist Manifesto*.

Novelty is not solely a function of the positive and assertive elements of a theorist. The innovations in thought associated with such men as Marsilius, Hobbes, Rousseau, and Marx came fully as much from what they rejected and silently omitted at the level of fundamental unifying assumptions as from what they advanced as new and different. Marsilius was not being original when he roundly condemned the papacy, nor was Hobbes when he underscored the role of fear; and, as Lenin once testified, most of Marx's leading ideas could be traced to previous writers. Whatever the truth of Whitehead's dictum that "creativity is the principle of *novelty*," [21] in the history of political theory, genius has not always taken the form of unprecedented originality. Sometimes, it has consisted of a more systematic or sharpened emphasis of an existing idea. In this sense, genius is imaginative recovery. At other times, it has taken an existing idea and severed it from the connective thread that makes an aggregate of ideas an organic complex. A connective thread or unifying principle not only integrates particular ideas into a general theory, but also apportions emphasis among them. If the unifying principle should be displaced, propositions within the complex which theretofore were commonplace or innocuous suddenly become radical in their implications. Thus there was all the difference in the world between saying, as Aquinas had, that the temporal ruler ought not to be under the coercive force (*vis coactiva*) of the law, and asserting, as Marsilius did, that the power of the political order ought not to be hindered by any human institution. The one statement occurred in a completely integrated complex wherein religion was considered as directive over all other human activities and the Church, as the institutional guardian, was established to protect and advance the unifying assumption of the Christian religion. Marsilius' statement, on the other hand, formed part of a systematic argument which, although it left untouched the content of Christian doctrine, aimed at reducing the independence of its institutional guardian, thereby releasing the political order from any external check.

When a unifying assumption is displaced, the system of ideas is thrown out of balance; subordinate ideas become prominent; primary ideas recede into secondary importance. This is because a political theory consists of a set of concepts — such as order, peace, justice, power, law, etc. — bound together, as we have said, by a kind of notational principle that assigns accents and modulations. Any displacement or significant alteration of the notational principle or any exaggerated emphasis on one or a few concepts results in a different kind of theory.

The originality of a particular political philosopher is assisted from another direction. Just as history never exactly repeats itself, so the political experience of one age is never precisely the same as that of another. Hence, in the play between political concepts and changing political experience, there is bound to be a modification in the categories of political philosophy. In part this accounts for the frequency with which we encounter the spectacle of two political theorists located at different points in history, using the same concepts but meaning very different things by them: each is responding to a different set of phenomena. The result is that each important political philosophy has something of the unique about it as well as something of the traditional.

This can be summed up in another way by saying that most formal political speculation has operated simultaneously at two different levels. At one level every political philosopher has concerned himself with what he thinks to be a vital problem of his day. Few writers have surpassed Aquinas in appearing to view political problems *sub specie aeternitatis,* yet he managed to discuss the issue most agitating his contemporaries, that of the proper relationship between spiritual and secular powers. No political thinker concerns himself exclusively with the past any more than he seeks to speak solely to the distant future; the price in both cases would be unintelligibility. This is only to say that every political philosopher is to some extent *engagé* and every work of political philosophy is to some extent a tract for the time. At another level, however, many political writings have been intended as something more than *livres de circonstance;* they have been meant as a contribution to the continuing dialogue of Western political philosophy. This explains why so often we find one political thinker belaboring another who has long since died. John Adams, in *A Defense of the Constitutions of America* (1787), could still work himself into a bad temper over the ideas of the relatively obscure seventeenth-century pamphleteer Marchamont Needham. Again, John Locke's *Two Treatises of Civil Government* is commonly used by every textbook writer as an example of political literature contrived to rationalize a particular event of his own day, the Glorious Revolution of

1688. Yet a careful reader cannot fail to see that Locke had also tried to refute Thomas Hobbes, whose writings had been largely concerned with another revolution which had taken place a half-century earlier. Finally, one may point to the storm of controversy aroused in recent years by Karl Popper's polemic against Plato.

It might be said that these illustrations are misleading in that the political thinkers in question have not been concerned to contribute to the tradition of Western political speculation, but rather a goodly share of their energy has been devoted to refuting certain ideas that appeared to them to possess a persistent and contemporaneous influence. The reply to this is simple: isn't this, by admission, the very definition of a political tradition, "a persistent and contemporaneous influence"? Doesn't a contribution usually take the form of a "correction" of a traditional error without seeking the overthrow of the whole? To put it another way, when a critical political thinker turns to analyze a persisting idea from the past, he involves himself in a rather complex process. As a thinker, who is himself situated at one point in time-space, he becomes engaged with ideas which are, in turn, reflective of a past time-space situation. Moreover, the ideas in question are similarly related to previous political thought and its situations. In addressing himself to persisting ideas from the past, a political philosopher unavoidably infects his own thought with past ideas and situations that have been similarly implicated with their own precedents. In this sense, the past is never wholly superseded; it is constantly being recaptured at the very moment that human thought is seemingly preoccupied with the unique problems of its own time. The result is, to borrow Guthrie's phrase, a "coexistence of diverse elements," [22] partly new, partly inherited, with the old being distilled into the new, and the new being influenced by the old. Thus the Western tradition of political thought has exhibited two somewhat contradictory tendencies: a tendency towards an infinite regress to the past and a tendency towards cumulation. Or if the latter sounds too much like the idea of mechanical progress, we can say that there has been a tendency towards acquiring new dimensions of insight.

One way to illustrate these two tendencies would be to take the classical idea of *fortuna,* or chance, and see how it was critically handled, first by St. Augustine and then by Calvin, who lived more than a thousand years later and yet had been deeply influenced by Augustine's thought. To Thucydides, Polybius and the Roman historians generally, *fortuna* had stood for the unpredictable element in human history, the intrusion that upsets the best laid plans and calculations.[23] With sure instinct Augustine singled out this idea as being representative of the classical spirit that Christianity had to overcome. He argued that this notion had been superseded by the Christian knowledge of a God who guided both nature and history towards a revealed end.[24] But, as Calvin acutely noted later, the Christian notion of a divine providence, far from eliminating *fortuna,* had really incorporated it. For unpredictable *fortuna,* it had substituted inscrutable Providence.[25] Yet Calvin's concern in this matter was not to help Augustine refute the classical pagans, but to attack the Renaissance humanists of his day who had revived the same classical idea that Augustine had attacked in the first place. In this example, we see two parallel continuities, the classical-Renaissance notion of *fortuna* and the Augustinian-Calvinist rejection of it in the name of a higher *fortuna.* Beginning with Augustine, each of the participants in the dialogue had built on his predecessors, and each had added a distinctive element, a different dimension. The moral of all this is contained in the lines from Eliot:

> Time present and time past
> Are both perhaps present in time future,
> And time future contained in time past.
> If all time is eternally present
> All time is unredeemable.
>
> . . . And do not call it fixity,
> Where past and future are gathered . . .[26]

The ideas and concepts that have been refined over the centuries ought not to be viewed as a fund of absolute political wisdom, but rather as a continuously evolving grammar and vocabulary to facilitate communication and to orient the understanding. This does not mean that the legacy of ideas contains only truths of no more than passing validity. It does mean that the validity of an idea cannot be divorced from its effectiveness as a form of communication.

The functions performed by a tradition of political thought also provide a justification for the study of the historical development of that tradition. In studying the writings of Plato, Locke, or Marx, we are in reality familiarizing ourselves with a fairly stable vocabulary and a set of categories that help to orient us towards a particular world, the world of political phenomena. But more than this, since the history of political philosophy is, as we shall see, an intellectual development wherein successive thinkers have added new dimensions to the analysis and understanding of politics, an inquiry into that development is not so much a venture into antiquarianism as a form of political education.

❦ TWO ❧

Plato:

Political Philosophy versus Politics

*. . . to reproduce by deliberate art what has thus been apprehended, and
"to fix in lasting thoughts the wavering images that float before the
mind."*

SCHOPENHAUER

I **The invention of political philosophy.** As we have suggested in the previous pages, political philosophy and political nature have a history; each may be said therefore to have a beginning. Questions concerning origins, however, are of antiquarian importance, except as origins may have influenced later developments. In the case of political philosophy, its origins are so significant that one can say, with very little exaggeration, that the history of political thought is essentially a series of commentaries, sometimes favorable, often hostile, upon its beginnings.

It is to the Greeks that we are indebted for the invention of political philosophy and for the demarcation of the area of political nature. Prior to the development of Greek philosophy in the sixth century B.C., man had

28

thought of himself and of society as integral parts of nature, as subject to the same natural and supernatural forces. Nature, man, and society formed a continuum. All enjoyed a shared stability and all suffered from the violence of angry gods. In this prephilosophical age, the explanation of both natural and social events took the form of "myths." Men were concerned not with "how" things operated but what superhuman agency was directing them.[1] Political phenomena remained undifferentiated from other phenomena, and political "explanation" as a separate form of thinking was unknown.

The first step in the long process of creating political philosophy occurred when man's attitude towards nature underwent drastic revision. This was the great achievement of the Greek philosophers of the sixth and fifth centuries B.C. They approached nature as something comprehensible to the human intellect, something to be explained rationally without recourse to the whims of the gods.[2] Once this step had been taken, the way was cleared for a rational explanation of all phenomena, political and social, as well as natural. At this stage, however, the Greek thinkers drew no clear distinction between physical nature and society; both areas were governed by the same "laws." Thus for Empedocles the tensions of Love and Hate (or Strife) constituted the dynamic principle at work throughout all of creation.[3] In this, as well as in other pre-Socratic philosophies, the multiplicity of conflicting things was believed to be merely surface to their essential unity; hence, the explaining principle was not to be derived from a knowledge of many "types" of phenomena, but from the perception of the underlying unity of warring opposites.[4] This idea of a principle common to nature and society appears in the fragments of Heraclitus: "Homer was wrong in saying: 'Would that strife might perish from among gods and men.' He did not see that he was praying for the destruction of the universe; for, if his prayer were heard, all things would pass away . . ."[5] In another fragment we find: "Therefore one must follow (the universal Law, namely) that which is common (to all) . . . we must base our strength on that which is common to all, as the city on the Law (*Nomos*), and even more strongly. For all human laws are nourished by one, which is divine. For it governs as far as it will, and is sufficient for all, and more than enough."[6]

It is not particularly important for our inquiry whether the Greeks first arrived at a philosophy of nature by way of reading political and social concepts into the natural world, or, conversely, whether their social and political ideas were derived from prior reasonings about nature.[7] The essential point is that in early Greek philosophy the emergence of political philosophy and of a special field of politics was obscured by the attempt to include all phenomena within "nature" and to explain their workings by a common unifying principle. Therefore, our question is not whether the Greeks read society into nature or vice versa, but when they hit upon the differences between the two.

Some light is shed on this latter problem by the discussion in Plato's dialogue *Phaedo*. In the early part of the dialogue, Socrates described how his search for truth had caused him to turn eagerly to the ideas of the earlier "nature philosophers." Instead of intellectual certainty he found only deep disappointment, and as a result his curiosity was turned from nature to man and society.[8] The significant point in Socrates' account was that the change in philosophical outlook was the result of the kind of questions that he posed and which the older "nature" philosophy could not answer. His complaint was that if philosophy intended to explain the nature of the cosmos, then it must perforce explain the nature of the order of the best. If, for example, the earth were declared to be at the center of the universe, then it was incumbent upon the philosopher to demonstrate why this was the best arrangement; that is, why the good had an obligatory power.[9]

Although Socrates' criticism may strike the modern reader as curious, the significant aspect of it lay in the method that Socrates was using. Where the nature philosophers, like Anaxagoras, had been intent on demonstrating the logical necessity behind their world-views, Socrates had approached the problems of philosophy in essentially ethical terms. In other words, his method was really adapted to eliciting answers about man and society, and not about nature. Political philosophy emerged by way of an ethical question which nature could never answer; the problems of men were not strictly coterminous with the problems of nature.

Socrates was not, however, the first to point to the possibility that society and man might be explained by principles different from those operating in nature. Actually it was the fifth-century Sophists, the bitter enemies of Socrates and Plato, who were the first to extricate politics from nature and to raise the assumption that the "political" constituted a definable field of inquiry. These distinctions were implicit in the claim of the Sophists to teach men the art of politics independent of any cosmogony. In a fragment of the Sophist Antiphon, there is preserved a clear statement of the distinction between politics and nature. Antiphon followed the current antithesis between "nature" and "convention" (*physis* and *nomos*) in order to contrast the conventional, legal justice embodied in the prevailing political arrangements with the justice decreed by nature:

Justice in the ordinary view consists in not transgressing or rather, in not being known to transgress any of the legal rules of the State in which one lives as a citizen. A man, therefore, would practice justice in the way most advantageous to himself if, in the presence of witnesses, he held the laws in high esteem, but, in the absence of witnesses, and when he was by himself, he held in high esteem the rules of nature. The reason is that the rules of nature are inevitable and innate; and again that the rules of the laws are created by covenant and not produced by nature, while the rules of nature are exactly the reverse.[10]

If, for the moment, we leave to one side this attack directed against the political order in the name of nature, we are better able to see the important assumptions on which Antiphon's criticism rested. These were: that the political order had become removed from nature; and that its very separateness allowed men to perceive in what respects the political had become separate. By contrasting the conventions of political society with the principles of nature, Antiphon was implicitly allowing that the political order could be distinguished; that the phenomena of politics possessed an identity of their own; and that the political observer himself could gain a measure of detachment. Antiphon was moving in the right direction, but, unfortunately, he drew the wrong conclusions. It does not necessarily follow from the conventional basis of political rules that they are false or disadvantageous to man; or that human agreement to them cannot provide the sanctioning element previously sought in nature.

In disengaging the political from the natural order, the Sophists were, in one sense, following the path of the earlier nature philosophers. The great contribution of the latter had been to approach the external world naturalistically; that is, as an order comprehensible to human reason and not as a mixture of natural and supernatural elements which defied rational explanation. This, in turn, was accompanied by still another claim: that the observer could, so to speak, "get outside" the object he was describing. But at this point certain differences, which were to assume great importance later, began to appear. The detachment of the nature philosopher consisted in his viewing nature as something to be understood, but not necessarily as something to be controlled. This form of detachment was not taken over by political philosophy. Instead, as the philosophy of Plato shows, the "nature" of politics was to be viewed as manipulatable, as a bundle of forces from which order could be fashioned. In this respect, political philosophy was to be armed with a bolder assumption than the scientific inquiry of that time.

This becomes clearer by noting a second ingredient in the detached attitude of the nature philosophers. They had grasped the idea that external objects possessed a nature of their own which was in some respects foreign to the nature of man. Moreover, these objects were neither sympathetic nor hostile to man; they were indifferent. But if the idea of a neutral order where the categories of human aspiration were irrelevant could be accepted as a postulate of scientific inquiry, its rejection at the hands of Greek political thinkers marked an important early separation between scientific and political modes of thought. In confronting the world of nature, man might be at once resigned and curious, for this was an order he could neither create nor change. But in the world of politics, a strongly anthropomorphic attitude prevailed: man could be the architect of order. The political world, in short, was amenable to human art.

These political ideas naturally evoked a host of questions: if the political world were distinct, did this mean that it was fully autonomous, unconnected with a universal moral order? how did man go about ordering this world? did it require a particular kind of knowledge? It was around these and similar questions that Plato constructed the first comprehensive political philosophy. Two aspects of this philosophy will be emphasized in our discussion. First, Plato delineated a remarkably clear theory of the political, one that strongly governed the thinking of later political writers. At the same time, his method of argumentation, as well as the motivation behind it, consistently tended to obscure the distinctiveness of the political. Second, Plato stated in classic terms the case against "politics." Although there were later writers who objected strenuously to his argument, there were few who ignored it.

Leaving aside for the moment this second aspect, Plato's inquiry into the nature of the political was governed by a belief that the political must first be differentiated from the other dimensions of life. This was clearly his intent in the dialogue *Politicus* where he undertook to distinguish the true art of the statesman from the shams of the "politician" and to establish the superiority of the political art over all of the other arts necessary to the life of the community:

> Where shall a man find the way of the Statesman then? For we must distinguish this path from all the rest by setting upon it the special sign of its distinctive form.[11]

What was truly "political" was the "art of responsible charge of a whole community" according to an absolute standard.[12]

There is an art which controls all these [other] arts. It is concerned with the laws and all that belongs to the life of the community. It weaves all into its unified fabric with perfect skill. It is a universal art and so we call it by a name of universal scope. That name is one which I believe to belong to this art and to this alone, the name of "Statesmanship." [13]

These remarks also contained the intimation of an idea that Plato developed at length in the *Republic* and later in the *Laws*, one that set forever the stamp of his genius on the nature of political philosophy. It can be put simply: he taught later writers to think of political society as a coherent, interconnected whole; he was the first to view political society in the round, to view it as a "system" of interrelated functions, an ordered structure. This seems such a commonplace to us now, educated as we are to think in terms of structural-functional analyses, that the breath-taking advance represented by Plato's insight is apt to be overlooked. But prior to Plato, writers had dealt only with fragmentary aspects of political society, concentrating perhaps on the qualities needed by a ruler or the duties of the citizen. Political speculation had not yet reached the level of conceptualizing political institutions, procedures, and activities as a system dependent upon the performance of specified functions or tasks. In short, Plato was the first to picture political society as a system of distinctive or differentiated roles. Whether it was the role of philosopher-statesman, auxiliary, or producer, each represented a necessary function; each was defined in terms of its contribution to sustaining the whole society; each bore rights, duties, and expectations which provided definite guides and signposts for human behavior and defined the place of the individual within the system. The harmonization and integration of these roles made of political society a functioning, interdependent whole. To maintain it required a sharp demarcation among the three classes of the community, careful training of each member in his specialized skill and, above all, the restriction of the individual to one function: there must be no confusion of roles, no blurred identities.

From Plato onwards, one of the distinctive marks of political philosophy was its approach to political society as a functioning system. Although Plato may have exaggerated the possibilities of a society's achieving systematic unity, the greatness of his achievement was to point out that in order to think in a truly political way, one had to consider society as a systematic whole.

Although Plato insisted upon the special identity of the political order, he was equally emphatic in denying its autonomy or moral isolation.

And philosophers tell us, Callicles, that communion and friendship, and orderliness and temperance and justice bind together heaven and earth and gods and men, and that this universe is therefore called Cosmos or order, not disorder or misrule.[14]

The famous myth of the Age of Kronos, which Plato used in *Politicus,* underscored his belief that the political order was to be viewed as a part of a meaningful, moral universe. At the same time, however, he also used this myth to emphasize the distinctiveness of the political order by warning against a confusion of the political order with the divine. During the Age of Kronos, "God was supreme governor in charge of the actual rotation of the universe as a whole, but divine also and in like manner was the government of its several regions; for these were all portioned out to be provinces under the surveillance of tutelary deities." [15] But with the dramatic reversal of the cosmic cycle — "there is an era in which God Himself assists the universe on its way and guides it . . . there is also an era in which he releases this control" [16] — the divine power had let go the leading strings controlling human affairs and men were largely on their own. The political order took shape and identity only when the divine governance had been relaxed. "When God was Shepherd there were no political constitutions . . ." [17]

Yet this apparent separation of the political from the divine was only preliminary to Plato's attempt to recapture the divine principle. It was for this end that he fashioned an alliance between the divine principle represented by philosophic wisdom and the exercise of the political art:

When the supreme power in man coincides with the greatest wisdom and temperance, then the best laws and the best constitution come into being; but in no other way.[18]

II **Philosophy and society.** This takes us to the heart of Plato's conception of political philosophy. The ideas of Plato provide the first full mirroring of the dramatic encounter between the ordering vision of political philosophy and the phenomena of politics. Never has the art of ruling been clothed in a higher dignity: "What art is more difficult to learn? But what art is more important to us?" [19] Never have the claims of political philosophy been advanced in more sweeping fashion: it "will not only preserve the lives of the subjects, but reform their characters too, so far as human nature permits of this." [20] And never has it been more strongly insisted that the rightful place of political philosophy ought to be at the throne of political power: ". . . the human race will not see better days until either the stock of those who rightly and genuinely follow philosophy acquire political authority, or else the class who have political control be led by some dispensation of providence to become real philosophers." [21]

If, however, political philosophy were to fulfill this architectonic role, two prior assumptions about the nature of politics had to be accepted. The whole range of political phenomena must be considered fully comprehensible to the human mind and malleable to human art. There must be no doubts, such as those expressed by Santayana, of the wisdom of trying "to harness this wild world in a brain-spun terminology." [22] If there existed a true pattern for the whole life of the community, and if political philosophy possessed the true science that could transform a diseased polity into a thing of beauty and health, then it must be assumed that the concepts and categories of philosophy could comprehend and penetrate to all of the varied aspects of political and social phenomena. Similarly, if it were claimed that through the master science of political philosophy the political order could be shaped by an eternal truth, then the materials of that order must be highly plastic to the impress of the right design.

Thus from the very beginnings of political philosophy, a duality was established between the form-giving role of political thought and the form-receiving function of political "matter." Political knowledge, like all true knowledge, was essentially a science of order, one that traced the proper relationship between men, indicated the sources of evil in the community, and prescribed the overarching pattern for the whole. It aimed not at describing political phenomena, but at transfiguring them in the light of a vision of the Good. The two words, *eidon* and *idea,* which Plato used to represent the eternal objects of knowledge, both contained the root-meaning of "vision." The effect of this was to impart to political philosophy a projective quality. The political philosopher, by an act of thought, strove to project a more perfect order into future time. "In dealing with a plan for the future . . . he who exhibits the model on which an undertaking should be fashioned should abate nothing of perfect excellence and absolute truth . . ." [23] Thus at the center of the enterprise of political theory was an imaginative element, an ordering vision of what the political system ought to be and what it might become. In later centuries, other political thinkers, such as Hobbes and Comte, recurred to this notion of thought as the ordering agency of political life, but no one has ever surpassed Plato in insisting upon the moral urgency and centrality of political vision:

There can be no question whether a guardian who is to keep watch over anything needs to be keen-sighted or blind. And is not blindness precisely the condition of men who are entirely cut off from knowledge of any reality, and have in their soul no clear pattern of perfect truth, which they might study in every detail and constantly refer to, as a painter looks at his model, before they proceed to embody notions of justice, honour, and goodness in earthly institutions or . . . to preserve such institutions as already exist? [24]

The element of political imagination, as developed in Plato's thought, was never intended as an exercise in utopia-building. The spirit of playfulness that marked many of the dialogues, those moments where Plato appeared astonished at his own boldness, and, at the opposite extreme, those passages brooding with disillusion — none of these moods displaced his basic conviction that men could effect a junction between truth and practice. Towards the end of his life, he did despair of seeing the ideal polity take hold in an actual society, yet he still insisted that there could be no marked improvement in existing polities unless men had an ideal pattern at which to aim. Political knowledge of the best remained absolutely essential if men were to share even that slight participation in reality allowed by the gods.[25] The shortcomings of the existential order of things did not destroy the claim of political philosophy to being a severely practical enterprise of the most serious kind. Political science was "the knowledge by which we are to make other men good." [26] Its ultimate ministry was the human soul. Statecraft was, in Samuel Butler's word, "soul-craft"; and the true ruler, an architect of souls.

The task of fashioning souls was not to be accomplished, however, by the ruler working directly on the human psyche. The essential problem was to establish the right influences and the most salutary environment wherein the soul could be attracted towards the Good. Plato, unlike some later Christian thinkers, never believed that the soul could be perfected in defiance of the surrounding political and social arrangements. In a society where naked ambition, acquisitiveness, and cleverness were encouraged, the best of characters could not remain uncorrupted.[27] Regeneration, like its opposite, was a social process, and the saving political knowledge had to be as wide-ranging as the life of the community itself. From this it also followed that the sphere of the political art was coextensive with all of the influences, public and private, that affected human character.[28]

The creation of a rightly ordered society promised the solution of still another problem, one that was intimately related to the other goals of moral regeneration and political stability. Some of the most moving passages in the dialogues occur where Plato reflected upon the deep antagonism existing between philosophy and society. It was not only that the practices of society were in fundamental contradiction to the teachings of philosophy; the real crime of society was to make a life devoted to philosophy impossible, or, at best, hazardous. Given the shape of existing societies, to pursue a life of philosophy was to invite martyrdom. Where the philosopher was not scorned, he was humiliated, as Plato had been by the tyrant Dionysius; where he was not humiliated, he was corrupted, as Alcibiades and Critias had been; where he could not be corrupted, he was condemned to death, as Socrates had been. We moderns need only substitute the "intellectual" for the philosopher, and we have a timeless document portraying the lot of the intellectual in society: rejected, enticed, never fully accepted, a lonely figure whom Plato compared to a traveller taking shelter under a wall from the swirling storm, "content if he can keep his hands clean from iniquity while this life lasts . . ." [29] To make a world safe for philosophy was as fully important a motivation in Plato's political theory as the reform of society and the moral improvement of its members. In fact, all three purposes were intertwined. For if the features of Plato's society appear harsh, and if the moral and intellectual stature of many of its members seem stunted, this was not the revenge of an intellectual nursing the angry hurts inflicted by society. All of these were the outcome of a deep conviction that a city of reason ruled by philosophy would be the salvation, not only of philosophers and philosophy, but of all its members. The fate of philosophy and the fate of mankind were as closely united as the twins of Hippocrates who flourished and suffered as one. A city hospitable to philosophy, *ipso facto,* would be a city following the principle of virtue and developing the best in its members.

The common assumption underlying Plato's strictures against existing societies, as well as his schemes for political regeneration, was that any political system, good or bad, was the direct product of the beliefs held by its members. This conviction concerning the sovereign role of beliefs was supported, in Plato's eyes, by the activities of the Sophists in the democratic politics of Athens. In undertaking to instruct men in the techniques of political success and in promising to outfit men for coping with the demands of "real" life, the Sophists, in effect, were asserting that they possessed a form of true knowledge. The assertion, Plato insisted, was a serious one, for it advocated that men reorder their behavior according to certain beliefs. It followed, whether the Sophists recognized it or not, that they had implicitly assumed a responsibility for the stability of the political order and a responsibility for the human soul. The superficiality of their teachings, however, had led only to confusion — confusion in the city and confusion in the soul.[30] More precisely, there had been disorder in the city and in the lives of the citizens because in both cases the Sophists taught not knowledge, but mere "opinion" (*doxa*). Disastrous as this experience had been, it testified, nevertheless, to the supreme importance of beliefs. If the power of mere opinion could create so much harm, then, Plato reasoned, true belief might work just as powerfully in the opposite direction. Here was further support for the proposition that political philosophy was a pursuit of the utmost urgency and practicality.

Plato's belief in the practical character of political philosophy received its classic expression in the dictum concerning the necessity for rulers being philosophers or philosophers, rulers. Yet in the dialogue *Politicus,* there was a still more striking assertion, that the political philosopher was deserving of the title "statesman" even though he might never possess the reality of political power.[31] From one angle this could be taken to mean that the basic distinction lay between those who had the true political knowledge and those who, like the Sophist and the "politician," had only a pretense of knowledge. In this sense, the true philosopher and the true statesman were alike. Considered from another angle, however, Plato was saying something much more significant about the nature of political philosophy. To grasp the true idea of political theory was to attain an intellectual position wherein the chaos of political life had been remoulded by the informing vision of the Good.[32] By virtue of the transforming power of political theory, the philosopher had already accomplished in thought what the ruler in practice had yet to do: he had cured the ills of the community and ordered it to a pattern of perfection. If, then, the drama of political transformation had been enacted previously at the level of mind, and if the philosopher possessed the knowledge whereby this drama might be enacted in actual political life, the Platonic alliance between philosophy and political power appears in a different light. The philosopher acquiring power or the ruler acquiring philosophy did not symbolize a harnessing of opposites but a blending of two kinds of power, a joining of complements. The perfect form of political power was to be achieved by a combination of the two, the power of thought prescribing the right pattern, the power of the ruler effecting it. In contrast, the commands of the tyrant or the persuasive arts of the political rhetorician were denied to be true forms of power. By definition, a power ought to bring some good to its possessor, but this occurred only when he had a true knowledge of the good and the just towards which to direct his power.[33]

Now in Plato's general philosophy, true knowledge exhibited certain general characteristics, and these exerted a profound influence over the categories which he attached to political thought. These characteristics were summed up in his conception of the nature of the true model: "Whenever the maker of anything looks to that which is unchanging and uses a model of that description in fashioning the form and quality of his work, all that he thus accomplishes must be good. If he looks to something that has come to be and uses a generated model, it will not be good." [34] Genuine knowledge, then, was derived from the stable realm of immaterial Forms.[35] The world of sense and matter, in contrast, was a world in movement, always in flux, and therefore unable to rise above the plane of "opinion" to that of knowledge; it was a world filled with maddeningly elusive half-truths and distorted perceptions. Each of these realms was to be approached in a different way, for each had its own set of categories. In the one case, the categories were shaped to express certainty, repose, permanence, and an objectivity unaffected by the vagaries of human taste; the sensible world, on the other hand, was to be understood through categories adapted to its nature, categories of uncertainty, instability, change, and variety. The categories descriptive of the Forms we might call "categories of value," while those relating to the world of sense perception, "categories of disvalue."

When carried over into political theory, the categories of disvalue were at once descriptive and evaluative of the existential world of politics, while the categories of value were indicative of what that world might become under the guidance of philosophy. Stability, timelessness, harmony, beauty, measure, and symmetry — all of these categories derived from the nature of the Forms were to be the angles of vision, the enclosing moulds for capturing political phenomena and reducing them to the proper shape. Thus the immutability of the Forms — "ever to be the same, steadfast and abiding, is the product of the divinest things only" [36] — was translated into the political category of stability; its final issue was the principle that "any change whatever, except from evil, is the most dangerous of all things." [37] Again, since knowledge of the Forms represented an insight into eternal beauty, the political order was to be transformed in the light of aesthetic categories: ". . . the true lawgiver aims only at that on which some eternal beauty is always attending . . ." [38] And as a final example, the perfect unity and harmony exhibited by the Forms had their political counterparts in Plato's obsessive preoccupation with the unity and cohesion of the city:

> Does not the worst evil for a state arise from anything that tends to rend it asunder and destroy its unity, while nothing does it more good than whatever

tends to bind it together and make it one? . . . And are not citizens bound together by sharing in the same pleasures and pains, all feeling glad or grieved on the same occasions of gain or loss; whereas the bond is broken when such feelings are no longer universal, but any event of public or personal concern fills some with joy and others with distress? [39]

III **Politics and architectonics.** Although Plato has commonly been regarded as the archetype of the political thinker who has his feet planted firmly in the clouds, the recognition of "politics" was indicative of Plato's strongly empirical vein. It was here that he spoke directly to the Greek political experience. Conflict and change, revolution and faction, the dizzy cycle of governmental forms — these were not the invention of philosophical fancy but the stuff of Athenian political history. Moreover, the dimension of "politics" had been further broadened by the establishment of democratic institutions and practices during the fifth century. As new groups were granted the privileges of citizenship, which included the right to deliberate in the public assemblies and law courts, the circle of political participation was widened and thereby the element of "politics" became more pervasive. Accordingly, the "politician" made his appearance, the skilled manipulator who fashioned power from the grievances, resentments, and ambitions festering the community. With him came the Sophists, the logical accompaniment to democratic participation, promising to instruct men in the art of political persuasion.[40]

The intensity of factional strife, the conflict between social classes, and the loss of confidence in traditional values had worked to create a situation where the political order appeared forever to tremble on the brink of self-destruction.

> After a contest for office, the victorious side engrosses the conduct of public affairs so completely . . . that no share whatever of office is left to the vanquished, or even to their descendants; each party watches the other in jealous apprehension of insurrection . . . Such societies . . . are no constitutional states . . . men who are for a party, we say, are factionaries, not citizens, and their so-called rights are empty words.[41]

In this competition for power, woven out of rival ambitions and jarring interests, lay the disturbing factor of "politics," the source of instability and change, and the inevitable product of a condition where political forms and relationships were allowed to flourish with a minimum of preconceived direction and a maximum of spontaneity. The prevalence of politics had dissolved political life into a "whirlpool," an "incessant movement of shifting currents." [42]

For Plato, the flux of political life was symptomatic of a diseased polity; the spontaneity, variety, and turbulence of Athenian democracy, a contradiction of every canon of order. Order was the product of the subordination of the lower to the higher, the rule of wisdom over naked ambition, and of knowledge over appetite. Yet in existing polities, a ruling group would base its credentials to rule on anything but wisdom — on birth, wealth, or democratic right. At every turn, the world of politics violated the dictates of the world of Forms. Where the world of Forms marked the triumph of unchanging Being over the flux of Becoming, the immutable nature of the Good over the ever-changing world of appearances, actual political practice was plagued by constant innovations as first one class, then another, tinkered with the constitution, altering here, modifying there, but never establishing the basic arrangements on a secure basis. Again, where the realm of Forms testified to a truth of majestic simplicity, existing independently of human tastes and desires, political life followed a frenzied path from one "opinion" to another, sampling first this, then that way of life, and finding rest only in a scepticism about all political values. Where the Idea of the Good taught the necessity of a harmonious mixture unstreaked by faction,[43] a necessity that reappeared in the imperative that the best polity was one that insured the happiness of the whole and not the disproportionate advantage of the part, existing regimes were torn by the bitter struggles between groups and classes, each straining to impose its special advantage.[44] Where the true pattern was a design of beauty, a whole where each part had been shaped to symmetry and softened by temperance — characteristics that pointed to the conclusion that "happiness can only come to a state when its lineaments are traced by an artist working after the divine pattern" [45] — actual political institutions were disfigured by an ever-changing ugliness and distortion as successive ruling groups tipped the scales in their own favor. Where the world of the Forms knew only regular, ordered motion, the political condition was one of random movements, jerking this way and that, as the wild energy of demagogues and revolutionaries seized the *polis,* or as a tolerant democracy allowed its citizens a limitless freedom to follow their own preferences.

As a kind of standing antithesis to the world of Forms, the world of politics testified to what life was like when it was unredeemed by that vision that "sheds light on all things." [46] Without an illuminating vision of the Good, the members of a community were condemned to live in a cave of illusions, vainly following distorted images of reality and ceaselessly driven by irrational desires. A visionless life further gave rise to struggles that wracked the community, for "all goes wrong when, starved for lack of anything good in their own lives, men turn to public affairs hoping to snatch from thence the happiness they hunger for. They set about fighting for power, and their internecine conflict ruins them and their country." [47] Far from being a "real" world, political societies dwelt in a shadowy realm, a dream world "where men live fighting one another about shadows and quarreling for power, as if that were a great prize . . ." [48]

At this point we must pause to consider some of the implications of Plato's argument. In particular we must ask: what meanings has he fastened upon "politics" and the "political"? Stated in summary form, Plato understood *political* philosophy to mean knowledge pertaining to the good life at the public level and *political* ruling to be the right management of the public affairs of the community. One may quarrel with Plato's definition of the good life and with his conception of rulership, but it is difficult to deny that Plato displayed a sure sense that the political, whether it be philosophy or ruling, has to do with what is public in the life of a society. This cannot be said, however, of his conception of "politics." Plato understood "politics" largely in the sense that I have used it earlier. He was aware of the struggle for competitive advantage, of the problem of distributing the good things of life among the various groups in society, and of the instabilities engendered by changing social and economic relationships among the members. He chose to treat these phenomena as the symptoms of an unhealthy society, as the problem against which political philosophy and the political art had to contend. Political philosophy and ruling alike had as their objectives the creation of the good society; "politics" was evil, and hence the task of philosophy and of ruling was to rid the community of politics. Thus the Platonic conception of political philosophy and ruling was founded on a paradox: the science as well as the art of creating order were sworn to an eternal hostility towards politics, towards those phenomena, in other words, that made such an art and science meaningful and necessary. The paradox had serious consequences for both thought and action. A science that is at odds with its own subject-matter, one that tries to get rid of the distinctive context in which the problems of that science take shape, is an instrument ill-adapted for theoretical understanding. Similarly, action designed to extirpate what are the inescapable givens of social existence will be driven to using the harsh methods that Plato himself grudgingly admitted were necessary. These criticisms suggest that the central weakness in Plato's philosophy lay in the failure to establish a satisfactory relationship between the idea of the *political* and the idea of *politics*. The problem is not how the one can eliminate the other, but rather how can we gain the necessary knowledge of politics to enable us to act wisely in a context of conflict, ambiguity, and change?

In this connection, Plato's fascination with the art of medicine leads to a quite misleading analogy: the body politic does not experience "disease," but conflict; it is beset not by harmful bacteria but individuals with hopes, ambitions, and fears that are often at odds with the plans of other individuals; its end is not "health," but the endless search for a foundation that will support the mass of contradictions present in society. Unless the distinctively political context is preserved, political theory tends to vanish into larger questions, such as the nature of the Good, the ultimate destiny of man, or the problem of right conduct, thereby losing contact with the essentially political questions that are its proper concern: the nature of political ethics, that is, right conduct in a political situation, or the question of the nature of the goods that are possible in a political community and attainable by political action. Similarly, the neglect of the political context is likely to produce a dangerous kind of political art, especially when it is motivated by an animus against "politics." The art of ruling becomes the art of imposition. A truly political art, on the other hand, would be one framed to deal with conflict and antagonism; to take these as the raw materials for the creative task of constructing areas of agreement, or, if this fails, to make it possible for competing forces to compromise in order to avoid harsher remedies. The business of the political art is with the politics of conciliation; its range of creativity is defined and determined by the necessity of sustaining the on-going activities of the community. Its restless search for conciliation is, at bottom, inspired by a belief that the art of imposition ought to be confined to those situations where no other alternative exists.

Implicit in the politics of conciliation is a notion of order markedly different from that held by Plato. If conciliation is a continuing task for those who govern — and the nature of "politics" would seem to dictate that it is — then order is not a set pattern, but something akin to a precarious equilibrium, a condition that demands a willingness to accept partial solutions. For Plato, however, order was in the nature of a mould shaped after a divine model; a concept to be used for stamping society in a definite image. But what kind of an order could issue from a political science dedicated in large measure to the eradication of conflict; that is, to the elimination of politics? If order could only flourish in the absence of conflict and antagonism, then it followed that the order thus created had surrendered its distinctively political element; order it might be, but not a "political" order. For the essence of a "political" order is the existence of a settled institutional arrangement designed to deal in a variety of ways with the vitalities issuing from an associated life: to offset them where necessary, to ease them where possible, and, creatively, to redirect and transmute them when the opportunity allows. This is not to say that a society cannot achieve order by imposition, but only that such a society is not "political." It also follows from this conception of a "political" society that the art of politics ought to proceed on the assumption that order is something to be achieved *within* a given society; that is, between the various forces and groups of a community. The ideal of order must be fashioned in the closest connection with existing tendencies, and it must be tempered by the sober knowledge that no political idea, including the idea of order itself, is ever fully realized, just as few political problems are ever irrevocably solved.

Plato, however, was convinced that the political realm was inherently prone to disorder and that the contraries of disorder — stability, harmony, unity, and beauty — would never develop out of the normal course of political events. They did not exist immanently within the materials of politics, but had to be brought in from the "outside." "The virtue of each thing, whether body or soul, instrument or creature, when given to them in the best way, comes not to them by chance but as the result of the order and truth and art which are imparted to them . . . And is not the virtue of each thing dependent on order or arrangement?" [49] Order, in all of its facets of harmony, unity, measure, and beauty was the positive creation of art; and art, in turn, was the province of knowledge. Political order was produced by an informing vision which came from the "outside," from the knowledge of the eternal pattern, to shape the community to a pre-existent Good.

The outside vision was of crucial importance to Plato's distinction between the true statesman and the philosopher, on the one hand, and the politician and the Sophist on the other. In the dialogue *Gorgias,* the great political leaders of Athens, such as Themistocles, Cimon, and Pericles, were severely criticized on the grounds that they had failed in the supreme test of statesmanship, the improvement of the citizenry. The reason for their failure, as well as the explanation of their power, was attributed by Plato to a false view of the political art. They had been content to manipulate and play upon the desires and opinions of the citizens. They had never risked the loss of power and esteem by attempting to transmute popular wants and opinions into something loftier; nor had they been willing to impose a correct but unpopular policy. The result was not only a degraded citizenry, but the degradation of the leaders as well:

> But if you suppose that any man will show you the art of becoming great in the city, and yet not conforming yourself to the ways of the city, whether for better or worse, then I can only say that you are mistaken, Callicles; for he who would deserve to be the true natural friend of the Athenian Demus . . . must be by nature like them, and not an imitator only.[50]

The true statesman, on the other hand, looked not to "politics" for his inspiration, but to the true dictates of his art; he sought not for the clever combination of existing political tendencies but for their transformations:

> [The older crop of politicians] were certainly more serviceable than those who are living now, and better able to gratify the wishes of the State; but as to transforming those desires and not allowing them to have their way, and using the powers which they had, whether of persuasion or of force, in the improvement of their fellow-citizens, which is the prime object of the truly good citizen . . . they were [not] a whit superior to our present statesmen . . .[51]

The crucial difference between the "democratic" leader and the Platonic ruler centers around the constituency that each "represents," or, if this word suffers from later associations, the constituency to which each is responsive. The popular leader owed his power to an ability to sniff the moods and aspirations of the populace, to juggle a wide variety of variables, and to strive for the *ad hoc* solution. His constituency, in short, was the community: its wants, demands, and humors insofar as these had political manifestations. His "virtues" were agility, shrewdness, and a calculating eye for the changing disposition of political forces within the community. Even in the hostile pages of Plato, he emerges as the true "political" man, the leader whose problems are defined by the ever-changing patterns of "politics" and whose knowledge is pragmatic and empirical, because he aims not at pursuing an absolute principle but at discovering a policy whose duration depends on the alignment of political forces at any moment. His was the politics of reconciliation, sometimes of the crudest sort. As a politician, his existence became possible only under certain conditions, such as when men were exhausted by bitter conflicts over principles; or when they had ceased to believe in immutable truths; or, finally, when they are, as Balfour put it, "so at one they can safely afford to bicker."

In contrast, the Platonic ruler had a different constituency, for he was not first and foremost a "political man" but a philosopher endowed with political power. As a philosopher, his loyalty was to the realm of truth, "a world of unchanging and harmonious order." As a ruler, he had an obligation to bring the community into a closer approximation with that realm, "to mould other characters besides his own and to shape the patterns of public and private life into conformity with his vision of the ideal." [52] Yet, in the Platonic formulation, there could be no conflict of interest or duty between the two roles. The ruler, in following the true art of statesmanship, was conforming to the knowledge made possible by philosophy and discharging the obligation of the philosopher to pursue the truth. And in following the dictates of his art, rather than the wishes of the community, the philosopher qua ruler satisfied the demands of rulership, because the ends of his art coincided exactly with the true interests of the community. His constituency was not the community, that is, it was not a political constituency that claimed his loyalty, but rather the Idea of the good community. "An art is sound and flawless so long as it is entirely true to its own nature as an art in the strictest sense . . ." [53]

This aspect of constituency becomes clearer when it is related to the motivations of the Platonic ruler. In the Platonic scheme, the community occupied a middle position between the impulse motivating the ruler and the pattern of the Good at which his art was aimed. The true ruler was inspired by an urge which, in the single role of philosopher, he could not satisfy; not merely to know the real, but to bring it into existence, to shape political actualities to conform with the divine pattern. The community supplies the aesthetic medium for the satisfaction of this impulse towards beauty. The motivation of the ruler, then, was not that of the politician — to retain power and to enjoy the prestige and rewards of office — but that of the aesthetician seeking to impress on his materials the image of perfect beauty. The aesthetic element in the political art connoted form, determinate shape, rational harmony, and all that was antithetical to the untidiness, dissymmetries, and moral ugliness of "politics." Its triumph was the victory of the Apollonian principle of harmonious order over the Dionysiac tendencies of political life. [54]

These considerations were further pointed up by the analogies drawn by Plato between the ruler and the physician, weaver, and artist. [55] The practice of each of these arts involved three elements: the active agency of the skilled practitioner; the Idea at which he aimed, such as health or beauty; and the passive material receptive to the impress of the Idea. The materials in each case possessed no "claim" of their own, because the only way that the sick body, the unshaped marble, and the unwoven strands could attain their respective ends was through the skilled art of the practitioner. The criteria for judging the product of each art were dominantly aesthetic: harmony between the parts; symmetry of proportion; a moderate blend of diversities. All of these aspects, in turn, were carried over by Plato into his conception of rulership. Like the artist, the statesman too was inspired by a pattern of beauty, which issued in the impulse to create an ordered harmony by assigning the "parts" of the community to their rightful functions. Harmony of the whole, unity of design, and the shunning of extremes — all of these became imperatives governing the actions of the statesmen as well as prescriptions for the institutions of society. The end of the royal art was the greatest of all human achievements, a community bound together in

> a true fellowship by mutual concord and by ties of friendship. It is the first and best of all fabrics. It enfolds all who dwell in the city, bond or free, in its firm contexture. Its kingly weaver maintains his control and oversight over it, and it lacks nothing that makes for human happiness so far as happiness is obtainable in a human community.[56]

Like any skilled practitioner, the ruler was justified by the end of his art in removing the obstacles that blocked the way to the realization of the true Form. Just as the physician might be compelled to amputate a member to preserve the body or the weaver to discard defective materials, so the ruler could purge the body politic of its deformed "members" by whatever means suitable.[57]

This concern with the condition of the "materials" of art led Plato to strain to the utmost the analogy between the ruler and the other skilled professions. No art could be fully realized and no aesthetic impulse truly satisfied if the materials were resistant to the "design of pure intelligence." [58] When translated into political terms, this meant that the "royal weaver" ought to take special pains in selecting the human nature from which the bonds of community were to be woven. He could not combine the bad with the good — for this would issue in a product both useless and ugly — but the various forms of virtue, such as courage and moderation, were the proper materials. The other human characters were to be discarded; that is, put to death, expelled, or so severely disgraced as to be deprived of any influence.[59]

This quest for the suitable materials was essentially a search for a political *tabula rasa,* and in the *Republic* Plato made it a necessary condition for political success that all of the members of the community who were over ten years old ought to be banished; the remainder would be shaped and moulded

to the desired form by the institutions of society, especially by the educational system.[60] Then and then only would the political artist be able to
paint with a free hand on a fresh canvas:

> He will take society and human character as his canvas, and begin by scrap-
> ing it clean. That is no easy matter; . . . unlike other reformers, he will
> not consent to take in hand either an individual or a state or to draft laws,
> until he is given a clean surface to work on or has cleansed it himself.[61]

The search for a fresh beginning also preoccupied Plato in his latest work,
the *Laws,* which many commentators still persist in regarding as a more
"practical" political scheme. In this dialogue, he confronts the imaginary legislator with a choice: will the art of the legislator function more effectively
in an established society where it could capitalize on the existing sense of
community created by a common language, laws, worship, and a spirit of
friendship developed over a long period of living together, or would the
chances for success be greater if the legislator were to sacrifice these advantages of a going concern and seek instead the fresh situation where the dis-
advantages of a going concern would also be absent? Any society which
lacked the informing hand of the philosopher-ruler would be etched instead
by entrenched interests, standing antagonisms, and engrained superstitions.[62]
It would, in short, present an unaesthetic medium, as well as a less plastic
material. It is not surprising that before the dialogue had progressed very far
one of the participants bursts in to announce — with something of the style
of second-rate melodrama — that he had recently been commissioned to draw
up a constitution for a new colony. Here, *mirabile dictu,* was the great opportunity of a "clean" political situation, one devoid of the blemishing dis-
proportions of wealth, debt, and the resulting social antagonisms.[63] All that
was lacking was the master hand to shape the receptive materials to order.
But instead of the philosopher educated for political power, which had been
the motif of the *Republic,* Plato advocated a philosopher-legislator who would
act vicariously through the agency of a young and pliable tyrant; that is, a
kind of idealized Dionysius. It was, however, the same formula of absolute
power yoked to absolute knowledge.[64]

Once the proper situation had been defined, the political art could then
set about constructing institutional arrangements. The detailed prescriptions
concerning political institutions, economic arrangements, the family, education, religion and cultural life, which were so prominent in the political
dialogues, were governed by two broad objectives. The first was to establish
points of political fixity or unalterable fundamentals capable of withstanding

the pressures of political change. Included among these points of rigidity were the size of the *polis* itself, its population, the structure of vocations, the institutions of property, marriage, and education, and moral and religious doctrines. When taken together, these various topics constitute a kind of catalogue of the areas of community life with the greatest potentialities for causing political disorder.[65] They were, in short, the main sources of political disagreements and conflicts. By attending to their close regulation, it would be possible to regularize human behavior and to eliminate, as far as possible, its unpredictable elements. In this way, the stability and unity reflective of the ideal pattern of community would be reproduced at the human plane.

The obverse side of these political fundamentals was more positive. They were the means for enabling the community to approximate the pattern of the Good, to become a medium for the expression of an eternal truth. This conception logically excluded the notion that the political fundamentals of a community constituted an index of agreements among the members. For in this latter view, the community in its political organization was the expression of a social consensus which, by its nature, would fall short of speculative truths.

One of the major techniques for establishing points of fixity was mathematics. If social stability and coherence were important goals, what could be a more suitable basis for political action than that knowledge that dealt with fixed objects of unrivalled symmetry and consistency?[66]

> The legislator must take it as a general principle that there is a universal usefulness in the subdivisions and complications of numbers . . . All must be kept in view by the legislator in his injunction to all citizens, never, so far as they can help it, to rest short of this numerical standardization. For alike in domestic and public life and in all the arts and crafts there is no other single branch of education which has the same potent efficacy as the theory of numbers . . .[67]

This belief, that the political art could transfer the properties of numbers to society and thereby create a more harmonious and regular life, was particularly influential in the political scheme described in the *Laws*. For example, the citizen-body was to be fixed at 5040 because this figure represented not only the optimum size, but also the most useful basis for political calculations. As the figure with "the greatest number of successive divisions," it could be used to divide the citizens for purposes of war, peace, taxation, and administration. By the use of numbers, then, the life of the community would come to reflect the mathematical properties of stability and precision.

But if the one objective was to create points of political fixity, the other was dictated by the contrasting consideration of providing for movement in the social body. It must, however, be a controlled motion: "order in movement is called rhythm." [68] Accordingly, the life of the community ought to express a kind of rhythm, a harmonious movement reflective of its best ideals. "The whole life of man stands in need of rhythm and harmony," and a soul conditioned to rhythmic patterns of ordered harmony was most likely to be drawn "into sympathy and harmony with the beauty of reason." [69] Thus in prescribing the forms of music that were to be admitted into the educational schemes, the public drama, and the religious festivals, art was to assist the aesthetic impulse by transcribing rhythm into the life and character of the community. In the *Republic,* Plato had relied primarily on the ordered structure of classes, where each member contributed a single function to the ordered harmony of the whole — and here justice touched rhythm — but in the *Laws* rhythm was used as a device for social integration as well. [70] The close attention to musical and poetic style, which had been prefigured in the *Republic,* was given a wider meaning in the *Laws,* in keeping with the more enlarged conceptions of unity and harmony that characterized the later dialogue. Whereas the earlier preoccupation had been almost exclusively directed at the unity prevailing in the ruling elite, now, in the absence of a clearly defined governing class living a common life of austerity, a whole community had to be integrated. Towards this end, the life of the community, down to its most intimate aspects, was to be given a common rhythm and ordered motion. Religious rites were to be celebrated at fixed intervals, thereby giving a kind of solemn periodicity to existence; public festivals were to be governed by a set calendar, thus providing regular occasions for the controlled release of popular emotions and enthusiasms; marriage was to be solemnized by annual festivities designed to impress on the participants the public significance of the institution. Out of these regulations, there emerged a triple relation between numbers, rhythm, and order which bound the community to the rhythm of the cosmos itself:

> The grouping of days into monthly periods, and months into years in such fashion that the seasons with their sacrifices and feasts may fit into the true natural order and receive their several proper celebrations, and the city be thus kept alive and alert, its gods enjoying their rightful honors and its men advancing in intelligence of these matters. [71]

IV The search for a selfless instrument. One measure of Plato's influence on Western political thought is the persistency with which later thinkers have clung to the Platonic categories. At almost any given period, it is possible to point to influential theorists who have accepted the belief that "harmony," "unity," "temperance," and "fixity" were not only the fundamental modes of political analysis but the most desirable attributes of a political regime and the fundamental ends of political action. Those political thinkers who have staked out a different path, like Polybius, Machiavelli, Locke, or the authors of the *Federalist Papers,* have, at best, been accorded a certain nuisance value, or relegated to the second rank reserved for unsystematic or untidy theorists. Yet the real problem presented by these anti-Platonists cannot be so easily dismissed. It is the problem of whether the political association has any necessary connection with an eternal truth; or, to say the same thing somewhat differently, whether the sustained pursuit of an ultimate truth does not of necessity destroy the peculiarly political quality of the association.

In directing the political association towards eternal Goods, Plato managed to preserve at least one distinctive aspect of that association. In emphasizing that it ought to be a community in sharing certain common benefits and in his denunciations of all attempts to exploit the political arrangements for the benefit of particular individuals or groups, he had made clear the peculiarly "public" element in political decisions.[72] If one function of political rule was to insure a "public" quality to decisions concerning common benefits, the political association could be partially, although not exhaustively, defined as a community that shared these benefits. It was this qualification on Plato's part, that the notion of the political association could not be exhausted by the benefits derived from a common life, that threatened the political character of the association. The Good at which the Platonic community aimed was in no way dependent on the community, nor was it in any real sense a matter for political decision.

By insisting that the political order must be linked to a transcendent order, Plato could afford to ignore some of the most pressing issues of a truly political character. To be more precise, he succeeded in hollowing out the political content from some basically political conceptions so that they became, if we may put it this way, dangerously irrelevant. This can be shown if we examine Plato's treatment of three basic political ideas: the idea of political obligation, the political community, and the nature of political rule.

Because of the dominating position which he assigned to knowledge, obligation was not a peculiarly political problem for Plato. The knowledge of the Good, which it was the function of the ruler to apply to the community so as to bridge the gap between political existence and true reality, was not really a form of political knowledge at all. It was not a knowledge concerning political matters, such as conflict between groups, the operation of political institutions, the art of leadership, or the problem of when to act and when not to act;[73] rather it was an extra-political knowledge which the ruler came to know, not by observing or acting in politics, but by an education that covered every important subject except the political one. At the same time, Plato maintained that the political association formed a proper vehicle for the realization of the ultimate good. Why was this true? Plato's answer was that the Good was a true good for everyone; that is, it represented the true interest of each. Moreover, since no one would ever knowingly refuse to follow his own true interests, it followed that an art, like the political, which was based on a knowledge of man's true interest, could never injure anyone as long as it was being faithfully observed.[74] Once political authority was armed with this kind of knowledge, it became irrelevant to ask why a subject was obligated to obey its commands. To pose the question in this context would be comparable to asking men to choose between salvation and damnation; it would be neither a question with a real choice, nor a question that was properly political.

The problem of political obligation emerges when conflicting considerations are recurrent, when it is seen that the acceptance of authority involves the individual in a real choice between competing goods, as well as competing evils. Interestingly enough, this had been brought out by Plato himself in the dialogue *Crito*. The condemned Socrates is faced with the choice of escaping the unjust judgment of the city or of taking the hemlock. Suppose he were to take the first alternative, what would be the reply of the city that had wronged him and was now to deprive him of life itself?

> Tell us, Socrates, what are you about? are you not going by an act of yours to overturn us — the laws, and the whole state, as far as in you lies? Do you imagine that a state can subsist and not be overthrown, in which the decisions of law have no power, but are set aside and trampled by individuals? . . . Since you were brought into the world and nurtured and educated by us, can you deny that you are our child and slave, as your fathers were before you? . . . And because we think it right to destroy you, do you think you have any right to destroy us in return? . . . Will you then flee from well-ordered cities and virtuous men? and is existence worth having on those terms? [75]

In making the possibility of injustice the price of civilized living, a genuine problem of political obligation was posed, but in the later dialogues, such as the *Republic* and the *Laws,* it was replaced by a problem of another order: what was the obligation of the philosopher to society? Plato's answer, that the philosopher had an obligation, one that he could be compelled to fulfill only in a society that had encouraged the development of the philosopher, was not an answer to a political question. Political obligation concerns man in his capacity as citizen; whether he is an artisan, a doctor, or a philosopher is not strictly relevant. As a doctor, for example, he may have a duty to his patients or to "society," but in any case, it is not a political duty. The issue of political obligation, then, is not one concerning the philosopher as a citizen, but the citizen who may incidentally be a philosopher.

Plato was led to formulate the question of obligation in terms of the philosopher because of his own belief, mentioned earlier, that the interests of the philosopher and the true interests of society were synonymous. Once the premise was adopted that the true interests of all classes and individuals would be satisfied when society and philosophy were no longer in conflict, then the task became one of insuring that society was ruled by philosophy; that is, ruled not by men but by the principles of true knowledge. But since it was impossible to escape government by men, the primary aim of all social arrangements, and especially of the educational institutions, was to create an elite which would rule not as ordinary men but as selfless instruments.[76] This dream of a vision armed with power, of a small group whose special excellence and knowledge coincided with the good of the whole society, is one that has assumed a variety of forms in the history of political thought. It had been latent in the familiar Greek idea of the Great Legislator, an idea that had fused together myth, legend, and memory to create the archetype of the political hero, the symbol of what uninhibited greatness might accomplish. From the great deeds attributed to a Draco, Solon, Lycurgus, and Cleisthenes, there was drawn the towering figure of the law-giver, sudenly intruding to save the disintegrating life of the *polis* and to re-establish it on a fresh foundation.

The notion that the image of the good society might be so deeply etched into political realities by the hand of a great statesman as to withstand almost indefinitely the eroding forces of conflict and disruption was one that Plato also seemingly shared. In reality, however, he added a new element which was to have a profound impact on later thought. This was the conception of the ruler as the agent of a divine and timeless idea, "in constant companionship with the divine order of the world," and not merely a man of surpassing wisdom or virtue. His task was to mediate between divinity and society, to transform men and their relationships, and to make human society in the image of the divine exemplar. This notion of the ruler as the political embodiment of a *logos* was revived in Hellenistic thought where the king was viewed as the transmitter of a life-giving force, infusing a new élan into men and revitalizing their communities. The ruler, declared Ecphantus, "in so far as he has a sacred and divine mentality he is truly a king; for by obeying this mentality he will cause all good things, but nothing that is evil." [77] Early Christian writers, such as Eusebius, Arian, and Cyril of Jerusalem, carried forward the ancient idea that the good ruler ruled his realms as God ruled the universe, and that the ruler who subordinated himself to the truth announced by Christ could act as a holy instrument in purifying society.[78]

In terms of later political thought, it is important to separate and distinguish some of these tangled skeins, because not all of the later writers visualized the Great Legislator or the Divine Ruler in the same way. Some later writers, such as Machiavelli and Harrington, recurred to the old notion of the great law-giver, but they viewed the legislator not as the agent of a divine idea but as a man of intelligence blessed with a golden opportunity.

> As no man shall show me a Commonwealth born straight, that ever became crooked; so no man shall show me a Commonwealth born crooked that ever became straight . . . a Commonwealth is seldom or never well turned or constituted, except it have been the work of one man.[79]

Others, like James I of England and many of the Royalist writers who supported his cause, disclaimed the argument from the intellectual virtue of the ruler, as well as the conception of the ruler as the intermediary of the *logos*. They were content to claim that kings had been sent by God to supply the political universe with the same kind of direction and control that God displayed in His cosmic realm. Like God, the King was an unmoved mover.

Many of these strands were gathered together in Rousseau's attempt to combine the notion of the Great Legislator with a new vision of the community as the active medium for the expression of the *logos*. To the Legislator was assigned the task of preparing the way for the *logos* by instilling in the citizenry an awareness that each is "part of a greater whole from which in a manner he receives his life and being." [80] But the *logos* itself is only expressed through the will of the members when, and only when, that will fulfills the criterion of generality; when, that is, the individuals transcend their private selves to will the general good of the society. The political order was, in short, potentially self-redemptive. These ideas were given a different form when Marx transferred the actualization of the *logos* from society to a class. The triumph of the proletariat was to mark the realization of a truth that had been immanent in history. When it became necessary to find a more catalytic agent of the *logos,* Lenin advanced the theory of the selfless revolutionary elite. The cycle was now complete, for in the Leninist theory of the Party that guides and prods a lethargic proletariat, we find faint echoes of the divine ruler of Hellenistic thought who labors to infuse into men a *logos* of which they are only dimly conscious.[81]

V The question of power. In order to understand Plato's relationship to these ideas, we must bear in mind the two considerations which governed his choice of the philosopher as the selfless instrument of a divine truth. One was the conviction that no political order could long endure unless its rulers sought to govern in the interests of the whole community. The other related to Plato's deep and abiding suspicion of absolute power, a consideration that has been frequently passed over by Plato's critics.[82] Plato's argument for entrusting the philosopher with absolute power did not originate in a naïve attitude towards the temptations of power, much less in the secret craving for *étatisme*. It came, instead, from two entirely blameless aims, the good of the whole and the avoidance of tyranny. In the figure of the philosopher-statesman these two objectives were to be reconciled. As a philosopher the ruler possessed a knowledge of the true ends of the community. He was the servant of a truth untouched by his own subjective preferences or desires; of a truth he had discovered but not invented.[83] At the same time, the character of the ruler was to be tempered by influences that would supplement the discipline of philosophy, by strict control over education, family life, living arrangements, and property. These were intended as part of a conditioning in self-denial and austerity which would produce selfless rulers, impervious to those temptations of power and pleasure that goaded the tyrant beyond endurance.

> . . . Whom else can you compel to undertake the guardianship of the commonwealth, if not those who, besides understanding best the principles of government, enjoy a nobler life than the politicians and look for rewards of a different kind? [84]

The real difficulty, Plato suggested, would lie in persuading the philosophers to abandon their contemplation of eternal objects for a turn of duty in the "cave" of politics. Yet the reluctance of the philosopher would be proof of his selflessness, and his ultimate commitment to philosophy the guarantee of his disinterestedness. "You can have a well-governed society only if you can discover for your future rulers a better way of life than being in office . . ." [85] That the very loftiness of the philosophic life might leave the future ruler ill-equipped for the rough-and-tumble of political life was a thought which Plato never seriously entertained.

The beneficence of Plato's ruler was not the product of a passionless nature. The philosopher by definition had a "passion for wisdom" which could not be stilled until he had come to know the essential nature of each thing. [86] His was the only vocation where "acquisitiveness" could be allowed, because the knowledge of the Good for which he strove was a type of knowledge that contained inherent limits; that is, a knowledge of the Good, by definition, did not entail knowledge for evil. Unlike those who panted after wealth and power, the lover of wisdom was not in competition with his fellow-citizens, nor did he gain his ends at the expense of his neighbor's. His was the only appetite that benefited the community as a whole. Whereas in most polities the political contests arose out of a competition for the limited goods of power, office, wealth, and prestige, the Platonic rulers would direct their acquisitive instincts toward the inexhaustible and immaterial goods of knowledge. The realm of philosophy knew no "politics"; ambition had been sublimated into the quest for wisdom.

The passionate nature ascribed to the philosopher throws an interesting light on Plato's conception of the community. The philosopher's quest for knowledge was fired by *eros,* and this deep longing of the purified soul not only drove the philosopher to seek unity with knowledge but also created a deep bond with those dedicated to a similar end. Yet while the seekers of knowledge were thus unified by a common impulse, the unity of the society at large was a vicarious benefit of the philosopher's search. Thus *eros* might bind philosophers together, but not them to the community, or the members of the community to each other. It required the Christian notion of *agape* before there could be an idea of love as a force fusing together a community. [87]

It was also Plato's belief that a selfless ruling group, dedicated not to politics but to philosophy, would solve the problem of absolute power. In existing societies, where the rulers were selected by irrational methods, absolute power was bound not only to corrupt the rulers, but to degrade the citizenry as well. The citizen of the Platonic community, however, would be benefited by the exercise of absolute power, because, in the last analysis, he would be compelled and controlled not by a personal power but by the impersonal agents of a timeless truth. The subject was to be under "the same principle as his superior, who is himself governed by the divine element within him." [88] The truth superior over ruler and ruled alike was by definition in the true interests of both. Since no man seeks to will other than his true interests, it followed that no man's will was being compelled when it was made to conform to these interests. The political principle that flows from these considerations is that when political power is joined to knowledge it loses its compulsive element. In this way, political power becomes etherealized into principle.

This argument also held some important implications for the community. By transforming power into principle, Plato could define the citizen as one who shared in the benefits flowing from that principle. This stands in contrast to the Aristotelian notion of the citizen as one who shared in the power of the *polis*. In Plato's scheme, there was no power to share; what was sharable was the Form of the Good written into the structure of the community. The results of this line of argument were two-fold: the idea of citizenship was severed from the idea of meaningful participation in the making of political decisions; and the idea of the political community, that is, a community that seeks to resolve its internal conflicts through political methods, is replaced by the idea of the virtuous community devoid of conflict and, therefore, devoid of "politics." Plato did not deny that each member of the community, no matter how humble his contribution, had a right to share the benefits of the community; what he did deny was that this contribution could be erected into a claim to share in political decision-making.

This marked one of the crucial points at which Aristotle diverged from his master. In rejecting Plato's sharp demarcation between an active ruling group and a politically passive community, Aristotle came closer to the practice of Athenian democracy where the basic distinction had been between those who were citizens and those who were not. This is not to make of Aristotle a partisan of democracy, but rather to insist on the significance of his returning to the notion that the political community was synonymous with the whole of the citizenry. A citizen, in Aristotle's definition, was one who participated in legislative and judicial deliberations. [89] The claim to participate flowed from the contribution made by the citizen to the true end of the political association. What saved this definition from the narrowness of Plato's was the tolerant admission by Aristotle that there were several kinds of goods proper to a political community. Neither knowledge nor virtue, much less wealth or birth, were defensible foundations for an exclusive claim to political power. [90] Goodness might have a higher claim than any other virtue, yet the nature of the political association was that of a self-sufficient whole, and this end of self-sufficiency was possible only through diverse contributions. The claim to participate, therefore, arose from a person's contribution to the civilized life of the community. From the citizen's point of view, however, it represented something more. Citizenship connoted the right of an individual to live in the only form of association that allowed him to develop his capacities to the fullest. In this sense, participation was a claim flowing from the nature of man. In Aristotle's words, man was born for citizenship.[91]

Plato's criticism of political participation grew directly out of his distinction between political knowledge and political "opinion." In the Platonic scale, "opinion" occupied an intermediate position between knowledge and incorrect belief. It was a compound of half-truths and correct beliefs imperfectly understood. It also represented the sort of crude notions carried around in the head of the average person. To allow the average person to participate in political decisions was to pave the way for government by "opinion." In other words, "opinion" did not constitute a relevant form of political knowledge; this could come only from a true science of politics.

VI **Political knowledge and political participation.** Plato's distrust of political participation, then, rested on a definite notion of what constituted a relevant source of political knowledge. If a case is to be made for popular participation, it would have to be shown that Plato's conception of political knowledge was unduly narrow and that a more adequate conception, one that would be more in keeping with the nature of political decisions, is directly connected to a more inclusive scheme of participation. The first thing to be noted is that Plato vastly exaggerated the degree of precision that political knowledge might attain. The belief that political science was a body of absolute knowledge was closely connected with the static character that Plato attributed to the objects of knowledge; there could be no valid knowledge where the objects of thought were changing and lacking in proportion. Conversely, because the true objects of thought were fixed, unchanging, and symmetrical, it was possible for thought to achieve an absolute precision and accuracy. But Plato's argument about the absolute character of political knowledge was not the consequence of a close examination of politics or of political situations, but was drawn from other fields, from mathematics or the skilled arts, like medicine or weaving or piloting. This is not to say, as some writers have, that Plato was singularly blind to political experience; this would be to ignore not only Plato's personal acquaintance with the political personalities and problems of his own day, but also the way in which this experience is reproduced at many points in the dialogues. The contention, instead, is that his notion of an absolutely valid political philosophy was not, in the first instance, shaped by the nature of political phenomena. It was inspired by the impressive precision attained in science, mathematics and medicine. But if one were to assert that the possible precision in a particular discipline is conditioned by the nature of its subject-matter, then a certain humility is in order. At no time in the history of political thought has this point been made so tellingly as by Plato's greatest pupil:

> Our discussion will be adequate if it has as much clearness as the subject-matter admits of, for precision is not to be sought for alike in all discussions, any more than in all the products of the crafts. Now fine and just actions, which political science investigates, admit of much variety and fluctuation of opinion . . . We must be content, then, in speaking of such subjects and with such premises to indicate the truth roughly and in outline, and in speaking about things which are only for the most part true and with premises of the same kind to reach conclusions that are no better . . . It is the mark of an educated man to look for precision in each class of things just so far as the nature of the subject admits; it is evidently equally foolish to accept probable reasoning from a mathematician and to demand from a rhetorician scientific proofs.[92]

Aristotle's remarks are all the more significant when placed in the context of a philosophy that stressed growth, change, and movement. Although the Aristotelian universe was one wherein purpose (*telos*) was writ large, it was still a universe full of the tensions and striving summed up in the idea of potentiality (*dynamis*). Nature itself was defined at one point as "a principle of motion and rest, in respect of place, or of growth and decrease, or by way of alteration."[93] Within this framework, political science was conceived as an art that assisted and completed nature. At the same time, however, it was a practical and not a purely theoretic science. Its end was action, but action within a situation fraught with change, accident, and contingency.[94] To expect mathematical precision in political theory was foolish, and to arm the practitioners of political science with absolute power was dangerously arrogant.[95]

Once the incomplete nature of political science is established it becomes possible to question the Platonic position from another side. Plato argued that the only relevant political knowledge was that possessed by a trained elite. From one point of view, this position is unassailable: expert knowledge is the preserve of the few. Yet the problem is more complex than this. It is whether expert knowledge is the only relevant form of knowledge for making political judgments. The problem, then, turns on the nature of a political judgment. What are the criteria of a political judgment? Do these criteria demand the admission of two kinds of political knowledge, one popular and the other expert, both of which are relevant and neither of which is sufficient by itself? Some answer to these questions is provided if we return to Plato's notion of "opinion" and try to reformulate it. His hostility towards "opinion" was, as we have noted, bound up with the conviction that a true political judgment was one deriving from a special insight into the eternal Forms of knowledge. In opposition to this, the argument here is that this is not a type of political judgment at all. The issue is not the existence of an immutable truth, nor whether men can make judgments derived from that source, but whether this kind of truth and judgment has any relevant connection to the special nature of the political association. If one of the main functions of the political association is to render "public" judgments in those situations where the plans, aspirations, and claims of its members are in conflict; and if, at the same time, it is an association that desires to retain a sense of community among its members — if, in other words, it is to be not only a community of well-being but of belonging — then there must of necessity be some clearly defined procedures whereby the "opinions" of the membership may be incorporated into the decisions affecting that community.

Potentially, opinions are the means for enhancing the politicalness of the society if they can be made to express a sense of involvement on the part of the members. What is all-important politically is not that the individual member formulate notions about his personal needs or hopes, but that he express a "public" opinion. This is possible if he comes to recognize that his personal life is implicated with the functioning of the political society; if, in other words, he perceives a relation between what is troubling him as a person and what the society is seeking in terms of general goals and purposes. This perception of the connection between what is private and what is public, between a "particular" opinion and a "public" opinion, represents the first awkward step towards political consciousness, because the member is required to state private needs, grievances or aspirations in a public manner. In other words, an opinion becomes politically relevant when it transcends the merely private concerns of the individual, when it can be related to what is general and shown to be a common problem.

This notion of the function of "opinions" can be enlarged by acknowledging Aristotle's insight that among the most important and exacting tasks of government in a civilized society is the distribution of various goods, such as public office and power, social recognition and prestige, wealth and privilege.[96] The question posed by the distributive role of government is: from what elements ought a judgment about distribution be fashioned? In maintaining that community "opinions" ought to be a vital element, the central issue does not revolve around the truth or falsity of these opinions, but around the special kind of rationality demanded of a judgment that is to apply to the whole community.

What, then, are the criteria governing a political judgment? What qualities distinguish a "political" judgment from other kinds of judgment? One possible way of answering these questions is to ask whether the adjective "political" has had a more or less stable meaning throughout the tradition of Western political thought. In later pages, it will be shown that this has been the case, but here we shall only state that the "political" has been employed repeatedly to designate what is "public." The "public" quality of a judgment has had two senses: a judgment, a policy, or a decision has been considered as truly public when expressed by an authoritative person or persons, that is by an authority recognized by the community; secondly, a judgment has been accepted as genuinely public when it appears to possess a general character, for only what is general is capable of application to the society as a whole.

Now the search for generality soon leads to a further criterion, because the formulation of a general policy or judgment attempts to find a rule applicable to all in roughly the same way, but persons and situations are so varied that the attempt must either be given up or the formulation must be somewhat crude and oversimplified. This is the basic dilemma of political judgments: how to create a common rule in a context of differences? The dilemma cannot be overcome, but what is possible is to lessen the crudities of the judgment. It is this hope that has inspired the third criterion of "political comprehensiveness."

To satisfy the criterion of political comprehensiveness a judgment has to be evaluated in the light of questions like the following: is the judgment, in its factual aspects, attentive to the actual tendencies of political forces, such as the attitudes and strategies of active social groups, the state of economic relationships, and other politically relevant factors? and is the judgment one that will be in accord with the dominant values held by the major groups in the society?

Procedures of this kind obviously encourage a strong element of expediency in political judgments, and expediency is usually regarded as having at least a faintly immoral quality about it. It connotes a departure from a known standard of right. Granting that a political judgment may be expedient in this sense, the question is: why does it happen so frequently? One answer is that political actors develop a blunted moral sense and are quite willing to sacrifice moral niceties in order to retain power and prestige. But this is a poor explanation, because it does less than justice to the anguish of the political actor who earnestly seeks to do right but finds that other considerations intervene. What I am suggesting here is that expediency is largely the result of the old problem of trying to establish a uniform rule amidst a context of differences. It is this that frequently leads to concessions and modifications in a policy. The reason is not simply that it is a good thing to formulate policies that will reflect a sensitivity to variations and differences throughout the society, but rather that a political society is simultaneously trying to act and to remain a community.

These considerations permit us to see more clearly the connection between political decisions and political participation or citizenship. The numerous acts whereby the citizen takes part in the political processes of the society help contribute to the comprehensiveness, and generality, of decisions; they are the methods for expressing the differences resident in society and thus make it possible that better informed judgments will emerge. Unfortunately, however, this does not solve the problem of action, for the unescapable fact is that, inevitably, any significant public policy or judgment directly benefits some more than others; a program of free lunches for school children is of more immediate benefit to the children and their families than it is to the bachelor who pays taxes to support the program. As both Plato and Aristotle recognized, political decisions are rarely of a general kind in the sense that the individuals or groups affected are treated exactly the same.[97] Policies concerned with benefits, such as public payments to the poor, or with burdens, such as taxes or military service, must of necessity be based on some discriminatory scheme of classification. From this viewpoint, general agreements are necessary preludes to discrimination; they supply the vital acquiescence that enables the political art to fashion "rational" schemes of classification; that is, discriminations that will be sensitive not only to technical problems but to their political consequences as well.[98] Participation is the basic method for establishing areas of agreement or political consensus.

For these reasons it is fatuous to assert, as one recent writer has, that "agreement may produce peace but it cannot produce truth."[99] The agreement that issues from participation is not intended as a symbol of truth but as a tangible expression of that sense of belonging which forms a vital dike against the forces of *anomie*. In its political aspect, a community is not held together by truth but by consensus. The range and nature of the consensus that a society arrives at exerts a strong and often determining influence upon the particular decisions made by a society, causing a modification in both means and ends different from what an "objective" or purely technical judgment might dictate. This gives to political judgments a character different from that of a "true" philosophical or theological proposition. In large measure, a political judgment is usually "judicial" in quality; that is, for the most part it involves a judgment concerning conflicting claims, all of which possess a certain validity. As Aristotle shrewdly pointed out, there is no problem of political judgment when one claim alone is admitted to be valid and enthroned above all the rest. The result of this condition, however, is that the political association is replaced by the state of siege.[100] But once the political association is defined as a compound of many diverse parts, and once it is allowed that these "parts" will have different opinions, interests, and claims, the politicalness of the judgment will depend on a sensitivity to diversities. A political judgment, in other words, is "true" when it is public, not public when it accords to some standard external to politics.

VII The limits of unity. Given the nature of political judgment, a quite different light is cast upon the art of political rule and its relation to unity. Plato had insisted upon the totality of unity. In the *Republic,* unity derived primarily from the virtue and wisdom that bound together the ruling groups and flowed from there to the rest of the society; the second great source of unity was provided by the ordered structure of functions assigned to each individual. In the *Laws,* the end of total unity remained the same, but there was less reliance upon a small elite as the conduit through which the forces of unity flowed to the remainder of the society. By means of meticulous legal regulations, which were to be preserved unalterably, the whole range of human existence was to be shaped towards unity. The difference in method between the two dialogues does not destroy the essential similarity in approach; in both cases unity was conceived to be the product of an imposed vision. The vision of the Good, whether it was located with the philosopher-statesman or written into the fabric of the laws, decreed that the aim of the ruler's art was to nurture souls, an aim that could be attained only if the community were at one in feeling and sentiment.

The Platonic conception of unity was criticized by Aristotle on the grounds that it had mistaken mere unison for harmony. A political association, Aristotle wisely noted, could become so unified that it would cease to be a political association.[101] Although Aristotle did not surrender the essentially Platonic belief that the political community ought to aim at the highest good, the significant point is that this belief was also accompanied by the idea that there were other goods that the community ought to recognize and promote. In this view, the political art is concerned to combine and mediate among the various goods that contribute to the self-sufficiency of the whole. Accordingly, while justice remains the ordering principle of the political association, justice itself has been widened to embrace the notion of political conciliation.[102] The political art has to do with the reconciliation of a wide range of valid claims.

Before we can push past the point reached by Aristotle and ask whether it is not to inflict the political order with an impossible task when it is burdened with ministering to the souls of its members, it is first necessary to clarify the notion of political unity implied by the foregoing. Plato was correct in emphasizing that a common set of values and purposes was necessary if a society was to express its solidarity and to act purposefully.[103] It does not follow, however, that this aspect of unity must be extended to every aspect of life or even to every important aspect of life. Unity, in short, is not synonymous with uniformity, as Plato was inclined to think that it was. The basic political importance of unity is that it is economical of a society's energies. An area of unity, such as in religion, economic arrangements, or political rights, symbolizes an area of agreement, or at least of acceptance, which no longer troubles a society. Energy and thought, therefore, can be directed at those matters where disagreement and conflict exist. To put it somewhat differently, an area of agreement provides the foundation for statecraft; it permits political authority to deal with areas of difference with the assurance that some problems have been temporarily solved. The metaphor might be slightly altered to point to one other contribution of unity; that is, it serves as a stepping stone from an area of agreement to one of disagreement. A society that agrees on some matters is more likely to accept policies dealing with more controversial subjects. In this way, it affords to government a certain amount of room for maneuver. When a measure of unity exists, government can engage in the fine art of accommodating the continual thrusts of groups and can embark on a sensitive exploration of those areas where the community can be made to "give" without snapping, where some groups will tolerate distasteful policies because there are so many other matters on which they are at one with the rest of society.

Finally, unity is a necessary precondition for that most demanding of the political arts, the knowledge when not to act — *quieta non movere*. Like any human organization, a government has a limited amount of energy. When it is extended too far, when it tries to do too much, it trails off into impotence. This means that one of the continuing tasks of statecraft is to discover at what points disagreement, conflict, and variety may be tolerated without their endangering the supporting framework that makes waywardness possible. Any society, in other words, tends to be a collection of imperfectly integrated particularities. As Hobbes later pointed out, the interaction of the particular purposes of individuals and groups within a situation of limited goods was bound to eventuate in conflict. Alongside the scarcity of goods was their relativity. Wealth, status, and privilege hold no meaning in society except on a comparative basis; there would be no bourgeoisie in the absence of a proletariat or an aristocracy, and no *droit de seigneur* without the *gabelle*. The relativity of social goods creates a condition where both the preservation of existing expectancies and the satisfactions of fresh demands can only be met at the expense of less favored groups. Moreover, the sources of conflict are enlarged by other factors that were operative in Plato's day and are with us still. At various stages of their development, Western societies have been afflicted by strains and upheaval which no one plans or intends. Cumulative disturbances, such as those which were registered in ancient Greece — war, colonization, monetary changes, technological innovation, economic depression, class dislocation, and the unsettling effects of contacts with different cultures — help to exacerbate the tensions and antagonisms already existing in society.

Given these considerations, it was highly improbable that a "logic" for politics could be fashioned from the Platonic categories of beauty, fixity, or harmony, much less from the concept of a unity unmarred by contradictory elements. The final term of a political logic is not q.e.d., because finality is the most elusive quality of a political solution. The order of problems with which political judgment has to deal is concerned with the achievement of tentative stabilities within a situation of conflict. Hence an adequate political logic must be framed to cope with contraries and dissymmetries arising out of a mobile and conflict-laden situation. Its tutelary deity is Proteus, not Procrustes.

A logic of this kind would be warranted by the ample evidence provided by Western political societies for the proposition that contraries and conflicts have been able to coexist almost indefinitely without destroying the necessary unity of a society. Men of the same society have disagreed about the nature of the gods, the distribution of economic rewards, political arrangements, and the nature of the good; and yet such conflicts have not always issued in social and political upheaval. The reason for this has been two-fold: the existence of substantial areas of agreement which have offset the centrifugal forces and, secondly, the ability of rulers to confine conflicts to their narrowest possible dimensions. To elaborate this last point a little more, political rule tends to be less effective over a long pull when it follows the simple policy of repressing conflicts. It has been most successful when it has pursued a policy of preventing potential sources of conflict from feeding each other. The danger point is not the existence of economic conflict, political grievance, or religious disagreement, but the convergence of these frustrations, such as happened in the religious wars of the sixteenth century and the English Civil Wars of the next century. The art of governance, then, must be aimed at achieving temporary stabilities and partial syntheses; at equilibrating some social forces, while carefully tolerating others. The art of the statesman is the art of dealing with the incomplete. For this reason, the Platonic conception of the ruler who imposes a unified vision is fatally defective to the ruler's art. The very completeness of the vision would inevitably tend to provoke extreme reactions which would fatally weaken the unity it was intended to insure. Philosophic and religious differences would become heresies; political disputes a sign of sedition; and economic conflicts a contest between vice and virtue. At the same time, the resolution of such conflicts would be more difficult by reason of the special knowledge upon which unity was supposed to rest. A knowledge cannot be at one and the same time accessible to the few and yet serve as the vital bond holding the entire community together. The principles of belief that cement a community together must be shared; they must be a "public" kind of knowledge.

VIII The ambiguities of Plato. In the preceding pages, the political ideas of Plato have been selected to illustrate a certain perspective on political phenomena. In using Plato as a "type," there has inevitably been a certain amount of distortion, for a philosophy so subtle, so full of irony and poetry, cannot but be streaked by twists and sudden turns which cut athwart the main tendencies. The greatest mistake a student can make is to assume that Plato, like Aquinas or Hobbes, was a thinker severely and angularly systematic. In Plato we confront a thinker with his full share of doubts, ambiguities, and anguishing dilemmas:

> . . . Wandering between two worlds, one dead,
> The other powerless to be born . . .[104]

We have already pointed out that Plato was troubled by a very lively fear about the abuse of political power. Surely this was uppermost in his mind when time and again he recurred to the theme that the greatest of all evils was to inflict injustice — a strange position for one who is reputed to be a totalitarian.[105] It is possible, too, to interpret the device of the "royal fiction" or lie as an attempt on Plato's part to limit the use of violence by resorting to deception.

Taken in the round, Plato's writings were not an unvarnished *apologia* for despotism, but a body of ideas with an unresolved contradiction. He was convinced that philosophy contained the saving knowledge that alone could bring happiness to society, yet he remained painfully aware that knowledge could only be translated into practice by the method he distrusted most, an act of power. Although he tried to resolve these two beliefs in the idea of the philosopher-king, he remained distinctly apprehensive over any lesser arrangement. He knew too well the meaning of power.

In the *Laws,* the ambiguities become more pronounced. The need for knowledge was expressed with the same urgency as before, but it is accompanied by a greater emphasis on the value of moderation in all things, including intellectual pursuits:

> . . . If any one gives too great a power to anything, too large a sail to a vessel, too much food to the body, too much authority to the mind, and does not observe the mean, everything is overthrown, and, in the wantonness of excess runs in the one case to disorders, and in the other to injustice, which is the child of excess. I mean to say, my dear friends, that there is no soul of man, young and irresponsible, who will be able to sustain the temptation of arbitrary power.[106]

This theme is reflected also in the constitution of the *polis* which is to be a blend of democratic liberty and the wisdom found only in the one or few. Concessions are made also to the knowledge that comes from experience; to the necessity for making some gestures towards satisfying popular opinion; to a wider conception of political participation; and to the principle of the accountability of the magistrates. All of these tendencies, unfortunately, were offset by the cramping rigidities of legal controls and the reappearance of the philosopher-rulers in the form of the Nocturnal Council. The political system depicted in the *Laws,* may, by courtesy, be called a *Rechtsstaat,* as one commentator has urged, yet it would be more accurate to call it a frozen *Rechtsstaat.*

More striking than any other ambiguity was an essentially tragic theme which intruded like an alien visitor to darken a scene made bright by the promise of a saving knowledge. Coupled with the conviction that human reason could aspire to absolute and immutable truth was the conflicting conviction that once men had joined practice and theory, once the pattern of perfection had become embodied in actual arrangements, an inevitable process of deterioration set in. The works of men were powerless to escape the dissolving taint of sensible creations.[107] A cycle of creation, decay, and dissolution ruled the world with an iron grip, and only at rare intervals could the art of men intervene to wrest one brief moment of seeming immortality. Even the best of constitutions, such as that sketched in the *Republic,* was not immune:

> Hard as it may be for a state so framed to be shaken, yet, since all that comes into being must decay, even a fabric like this will not endure for ever, but will suffer dissolution.[108]

The concluding note of Plato's political science is not of an unlimited arrogance that man can fashion a polity untouched by time, but of a heroism chastened by the foreknowledge of eventual defeat. It is, in Shelley's words, "Eternity warning Time."

✑ THREE ✑

The Age of Empire:
Space and Community

Will you take your children into Thessaly and deprive them of Athenian citizenship?

PLATO

I am a citizen of Greece.

LYSIAS

You are a citizen of the universe . . .

EPICTETUS

I **The crisis in the political.** Much has been written by modern scholars about the failure of classical political thought to transcend the narrow unity of the city-state. It has been alleged that the ideas of Plato and Aristotle were so closely bound to the fortunes of this tiny political entity that, when the *polis* gave way to the larger empires of Macedonia and Rome, the parochial assumptions of their ideas were exposed: assumptions about the racial homogeneity of the population, the optimum size of the political community, and a social structure that would allow a small part of the population sufficient leisure for political affairs. There is no question that these beliefs made classical political thought appear hopelessly municipal in an era where the conditions of existence were imperial. A comparable indictment was later

69

laid against Rousseau. He was charged with favoring a political model based on the Genevan city-state at a time when the nation-state was everywhere taking hold. Yet in the cases both of Rousseau and of Plato and Aristotle this kind of easy criticism misses the mark. The essential questions raised by these political thinkers were: how far could the boundaries of political space be extended, how much dilution by numbers could the notion of citizen-participant withstand, how minor need be the "public" aspect of decisions before the political association ceased to be political?

Looked at in this way, the political thought of Plato and Aristotle suffered not so much from being parochial as from being strongly political. The association that they had in mind was "political" for several reasons. It served needs that no other association could; it was reflective of a part of the individual's life that he lived in common with other men; it was a whole compounded of measurable contributions made by its members, and hence its quality was no better or worse than that of its citizens. In short, the association was political because it dealt with subjects of common concern, and because all of the members were implicated in a common life. As Aristotle had remarked, it was quite possible to enclose the whole of the Peloponnese by a single wall, yet this would not create a *polis*.[1]

Even before the death of Aristotle in 322 B.C., the classical concept of the "political" was being undermined by a new set of conditions. The emergence of the Macedonian Empire in the fourth century inaugurated an era of large-scale organization which later reached its fullest expression in the Roman world-state. During this period, the tradition of Western political thought underwent a transformation that resulted in drastic modifications of the notational principles governing the accents of classical political philosophy. New priorities appeared, emphases were redistributed, and the phenomena of political life were surveyed from an altered perspective. Yet the political thought of the Hellenistic and Roman period retained much that was familiar. The legacy of Plato and Aristotle was preserved while being modified; a tradition of political thought was in the making.

Although a comprehensive analysis of these developments is impossible within the limits of the present study, the main theme of the relationship between politics and political thought can be illuminated by emphasizing a few selected problems. The method to be followed will be topical rather than chronological. The first problem chosen is the revolutionary challenge to political thought posed by the fact that the *polis* had ceased to be *the* politically significant unit. It was overlain by giant state forms which lacked the attributes of strongly political societies and which, when judged by the canons of classical political thought, appeared as monstrous aberrations. The growing disparity between the new actualities of political life and the political criteria of classical Greek thought provoked an intellectual crisis which persisted down to the advent of Christianity. Beginning in the Hellenistic age the attempt was repeatedly made to adjust the categories of political thought to the unprecedented situation where masses of men, scattered over great distances and differentiated by race and culture, had been gathered into a single society and governed by a single authority. This continuity of preoccupation with the nature of the political in an age of empire will be traced from the philosophic theories of the Hellenistic period down to the Roman writers of the early Christian era.

The second broad problem that I have singled out pertains to the politics of the Roman Republic during the period from roughly 150 B.C. to the establishment of the Augustan Principate in 27 B.C. The expansion of Rome from a typically small city-state to a huge empire was primarily accomplished during the days of the republic. The attempt to govern this enormous space while retaining the values and institutions of a small political community imposed severe strains on the system. At the same time, the tension between the demands of space and the design of institutions was accompanied by an intensification of political conflict and rivalry. By examining the response of Roman writers to this situation, it is possible to expose with a sharper emphasis some of the implications of certain political problems that had been obscured by the homogeneity of the Greek *polis:* problems of the admissible limits of political conflict, the role of institutions in containing and ordering these conflicts, and, above all, the implications of conducting politics on the basis of interests.

Before turning to these problems, a brief word on some special difficulties for the study of Roman political ideas. Although there is no dearth of material for the student of Roman political practices, the student of political ideas must deal with a period notoriously lacking in great political thinkers. To compound the difficulty, what little there was in the way of systematic theory proves on closer analysis to be more often Greek than Roman in origin. But if the absence of systematic thought is considered along with the universally acknowledged contribution of Rome in the fields of law and political institutions, the combination of the two suggests, not that we ignore Roman political thought, but that we handle it differently than we would a formal system such as Plato's. More concretely, it means that we take seriously the commonplace judgment that the Romans were a "practical" rather than a theoretical people, or, to state the matter more correctly, that they were a people whose political thinking was centered upon questions of immediate action.

II **The new dimensions of space.** In the course of a long speech contained in the *Annals,* Tacitus has Tiberius explaining the contrast between the moral austerity of the old Rome with the profligacy of contemporary society by saying that in the old days self-restraint was practiced "because we were all members of one city. Not even afterwards had we the same temptations, while our dominion was confined to Italy." [2] This allusion to the loss of civic intimacy consequent on the expansion of the Roman Empire can serve as introduction to one of the great problems of post-Aristotelian political thought, the theoretical implications of the new spatial dimension. The philosophical issues that accompanied the appearance of large governmental units concerned both the relevancy and the validity of the classical meaning of "political." The etymological meaning of political had been "concerning the *polis*," while in terms of political philosophy it had related to the knowledge and actions that would help or harm the community. Yet the main point was that in Greek thought the concept of the political had become identified with the determinate spatial dimension of the *polis.* The rigid limits that Plato and Aristotle had set for the size and population of their ideal cities and the detailed attention that they devoted to matters of birth control, wealth and commerce, colonial and military expansion were part of their belief that the life of the *polis,* which they considered synonymous with its political character, could be articulated only within the narrow confines of the small city-state. This total absorption with a small, highly compact community imparted to Greek political thought a nervous intensity which contrasts sharply, for example, with the mood of later Stoicism which leisurely, and without the sense of compelling urgency, contemplated political life as it was acted out amidst a setting as spacious as the universe itself. Greek thought had been intense because it had accepted the challenge of prescribing actions for a political condition that was at once tightly packed yet highly volatile. This is easily sensed in Plato's critical analysis of democracy. Despite the humorous vein that colored his description, he was obviously and deeply disturbed by democracy's extreme social mobility, the release of destructive energies that followed in its wake, and the system of lot and election that seemed intent upon making instability a permanent feature of political life. Accordingly, Plato's solution, in part, was shaped to overcome the jostling anarchy unendurable in a crowded political condition. By clearly defining the functions that each class was to discharge, by discouraging movement from one class to another, the new structure of political space would be protected from random movements.

The highly developed consciousness of political space in Greek philosophy was the direct reflection of an actual political world wherein a multitude of small independent cities, driven by the dynamics of ambition, class struggle, population pressures, and economic disequilibrium impinged upon each other and found it difficult to act without colliding.[3] This sense of being hemmed in was written large in Greek politics in the attempts to ease internal pressures by establishing colonies, exploring new commercial routes, or developing imperial dependencies. On the other hand, it was significant that what little discussion was given by Plato and Aristotle to the problems of foreign policy and interstate relations took the form of a warning about the moral consequences of war and expansion, especially as these were directed against other Greeks.[4] That the reaction of the two greatest Greek thinkers should have been a moralistic one was evidence of the deeply introspective quality of Greek political thought, of its tendency to turn all political problems inward. Fear and suspicion of the "outside" was the psychological accompaniment of an inability to think politically in terms of an area broader than the *polis*. By refusing to seek solutions through the redefinition of political space, the Greeks were thrown back to containing the vitalities of political life within suffocating limits. The result was a species of theory filled with tensions, tensions created by economic conflicts, the growing demand for extension of political rights, and the circle of rival cities pressing on the outer edges of the *polis*.

On the institutional level, some attempt at reconstructing the spatial dimension of political life was made through the experiments with federal organizations and other systems for concerting the military and diplomatic efforts of several allied cities.[5] Some of these progressed to the point of breaking down the rigid conceptions of citizenship. Thus under the arrangement called "isopolity," a citizen of one city enjoyed citizenship in all of the member cities; in another form of federation, "sympolity," the citizen of the individual city also possessed membership in the federal union. Important as these experiments are in reminding us of the transitional phase occurring between the decline of the *polis* and the appearance of the Macedonian world-monarchy, their failure to attain theoretical embodiment indicates that they lay outside the meaning of "political" as it had come to be defined by the major writers. Examples of leagues, alliances, and confederations can be found as far back as the sixth century B.C., yet none of this experience was embodied in Platos' thought. Again, as is well known, Aristotle's association with the empire-builder Alexander left little impression upon the Peripatetic philosopher.[6] The reason for this is not that these philosophers were obtuse, but rather that, according to the form given political philosophy at the Academy, these broader political arrangements did not appear to raise genuine philosophical issues. The practice of federalism, for example, called for a knowledge of techniques: how to conduct a foreign policy representing several states instead of one? what standard ought to be used in assigning representatives to the deliberative and executive organs? how to apportion taxation and administer a common treasury? Important and significant as these questions were, they did not seem to go to the root of the problem as it had come to be defined in political philosophy; that is, what is the nature and quality of the life that men could attain in a political association? In other words, it was assumed that questions of techniques constituted second-order problems which could be discussed and acted upon without seriously disturbing the first-order problems. This is precisely what occurred in these experiments. They never succeeded in dislodging or modifying the political, social, and cultural primacy of the *polis*.

The identification of politics with *paideia,* that is, with the moral and cultural education of the membership, and the corollary belief that the extension of the *polis* meant the destruction of the only dimension within which the *paideia* of the members could be furthered, were tested during the fourth century when Persian and Macedonian pressures began to awaken the Greeks to the realization that internecine warfare among the Greek cities had exposed the entire Hellenic world to outside domination. Among the dramatists, political writers, and politicians, there appeared a growing consciousness of the unity of Hellas.[7] Yet Panhellenism, too, was unable to modify the stubborn conviction that political space could never be divided in any meaningful way except according to the specifications of the moral mission of the *polis*.

Nevertheless, there were minor political writers, such as Gorgias,* Isocrates,** and Demosthenes,† who sought to arouse the Greeks to the urgent

---

* Gorgias (*cir.* 480-380 B.C.) was born in Sicily and achieved prominence as a sophist and rhetorician. He was one among several writers urging Panhellenism.

** Isocrates (436-338 B.C.) was a famous Athenian orator and rhetorician who had studied under Gorgias and Socrates. Although not a profound thinker, he had recognized, nevertheless, the need for constructive action to deal with the incessant conflicts among the Greek city-states. He had argued that unity of policy was possible because of the common culture shared by the Greeks. On this basis, he championed a common foreign policy against the Persians.

need of overcoming the rivalries engendered by city-state particularism. It was significant, however, that all of these writers were rhetors or sophists; that is, they belonged to the groups that traditionally were concerned with techniques and means, and none of them appears, on the basis of the surviving evidence, to have raised the fundamenal theoretical implications consequent upon these experiments in a wider unity. Isocrates, for example, had been conscious that the supreme difficulty lay in the way that political space had come to be organized: "It is the polities by which they govern their states that have divided most of them." [8] Although Isocrates was able to project the idea of an Hellenic unity — "the title 'Hellenes' is applied rather to those who share our culture than to those who share a common blood" — it was in no sense a picture of a new kind of political society. The distinctive identity of each city was to be retained, and the only problem was to persuade the other cities that to Athens belonged the rightful hegemony over the whole. The whole argument rested on the belief that if the destructive energies of the Greeks were turned against an outside power, in this case Persia, there would be no need to alter the existing way of life in the separate *poleis*.[9] That the Panhellenic sentiments voiced by Isocrates rested on nothing more substantial than a fear of the Persian barbarians was revealed in the despair that later led him to appeal to Philip of Macedon to rise to that sense of Greekness which the Greek cities themselves lacked:

> While it is only natural for the other descendants of Heracles, and for men who are under the bonds of their polities and laws, to cleave fondly to that state in which they happen to dwell, it is your privilege . . . to consider all Hellas your fatherland . . .[10]

In resigning to Philip the final hope of Greek unity, Isocrates confessed the failure of classical political thought to translate a broader cultural unity into political terms. As long as the political remained identified in men's minds with an intensive participation in a life of common concerns, the theoretical proposals of Isocrates and Demosthenes for a united front among the Greek cities and the practical experiments with sympolities could not compete for men's political loyalties. Although the life of the Greek cities continued in active fashion long after the Macedonian conquest of the fourth

---

† Demosthenes (*cir.* 384-322 B.C.), the famous orator, sought to arouse the Greeks against the aggression of Philip of Macedon. After the Greek defeat at Chaeronea in 338, accusations were brought against Demosthenes and he was imprisoned. He later escaped and returned, following the uprisings against Macedonian rule (323). The Macedonians, however, restored their control and Demosthenes committed suicide.

century, the realities of existence were such as to demand a complete rethinking of the nature of the political. Alexander might allow the Greeks an impressive measure of independence and the Achaean League of the third century might stand as evidence that Greek political inventiveness had not been
exhausted, yet the central fact from the death of Alexander (323) to the final
absorption of the Mediterranean world into the Roman Empire was that
political conditions no longer corresponded to the traditional categories of
political thought. The Greek vocabulary might subsume the tiny *polis* and
the sprawling leagues of cities under the single word *koinon*, yet there could
be no blinking the fact that the city denoted an intensely political association
while the leagues, monarchies, and empires that followed upon the decline
of the *polis* were essentially apolitical organizations. Hence if the historical
task of Greek political theory had been to discover and to define the nature
of political life, it devolved upon Hellenistic and later Roman thought to
rediscover what meaning the political dimension of existence might have in
an age of empire.

In large entities like the empire of Alexander, the monarchies of the Seleu-
cids, Ptolemies, Antigonids, and the Roman Empire, the methods of generating loyalties and a sense of personal identification were necessarily different from those associated with the Greek idea of citizenship. Where
loyalty had earlier come from a sense of common involvement, it was now
to be centered in a common reverence for power personified.[11] The person
of the ruler served as the terminus of loyalties, the common center linking
the scattered parts of the empire. This was accomplished by transforming
monarchy into a cult and surrounding it with an elaborate system of signs,
symbols, and worship. These developments suggest an existing need to bring
authority and subject closer by suffusing the relationship with a religious
warmth. In this connection, the use of symbolism was particularly important,
because it showed how valuable symbols can be in bridging vast distances.
They serve to evoke the presence of authority despite the physical reality
being far removed. At the same time, symbols are an invaluable means for
communicating a common set of meanings at an elementary level. It is not
surprising that the Romans found need for a large number of authority-sym-
bols. The *fasces, lituus, toga praetexta,* and the systematic use of the coinage
system[12] as a means of political propaganda were important techniques aimed
at overcoming distance.

The personification of authority and the resort to symbolism during the
Hellenistic and Roman periods were dictated not only by the heterogeneity
of the constituencies, with their vast differences in culture and political so-

phistication, but also by the need to combat the increasingly abstract character of political life. With the development of imperial organization, the locus of power and decision had grown far removed from the lives of the vast majority. There seemed to be little connection between the milieu surrounding political decisions and the tiny circle of the individual's experience. Politics, in other words, was being conducted in a way incomprehensible to the categories of ordinary thought and experience. The "visual politics" of an earlier age, when men could see and feel the forms of public action and make meaningful comparisons with their own experience, was giving way to "abstract politics," politics from a distance, where men were informed about public actions which bore little or no resemblance to the economy of the household or the affairs of the market-place. In these circumstances, political symbols were essential reminders of the existence of authority.

Growing distance also called for new methods of political control. The great achievements of the Romans in jurisprudence and in organizing and administering a far-flung empire were, in reality, clear testimony to the formalism of political life, to the need for putting a large number of individuals into general and therefore manageable classifications, and for settling the rules and regulations that were to govern the relationships among strangers. The megalopolis had displaced the *polis,* and in this new spatial dimension the old notion of the political association, as sustained by a friendship among familiars, appeared anachronistic.[13] The concept of the political community had been overwhelmed by the sheer number and diversity of the participants. These changing conditions were pointed up by the kind of appeal made by Roman leaders to some rebellious Gauls of the first century A.D.:

> There is no privilege, no exclusion. From worthy Emperors you derive equal advantage, though you dwell so far away . . . Endure the passions and rapacity of your masters, just as you bear barren seasons and excessive rains and other natural evils.[14]

III **Citizenship and disengagement.** If political activity had ceased to be a significant mode of human experience except for the very few, what was the meaning of membership and wherein did the political element reside? Although the new power organizations that controlled the Hellenistic and Roman worlds had lost some of the old political qualities of the *polis,* they had not ceased from making many of the same demands on their members. If anything, the nature of membership had become an even more pressing question, because men were now being asked and compelled to co-operate, sacrifice, and serve in the name of an association of which they were parts only in a formal and sometimes, as in the Roman grants of citizenship to distant peoples, in a fictional sense. The roots of this problem of member-ship lie deep in the Hellenistic age and, more specifically, in the critical at-tacks of the Cynics, Epicureans and early Stoics upon the customary ties and relationships that had defined the individual's status and role in society. The Cynic school, which had flourished in the last half of the fourth century B.C., asserted that the "conventional" values represented in the life of the com-munity by the laws, customs, institutions, and class structure could no longer be shrugged off as harmless irrelevancies or annoyances. They must be classed instead as positive impediments to the attainment of virtue and ought therefore to be rejected. In this respect, the difference between the Cynics and Epicurus (*cir.* 341-269 B.C.) was the difference between a big "no" and a small "yes." Although the Epicureans were willing to grant some utility to the political order, they, too, set about whittling down the claims of family, so-ciety, and political life until all that remained was the irreducible minimum necessary to sustain peace. "If the good is different from the noble and just," a later Stoic wrote, "then father and mother, country and all such things disappear." [15] As the old ties were successively cast off by these philosophies, the outline of the individual person emerged with startling clarity.

Political disengagement had been foreshadowed in the sixth book of Plato's *Republic* and counseled again in his *Euthydemus,* yet it is essential to dis-tinguish a minor theme from what became the *leitmotif* of the philosophies that appeared towards the end of the fourth century B.C. The strong elements of despair and withdrawal that colored Cynicism and Epicureanism were nourished by an anti-political impulse which could not be concealed by their temporizing and grudging acknowledgment of some utility in a political order.[16] The advice of Epicurus, "we must free ourselves from the prison of affairs and politics," [17] was not the premise but the conclusion to the belief that the individual not only had a life of his own independent of the polit-ical association, but that this was the most significant and valuable part of his life. "A man must prepare himself for solitude too — he must be able to suffice for himself, and able to commune with himself." [18]

Thus the formula read: a minimal commitment to an association of limited value. It was a far cry from the Socratic view of political obligation as based upon the positive civilizing function of the *polis* to the Epicurean conception of society as bound together by a social contract guaranteeing only that "men shall not injure one another or be injured." [19] This was but one indication of the extent to which post-Aristotelian thought had begun to nibble away at the political assumptions of the preceding age. Epicurean and Cynic alike questioned the supposedly close connection between the virtue of the political association and the virtue of the individual, between the conditions of communal order and the discovery of the self. In the Epicurean argument, the collapse of the *polis* and the accompanying uncertainties that followed upon the Macedonian triumph were taken as proof of a cosmic disinterest in the destiny of man. If the gods had been truly concerned with man's welfare, they would not have allowed the cities to disintegrate to a point where municipal life verged on a state of nature. If men could not trust in the divine agency of the gods, and if human perfection were no longer possible within the *polis,* the only conclusion seemed to be that man's fate was solely a personal matter.

By dismissing the cosmic and communal props to morality, the Epicureans opened the way to a radical individualism grounded in self-interest and directed towards self-sufficiency. Happiness was viewed as a matter of individual definition, and any a priori commitment of a civic or political kind carried the initial suspicion of being a snare designed to trap the individual and to make him conform to a public definition of happiness.

Yet the old idea, that man owed an allegiance to the order of relationships supporting his existence, was too deeply rooted, and it fell to the Stoics to work out a new formula of membership.[20] This was no easy matter, for it involved positing a form of order acceptable to the newly self-conscious individual yet durable enough to survive a society of non-communing members. The effect of the Cynic and Epicurean attack had been to dissolve political relationships into a condition of "political nature," into mere phenomena without stability or inner coherence, into the political counterpart to a purposeless universe. The response of the Stoics was dictated by the need to ease men's fears and uncertainties, and this they tried to do by summoning men back to membership. Men were enjoined to follow nature; that is, to identify themselves with the immanent reason or *logos* pervading the universe:

> O thou who over all dost hold
> Eternal dominance, Nature's author, Zeus,
> Guiding a universe by Law controlled.[21]

All of creation was pictured as forming an order, a rationally integrated scheme wherein the several parts contributed their function to the ensuing harmony of the whole. To become a member of the universal society meant fulfilling the obligations inherent in one's social position — a sort of "my station and its duties" philosophy. From this medley of contributing parts would issue a universal "sympathy," a bond of unity binding all together as tightly as the Platonic city: "we are the parts of one great body." [22] Thus the authentic relationships lacking in the existential political societies were re-created in the image of a larger order; the natural order was not only a realm of value, but also a society, indeed the highest form of society:

> When a man has learnt to understand the government of the universe and has realized that there is nothing so great or sovereign or all-inclusive as this frame of things wherein man and God are united . . . why should he not call himself a citizen of the universe and a son of God? [23]

The undeniable contribution of Stoicism to Western notions of equality, freedom, and human dignity makes it difficult for a critic to appear other than carping and ungenerous. Consequently, most criticisms of Stoicism have been content to draw attention to the incongruity between the Stoic appeal to universal values of reason, equality, and freedom, on the one hand, and, on the other, the strain of intellectual snobbery that tended to restrict membership in the universal society to an elite of the "lofty, free, unhindered, untrammeled, trustworthy, and self-respecting," a kind of invisible church of rational beings. Strictures of this kind, however, do not go deeply enough, for the difficulty inherent in the Stoic teaching is not exposed by drawing out either its logical contradictions or by pointing an accusing finger at its intellectual elitism. Rather the shortcomings of Stoicism stemmed from the intellectual fuzziness surrounding its conception of the nature of political society. This can be indicated by turning to a classic statement by Marcus Aurelius (121-180 A.D.) of the Stoic ideal of the universal society:

> If our intellectual part is common, the reason also, in respect of which we are rational beings, is common; if this is so, common also is the reason which commands us what to do, and what not to do; if this is so, there is a common law also; if this is so, we are fellow citizens; if this is so, we are members of some political community; if this is so, the world is in a manner a state. For of what other common political community will any one say that the whole human race are members? . . . from this common political community comes also our very intellectual faculty and reasoning faculty and our capacity for law; or whence do they come? [24]

The relevant query here is not to ask how these ideas have contributed to later notions of an international society, but rather to ask the same question which ought to be directed against modern advocates of a world-community; namely, in what sense, if any, can these ideas be said to have expressed a politically meaningful conception of society? True, the Stoics employed the old familiar language of political theory: a fellowship of citizens, the bond of law, and the need for order and unity. But political language alone does not constitute a political theory, any more than the existence of "internal politics" in churches, trade union, business corporations, or universities makes these groups identical in nature to a political society. To qualify as political, language must serve as a medium for expressing a theoretical conception that is itself political. This Stoicism failed to do, and for two basic reasons. First, its philosophic outlook was not derived from a positive view concerning the nature of a truly political order, but from a conclusion about its insufficiency. The Stoic commitment was towards a society which lay outside politics. This was related, in turn, to the second fundamental weakness; namely, the ambiguity resident in the conception of the universal society. The Stoics had argued from an idea about the order of nature, that is the harmony of a rationally integrated universe, to a notion of an ideal society embracing all of creation. This produced a theory that rested upon a serious confusion of contexts, the one a context of natural objects, the other a context of human beings. The end result was a bastardized conception whereby nature was interpreted politically and, on this basis, men were entreated to identify themselves politically with nature.[25] What the Stoics had done was to extract certain ideas previously connected with the political order and to transfer them to the natural order. Universal "citizenship," natural "law," and "justice" were seriously claimed as attributes of this latter order, and men were exhorted to extend their allegiance to the cosmos as though it were a true society. But, as Professor Gilson has wisely said, identification with the cosmic harmony "could be performed as an act of wisdom, but not as an act of citizenship." [26] In other words, the universal society was not and could not be a true political society for the very reason that it lacked any semblance of the political relationships that made "citizenship" a meaningful category.

In retrospect, then, the important development that had taken place in political thought since the time of Aristotle had come down to this: the distinctively political elements in political philosophy had become swallowed up in an undifferentiated whole. The terse epitaph was supplied by Marcus Aurelius: "the poet says, Dear city of Cecrops; and wilt not thou say, Dear city of Zeus." [27] It was not that political philosophy had regressed to a pre-Platonic stage where the distinction between nature and political society had become blurred, but rather that philosophy had socialized and politicized nature while denaturing the political.

Although it is customary to distinguish various periods in the development of Stoicism and to point out that the thinkers of the Middle Stoa (second and first centuries B.C.) modified the apolitical tendencies of the early teaching

and fashioned a doctrine more suitable to the needs of Roman life, it seems
to me truer to say that Stoicism always retained in some measure the anti-
political bias of its origins. Although it had sprung from dominantly Greek
modes of thought, it did not carry the imprint of the intensely political world
of Thucydides, Plato, and Aristotle, but of the Hellenistic world where absolute monarchy had withered the roots of political participation and imperial organization had made a mockery of the educative mission of the
polis. Yet this philosophy found its way to Rome towards the beginning of
the second century B.C. and there it influenced several eminent public men,
such as Scipio Africanus minor and M. Porcius Cato. Its stern morality of
probity, fairness, and austerity seemed ready-made for a political system that
desperately needed a code of conduct for public magistrates and administra-
tors. Moreover, the Stoic model of a universal society, built on a fine contempt for the parochialisms of race, class, and nation appeared to coincide
nicely with the Roman world-state. For all of these seeming congruities, however, Stoicism became the natural complement to Rome only when that
society had become so exhausted by internal conflicts and distended by imperial conquests that it had lost the basic determinants of a political community. The tension between philosophy and society was abolished under the
happy coincidence that both were apolitical.

Something of this is to be glimpsed in the values of Roman public life that
Stoicism helped to support: *gravitas, constantia, disciplina, industria, clementia, frugalitas*.[28] Here was an ethic that was not so much derived from
political life as one intended to protect the participant against its temptations. At bottom, it reflected the conviction that the bureaucratized and highly
impersonal public life of the Empire had only the slenderest ties with man's
potentiality for moral development. Public office and political participation
became something it had never been for the Greeks, a stern duty requiring
an elaborate justification. Under these circumstances the best that philosophy
could produce was an ethic of public service, a joyless bureaucratic morality.
Perhaps it had not been a simple philistinism but an instinct for the political
which had let the Senate, shortly after the Stoic Crates had begun to lecture
at Rome, to issue a decree expelling philosophers (161 B.C.).[29]

IV   **Politics and the Roman Republic.** Almost two centuries before
Augustus succeeded (in the words of Tacitus) in subjecting a
world "wearied by civil strife" to near absolute control, the Romans had
known one of the most intensive political experiences of any Western people.

In the brief period from the middle of the third century to about the middle of the first century B.C., the Romans had not only to cope with the social and economic problems familiar to the ancient world generally, but to subdue and govern an enormous stretch of territory, containing a wide variety of cultures, and to attempt all of this through a set of political arrangements intended rather for a city-state than an empire. Polybius might marvel at the wonderful way in which Roman institutions were adapted for this imperial task, but in the end the republican system proved unable to sustain its enormous burden. Before this magnificent failure, however, the Romans had presided over an unprecedented experiment in managing the dynamics of politics through institutional forms and in exploring the outer limits of political conflict. The system itself was not democratic in the older Greek sense, and the active conduct of affairs always remained in the hands of a relatively closed oligarchy. It is also true that legal niceties were not always observed and that the great struggles of the first century exposed the largely formal quality of Roman constitutionalism. Nevertheless, after all of the necessary qualifications have been made, the fact remains that the Romans did try to accommodate political vitalities in a new way and, in so doing, made a considerable contribution to political practice and one that had important implications for political theory.

In the first place, the Romans showed the role that institutions might play in giving shape and direction to society. Roman society was sharply differentiated into several social orders — patricians, plebs, clients, freedmen, *equites* — and these were structured into several gradations of classes and centuries, each with its own rights and obligations. These social arrangements, in turn, were meshed with the system of assemblies, elections, and military organization. Although the interplay between social structure and political institutions did not always function smoothly or effectively, it did useful service in keeping the political system sensitive to changing social pressures and it did help to direct political behavior along fairly orderly lines. Cicero's bias was evident in his remark that "when the people are divided according to wealth, rank, and age, their decisions are wiser than when they meet without classification in the tribes," [30] yet it was based on a sure recognition of the role of institutions in defining and ordering an important segment of the community.

The political institutions themselves, that is the system of assemblies, executive offices, courts, and the Senate, formed a complex mechanism that provided both an outlet for, and a restraint upon, the dynamics of class conflict, group rivalries, and personal ambitions. Polybius and Cicero were mistaken in trying to explain the genius of the system in terms of a neat balance of forces, but they were basically correct in drawing attention to the fundamental importance of institutions in legitimizing political conflict among diverse forces and interests in Roman society.

There were other lessons to be derived from institutional politics. One of the most important is related to the type of leadership possible when politics is conducted through institutional forms. Greek political thought had largely conceived leadership in terms of a political hero whose task it was to fabricate the institutions of society and to leave behind a political order bearing the impress of a single personality. In contrast, the Romans viewed leadership as a political activity that must conform to pre-established institutional requirements. They sensed that institutions function as a kind of common denominator of action, requiring the political actor to respect established conventions and settled expectations. The effect of these conformities was to level individual greatness, or rather to identify it with the political system itself. The limits placed upon leadership by institutional requirements also exerted a significant effect on the nature of political action. An institution, such as an assembly or an administrative body, is a complex of human actions that must be integrated and coordinated if a decision is to emerge. At best, coordination tends to be imperfect, and, consequently, the objectives of action are rarely achieved in a direct way. Political action, in other words, becomes indirect in character: between the word and the deed stands the distorting medium of institutions.

In the political thought of the period, these characteristics of institutions were expressed through an implicit criticism of Platonism. The role of institutions in legitimizing conflict, in levelling political greatness to conform to the requirements of institutional politics, in making political action indirect, all served to raise questions about the Platonic conception of the political act as one whereby a superhuman intelligence, working directly on its "materials," transformed a whole community. Towards this union of architectonic knowl-edge, individual greatness, and political power, Roman thought expressed a deep and very Burke-like suspicion:

> Cato [according to Cicero's report] used to say that our constitution was superior to those of other states on account of the fact that almost every one of these commonwealths had been established by one man . . . On the other hand our own commonwealth was based upon the genius, not of one man, but of many; it was founded, not in one generation, but in a long period of several centuries and many ages of men. For, said he, there never has lived a man possessed of so great genius that nothing could escape him, nor could

the combined powers of all the men living at one time possibly make all necessary provisions for the future without the aid of actual experience and the test of time.[31]

These ideas were put into more systematic form by Polybius, (*cir.* 200-120 B.C.) who, although a Greek by education, had acquired an intimate knowledge of both Greek and Roman politics. While admitting that some of the Greek constitutions were good evidence of what a single intelligence might accomplish, Polybius maintained that the Roman example showed that there was another kind of political knowledge, not one based on "any process of reasoning" but rather on the experience gained from "many struggles and troubles." [32] When the major principles of Polybius's thought are gathered together — the turn towards a pragmatic form of knowledge, the contempt for theories of ideal states, the use of an historical method, and, above all, the belief that the future could be predicted from a correct reading of the past — the result was to give a new direction to political theory. "In the first place," Plato had declared, "let us try to found the State by word." [33] Now, however, political theory, like political action, was to become more indirect in nature. Instead of seeking a vantage point "outside" political phenomena, one that would enable thought and action to impose a pattern on the whole, political theory was to occupy an observation point within phenomena, content to report the drift of events rather than to master them, and to resign itself to a world ultimately unconquerable:

> [Just as] the sole test of a perfect man is the power of bearing high-mindedly and brave the most complete reverses of fortune, so it should be in our judgment of states.[34]

Similarly, Plato's deep bias against political conflict and the general Greek tendency to treat disorder as symptomatic of a diseased polity[35] were at odds with the phenomenon of intense political rivalry that characterized Roman public life in the two centuries preceding the Principate. The Romans had tested and perfected almost every technique of political management: the conscious manipulation of the masses by means of public spectacles and demonstrations and the exploitation of the symbols of religious and political belief. They had reduced political strategy to a fine art; coalitions among interest groups and the tactic of wooing the supporters of rival groups formed the basic behavior pattern in Roman politics. At the same time, the seamier side of politics was also practiced with great skill — patronage, bribery, vote-buying, tampering with electoral bodies, and the sale of public contracts. Elections themselves were highly organized affairs wherein candidates would canvass (*petitio*) the electorate, dispatch their election agents (*divisores*) to solicit the vote and to distribute bribes.[36] In view of the pervasiveness of politics at Rome, it is not accidental that modern students of Roman history have felt justified in analyzing these developments with the aid of concepts like "parties," "pressure groups," and "machines." [37] Although these notions court the danger of anachronistic interpretations, their use testifies to a felt need to find concepts that will do justice to the politics-ridden quality of the subject-matter.

During the republican period, political activity took the form of group politics wherein rival oligarchies, drawn from largely the same social strata, competed for office, prestige, and power. The famous struggles between the plebs and the patricians and, later, between the *optimates* and *populares,* were essentially contests between rival groups of the nobility. Although they rarely scrupled to bid for mass support, they never surrendered control of the game. The nuclear center in these struggles was the great families, such as the Fabii, Aemilii, and the Claudii, who succeeded in establishing virtual monopolies over certain offices, like the consulate and censorship, and fought always to restrict membership in the Senate to their own strongly inbred group. To preserve and extend their influence, the great houses entered into alliances with lesser families; marriages and adoption became highly refined forms of political strategy.

This shift towards interest as the basis of politics was further registered in a changing conception of virtue. Friendship (*amicitia*) was purged of the disinterestedness ascribed to it by Aristotle and made to accord with the group politics described earlier. The extent to which the idea of friendship was converted into an instrument of political strategy is apparent in Cicero's effort to patch up his differences with Crassus; his letter of friendship, he wrote, should be considered as a treaty (*foedus*).[38] The virtue of *liberalitas,* too, was defined with an eye towards its political uses. According to Cicero's interpretation, it had to do with the prudent management of one's resources so that one's friends could be benefited. "The common bonds of society will be best strengthened if kindness is extended to those nearest us." [39] In keeping with this mood, justice was treated as a useful type of knowledge for eliciting the cooperation of others in supplying our own wants "in full and overflowing measure." At times Cicero's discussion of justice in *De officiis* seemed wholly absorbed with the intriguing problems of why some men will voluntarily work to advance the interests of another man and what techniques were best suited for securing this kind of support.[40] The modification of the virtues was further bound up with the activism that pervaded Cicero's philosophy — *virtus in usu sui tota posita est* — and formed the logical accompaniment to the emphasis on interests. "The first care" of those who administered the commonwealth was to see that "everyone shall have what belongs to him and that private citizens suffer no invasion of their property rights by act of the state." [41] Since "public actions have the widest sphere and affect the lives of the most people," the highest form of virtuous action was not to be located in philosophic contemplation, as Plato and Aristotle had held, but in governing a state. "Action is chiefly employed in protecting human interests; it is indispensable to human society and holds, therefore, a higher rank than mere speculative knowledge." [42] Nothing was more revealing of the distance between Cicero and Plato than the anguish experienced by the Roman because banishment from active politics had driven him to the vocation of philosopher; the difficulty envisioned by Plato would be to force the guardians to lay aside philosophy for governing.

V **The politics of interest.** The importance that interest had assumed in Roman political practice and thought added a new shade of meaning to politics and heightened the distinctive character of political action. The Romans had realized instinctively that the legitimizing of interest not only entailed a limited form of action, a kind of domestic diplomacy, but that the multiplicity of interests presupposed as well the incomplete character of solutions to political issues. If political activity was centered around interests, the attendant problems had to be resolved on the same basis; that is, on the basis of claims that conflicted precisely because each claim had a particularity that set it off from other claims.

> Harmony is very easily obtainable in a state where the interests of all are the same, for discord arises from conflicting interests, where different measures are advantageous to different citizens.[43]

The rivalries for power and advantage taught the Romans something else about the odd status of a political problem. The common spectacle of competing groups, each headed by experienced leaders with roughly the same patriotic motives, yet each asserting a different policy for the same problem, could not help but raise questions about the nature of the problem itself. What was it about a political problem that provoked a variety of proposals, each often inconsistent with the other? The most frequent answer, that given by Plato among others, was to reject the question as specious and to claim instead that when men gave different answers to the same problem the cause lay not in the problem but in their knowledge about it. Nevertheless, the mere fact that a political society can withstand rivalry among groups and survive, even flourish, amidst the quick changes from one policy orientation to another, raises the possibility that the status of political issues is *sui generis*. The Roman historian Sallust remarked that after decadence had set into Roman society "it was the commonwealth in its turn that was enabled by its greatness to sustain the shortcomings of its generals and magistrates." [44] This does not imply that a political society can withstand any number of fantastic remedies and incompetent leaders, but it does hint at the presence of certain types of conditions that operate either to offset the effects of different and alternating policies or else restrict the range of possible remedies that might be advanced. In the first case, that of offsetting conditions, one might argue that a society that enjoys continued and expanding economic prosperity, such as Rome enjoyed as a result of her imperial position, or Britain later experienced in the nineteenth-century phase of the Industrial Revolution, or the United States today — under these conditions a society can absorb a good deal of experiment and alternation in policy, some of it even foolish and uninspired. In the second case of conditions that serve to limit the range of remedies, a kind of "political rationality" develops when contending groups are exposed to similar education and experience; they gradually come to accept the same set of values, regardless of how lofty or ignoble they may be. Even a band of thieves, Augustine remarked later, must recognize certain limits if the group is to survive. When political competition takes place within a setting where some agreement exists concerning the rules and the general meaning of distributive justice, the groups involved come to see the world in much the same light. [45] Although there may be disagreement over remedies, there is usually agreement over what are the problems. Moreover, since each group is bidding for the support of the same constituency, it is compelled to try to woo the supporters of its rivals by adopting a largely similar program with only slight changes of emphasis. At the same time, rivalry on these terms means that certain alternatives are naturally excluded because, under the existing prerequisites of successful political action, their realization is impossible.

Whether the factors contributing to rational political behavior be in the nature of basic laws, fundamental conventions, or a common political morality, their continued observance implies that politics has not as yet been reduced completely to a matter of interest. That is, the obligation of the competing groups to adhere to the basic rules means nothing less than obeying the rules even when particular interests or ambitions are not always being served. The question of whether an obligation is present when one's interests are *never* served by the system of rules is of a different order. This extreme condition aside, when the interest motive is admitted into politics the real danger does not reside in any moral depravity consequent on the pursuit of so-called materialistic ends; man's history has not been a pretty record when he has fought for "ideal" ends. The real danger comes when politics is reduced to nothing but the pursuit of interests, when no controlling standards of obligation are recognized.

The perfect example of this is provided by Cicero's formula for halting the gradual erosion of the constitutional system. He urged a *concordia ordinum* among the "best" elements in Roman society, an alliance of the *optimates* against the *populares*.[46] But the proposal was futile inasmuch as no such alliance was possible except on the basis of interests; the only basis capable of uniting some men was one that divided them from others. This dilemma, however, was not the result of accident, but the inescapable consequence of the basic principle that, according to Cicero, underlay the Roman system. The main reason for establishing a commonwealth had been interest; that is, man's desire to keep what was his own:

> Although mankind were associated together with the help of nature, yet it was the hope of retaining their property that led them to seek the protection of cities.[47]

Cicero's lament, "some belong to a democratic, others to an aristocratic party but few to a national party," was merely a rhetorical escape; interest is not to be conjured away by calling it "national" or locating it in some mysterious realm above politics.

Towards the middle of the first century B.C., the limitations of the politics of interest began to become apparent. Imperial expansion, the enormous flow of wealth into Rome, the seemingly endless opportunities for political ambition intensified the pace of politics and made men impatient with traditional restraints and customary procedures. The fluidity of the situation allowed the political adventurer to circumvent the long and arduous haul up the several rungs of office prescribed by the *cursus honorum*. "Many have thus perished," Tacitus wrote, "even good men, despising slow and safe success and hurrying on even at the cost of ruin to premature greatness."[48] The violence of party struggle grew, placing an unbearable strain on constitutional processes. The ground-rules of political life, which Cicero had defined as equal protection before the law and the common recognition of law as the inviolable bond of society (*lex sit civilis societatis vinculum*),[49] steadily lost their meaning. Ter-

ror, proscriptions, confiscation of the opposition's property, and the growing
reliance on private armies became the prevailing techniques. Politics had
passed from rivalry to warfare. The frequent pleas voiced by a Cicero or Cato
for the revival of the old values and virtues sounded hollow, because the
long schooling in interest-politics had conditioned the Romans to distrust
their own political vocabulary. Cato's complaint, that "we have long since
lost the true names for things," [50] was part of the evidence that the crucial
words communicating the Roman political consensus, *libertas, auctoritas,
pietas, mos maiorum,* had for so long been manipulated as party slogans that
they seemed more a disguise for than an indicator of reality. As men came
to distrust the formalities of politics, they began instinctively to be on the
alert for the interest "behind" high-flown phrases, the "true" motive concealed beneath public pieties. "Under the pretence of the public welfare,"
Sallust noted, "each in reality was working for his own advancement." [51]
The Romans had learned the hard truth of Aristotle's dictum that when particular "ideologies" prevail, when public meanings appear determined exclusively by the interests of those having sufficient power to impose their particular interpretations, then it becomes extremely difficult to maintain a consensus. A society, however, cannot long endure uncontrolled political conflict
and the inevitable reaction is to demand peace at any price. "Custom or law
there was none," wrote Tacitus, until society, exhausted by the violent politics
of the late republic, found refuge in a regime pledged to the elimination of
all but the most controlled political activity. The Augustan Principate was
summarized by Lucan in words that served also as the epitaph of Roman
politics: *"Cum domino pax ista venit."* [52]

VI **From political association to power organization.** The declining
significance of popular participation, the losing struggle to maintain republican institutions, the ingenious use of a constitutional façade to
conceal the emergence of monarchy, and the growing importance of bureaucracy were evidence that men were now being governed by a power organization rather than a political association. In stressing the power character of the
new political organization, I am not contending that prior to the age of
empire men had refused to recognize that power was an essential part of
governing. All that is suggested is that power assumed a pre-eminence as the
distinguishing mark of government primarily because the other factors in
political society were being reduced to secondary importance. Plato and

Aristotle had appreciated the phenomenon of power, but had inserted it within a context of controlling considerations. In their view, the political association existed to serve the material and cultural needs of the members, and although power was necessary to coordinate and direct human activities in order that these needs would be best satisfied, it did not follow that power was the central mark of an association composed of contributing parts. When these considerations lost their compelling force, however, the way lay open for considering power the central political fact. The transition to the new view of power had been clearly registered in the political thought of Polybius. His *Histories* sought to account for the rapid emergence of Roman supremacy, and, as he admitted, the controlling conception in his study was the nature of power: "how it was and by virtue of what peculiar political institutions that in less than fifty-three years nearly the whole world was overcome and fell under the single dominion of Rome, a thing the like of which had never happened before." [53] From here Polybius was led to ask questions about the nature of power: what were the causes of the military successes and political expansion of Rome? why had she succeeded where other states had failed? was there a regular pattern to the waxing and waning of various types of states? And when Polybius had found his answer it turned out to be a prescription for the right organization of power by means of an institutional balance.

The power nature of the new organizations was reflected in the turn taken by the later Roman conception of citizenship. At Rome the category of citizen was highly prized, but after the brief period of republicanism had passed, the citizen of the Principate and Dominate came to be regarded less as a participant than as a subject; that is, as one who obeyed the commands of authority. At the same time, the psychology governing the possession of rights was dictated as a response to power. To compensate for the loss of identity with the community, men looked to legal guarantees against the community. In Cicero's revealing definition, "the peculiar mark of a free community" consisted of the principle that it was illegal to violate the civic privileges or private property of an individual except by the decisions of the senate, the people, or an appropriate tribunal.[54] Henceforth the element of participation became of secondary importance,[55] and the operative role of citizenship was to provide the only common status or meeting ground for men who were otherwise sharply distinguished by social, economic, religious, and cultural differences. What was political about citizenship was its role in overcoming heterogeneity, numbers, and space. The dramatic event that underscores this change was when Paul, the apostle of a persecuted and hostile sect, demanded of the centurion, "Would you scourge a man who is a Roman and uncondemned?"

If we ask: what was the intellectual response to the primacy of power? the answer is that nowhere was the failure of political philosophy more effectively demonstrated than in its inability to account, in political terms, for this central fact in the political life of these centuries. Confronted with power, one impulse of political philosophy was to flee and seek refuge in a "golden age" located somewhere in the prepolitical past. In numerous writers we find this idea, but the significant point is that they pictured mankind in a society that had been purged of all political marks: neither law, coercion, property nor conflict had existed in the state of political innocence.[56] Another and far stronger impulse, but one that was equally apolitical, was to suffuse power with religious symbols and imagery. Not the naturalism of a Polybius but a supernaturalistic view of power was dominant throughout much of the Hellenistic period and again in the centuries following the establishment of the Augustan Principate. This was a certain sign that men had come to look towards the political regime for something over and above their material and intellectual needs, something akin to salvation. If men could not flee from power to the golden age or to the universal city of reason, they would interpret it differently, treating it as the saving force that sustained the political world. As far back as Hellenistic times, the theories of kingship had revealed a trend in which the ruler stood as the symbol of the fears and yearnings of the politically disinherited.[57] In the writings of the period, the other elements of a political theory receded to the background and the ruler stood alone and remote. The fate of the body politic was resigned to the moral character and foresight of its governing head. He was the sole instrument of the divine *logos,* of that saving force which, by his mediation, could regenerate society and its members; he alone could rid the world of conflicts and make it a replica of the divine *homonoia;* he must, therefore, be worshipped by the names of Savior, God Manifest, Benefactor, and Creator.

These same themes were picked up again by the poets of the Augustan age, Virgil and Horace, who wove them into quasi-religious patterns. Augustus was depicted as a political savior who had come "to succor a ruined world" and to transform "an age of violence" into one of peace.[58] While the poets succeeded only in decking absolutism with pretty myths, philosophy, although less graceful, was equally futile. If we take Seneca's *De Clementia* as representative, we find that absolutism has paralyzed the ability of philosophy to do more than offer comfort. The whole of Seneca's political world was dwarfed by the towering figure of the absolute ruler and completely dependent on his merest whim:

> All those many thousands of swords which my peace restrains will be drawn at my nod; what nations shall be utterly destroyed, which banished, which shall receive the gift of liberty, which have it taken from them . . . this is mine to decree.[59]

The emperor was "the bond by which the commonwealth is united, the breath of life which these many thousands draw," and without him the whole society would rush to its own destruction. Before this terrible power, the proud tradition of philosophy was reduced to a groveling helplessness; nothing remained except for Seneca to beseech Nero to temper his absolutism by mercy (*clementia*).[60] This belief in a political savior, as well as the persistent attempts to assimilate the ruler to a deity and to describe the government of human society as analogous to God's rule over the cosmos, were themes reflective of the degree to which political and religious elements had become deeply intermixed in men's minds. In a variety of ways, in the conception of the ruler, subject, and society, the "political" quality was becoming indiscernible. At the same time, from the fourth century B.C. until well into the Christian era, men repeatedly thought of the Deity in largely political terms. Thus the paradoxical situation developed wherein the nature of God's rule was interpreted through political categories and the human ruler through religious ones; monarchy became a justification for monotheism and monotheism for monarchy.[61] In the dialogue *Octavius,* composed by the Christian writer Minucius Felix in the third century A.D., one of the speakers says, "Since you do not doubt the existence of providence, surely you do not think we need inquire whether the heavenly kingdom is governed by the rule of one or the control of a number." The final touch to these confusions of vocabulary was supplied by another Christian, Justin Martyr, in his *Dialogue.* The value of philosophy was defended by the remark, "Don't philosophers make all their discussions about God, and aren't they always asking questions about his foresight and monarchy?"[62]

VII **The decline of political philosophy.** In looking back on the kinds of political speculation that had followed the death of Aristotle, it is evident that the apolitical character of life had been faithfully portrayed, but no truly political philosophy had appeared. What had passed for political thought had often been radically apolitical; the meaning of po-

litical existence had been sought out only in order that men might more
easily escape from it. It was not that the Hellenistic philosophies had criticized the existing political societies, or even that they had pointed their
thought towards a transcendent society, but rather that they had reacted to
the growth of large-scale, impersonal societies by projecting a picture of a
society without any discernible limits at all. The decline of the *polis* as the
nuclear center of human existence had apparently deprived political thought
of its basic unit of analysis, one that it was unable to replace. Without the
polis, political philosophy had been reduced to the status of a subject-matter
in search of a relevant context. Instead of redefining the new societies in
political terms, political philosophy turned into a species of moral philosophy,
addressing itself not to this or that city, but to all mankind. When Eratosthenes advised Alexander to ignore Aristotle's distinction between Greeks and
barbarians and to govern instead by dividing men into "good" and "bad,"
this marked not only a step towards a conception of racial equality, but a
stage in the decline of political philosophy. Aristotle's distinction had been
derived from an essentially political judgment about the competence of non-
Greeks to undertake political responsibilities.

> The people of northern Europe, he noted, have retained their freedom, yet
> they exhibited no capacity for political development or for governing others.
> The Asiatics suffered from a servile spirit, and hence they remained subjects
> and slaves.[63]

Eratosthenes' advice indicated that political thought, like the *polis* itself, had
been superseded by something broader, vaguer, and less political. The "moral"
had overridden the "political," because the moral and the "good" had come
to be defined in relation to what transcended a determinate society existing
in time and space. Seneca's suicide was the dramatic symbol of the bankruptcy
of a tradition of political philosophy that had exchanged its political element
for a vapid moralism.

FOUR

The Early Christian Era: Time and Community

. . . Ye are no more strangers and foreigners, but fellow-citizens with the saints . . .

. . . Our commonwealth is already existing for us in heaven . . .

ST. PAUL

I **The political element in early Christianity: the new notion of community.** The troubled centuries that followed the establishment of imperial monarchy at Rome found the tradition of Western political thought at its most impoverished. There had been failure all along the line: failure to face the implications of concentrated power, failure to indicate ways and means for recapturing a sense of participating membership, and failure to preserve the distinctive integrity of political knowledge. Hellenistic and Roman thinkers had struggled to account for the new magnitudes of politics, the extension of space, the centralization of power, and the unprecedented enlargement of the constituency, but in the end they had confessed to being unable to supply new theoretical constructs that were both political and intelligible. The attempted ordering of political phenomena through cosmological categories suggests that the newly enlarged magnitudes of politics had so far outdistanced the political understanding that only cosmic concepts appeared pertinent.

The reconstruction of political thought proved to be a long and arduous process extending over several centuries and manifesting odd twists and turns. It was a process that began in paradox and ended in irony. With the default of philosophy, it fell to Christianity to revivify political thought. This may seem paradoxical in the light of the common belief that in its early phase Christianity professed a resolute indifference to political and social affairs and its followers appeared absorbed in "otherworldly" concerns. Admittedly, there is no difficulty in mustering evidence to show that in the first two centuries the Christians believed political affairs highly irrelevant to the fundamental problem of human existence. Their hopes were high that the "last days" were imminent, hence what need was there for Christians to turn to politics when the political order was part of a scheme destined to disappear in the Apocalypse? Had not Jesus declared, "My kingdom is not of this world . . . Let those who mix in the world live as if they were not engrossed in it, for the present phase of things is passing away"?[1] Moreover, the apolitical direction of early Christianity seemed further confirmed by the way in which it gradually established an identity distinct from Judaism. For the religious experience of the Jews had been strongly colored by political elements; church and nation had been a single concept. The terms of the covenant between Jahweh and his chosen people had often been interpreted as promising the triumph of the nation, the establishment of a political kingdom that would allow the Jews to rule the rest of the world. The messiah-figure, in turn, appeared not so much as an agent of redemption as the restorer of the Davidic kingdom.[2] In the early Christian teaching, however, the rejection of Jewish nationalism — "neither Greek nor Jew, circumcision nor uncircumcision" — and the dramatic refusal of Jesus to accept the role of messiah-king, added a further consistency to the claim of the new movement to be above politics.[3]

Given these strongly apolitical tendencies, the thesis that the new religion contributed substantially to the revitalization of political theory can be sustained only by adopting a somewhat unorthodox approach. Most discussions begin by accepting in a literal fashion the Christian claim to being a politically undefiled movement. This leads to a kind of Hegelian interpretation in which the numerous contacts between the new sect and the political order are viewed as a dialectical encounter in which the purely political thesis meets the purely

religious antithesis. In the present chapter, I shall take issue with this interpretation. The significance of Christian thought for the Western political
tradition lies not so much in what it had to say about the political order, but
primarily in what it had to say about the religious order. The attempt of
Christians to understand their own group life provided a new and sorely
needed source of ideas for Western political thought. Christianity succeeded
where the Hellenistic and late classical philosophies had failed, because it put
forward a new and powerful ideal of community which recalled men to a
life of meaningful participation. Although the nature of this community
contrasted sharply with classical ideals, although its ultimate purpose lay
beyond historical time and space, it contained, nevertheless, ideals of solidarity and membership that were to leave a lasting imprint, and not always for
good, on the Western tradition of political thought. At the same time, the
movement quickly evolved into a more complicated social form than a body
of believers held together in fervency and mystery; the mystic community
was soon encased in its own structure of governance. This, as we shall see,
provoked new problems equally pertinent to political thought.

There was irony too in these developments. The remarkable spread of
Christianity and the evolution of its complex institutional life were accompanied by a politicization of the Church, both in behavior and in language,
which had the unintended effect of continuing the political education of the
West. In pursuing religious ends, the leadership of the Church was compelled
to adopt political ways of behavior and political modes of thought. The long
tradition of civility which was built up "inside" the Church, and which became all the more important as the Church acted as residuary legatee of the
Roman Empire, put the West eternally in debt; for the experience meant
nothing less than that political ways of thought and action were preserved.
The irony, however, lies in the fact that the Church paid a price, one that was
strictly exacted at the Reformation, of a loss in religious vitality. The weakening of the Church not only allowed temporal rulers to establish their freedom
of action and to prove how well they had learned their political lessons, but
the politicization of religious thought, which had all along accompanied the
merging of the purely religious identity of the Church into a politico-religious
compound, opened the way for the development of an autonomous body of
political theory which a compromised theology could not contain.

These developments had their beginnings in an event that is often overlooked in political theory but was crucial from the viewpoint of the early
Christians. The drama of the Crucifixion had been enacted against a political
backdrop; the Lord of the Christians had been put to death at the command

of a political regime.[4] This act made it impossible for Christians to take a strictly neutral attitude towards the political order. In addition, the complicated view that the Christian took of his own condition compelled him to confront the political order. Although he expressed a contempt for the "world" and his conviction of its impermanency was strengthened by periods of Roman persecution, his outlook was not comparable to the classical cult of withdrawal where the wise man searched for a fortress of impregnable virtue to withstand the buffets of chance and fate. Instead the Christian's political attitudes were born of tensions inherent in the nature of the summons laid upon him. He was being called upon to struggle for a new life while entrapped within the old. The result was a continuing tension between the untransfigured realities of political and social existence and the promise of "new heavens and a new earth wherein dwelleth righteousness." [5] At times the tension was snapped in an ecstasy of millenarianism, and men looked hopefully towards "the last hour" which would put an end to the evils and injustices of political and social life.[6] Yet the uncertainty surrounding the second coming of Christ made it inevitable that Christians would have to seek some modus vivendi with the world of magistrates, tax collectors, and law courts. One expression of this was Paul's distinction between the obligations owed to political authority and those reserved for God.[7] In exhorting Christians to render to Caesar the things which were due him, Paul did not mean to imply that civic loyalties were wholly separate from religious loyalties and that, consequently, the political order existed in tarnished isolation from the rest of God's creation. The critical significance of the Pauline teaching was that it brought the political order within the divine economy and thereby compelled its confrontation by Christians:

> For by him were all things created that are in heaven, and that are in earth, visible and invisible, whether they be thrones, or dominions, or principalities, or powers: all things were created by him and for him.[8]

Despite Paul's attempt to accommodate the political order within the Christian scheme of things, there were powerful forces operating within early Christianity which inhibited a total integration. A sense of political estrangement persisted. That Paul felt it necessary to come down heavily in defense of political authority — "the powers that be are ordained of God . . . whosoever therefore resisteth the power, resisteth the ordinance of God . . . wherefore ye must needs be subject, not only for wrath, but also for conscience sake" [9] — was evidence of a deep unease in the relationships between the Christians and the political order.[10] This is to be explained partly by the psychological difficulties experienced by a beleaguered and persecuted sect in a hostile society. Paul would not have had to put the case for political obedience in such emphatic language had the Christians felt a natural and spontaneous loyalty to their Roman rulers.

Psychological explanations aside, however, the ambivalent political strains of limited commitment and ultimate disengagement can be understood more fully in terms of other considerations. In the first place, the Christian political attitude expressed the mentality of a group that regarded itself as being outside of the political order. Irrespectively of how often the early leaders pleaded for the faithful to obey their political rulers or how strongly they insisted upon the sanctity of social obligations, they could not dispel the impression of an unbridgeable distance between the point from which Christians surveyed political affairs and the actual locus of affairs. "And be not conformed to this world, but be ye transformed by the renewing of your mind . . ." [11] This attitude must not be understood as mere alienation or the expression of an unfulfilled need to belong. Nor is it to be accounted for in terms of the stark contrasts that Christians drew between eternal and temporal goods, between the life of the spirit held out by the Gospel and the life of the flesh symbolized by political and social relationships. What is fundamental to an understanding of the entire range of Christian political attitudes was that they issued from a group that regarded itself as already in a society, one of far greater purity and higher purpose: "a chosen generation, a royal priesthood, an holy nation, a peculiar people . . ." [12]

All of these components in the Christian political complex were nicely illustrated in the thought of Tertullian.* There was the sharpened sense of separateness from the political order: "the fact that Christ rejected an earthly kingdom should be enough to convince you that all secular powers and dignities are not merely alien from, but hostile to, God." There was also the confidence that came from being a member of a better society:

> We are a body knit together as such by a common religious profession, by unity of discipline, and by the bond of a common hope . . . Your citizen-

---

* Tertullian (cir. 160-220 A.D.) has been called, next to Augustine, "the greatest theologian of the patristic period." Born into an African and pagan family, he received a legal and classical education which left a lasting mark on his thought even after his conversion. He quickly became one of the most effective apologists for Christianity during its period of persecution and was the first Christian theologian to write in Latin. Later he joined the Montanists, a rigorist and "enthusiastic" sect, and turned his talents against the Church. Eventually he broke with Montanism to form his own sect. Despite his association with heresies he made lasting contributions to Trinitarian and Christological doctrines.

ship, your magistracies, and the very name of your *curia* is the Church of Christ . . . You are an alien in this world, and a citizen of the city of Jerusalem that is above.[13]

At the same time, there was the reluctance to withdraw totally, to deny that Christians were part of the society "outside": "We live with you in this world, not without a forum, not without baths, taverns, shops . . . and other places of intercourse. Moreover, we sail with you, serve in your armies, work with you in the fields, and trade with you." [14]

In later pages, we shall try to indicate more fully the "political" nature of this community: how Christians came to express their common life through an increasingly political vocabulary and how the church, in developing many of the attributes and facing many of the same problems usually considered to be peculiarly political, eventually came to rate its own communal life as inherently superior to a political society, not simply by the obvious standard of spirituality, but by *political* and *social* criteria. In other words, political society was to be challenged on its own grounds by a church-society which had become, in Newman's phrase, a "counter-kingdom." At this point, however, we are concerned only to emphasize that the Christian understanding of the outside political order, the way they viewed the scope of its powers, the extent of its legitimate obligations, and its over-all utility, was not the expression of the frustrated longings of some disinherited souls in search of community, but of a group whose solidarity was assured by a profound sense of membership:

> Christians are not distinguished from the rest of mankind by country or language or customs . . . While they live in cities both Greek and oriental . . . and follow the customs of the country . . . they display the remarkable and confessedly surprising status of their [own] citizenship. They live in countries of their own as sojourners. They share all things as citizens; they suffer all things as foreigners . . . They pass their life on earth; but they are citizens in heaven.[15]

The Christian conception of the nature of their community was to have far-reaching effects upon later social and political ideas. A whole range of traditional categories was upset or modified, categories relating to membership, social unity, the kinds of purposes that could be achieved in common, and the relationships that ought to hold between leaders and members. The first aspect to be noted is that Christian writers looked upon Christ as an architect of community, "the new law-giver" in Justin Martyr's words. According to Origen,* Christ "began a weaving together of the divine and human nature in order that human nature, through fellowship with what is more divine, might become divine . . ." [16] Yet the transcendental quality attaching to Christ sharply separated His labors from those of the great legislator portrayed in the classical tradition. This contrast was heightened in the basic elements singled out by Christians to mark the peculiar identity of their society. They borrowed the old classical analogy between a body politic and an organic body, with its intimations of oneness and mutual interdependency, but they suffused it with mystical and emotional qualities alien to classicism:

> For as the body is one, and hath many members, and all the members of that one body, being many are one body; so also is Christ. For by one Spirit we are all baptized into one body . . . [17]

At its deepest level, then, the community was founded on the mystery of the *corpus Christi*. The symbol of community was the sacrament of the Eucharist whereby the believer took in the life-giving substance of Christ's body. In partaking of the "medicine of immortality," as Ignatius** called it, each individual formed a part of a community of true communicants, sharing together the promise of eternal life.[18] Their common membership was further symbolized by baptism, which marked their entry into the new fellowship; by the comunity meal of the Lord's supper,[19] which contrasted so sharply with the rationalistic proposals for common dining in Plato's *Laws* and Aristotle's *Politics*; and by the constant effort of the members to emulate their Master whose death itself had a social meaning: "I am making up in my own flesh the deficit of Christ's suffering for His Body which is the Community." [20] Just as Christ had died out of love for mankind, so the new community was bound together, each member to the other, by affective ties which expressed an emotion unknown to the Greek idea of a community of friends:

> We know that we have passed from death into life, because we love the brethren. He that loveth not his brother abideth in death.[21]

---

* Origen (*cir.* 185-254 A.D.) was born in Egypt and educated at Alexandria. He is considered the greatest Greek apologist for the Christian religion. Educated in classical philosophy, and especially in its Neoplatonist version, he labored to fashion out of Platonism and Christianity a philosophical theology. Although many of his doctrines were subsequently declared heterodox, his influence on later theological doctrines was profound.

** Ignatius (*cir.* 37-107 A.D.) is included among the Apostolic Fathers. The many letters that he wrote placed great emphasis upon the unity of the Church and the authority of the bishops and clergy. He became Bishop of Antioch and, according to one tradition, he was killed after being condemned by the Emperor Trajan.

Although these were notions intended to define the nature of the new society, as well as to educate Christians to an understanding of their own community, they could not fail to have disturbing effects on traditional political
ideas. One example of this was the impact on the idea of political obligation.
Too often most discussions have fastened on the conflict created by the Christian belief that the limits of political loyalty were to be determined in the light
of a higher duty to God. Undoubtedly this introduced a conception radically
different from that of antiquity, but the truly revolutionary aspect was that
the Christian could approach the question of political obligation in a way
that classicism never could. For the Greeks, the question did not involve
a meaningful choice, because political membership was treated as an overriding necessity — excepting, as Aristotle had noted, only beasts and gods.
So powerful was the classical belief in the intimate connection between human perfectibility and the political order whose province it was to sustain
the appropriate conditions that, although a question of ethical duty might be
provoked by this or that law or by the nature of a perverted regime, such as
a tyranny, rarely were doubts raised about membership in political society
per se. Even though the Stoic might simulate allegiance to a universal society
of rational beings, they never argued that in cases of conflicting loyalties there
existed a genuine alternative to the political order. The Christian, on the other
hand, could entertain meaningful doubts about political obligation and membership, because his response was not governed by a hard choice between
membership in a political society and membership in no society at all. He
could choose because already he belonged to a society that surpassed any
existing one in the things that mattered most; he belonged to a society that
was "an outpost of heaven." Thus it was the early Christians who, for the
first time, converted disengagement into a fundamental challenge to political
society. In place of the protesting individual Cynic or Stoic, the political order
faced an unprecedented situation where the politically uncommitted had
been gathered into a determinate society of their own and where political
disengagement went hand in hand with the rediscovery of community, albeit
one pitched to a transcendent key.

The obvious query that arises at this point is, if the early Christians considered their own society superior, why were their leaders constantly reminding the members to discharge their civic duties, engage in normal social relationships, and support the political order in most matters? There are, of
course, some obvious answers. Survival dictated that an unpopular sect not
go out of its way to provoke public authorities. Again, there is little evidence
to indicate that Christians looked upon their society as replacing all of the

functions carried on in the "other" society. When Paul warned against "going to law before the unjust, and not before the saints," he meant only that Christians could resolve their controversies inside the group; he did not mean that Roman tribunals had been superseded in all matters by Christian procedures. But there was, I think, a far more significant reason why Christians felt drawn towards political commitment; this was the element of fear. To refuse civic duties, to withdraw from social functions meant, as was soon recognized, an inevitable weakening of the order that maintained peace and the arts of civilization. This belief, that the Roman Imperium was all that stood between civilization and anarchy, was not original with the early Christians. It formed, instead, a continuation of an old theme which had been prominent, for example, in the literature of the Augustan age. Virgil, Horace, Tacitus, and, later, Seneca constantly invoked the frightened imagery of a tottering world whose sole salvation depended on the *providentia* of its ruler.[22] The emperor came to be praised as the *restitutor orbis,* the rejuvenator of a dying system. Although the bitter rivalries among the political factions of the late republic undoubtedly contributed to these apprehensions and made men ready to reverence authority, these tendencies were hurried along by the growing threat of barbarian pressures at the extremities of the Empire. The barbarian invasions shocked the Romans into a fearful consciousness of an "outside," of a restless and alien force, constantly probing for weakness and threatening to engulf the civilized world.

> O, forge anew our edgeless swords
> On other anvils, to be bared
> Against the Huns and Arab hordes! [23]

Fear and a sense of the fragility of power were written large into the early Christian attitude as well. Again, our best witness is Tertullian. Despite his extreme doctrinal views and his later association with the Montanist heresy, his early works faithfully represented the Christian attitude towards the Roman Empire. Writing as he did during a period of severe persecution, there was no reason for him to feel kindly towards the political order. Nevertheless, despite frequent expressions of hostility towards political life, he saw no contradiction in Christians praying for the continued power of Rome. "We pray," he protested, "for Emperors, their ministers, for the condition of the world, for peace everywhere, and for the delaying of the end." [24]

This last phrase, "the delaying of the end," illustrated the paradox at the heart of the Christian attitude towards the world. On the one hand, a genuine recognition that the new sect was implicated in the fate of the political order:

> When the Empire is shaken, all of its parts are shaken also, hence even though we stand outside its tumults, we are caught in its misfortunes.[25]

On the other side, the strongly running current of chiliasm, which Tertullian shared, encouraging Christians that the end was imminent, that the cataclysm preceding Christ's return was happening before their eyes in the form of Rome's disintegration. In the contest between these two contraries, one pulling Christians towards the defense of the political order, the other causing them to exult at its imminent demise,[26] millenarianism was defeated; the thought of existence without the securing power of the political order was too much to bear. Men feared a return to "political nature" more than they loved the Apocalypse, and when, after the second century, the Church itself developed a vested interest in delaying the millennium — one expression of this being that among the sects branded as heretical several held to a fervently eschatological outlook — the stage was set for the development of a tradition of Christian writers feeling a deep sense of involvement in the fate of the Empire. Jerome* and Lactantius** for example, vividly reflect the shock at the crumbling of Roman power,[27] and Augustine's *De Civitate Dei,* perhaps the greatest of all Christian writings, was a direct response to the sack of Rome in 410.

The presence of an unknown "outside," the fear of an intruding force which would dissolve the web of political and social relationships, had been, as we have seen, a constituent element in Western political thinking as far back as the time when the Greeks had become conscious of the Persian Empire. From that time forward, the intellectual response has been that the "outside" posed the danger of a return to a condition where political relationships and the accustomed course of phenomena lose their coherence and lapse into a state of disconnectedness, a state of political nature. Consequently,

---

* Saint Jerome (340-420 A.D.) was one of the important Latin Fathers. He was born of a wealthy Christian family and thoroughly educated in classical rhetoric and philosophy. He wrote voluminously and is best remembered for his superb translation of the Bible into Latin.

** Lactantius (*cir.* 240-320 A.D.) was a North African by birth and became one of the major Christian apologists for the Empire. He spent his life as a teacher and writer. In the former capacity he served Constantine's son Crispus. In his writings, the most important being the *Divinae Institutiones,* he sought to persuade the educated of the truth of Christianity. The purity of his style was such that he is often called "the Christian Cicero."

political thinking has striven to render the situation intelligible by demarcating the boundary between the coherent and the incoherent, to encase the former within a conceptualized structure sufficiently sturdy to withstand the fears aroused by the unknown. In later pages, we shall examine the culminating effort of early Christianity, as represented by Augustine's concept of *ordo*, to extend regularity, not only to political affairs, but to all of creation and to all of human history. The impulse towards theoretical order has, however, taken several forms. During the early Middle Ages, it was expressed by the claim of the popes to be *caput totius mundi*; that is, to be governing heads of a world that seemingly knew no outside. More modest, but perhaps the more significant on that account, was the notion of *Europa* which emerged in fitting complement to the Church's consecration of Charlemagne's rule. *Europa* was conceived as a distinct unity whose identity was defined by a common faith and whose existence was secured through the common governance of emperors and pope.[28] Whether men wrote of an *imperium christianum*, a *regnum Europae*, or later of a *societas christiana*, there was the same impulse to separate the known securities of the "inside" from the dark and threatening forces of paganism, heresy, and schism which lay beyond the perimeter. Nor is it difficult to find in modern political literature continuities with this type of thinking. It is sufficient to recall Burke's characterization of the French revolutionary government as breaking its "great political communion with the Christian world" and adopting a political foundation "fundamentally opposite to those on which the communities of Europe are built."[29] And the same theme has recurred in twentieth-century writings concerned with the challenges of Communism, Fascism, and Asian nationalism to the common set of cultural values associated with the "West."[30]

II **The Church as a polity: the challenge to the political order.** The recognition on the part of the early Christians that the Roman Empire constituted a bulwark of civilization did not, however, dissolve fully the inherent tensions between Christianity and the political order. Christians might feel gratitude to the Roman legions for securing the frontiers and to Roman officials for administering justice, yet gratitude could not compete with the Christian allegiance to the church-community. The discrepancy in value between the two societies constitutes only a part of the Christian position; for although they accounted the church-community superior they did admit that the political order was valuable for serving the ends of peace and maintaining the conditions of social life. As Augustine later allowed, even a society "alienated from the true God" contained a measure of worth.[31] Out of these considerations there issued the Christian estimate of the political order as a second-best arrangement, inferior to the promised city "which cannot be moved," [32] and necessarily condemned to rely on coercion rather than love. It was primarily for this reason, that is that the political order epitomized coercive power, that it could never rival the society of believers. This judgment had been passed by Paul in *Romans* when he had laid special emphasis upon the repressive nature of political authority: "he is the minister of God, a revenger to execute wrath upon him that doeth evil." [33]

In previous pages we have seen how the classical tradition had always struggled to show that the political order comprised more than mere power, that it was a complex of functions contributing positively to man's development. What Christianity succeeded in doing was to equate the political order with power and then, without conscious predesign, to transfer to their own society many of the attributes previously associated with the political order, including the element of power. "We also rule," declared Gregory Nazianzen.* "It is a rule that is more excellent and more perfect, unless the spirit is to be subjected to the flesh and the heavenly to the earthly." [34] The politicizing of the Church which paralleled the diminution of political qualities attributed to the political order was bound up with changes occurring in the life of the Church. By the end of the second century it had ceased to be a loose association of believers, bound together by ties of doctrine and the vague primacy of the early apostles, and had become instead an institutionalized order.[35] The appointment of its officers had been placed on a regular basis; the creed had become more formalized; a hierarchy of authority had developed; there were extensive properties to be managed; and a measure of uniformity had to be achieved among the scattered churches. The change from a spontaneous group life to a more formal ecclesiastical polity testified that the logic of order, like the fervor of belief, had its own imperatives. Although the primordial unity of Christian society had rested upon a unity of belief, it was gradually realized that a believing society did not differ from any other kind of society in its need for leadership, governance, discipline, and settled procedures for conducting its business. A passage from Origen, which deserves lengthy quotation, makes it apparent that the increasingly political character of the Church had made men conscious of the parallel with political societies, and that, far from being alarmed by the

---

* Gregory Nazianzen (329-389 A.D.), one of the "Cappadocian Fathers," was highly influential in the defense of the Nicene Faith and served as Bishop of Constantinople.

comparison, the response was to proclaim superiority of the Church, as a polity, over other political entities:

> The church (*ecclesia*) of God, let us say in Athens, is quiet and steadfast, as wishing to please God who is over all things; but the assembly — also called an *ecclesia* — of the *people* of Athens is full of discord, and in no way comparable to the Church of God in Athens. The same is true in . . . Corinth . . . Similarly, if you compared the Council of the church of God with the Council of any city, you would find that some of the councillors of the church are worthy, if there be such a thing as a city of God for the whole world, to join in the government of that city . . . you have only to compare the ruler of the church [i.e. the bishop] in each city with the ruler of the people in the city, in order to see that . . . there is a real superiority, a superiority in progress towards the attainment of virtue, when measured against the behavior and manners of the councillors and rulers who are to be found in these cities.[36]

Even in the early years there was evidence that the believers had realized that a kind of latent power inhered in the Church. This was identified with the miraculous workings of the Holy Spirit, indwelling in a congregation and heightening the solidarities of doctrine and ritual.[37] By the second century, however, the power of the group was coming to be associated with unity and uniformity; that is, with those qualities that had been central to the inquiries of classical political thought:

> And do not try to think that anything is praiseworthy which you do on your own account: but unite in one prayer, one supplication, one mind, one hope . . . When you meet frequently the forces of Satan are annulled and his destructive power is cancelled in the concord of your faith.[38]

When this point had been reached, the task of preserving unity led to other problems equally political in nature, such as the proper obedience to be rendered authority and the disciplinary instruments needed to insure conformity. In an argument no different from that commonly used to support political obligation, Ignatius pointed out how the office of bishop served to enhance the power of the group and that, therefore, the believer-subject must obey unhesitatingly:

> If the prayer of "one or two" has such power, how much more that of the bishop and all the church . . . Let us then be careful not to resist the bishop, that through our submission to the bishop we may belong to God . . . Let no one do anything that pertains to the church apart from the bishop . . .[39]

This shift in the center of gravity from the community to its leaders was summarized in the next century by Cyprian* in words that clearly revealed the degree of politicization that had crept into Christian modes of life and thought:

> The episcopate is one; the individual members have each a part, and the parts make up the whole. The Church is a unity . . . the Church is made up of the people united to their priest as the flock that cleaves to the shepherd. Hence you should know that the bishop is in the Church and the Church in the bishop, and that if any one be not with the bishop he is not in the Church . . . the Church is one and may not be rent or sundered, but should assuredly be bound together and united by the glue of the priests who are in harmony one with another.[40]

All that remained to round out the theory of authority was to give it a temporal depth, and thereby a legitimacy, comparable, say, to the hereditary principle in politics. This was supplied by the idea of apostolic succession which sanctioned power in the name of an unbroken chain of continuity, linking present office-holders with the primitive apostles:

> Age has succeeded age, bishop has followed bishop, and the office of bishop and the principle of church government has been handed down, so that the Church is established on the foundations of bishops, and every act of the Church is directed by those same presiding officers.[41]

These political tendencies were strikingly confirmed from another quarter. As the early Church became more routinized, developing settled ways of behavior, fixing points of doctrine, and evolving an hierarchical system of offices, it encountered a serious dilemma. On the one hand, it sought to develop doctrine and ritual in a way that would promote the widest possible unity consistent with truth; on the other hand, since this called for accommodating a wide variety of views at a time when doctrine and ritual had not fully matured, it was inevitable that the Church would be criticized by purists and accused of departing from the original legacy. The dilemma was that of any expanding organization; its size, complexity, and the variety of its constituents made it very difficult for it to continue making decisions without outraging a part of its membership. At the same time, the resentments thus provoked inevitably undermined the unity and consensus of the

---

* Cyprian (cir. 200-258 A.D.) achieved wealth and status as a lawyer before his conversion in 246. His great talents as an administrator were quickly recognized and he was made a bishop. His writings contributed one of the most comprehensive early theories of the nature of the Church.

community, thereby helping to destroy the conditions for effective action. As a result, the Church was plagued by a succession of internal dissensions which its organizational imperatives could not tolerate; the categories of schism and heresy were born, and their shape was conditioned in no small degree by the fact that the Church was deeply involved in the circular dilemmas of political types of decision-making.[42]

It is not our purpose to examine the range of issues provoked by these dissident movements, but to fasten attention on one aspect: that an important part of their grievances was directed at what we have called the "political" qualities of the Church. This was particularly marked in the case of Montanism,* which began in the middle of the second century and continued into the third when it attracted its most famous convert, Tertullian; and it formed a significant element in the Donatist** schism of the fourth century. The anti-politicism of these movements consisted in their rejection of just those aspects of the Church that were distinctively political. The dissidents protested that the true nature of the Church could not be reconciled with a decision-making organization resting on a sharply defined concept of authority, instruments of power for enforcing discipline and uniformity, a bureaucratic hierarchy designed to govern and administer a scattered constituency, and techniques of compromise, such as church councils and synods, to facilitate the Church in juggling its many contradictions of love and power, truth and solidarity, transcendent goal and worldly involvement.

This whole politico-religious complex was attacked at several crucial points by the dissenters with the result that the Church was driven to a deeper understanding of the political elements in its own make-up. In the first place, the rebels often expressed a view of history and time which, by its radicalism, pointed up the degree to which the Church had tamed and modified the primitive, chiliastic view of time to accord with the needs of an institutionalized order. The spokesmen of the Church sensed the inherent antagonism between the assumptions underlying an ordered structure, with its developing sense of tradition and reliance upon routine, and the assumptions of

---

* Montanism was a movement of the last half of the second century. It was characterized by a strong belief in the imminence of the Apocalypse and its outlook was colored by enthusiasm and asceticism. It was eventually condemned by the Church.

** Donatism was a fourth-century schismatic movement. African in origin, it was distinguished by rigorism, a "perfectionist" theory of the Church, and by the teaching that sacraments administered by an impure minister were invalid. At times members of the movement resorted to violence, and strong overtones of African nationalism were also evident.

those who had grouped together in the expectancy that the destruction of the world was imminent. Thus the contrast in conceptions of time was logically accompanied by opposing estimates of the worth of institutional arrangements. On the one hand, there was the high excitement generated by the belief in an impending apocalypse, an irruptive view of time: Christians, Tertullian declared, need no longer obey the biblical injunction to increase and multiply, for the last days were impending.[43] On the other side, there was the contrast of the unruffled, measured outlook of a large organization, sophisticated rather than primitive, viewing time as a gradual, smooth unfolding in the tempo of Elgar's *Pomp and Circumstance*. For the latter, time had to be adjusted to institutional life; to the former, institutions had shriveled to a trifling concern before the impending climax of history. If, as the chiliasts believed, the Apocalypse was near at hand, the "true" Church must be readied for the final test. Its membership must be rid of the tares and made a truly holy society, "without spot or wrinkle." Since the existing Church was one where "the Antichrist baptizes in the name of Christ, the blasphemer calls upon God, the profane person administers the office of the priesthood, the sacriligeous person establishes an altar," it behooved the true believers to break off communion, "to flee from and avoid, and to separate ourselves from so great a wickedness." [44] Thus like the style of argument used by later political as well as religious radicals — the Anabaptists, the English Puritans, the Levellers, Tom Paine, and Rousseau — these early dissenters hearkened back to a society at once simpler, purer, and undisfigured by distinctions of status or the tortuous methods of organizational decision-making. Tertullian's protest, "Are not even we laymen priests?" and its subversive conclusion that "you both offer and baptize, and are a priest alone for yourself," [45] carried the genuine accents of radicalism, its belief that virtue is stifled by institutions, that a mass of graduated intermediaries has been unnaturally inserted between the individual and the life-giving spirit he seeks. "Did God speak to Moses to speak to Jean-Jacques Rousseau?"

As in so many later forms of radicalism, "enthusiasm" ran high in these early movements.[46] Not the stately pondered decisions of ecclesiastical councils, but the sudden, spontaneous revelation of the private believer was taken as the mark of religious authenticity. This same temper was apparent later when, for example, the English Levellers appealed to the private judgment of the individual citizen: "every man that is to live under a government ought first by his own consent to put himself under that government"; or when Paine proclaimed the superiority of a system based on the spontaneous desire of each to satisfy his interests over one where prescription and hereditary right had etched things in a way outrageous to common sense. In the case of the early Christian radicals, what they wanted was not a bureaucratic but a pneumatic society, a society of ascetic spirits, undifferentiated by rank or authorities, held together, not by power, but by truth, and forever trembling with an explosive intensity.[47]

Anti-politicism was in evidence, too, during the great fourth-century controversy over the sacraments. One of the important issues, if we may simplify, was whether the sacraments administered by a bishop of dubious orthodoxy were invalidated by reason of his moral or religious deficiencies. The official position, as formulated by Optatus,* was that the sacraments were holy in themselves and not because of the men who administered them: "The Church is one, and its sanctity is derived from the sacraments, not weighed on the basis of pride in personal achievements."[48] The Donatists, on the other hand, contended that the worth of the sacrament was destroyed if the bishop were immoral or heretical. On its face, this dispute might seem a strictly theological matter of no political relevance. In actuality the reverse was true. The Donatists, in effect, were attacking the Church's conception of the transforming power of office. For the Church, the divine promise had been located only in the life of the religious society over which it presided; divine grace was expressed through its institutions. It followed that the personal sanctity of a bishop was subordinate to whether he had been duly invested with the authority of office.

That the Church should have taken this positon was some indication of the distance it had traveled since the days when it had been a spare organization of believers seeking to imitate the life of Christ. In keeping with the institutional behavior now demanded, the leaders no longer based their superiority, as of old, on the grounds that their actions were in *imitatio Christi,* but rather on the fiction of representativeness; that is, on the performance of an institutional function and the authority that accompanied it:

> The invariable source of heresies and schisms is in the refusal to obey the priest of God [the bishop], the failure to have one in the church who is looked upon as the temporal representative of Christ as priest and judge.[49]

The emphasis on authority indicated, too, the rejection of the Montanist and Donatist contention that the Church ought to be a holy community of the pure. In Augustine's formulation of the "official" position, the membership of the church-society was a mixture of sinners and saints, yet this did

---

* Optatus (fl. 370 A.D.) was an African bishop. Except for his attacks on the Donatists, little is known about him.

not undermine its authority or its holiness, because these were not gifts of the members but of Christ.[50] It followed from the mixed nature of the membership that authority and discipline, order and hierarchy were all the more necessary.

The natural accompaniment to these political manifestations in the Church was an increasing resort to essentially political modes of thought. Again the roots lie deep in the early beginnings of the movement. A hint is contained in the way that Christ was addressed by some of his followers as "king." Similarly, in the confession of the primitive church, the response, "Jesus is Lord," was squarely in the tradition of the patriotic confessions employed in the imperial cultus.[51] In the *Epistle to the Hebrews,* strong political overtones were in evidence: Jesus is given a throne and sceptre by God; through his faith he proceeds to political triumphs, subduing kingdoms and bringing righteousness; and the crowning fulfillment lies in the promise of "a kingdom which cannot be moved." [52] Again, St. Paul, in writing of the ultimate "community" in heaven, reverted to the Greek *politeuma,* a word rich in political associations; and when he went on to declare that the faithful, by virtue of their membership in the *politeuma,* were joined with the saints in heaven, the word he used was *sympolitai;* that is, fellow-citizens.[53] So accustomed did men become to sliding back and forth between political and religious usages that a scriptural text, like *Romans* xiii:2, which had been employed to enjoin political obedience — "whosoever therefore resisteth the power, resisteth the ordinance of god" — was turned by St. Basil* to magnify church authority: "those who do not receive from the churches of God what is commanded by the churches resist the ordinances of God." [54]

Recent scholarship has carefully investigated much of the Christian vocabulary and conceptual forms of the first five centuries and has produced persuasive evidence of the depth to which political ideas had penetrated theology. This in itself is not surprising. We have already pointed out that during the Hellenistic period political concepts had merged with ideas about nature and deity; hence the age in which Christianity first appeared was one in which the distinctiveness of political thinking had already been severely compromised. When Christians began to systematize their beliefs about the nature of God's rule, Christ's relation to the society of Christians, and the character of the Christian community, they could not avoid expressing their thoughts through prevailing ideas about the nature of the emperor's office,

---

* Saint Basil (*cir.* 330-379 A.D.) was famous for his formulation of the rules of monastic life. He held the bishopric of Caesarea and wrote vigorously in the defense of the Nicene formula.

the role of the citizen, and the function of a governing power. In describing God's nature, Origen paints a picture of an imperial monarch who governs the vast stretches of his domain without "ever leaving his home or deserting his state." Again, Lactantius discusses the question of "whether the universe is governed by one God or many" in the same manner that a classical political writer would have discoursed on the advantages of monarchy over government by the few or many.[55] Even in such unpromising subjects as Christology and Trinitarianism the political element was never far beneath the surface. Origen had Christ appear as a political savior, sent to rescue men from the final perdition and to revive the strength of rulers and ruled; to "restore to men the discipline of obedience, to the ruling powers the discipline of ruling." Tertullian turned to a familiar theory of monarchy in order to explain the role of the Father in the trinitarian formula, and in one of the early writings of Athanasius,* the *logos* was compared to a king presiding over the founding of a city; elsewhere he likened the *logos* of the Father to a power which ruled the cosmos by a nod, causing all things to fall into order and to perform their functions.[56]

What the foregoing suggests is that, as the Church evolved a political structure, it became increasingly natural for its spokesmen to fall into political modes of expression. This tendency was further supported by the fact that many of the leading churchmen had been educated in classical philosophy and rhetoric, disciplines in which the political element had been prominent. In view of the infusion of the political into church life and thought, was it accidental that the Church declared heretic the Tertullian who most concisely epitomized both the anti-political and anti-philosophical temper of a by-gone phase: "There is nothing more alien to us than politics . . . What is Athens to Jerusalem, the Academy to the Church?"[57]

III **Politics and power in a church-society.** After sketching the various features of the political profile of the Church, including the development of a political vocabulary, there remains the problem of whether the church-society could be said to be "political" in the far more significant sense of having to cope with situations comparable to those faced by any political

---

* Athanasius (*cir.* 296-273 A.D.) was the leader of those churchmen who defended the formulas of the Nicene Council against the attacks of Arius. The doctrinal contribution of Athanasius to the Nicene Faith was instrumental to its success. Throughout his life he was frequently exiled as a result of the intrigues of his enemies.

society. In other words, was the Church compelled to face the problems of "politics"? Earlier in our discussion "politics" was located in the situations of conflict and rivalry which crop out in society and call for the use of distinctive techniques of ruling, such as compromise, conciliation, the art of distributing various kinds of social goods, and, when necessary, the application of force. If we apply this conception to the Church, a surprising amount of politics is evident. To be sure, allowance has to be made for a certain refraction that occurs when political matters are passed through the different medium of religion, yet there is abundant evidence that the Church had continually to face political situations and that it responded to these in a political way. Although it might be said that political characteristics tend to become the properties of any large organization, enough has been stated already to indicate that these characteristics were not fortuitous products, happening to result because the Church had adopted a settled organization, but rather the logical consequence of latent political motivations and of the kinds of problems confronted. A remark by Chrysostom* illumines these tendencies: "Nothing will so avail to divide the Church as love of power." [58] This warning, which can be duplicated by many others, suggests that the Church was acting politically, rather than the different conclusion that some of its actions appeared akin to political behavior.

The most extreme form of political conflict was experienced in connection with the phenomena of schism and heresy, yet there were other, less spectacular, but equally political rivalries which plagued the life of the society during the formative centuries. For example, the contest over appointments to high ecclesiastical office was not greatly different from the usual rivalry for political positions. Again, the growing superiority of the bishop of Rome created national resentments among the churches in Antioch, Africa, and elsewhere with the result that the "central government" had to make concessions of various kinds — concerning finances, appointments, or local autonomy — which would satisfy local sentiments. The Donatist schism, for example, had drawn strength from the resentment felt by African Christians towards "outside" interference from Rome. Finally, the growth of an ecclesiastical bureaucracy, coupled with the federalism of the early church, created endless jurisdictional disputes of a type common to any political organization. We can summarize these considerations by saying that the Church, like

---

* Saint John Chrysostom (*cir.* 347-407 A.D.), a Greek Father of the Church, was famed as a reformer, a brilliant stylist, and strong opponent of allegorical and theological interpretations of scripture. He has been called the "greatest of Christian expositors."

any political order, had to face political problems at two levels, each of different intensity. At one level, that of primary or "first-order" conflict, it had to contend with disputes directed at fundamental principles of doctrine or organization. This occurred in the case of schisms and heresies where the Church was faced with the alternatives either of making concessions on fundamental matters, and thereby altering its own identity, or of extirpating the dissidents. At the other level of secondary conflict, such as that provoked by rival claims to a bishopric or by jurisdictional disputes, the issues could be resolved without touching the essential principles of the church-society.

The distinction between primary and secondary conflicts can be put in another way which draws out some further implications. Secondary conflicts of the kind mentioned above revolve around objects of scarcity: the demand for offices, honors, and money exceeds the supply. Consequently, the same problem of distributing scarce goods, which we have earlier noted in connection with political regimes, appears also in an ecclesiastical polity. The case of primary conflicts, however, is less straightforward, and there are further complicating elements in a church-society because of its claim to be based on truths that admit little leeway in interpretation. In the latter sense, the good symbolized by the Church is boundless and, therefore, unsusceptible to the sort of conflicts engendered by scarcity or by the thorny question of relative distribution which appears when social status, wealth, or preferment are at issue. At the same time, the Church also acts as guardian of a uniform truth which is conceived as being coextensive with the Church. This was the essence of Cyprian's formula, and it has remained the distinguishing claim of the Church over the ages: *extra ecclesiam nulla salus,* no salvation outside the Church. Thus the good administered by the Church was inexhaustible, but only within the confines of the Church. There could be no spiritual life outside; a schismatic group might perform the same rituals and utter the same words, but no efficacy attached to the ceremonies for they lacked the sanctifying holiness present in the life of the Church. "The Holy Spirit is one, and cannot dwell within those outside the community." [59]

The issues provoked by schism and heresy, by virtue of the fact that they touched upon fundamental principles, had the effect of deepening the political consciousness of the early Church and forcing it to defend its unity by methods comparable to those used by a political order. Although a distinction between schism and heresy was recognized after the second century, the early Church tended to treat both as raising conflicts of first-order significance. "It is not a different faith but the broken fellowship of communion

which makes schismatics." Or in the later definition by Isidore of Seville,*
"Schism is named from the rending of minds. For with the same worship and
rites it believes as the rest; it delights simply in the division of the congregation." [60] Against these threats the Church emphasized the importance of
unity, which it defined in terms of a uniform communion permitting only
minor differences. Just as a political order is led to distinguish between per-
missible and non-permissible forms of behavior and thought, and to decide
when disagreements become sedition, the Church, too, had to practice the
fine art of drawing lines. This had the effect of placing dissident groups,
whether of the latently or openly schismatic variety, in the same position as
a political faction. That is, the nature of unity in a religious society rested
upon uniformity, and hence any group that challenged the elements of uniformity became a divisive force. Words like *factio* and *stasis* crept into the
vocabulary of the Church, and controversies over doctrine, organization, or
appointments were fought out by organized groups, such as the one that
existed in the fourth century at Antioch over the *homoiousion* dispute. These
conflicts reproduced another form of behavior identical to that in political
societies when groups struggle to make their partial position or interest identical with the whole, and to have the seal of "public" authority affixed to their
viewpoint. The response of the Church was politically revealing in that it
exhibited a far greater elasticity in crucial matters than one might expect.
An impressive set of techniques of compromise and negotiation were employed to explore avenues of conciliation. Synods, councils, conferences, and
other methods for reaching agreement became political arts shaped to deal
with situations not covered by tradition, revelation, or the inspired literature
of the Church.

From the point of view of the schismatic, the decision that he had to make
formed a striking parallel with that facing a citizen who refuses to obey the
law. Apostasy is rebellion written in a theological key. Although the rebel
might claim that the official Church was no longer the "true" Church, he
could not avoid having to decide at what point he could no longer obey
without doing violence to his religious and moral scruples. Once this point
was reached, a host of other questions assailed him: how did he know that
his judgment was infallible? what effect would his disobedience have on the
Church? how was the truth which he defended to be weighed against the
evils which necessarily followed from disobedience to authority? was it

---

* Isidore of Seville (*cir.* 560-636 A.D.), author of the encyclopedic *Etymologiae*,
was famed both for his learning and his organizing abilities in helping to spread
Catholicism in Spain.

justifiable to rebel over a few points when one was in agreement with so much else? [61]

On its side, the Church had to face squarely the problem of coercion. St. Basil might describe the Church as "an evangelical and guileless polity," but its spokesmen quickly recognized that innocence was of no avail when the principle of ecclesiastical authority was being challenged by "mad dogs who bite secretly." [62] Beginning with the conversion of Constantine in the early fourth century and continuing throughout the next, Christianity frequently appealed to secular authorities for aid. One of the charges laid by the Donatists against the Roman Church was that the latter had called for the intervention of secular power into religious controversies. In attempting to justify this course, the Church apologists were compelled to examine the nature of power and the implication of its uses by an organization that professed virtues at the opposite extreme from coercion, virtues such as love, charity, and humility. There was little attempt on the part of these early Christian writers to dodge the issue, as later papal apologists were wont to do, by pointing out that the dirty business of punishment belonged to the temporal order, and that, therefore, while the Church defined religious crimes, its hands remained unsoiled by power. Instead, spokesmen like Augustine met the issue directly: how could a society based on belief, that is on the inner convictions of the members, justify the use of compulsion? The central issue was not so much whether the enforcement of legal penalties could direct external behavior; the church-society demanded believing adherents, not outward conformists. What, then, were the dynamics of power that enabled it to induce or compel a change of heart, a reorientation of belief towards the good?

By putting the question in this way, we are able to see the radical aspect to the Christian teaching on power. The source from which power drew its strength was fear, not the fear of the righteous, for whom the application of power was irrelevant, but rather the fear of the unrighteous:

> For rulers are not a terror to good works, but to the evil. Wilt thou then not be afraid of the power? do that which is good, and thou shalt have praise of the same: For he is the minister of God to thee for good. But if thou do that which is evil, be afraid . . .[63]

This early formulation identifying power with fear was perpetuated by later writers. Thus in the *Adversus Haereses,* written by Irenaeus* about

---

* Irenaeus (*cir.* 130-200 A.D.) has been described as "the first biblical theologian." He was a staunch opponent of Gnosticism and defended scriptural revelation and the primitive Christian view of history against esoteric teachings.

185 A.D., it was declared that originally fallen man existed in a condition of violence, but, unlike the later Hobbesian state of nature, there was no sense of fear to force men to ponder the way of escape. It required instead an act of divine intervention; God had to send government and law so that men might know fear and be receptive to obeying.[64] But this still left the basic question unresolved: was government simply a negative, repressive force, or could it exploit fear for creative ends? This next step was hinted at in Tertullian's cryptic formulation, *"Timor fundamentum salutis est,"* fear is essential to salvation.[65] Although Tertullian did not have in mind the use of political power, this became less important as the Church began to evolve its own forms of control, including the ultimate weapon of excommunication. In a society of believers there could hardly be any greater way of inspiring terror than to threaten men with separation from the life-giving communion. As Cyprian warned, under the old law the Jews had used the temporal sword to slay those who had rebelled against the authority of the priests, but now the religious rebel was cast out of the Church; that is, slain by the spiritual sword.[66]

By the time Augustine wrote, there had been almost a hundred years of experience with the use of secular power to support religious belief. His views were all the more significant because originally he had doubted the efficacy of force in changing convictions. The Donatist schism caused him to alter his position and to re-evaluate the matter. He held that coercion in itself was not evil; everything turned on the object towards which men were compelled. Admittedly, the application of power could not directly create true believers out of heretics and schismatics, but it could instill a salutary fear, a provoking stimulus forcing them to reconsider their own beliefs in the light of the truths to which they were being made to accede.

> When the saving doctrine is added to useful fear, so that the light of truth drives out the darkness of error, and at the same time the force of fear breaks the bonds of evil custom, then . . . we rejoice in the salvation of the many who bless God with us.[67]

To a surprising degree, Augustine rested the case for compulsion on pragmatic grounds. Since persuasion had proved unavailing in inducing the vast majority of men to enter the Church, sheer numbers could be brought in only by power, and hence the pragmatic test: did coercion in fact increase the number of Christians inside the Church? [68]

This tough-minded view of power seems incongruous in the great exponent of Christian love.[69] Yet the paradox is an important one, because it shaped a theory of power that has exerted a powerful influence in the West. Augustine consistently held that love and power were not of necessity mutually inconsistent: "righteous persecution" must be distinguished from "unrighteous persecution." Compulsion was righteously used when it was informed and motivated by a spirit of charity; to neglect those souls who had strayed from correct belief was a greater cruelty than punishment, because it forever condemned them to darkness. "Terrible but salutary laws" administered in a "spirit of love," and a deep concern for the souls of others, took the stigma from power. In short, love dictated compulsion.

Although there were some precedents for this notion in the Hellenistic and Roman tradition, where the emperor had been pictured as a kindly father who reluctantly chastised his child-like subjects for their own good, these had lacked the powerful passions and sentiments of Christian love. Power and compassion, the use of violence against persons with whom the power-wielder was implicated and interconnected by the mysteries of the faith, this was something new and frightening. Unlike Dostoyevsky's Grand Inquisitor who, readily admitting that his role was not that of the sweet and gentle Jesus, eventually drives the Savior away, the Augustinian power-holder had blended the two roles leaving no appeal from power to love.

Augustine was prepared to go even further in defending the use of power. Unity, he argued, was an essential quality of society, because it contributed to that condition of peace which made a Christian life possible. If unity was a good, Augustine reasoned, then even enforced unity possessed some value; and, since there could be no higher unity than that based on a common set of beliefs or "precepts of agreement," it was legitimate to enforce temporal penalties on behalf of true belief. Why should a man be allowed to enjoy the protections of the law and the benefits of society, and be free to sin? [70] With this the Western political tradition was brought to the edge of a definition of the political community which was to bedevil men with countless theoretical and practical difficulties down to the end of the seventeenth century: the definition of the political community as a unity of like-minded believers.

IV   The embarrassments of a politicized religion and the task of Augustine. Once the Church had accepted power as a legitimate instrument for advancing its ends, it faced the danger of losing its distinctive identity in an argument that proved too much. To the early Christians one of the main distinctions between the political and religious orders was that the latter alone controlled the practices of redemption. The peace, order, and prosperity maintained by government did not advance the salvation of the believers or invade the monopoly of the means of grace held by the Church. Yet if it were admitted that power could promote the divine mission of the Church, and if at the same time the state was viewed as the supreme embodiment of power, the unique character of the church-society would thereby be compromised.

The threat to identity had appeared in the fourth century when Christianity faced the great temptation, that of relying on a friendly government for support and accepting the use of political power to forward the universal mission of the Church. After the Roman policy of intermittent persecution had failed to check the rapid growth of Christianity, the state suddenly switched to the more benevolent and dangerous method of favoring the new religion. With the triumph of Constantine in the West (312 A.D.), Christianity entered into a novel and difficult stage, a kind of *scandale du succès* in which the status of a disreputable and harried sect was changed dramatically into a privileged position, that of the official state religion. The nature of Constantine's conversion is a vexed issue which need not detain us, for the important point was that his policies retained much that was reminiscent of older modes of thought concerning the relationship between religion and the political order. The danger came not so much from the favored position enjoyed by Christianity, but rather from its being converted into a chosen instrument for political regeneration, a "civil religion" shaped to the old classical model.

The suddenness of the developments found some of the Christian leaders unprepared and able to see only the great advantages in having the state actively promoting the faith. To some churchmen it seemed like a sign of speedy fulfillment of the divine promise that the religion which was meant for all mankind should now be linked to the imperium whose power seemingly stretched to the ends of the earth. Thus two pressures converged: the Christian one that aimed at the conversion of society and the political one that sought to harness this new *élan vital* for political ends. In Eusebius of Caesarea* a spokesman appeared voicing the rhetoric of the holy alliance. He did not hesitate to identify the fortunes of Christianity with the existing

---

* Eusebius (264-340 A.D.) was one of a distinguished line of Christian scholars at Alexandria. He became Bishop of Caesarea and later the advisor of Emperor Constantine. He is chiefly remembered for his formulation of an ideology that justified the alliance between Christianity and the Empire.

political arrangements, even to the point of inferring that Constantine had been sent by God for the special purpose of verifying the promise of Christ.

> . . . By the express appointment of the same God, two roots of blessing, the Roman empire and the doctrine of Christian piety, sprang up together for the benefit of men . . . [With the reign of Constantine] a new and fresh era of existence had begun to appear, and a light heretofore unknown suddenly dawned from the midst of darkness of the human race: and all must confess that these things were entirely the work of God, who raised up this pious emperor to withstand the multitude of the ungodly.[71]

The desperate wish to lessen the appalling distance between the Kingdom of God and the society of man encouraged a belief that the emperor represented a divine instrument of the *logos* and the political order a convenient vehicle for spreading Christian truth; yet when the wish took the practical shape of an alliance between church and state, it posed a real danger that the distinctive identity of the church-society would be lost. This was the fear that had moved Donatus to protest, "What has the emperor to do with the Church?" And it could hardly be said that the reply of Optatus was reassuring: "The *respublica* is not in the *ecclesia,* but the *ecclesia* is in the *respublica,* that is, in the Roman empire." These conflicting attitudes were but the partial expression of a developing crisis occurring within Christianity and demanding some answers to a whole range of delicate issues: how could Christianity support the state and be supported by it and yet avoid becoming merely another civic religion? what was the identity of the state in an historical situation where the Church had grown steadily more political in organization and outlook? what was the identity of the Church when the state undertook to advance the faith and police the behavior of the believers? could this hurry the last Judgment? where did both the Church and the political community stand in relation to the time-dimension of history?

The most comprehensive attempt at dealing with these problems is to be found in the writings of St. Augustine (354-430), the first and perhaps the greatest of Christian synthesizers. The significance of his work was not that it solved any of the political ambiguities in Christianity but rather that it supplied a depth and sharpness which rooted them more firmly into the Western tradition. He made the supreme effort to etch in the sharpest possible relief the *religious* identity of Christianity, its way of life and mission, its complex nature as an existential society as well as an intimation of a celestial society, its involvement in history and its ultimate triumph over time. Yet the ambiguities persisted; he recognized that at the existential level the Christian was politically implicated and crucially dependent on political society, so much so that the Augustine who could write of the notion of love (*amor*) with an unmatched passion and profundity was also the theorist of power, supplying the most persuasive case for coercing men's minds. These were ambiguities deeply rooted in Augustine's own life and personality; almost everything that he wrote carries the tensions of a passionate mind longing to rise above finite existence, "and by the continued soaring of the mind, to attain to the unchangeable substance of God." Yet he was also the ecclesiastical administrator, compelled to exercise power and to hand down judgment and punishment.

The culmination of this system, woven of the most exquisite contraries, found expression in the vivid symbolism of the two cities, of the holy society sustained by Christian *caritas* and the "minimum society" rent by human *cupiditas*:

> Two cities have been formed by two loves: the earthly by the love of self, even to the contempt of God; the heavenly by the love of God, even to the contempt of self. The former, in a word, glories in itself, the latter in the Lord . . . In the one, the princes and the nations it subdues are ruled by the love of ruling; in the other the princes and the subjects serve one another in love, the latter obeying, while the former take thought for all.[72]

It is important not to be misled by the powerful antithesis of the two cities into concluding that Augustine was interested in manipulating the political order only as a convenient foil for the superiorities of the Church and the glories of the celestial city. Augustine could dwell on the bitter quarrels that racked the earthly city and could speak of a deep enmity between the two cities, but he was also prepared to allow that society was natural to man, that far from being an unmitigated evil, it was "better than all other human good," and that even a society "alienated from the true God" possessed a degree of value.[73]

Once the complexity of Augustine's ideas is recognized and it is understood that the promise of a heavenly city was not taken by him to mean that the political order had shrunk to insignificance, then we can better appreciate that the dualism of the two societies functioned to establish the identity of the political as well as the religious order. The intricate pattern of religion and politics, intersecting but not absorbing, was fashioned to teach that the political and the spiritual were distinctive, however complementary they might be at certain points; that while each ought to benefit the other, neither could achieve the other's salvation; and since it followed that the one ought not to be judged totally by the mission of the other, each had to be understood to an important degree in its own terms.[74]

This can be stated differently by saying that Augustinianism contained a strong dialectical element in which the polarities of good and evil, flesh and spirit, Church and political society were lodged within a comprehensive and powerfully structured order which contained and directed these dynamics toward their predestined end. On the one side, the theory of antitheses meant, in its political bearing, that the political order, for all of its utility, was never exalted but only reprieved. On the other, the theory of *ordo* worked to knit the political into a cosmic whole, a gradually ascending hierarchy of ends, each of which was served by an appropriate order of power and authority. "Order is the distribution which allots things equal and unequal, each to its own place." [75] It was an hierarchical and distributive principle written into the very fabric of creation and animating things high and low, rational and non-rational, free and enslaved, good and evil. Its sustaining principle was love, the love of God for his creatures, the love of man for his fellows. *Ordo est amoris*.[76] When each creature within the universal network fulfilled its proper function, then order issued in peace. A perfect and total *ordo* rested on a congeries of supporting orders:

> . . . The peace of the household is ordered agreement of those who dwell together, whether they command or whether they obey; the peace of the city is ordered agreement of its citizens, whether they command or whether they obey; the peace of the heavenly city is the fellowship of enjoying God and enjoying one another in God, a fellowship held closely together by order and in harmony; the peace of all created things is the tranquillity bestowed by order . . .[77]

V The identity of the church-society reasserted: time and destiny. The idea of *ordo,* however, was more than the vision of an hierarchic universe, stable, compact, and seemingly static, wherein the manifold diversities of existence had been blended into an harmonious whole. The order of creation was a pulsating one which contained a thrust, or "set," written into its being. It was a unity pointing towards consummation at the end of time. In the Augustinian conception of time one of the most original and significant contributions of Christian thought was given its classic statement.[78] There were enormous political implications in the new notion of time, implications which did much to delineate the contrasts between the classical and Christian attitudes towards political problems. Among many classical writers time had been conceived in terms of cycles which closely resembled nature's seasons of growth and decay, regularity and repetition: "Things which are to be do not spring suddenly into existence, but the evolution of time is like the uncoiling of a hawser: it creates nothing new and only unfolds each event in its order."[79] To the Christian, with his belief that time was building towards a unique and shattering climax, the classical notion of an eternally recurrent cycle governing human affairs, a rhythm which began in hope and ended in despair, seemed a mockery of both God and man. "What wonder is it," wrote Augustine, "if, entrapped in these circles, they find neither entrance nor exit?"[80] Christianity broke the closed circle, substituting a conception of time as a series of irreversible moments extending along a line of progressive development.[81] History was thus transformed into a drama of deliverance, enacted under the shadow of an apocalypse that would end historical time and, for the elect, bring a halt to suffering. Buoyed by this "assurance of things hoped for" and secure in the knowledge that "the mystery which had been hidden for ages and generations has now been revealed to the saints," the Christian could anticipate what the classical mind had feared, the unfolding of future time. The future had become a dimension of hope:

> As, therefore, we are saved, so we are made happy by hope. And as we do not as yet possess a present, but look for a future salvation, so it is with our happiness . . . for we are surrounded by evils, which we ought patiently to endure, until we come to the ineffable enjoyment of unmixed good; for there shall no longer be anything to endure.[82]

All of these ideas spelled a new temporal dimension for the political order. In the providential plan controlling human destiny, it was the church-society that was the sanctified means. One of the striking aspects of classical thought had been that time had been conceived in largely political terms, as witness Plato's myth of Kronos and Polybius's cyclical theory of government. Political forms were treated as the media through which the processes of time and history were revealed. The new time-dimension, however, was both unpolitical and anti-political: unpolitical in that the vital moments of meaning (*kairoi*) in time, such as Creation, Incarnation, and Redemption, lacked any essential connection with political matters; anti-political in that political society was implicated in a series of historical events heading towards a final consummation which would mark the end of politics. From the Christian viewpoint the central issue was whether man and society would serve the ends of eternity or be satisfied with the transient goods that existed in time.

The new political criteria, as crystallized by Augustine, could be read in this way: to the degree that a political society promoted peace it was good; to the degree that it embodied a well-ordered concord among its members it was even better; to the extent that it encouraged a Christian life and avoided a conflict in loyalties between religious and political obligations, it had fulfilled its role within the universal scheme. The highest aspiration of political society was satisfied if it permitted those of its citizens enrolled in the *civitas dei* to pursue salvation unhindered by political distractions.

> The earthly city, which does not live by faith, seeks an earthly peace, and the end it proposes, in the well-ordered concord of civic obedience and rule, is the combination of men's wills to attain the things which are helpful to this life. The heavenly city, or rather that part of it which sojourns on earth and lives by faith, makes use of this peace only because it must, until this mortal condition which necessitates it shall pass away. So long as it lives like a captive and a stranger in the earthly city, though it has already received the promise of redemption, and the gift of the Spirit as the earnest of it, it makes no scruple to obey the laws of the earthly city, whereby the things necessary for the maintenance of this mortal life are administered; and thus, as this life is common to both cities, so there is a harmony between them in regard to what belongs to it.[83]

In Augustine's system the *civitas terrena* was not intended to represent in an exact way the political community any more than the *civitas dei* was synonymous with the Church. Rather the *civitas terrena* was a universal category imaginatively constructed to illustrate that type of life that contrasted most sharply with the *civitas dei*. Nevertheless, both the *civitas terrena* and the *civitas dei* were related in a special way to the political community, for the political community contained individuals typifying the antithetical ways of life associated with both of these cities. The political order, then, occupied a kind of intermediate plane where the two antithetical symbolisms intersected. The collective life of the political community was carried on amidst a deep tension between the naturalism of the daily activities of the community and the supernaturalism of the City of God.

Among classical writers, the radical plurality of human needs and aspirations had created the functions and justified the status of the political community. The satisfaction of these needs through the organization of a division and coordination of labor set the problem of political rule and political wisdom. Augustinianism, however, implied a contrary proposition: the highest, and therefore the most fundamental, needs of man were precisely those which no human society could ever satisfy. Ethical concerns no longer re-volved on a socio-political basis, but on the extra-political claims of the soul.

> [Christians] will not refuse the discipline of this temporal life, in which they are schooled for life eternal; nor will they lament their experience of it, for the good things of the earth they will use as pilgrims who are not detained by them, and its ills either prove or improve them . . . Incomparably more glorious than Rome is that heavenly city in which for victory you have truth; for dignity, holiness; for peace, felicity; for life, eternity.[84]

If, however, the political order were found wanting when judged against the dimension of eternity, how was it possible, within the Christian cate-gories, to treat of that middle area where political existence shaded into a realm of purposes, such as law, justice, peace, security, economic welfare, and a sense of community — all of which were significant without being ultimate?

This problem assumed central importance in Augustine's famous dis-cussion of whether the Roman state could be considered a true common-wealth. It provided a classic example of how the Christian adopted the older political concepts only to transform them. Augustine took Cicero's definition of a *respublica* — an association based on a common agreement concerning right and on a community of interests — and then raised the question of what conditions a commonwealth must satisfy before it could be considered "just." Now the classical political writers, such as Plato and Aristotle, did not deny the existence of an absolute justice, but they did assume that an inquiry into the relationship between the "political" and the "just" ought to be directed at the kind of justice that was relevant to the peculiar nature of the political community. Augustine, however, followed a quite different method. Instead of seeking to discover what kind of justice a political order was capable of, he argued that Rome could never qualify under the Ciceronian definition because "true" justice had never been recognized. "Justice which is true jus-tice resides only in that commonwealth whose founder and governor is Christ." [85] But this conclusion obviously turned on a different definition of justice and a different conception of commonwealth than that of classicism, a definition of Christian righteousness founded on the love of God, and a conception of a commonwealth transcending any human city.

It is a mark of Augustine's greatness that he was sensitive to the limita-tions inherent in this procedure. "If you adopt other and more acceptable definitions," then "in her own way and within a limited degree Rome was a commonwealth." [86] What other definition was possible and to what extent could a non-Christian society qualify as a commonwealth? Augustine responded with a definition remarkable for its naturalism: "A people is a gathering of a multitude of rational beings united in fellowship by sharing a common love of the same things." [87] This presented a striking contrast to the moral rigidity of the first definition where "true" justice had been restricted to the City of God and where every political society, past, present, or future, could be found deficient. This did not mean that the first definition was abandoned; it served instead as an absolute standard of justice. On the other hand, the naturalistic definition pointed to the possibility of establishing a gradation of *civitates*. The evaluation of a particular political order would then depend on the quality of the objects to which the "common love" was attached.[88] It also implied a more empirical temper since it presupposed some kind of investigation into the actual values sought and realized by a particular order. Above all, it allowed any political society that had succeeded in establishing order and peace to qualify in some measure, no matter how limited, as a commonwealth.

VI **Political society and church-society.** The estimate of the political order, as it finally took shape in Augustine's thought, was a complex one. It was acknowledged that a pagan order was valuable, if only for the minimal conditions of peace that it secured. On the other hand, even if a political society were dedicated to Christian ends and administered in a Christian spirit, it could never, as a society, know salvation or serve as the instrument of divine fulfillment. These limitations were inherent in the conception of history which, in its most fundamental meaning, had rendered the political order irrelevant and, ultimately, obsolete. The reorientation of time away from a political focus automatically excluded some of the boldest themes of classical political thought. One of the first casualties was the notion of political action as heroics. The political hero of classicism had presupposed that history was plagued by an unpredictable element which defied human forethought.[89] While the existence of chance or *fortuna* worked to make political achievements unstable and fleeting, it was also a challenge calling for heroic abilities. Politics was thus the sport of supermen who matched their skills against the incalculable whims of fortune, sustained only by the hope of shoring up a temporary island of achievement against the corrosive flow of time.

In the Christian view of history there was no place for *fortuna* and, by the same logic, none for the political hero. In his stead appeared the "Christian prince," a far different type of actor who found no exhilaration in political

challenge, merely weary duty, supported only by the hope of some day joining the truer kingdom. He was not the political hero, but the martyr-prince,
struggling "to make power the handmaid of God's majesty," but always with
something of the sweet sadness and resignation that had colored the musings
of Marcus Aurelius.[90]

The Augustinian conception of time, with its emphatic distinction between what was possible in history and what was reserved for eternity, also
condemned the classical quest for the ideal polity as an irreverent and proud
ambition. The promise of eternity was reserved exclusively for the *civitas dei.*
In the depreciation of the mission, efficacy, and moral status of the political
order, Christianity was faced with the temptation of substituting the church-
society in its stead, making of it an idealized political form which could satisfy the potentialities denied temporal societies. Was the Church, in other
words, to be viewed as a kind of etherealized version of the absolutely best
form of society, a christianized *Republic?* The answer is complicated by the
fact that almost from the beginning Christian writers had attributed at least
three distinct meanings to the notion of the Church. One of these referred to
the local organization, as in the phraseology of the first *Epistle of Clement:*
"The church of God which sojourns in Rome greets the church of God which
sojourns in Corinth." Secondly, there was the Church universal, which embraced the whole body of believers irrespective of locality. Finally, there was
the Church transcendent, the holy city, the final destination of those who
had been saved. The first and second meanings were later formalized into
the notion of the "visible" Church, an organized and institutionalized society
possessing the marks of power and authority which we have discussed earlier.
In the third definition, the "invisible" Church was not to be identified with
any earthly embodiment; it was a society of the blessed and consequently
had no need for the weapons of discipline and coercion.

Although we have oversimplified these distinctions and lent them a sharpness that was lacking in these early centuries, they do allow a better insight
into Augustine's ideas on the Church. There has been disagreement among
commentators on this topic, largely because Augustine did not always observe a sharp distinction between the visible and invisible Church.[91] Without
entering into the niceties of the matter, it is evident that Augustine did not
conceive of the visible Church primarily in terms of a power structure or
governing order. The conception uppermost in his mind was that of a community or society; that is, an association wherein power was not the constituent element of cohesion. In two of his favorite symbols, the Church was
likened to a mother and a dove.[92] These are not the language of power. This

is not to say that he advocated a "weak Church" theory, for his ideas on baptism, the ministry, doctrinal authority, and unity refute this.[93] It is difficult, nevertheless, to elicit from Augustine's writings the later political profile of a compact hierarchical structure of ecclesiastical power and authority. In other words, the visible Church did not surpass the political order on "political" grounds but by reason of its superior mission. Moreover, it could not be identified with the absolutely best form of society, for the mixed purity of its membership, some destined for salvation, others for damnation, rendered it inferior to the holy society. Similarly, the doctrine of predestination imposed clear limits on the power of the visible Church; the elect and the damned were singled out by an act of God, not of the Church.

Oddly enough, it was the *civitas dei,* the mystical society stretching over past, present, and future and defying identification with any visible institutions, that presented the most challenging parallel with political society. We have already noted that in early Christian thought there had been a tendency to associate the political order with compulsion and, on this basis, to contrast it unfavorably with the spontaneous solidarity of the society of believers. But this contrast became less impressive when the Church developed its own system of coercion. To preserve the superior identity of the Church required a conception of the Church as a coercionless society. This was crystallized in Augustine's *civitas dei.* In describing the two cities Augustine employed language and concepts in such a way as to drain off, so to speak, the divine elements, which both classical and early Christian thought had attributed to political society, and to rechannel them to the *civitas dei.* There persisted a strongly artificial and alien quality to political authority, Augustine declared: artificial in that God had intended men to have dominion over dumb animals but not over each other; alien, because in the last analysis the brief span of human existence made it irrelevant "under whose government a dying man lives, if they who govern do not force him to impiety and iniquity." [94] The depreciation of the political order left it vulnerable to challenge on *political* grounds by the *civitas dei.* Thus a political society could expect to be ruled alternately by good and bad rulers, but the City of God would never have any but the perfectly good rule of Christ. It followed that the bond between ruler and ruled in the one city was vastly superior to that which the other city might attain. Where the members of the heavenly city were knit together by a good that was truly common, the earthly cities were necessarily divided by the multiplicity of private goods and interests. In the one city conflict had been eliminated; in the other it was an inevitable accompaniment to the condition. At best, therefore, the earthly society might achieve but a well-ordered diversity, an unstable blend of good and evil; the *civitas dei,* on the other hand, enjoyed an unblemished harmony and order. Thus the heavenly city was not the negation of the political society but a perfecting of it, a transmuting of its attributes to a glory that the former would never know. Its fulfillment at the end of history marked the highest fellowship of which creation was capable, a *socialis vita sanctorum.*[95]

The crux of these contrasts lay in the inference that the *civitas dei* was more perfectly "political" primarily because it was more perfectly "social." The superiority of the "social" category over the "political" was a fundamental proposition in Augustine's thought. The one connoted harmonious fellowship, the other conflict and domination. The conclusion that flowed from this was that the more closely the political order approximated a Christian life, the less political it became. The conflicts that were the *raison d'être* of political authority would diminish in proportion as the society became truly christianized. At the same time, the "social" character of the order would be enhanced. This explains why the "political" was of less consequence than the "social" for the true Christian: while in the political order, he was not of it. His real membership was in the society of the elect, a life so far transcending the political order that it could be said to form one society with the angels.[96]

This notion that there was something more divine and natural about social relationships has cropped up repeatedly in later thought. Even though Aquinas later defined man as *naturale animal sociale et politicum,*[97] the belief persisted that society represented a spontaneous and natural grouping, while the political stood for the coercive, the involuntary. Curiously enough, the superiority of the social over the political found its fullest expression in the late eighteenth century. Tom Paine, for example, put it this way:

> Formal Government makes but a small part of civilized life; and when even the best that human wisdom can devise is established, it is a thing more in name and idea than in fact. It is to the great and fundamental principles of society and civilization — to the common usage universally consented to, and mutually and reciprocally maintained — to the unceasing circulation of interest, which passing through its million channels, invigorates the whole mass of civilized man — it is to these things, infinitely more than to anything which even the best instituted Government can perform, that the safety and prosperity of the individual and of the whole depends.[98]

Nor has the antinomy been laid to rest by more recent thought. The classical liberal economists, as well as Saint-Simon, the father of modern managerialism, accepted the notion of society as a spontaneous grouping but identified it with economic activities and relationships. Government, or the political, on the other hand, was pictured as an artificial controller whose existence was tolerated only to the extent that it secured the conditions making for spontaneity. This line of thought has also been retained by modern liberals. Thus Sir Ernest Barker defines "society" as "the whole sum of voluntary bodies, or associations, contained in the nation." In contrast to the "social" and "voluntary" character of society, the "state" "acts in a legal or compulsory way . . ." [99] Marxism, on the other hand, depicted the state as a power "above society and alienating itself more and more from it." Ultimately the proletarian revolution would destroy the state by a final act of force and thereby prepare the way for a society without conflicts or compulsion, a true *civitas humanitatis*.[100]

V II The language of religion and the language of politics: footnote on mediaeval Christian thought. Augustine's emphasis upon the social side of the Church pretty well summarized the Christian outlook of the first five centuries. The Church, he wrote, "is better than a society, . . . it is a fraternity." [101] Although, as we have pointed out, the power-profile of the Church was becoming more evident as time went on, it was not until the subsequent mediaeval period that the organizational, coercive side, that is, the Church as a rationalized ecclesiastical polity, came to predominate over the social or communal side. Consequently we can find at various times throughout the Middle Ages an undercurrent of unease fed by the Church's attempt to maintain a double identity: on the one side, the Church as the governing organ of Christendom; on the other, a society of believers who, in their mystical unity, were members of a living body following a common life inspired by the love of Christ. These two conceptions did not easily co-exist, and out of their commingling emerged a somewhat confusing image of an imperial power organization which professed also to be a community. The significance of this dual nature is that it expresses the quandary of most modern societies. Moreover, this similarity between the Church and modern political societies is not fortuitous. In both instances the force fusing the members into a solidary whole has been a mystical, non-rational one. In temporal societies it has been the force of nationalism; in the church-society it has been the sacrament of symbolic communion which joins the members to the mystical body of Christ.[102] The religious element in national sentiment can be exposed more clearly by indicating briefly the changes that the *corpus mysticum* idea underwent and how these were reflected into political thought.

The term itself, *corpus mysticum,* is uniquely Christian and without a biblical background.[103] It did not come into usage until the ninth century and at that time its meaning was strictly sacramental, referring to the Eucharist and not to the Church or to any notion of a society of Christians. By the administration of the sacrament the host was consecrated and incorporated into the mystic body of Christ.

As a result of the doctrinal disputes raised by Berengar, the mystical element receded, and the doctrine of the real presence of the human Christ replaced it. The *corpus mysticum* was now called the *corpus Christi* (or *corpus verum* or *corpus naturale*). This, however, was preliminary to the socializing and politicizing of the concept of the *corpus mysticum,* for after the middle of the twelfth century, the *corpus mysticum,* which had previously been employed in sacramental usage to describe the consecrated host, was now transferred to the Church. The mystical force and passion surrounding the old notion was brought to sustain the whole society of Christians and its power structure. In the papal bull of *Unam sanctam* (1302), the Church was described as *unum corpus mysticum cuius caput Christus,* one mystical body whose head is Christ.

Whereas classical political thought had ascribed a close, solidaristic nature to the political community, it had never conceived of it as a mystic body cohering around a godhead. But Christianity helped father the idea of a community as a non-rational, non-utilitarian body bound by a meta-rational faith, infused by a mysterious spirit taken into the members; a spirit that not only linked each participant with the center of Christ, but radiated holy ties knitting each member to his fellows. The Christian community was not so much an association as a fusion of spirits, a pneumatic being. This comes out clearly in a passage from Aquinas. After defining the sacrament of baptism as the method by which a man becomes a participant in ecclesiastical unity, Thomas described the nature of this sacramental society:

> . . . Life is only in those members that are united to the head, from which they derive sense and movement. And therefore it follows of necessity that by Baptism man is incorporated in Christ, as one of his members. — Again just as the members derive sense and movement from the material head, so from their spiritual Head, i.e., Christ, do members derive spiritual sense consisting in the knowledge of truth and spiritual movement which results from the instinct of grace.[104]

However, secular writers were not slow in perceiving the enormous emotional force that lay behind the idea of the *corpus mysticum.* By the middle of the thirteenth century one of them defined a people as "men assembled into one mystical body" (*hominum collectio in unum corpus mysticum*). Later writers, such as the Englishman Sir John Fortescue, tended to employ the phrases *corpus mysticum* and *corpus politicum* indiscriminately to designate a people or a state.[105] Something of this notion was later recaptured in Rousseau's conception of the community. Here, too, the members were suffused by a common spirit which drew them into the closest communion and dependency and expressed in the sharpest possible terms the distinctive identity of the whole. The ancient words of Cyprian, *extra ecclesiam nulla salus,* found their appropriate echo in Rousseau's dictum, *"sitôt qu'il est seul, il est nul,"* as soon as he is alone, man is nothing.[106] In accepting the bonds of civil society, each individual

> deprives himself of some advantages which he got from nature, yet he gains in return others so great, his faculties are so stimulated and developed, his ideas so extended, his feelings so ennobled, and his whole soul so uplifted, that, did not the abuses of this new condition often degrade him below that which he left, he would be bound to bless continually the happy moment which took him from it forever, and, instead of a stupid and unimaginative animal, made him an intelligent being and a man.[107]

These ideas of the redemptive community and the "new man" that issues from it recurred in the romantic and nationalistic literature of the nineteenth century. Articulate writers, voicing the loneliness of large and increasingly impersonal societies, clutched for ideas of a close communion which would turn highly utilitarian political organizations into vibrant communities and its apathetic citizens into fervent communicants.

> A country must have a single government. The politicians, who call themselves federalists . . . would dismember the country, not understanding the idea of Unity . . . What you, the people, have created, beautified, and consecrated with your affections, with your joys, with your sorrows, and with your blood, is the city and the commune, not the province or the state . . . A country is a fellowship of free and equal men bound together in a brotherly concord of labour towards a single end . . . The country . . . is the sentiment of love, the sense of fellowship which binds together all the sons of that territory.[108]

Although the mystical element furnished the basic ingredient of cohesion to the society of believers, it, no more than nationalism, could supply a rationale for coercive power. But what it did do was to shape the outlook of the members in a way that made them receptive objects of power. There was only one sense in which the sacramental bonds created an equality among the participants, and that was an equality of mutual subservience. Again, the anticipation of nationalism was striking; neither the *mystique* of the *corpus Christi* nor the *mystique* of the nation could admit an equality of claims on the part of each member against the others. To exploit the *mystique* of equal subservience was the task of papal writers of the Middle Ages, and they accomplished it in a most ingenious way. To establish the superiority of the Church and its governing head over temporal rulers they shifted the emphasis from the *mysticum* aspect to the *corpus* itself; like any body the Church needed a directing head, a prime mover who would impart a regular and purposeful motion to the whole.[109] Thus by giving a political twist to Aristotelian physics, the papal case could now exploit both sides of the Church's nature; the *corpus mysticum* idea could be used when there was need to emphasize the cohesion and unity of the society of believers, while the analogy with the physical body provided a defense for the position of the pope as the directing head. The one was essentially an argument for community, the other an argument for authority and power.

This notion of a society that was at once a mystical community and a structure of power was strongly suggested in St. Thomas's theory of the sacraments. Of all of the sacraments, he asserted, the Eucharist was the most important. "The reality of the sacrament is the unity of the mystical body, without which there can be no salvation; for there is no entering into salvation outside the Church . . ." It was the means for aggregating men into ecclesiastical unity, because the Church itself was identical with the mystical body of Christ. "The common spiritual good of the whole Church is contained substantially in the sacrament itself of the Eucharist." [110]

It remained for Thomas to connect the communal foundations prepared by the Eucharist, and further strengthened by Baptism and Confirmation, with the element of power. This was furnished by his conception of the sacrament of Order which dealt with the various offices and functions of the ecclesiastical hierarchy. Significantly, Thomas insisted that this sacrament, above all others, was most closely connected with the Eucharist. Order was the grand remedy against "divisions in the community," [111] the preservative of the mystical unity against schism and heresy. Order, therefore, required power, and order within the Church was concerned with the various gradations of power. "Each order sets a man above the people in some degree of authority directed to the dispensation of the sacraments." [112]

The political quality of the argument has an important bearing not only for interpreting the political philosophy of Aquinas, but also for understanding the effect on the Western tradition of this mixture of religious and political elements. Most political commentaries on Aquinas have concentrated on explaining how the Aristotelian revival of the twelfth century stimulated Thomas to revise the widely held Christian idea that the political order was rooted in man's depravity. Although it is undeniable that the political thought of Aquinas contained an important restatement in Christian terms of the classical belief in the dignity of the political community, the impression is created that the political element was restricted mainly to those parts of the Thomistic system that dealt with matters of government. What is most striking is the degree to which the concepts and vocabulary of politics had penetrated not only to Thomas's theory of the Church, which is not surprising, but also left a distinct imprint on his theology. Whether he was discussing the nature of the Divine Providence, the status of angels, the Church, or the sacraments, essentially political categories were recurrent: authority, power, membership, community, common good, law, and monarchical rule.

The primary medium through which the "political" was diffused throughout the Thomistic system was the notion of "order." This was the conceptual center that served to organize the realms of being. Since it was a concept heavily charged with political connotations, the realms themselves tended to assume a political character. "Divine providence imposes an order on all things and manifests the truth of the Apostle's saying: 'All things that are, are set in order by God' (*Romans,* xiii:1)." [113] "Order principally denotes power" and "power properly denotes active potentiality, together with some kind of pre-eminence." [114] God, angels, the Church, man, nature, and even the demons were implicated in a series of governed relationships which served to articulate the distinctive identity of each within the soaring hierarchy of creation.

> . . . One hierarchy is one principality — that is, one multitude ordered in one way under the government of one ruler. Now such a multitude would not be ordered, but confused, if there were not in it different orders. So the nature of a hierarchy requires diversity of orders . . .
>
> But although one city thus comprises several orders, all may be reduced to three, when we consider that every multitude has a begnining, a middle, and an end. So in every city, a threefold order of men is to be seen . . . In the same way, we find in each angelic hierarchy the orders distinguished according to their actions and offices, and all this diversity is reduced to three — namely, to the summit, the middle, and the base.[115]

Since each order was essentially a form of governance, it required a governing head to impart regularity and directed motion to the whole in accordance with the laws appropriate to the particular order.

> . . . Law denotes a kind of plan directing acts towards an end. Now wherever there are movers ordained to one another, the power of the second mover must needs be derived from the power of the first mover, since the second mover does not move except in so far as it is moved by the first. Therefore we observe the same in all those who govern, namely, that the plan of government is derived by secondary governors from the governor in chief. Thus the plan of what is to be done in a state flows from the King's command to his inferior administrators; and again in things of art the plan of whatever is to be done by art flows from the chief craftsman to the under-craftsmen . . . Since, then, the eternal law is the plan of government in the Chief Governor, all the plans of government in the inferior governors must be derived from the eternal law.[116]

The maintenance of these hierarchies of structured differences demanded power, as did the direction of each towards its proper end. A model of the right order existed for each ruling head to follow, and the task of every governor was to imprint the exemplary pattern on his subjects in much the same way as the Platonic ruler had been instructed to inform the "matter" of his community.[117] Like the Platonic guardian, the priest too was to be a selfless instrument, advancing the welfare of others while serving as the agent of a timeless idea. Yet in one crucial respect the priest was quite unlike the Platonic ruler and far more powerful: the power and authority of the priest did not rest on the uncertain base of personal merit, but on the solid bedrock of the most durable and powerful institution ever created in the West. It was not the private moral character of the priest or bishop that counted, but rather their "public" status as authorized agents of an institutionalized order. The inherent power and dignity of these offices was such that no personal failing could detract from the saving potency of the function; the mass performed by a sinful priest, for example, was no less efficacious than that of a good priest. The power that he wielded was not personal but functional.[118] More specifically, the power of priest and bishop was that of a representative; that is, one who was empowered to act in place of or on behalf of another. Thus in ministering the Eucharist the priest acted in the place of Christ, while the bishop, in acting upon the mystical body of the Church, was exercising a power on behalf of Christ.[119] It was a theory of representation, but of a limited type. The responsibility of the agent lay to a higher authority and ultimately to a form of truth. The ecclesiastical official, like the political ruler, existed to promote the good of those subject to his authority; that is, the good of his "constituents." But unlike the ruler, the power of the ecclesiastic was exerted over a constituency that could only be the object and never the source of authority.

These considerations of language, concepts, and style of thought should give pause to the usual view held concerning the fate of political thought during the Christian centuries. Every schoolboy comes to learn a list of dualisms purporting to describe mediaeval ways of thought: "secular" and "spiritual," "nature" and "grace," "faith" and "reason," "Empire" and "Church." These catchwords, in their application to political affairs, have encouraged the notion that the mediaeval mind drew such sharp distinctions between spiritual and political matters as to create two contrasting realms of discourse and action, existing side by side and occasionally converging for the sole purpose of abusing and misunderstanding each other. Another impression is that political thought diminished in importance during these centuries, becoming a mere handmaiden to theology, the new queen of the sciences. In this view a loss of status automatically implies a loss of vitality.

From this simple picture of things, it is easy to pass to the conclusion that Machiavelli and the writers of the Italian Renaissance "saved" political philosophy by dismissing from it all Christian objectives and presuppositions. This, however, is to misunderstand the character of mediaeval political thought and, as we shall see, to underestimate the revolution accomplished by Machiavelli. In actuality, political thought was nourished and extended during the Middle Ages, and nowhere is its political quality better demonstrated than in the kinds of arguments and vocabulary employed by papal writers during the long controversies between the papacy and secular writers. All of the major categories of political and legal thought were explored in the effort to defend the cause of the Church: the legitimacy of the derived powers of the popes; the necessity for a directing authority within the Christian society; the scope and limitations of papal rulership and its relationship to various forms of law; and the nature of the obedience demanded of its subjects. As one reads the voluminous polemics of the age, it is difficult to evade the conclusion that there was little to distinguish the papal arguments from purely political ones. Save for certain important premises derived from Christian sources, the propositions and conclusions contain very little that justifies their being treated as peculiarly religious or Christian. This is not to belittle the subtlety or profundity of the case, but only to emphasize its strongly political character. Consequently, when emperors and national monarchs came to challenge papal claims, the situation is not to be likened to one where secular rulers and their champions put forward a "political" theory to defend a "political" position, while the papalists opposed them with esoteric arguments drawn from the mysteries of revealed religion. In reality it was a situation where one political theory, which often frantically sought to bolster its cause by borrowing religious ideas from its opponents, was pitted against another political theory which spoke in the name of an organized religion that had become deeply politicized in thought and structure. For example, one of the fundamental contentions advanced by papal writers was that governance was not the monopoly of the political order. This was often couched by saying that inferiors ought to be ruled by superiors, but, as the following quotation from a fourteenth-century papal apologist, Aegidius Romanus, makes clear, the significant point is the assumption that centuries of thought and experience had made natural; namely, that the two orders of Church and political regime could be profitably compared because both were orders of government:

> Inferior bodies . . . are ruled through superior bodies, and the grosser through the more subtle and the less potent through the more potent . . . And what we see in the order and government of the universe we ought to copy in the government of the commonwealth and in the government of the whole Christian people. For the same God Who is universal ruler of the whole machinery of the world is special governor of His church and those who believe in Him.[120]

We can summarize the foregoing pages on the Christian encounter with politics by saying that Christian learning, far from obliterating a tradition of political thought, had revitalized it: *gratia non tollit scientiam politicam sed perficit.* The supreme irony of this development was that it helped prepare the way for the emancipation of political theory from its servitude to theology. For although the categories of religion were becoming highly politicized, the reverse was not true of political theory. As the political ideas of Aquinas showed, Christian writers were largely content to point the traditional concepts of political theory towards distinctively Christian ends, but without destroying the content of the concepts themselves. The political order, for example, was declared to be necessary for the attainment of the highest earthly good, although it could never effect the supreme good. But inasmuch as classical political thought had never entertained the notion of the political order as preparing mankind for some suprahuman good, its categories of thought could be retained, and the basic problem became one of insisting upon the point at which classical notions no longer held good.

At the same time that traditional political ideas were being preserved insofar as they were used to explain essentially political phenomena, theological categories became increasingly infected by political notions; political ideas were pressed to explain grace as well as "nature." Now in a situation where theology had become compromised by its politicalness and political theory proper remained largely unchanged, it is not surprising that the attempt of mediaeval writers to assert the superiority of the spiritual realm over the temporal — an attempt perfectly in keeping with Christian postulates — should have produced, as far as the status of political theory was concerned, an opposite result to that intended. One would naturally expect that the assertion of the superiority of sacerdotal over temporal authority would lead also to the submergence of political theory beneath theology, and to the eventual obscuring of things political. Instead, the identity of political theory and the integrity of its subject-matter were disclosed more clearly. For when a point of view, which professes to be spiritual but is in fact highly sophisticated politically, tries to draw rather sharp lines between the political and the religious, it succeeds, not in subordinating the political to the religious, which at best can only be a short-run achievement, but in preserving the identity of the political. In insisting, as Thomas did, upon the vital role of the political order, in seeking to define the distinctive laws by which it was ruled, the unique common good which it served, and the kind of prudence proper to its life, there was a heavy price to be paid, even though the terms were not fully revealed for several centuries. Thomas had not only restored the political order to repute; he had given it a sharpness of identity, a clarity of character, that had been lacking for several centuries. The "political" might be enclosed within the soaring architecture of creation, but it had not been swallowed up. Creation itself was a structure, a complex, institutionalized order composed of regularized processes and governing authorities. In this respect, Thomas merely capped off a long development that had been growing steadily almost since the emergence of Christianity; without a conscious intent to do so, Christianity had once more taught men to think politically. When this was accompanied by a growing appreciation of the identity of the political order, the way had been prepared for Machiavelli's reassertion of the radical autonomy of the political order.

Before turning to Machiavelli, however, it is necessary to examine the last sustained attempt at establishing a distinctive religious perspective on politics. The Protestant Reformation deserves a place in this study on several accounts. It began, with Luther, as an attempt to depoliticize religious thought and ended, with Calvin, in the readmission of political elements into religion.

It began with an assault on the ecclesiastical polity that was the mediaeval Church and, after passing through a phase of deep hostility towards institutionalism, ended with the construction of the granite edifice of Geneva. It invented the "tender conscience" which was to disturb Western societies for at least two centuries and then it frantically sought a discipline to control its creation. It often fell to preaching a doctrine of a spiritual kingdom aloof from the political society, yet it often yielded to the tempting vision of a New Jerusalem which would be imposed on the old society.

❧ FIVE ❧

Luther:

The Theological and the Political

All terms become new when they are transferred from their proper context to another . . . When we ascend to heaven, we must speak before God in new languages . . . When we are on earth, we must speak with our own languages . . . For we must carefully mark this distinction, that in matters of divinity we must speak far differently than in matters of politics.

LUTHER

I   **Political theology.** In its theology and philosophy, the mediaeval mind displayed a fondness for making complex distinctions which later ages have found both admirable and annoying, admirable because of the analytical subtleties that were developed and annoying because of the seemingly trivial subjects that were discussed. What was most impressive about this penchant for distinction-making, as well as what gives it an appeal for many moderns, was that most mediaeval thinkers could assert fine and even sharp distinctions between matter and spirit, essence and attribute, faith and reason, spirituality and temporality, without dissolving irrevocably their connective tissues. Things might be sharply defined and analytically distinguished, yet this was not taken as evidence of a want of coherence. To an age that distrusted discontinuities, identity, even of a highly distinctive kind, did not denote isolation or autonomy.

In keeping with this vein, mediaeval historians have warned us against reading modern antitheses, like "church" and "state," into mediaeval thought. Most mediaeval thinkers assumed that *regnum* and *sacerdotium* formed complementary jurisdictions within the *respublica christiana*. Yet the running disputes between the papacy and temporal rulers over such matters as the taxation of the clergy and investiture of bishops should give pause to those who believe that an agreement about fundamental values and assumptions *ipso facto* eliminates the possibility of bitter conflict. One might just as easily conclude from the mediaeval experience that disputes tend to become more embittered when each side is intent on capturing the same symbols of authority and truth; common ground and battleground can become interchangeable.

From the discussion of the preceding chapter, we can see that the common outlook that informed the mediaeval approach to problems of religion and politics derived its strength from more than a shared set of religious beliefs and habits. It was supported also by the way in which political and religious concepts had come to influence each other. This, in turn, faithfully reflected the realities of mediaeval life where the political and the religious were subtly interwoven. But the great issue that arose near the end of the Middle Ages concerned the fate of these mixed and interdependent moods of thought in a world where national particularism had visibly shaken assumptions about the universal society of Christendom. The end of the alliance between religious and political thought was foreshadowed in the fourteenth-century figure of Marsilius of Padua. What could have been more mediaeval than the opening promise to discuss the "efficient cause" of laws? But the tone changes abruptly and Marsilius announces that he is not going to treat the establishing of laws by any agency other than the human will; that is, he is not interested in God's role as prime legislator. "I shall treat the establishment of only those laws and governments which spring directly from the decision of the human mind."[1] Yet Marsilius, for all of his radicalism, still retained strong traces of the mediaeval outlook, and it is to the sixteenth century that we must turn in order to discover a revolution in political thought comparable to, and reflective of, what had occurred on the actual plane of political organization.[2] In the two great impulses of Protestantism and humanism, we find the vital intellectual forces that dissolved the common outlook achieved by the mediaeval mind. Each in its own way worked towards a more autonomous political theory and one that was more national in orientation. On the one side, the contribution of Luther and the early Protestant Reformers was to depoliticize religion; on the other, that of Machiavelli and the Italian humanists worked to de-theologize politics. Both sides served the cause of national particularism.

II **The political element in Luther's thought.** The impulse towards disengaging political elements from religious modes of thought had its ultimate origins in Luther's fervent belief that "the word of God, which teaches full freedom, should not and must not be fettered." [3] This quest for the "real" in religious experience eventually drove Luther into bitter opposition to what he considered as the two main enemies of religious authenticity: the hierarchically organized power structure of the mediaeval Church and the equally complicated subtleties of mediaeval theology. In both areas, Luther's basic urge was towards simplification: pure truth was to be uncovered by sloughing off the man-made complications which had accumulated over time. Characteristic of this "simplistic imperative" were Luther's attacks on the confused state of marriage laws:

> . . . Any and all of the practices of the Church are impeded, and entangled, and endangered, on account of the pestilential, unlearned, and irreligious, man-made ordinances. There is no hope of a cure unless the whole of the laws made by men, no matter what their standing, are repealed once for all. When we have recovered the freedom of the Gospel, we should judge and rule in accordance with it in every respect. [4]

In its broad outlines, Luther's case implied more than a return to a primitive purity in doctrine and ritual. Its main thrust was directed against ecclesiasticism and scholasticism; that is, against a church structure whose hierarchical principle and temporal entanglements had left a strongly political mark on the life of the Church; and against a mode of thought that had become imbued with political overtones. Consequently, as Luther developed his ideas on doctrine and the nature of the Church he moved steadily in the direction of reducing the political elements in both subjects. In the end he succeeded in creating a religious vocabulary largely devoid of political categories. [5] Yet, and this is the paradox, it was this depoliticized religious thought that was to exercise a profound influence in the later evolution of political ideas; the more heavily political formulations of Catholicism, on the other hand, exerted little effect except by way of hostility.

The importance of Luther in the history of political thought resides in more than his attack on political theology. He also elaborated an important set of political ideas about authority, obedience, and the political order which were so closely related to his religious beliefs as to point to the conclusions that his political ideas presupposed his religious beliefs in a peculiar way. It was not that Luther's political ideas were logically deducible from his religious premises, or that both formed part of a unified system. Rather, Luther's theology "fed" his political ideas in the sense that what he eliminated from the Church in the way of power and political patterns he was compelled to reassert in his conception of temporal government. More succinctly, Luther's political authoritarianism was the product of the anti-political, anti-authoritarian tendencies in his religious thought. The shape of his political thought was determined in large measure by the basic aim of reconstructing theological doctrine. But, as we have noted, one consequence of the critical destructiveness which accompanied this effort was to depoliticize religious categories. Not only did this have a profound effect on theology, but it had important political repercussions as well. The political elements which had been rejected in matters of dogma and ecclesiology could now be more wholly identified with the concerns of political thought. The effect of this was to be far-reaching, even though Luther had not intended it; for the necessary precondition for the autonomy of political thought was that it become more truly "political." That the independence of political thought involved more than a matter of theoretical interest is evidenced by the fact that these developments were accompanied by practical actions on Luther's part which pointed in the same direction. The autonomy of political thought, now rid of the enclosing framework of mediaeval theology and philosophy, went hand in hand with the autonomy of national political power, now unembarrassed by the restraints of mediaeval ecclesiastical institutions.

Before turning to these problems, a preliminary difficulty must be disposed of. It has been argued by some commentators that Luther's thought, from beginning to end, was motivated solely by religious concerns and that, therefore, his outlook was fundamentally non-political. In the words of one recent writer, Luther "was first of all a theologian and a preacher," hence "he never developed a consistent political philosophy and knew little about the theories underlying the formation of national states in western Europe." [6] Although it would be fruitless to deny the primacy of theological elements in Luther's thought, it is misleading to conclude on that account that politics was an alien concern. Luther himself held no such modest view of his own political acumen. Prior to his own writings, he declared, "No one had taught, no one had heard, and no one knew anything about temporal government, whence it came, what its office and work was, or how it ought to serve God." [7] Underlying this exaggeration was the implicit assumption that a religious reformer could not avoid political speculation. The extraordinary intermixture of religion and politics in that period compelled him to think about politics and even to think politically in religious matters. It was at once Luther's insight, as well as the source of a good many of his later difficulties, that he understood that religious reforms could not be undertaken in utter disregard of political considerations. It was exactly this lesson that many of the sectarians ignored at great cost. The problems in Luther's political thought were not the product of a monumental indifference toward politics, but arose from the "split" nature of a political attitude which oscillated between a disdainful and a frenetic interest in politics and sometimes combined both.

Although the historical entanglements of politics and religion in the sixteenth century contributed in no small measure to Luther's political consciousness, an even more influential factor lay in the nature of the religious institutions that he attacked. His great anti-papal polemics of 1520 were directed against an ecclesiastical institution that, to the sixteenth-century mind, had come to epitomize organized power. The nature of the papacy invited an indictment framed in political terms, and in this stage of its development, Luther's ecclesiology retained important political elements. His writings of 1520 provide impressive evidence that he clearly recognized the issue to be one involving the power of an ecclesiastical polity. In the first place, the vocabulary employed was heavily sprinkled with phrases and imagery rich in political connotations. The sacramental practices of the priesthood were attacked as "oppressive" (*tyrannicum*) in that they denied the believer's "right" (*ius*) to full participation. The papacy was denounced as the "tyranny of Rome" (*Romanam tyrannidem*), a "Roman dictatorship" (*Romana tyrannis*), to which Christians ought to "refuse consent" (*nec consentiamus*). The demand was then raised for the restoration of "our noble Christian liberty." "Each man should be allowed his free choice in seeking and using the sacrament . . . the tyrant exercises his despotism and compels us to accept one kind only." [8]

The political note became more pronounced as Luther went on to accuse the papacy of ecclesiastical tyranny: the papacy had arbitrarily legislated new articles of faith and ritual. When its authority had been challenged, it had sought refuge in the argument that papal power was unbound by any law. Moreover, the temporal pretensions of the papacy had not only endangered the spiritual mission of the Church, but had damaged the effectiveness of secular authority as well by confusing secular and spiritual jurisdictions. [9] The usurpation of temporal power had permitted the popes to advance their temporal claims under the guise of a spiritual mission, and, at the same time, to pervert their spiritual responsibilities by treating them politically. On this latter score, the sale of indulgences, the annates, the proliferation of the papal bureaucracy, and the control over ecclesiastical appointments had as their objective, not religious considerations, but the enhancement of the political power of the papacy. The pope had ceased "to be a bishop and has become a dictator." [10]

During these early years Luther was prepared to accept the perpetuation of the papacy on a reformed basis. His criticisms were founded on the assumptions that religion and politics constituted two distinct realms within the *corpus christianum;* that each realm required its own form of ruling authority; and that although rulership might be either of a religious or of a political type, it ought not to be both. Despite these distinctions, Luther's program for papal reform carried strong political overtones in that it was basically a demand for ecclesiastical constitutionalism and owed not a little to conciliarist inspiration. [11] The pope was to exchange the role of despot for that of constitutional monarch. Henceforth his power was to be bounded by the fundamentals of Christianity, and he could no longer legislate new articles of faith. Thus the teachings contained in Scripture were to be observed in much the same way as a fundamental law; they performed the function of a doctrinal constitution limiting the power of the popes. [12] To the papal argument that such institutional tinkering was blasphemous in that it would allow unclean hands to tamper with a divine institution, Luther responded that the papacy itself was of human fabrication and hence susceptible of improvement.

The political element in Luther's case received further emphasis in the remedies he prescribed for dealing with a pope who refused to recognize the bounds of his authority. If a pope persisted in violating the clear injunctions of Scripture, then Christians were obligated to follow the fundamental law of Scripture and to ignore the papal commands. [13] Parenthetically it should be noted that this was the same formula employed later by Luther in dealing with secular rulers whose commands ran counter to Scripture. But in one particular Luther was prepared to counsel measures more drastic than anything he proposed against secular rulers. In an argument more political than scriptural, he contended that the papacy might be forcibly resisted. "The Church has no authority except to promote the greater good." If any pope were to block reforms, then "we must resist that power with life and limb, and might and main." [14]

Although Luther later retracted this and other more sanguinary exhortations,[15] the political element reached a climax when Luther prescribed for the condition *in extremis* where the papacy blocked all efforts towards reform. Secular authorities possessed the right and the responsibility to initiate the processes of reform:

> Therefore, when need requires it, and the pope is acting harmfully to Christian wellbeing, let any one who is a true member of the Christian community as a whole take steps as early as possible to bring about a genuinely free council. No one is so able to do this as the secular authorities, especially since they are also fellow Christians, fellow priests, similarly religious, and of similar authority in all respects.[16]

Despite the acerbity displayed in Luther's writings of this period, their revolutionary quality was blunted by the reliance on conciliarist arguments. He looked to a combination of secular initiative and conciliar reforms to restore the purity of the papacy. In place of papal supremacy he relied partly on the older notion of the conciliarists that the Church was a *societas perfecta,* a self-sufficient society containing its own authority, rules, and procedures for regulating the common spiritual life of its members. According to this conception, essentially Aristotelian and political, the Church contained within itself the necessary resources for remedying any ills or grievances that might afflict it.

These conciliarist arguments worked to obscure two emergent aspects of Luther's thought: the reliance on secular authority and the bias against institutions. As long as Luther placed his hopes in a Church council as the agency of reform, the secular ruler was reduced to secondary importance. But once this avenue of reform was closed off, the choice was automatically narrowed down to the secular ruler. When this stage was reached, the idea of the Church as a *societas perfecta* was dropped; the revitalization of its spiritual life was now held to depend on an external agency. In other words, as Luther's Church became less political in concept, it became increasingly political in its dependency on secular authority.

As long as Luther adhered to a conciliarist position, and as long as he attributed some utility to the papacy, the revolutionary quality of his theory of the Church would remain muted. But once he had broken with pope and council, the doctrine of the "priesthood of all believers" would assume central importance and the Lutheran conception of the Church would become clearer. Both of these developments, the reliance upon secular rulers and the Lutheran idea of the Church, were interrelated dialectically, in that Luther's quest for the "real" in religious experience led him to dismiss ecclesiastical institutions and to magnify the political institutions of the ruler. It is only partly correct to attribute Luther's emphasis on secular authority to the desperate plight of a reformer who had no alternative but to appeal to that quarter. Nor is it correct to view his extreme utterances during the Peasants' War as marking a sudden discovery of the absolute power of secular princes. There is sufficient evidence to indicate that he held a high opinion of secular authority before the peasant outbreaks. Instead, the emphasis on secular power should be viewed as the outgrowth of the deepening anti-political radicalism of his religious convictions, which, by assigning exclusive rights over the "political" to temporal governors and by minimizing the political character and ecclesiastical power of the Church, opened the way for a temporal monopoly on all kinds of power.

Once this is grasped, Luther's later dilemma becomes more understandable; the secular powers, whose assistance he had invoked in the struggle for religious reform, began to assume the form of a sorcerer's apprentice threatening religion with a new type of institutional control. The sources of this dilemma lay in the disequilibrium which had developed between his theory of the Church and his theory of political authority. In the early years of his opposition to the papacy, he did not disavow the central argument of the papalists that spiritual affairs required a ruling head. Thus, although he disagreed with the papalists over the nature of that office, his thinking preserved the mediaeval tradition of a distinctive set of ecclesiastical institutions which might offset the thrusts of temporal powers. But as his views matured into a flat rejection of the papacy and of the entire hierarchical structure of the Church, the whole idea of a countervailing authority was naturally dropped. The tie between religious beliefs and religious institutions was severed; at this stage of his thought, Church organization was regarded as an impediment to true belief. Concurrently with these developments in Luther's conception of the Church, his doctrine of political authority had evolved towards a more enlarged view of the functions and authority of rulers. The rulers were now entrusted with some of the religious prerogatives previously belonging to the pope.[17] Thus while institutional authority was being undermined in the religious sphere, it was being underscored in the political.

It was at this point that the supreme difficulty arose. In his later years, Luther began to pay increasing attention to the need for religious organization, a need that he had earlier minimized. But for practical reasons this could not be accomplished except by calling in the secular authorities whose power he had consistently exalted. The institutional weakness of the Church made it no match for the secular power that Luther had rationalized. The end-product was the territorial Church (*Landeskirche*).

Luther's elevation of political authority, then, was closely connected with his idea of the Church. The latter, in turn, was an outgrowth of his conception of religion; hence something must be said about his religious doctrines and their bearing upon his ecclesiology and politics.

In Luther's theology the supreme vocation of man consisted in preparing for God's free gift of grace. Religious experience was located around an intensely personal communication between the individual and God; the authenticity of the experience depended upon the uninhibited directness of the relationship. Good works, therefore, were unavailing unless informed by God's sanctifying grace. "Good and pious works can never produce a good and pious man; but a good and pious man does good and pious works." [18] Similarly, the ministrations of an ecclesiastical hierarchy and the full sacramental system were both useless and dangerous; they only multiplied the intermediaries between God and man and raised the inference that there existed a substitute for faith. In sum, everything that stood between God and man had to be eliminated; the only true mediators were Christ and Scripture.

Against this backdrop, Luther's famous metaphor of the "three walls" surrounding the papacy was symbolic of the dominant driving force in his religious thought: the compulsion to erase and level all that interfered with the right relationship between God and man. The significance of this "simplistic imperative" lies in the variety of ways in which it was expressed: political, intellectual, as well as religious. Intellectually it took the form of a nearly total rejection of the mediaeval philosophical tradition. It was not a rejection steeped in ignorance, but one flowing from a deep conviction that centuries of philosophy had worked to pervert the meaning of Scripture and to support the pretensions of the papacy.[19] The influence of Aristotle was declared to be pernicious; the Christianized Aristotelianism of Aquinas was condemned as an "unfortunate superstructure on an unfortunate foundation." [20] Impatient with the "Babel of philosophy," with its endless and subtle disputations concerning substance and accidents, Luther called for a return to the unglossed wisdom of Scripture and the Word of God.[21] In this connection, his radicalism was also turned against the *corpus* of traditional knowledge represented by the teachings of the Church Fathers, the pronouncements of the councils, and the doctrines of the canonists. The significance of the attack can best be grasped if it is recalled that mediaeval Church doctrine, formal theology, and philosophy had become deeply impregnated with political strains.

It was not accident, but a kind of unerring instinct, that led Luther to group together philosophers, canonists, and theologians, for the extent to which each had incorporated political concepts was largely a matter of degree. From this point of view, then, Luther's attack had the effect of dissolving the alliance between religious and political thought.

One important indication of this trend in Luther's thought is provided by a contrast between his theory of the sacraments and that held by a mediaeval theologian like Aquinas. One of the most striking aspects of Thomas's discussion of the sacraments was its doubly political character; the language and concepts evoked a strongly political imagery, and the nature of the sacraments was defined so as to strengthen the political character of the Church and its priesthood. The sacraments, he declared, were to be understood as more than a sign or symbol; they were a form of power (*vis spiritualis*) which imprinted a certain character on the recipients; the grace that informed the soul was an infused grace (*gratia infusa*). The "power-nature" of the sacraments also had an important bearing on the role of the priests. The sacrament of ordination established a necessary and salutary inequality of some men over others; the superior excellence of the priesthood was essential to the perfection of the laity. Ordination also conveyed a power (*potestas*) to the priest to consecrate; that is, to use his divine power to effect a miraculous change in the eucharistic elements of the Mass. Grace thus becomes restricted to a sacramental grace, and it is this alone that justifies men.[22]

In Luther's conception, however, these politically suggestive aspects were dropped. Grace was not something administered or infused by the impersonal power of an intermediary. It was the free gift of God, the promise of forgiveness and reconciliation to the repentant sinner. Significantly, Luther reduced the number of sacraments, and among those eliminated was the sacrament of ordination and its accompanying intimations of hierarchy. In subsequent pages we shall further examine the decline in political status of the Lutheran ministry, and here we need only note that this was augured in Luther's doctrine concerning the relationship between the sacraments and the believer's state of grace. By insisting upon justification by faith, the power element in the sacraments was diminished in importance and the political overtones practically eliminated. This was clearly registered in some words of Melancthon which can be taken as marking the epitaph of mediaeval political theology:

Sacraments do not justify . . . Thou mayest be justified, therefore, even without the sacrament; only believe.[23]

A second example of the depoliticizing tendencies in Luther is furnished by his conception of the Kingdom of God. From the very beginning, Christian exegetes had resorted to political concepts to define the nature of God's power and the rule of Christ, and as far back as Eusebius we find an argument in which monotheism and monarchy mutually justify each other. All of these tendencies, however, were resisted by Luther. In repeatedly insisting on a sharp demarcation between the Kingdom of God and the kingdom of the world, he inserted, in effect, a restraining wedge between the two realms which prevented any easy transposition of categories. On the one side stood the Kingdom of God, composed of believing and practicing Christians, earnestly seeking the Word of God and the Spirit of Christ; on the other, the kingdom of the world where temporal government ruled over those non-Christians and lukewarm believers who required a coercive and restraining power to keep them within decent bounds.[24]

Although the antitheses between these two realms were manifested in several ways — by their contrasting ways of life, by the ethic that prevailed in each, and by the ends pursued — there was one aspect particularly germane to this study. Only one kingdom, that of the world, possessed any political attributes connecting it to the ordinary meaning of kingdom. Here alone was repressive power, law backed by coercion, and all of the other elements of governance. Luther's conception of Christ's rulership, on the other hand, lacked any important political qualities. From the outset he insisted that Christ's vocation had been eminently non-political, and he carried over this notion into the discussion of the role of priests and bishops within the Church.[25] The apolitical nature of Christ's kingdom was made possible not only because coercion and law were unnecessary for Christians, but also because the abolition of the hierarchical principle had destroyed the rationale for distinctions of power and authority among believers.[26] Climaxing these notions was Luther's strong warning that men could not be hurried or pushed into salvation by the use of power. Even in God's Kingdom the central fact was not His power, but His Word:

No one shall and can command the soul, unless he can show it the way to heaven; but this no man can do, only God. Therefore in matters which concern the salvation of souls nothing but God's Word shall be taught and accepted.[27]

III **The bias against institutions.** One product of this revolt against the authority of philosophy and the Catholic conception of an accrued historical wisdom, painstakingly built up through centuries of interpretation, was a pronounced streak of religious primitivism which flaunted simple faith against philosophical complication and was prepared to break "the images of ancestral wisdom" in the name of a return to original Christianity. These aspects of Luther's thought took on additional dimension when, with the battle cry of *"sola Scriptura"* and *"sola fide,"* he carried the assault directly against the mediaeval conception of the Church. Again the emphasis was put on leveling the "walls" that stood between the believer and the object of his beliefs. The whole of the ecclesiastical hierarchy, with its subtle gradations of authority and function, was to be razed. Since the plain meaning of Scripture could be understood by the average man, sacerdotalism was superfluous; there could be no distinctions among believers:

> We all have the same authority in regard to the Word and sacraments, although no one has a right to administer them without the consent of the members of his church, or by the call of the majority (because, when something is common to all, no single person is empowered to arrogate it to himself, but we should await the call of the Church) . . . When a bishop consecrates, he simply acts on behalf of the entire congregation, all of whom have the same authority. They may select one of their number and command him to exercise this authority on behalf of the others.[28]

The radical egalitarianism implicit in the doctrine of the priesthood of the believers was not dictated by any necessary relationships among the believers themselves. Rather, it grew out of Luther's conviction that faith could be attained only by individual effort and that, therefore, the "Christian liberty" of the believer must be unbound by externals. Faith could not be created or instilled by an external agency, whether sacerdotal or political; it was an inward disposition of the individual inclining him towards God.[29] The reward of faith was membership in the invisible communion of Christians, the *corpus mysticum* ruled by Christ:

> There is no superior among Christians, but Christ Himself and Christ alone. And what kind of authority can there be where all are equal and have the same right, power, possession, and honor, and no one desires to be the other's superior, but each other's inferior? One could not establish authority where there are such people, even if one would, since their character and nature will not permit them to have superiors, for no one is willing or able to be the superior.[30]

The "true" Church, then, was not to be located in any physical assemblage of offices, nor was it to be identified with any hierarchical institution. The Church consisted simply of "an assembly of hearts in one faith . . . This unity is of itself sufficient to make a Church." [31]

In this notion of the Church there was one aspect that bore a striking affinity to a theme discussed earlier in connection with Augustine. This is the notion emphasizing the social nature of the Church. The Church emerges as a spontaneous, joyful — *"nun freut euch lieben Christen gemein"* — and largely coercionless society, one which culminates in the invisible society of saints where "all have all things in common." [32] The dialectical antithesis to this condition is temporal government that rules its society by domination and power. Thus on the one side was a society without government, on the other a government without a true society or fellowship. This emphasis on the fellowship of the believers was rooted in an antipathy towards power which formed one of the basic characteristics of the Lutheran church-society, underlining once more the apolitical tendency in the new ecclesiology.

Implicit in Luther's theory of the church-society were some novel and far-reaching implications. He was advancing the radical proposition that a society could not only retain its identity without the power of a visible, directing "head," but that the perfection of its nature demanded that it be acephalous. This assertion, that a society could be tightly knit and cohesive, yet remain headless, ran counter to one of the common assumptions of much of classical and mediaeval thought, that any society or order presupposed a directing head, a central source of impulse. There was also Luther's equally disturbing claim that a society could flourish and express its identity without relying upon a hierarchical principle. As far back as Plato and Aristotle, philosophers had contended that there could be no right order of any kind unless the "lower" were subordinated to the "higher," the "inferior" to the "superior." In opposition to this long-standing belief, Luther revived the radical notion of Christian membership: to be a Christian meant to occupy a status that was at once more elevated than any other, yet those who did occupy it entered into a condition of equality each with his fellows.

> . . . We are not baptised unto kings, princes, or even unto the mass of men, but unto Christ and unto God himself; neither are we called kings, princes, or common folk, but Christians.[33]

This equality of condition, however, did not carry the same meaning as in later democratic thought; that is, the idea of an equality of claims or rights. Rather it meant something at once more provocative and ominous: an equality of mutual subservience where "no one desires to be the other's superior, but each the other's inferior." [34]

Luther's rejection of the two principles of monarchy and hierarchy, insofar as these applied to ecclesiastical matters, marked also an important stage in the destruction of certain forms of political imagery. The notion of society as forming a huge pyramid, wherein the power assigned each layer was in an inverse proportion to the length of the layer, was cast aside for the flattened imagery of a society where, ideally, the members were equal. This raises the question of what the role of the ministry was to be in the new Church; if Luther had felt compelled to smuggle back some elements of papal power, this would have been registered in his doctrine of the ministry. Although Luther consistently denied that the equality of the believers obviated the necessity for a trained ministry, this denial in no way presaged the reintroduction of political elements into the Church. The priesthood, as Luther emphasized, did not denote power or authority but "office"; that is, a defined function.[35] This meant the transformation of the mediaeval priest into a minister, an agent who administered, expounded and explained the Word.[36] This loss in status was accompanied by a drastic change in the relationship between minister and congregation. Unlike the priest, the minister could not draw upon the mysterious sources of authority flowing from a centuries-old tradition. Stripped of the *mystique* of office, the minister faced his congregation as a *primus inter pares*. The office itself was no longer consecrated by the representative of a powerful ecclesiastical institution; it was derived from the consent of the *pares*. Since the minister was the creature of consent, not of authority, he could be removed from office by those who had selected him.[37]

In depoliticizing the ministry, however, Luther had inserted some broad hints concerning the congregation which were to be caught up in the thought of the radical sectarians of the sixteenth and seventeenth centuries and through that medium were to have a decisive influence on democratic theories. In other words, while ejecting some political elements from his theory of the Church, especially those that came to be embedded in the idea of an ecclesiastical hierarchy, Luther had also ended by adopting others. For example, underlying the equality of the believers and the minimal role of the ministry were certain assumptions about the capacity of the believers to recognize truth, assumptions that seemingly echoed Aristotle's defense of the citizen's ability to judge:

> . . . Each and all of us are priests because we all have the one faith, the one gospel, one and the same sacrament; why then should we not be entitled to taste or test, and to judge what is right or wrong in the faith? [38]

From this followed Luther's demand that the "second wall," symbolizing the papal claim to be the final interpreter of doctrine, be swept aside. The papal position, as Luther instinctively recognized, was grounded in a kind of Christianized Platonism which asserted that disputed truths could be resolved only by a specially endowed intelligence.[39] Against this "aristocratic epistemology," Luther advanced a "democratic" one which matched the uncomplicated "simple faith" of the people against the subtleties of theologians and averred both the right and the ability of the congregation to judge religious teachings.[40] He adopted this position partly from a profound conviction concerning the primacy of the direct communion between God and the individual soul, and partly from a conviction that the individual conscience could not be forced into salvation by an outside human agency. Although Luther later modified his optimism about the capacities of the average believer, his early statements lent a powerful stimulus to the currents that culminated in congregationalism. They also held far-reaching implications for political thought. Latent in this conception of a cohesive religious fellowship which could decide and act without the aid of any hierarchy was the further idea of a community that could express a truth. This represented something more than the Aristotelian notion about the superiority of a pooled judgment contributed by the citizenry. The Lutheran conception did not involve a judgment at all; it did not relate to contingent matters, but to fundamental truths; it was not the product of diverse talents and experience, but of an inner knowledge common to a body of communicants.[41]

IV The status of the political order. Nostalgia for the apostolic simplicity of the primitive Church did not blind Luther to the fact that a near-anarchistic form of church organization was an inadequate prescription for an actual congregation whose members dwelt in varying states of grace and faith. At an early stage in his writings, he began to elaborate the distinction between the "visible" and the "invisible" Church. The former consisted of those Christians whose weak faith necessitated a visible form of organizational structure. Unity had to be created externally by human art. The "invisible" Church, in contrast, derived its unity from faith; it was largely independent of organization and regulations.[42]

In his later years, Luther came to be more impressed with the value of "distinguishing marks," even for the invisible Church.[43] This was less significant, however, than his growing reliance upon secular authority to police the visible Church and to insure a degree of religious uniformity. Given this development, the Lutheran conception of political authority assumes crucial importance; for a religion that had denied itself the power of an ecclesiastical organization was now confronted by, and invited the assistance of, political rulers who were unhampered by the traditional restraints of religious institutions. To appreciate the new theoretical setting within which temporal authority was now to operate, something must be said concerning earlier Christian attitudes towards the political order and the office of ruler.

From its early beginnings, the Christian attitude concerning politics had been complicated by a persistent impulse towards disengagement from the world. The scriptural warning that "My Kingdom is not of this world" was later systematized by Augustine into the tense symbolism of the *civitas dei* and *civitas terrena*. Despite the impressive effort of Aquinas to fashion a comfortable accommodation between the political order and the divine, the mystics and the monastics survived as eloquent witnesses to the strain of *incivisme* in Christianity.

In Luther, the impulse towards disengagement took a quite different form. Where Augustine had relied upon the Church as the main aid to individual salvation and had relegated the state to the role of guardian of order, Luther felt constrained to call upon secular power to help Christian souls in gaining release from the tyranny of the organized Church.[44] One fundamental reason for the different roles assigned government by Augustine and Luther is to be found in the different historical positions occupied by each. Augustine's thinking was deeply tinged by the millennial hopes common in the early centuries of the Christian era. It was natural for him to adopt a time-perspective oriented towards the future. Although, in contrast to the expectancies of some of the early Christians, Augustine minimized the imminence of the millennium, the notion of a future pregnant with the promise of deliverance remained a vivid element in his thought.[45] The thousand years intervening between Augustine and Luther could not but have a sobering effect on Christian optimism. What had been a beckoning future for one became, for the other, an interminable present calling for a certain resignation on the part of the believer. The muted chiliasm of Luther contributed in an important way to his marked antipathy for history. After the days of apostolic simplicity had been passed, history had become a record of the degradation of the Word. Consequently, the theological and ecclesiastical legacy of these centuries must be dismissed. On the basis of these beliefs, Luther's time-perspective was reflective of a compelling urgency to return to a more primitive state of Christian perfection; it was a part of a radicalism oriented towards recapturing the authentic Christian elements of the distant past.

These contrasts in time-perspectives were closely related to some important differences in the political ideas of Augustine and Luther. Although Augustine had punctured the classical notion of the autonomy and self-sufficiency of the political order, he had not left the political order dangling in limbo. It was an integral part of the whole *ordo* of creation and contributed its share towards the preservation of the total harmony. For Augustine, the concept of a divine order symbolized more than an ingenious blend of diversities; it was a *concordia* dynamically oriented towards perfection. Accordingly, the political order, integrated as it was into a cosmos full with meaning and direction, acquired a rooted stability, a sustenance drawn from the nature of creation itself. Thus, even though the political community was destined to be superseded at the climax of history, until that time it participated in the perfection written into the very essence of things.

Luther, however, departed significantly from the Augustinian conception of *ordo*. For Augustine, *ordo* had operated as a principle immanent in the whole of creation; therefore, any association, even a non-Christian one, possessed value to the extent that it secured peace and tranquillity. Luther, on the other hand, reduced "order" from an immanent to a formal principle without real viability:

Order is an outward thing. Be it as good as it may, it can fall into misuse. Then it is no longer order but disorder. So no order has any intrinsic worth of its own, as hitherto the Popish Order has been thought to have. But all order has its life, worth, strength, and virtue in right use; else it is worthless and fit for nothing.[46]

In abandoning the concept of *ordo* as the sustaining principle within a larger pattern of meaning, Luther deprived the political order of the moral sustenance flowing from this more comprehensive whole. The lack of integration between the political order and the divine order produced a marked tension within Luther's conception of government. The political order appeared as a distinctly fragile achievement, precarious, unstable, and prone to upset. At the same time, the vulnerability of this order created the need for a powerful, repressive authority. In other words, it was not the political order itself that was sustained by a divine principle; it was the secular power upholding order that was divinely derived. It was no idle boast of Luther's to assert that he had praised temporal government more highly than anyone since Augustine.[47] Such praise was necessary once the political order had been extracted from its cosmic context. The divine element in political authority was inevitably transformed from a sustaining principle into a repressive, coercive one.

Luther's attachment to temporal authority, then, was not the product of a particular stage in his development, but was rooted in the conviction that the fallen world of man was fundamentally orderless. Order had to be imposed:

> Let no one think that the world can be ruled without blood; the sword of the ruler must be red and bloody; for the world will and must be evil, and the sword is God's rod and vengeance upon it.[48]

Significantly, Luther singled out, as the first "wall" to be leveled, the papal claims to temporal jurisdiction. His logic here displayed the same impulse as his religious theorizing: just as the believer's free access to Scripture was to be secured from papal interference, so the secular ruler was to be unhampered in his efforts to achieve order:

> . . . The social corpus of Christendom includes secular government as one of its component functions. This government is spiritual in status, although it discharges a secular duty. It should operate, freely and unhindered, upon all members of the entire corpus, should punish and compel where guilt deserves or necessity requires, in spite of pope, bishops, and priests; and whether they denounce or excommunicate to their heart's desire.[49]

The long scholarly disputes over whether or not Luther preserved the mediaeval conception of a *corpus christianum* have served to obscure the profound changes he made in the content of that concept.[50] The emphasis on secular authority was accompanied by other doctrinal changes which enhanced that authority still further. At the same time that Luther was undercutting the sacerdotal hierarchy by the idea of the priesthood of all believers, he was elevating the status of rulers by clothing it with a sacerdotal dignity: rulers "are priest and bishops too." [51] The sharp line between clergy and laity was erased, and priest and peasant were placed on a level of equality in relation to secular jurisdiction.[52] The estate of Christendom had fallen to new trustees: the princes "discharge their office as an office of the Christian community, and for the benefit of that community . . . Each community, council, and administration has authority to abolish and prevent, apart from the knowledge or consent of pope or bishop, anything contrary to God, and hurtful to man in body and soul." [53]

The practical significance of the role assigned to political authority lay not so much in its broad mandate, nor in its responsibilities for religious reform, but rather in the fact that its power was now to be exercised in a context where papal institutions had been deprived of divinity and power. The secular ruler alone derived his powers from God; the power of the papacy, in contrast, had resulted from strictly human contrivings, or, worse, from the machinations of the Antichrist.

V **The political order without counterweight.** Luther's view of political authority was not all of one piece; it varied depending on whether the issue was primarily religious or political. When temporal government was called upon to assist in furthering religious reforms, it was viewed as a positive and constructive agency. But in its more secular and political role, government appeared as essentially negative and repressive. In the one area, it was treated as the sole alternative for initiating reform; in the other, as the sole alternative to anarchy.[54] The link that bound together the two views of political authority was Luther's demand that rulers be released from pre-existing restraints in order to accomplish their work. We have already examined this element in connection with Luther's attack on the papacy; it reappeared when he considered the secular activities of government. Finding the same confusion and complexity in the laws of society as had prevailed in religious matters, Luther advocated a characteristically simple and radical solution:

> . . . The body politic cannot be felicitously governed merely by rules and regulations. If the administrator be sagacious, he will conduct the government more happily when guided by circumstances rather than by legal decrees. If he be not so wise, his legal methods will only result in harm, since he will not know how to use them, nor how to temper them to the case in hand. Hence, in public affairs, it is more important to make sure that good and wise men are in control than that certain laws are promulgated. Men of this kind will themselves be the best of laws, will be alert to every kind of problem, and will resolve them equitably. If knowledge of the divine laws accompanies native sagacity, it is obvious that written laws will be superfluous and noxious.[55]

The only restraints operating on the ruler, other than those of his own conscience, came from the exhortations of the ministers; since the ministers no longer spoke as the representatives of a powerful ecclesiastical establishment, the effectiveness of this restraint would be problematical.

Although some commentators have shown that Luther never intended to emancipate the secular authorities from the dictates of natural law and reason, this proves only that Luther was not Machiavelli. For the point is that natural law becomes a mere set of moral homilies when it is translated into a context where the power of the rulers alone has been elevated above all other institutional rivals and where allegiance to the other great power institution has been condemned.

The situation thus created was ripe for a collision between the two entities that Luther, by analogous arguments, had sought to set free. On the one hand there was the secular ruler, unrestrained by the pressures of competing institutions, and on the other the Christian congregation seeking divine grace, unaided and unguided by sacerdotal institutions. Luther, however, often wrote as though the former never presented a threat to the latter. The true believer was a subject of the Kingdom of God, where Christ alone rules. "Therefore, it is not possible for the secular sword and law to find any work to do among Christians, since of themselves they do much more than its laws and doctrines can demand." [56] If all men were to become true Christians, secular government would be unnecessary. Government was justified by the existence of the large masses of the unrighteous and unregenerate; in the absence of coercion, men would be at each other's throats and society in chaos. "For this reason God has ordained two governments; the spiritual, which by the Holy Spirit under Christ makes Christians and pious people, and the secular, which restrains the unchristian and wicked so that they must needs keep the peace outwardly, even against their will." [57]

Even if the secular rulers, whose characters Luther frequently criticized, were to overstep their bounds and issue commands contrary to Scripture, no real harm could be done to the true Christian. Government, laws, and the ways of society could affect the physical goods of man, but never the vital center of his soul:

> When we consider the inner, spiritual man and see what belongs to him if he is to be a free and devout Christian, in fact and in name, it is evident that, whatever the name, no outer thing can make him either free or religious. For his religion and freedom, and moreover, his sinfulness and servitude, are neither bodily nor outward.[58]

"Christian liberty," then, was the state enjoyed by the believer who had severed his external dependencies and had oriented his soul towards a complete submission to God. Although he could be expected to do more than his social and political obligations required, his ultimate salvation was in no way implicated in the world; his good works in the world were the consequence of his faith, and his faith could never be the result of his works. "You have the kingdom of heaven; therefore you should leave the kingdom of earth to any one who wants to take it." [59]

The doctrine of Christian liberty was modified by Luther in the light of his experiences during the Peasants' War. The basic question raised at that time was whether the spread of lawlessness might eventually undermine the peace of the faithful and thereby interfere with the quest for salvation. The pressure of events forced Luther to soften the distinction between the Kingdom of God and the kingdom of the world. If the rebellious peasants were to gain the upper hand, "both kingdoms would be destroyed and there would be neither worldly government nor Word of God, but it would result in the permanent destruction of Germany . . ." [60] If both the Kingdom of God and the kingdom of the world possessed a common need for order, as Luther admitted, then the true believer could not be as indifferent towards the political order as the doctrine of Christian liberty implied. Religion and politics were more closely intertwined than the theory of the two kingdoms inferred. Luther's theory of government, then, came down to this: temporal authority could insure outward peace for the true believer; it could never affect his internal virtue. For the unbeliever, government could impose external order and external virtue. Government existed "in order that the good may have outward peace and protection; and that the wicked may not be free to do evil, without fear, in peace and quietness." [61]

Certain confusions began to appear in Luther's thought, however, when he attempted to relate his doctrine of government to the problems of obedience and freedom of conscience. Sometimes he argued that authority could not coerce the consciences of the believers; and this was consistent with his teaching that externals could not affect the liberty of the Christian man. At other times, he insisted that government ought not to coerce consciences. This could only mean logically that freedom of conscience was useful primarily for the unrighteous who might some day be led back to the fold.

The same difficulty reappeared when Luther allowed that men need not obey when a ruler commanded contrary to the teachings of Scripture. [62] But this could involve only the true believer, for he alone possessed a conscience guided by Scripture. At the same time, he alone owned a conscience that could not be harmed by external actions.

The contradictory elements were present in other aspects of Luther's teaching on this same general subject. Earlier he had urged that the secular rulers apply force against the papacy, yet he overwhelmingly maintained that secular rulers ought not to be resisted for any cause. Thus political authority might resist religious authority on either political or religious grounds, while religious authorities might never resist political authority on either religious or political grounds. The final incongruity appeared during the Peasants' War when Luther advocated the right of anyone to kill a rebellious peasant. Thus a rebel might be slain by anyone, a tyrant by no one.[63]

VI **The fruits of simplicity.** Luther has frequently been criticized by later writers for promoting the cause of political absolutism. Figgis, for example, coupled Luther with Machiavelli and treated their ideas as two sides of the same coin.[64] Although this view is correct in emphasizing the extreme lengths to which Luther went in releasing temporal rulers from previous restraints, it tends to view the problem primarily in terms of moral and religious restraints. Actually, Luther consistently upheld the right of Christians to rebuke the excesses of princes, and his own writings testify to the extent to which he followed that advice. If we are to look for the fundamental weakness in Luther's thinking, it is to be sought in his failure to appreciate the importance of institutions. His obsession with religious simplicity caused him to ignore the role of religious institutions as political restraints. The social consequences of a weakly organized religion were apparent in his own day. At moments of political and social crisis, he was unable to appeal to any effective religious organization to act as mediator. During the Peasants' War, he was compelled to entrust the whole cause of peace to the princes, despite his own conviction that all of the wrongs were not entirely on one side. In trying to get out of this predicament, Luther succeeded only in making the Christian ethic appear irrelevant to the logic of the political order: "the sayings on mercy belong in God's kingdom and among Christians, not in the kingdom of the world . . ."[65]

The quest for simplicity also had its effects when Luther considered political institutions. Here it took the form of accepting authority rather than rejecting it. From a few ingenuous ideas about authority, order, and social classes, Luther fashioned a political doctrine of stark simplicity, unrelieved by the shadows of qualification. It was designed essentially to impress on princes the desirability of paternal rule and on subjects the wickedness of disobedience. Just as his religious teachings emphasized the single relationship of a believer who throws himself on God's mercy, so the political order was stripped of nearly all except the single relationship between ruler and ruled. In both cases the moral impotence and sinfulness of man were the source of his dependence. But the peculiarity of the relationship between political superiors and their inferiors was that so much of it remained unpermeated by religious values. Religious considerations entered only at the extremities of the relationship; the ruler held his authority from God, while the subject was under a divine injunction to obey rulers in every conceivable *political* circumstance. No provision was made for the other complex relationships in a political order. The political relationship, like the religious, was a personalized rather than an institutionalized one. These ideas marked the eclipse of the mediaeval conception of a political society with all of its rich suggestion of a corporate whole knit together in a common involvement. There was no counterpart in Luther's thought to the ideal monarch of Aquinas who looked upon his subjects *sicut propria membra,* as members of his own body.[66] Instead Luther's ruler was cut in the image of an Old Testament God, angry and vengeful, yet softening his wrath by a paternal concern. This growing alienation between political authority and the society over which it ruled was further enhanced by the fact that society itself was no longer pictured through categories colored by the *corpus mysticum* idea. The promise of a society founded in fellowship had been reserved exclusively for the church-society. Moreover, the common love of Christ which pervaded the membership of this more perfect society created in it an inner dynamism, a capacity for self-generated movement which was lacking in an unsanctified society. Political society was not pervaded by love, but by conflicts which vitiated any possibility of a common life and incapacitated the whole from acting in unison. The inability of political society to generate its own actions provided the justification for the overweening position of the temporal ruler; his absolute power was the logical remedy for a depraved society which urgently needed control but was helpless to provide it; his position outside and above society merely dramatized the malady of a body whose sole movement was the shudder of convulsive conflict.

In this connection, Luther's doctrine of Christian liberty and his defense of disobedience on religious grounds did little to redress the balance against the secular ruler. Both of these ideas had been hollowed of their political content. "True" liberty had been transformed into an internal state of faith, while obligation was disconnected from political relationships and made to apply solely to religious issues; in political matters, men had to obey unquestioningly.

The foregoing points to the conclusion that the problem presented by Luther was not one arising from the divorce between politics and religious values, but from the political irrelevancy of the Christian ethic. Although Luther certainly assumed that Christian values, such as love, neighborliness, and charity, would exercise a salutary influence in society and politics, he failed to show their viability in dealing with problems other than those located at the elementary level of the household and the neighborhood. The Christian ethic might well be applicable at the intimate, personal level, and yet be quite irrelevant for the relationships created by a complicated political order. Luther remained unaware of this difficulty, because he reduced political relationships to a single form. Something of the political inadequacy of the Christian teaching was glimpsed by Luther himself. In the tract *On Trading and Usury* (1524), his argument began by laying down the strict Christian teachings on the subject; soon, however, he was led to admit that the Christian ethic was of little utility here inasmuch as most members of society did not act as Christians. His solution was to abandon the Christian argument and to invoke, instead, the coercive arm of government. The argument ended on the note that the world would be reduced to chaos if men tried to govern by the Gospel.[67]

These doubts about the political effectiveness of Christian teachings had their roots in the fundamental ambiguity characteristic of the thinking of many of the early Reformers. On the religious side they advocated the most uncompromising and radical reforms, while on the political side they enjoined quietism. Luther, for example, vehemently rejected any hierarchical distinctions among Christian believers; yet he assumed that a social hierarchy was natural and necessary.[68] He eloquently defended the sanctity of the individual conscience; yet he unhesitatingly accepted the institutions of serfdom. He admitted that some of the grievances of the peasants were justified, but counseled the peasant against attaching much value to material concerns. He was willing to raise fundamental questions about every form of religious authority, but towards political institutions he was quite unsceptical, even when he doubted the morals and motives of rulers. His thought represented a striking combination of revolt and passivity.

✒ SIX ✑

Calvin:

The Political Education of Protestantism

*If you are walking westward . . . you forfeit the northern and eastward
and southern direction. If you admit a unison, you forfeit all the possibilities of chaos.*

D. H. LAWRENCE

I **The crisis in order and civility.** The political problem bequeathed by
Luther and nourished by the radical sects of the Reformation centered
around a developing crisis in the concept of order and in the Western traditions of civility. The criticism of the papacy by the early Reformers had
really amounted to a demand for the liberation of the individual believer
from a mass of institutional controls and traditional restraints which hitherto
had governed his behavior. The mediaeval Church had been many things,
and among them, a system of governance. It had sought, not always successfully, to control the conduct of its members through a definite code of discipline, to bind them to unity through emotional as well as material commitments, and to direct the whole religious endeavor through an institutionalized

power structure as impressive as any the world had seen. In essence, the Church had provided a rationalized set of restraints designed to mould human behavior to accord with a certain image. To condemn it as the agent of the Antichrist was to work towards the release of human behavior from the order which had formed it. This liberating tendency was encouraged by one of the great ideas of the early Reformers, the conception of the Church as a fellowship bound together by the ties of faith and united in a common quest for salvation. This emphasis on community represented a latter-day version of the theme already discussed in connection with early Christianity, the superiority of a "social" form over a "political" form, of a voluntary fusion of members over a society subjected to externally enforced norms:

> *Communicare* means to take part in this fellowship, or as we say, to go to the sacrament, because Christ and all saints are one spiritual body, just as the inhabitants of a city are one community and body, each citizen being a member of the other and member of the entire city . . . In this we are all brothers and sisters, so closely united that a closer relationship cannot be conceived . . . no other brotherhood is so close . . .[1]

The difficulty, however, was that the *Genossenschaft* idea lacked the complementary notion of the Church as a *corpus regens,* a corporate society welded together by a viable structure of power. It inferred that men could be fashioned to live in an orderly community without the serious and consistent application of force, that they could be members of a group that was social yet not political, and that their "other" roles as members of a political society involved activity in itself inferior. These tendencies were to be found in their most extreme form in the Anabaptist movement which developed contemporaneously with Lutheranism. The dominating obsession of the Anabaptists was with preserving the purity of their church in the midst of a contaminating world. They sought to achieve this end by separating their community from the world and by denying that their members owed any obligations to the political order. The "social" nature of their communion, in other words, was to be maintained by avoiding contact with the "political" outside.

In this connection the brief and violent Anabaptist dictatorship established at Münster had an affinity with the basic outlook of the movement, even though the dictatorship contradicted the Anabaptist ideal of non-violence.[2] The followers of Thomas Muentzer were motivated by the same hatred of the world, by the same anti-political impulse present in the more peaceful version of Anabaptism. Instead of rejecting evil and seeking escape from the world, the Muentzerites reacted in much the same manner as some of the fringe groups of seventeenth-century Puritanism: they fought with a "holy violence" to overcome the corrupt world, to root out its vicious elements, and to reshape it in the image of a pure communion of saints.[3] Whether peaceful or bloody, the anti-political impulse was common to this mentality.

Luther, as we have seen, had come to acknowledge that, because of its mixed membership, the visible Church was a defective society and hence in need of disciplinary mechanisms. The paradox of his thought, however, was that, on the one side, he was suspicious and often contemptuous of political institutions and personalities and yet, because he identified the church-society with a voluntary union bound by love, faith, and the worshipped presence of Christ, he was compelled to invite the suspect political order to police the holy community. The reason for this lay in his conception of the Church as an essentially "social" unity; because it was a brotherhood, it could not generate power, domination, and authority. Secular government thus stood alone, but undignified, as the sole embodiment of an effective ordering discipline; it was the major cohesive force in society. Despite its practical importance, the political province was not that of Christian virtue, but of coercion and repression. The ruler was not so much the agent for the common purposes of the community as a kind of high priest presiding over profane mysteries. In short, hostility towards the political order was also a part of Luther's outlook.

The result of these ideas was to jeopardize a whole tradition of order and civility, for, clothed as they were in the language of religion, and aimed as they were at an audience that took religion seriously, they could not fail to impress a set of attitudes that would have profound repercussions on the political behavior and outlook of their followers. In the midst of this developing crisis, Calvin put forward a system of ideas which stemmed the flight from civility. On the political side, he worked to restore the reputation of the political order, to remind Protestant man of the political side of his nature, and to instruct him in the rudiments of a political education. To achieve these purposes, Calvin had to break with Luther's teaching that government was a mighty engine of repression and the political order superfluous for the Christian man.[4] On the religious side, Calvin's ecclesiology was a systematic elaboration of the principle that a church-society would remain incomplete and ineffective if it did not possess an institutional structure that could articulate its life. A gathered community of believers was not enough; the additional element of power was needed to insure the coherence and solidarity of the group. The difficulties encountered by Lutherans and Anabaptists were to be overcome by the essentially political remedy of an ecclesiastical polity. The Lutheran church appeared increasingly vulnerable to political pressures, while the Anabaptist congregations seemed to have escaped the world only to be troubled by internal disorders. Thus the one church was plagued by political interference, the other by the confusions of congregational democracy. To meet these problems, Calvin proposed that the best church polity should aim at self-sufficiency, but without divorcing itself from the life of political society; it should follow the Reformation principle of bringing the members into the active life of the church, but without entrusting them with the close supervision of affairs; it should provide for strong leadership and direction within the church, but without restoring the pope. In tracing out a solution in these terms, Calvin produced a political theory of church government.

Although it would be extreme to conclude that Calvin presided over the "liquidation of the Reformation,"[5] there can be no denying that his emphasis on structure and organization, on controlling the impulses liberated by the Reformation, inaugurated a new phase of the movement. The individual was to be reintegrated into a double order, religious and political, and the orders themselves were to be linked in a common unity. The discontinuity between religious obligations and restraints and their political counterparts was to be repaired; Christian virtue and political virtue were to move closer together. The order that emerged was not a "theocracy," but a corporate community that was neither purely religious nor purely secular, but a compound of both.

II **The political quality of Calvin's thought.** The restorative work of Calvin was most clearly displayed in his theory of the church, for it was in this area that the anti-institutional bias of the early Reformers had been most evident. In his theory, the idea of the church had two aspects, the church visible and the church invisible. The latter he defined as "the society of all the saints, a society spread over the whole world, and existing in all ages, yet bound together by the one doctrine, and the one Spirit of Christ. . . ."[6] The visible church, on the other hand, stood as a concession to human frailty. Since it included "many hypocrites" and many members of varying degrees of faith, its existence was attended by more tangible marks than the preaching of the Word and the administration of the sacraments. Its location was not universal but specific; its unity was not guaranteed by grace, but required a definite and insuring structure of offices; so its concord was not spontaneous, but was the calculated product of discipline. The visible church, in short, was a kind of second-best form of church polity accommodated to the weaknesses of man's nature. At the same time, Calvin repeatedly warned that the disparities in perfection between the visible and the invisible church could never justify men in forsaking the visible form out of a desire to avoid contamination. "A departure from the church," he declared, was a "renunciation of God and Christ," "a criminal dissension." [7] Just as Aristotle had believed that every imperfect polity was capable of being improved, so Calvin believed that every visible church could be reformed by judicious measures.

The end at which such measures should aim was unity. This was the distinguishing mark of any society, visible or invisible, religious or civil. The solidarity of each type of society, however, was differently expressed. The unity of the invisible church, for example, was not the product of human art, but the result of the secret election of God which had predestined the membership for salvation. The unique destiny of the saints, however, did not detract from the fact that they lived a social life. In their communion they formed a universal society; the bonds of community came from a common love of Christ. [8]

For the visible church, too, Christ served as the central point of loyalty, the object of continual and ultimate commitment from which the unity of the whole derived. The force that conserved the society of believers was not produced from the controlling center of a pope who acted as trustee for the *corpus christianum*. Instead the cohesive force came from a mystical spirit working through the members who had joined with Him to form a *corpus mysticum*. [9] In the sacrament of the Last Supper, the society possessed a unifying symbolism, which not only pointed towards the divine element that lay at the vital center of society, but towards the sustaining principle of love that nourished the common identity of the members. The sacramental rite signified a common good which the participants shared with, and through, Christ. And the common love of Christ became the actuating principle compelling the participants to share this good with their fellows; they could not love Christ without loving each other; and they could not injure each other without injuring Christ. [10]

The second primary bond that worked to unify the visible society was of a doctrinal kind. Through the constant preaching of the ministry and the arduous effort of the members to model themselves to an image of perfection, the teachings of Scripture would come to penetrate and infuse the most intimate areas of human conduct.

But although the preaching of the Word and the sacramental rites were sufficient to establish the existence of the invisible society, the visible society, containing as it did members in varying states of belief and unbelief, required additional aids. Unlike the invisible society, the visible lacked the unity of a common destiny; hence it had to create its unity by means of a coercive structure. Stated somewhat differently, the sacraments and the Word could provide a "social" unity for the visible church, but they could not provide the ecclesiastical government, the element of power, which was necessary for dealing with the heterogeneous nature of the members. The disparate character of the membership, some destined for salvation, others for damnation, could be moulded to unity only by a definite set of controlling institutions, an ecclesiastical polity designed to spread and enforce the Word, effect order, promote cohesion, and insure regularity in church decisions. In sum, the visible church had to be equipped with the proper instrumentalities of power.

To the extent that the visible church required institutions, laws, and governing officials, it belonged to the realm of human art; and to that extent, it challenged the ecclesiastical legislator to make of it *une église bien ordonnée et reglée*. Although it could never achieve the perfection of the invisible society of the elect, it might aspire to a special excellence of its own. At the same time, the architect of the church did not have a perfectly free hand in executing the grand design. He was limited by the injunctions of Scripture and by the reverence that ought to be accorded a divinely ordained institution. He did not create the idea of the church or its purposes. His task was to imitate, as far as the puny art of man allowed, the divine order that controlled the universe; to blend diversity into ordered harmony and individuality into a common good; to arrange the institutions and offices of the church so that the whole would function with the coherence of a living body.[11]

In drawing attention to the structure of the church, its "constitutions" and "offices," Calvin was rediscovering what the Roman Church had always practiced and the early Reformers had nearly always forgotten: that a religious society, like any other society, must find support in institutions; and that institutions, in turn, were aggregates of power. Many of the Reformers, in their eagerness to condemn the "worldly power" of the mediaeval Church, seemed to believe that there was another kind of power, "spiritual" power, which ought to be the proper mode for expressing the authority of a religious society. Luther, for example, always drew a sharp contrast between the two forms of power, "spiritual" and "secular," and emphatically denied that there were any elements common to both.[12] "Spiritual" power emerged as something *sui generis*. It was visualized as a form of suasion over the consciences of the believers. It was the kind of influence represented by the ministerial functions of preaching and discipline. The extent to which "spiritual" power was "inner-directed" was best represented by Luther's teaching on the church's power of excommunication or the ban. He insisted, first, that this power, while it could be used to banish members from the fellowship of the church and its sacraments, could not carry with it any civil disabilities or penalties.[13] Again, while the ban could exclude an individual from the "outward, bodily and visible fellowship," it could not affect "truth and righteousness [which] belong to the inner spiritual fellowship . . . they dare not be surrendered for the sake of the external fellowship, which is immeasurably inferior, nor because of the ban." [14] Thus Luther's belief in the superiority of religious truth and faith over institutional forms helped to transform the concept of "spiritual" power from what it had been in the mediaeval Church. It surrendered its commanding, coercive, and final character and took on what Hobbes would have called a "ghostly" form.

In Calvin's case, however, the rediscovery of institutional life led to a rejection of the antithesis between the two types of power and of the assumption that underlay it. Civil government and ecclesiastical government did not symbolize distinctions of kind, but of objectives. Their natures, therefore, were more analogous than antithetical. A spiritual polity (*spiritualis politia*) bore the same necessary relation to the life of the church as the civil government to the life of civil society.[15] The governors of the church, too, must be well-versed in "the rule and law of good government," because such knowledge was essential to preserving any kind of order. Order, which Calvin defined as "a well-regulated polity, which excludes all confusion, incivility, obstinacy, clamours, and dissensions," was therefore a central objective of religious as well as civil polities.[16]

In Calvin's view, order was not a self-sustaining condition which, when once established, would continue from the momentum of its own perfection. It required a constant exercise of power. Just as the order of the universe was preserved by an active God so the human order must be supported by a steady force if its coherence was to be maintained.[17] Wherever there was order, there was power. Hence the kind of power that sustained a religious order might carry the adjective "spiritual," yet this did not transform it into a species of compulsion radically different from that present in the civil order. Spiritual power, in other words, constituted a specialized, not an etherealized, aspect of power applied to religious ends.

Admittedly Calvin frequently appeared to be arguing a sharp antithesis between secular and spiritual power; it was, he declared, "a Jewish folly" to confound the two. Spiritual government was concerned with "the inner man" and with his preparations for eternity; civil government, on the other hand, regulated "external conduct" and "the concerns of the present state." [18] Nevertheless, if Calvin's distinctions are examined more closely it becomes apparent that the difference between the two powers was not one of substance but of application. In a highly revealing passage in the *Institutes,* Calvin remarked that "it was usual" to distinguish the two orders by the words "spiritual" and "temporal"; and, while this was proper enough, he preferred to call *"l'une Royaume spirituel, et l'autre Civil ou politique"* (*regnum spirituale, alterum regnum politicum*).[19] In avoiding the usual pejorative contrast between "spiritual" and "secular" and by declaring each of them to be a *regnum,* Calvin was pointing to the fact that the coercive element was common to both governances. The differences between them lay in their range of objects or jurisdiction.

That spiritual power did not represent a difference in kind is further supported from another direction. One of the primary motives that had led Calvin to draw the distinction in the first place had been polemical. He had sought to defend power against those who had rejected it in the one form or the other. On the one hand, some of the radical sectarians, in the name of "Christian liberty," had taught that the true believer was totally absolved from the commands of political authority. At the other extreme, and equally dangerous in Calvin's eyes, were "the flatterers of princes" who would have so magnified the power of civil magistrates as to destroy the integrity of the spiritual power. Against the one extreme, Calvin asserted the value of the civil order for all men and its right to command Christians in particular; against the other, he affirmed the independent power of the church and its claim to a distinctive jurisdiction. In short, Calvin's distinction between the two powers was intended to preserve the power of each and to refute the notion that spiritual power was merely a form of insubstantial persuasion. Moreover, when Calvin defined the spiritual government as the means whereby "the conscience is formed to piety and the service of God" and the civil government as that order that "instructs in the duties of humanity and civility," he did not mean that the spiritual government alone was concerned with conscience while the political government alone regulated "external" conduct. As we shall note later on, the civil government was concerned with conscience, but of a different kind. It had a positive duty to promote and shape a "civic conscience," or what the ancients had called "civic virtue." Conversely, the spiritual government, in discharging its functions of preaching and instruction, was also expected to help form civil manners, to correct "incivility," in short, to influence "external" conduct. The conclusion towards which all these considerations pointed was that "man contains, as it were, two worlds, capable of being governed by various rulers and various laws."[20] In both worlds Calvin conceived man to be a creature of order, subjected to restraints and controlled by power.

Calvin divided the power of the church into three aspects. The first, the power over doctrine, was limited by the injunction that "nothing ought to be admitted in the church as the Word of God, but what is contained first in the law and the prophets, and secondly in the writings of the apostles. . . ."[21] But in its relationship to the members of the church it took on a more positive aspect. The power to preach and expound an unchanging body of truths was a method for strengthening the collective identity of the community by keeping before the members the object of the common allegiance.

Closely connected with this theme was Calvin's insistence that the interpretation of Scripture be confined strictly to the appropriate officers of the church. Here Calvin was motivated to some degree by the threat to unity present in the Reformation principle of putting the Bible in the hands of Everyman. This might lead, as Calvin well recognized, to as many private images of God as there were believers. Hence Calvin's insistence on the primacy of a uniform public truth, and the centralization of its interpretation in the ministry had a social as well as religious purpose: to preserve the communal foundations of belief against the disintegrating effects of private visions.[22]

The second aspect of ecclesiastical power centered in the ability to make laws (*in legibus ferendis; ordonner loix et statuts*). In his discussion of this power, Calvin was at his subtlest and most legalistic. He wanted to discredit the papal use of the legislative power without discrediting the power itself. In line with the first objective he contended that the papacy had abused the legislative power by enacting new rules of faith which had created unnecessary anxieties for believers. The popes, in other words, had trenched upon the sanctity of the individual conscience. In the course of Calvin's argument the claims of conscience came to be clothed with an almost sovereign immunity. Since Christ had been sent to free the Christian conscience from the burdens of error and superstition in order that men might more easily accept His teachings, it followed that "in matters that were left free and indifferent" no authority could legislate new barriers between the believer and the scriptural promise. "Our consciences have to do, not with men, but with God alone."[23]

Having demolished the Roman case, Calvin could only salvage the same power for his own church by modifying the dogma of conscience. For this purpose the proper starting point was not conscience but order. "In every human society some kind of government is necessary to insure the common peace and maintain concord." The nature of government required "some settled form" or procedures to expedite its transactions "decently and in order." But militating against any settled arrangement were such vagaries as the "diversity in the manners of men," the "variety in their minds," and the "repugnance in their judgments and dispositions." To overcome these anarchic forces, laws and ordinances were needed as "a kind of bonds," and once these controls had been established their existence would play a vital part in preserving the order of the church. "The removal of them would unnerve the church, deface and dissipate it entirely." Thus the legislative power, while not essential to the salvation of the believer, was fundamental to the preservation of the religious society. It was rescued by Calvin, not for the sake of the individual conscience, but for the sake of protecting the community against the strayings of the liberated conscience.[24]

The third aspect of the church's power, and "the principal one," was jurisdiction. This power was "nothing but the order provided for the preservation of spiritual polity." [25] Its scope extended from the humblest member of the congregation up to the highest political officers. Its pre-eminence came from the fact that it dealt with the most fundamental problem of order, namely, the discipline of the members.

> For, if no society and no house . . . can be preserved in a proper state without discipline, this is far more necessary in the church, the state of which ought to be the most orderly of all. As the saving doctrine of Christ is the soul of the church, so discipline forms the ligaments which connect the members together, and keep each in its proper place . . . Discipline, therefore, serves as a bridle to curb and restrain the refractory, who resist the doctrine of Christ; or as a spur to stimulate the inactive; and sometimes as a father's rod with which those who have grievously fallen may be chastised in mercy, and with the gentleness of the Spirit of Christ.[26]

Calvin's emphasis upon discipline makes it obvious that he saw in it another method for controlling the liberated conscience.[27] By means of discipline the believer was to be reinserted into a context of restraints and controls; he was to be reshaped into a creature of order. This was to be accomplished by minutely regulating his external conduct and by indoctrinating him in the basic teachings of the religious society. And buttressing this comprehensive system of controls was the supreme sanction (*severissima ecclesiae vindicta*) of excommunication. In Calvin's system, excommunication implied a great deal more than the mere severance of external ties. The expelled were condemned to a life without hope, a life outside the circle of fellowship:

. . . There is no other way of entrance into life, unless we are conceived by [the church], born of her, nourished at her breast, and continually preserved under her care and government until we are divested of this mortal flesh and "become like the angels" . . . we must continue under her instruction and discipline to the end of our lives . . . Away from her bosom there can be no hope of remission of sins or any salvation . . . It is always fatally dangerous to be separated from the church.[28]

Although Calvin denied that the power of jurisdiction was comparable in coercion to the punishing sword of the state, it is difficult to see how a power that could expel the already anxious believer from the circle of the faithful was in any way inferior to the strongest weapons at the disposal of civil rulers. The severity that marked this power was attributable not to any "Catholic" tendencies in Calvin's thought but to political ones; for it testified to his conviction that the problem of order was crucial. The solution, according to Calvin's logic, demanded the use of positive power on the part of the church in order to refashion Protestant man into a creature of order, or more accurately, to make him conform to a Christian image of civility.

The contrast between this conception of the role of the church and Luther's was not produced simply by Calvin's willingness to restore a three-term relationship of God-church-believer for the simpler notion of Luther. The real contrast took shape from Calvin's effort to recapture an older conception of the community as a school of virtue and the vital agency for the realization of individual perfection. If we compare, for example, Calvin's symbolism of the mother-church with the passages in Plato's *Crito* where Socrates declares he would rather take the hemlock than betray the *polis* that has nurtured him to dignity, a striking similarity in outlook emerges. This is not to say that Calvin, as the respresentative of sixteenth-century French humanism, was intent on reviving in some mimetic sense the classical conception of the community. It is only to indicate that Calvin's conception of a church-society stood as the culmination of a long intellectual heritage, extending back to the beginnings of Christianity, whereby the idea of the community as the custodian of virtue had been translated from a political to a religious setting. The church and not the city became the vital medium for human improvement, the symbol of human destiny: "to the end of time," wrote Augustine, "as a stranger upon the earth, suffering the persecutions of the world and receiving the consolation of God, the Church travels onwards." [29]

Although Calvin retained the Christian idea of the superior virtue of religious society, he reformulated it in a way that was different from both the mediaeval and the Lutheran conceptions of the church. In adopting the

Lutheran idea of a community-in-fellowship, Calvin departed from the dominant mediaeval tradition; in enveloping that community within a structure of power he departed from Luther. The final result pointed at a church that was to be something more than a community and something more than a christianized *polis*. At its deepest level, the church cohered as a *corpus mysticum,* but on top of this mystic foundation Calvin erected a set of institutions to articulate and enforce a distinctive way of life. The tight corporate quality of the whole recalled the ancient *polis,* yet the underlying element of mystery was a reminder of that transcendent strain utterly alien to the classical community. The church heralded the triumph of God — and here Calvin followed an old Christian belief; it pointed towards a perfection in eternity, and not within the time-space limits of the *polis*. Citizenship in the church-society did not connote participation in offices, but participation in a pilgrimage that would ultimately transcend history.

Despite the fact that Calvin placed a high value on community life and the institutions of the church, he was not insensitive to the danger that institutional means might become elevated into ultimate ends. As a safeguard against this possibility he insisted that the power of the church was limited, that the authority of the Scripture was superior to that of the church, and that faith stood above both men and institutions:

> Ours is the humility, which, beginning with the lowest, and paying respect to each in his degree, yields the highest honor and respect to the church in subordination, however, to Christ the church's Head; ours is the obedience, which, while it disposes us to listen to our elders and superiors, tests all obedience by the Word of God.[30]

III **The political theory of church government.** Calvin was particularly sensitive to the charge that, under the guise of attacking the papacy, he had reintroduced a new hierarchy. He tried to counter this by arguing that a church modeled on the *Institutes* could not be hierarchical because none of its offices could claim an authority independent of Scripture. Hierarchy, in his definition, was equivalent to arbitrariness; a chiseled edifice of offices was not bad in itself, as long as it did not culminate in a single, pre-eminent human authority. Calvin, in short, was not so much anti-hierarchical as anti-monarchical.

Of the major offices outlined by Calvin the two most important were the pastorate and the elders (*les Anciens*). Under the Genevan system the

Elders were laymen elected by the secular civic Council; together with a selected number of ministers, they formed the Consistory, the chief organ of church discipline.[31] The pastors were unquestionably the most powerful agency and the nerve-center of the whole system. They were to be nominated, in the first instance, by their fellow-ministers, and then passed on by the Council. The names that survived were then submitted to the congregation for its approval or rejection. These procedures provide a good illustration of the role allotted the congregation in Calvin's scheme: the membership could ratify or reject decisions; they could not formulate policy. Calvin looked upon the actions and the decisions of the church as being primarily institutional products. They were the results of prescribed procedures and of the actions of certain designated officers and agencies. Above all, these methods were the guarantee that order and regularity would prevail in church affairs; they were the alternatives to the confusion and disorder of popular control. The element in Calvin's church that most corresponded to popular participation occurred at what we could call the "social" or sacramental level. It was through the symbolism of the sacraments and the preaching of the Word, and not in the making of "political" decisions in the church, that the members enjoyed the shared intimacies of community.

These aspects of Calvin's system formed a sharp contrast to certain sectarian ideas — also hinted at by Luther on occasion — that the ministers of the church were agents of the community, hence subject to recall, and that some of the powers of the church, such as excommunication or expulsion, were to be wielded by the whole membership. For Calvin the powers of the church resided "partly" in the pastors and "partly" in the councils of the church. But the officers of the church, even though elected by some of the members of the congregation, were not to be considered agents of the community, but instruments of the Word of God the maker of all things (*instrumentorum artifex*).[32]

Although the role of the congregation was hollowed of most of its substance, the pastorate, as the symbol of the common social purpose — "the principal bond which holds the believers together in one body" [33] — was exalted:

> Here is the supreme power (*summa potestas*) with which the pastors of the church . . . ought to be invested: that by the Word of God they may venture to do all things with confidence; may constrain all the strength, glory, wisdom, and pride of the world to obey and submit to His majesty; supported by His power, may govern all mankind, from the highest to the lowest . . . may instruct and exhort the docile; may reprove, rebuke, and

restrain the rebellious and obstinate; may bind and loose; may discharge their lightnings and thunders, if necessary; but all in the Word of God.[34]

This last phrase — "all in the Word of God" — was the crucial qualification to Calvin, for it transformed what might have been a roving mandate into a species of limited power. Despite its central position in Calvin's scheme, the pastorate was not an office possessed of unlimited possibilities. It did not belong to that tradition wherein the holders of power might freely shape the passive mass of the governed, restrained only by the malleability of the human materials. In certain aspects Calvin's conception of the role of office in an organized community veered towards the Platonic tradition of the philosopher-ruler as the objective agency for an eternal truth which he served but did not invent. In its ideal form, the office of pastor, like that of the philosopher-ruler, remained undisfigured by the personality of the incumbent. A pastor who strayed beyond the objective teachings of Scripture profaned his office. The pastors were enjoined to "bring forward nothing of themselves, but speak from the mouth of the Lord" and "speak nothing beside His Word." [35] The pastor must labor, then, as a selfless demiurge, a dedicated artisan at the service of the Word. His power was not personal but institutional.[36]

Nevertheless, qualifications attached to Calvin's conception of this key office removed it at certain points from the Platonic tradition. The Platonic ruler symbolized the unbroken trinity of virtue, knowledge, and power; if perfect knowledge were perfect virtue, then these must be allied to perfect power. But Calvin's pastor was deficient in all three; the elect symbolized virtue, and there was no guarantee that the pastor qua pastor belonged to this group; greater knowledge of Scripture he might have, but it would have been blasphemous to assert that this represented a perfect knowledge; and although he possessed great power and influence over the congregation, he was far from having a monopoly in these matters. The pastor, in short, was a leader, not a ruler. It was the highest office possible in a community without a head, without a single human center of direction and control.

When this conception of the pastoral office is placed alongside the other elements of Calvin's ecclesiology, such as the passive role of the congregation and the repeated emphasis on institutional structure, and when these in turn are combined with his unvarying belief in the binding objectivity of Scripture, then the fundamental motivation becomes clear: to make of the church and its officers a selfless instrument for advancing the Word. So obsessive was this master-idea that in the end the church stands as a kind of granite edifice, an inhuman monument. Its structure has been built to anticipate and counter the threat of human discretion. Wherever the human element, like some wayward and mercurial spirit, sought escape from the institutional processes in order to assert its own individuality, it was met by Calvin, lying in wait with the exacting measure of Scripture.

The obverse side to Calvin's conception of the church was that it marked the Protestant rediscovery of the institutional dimension. In developing his ideas on this subject, Calvin touched upon a whole range of topics, including the nature of power, the functions of office, the bonds of community, and the role of membership. The totality of these problems constituted more than a theory of an ecclesiastical polity; it was nothing less than a comprehensive statement covering the major elements of a political theory. Here was a vision of a rightly ordered society and its government; here, in the sacramental mysteries and in the preaching of the Word, lay a new symbolism; a new set of sustaining "myths" to cement the society together; here, in the tight discipline enforced by the church, was the shaping hand to mould the members to a common outlook and instruct them in the lessons of a common good; and here in the promise of salvation was the perfecting purpose towards which the particular wills of the members were to be bent. The central message of the whole was of man's necessary relationship to a determinate order.

IV The restoration of the political order. The transition from Calvin's religious to his political thought was not abrupt. The same categories of analysis and modes of thought that had informed his religious writings are found in his political theory. For Calvin, political and religious thought tended to form a continuous realm of discourse. The major unifying element was the general concept of order which was a premise common to both religious and political society. This unity of outlook is worth emphasizing, because it is in sharp contrast to that of the early Reformers. In the thinking of Luther and the Anabaptists, the political and religious categories, far from being united by any internal connection, faced each other in a posture of dialectical tension. The hostility of many of the early Reformers towards the political order created a kind of fault line between their political and religious modes of thought. When they described the nature of the church or the holy life of the believers, their words and concepts evoked a picture of a good society, united in holy fellowship and living a life of harmony. But when they turned to consider the kingdom of the world, the categories shifted abruptly and the imagery darkened. For language and concept were no longer dealing with the church, the vessel of God's grace, but with the state, the weapon of His awful vengeance. Love, brotherhood, and peace, those immanent forces in the life of the church, trailed off into wistful hopes when confronted with political society. As part of the kingdom of the world, political society was a realm where conflict and violence rumbled below the surface, ready at any moment to erupt into bloodshed and disorder. Political authority naturally tended to be pictured as a mighty engine of repression — "smite and smite, slay and slay," Luther had exhorted the princes during the Peasants' War — designed to enforce peace and to protect the Christian remnant from the terrors of the world. Such a government aimed not at virtue, but at keeping men from each other's throats; mankind had never really given up the Hobbesian state of nature. In this view, an extreme tension persisted between the nature of man and the requirements of order. Political society marked a condition of "fallen nature" where sinful man strained impatiently at the restraints imposed by authority and restlessly searched for the chance to break through.

Yet it is a picture with a striking incongruity between the Christian cosmology and the Christian sociology, the one positing an omnipotent God ordering all of creation towards harmony, the other painting society as a dark, disordered mass trembling on the brink of anarchy and seemingly outside the beneficent order of God. In the thought of some of the early Reformers, political society could be likened to a realm where the cosmic writ did not run. But although the moral status of government had shrunk, its power had been exalted even to the extent of entrusting it with religious responsibilities.

The task Calvin undertook was to reconcile the several opposites created by the split-vision of the early reformers. He had to resolve the conflict between the Christian cosmology and its sociology; he had to re-establish the moral status of the political order, but without making it appear as a substitute for religious society; he had to soften the black-and-white contrasts between the two forms of society. The over-all method Calvin employed for bringing the two societies into some kind of congruence was to treat them both as subject to the general principle of order. Order became the common center to which the problems of the two societies, as societies, were to be referred. Political society was to be rescued from limbo by being restored to a wider, ordered frame. It was to become a part of the Christian cosmology. For Calvin, the governance of God was displayed in His total command over all that occurred within His domain: "not a drop of rain falls, but at the express command of God." [37] His mastery extended also to history and society; He visited judgment on the affairs of men, punishing the wicked, elevating the just and protecting the faithful. The plenitude of His power, therefore, excluded the disruptive influence of contingency and chance. He "regulates all those commotions in the most exact order, and directs them to their proper end." [38]

As part of this divine economy, civil government could no longer be viewed as a mere agency of repression or as "a polluted thing which has nothing to do with Christian men." [39] It had been designed by God to preserve and to improve the creatures with whom He had covenanted. Government was elevated into an educative agency "by which a man is instructed in the duties of humanity and civility, which are to be observed in an intercourse with mankind." [40] But if the function of government is raised above mere repression, then evidently the nature of man must contain something beyond an irrepressible inclination towards disorder. Although Calvin stood second to none of the Reformers in his low estimate of man's nature,[41] we find him, nevertheless, attaching an important qualification. The minds of men contained "general impressions of civil probity and order"; they exhibited "an instinctive propensity to cherish and preserve society." [42]

By returning to the older political tradition which had pictured man as a creature destined for order, Calvin was able to recapture for his own purposes the idea of political society as the fulfillment of certain desirable tendencies in men. Political society, far from being a Procrustean bed which cut ungovernable humanity to the pattern of obedience, was now advanced to a divinely ordained agency for man's improvement. "The authority possessed by kings and other governors over all things upon earth is not a consequence of the perverseness of men, but of the providence and holy ordinance of God." [43] Government was "equally as necessary to mankind as bread and water, light and air, and far more excellent." [44]

Concurrently with the restored status of political society and the reinvestment of man with a political nature, the ends of the political order took on a loftier dignity. The office of the magistrate aimed not merely at the preservation of life, but at "the enactment of laws to regulate a man's life among his neighbors by the rules of holiness, integrity, and sobriety." [45] Through the pursuit of these ends, the political order was linked with the higher purposes of religious society. Nevertheless, this union did not obliterate the integrity or the distinctiveness of the political order. It still had a unique role to play. It outfitted men with a type of civility and discipline that could not be gained elsewhere. The charge that Calvin was intent on stamping society with a Christian image, or on purging it of its distinctively political attributes, does less than justice to his basic intent. If the matter is analyzed merely in terms of certain "higher" and "lower" values, then there can be no denying that Calvin believed political society ought to promote the "higher" ends of Christianity — *ad majorem Dei gloriam*. To be a good citizen was not an end in itself; one became a good citizen in order to be a better believer. Nevertheless, the ends of political society were not exhausted by its Christian mission. Government existed to promote "decency" as well as "godliness," "peace" as well as "piety," "moderation" as well as "reverence." In other words, government existed to promote values that were not necessarily Christian, even though they might be given a Christian coloration; they were values that were necessary for order and, as such, a precondition for human existence. Civil government, then, was to promote the values that sustained order; it was to *civil*-ize men, or, in Calvin's words, "to regulate our lives in a manner requisite for the society of men, to form our manners to civil justice." It followed that, when the spiritual and the political jurisdictions were rightly constituted, the two orders were "in no respect at variance with each other." [46]

In a striking passage condemning the sectarian animus against the political order, Calvin summarized the value of political society and underscored its vital role in the Christian economy:

> For that spiritual reign, even now upon earth, commences within us some preludes of the heavenly kingdom, and in this mortal and transitory life affords us some taste of the immortal and incorruptible blessedness; but the end of this temporal regime is to foster and maintain the external worship of God, the pure doctrine and religion, to defend the constitution of the church in its entirety, to adapt our conduct to human society, to shape our manners in accordance with civil justice, to create concord among us, to maintain and preserve a common peace and tranquillity. All these things I confess would be superfluous if the kingdom of God, as it now exists within us, extinguishes the present life. But if it is the will of God that we should wander upon earth while aspiring towards our true country, and if such aids are necessary to our journey here; then those who would take them from man deprive him of his humanity.[47]

The values of unity and cohesion, so prominent in Calvin's discussion of the church, were evident also in his conception of the political community. The unity of the political order, however, was not that of the *corpus mysticum*. Political unity would draw sustenance and support from the mystic solidarity of Christians — "Christians are not only a body politic, but they are the mystical and spiritual body of Christ" [48] — but the more immediate source of cohesion would be in the political society itself.[49] There was a kind of natural unity arising from man's innate instinct towards an ordered life in society, and there was a kind of artificial unity which could be induced by the institutions of society. The full unity of the society was the product of an alliance between nature and art. For the individual member, it meant an education in order; that is, the acquisition of a set of civil habits which would simultaneously support civilized life and satisfy one of man's basic instincts.

Although civil law and political institutions were two of the main agencies of stability and order, these same ends were also served by the system of vocations. A graduated social hierarchy, clearly defined in terms of offices and obligations, was but the civil counterpart to the divine principle that sustained the universe. Far from being a divisive force, distinctions of status and eminence were not only inevitable, but, in a Christian society, salutary. They had been instituted by God to prevent men from wallowing in "universal confusion." They outfitted the individual with a sort of social map, a sense of direction "that he might not wander about in uncertainty the rest of his days." [50]

Man's education to membership in an ordered community was furthered from still another source. The life of the church was an intensely social one, and in the element of love, which bound the fellowship together, it possessed a powerful cohesive whose influence would carry over to blunt the sharp edges of the social hierarchy. Love became the basic fusing force which blended the private goods of individuals into a common good for the whole society:

> . . . No member [of the human body] has its power for itself, nor applies it to its private use, but transfuses it among its fellow members, receiving no advantage from it but what proceeds from the common convenience of the whole body. So, whatever ability a pious man possesses, he ought to possess it for his brethren, consulting his own private interest in no way inconsistent with a cordial attention to the common edification of the church . . . whatever God has conferred on us, which enables us to assist our neighbor, we are the stewards of it, and must one day render an account of our stewardship.[51]

V   **Political knowledge.** Calvin's claim that there was a kind of virtue attainable only in a political order raised still another set of problems. If virtue implied knowledge — and Calvin assumed with the ancients that it did — then was it possible to have political knowledge and, if so, how reliable was it?

Calvin agreed that there was such a form of knowledge. It was located in the province of "terrestrial knowledge" (*l'intelligence des choses terriennes*), a knowledge "which relates entirely to the present life" and "in some sense is confined within the limits of it." The highest type of knowledge was "celestial knowledge" which pertained to "the pure knowledge of God, the method of true righteousness, and the mysteries of the heavenly kingdom." [52] The inferiority of political knowledge was the result partially of its association with lesser objects and partially of its reliance on the imperfect instrument of reason. Reason, like the rest of man's nature, had been ineradicably corrupted by the Fall. There was, however, an important qualification: the corruptive effects of Adam's rebellion were partial, not total. Man's rational understanding had been crippled but not annihilated. "Some sparks continue to shine in the nature of man, even in its corrupt and degenerate state, which prove him to be a rational creature. . . ." Although reason could not lead man to spiritual regeneration or to "spiritual wisdom," it might usefully serve him in political society.[53]

Proof of a natural relation between reason and political life was to be found in man's "instinctive propensity towards civil society." "This," Calvin declared, "is a powerful argument that in the constitution of this life no man is destitute of the light of reason." [54] Man was not rational and therefore social; he was social and therefore rational. More important, Calvin claimed that reason could elicit political truths, an assertion that he supported by the writings of the classical pagan authors. Where Luther had venemously condemned the "harlot reason" and had likened previous political philosophy to an Augean stable awaiting only the broom of the Wittenberg Hercules, Calvin moved to restore something of the classical relationship between reason and politics and something of the reputation of the classical philosophers: "shall we deny the light of truth to the ancient lawyers, who have delivered such just principles of civil order and polity?" [55] Calvin strongly agreed that natural reason would play men false if they attempted to convert it into a vehicle of spiritual salvation, yet this did not prevent a kind of kinship between the political wisdom in the Christian precepts, such as that contained in the second table of the Decalogue, and the political insights of natural reason. Both types of wisdom had a common origin in the will of God. Thus the principles of reason were not to be viewed as a human invention *ab nihilo* but as deductions from the moral dictates that God had "inscribed" and "engraven on the hearts of all men":

Since man is by nature a social animal (*homo animal est natura sociale*), he is also inclined by a natural instinct to cherish and preserve society. Accordingly, we see that there are some general precepts of honesty and civil order impressed on the understanding of all men. For this reason there is no one who does not recognize that all human associations ought to be ruled by laws, and there is no one who does not possess the principle of these laws in his own understanding. For this reason there is a universal agreement among nations and individuals to accept laws, and this is a seed planted in us by nature rather than by a teacher or legislator.[56]

But since this universal moral law of conscience was too dim to illumine men's actions with any consistency, God had supplemented it by the Decalogue, which declared "with greater certainty what in the law of nature was too obscure . . ."[57] When thus reinforced by the Decalogue, the moral law could function as the Christian version of natural equity which was "the same for all mankind." It was to be the informing standard for a rightly ordered community, "the scope, and rule, and end of all laws."[58]

The qualifications that Calvin attached to the moral law were consistent with his conviction that a perfect knowledge of politics could not be achieved independently of the Christian teaching. Lacking the Christian wisdom, political knowledge possessed only a limited integrity of its own. The insufficiency of political reason in Calvin's system formed a logical parallel to the limited ends pursued by the political order itself. The sights of political society were pitched lower because the virtue at which it aimed was a virtue of the second order. The chief end of man was to know God, and to achieve this end men had to be regenerated — "depart from ourselves" and "lay aside our old mind, and assume a new one." But the task of fashioning the "new man" was not assigned to the political order. Its business was to shape men to the habits of civility and order; it could not cure souls. Just as rational knowledge was lower than celestial knowledge, and just as the ends of civil society were inferior to those of religious society, so civic virtue stood beneath the perfect virtue taught by Christianity.

But having noted these distinctions in values, it is important not to translate them into antitheses. Although Calvin believed that a Christian foundation was a prerequisite for a well-constituted civil polity, there was no equivocation on his part about the essential value of the polity itself.

VI Political office. The consistency of Calvin's political and ecclesiastical thinking was nowhere more clearly evidenced than in the discussion of the office and duties of the civil magistrate. The same impulse which had dictated Calvin's conception of the pastoral office reappeared in

the magistracy. Even the language he used to describe the civil governor —
"sacred ministry," "vicar of God," "minister of God" — left the unmistakable
impression that Calvin was less concerned to depict a political office as such
than to create a political analogue to the pastorate. In both cases, there was
a single-minded concentration on the impersonal nature of the office; that is,
on the institution. In both cases, the personality of the occupant was absorbed
into the office itself. Both magistrate and pastor were intended to be selfless
instruments of a higher purpose and subordinated to a written law. Where
the pastor was enjoined to add nothing of himself to the office or to the
preaching of the Word, but to be only *"la bouche de Dieu,"* the magistrate
too was to be depersonalized, but in relation to the civil law: "the law is a
silent magistrate, and a magistrate a speaking law." [59]

The parallel between the two offices was expressed in still another way.
Both were enveloped by an impressive *mystique* which aimed not only at
discouraging disobedience in the respective societies, but also at awing the
office-holder as well. Both of these elements were necessary to Calvin's theory
of political obedience. The distinctive emphasis of the doctrine lay in its insistence on active, affirmative allegiance to the ruler, and not merely on a
willingness to obey his commands. [60] The reverence of subjects towards their
ruler ought to be rooted in conscience, not fear. At the same time, however,
the loyalty of the subjects should be directed at the office rather than at the
individual magistrate. The civic commitment was institutional and not personal. At bottom this institutional allegiance ran to the broad purposes of the
society, to the civilized ends secured by the political order. Those who weakened the fabric of order were classed as "inhuman monsters," "the enemies of
all equity and right, and totally ignorant of humanity." [61]

For his part, the magistrate symbolized, not mere power, but the permanent
ends of society. His functions were to preserve order and a "temperate
liberty"; to enforce justice and righteousness; and to promote peace and godliness. [62] He did not stand as the representative of the interests or opinions
of particular groups, classes, or localities, but of a set of purposes which he
served but had not originated. And since none of these ends were possible
without order, the basic task of the magistrate was to insure that this condition prevailed. The pressing importance of order drew from Calvin the
admission that even tyrants "retain in their tyranny some kind of just government. There can be no tyranny which does not in some respects assist in
consolidating the society of men." [63] The tyrant was connected to the cause
of order by his mere possession of power. The price of cohesion and unity
was the active exercise of power, and this minimum condition could be ful-

filled by a tyrant. "There is much truth in the old saying that it is worse to live under a prince through whose levity everything is lawful, than under a tyrant where there is no liberty at all." [64] Even the lawful ruler must, therefore, assert his power affirmatively; had not Jeremiah urged "execute ye judgment and righteousness"?

Although at one level the allegiance relationship depicted by Calvin was essentially political between ruler and ruled, at another level it transcended the political and implicated both parties in a relationship with God. The ruler was a transient occupant of a divine office and owed a responsibility to God for the faithful discharge of his trust. On the other side, the subjects were bound to obey the commands of a divinely authorized agent. Allegiance, therefore, was both a political and a religious duty. At the human level, it supported the civilized ends of society; at the ultimate level, it was a search for a right relationship with God.[65]

In the case of the tyrant, the religious element was, in a sense, dominant. He was the agent of God's wrath sent to scourge the community for its sins; his coming ought to provoke a sense of collective guilt among the people, causing them to search their consciences for the sins they had committed.[66] The relationship between citizen and tyrant, then, belonged not to the political but to the "celestial" category, because the concept of sin, which connected tyrant and subject, was not a political conception at all.[67] And despite Calvin's intention of making obedience to tyrants appear more palatable, the effect of his reasoning was to underscore the extraordinary nature of tyranny and to isolate it from the normal political relationships. The tyrant might be elevated to a divine instrument sent *"pour châtier les péchés du peuple,"* [68] yet this very mission made him an essentially apolitical figure. Sin was a theological and not a political relationship.

This tendency towards placing the tyrant outside the usual political relationships cropped out again when Calvin came to consider the problem of obedience. In obeying the tyrant, the loyal subject was viewed as discharging an obligation to God rather than one deriving from the general ends of society. Obedience, however, was limited by the dictates of conscience, that is, by another extra-political factor. Although conscience created a direct relationship between the individual and God, and thereby circumvented the political relationship between subject and ruler, it offered, nevertheless, a powerful threat to the unlimited claims of the tyrant. Conscience was essentially a religious conception and owed its beginnings to religious controversies, but it could be turned to political advantage without straining its fundamental meaning. For, in one sense, conscience was a response to power;

it had to do with the individual as the object of compulsion in a governed order. Yet whether the protesting conscience felt imperiled by papal or civil power, it retained a saving relationship with God. In one sense, Calvin's "court of conscience" pointed the individual away from the "political"; in another, it was obviously designed for the politically involved citizen. The citizen who, on strictly religious grounds, disobeyed a command that ran contrary to Scripture was, in Calvin's view, not only fulfilling his obligation to God, but also reminding the ruler of the true nature of his office. Calvin's conception of resistance was that of a selfless service designed to preserve the integrity of political institutions from the errors of temporary office-holders.[69]

Although there was nothing novel in the proposition that scriptural injunctions prevailed over political commands, Calvin displayed a greater sensitivity than most of the Reformers to the political implications of religious resistance. It was this that eventually led him to formulate a theory of resistance which was political rather than religious in its motivation. He allowed that the estates or specially designated magistrates might "oppose the violence and cruelty of kings." By virtue of their position, these agencies had a positive obligation to protect popular liberties:

> If they connive with kings in the oppression of the humble people, their dissimulation is not free from nefarious perfidy, because they maliciously betray the liberty of the people, while knowing, that by the ordinance of God, they are its protectors.[70]

Near the end of his life, Calvin began to veer, hesitatingly to be sure, towards an acceptance of the idea that the coronation oaths and the laws of a country formed a system of agreements which might be defended against an arbitrary ruler:

> . . . Certain remedies against tyranny are allowable, for example, when magistrates and estates have been constituted and given the care of the commonwealth: they shall have power to keep the prince to his duty and even to coerce him if he attempt anything unlawful.[71]

Two aspects of this deserve underlining. First, Calvin's declaration that the estates and inferior magistrates were entrusted with a divine responsibility contrasts with Luther's tendency to elevate rulership above all other offices. Consistent with this had been Luther's strong scepticism concerning the legitimacy of the estates as restraining organs.[72] Calvin, on the other hand, by breaching "the divinity that doth hedge a king," had created a rival agency, armed with the only credentials that most men of the period would respect, a divine ordination. The second important aspect of Calvin's resistance theory was its mention of the strictly political ends served by the organs of resistance: the protection of "the liberty of the people," "the care of the commonwealth." The effect of this was to provide a balancing parallel to the theory of allegiance. For the same reason that men obey authority in order to preserve the civilizing purposes supported by the political order, so the specified organs of the community might have to disobey in order to preserve that order.

While none of these considerations worked to dislodge either the primacy of the religious motive in Calvin's thought or the priority held by spiritual values, they did signify his rediscovery of political complexity. More than any other contemporary Reformer, he was supremely sensitive to the plurality of relationships and obligations operating in a political community. Among most of the Reformers, the general tendency had been to reduce the manifold complexity of politics to a simple connection between ruler and ruled or between both of them and God. Calvin, however, avoided this simple explanation and emphasized instead the triangular relationship of ruler, people, and the law. The connecting link between ruler and citizen was not a direct one, but occurred through the mediating agency of the law.[73] From the standpoint of the ruler this had the effect of adding one more obligatory element to his office: he owed responsibilities to the people, to God, to the law, and to the whole range of purposes proper to a rightly constituted society. The sum total of these obligations formed a premise that made the act of resistance a logical possibility within the Calvinist system and not, as many later commentators would have it, a matter of geographical accident.

VII **Power and community.** Calvin's conception of the church and of civil society, taken together, marked the Protestant rediscovery of the idea of the institutionalized community. It had been the genius of early sixteenth-century Protestantism to create the notion of a cohesive religious association; but the failure to equip the religious fellowship with the necessary institutional structure had threatened the fellowship with dissolution from within and encroachment from without. Although there can be no denying that the institutional hostility of the early Reformers was nourished by a deep desire to prevent religious feeling from being stifled by ecclesiasticism, they failed to grapple with the fact that, as long as the church was bound to this world, it would have to face the threat of rival institutions powerfully organized. The strength of Calvin's position lay in its realization that the precondition for the survival of the community of believers was a strongly structured church government; a sense of institutions must be combined with a sense of community.

Similarly, where the early Reformers expressed an indifference to the political order or else viewed it solely as a repressive agency, Calvin reasserted its value and denied that its essence consisted in coercion. In short, Calvin's emphasis on a strong church and on the dignity of political society was designed for a double purpose: to make the church safe in the world and the world safe for the church. In reorienting Protestantism towards the world, Calvin stands as the Protestant counterpart to Aquinas. Like Thomas he labored to reintegrate the political order with the order of grace, but unlike Thomas he had the further task of showing that the church could contribute to the order of civil society without perverting its own nature. The ethos created by the church was to be a *civil*-izing one, one that habituated the liberated Protestant to a life under order and discipline. In Calvin's system the church became the agency for resolving the uneasy tension encouraged by the early Reformation belief that man was a divided being dwelling partly in a society of faith ruled by Christ and partly in civil society ruled by temporal authority. In resolving the bifurcated existence of man, Calvin returned to the substance, but not the form, of the mediaeval idea that human existence, whether lived at the spiritual or "material" level, was an existence pre-eminently social and ordered. No abrupt transition separated both aspects of existence, because in both of them man was a creature accustomed to the power and restraints of institutions and to a life of civility.

The result of these labors was not only to impart to Protestantism a depth of political understanding it had previously lacked, but to place the new movement on a more equal footing with the political sophistication of Catholicism. From the time of the first political repercussions of Protestantism, Catholicism had claimed to be more congenial to the requirements of civil society. In one sense this claim was profoundly true. Under the government of the Church the believer had been accustomed to the patterns of "civil" behavior enforced by Church discipline, and was therefore prepared for the life of civil society. Once this is recognized it is easy to see that the emphatic insistence of the early Reformers on an almost unqualified obedience to civil rulers was but a crude effort to overcome the political superiority of Catholicism. It was crude because it assumed that the habits of civility could be summed up so easily. Calvin's contribution was to see that the habits of civility needed by the church were also essential to civil life; the essential demands of order were the same for both societies. The interlocking of the religious and civil orders in Calvin's system was simply the fulfillment of two dominant impulses in man, one religious, the other social, and both united by the need for order.

Two elements in the Calvinist conception of order held radical implications for the future. The first was the notion that a society could be at once well-organized, disciplined, and cohesive and yet be without a head. Although all Protestants were necessarily anti-monarchical in their belief that a religious society could flourish without a papal monarch, Calvin was unique in being able to describe the institutional substitutes for the pope. The political application of these beliefs awaited the English civil wars of the seventeenth century, but the distaste for secular monarchy was already in evidence in Calvin's own writings.[74]

The other potentially explosive idea lay in Calvin's belief that a community rested on an active membership. The unity that flowed from participation was the Calvinist answer to the papal theory that unity could only be guaranteed by the single will of the pontiff. Moreover, participation was an equalizing conception because the nature of the good at which the society aimed was one intended for all the participants; the body of Christ knew no distinctions in value among the members. Once this concept of participation was given a political twist, it would be but a short step from Geneva to the English Levellers at Putney and Colonel Rainborough's claim that the "poorest he that is in England hath a life to live, as the greatest he . . . every man that is to live under a government ought first by his own consent to put himself under that government." [75] To view such a step as the radical transformation of essentially religious notions would be to miss the whole meaning of Calvin's system. It was a system that needed no "transforming" in order to bring out a political implication, because the political element had been present from the start. At the very moment that Calvin grasped the importance of order the political theme was incorporated into the main body of writings and reached its fullest expression in the Calvinist conception of the church-society. To the extent that the church was a governing order, fully institutionalized and equipped with power, it possessed many of the qualities of a political society.

If we accept the view that Calvin's notion of the church was in some degree a species of political theory, additional light can be thrown on the relationship between Christianity and the development of Western political thought. One of the most important effects of Christianity had been to discourage the classical quest for an ideal state. To the Christian persuasion, the attempt to build an eternal polity, untouched by the corrosions of time, had appeared as an act of *lèse-majesté,* an attempt to emulate the omnipotence of God. A writer like Aquinas, for example, might devote considerable attention to the best form of government, yet this was a far cry from the Platonic vision of a total regeneration of man through political means. The true Christian counterpart of the absolutely best societies projected by Plato and Aristotle was to be found in Augustine's City of God. The ideal society existed beyond and not within history; it was a society transcendental, not empirical. The powerful hold that this idea was to gain over the Western imagination had the effect of etherealizing the old classical idea of the best society into the idea of the Kingdom of God. Only occasionally did the older notion reappear in the sublimated form of More's *Utopia* or Campanella's *City of the Sun.*

In Calvin's writings, however, the idea of the best society re-emerged, but in a distinctively Christian rather than classical way. The church and the civil society were both viewed as social orders embodying certain values, yet the church was the better society on several counts. Its mission was loftier, its life more social, and its virtues of a higher dignity. The sacramental bond provided a kind of unity which the civil order could never attain: "every one imparts to all in common what he has received from the Lord." [76] In civil society, on the other hand, the necessary precondition was that "men should have peculiar and distinct possessions." [77] The ethical pattern, the *justum regimen,* of the one society was to be sought in Christ, while the other society could never aspire to a good greater than external piety. The one society aimed at salvation and repentance; it was *"un vray ordre";* the other was concerned only with the public side of man. The one, in short, was the good society, the other a necessary but inferior society.

But although the church stood as the better society in comparison to the state, the church itself was only the best realizable society, not the absolutely best. Above the visible society of believers was the church invisible and eternal, the pure communion of saints. When compared to this society, the visible church was a *"res carnalis"* confined within the limits of time and space. But although the best society could not be realized by men on earth, it was not entirely disconnected from what men could achieve. A rightly ordered church and civil society could follow the same doctrine that inspired the life of the saints; and if their endeavors fell short of the standard of the best society, they might still achieve something of inestimable value, a whispered intimation of immortality.

A few final words on the Reformers before turning to Machiavelli's political thought. In most accounts, the political philosophy of Machiavelli is depicted as startlingly modern in character; and what was omitted by Machiavelli is usually supplemented by drawing from Hobbes. Together they are taken as the symbols of modernity. In the following pages an attempt will be made to explicate the elements of modernity in both of these writers, but here I wish only to caution against exaggerating the contrast between them and the Reformers. In certain decisive respects the Reformers acted and spoke more towards the future than either Machiavelli or Hobbes.

To begin with, men like Luther, Zwingli, and Calvin were actors as well as thinkers; and in the former role they experimented with a mode of action suspect by both Machiavelli and Hobbes yet commonplace to modern times. They were all leaders of mass movements and, as such, among the first to attempt to catalyze the masses for the purpose of social action. When the Reformation leaders are viewed in this light, we are able to see how eminently suited were their techniques and doctrines to creating and encouraging popular action. The "priesthood of the believers" notion, for example, was marvelously successful in arousing the enmity of the followers against all forms of religious status; that is, of supplying a focus of hatred; and yet it also supplied a sense of elevated equality among the believers, an undifferentiated mass status.

Consider also how the sustained attempt at simplifying religious ideas to their basic essentials, the emphasis on faith or belief rather than rational knowledge, the translation of Scripture into the vernacular languages, all of these bear the earmarks of having been designed for mass action. Consider, too, the political implications of the Reformation as a broad movement of revolt directed against an established order, a revolt whose success depended upon radicalizing the masses into disaffection with existing authorities and institutions. The perfecting of the arts of popular leadership and the tendency to blur the line between systematic theology and popular ideology — it was as though the guardians had ventured to combine the roles which Plato had carefully distinguished: the thinker-statesman, for whom the public had to be shaped to the demands of truth, and the politician, for whom truth had to be accommodated to the mood and wants of the public.

Hardly a trace of these notions can be found in Machiavelli and Hobbes, and this despite the fact that they are usually considered the precursors of modern political thought. Their failure in these respects is as fully illuminating for what it tells us about modern political thinking as for what it tells us about Machiavelli and Hobbes. Although Hobbes, for example, was occasionally to voice the hope that political philosophy might be reduced to a few simple theorems, he and Machiavelli both remained faithful to the tra-

ditional distinction between the rigorous demonstrations appropriate to political knowledge and the crude catechisms suitable for the vulgar understanding. For all of their heresies, they remained stubbornly orthodox in
their belief that political philosophy represented a form of knowledge pertaining to the good of a whole society, not one tailored to appeal to the common intellect of the members.

The philosophical status assigned political knowledge by Hobbes was in
part a reflection of the different relationship he saw between thought and
action. Both he and Machiavelli remained unaffected by the great temptation
of modern political theory of converting political philosophy into a species
of popular ideology suited to the appetite and organizational needs of political mass movements. In the notion of what group they were writing for,
Machiavelli and Hobbes were distinctly pre-modern. The modern writer
tends to assume that the age-old problem of bridging the gap between theory
and practice can be accomplished by appealing to the dominant group in society. This means, in the modern era, an appeal to a popular audience. As
Rousseau recognized, "It is no longer a question of speaking to a small
number, but to the public . . ."

In contrast, the style and method of Machiavelli and Hobbes show them
to be strongly self-conscious that they were addressing a highly select audience. They spoke to their intellectual peers and directed their efforts at influencing the few who occupied the seats of power. This is to say that both
writers were at one with the classical and mediaeval traditions in holding
that since political action meant action by the one or few, there was a point
in hoping that the few would someday listen. It was this hope that kept alive
the enterprise of political knowledge as something to be *known,* not merely
believed. Much of modern political theory has looked towards a far different
audience; it has sought out, not the Borgias or the Cromwells, but the
"masses." In the spirit of Baudelaire, it sees in the masses "a huge reservoir
of electrical energy" waiting to be tapped; its aspiration is to rouse the sleep-
ing giant, cause him to exchange his supportive role for that of positive
agent. This approach implies not only a wholesale transformation of political
action, but of political philosophy as well. Political ideas come to be something to be *believed* rather than *known;* political philosophy ceases to be
philosophy and becomes popular literature; for belief, unlike knowledge,
thrives on a common mentality. In these matters Hobbes was hopelessly
classical, Luther ominously modern.

❦ SEVEN ❧

Machiavelli:

Politics and the Economy of Violence

This is the question finally at stake in any genuinely moral situation:
What shall the agent be? What sort of character shall he assume?

JOHN DEWEY

I The autonomy of political theory. The impact of the Reformation on the
Western European countries had resulted in a significant alliance, although not always on a self-conscious basis, between the groups advocating religious reform and those intent on furthering national independence. This had been facilitated by the tendency among the religious writers
of the last half of the sixteenth century to turn increasingly to consider political theories and problems. Calvin undertook to reintroduce political categories into church theory as the necessary accompaniment to a reintegration
of the political and religious orders. In England, Hooker supplied to Anglicanism a philosophy which extolled the intermingling of political and religious elements and accepted royal supremacy in ecclesiastical matters.

195

Ironically, the Puritans, whose concept of the "two kingdoms" Hooker had labeled subversive of the unity of political and religious life, became increasingly doubtful of their own distinction. In the next century they showed a startling talent for expanding the claims of the kingdom of grace, until the political order itself was temporarily under the domination of the saints.

The revival of the language of politics was also bound up with a growing sense of national identification on the part of Protestant apologists. The language of church theory, in particular, had to be recast to accord with the dissolution of the universal organization and the nationalization of religious life. These two developments, the reintroduction of political concepts into religious thought and the sense of national particularism, were summed up by Hooker near the end of the century:

> . . . As the main body of the sea being one, yet within divers precincts hath divers names; so the Catholic Church is in like sort divided into a number of distinct societies, every one of which is termed a Church within itself . . . A Church . . . is a Society, that is, a number of men belonging unto some Christian fellowship, the place and limits whereof are certain . . . For the truth is, that the Church and the commonwealth are names which import things really different; but those things are accidents, and such accidents as may and should always dwell lovingly together in one subject. Wherefore the real difference between the accidents signified by those names, doth not prove different subjects for them always to reside in.[1]

The growing merger of political and religious categories of thought was an intellectual footnote to the spread of political control over national churches. When these tendencies were joined to the growing strength of the national monarchies and to an emerging national consciousness, the combined effect was to pose a possibility which had not been seriously entertained in the West for almost a thousand years: an autonomous political order which acknowledged no superior and, while accepting the universal validity of Christian norms, was adamant in insisting that their interpretation was a national matter. But while Reformation Europe could accept the practice of an autonomous political order and disagree primarily over who should control it, there was greater reluctance to explore the notion of an autonomous political theory. As long as political theory contained a stubbornly moral element and as long as men identified the ultimate categorical imperatives with the Christian teaching, political thought would resist being divested of religious imagery and religious values. Even if men had been prepared to doubt the centrality of ethics to politics, even if like Sir Thomas Smith in the sixteenth century they were to wonder if the argument of Thrasymachus had been "so farre out of the way, (if it be civillie understood) as Plato would make it," [2] it is doubtful that political theory could have avoided the contagion of religious thinking. Like other forms of discourse, political theory is relevant only when it is intelligible. The intelligibility of a theorist's ideas depend upon his honoring the tacit conventions of his age, even when he has undertaken to explore their outer limits.[3]

In sixteenth-century Western Europe the price of persuasion was defined by an audience committed to religion. This had been further strengthened by the fact that, whatever support had been given religious reform by economic and national impulses, the most sustained attacks on the Middle Ages had been largely couched in the language of religion. It followed that the political theorist could not dismiss religion, but only take up different attitudes towards it. Before the conventions controlling political discourse could be altered, the intensity of religious conviction amongst the audience had first to be undermined by scepticism, indifference, and, above all, by decades of bitter and costly religious wars. Similarly, the practical relevance of political ideas was closely tied to religion, if for no other reason than that religious unrest presented one of the main threats to political stability. The new states of Europe might be politically autonomous in the practical sense of being independent of the control of religious institutions, but they could not afford to be indifferent towards religion. Moreover, for centuries now, Western political societies had relied on habits of civility whose content and sanctioning inhibitions were supplied by Christianity. As late as the eighteenth century, convinced Erastians, like Voltaire, were apprehensive of trying to govern a society in which the Christian ethic had lost its hold.[4] Nationalism and patriotism had not yet reached a position of being able to furnish from their own resources a code of civic conduct independent of religion. For all of these reasons the language and concepts of political theory, as they developed during the Reformation, could not break conclusively out of the circle of possibilities drawn by religious thought and religious problems.

If the promise of an autonomous political theory could not be fulfilled within the intellectual framework established by the Reformation, its evolution must be sought instead in a setting unruffled by religious upheavals and one wherein the conventions of discourse fashioned by the Middle Ages were being challenged by modes of thought other than theological ones. Such a situation existed in Italy during the sixteenth century. Here the energies of Italian intellectuals were being turned more and more to the exploration of new realms of inquiry without the distraction of endless religious polemics.

At the same time that the dominant intellectual outlook was no longer being shaped by religious influences, the power of religious institutions had begun to recede, or, more accurately, the power of the Church was significant not as an extension of its spiritual mission but for its role in the internal politics of the Italian peninsula. This conjuncture of factors created the opportunity for political phenomena to emerge more sharply and distinctly.

The lack of national unity, the instability of political life in the Italian city-states, and the easy access to status and power beckoning the political adventurer joined to render the political dimension of existence pervasive and compelling. To move on a thoroughly political plane necessarily called for casting off modes of thought inherited from an earlier age where politics had been tightly enclosed by a religious world-view. Almost a century before *The Prince* was written, a viable tradition of "realism" had developed in Italian political thought. While these writers of the early *quattrocento* had been mainly preoccupied with comparing the relative merits of monarchies and republics and with evaluating the life of action as against the *vita contemplativa* preached by the humanist sage,[5] the most significant aspect of the controversies was the absence of religious polemics which allowed the theorists to confront issues like order and power in almost strictly political terms.

In the political thought of Machiavelli these latent possibilities were taken up and made the basis for the first great experiment in a "pure" political theory. The manifesto which he drew for the new science reflected the belief that before political phenomena could be meaningfully analyzed, they must first be freed from the enclosing illusions woven by the political ideas of the past.

> And because I know that many have written on this topic [of the prince], I fear that when I too write I shall be thought presumptuous, because in discussing it, I break away completely from the principles laid down by my predecessors. But since it is my purpose to write something useful to an attentive reader, I think it more effective to go back to the practical truth of the subject than to depend on my fancies about it.[6]

Machiavelli's condemnation of the great political philosophies of the past was not prompted by any formal philosophical objections on his part. It was based instead on the belief that the concepts inherited by political thought had ceased to be meaningful because they no longer dealt with phenomena that were truly political. Where mediaeval political thought had made ecclesiastical institutions a major focal point of its inquiries and consequently had had its concepts imbued by religious imagery and ideas, Machiavelli contended that ecclesiastical governments were irrelevant to the proper concerns of the new science. Other critics of the papacy, such as Marsilius and Luther, had stigmatized it for being too political; but Machiavelli's charge was that it was not political enough to warrant the attention of political theory. In his biting words, such regimes maintain their princes in power regardless of "the way they act and live."

> These are the only princes who have states and do not defend them, sub-
> jects and do not govern them; yet their states are never taken away from
> them as a result of not being defended; and their subjects do not object
> because they are not governed; they do not dream of being alienated from
> the Church, nor can they be. These principalities alone, then, are secure and
> happy. But since they are protected by higher causes, to which the human
> mind does not reach, I will omit speaking of them; because, since they are
> maintained and set up by God, it would be the part of a presumptuous and
> conceited man to treat them.[7]

While it would make a nice point to discuss whether Machiavelli believed papal government to be beyond the reach of political theory or, instead, beneath its contempt, the important thing is that his antipathies were the outcome of a highly self-conscious notion of what matters were germane to political theory.[8] If political significance were denied the papacy, the language of mediaeval political theology became superfluous to the needs of the new science. In this respect political theory was to contribute to one of the fundamental tendencies of the Renaissance, namely, the proliferation of independent areas of inquiry, each intent on staking out its autonomy, each concerned to develop a language of explanation suited to a particular set of phenomena, and each proceeding without benefit of clergy. In the long run, this development presented a far more serious threat to the unified worldview of the Middle Ages than any number of anti-Christian crudities.

The break with mediaeval modes of thought has not been accounted by most modern commentators as the sole reason for acclaiming Machiavelli the first truly modern political thinker. They have rightly included his rejection of traditional norms, such as natural law, and the exploration of a pragmatic method of analysis concentrating almost exclusively on questions of power. We have added to these the suggestion that Machiavelli's modernity also lay in the attempt to exclude from political theory whatever did not appear to be strictly political. While religion was the most important casualty of the principle of exclusion, there were others equally significant, but of quite different types. In this connection it is worth examining Machiavelli's animus against hereditary rulers and his deep contempt for the nobility. The importance of this discussion does not relate to the language and concepts of the new science, but rather to its political and social biases. If the new science was hostile to hereditary princes and the aristocracy, it could not be accused of being a mere ideology designed for the purpose of rationalizing these particular interests. On the other hand, if the new science were to cut itself off from these two, in what quarter could it find allies for the task of reform? We can perhaps throw some light on these matters by examining Machiavelli's attitudes towards the nobility and the principle of hereditary rule.

The antipathy towards hereditary monarchs was bound up with Machiavelli's appreciation of the crisis which had been developing in the notions of authority and legitimacy. He sensed correctly that in recent centuries the rapid changes in institutional forms, social structures, and types of leadership had rendered older notions of legitimacy obsolete. A political world had emerged where the hereditary principle and most forms of traditionalism were steadily losing their hold. Despite the continued existence of viable hereditary systems, such as in France, Machiavelli contended that they held little relevance for political theory. "A new princely government," he wrote, "encounters difficulties," but "hereditary states, being accustomed to the family of their princes, are maintained with fewer difficulties than new ones." [9] Thus an hereditary system, which by definition presupposed a settled situation where the loyalties and the expectations of the subjects remained fairly constant, did not call for any special skill or knowledge and hence presented no real challenge to political science.[10] On the other hand, a newly acquired dominion was retained or lost strictly according to the ruler's measure of skill. The latter, then, represented a purer form of politics in that accidental factors played a minor role.[11] This difference was reflected also in the comparative possibilities for *virtù*. An hereditary prince had small opportunity for greatness, because glory was more possible in the gaining of power rather than in the inheriting of it. The hereditary monarch stood to suffer a "double disgrace" if "though born a prince, he loses his dominion because he is not prudent." Moreover, a prince who had enjoyed a long reign and who then suffered a sudden reverse was even denied the comfort of blaming his downfall on *Fortuna*. Lulled by security, he had patently failed to make adequate preparation for the political contingencies afflicting all regimes.[12] In contrast, the new prince had the chance of "double glory": he could found a new realm and experience the aesthetic exhilaration of stamping it with the impress of his own personality, something necessarily denied the hereditary ruler whose power depended on honoring existing arrangements.[13]

Disdainful of the hereditary principle, Machiavelli offered the new science of statecraft as the alternative to the old principle of legitimacy, boldly promising to make "a new prince seem to be an old one" and "immediately make him safer and firmer in his realm than if he had grown old in it." [14] To this extent the new science reflected an age of extreme social mobility, an "age of the bastards," as Burckhardt called it. In serving the new men as they scrambled for power, status, and glory, the new science worked as a great equalizer, elevating the comparative position of those who pitted ability against hereditary right.[15] This, incidentally, partially explains the great weight assigned to the military arts by Machiavelli: a knowledge of warfare, he explained, was of service not only to those who were born princes, but it "causes men to rise from humble positions to that [same] rank." [16]

In the new man, the political *arriviste,* Machiavelli painted a striking portrait of the figure which was to bedevil modern politics. The new man was the offspring of an age of restless ambition, of the rapid transformation of institutions and quick shifts in power among the elite groups. He symbolized, in brief, the flux of politics, its impermanency and its endlessly on-going character. In contrast, the hereditary ruler stood for the anachronistic principle that fixed situations and settled arrangements were of the essence of politics. At bottom, then, the bias of the new science towards the "new prince" and against the hereditary one was based on the belief that the former was a truer image of the nature of politics. But whether he was a more reliable agent for the application of the new science is a question which we shall reserve until after we have examined Machiavelli's case against the nobility.

"Human appetites," Machiavelli wrote, "are insatiable, for by nature we are so constituted that there is nothing we cannot long for, but by fortune we are such that of these things we can attain but few. The result is that the human mind is perpetually discontented . . ." [17] Machiavelli believed that this form of discontent was the particular vice of the nobles: nothing short of complete domination could satisfy them.[18] This, however, was no longer feasible for the reason that the long experience of civic freedom had encouraged the expectations of the average citizen to believe it right that his own desires should be treated equally with those of others. The interests and ambitions of both groups could not be harmonized, for one demanded preference, the other equality. This was not so much a logical contradiction as a political one. It was the nature of political action that it had to be undertaken in a limited "field" where the objects of interest and ambition existed in short supply. Unlike other fields of action, politics was plagued by the dilemma of limited goods and limitless ambitions.[19]

The problem of scarcity and ambition, which was to be put at the center of political theory in the next century by Hobbes, led, in turn, to the issue of inequality. Here again we find Machiavelli elaborating the attitude which was to characterize modern political theory: the new science was fundamentally hostile to social distinctions and to the aristocratic principle in particular. One of the indices of a corrupt society, in Machiavelli's view, was the existence of widespread social and economic inequality and of a parasitic gentry which refused its social duties and amused itself by frequent armed forays into the surrounding countryside, destroying and disrupting the peace. This antipathy towards the *gentiluomini* and *grandi* sprang partly from Machiavelli's republican belief that a condition of great inequality was prejudicial to a republic. But it was also favored by the view that simpler societies, like the German states, where equality prevailed, were more susceptible to the shaping hand of the new science.[20] The bias against the nobility held yet another implication which was more fully developed by Hobbes: that the qualitative kind of distinctions inherent in an aristocratic society were less congenial to the new science than a society where men could be analyzed as entities possessed of similar capabilities and outlooks. The great discovery of Machiavelli, as we shall note later, was that a uniform mass could be more easily analyzed in theory and more easily manipulated in practice than a differentiated social body.[21]

In later pages Machiavelli's orientation towards the mass will be more closely examined and we will try to show that it was accompanied by an increasing disenchantment with the new prince as an instrument of the new science. What ought to be noted here, however, is that these developments in no way spelled the "democratization" of political theory into a body of knowledge designed specifically to advance the interests of the people. Instead, the crucial characteristic of the new science was that it was detachable from the interests of any party. This had been made clear by Machiavelli in his Dedication to *The Prince*. After pleading that the novelty (*varietà*) and seriousness (*gravità*) of his topic might serve to excuse his presumptuousness in offering directives to princes, Machiavelli went on to compare the political writer to a landscape artist who could best execute his canvas by situating himself in the valley so that he might faithfully render the towering mountains; and, conversely, he could best sketch the valley by occupying the heights. In the metaphor the valley symbolized the people, the mountains the prince; the political theorist, as painter, was superior to both, moving with equal facility to either position, and capable of prescribing for one or the other.

This same point was made in a slightly different way in the *History of Florence*. Machiavelli's technique was to set out a situation where conflicting class interests were involved, and then, through the mouth of some partisan spokesman, proceed to argue the best case possible for each interested group.[22] Regardless of the party, whether proletarian or patrician, the versatility of the new science enabled it to enter imaginatively into any particular position, analyzing the problems as they appeared from that perspective and indicating the course of action which would satisfy the interest in question. Perhaps the most dramatic evidence of the ability of the new science to avoid "over-identification" with a particular constituency was provided by Machiavelli's analysis of various problems of international politics. Here, too, the new science showed itself capable of entering into any position, even of Italy's worst enemies, diagnosing the situation from that point of view, stating the alternatives, and prescribing the better moves.[23] It is easy to see from this why many critics have argued that Machiavelli fallaciously assumed international politics to be simply a chess game, thereby overlooking aspects which could not be reduced to these terms. But one might also suggest that this was inevitable, given the versatile and detached quality of the new science: for the essence of chess is that it is a science applicable to either side of the board. This can be put another way by saying that the vantage point which Machiavelli sought for political theory was to come from its being inspired by a problem orientation rather than an ideological orientation. A problem has several facets, an ideology a central focus.

We might summarize the foregoing remarks by saying that in Machiavelli's conception political theory could furnish a set of techniques useful to any group, but, as we have also seen, not every group was considered equally useful to the new science. Both considerations entailed certain types of commitments, and it is to these commitments and their interconnections that we now turn.

II The commitments of the political theorist. There exists a persistent image of Machiavelli as a clear-eyed realist, devoted to ridding political thought of fuzzy ideals, and possessed of no more moral passion than is found in the scientist's dedication to objective methods.[24] Admittedly Machiavelli supplies ample material for this portrait. His defiant announcement that he intended to blaze a "new route" in political analysis, one which would "get at the practical truth (*verità effectuale*) of the matter," has been accepted as the core of his system.[25] Nevertheless, certain doubts about this estimate are raised by the abrupt change in style which occurred in the last chapter of *The Prince*. The language was no longer that of realistic appraisal and detached advice, but of fervent nationalism which culminated in the plea for a crusade to unify Italy. Serious students have contended that the chapter constitutes a later addition to the main body of the text, yet this does not dispose of the fact that Machiavelli did write the chapter and that he never evinced any embarrassment for having included it in his pioneering work.[26] The last chapter can be regarded as gratuitous only by assuming that it is eccentric for realism and passion to be combined in a political theory. If the assumption is discarded, however, it is then possible to see that objective realism and passionate nationalism were the expression of two different kinds of commitments on Machiavelli's part. It then remains to explore not only their natures but also the kind of language appropriate to each.

As we have previously noted, when Machiavelli attempted to describe Italy's political ills, he took to employing the language of moral passion. Italy's condition, he wrote, was "more enslaved than that of the Hebrews, more oppressed than the Persians, and more scattered than the Athenians; without a head, without order, beaten, despoiled, lacerated, and overrun . . ."[27] The theme gathers power as Machiavelli, implicitly and apparently without conscious intention, adopts the language of religion: Italy, like the *corpus Christi,* has been condemned to suffering disunion that it might atone for the past sins of those whose existence it symbolized. It was "necessary" that, like the ancient nations, Italy suffer devastation and enslavement before being redeemed *(redenzione)*. Having evoked the image of the suffering body politic, Machiavelli then offered a kind of litany to the political savior on whom rested the hope of Italy's future redemption:

> And though before this, certain persons have showed signs from which it could be inferred that they were chosen by God for the redemption of Italy, nevertheless it has afterwards been seen that in the full current of action they have been cast off by Fortune. So Italy remains without life and awaits the man, whoever he may be, who is to heal her wounds . . . and cure her of those sores that have long been festering. She may be seen praying God to send some one to redeem her from these cruel and barbarous insults. [And then after urging that the deliverer need only follow the means advocated earlier, Machiavelli presents his own version of an Old Testament prophecy:] We have before our eyes extraordinary and unexampled means prepared by God. The sea has been divided. A cloud has guided you on your way. The rock has given forth water. Manna has fallen. Everything has united to make you great. The rest is for you to do.[28]

The vision is climaxed in the promise of the joyous reception awaiting the savior-prince (*redentore*), a promise of power and glory without Gethsemane:

> I am unable to express with what love he would be received in all the provinces that have suffered these foreign deluges; with what thirst for vengeance, what firm faith, what piety, what tears! What gates would be shut against him? what peoples would deny him obedience? what envy would oppose itself to him? what Italian would refuse to follow him? [29]

From the above it is apparent that older forms of religious emotion and language had been carried over and sublimated into the newer imagery of the nation. And following as they do the technical counsels offered in the preceding chapters of *The Prince,* the conclusion is suggested that the new political theory was not self-contained but drew its impulse from national inspiration, an impulse which Machiavelli could communicate only through the older language of religious emotion and thought. The religious element accompanying the new political theory was not confined solely to Machiavelli's nationalism, but reappeared in the notion of a vital principle inherent in political societies. A political society was classified by Machiavelli among those types of bodies which could escape disintegration only by repeating a certain ritual of renewal.[30] In the case of mixed or composite bodies — and here Machiavelli significantly lumped together republics and organized religious groups — renewal was attainable by recurring to the original principle. This could be done either by means of internal measures or by the shock of some external force. But over time the decay of these bodies could only be arrested by returning to their *archē* or fundamental principle. Machiavelli warned that in a republic it would be necessary to shock men back to a consciousness of the original basis of their polity and this ought not to be delayed more than ten years, otherwise corruption would have penetrated so deeply that the body politic would be beyond redemption.[31]

This notion of a revivifying principle was highly reminiscent of the eucharistic usages. Partly as a result of Machiavelli's influence it was carried into later political theory, particularly among constitutionalists. Harrington, who called Machiavelli "the only politician of later ages," argued that a republic which adhered to its basic laws would be assured of immortality.[32] The idea of fundamental law, which played so great a role in the political and constitutional debates in seventeenth-century England and to later ideas of a written constitution, has preserved the notion of a life-giving force whose observance guaranteed the continued strength of the body politic.[33]

We have suggested that there existed an important substratum of religious feeling and imagery in Machiavelli's thought and that this was most exposed when he wrote on the theme of national revival. But in those parts of his writings which were dominantly analytical or concerned with counsel, the language of religion was excluded. Hence while the cause of national revival formed a basic purpose for the realization of which certain means were pre-scribed, it did not function as an informing purpose coloring and infecting every aspect of his work. Machiavelli opened the significant possibility of a separation between the style of analytical political inquiry and that of basic purpose, each having its own vocabulary and concepts. But what had been a bare possibility for Machiavelli has today become an article of faith in most modern social sciences: the language of moral passion has been tagged as "subjective" or "emotive," and hence a less attractive subject for precise in-vestigation. This does not mean, any more than it did for Machiavelli, that the modern political scientist lacks a moral sense or a commitment to cer-tain values. Rather, as the following statement by contemporary political theorists shows, it is the status of political values that is significant:

> Our own values are those of the citizen of a society that aspires toward free-dom. Hence we have given special attention to the formulation of conditions favorable to the establishment and continuance of a free society . . . But we are not concerned with the justification of democratic values, their deriva-tion from some metaphysical or moral base. This is the province of political doctrine, not political science.[34]

But when beliefs are simultaneously relegated to the status of unexamined preferences and declared undemonstrable according to the most respected method of validation, their tendency is to become ritualistic dogmas. Just as Machiavelli had his unexamined beliefs — the nation-state, international anarchy, a kind of wage-fund theory of power — so the contemporary political scientist has his — democracy, a liberal theory of rights, an economic market partly free and partly controlled. It is not that these beliefs are bad or erro-neous, but that they are considered unexaminable in any rigorous sense with the result that their influence in dictating empirical or analytical inquiries is not always recognized.

If the preoccupation with analytical methods appears to have originated in some degree with Machiavelli, it becomes important to discover what kind of conviction or passion lay behind this commitment. This problem is, in a sense, founded on a paradox: having suggested that Machiavelli excluded basic values from the logic of inquiry, we are now asking whether his method of inquiry was supported by certain passionate convictions. What we have in his case is a passionate commitment to the vocation of political theorist and one which was strikingly illustrated in a passage from his correspondence:

> Fortune has decreed that since I cannot discuss silk-making or wool-manufacture, or profits and losses, I have to discuss matters of state. I must either make a vow of silence or talk about that subject.[35]

There were many other expressions testifying to a deep sense of dedication to the vocation of political theorist; *The Prince* itself was prefaced by the remark that the volume represented "all I have learned in many years and with many discomforts and perils." This sense of dedication was an essentially moral response inspired by a concern for man in an age of political corruption.

> [One] comes across nothing but extreme misery, infamy and contempt, for there is no observance either of religion or of the laws, or of military traditions, but all is besmirched with filth of every kind. And so much the more are these vices detestable [in] those who sit on the judgment seat, prescribe rules for others, and expect from them adoration.[36]

Implicit in this protest was the recognition of the epoch as a deeply politicized one where politics had become the major determinant of man's future. And the response of the engaged thinker who had "not been asleep or reveling in the fifteen years" that he had "devoted to the study of the art of the state," his *cri de coeur* was "I love my country more than my soul."[37]

Yet the moral sentiments underlying the new science were not inspired by patriotic motives alone, but were linked with Machiavelli's sensitivity to the anguishing elements in the political condition itself. We have become so accustomed to the portrait of Machiavelli as the sardonic confidential clerk that we have missed the pathos of his writings. His picture of Piero Soderini, the gonfalonier of Florence, is a nice example. Here was a gentle, well-intentioned man forced by the imperatives of politics to choose between the objective necessity of destroying his enemies or of observing legal niceties which would allow his enemies to destroy him. Being a good man, he chose the latter, thereby inflicting grave harm on his country and himself. Surely a condition which makes such choices unescapable has its share of anguish. Or, again, there was Machiavelli's famous maxim that a successful prince must be part lion and part fox, that is, courageous yet deceptive. Although this has usually been taken as a typical bit of Machiavellian immorality, it was really the argument of a moralist. His discussion began with the remark that in a corrupted age greatness could only be achieved by immoral means.

In such periods there were two methods of fighting which are clearly distinguishable: one by the laws, which was the way of civilized men, the other by force, which was the way of beasts. Both methods represented forms of combat, because both were a response to the fact that politics was a condition of conflict. The challenge was to reduce the area in which man must act the animal. For as long as the times remained corrupt, legal means alone were inadequate, hence political man, even if he had the best intentions, must be part beast in order to survive.[38] Machiavelli's advice, that the political actor may have to break his word, was not the product of a scepticism about the tenability of moral distinctions, but of a conviction that the imperatives of politics refuse any other alternative. Like Luther, Machiavelli's actor could do no other. And the moral pathos resided in a situation, not where the end justified the means, but where the end dictated means of a type which rendered both the wholly good man and the wholly evil one superfluous.

> But, to reconstitute political life in a state presupposes a good man, whereas to have recourse to violence in order to make oneself prince in a republic supposes a bad man. Hence very rarely will there be found a good man ready to use bad methods in order to make himself prince, though with a good end in view, nor yet a bad man who, having become a prince, is ready to do the right thing and to whose mind it will occur to use well that authority which he has acquired by bad means.[39]

Surveying politics from this vantage point, Machiavelli might well sign his letter to Guicciardini "Niccolò Machiavelli, *istorico, comico e tragico*." [40]

This sense of the moral dilemmas of politics had a direct bearing on Machiavelli's theory of violence and his conception of political ethics, both of which will be treated below. But here it might also be pointed out that moral anguish also led Machiavelli to redefine the kind of knowledge relevant to politics. Where the classical and mediaeval traditions had taken political knowledge to be a set of prescriptive remedies aimed at the steady elimination of evil from political society, the new science was grounded on the premises that the quantity of evil in the world remained fairly constant and that it was the peculiar nature of political action that it could not be dissociated from evil consequences — *le condizioni umane che non lo concentono*.[41]

> So that this is just one of those things in which evil is so closely associated with good, and so bound up are they one with the other, that it may easily happen that he who thinks he will get one, gets the other.[42]

In this vein, Machiavelli once wrote to Guicciardini, "I believe that the true means of understanding the road of paradise is to know that of hell in order to avoid the latter." [43] It was imperative, therefore, that the new science be a knowledge of a particular kind of good, but also of a particular kind of evil relevant to the political condition. None before had argued that it was the function of political knowledge to instruct rulers in the techniques of evil, because none had believed that wrongdoing was the price exacted by survival.[44] And while earlier writers had warned against the morally corrupting effects of exercising power, none, save Augustine, had asserted these evils to be inherent in the nature of political action. Thus the profile of the new political knowledge had its ambivalence of light and shadow: high exuberance at the possibilities of creative political action, but shaded by the sober realization that evil was implicated in the very nature of political creativity.

III The nature of politics and the categories of the new science. Most commentators, in striving to locate the modernity of the Florentine's thought, have mainly considered his method of analysis, especially as it dealt with the causal factors producing events.[45] Without disputing the importance of the problem, it is suggested here that this approach, by dwelling on the positive features of the "new route," has obscured some of the novel elements in Machiavelli's outlook. In his case novelty was not simply the function of certain positive and assertive elements in his theory, but was equally the product of certain significant omissions. When taken together, these spelled a new notational principle which established the identity and novelty of Machiavelli's thought. The supercession of one notational principle by another serves notice that a whole system of symbols, meanings, and feelings are being wholly or partially replaced. A single example, such as the contrasting treatment of the Romulus legend by Augustine and Machiavelli, provides a measure of the distance between one age and another. For Augustine the vile acts committed by Romulus in laying the foundations of Roman power constituted a political version of the drama of original sin: whatever the record of Roman imperial greatness, it carried the stigma of violence from beginning to end. Machiavelli was not ignorant of this charge, but argued that the ends of national greatness legitimized Romulus' deeds: crimes committed by political actors fell under the judgments of history not morality.[46]

A change of this magnitude was a sign that the old unifying principles no

longer made political phenomena appear intelligible and political action possible. It also marked the dissolution of the conceptual structures encasing
"political nature" and the exploration of new forms of meaning. One need
only compare the niched and ordered systems of mediaeval political theory
with the kind of language employed by Machiavelli's contemporary, Guicciardini, who felt compelled to describe the political condition through similes
drawn from wild and violent nature:

> The effects of the French invasion spread over Italy like a wildfire or like a
> pestilence, overthrowing not only the ruling power, but changing also the
> methods of government and the methods of war . . . everything was thrown
> upside down, as though by a sudden hurricane; the bonds which held the
> rulers of Italy together were broken, their interest in the general welfare
> extinguished. In looking around and noticing how cities, dukedoms and king-
> doms were shattered, each state became frightened and began to think only
> of its own security, forgetting that fire in the house of a neighbor could
> easily spread and bring ruin to himself. Now the wars became quick and
> violent, a kingdom was devastated and conquered more quickly than pre-
> viously a small village, the sieges of cities were very short and were success-
> fully completed in days and hours instead of in months; the battles became
> embittered and bloody. Not subtle negotiations and the subtleness of diplo-
> mats, but military campaigns and the fist of the soldier decided over the fate
> of the states.[47]

The older view of political nature, as a microcosm displaying the same
structural principles of order prevalent in creation as a whole, had been
shattered and political nature now lay exposed as orderless and near-an-
archic. The task of reconstruction was one which political theorists of the
past had also faced, and the creativity of a Plato or an Augustine had taken
the form of encompassing great disorder. The same experiment in order
was conducted by the Italian writers of the sixteenth century, men like
Machiavelli and Guicciardini, and the significance of their attempt was that
it was undertaken without the aid of the traditional guideposts which had
served the last several centuries. This has been made familiar to us by countless commentators who have emphasized the rationalism of the undertaking,
its quest for unifying laws which would explain political phenomena on a
matter-of-fact basis. Yet it is equally important to note that the response of
Machiavelli and Guicciardini to the disorder of politics contained important
non-rational elements. The picture that emerged from their writings was of
a political nature efflorescent with occult signs and mysterious portents, de-

cipherable by auguries, and haunted by unpredictable *Fortuna*.[48] It was, in short, a political universe inhabited at its very center by magic.

> The cause of such events should be discussed and explained, I think, by some one versed in things natural and supernatural, and this we are not.[49]

When rational explanation confesses its shortcomings and trails off into magic, it is a sign, not of atavism, but of a post-Christian phenomenon. Thought has been emancipated from the old cosmology yet it despairs of integrating political phenomena into a dechristianized universe.

It would be superfluous to document the turmoil of Italian politics which gave substance to the feeling that political nature had lost its coherence: this had been the constant theme of poets, historians, and political writers. In terms of political theory, what was desperately needed were new categories of intelligibility. This could come only through the formulation of a new language of politics and a new notational principle linking together the categories of analysis. Both of these presupposed a new political metaphysic.

One of the significant aspects of Machiavelli's political metaphysic was that it was unrelated to a systematic philosophy. Every effort made by later commentators to furnish him with one must of necessity produce an artificial picture of his thought.[50] To possess a political metaphysic without a philosophy may initially strike us as paradoxical or trivial, but these reactions are largely the result of our familiarity with modern or contemporary political thought which encourages us to expect political assertions unaccompanied by systematic philosophical support, and to be impatient when they are. Here we are the heirs of Machiavelli, for inherent in his "new route" to political knowledge was the claim that it was possible to say something meaningful about politics without constructing or even presupposing a philosophy. But in discarding philosophy, he was freed to create something new: a truly "political" philosophy which concentrated solely on political issues and single-mindedly explored the range of phenomena relevant to it.

The development of a political metaphysic, as part of a political philosophy, issues from the theorist's confrontation of political phenomena: what is the nature of political phenomena? how are they to be understood? what are the limits of the understanding and of human control? Machiavelli's approach to this matter, his conception of political nature, can best be understood by way of a question suggested by Plato: what would be the consequences for political thought and action if man's condition were that of permanent resident in the Cave? What would be the implications if a man's whole existence were defined by a world of fleeting sense impressions and phenomenal flux, a world having precious little in the way of a firm foundation for knowledge? As Machiavelli saw it, the world in which the political actor performed and the theorist prescribed was one where "all human affairs are ever in a state of flux and cannot stand still, either there will be improvement or decline . . ."[51] Political action took place in a world without a permanent basis for action, without the comforting presence of some underlying norm of reality to which men could adjust or from which they could draw firm rules of conduct. The further result was one which Plato had predicted: in a world of fleeting phenomena, the political actor would be led astray by illusions. But where Plato had sought escape to the clear world of essences, the new science chose to remain in order to analyze the nature of political illusions more closely. Machiavelli's treatment of illusions is so revealing of the new temper of political theory that it deserves to be examined at some length.

Men find it difficult, Machiavelli noted, to accept a world of becoming; they hunger for constants. This leads them to create an illusory world which is then treated as though it were a real basis for action.[52] In terms of human behavior this often took the form of clinging to certain habits despite their having been long outdistanced by the pace of events. Men preferred the security of a false world which was known to the anxieties of a "real" world wherein the painful task of readjustment had to be undertaken anew. At the opposite extreme from the conservative world presupposed by habit, were the forms of illusion springing from man's tendency to project a world distorted by his own excessive ambitions, hopes, or fears. And as if it were not enough that his passions should play him false, he must turn his intellectual talents to spinning utopian ideals wholly untested by experience. Man was truly *homo faber opinionum falsarum,* a spinner of fancies and illusions concealing the true nature of events. Even when men may try to be more "realistic" and refuse to act on any other basis than what they can actually see, they end up being trapped by their own overly simple view of reality. For, in Machiavelli's cryptic comment, while "everyone is equipped to see, few can understand."[53] There is nothing so deceptive in politics as mere appearance, whether it be the appearance of power, of reputation, great wealth, a large army, or a verbal promise. Even those who seek desperately to avoid the other sources of illusion, and try to base their judgments strictly on the consideration of consequences, can come to grief. Consequences can be as deceptive and misleading as any other phenomena.[54]

The symbol of man's illusions was the armed fortress. The fortress, in all of its seeming solidity, dramatized the false hope that there could be points of fixity, an unchanging basis of political and military security, in a restless world. But there is a further lesson to the symbol. Deceived by the impressive exterior of his fortress, the ruler comes to believe himself invincible and is tempted into cruel and extreme acts. The illusion of security thus releases the psychological springs of ambition and domination.[55] This example gives point to one of the principles of the new science: vice, in a political sense, is often the function of illusion, virtue the product of clear-sightedness.[56]

The prevalence of illusions did not lead Machiavelli into a crusade for a science which would dispel them. Instead the aim of the new science was to unmask those illusions which interfered with the proper ends of political action and, at the same time, to teach the political actor how to create and exploit the illusions which served these ends. In its unmasking role, political knowledge would allow men to cut through the mass of distortions preventing a true estimate of particular situations, distortions such as those worked by prejudice, false hopes, acquisitiveness, ambition, and common delusions about the power of money or the role of mere numbers in military campaigns.[57] The other role, that of instruction in the fine art of creating illusions, was aimed at inducing one's enemies to commit costly mistakes based on false estimates and calculations. By a variety of techniques — flattery, a misleading show of strength or weakness, false information, feints, etc. — a false world could be created which the opponent would accept as real. But this art had its predicament. Where the actors were all intent on creating false worlds, success depended not only on the ability to distinguish the true world from the false, but also in avoiding the trap of one's own deceptions.[58]

From Machiavelli's analysis of illusions we can see that the new science was more in the nature of a body of knowledge adjusted to a world of movement, rather than one aimed at freezing it. Moreover, while the sources of the endless movement of events lay partly in man's own deficiencies, some of which might be remedied by knowledge, there were other causes which could not be eradicated but only eased. First, capricious *Fortuna* constantly threatened the best laid calculations of art. Secondly, there was the instability which flowed from the intersection of human ambitions. At the level of the city the struggle for competitive advantage took the form of factional strife; throughout the peninsula it was the contest for mastery between princes, popes, and foreign rulers; on the international plane rival rulers ceaselessly probed each other's strengths and sought to exploit every show of weakness.[59] To create a political theory for a world of random movements, a task which had never been seriously undertaken before, meant surrendering certain kinds of inquiry because they no longer presented meaningful problems. In a world pulsating with change, there seemed to be little point in continuing the old quest for a motionless polity.[60] Likewise, there was a marked shift away from questions of legitimate authority, with their connotations of a stable political world, to questions of power, or the ability to exert mastery by controlling an unstable complex of moving forces. Similarly, the old values of *pax, ordo,* and *concordia* were treated by the new science not as ends, but as ironies: the nature of the political condition was such that good often issued in evil, order in disorder, culture in anarchy.[61] Moreover, the fugitive quality of events made it difficult to establish nice distinctions. The compulsions of the world were more often necessary than logical, and "necessity will lead you to do many things which reason does not recommend." [62]

But if political society were to be approached as a complex of volatile forces, then what of the traditional classical-mediaeval notion of an organic body politic? Instead of breaking with this idea, which accorded so ill with the bent of his thought, we find Machiavelli struggling to express himself through the old terminology. The result was not a sharply defined picture, but a series of palimpsests. At times he followed the old classical method of likening political society to an organic body and political knowledge to a medical science which prescribed periodic purges to rid the body of its distempers.[63] Again, Machiavelli fell into the mediaeval way of arguing that a political society resembled an organic body, and therefore required a directing head to coordinate the movements of its members.[64] But at other times there emerged a conception of political bodies easily translatable into the language of physics. A political society was a body possessed of an expandable mass and a fixed amount of energy; as such it existed for a definite duration, although there was no guarantee that the allotted span would be fulfilled. This was because it existed within a political universe of similar bodies constantly on the move and constantly impinging on each other. The resulting friction caused some bodies to lose their vital source of movement and hence their distinctive identities. They were soon absorbed into the orbits of other bodies.[65]

Given this complex political universe, the first problem was that of evolving a language of explanation which would faithfully portray the dynamic movement of events and yet provide directives. In history Machiavelli found such a form of explanation, for the virtue of the language of history was that while it described movement and change, it also assumed certain constant factors operating over time. History, in other words, captured the flux of events but at the same time established intelligible limits. Yet it did not follow that constancy was more "real" than change. In fact, the great innovation of

Machiavelli was to insist on the reality of movement and change, to adopt this as his basic unifying principle:

> The vicissitudes to which empires are subject cause them to pass from order into confusion, and afterwards to return once more to a condition of order. The nature of worldly affairs prevents their continuing on an even course; when they have arrived at their greatest perfection, decline soon sets in. Similarly, having been overcome by disorder, and reduced to the lowest state of depression, unable to sink lower, they must necessarily reascend; and thus from good they gradually sink into evil, and from evil return once more to good.[66]

The notion of time, as having its meaning in the ceaseless process of deterioration and renewal, departed sharply from the Christian idea of time as a gathering dimension guided by providence towards a culminating fulfillment. The vicissitudes of history depended on good and evil being constant quantities, varying only in their distribution. In ancient times *virtù* had been concentrated at Rome; after the fall of Rome it had been diffused in varying portions among several nations.[67] From this belief that history contained qualitatively superior periods Machiavelli drew the conclusion that the example of republican Rome provided later ages with a timeless model on which to base political action and institutions. The element of transcendence lay in the proven ability of the Romans to master events and this quality of mastery could, in turn, be extended to include any act of greatness, regardless of the era.

If history could furnish a stable body of knowledge transcending the flux of events, then there was hope of reducing the uncertainties of the political condition. This meant, in effect, a different answer for the same quest that had motivated the Greek philosophers and the Christian theologians. Instead of timeless reason and timeless faith, the "new way, as yet untrodden by anyone else," found its certainty in the timeless examples of greatness preserved in history. In the Preface to the first book of *The Discourses* Machiavelli developed this point through a lengthy comparison between the present state of art, medicine, and law on the one hand, and the poverty of political knowledge on the other. The former fields had succeeded in systematizing the distilled experience of the past, but in politics "one finds neither prince nor republic who repairs to antiquity for examples." The discrepancy between political and other forms of knowledge could be overcome, however, if men were to realize that ancient history contained practical lessons. To assume that these could not be imitated, to hold that past models of greatness were irrelevant to the present, was to argue that every situation in every age was unparalleled. It was "as if the heaven, the sun, the elements and man had in their motion, their order, and their potency, become different from what they used to be." [68] While this did not imply that political action ought slavishly to imitate the past or refuse to modify ancient precepts in the light of circumstances, it did mean that there existed a timeless body of examples, a set of models tested not so much by experience as by their historically demonstrated consequences.

The belief that historical examples contained politically relevant knowledge also had significant bearing for those engaged in political action. Although Machiavelli did not believe that political action could be reduced merely to following the examples of the ancients, the theory of imitation did suggest a radical break with the older notion that philosophical wisdom ought to be possessed by those engaged in politics. What was now implied was that political wisdom formed a body of knowledge external to the political actor, something which could teach him what to do in appropriate circumstances. But it was not a form of knowledge which he really knew in the way that Plato's philosopher knew reality; it was only a set of precepts which he had learned.[69]

The external character of political knowledge was related to Machiavelli's concept of politics. Except for those few occasions when fortune furnished the opportunity and the "matter" for the truly creative task of founding a new system, political action involved dealing with a mass of shifting components which could not be reduced to a settled form for any fixed length of time. The world of politics was an ambiguous one where "it is impossible to remove one inconvenience without another emerging," and where "one never finds any issue that is clear-cut and not open to question." [70] Political action, therefore, was essentially manipulative, not architectonic. Its aim was political mastery and not political sculpture. Political action could not, then, be a fusion of the personality of the actor with his materials; political phenomena existed to be mastered and controlled.

Mastery, in turn, meant getting on "top" of events by following the double strategy of creating reliable instruments of action, such as a disciplined army, and of making other political actors dependent on one's own will. When successful, this strategy was equivalent to Machiavelli's definition of political power: to possess power was to be able to control and manipulate the actions of others and thereby to make events conform to one's wishes. But by mastery Machiavelli did not mean, as some commentators have implied, mere technical efficiency.[71] The new science was intended as the basis for a new political ethic. Thus, to know the shape of events was to be in a position to exercise prudence or foresight; to select the type of action appropriate to a given situation was to possess a sensitive and discriminating intelligence which allowed for the weighing of several factors simultaneously, as well as a knack of imaginatively projecting possible consequences. The political condition demanded great resolution and decisiveness, because extreme and violent actions were often necessary.[72] There was call, too, for courage in facing unexpected disasters brought by *Fortuna*.[73] Above all, the political actor needed a temperament which could endure acting without the assurance of certainty:

> No state should believe that it can always make plans certain of success, it should expect to make only doubtful ones. For the course of human events teaches that man never attempts to avoid one disadvantage without running into another. Prudence, therefore, consists in the power to recognize the nature of disadvantages and to take the less disagreeable as good.[74]

The significant aspect of the moral qualities needed by Machiavelli's political actor lay in their fundamentally public or exterior character. They represented a mask which he must wear in his role as a public figure; they had no intrinsic value. Thus while the new science was the product of the moral commitment of the theorist — "it is the duty of a good man to point out to others what is well done, even though the malignity of the times or of fortune has not permitted you to do it for yourself" [75] — it assumed a purely political morality in those who were to practice its dictates because politics itself held only a necessary and not an ultimate value. The exteriorization of virtue was but the symbol of man's alienation from his political world. It was, ironically, the end product of centuries of Stoic and Christian criticism now couched in the language of realism.

IV Political space and political action. Machiavelli's conception of political space bore the imprint of an age where older arrangements of control had broken down and the resulting release of energies threatened to make the establishment of order impossible. The mediaeval structure had long since dissolved, erasing settled habits of conduct and leaving political space exposed to the converging lines of human ambitions. Here was the impression registered in Machiavelli's thought:

> Ancient writers were of opinion that men are wont to get annoyed with adversity and fed up with prosperity, both of which passions give rise to the

same effects. For, whenever there is no need for men to fight, they fight for ambition's sake; and so powerful is the sway that ambition exercises over the human heart that they never relinquish it, no matter how high they have risen. The reason is that nature has so constituted men that, though all things are objects of desire, not all things are attainable; so that desire always exceeds the power of attainment, with the result that men are ill content with what they possess and their present state brings them little satisfaction. Hence arise the vicissitudes of their fortune. For, since some desire to have more and others are afraid to lose what they have already acquired, enmities and wars are begotten, and this brings about the ruin of one province and the exaltation of its rival.[76]

Minds that knew no repose, ambitions that were boundless, an insatiable pride, a restless species of political man which, when not bedeviled by ambition, was stirred by sheer boredom — all of these considerations conspired to shrink political space, to create a dense and overcrowded world. A terrain with few areas open for unrestricted movement left one course for the politically ambitious: to dislodge those already occupying specific areas.[77] This found appropriate expression in the attention which Machiavelli's new science devoted to instructing the *novus homo* in the art of gaining as well as regaining power.[78] It was differently expressed in Machiavelli's disdain for hereditary governments. Such systems appeared as anachronistic because political space had become so well articulated through old laws, customs, and habits that the problem of boundless energies did not arise. As Machiavelli remarked, hereditary rulers had less reason and necessity for offending their subjects; all they had to do was to respect existing expectations. On the other hand, "nothing is more difficult to plan, more unlikely to succeed, or more dangerous to manage" than the creation of a new system.[79] The new ruler had to reorder political space by resettling the laws, uprooting old habits, and redefining the legitimate routes of ambition.[80] On a less heroic scale this same task confronted those political systems where corruption was not as deep-seated.

The case of the "normally" quiet republic provides a study illustrating the techniques for the redirection of human energies. The dilemma which arises in these states is that a peaceful condition frustrates the ambitions and talents of great men and, on the other hand, it encourages the small men to challenge the great. The latter are provoked to stir up trouble in the hope that a crisis will create a demand for their idle talents. The proper policy, Machiavelli advised, consists in keeping the citizenry poor and putting the state on a continual wartime footing so as to insure a steady need for the services of the great.[81]

There were other techniques as well for diminishing the threat of demonic energies: energies could be sublimated into economic pursuits and the arts; they could be redistributed by planting new colonies.[82] Yet limits existed on what the new science could do with an overcrowded condition. Fortunately, when the pressures within political space became too intense, nature provided a catharsis in the form of floods, pestilences, and famine:

> . . . When every province is replete with inhabitants who can neither obtain a livelihood nor move elsewhere since all other places are occupied and filled up, and when the craftiness and malignity of man has gone as far as it can go, the world must be needs purged . . . so that mankind, being reduced to comparatively few and humbled by adversity, may adopt a more appropriate form of life and grow better.[83]

The problem of space also brought Machiavelli to consider its relationship to expansionism and aggrandizement. Actions between states raised the same order of difficulties, because the same law of comparative advantage prevailed. An increase in one nation's power spelled a loss for someone else, as well as a general redistribution throughout the whole system of states. But if international instability was merely the extension of the pressures which disrupted internal politics, it was also true that conflict and aggressiveness among states, like the salutary conflict among domestic factions, could have a beneficial effect. In the first place, the choice, even for a peaceful republic, was not whether to expand or remain stationary, but how much to expand.[84] The necessity for *Lebensraum* was dictated partly by the need to divert the driving energies besetting internal politics, partly to protect the state from aggressive rivals, and, lastly, to maintain the civic *virtù* of the citizenry.[85] A world where states were constantly in motion denied the possibility of a republic's surviving unless it expanded also; even if by some miracle this imperative disappeared, the republic would then be plagued by the unsatisfied energies which had not been drained off by foreign wars.

All of these considerations joined to shape the focus of the new science: it was to concentrate on political actions occurring in overcrowded conditions. Unlike Plato, Machiavelli denied himself the escape of legislating for a new colony. And because the new science set for itself the task of writing on a badly scarred *tabula,* it could follow only to a degree the aesthetic impulse of classical political theory. Only a deeply corrupted political condition justified treating society as clay to be molded by the absolute power of a political artist. But in societies short of this condition, the aesthetic impulse had to find satisfaction in the calculating manipulation of political factors. For the new science did not deal with the static organism of classical and mediaeval theory, a *corpus immobile;* it dealt instead with volatile bodies in motion, bodies which consumed their rivals, *corpus vorans.*[86]

V **The economy of violence.** While there had been few political theorists before Machiavelli who would have contested the elementary proposition that "security for man is impossible unless it be conjoined with power," [87] there had been still fewer prepared to declare power the dominant mark of the state. Indeed, it has been and remains one of the abiding concerns of the Western political theorist to weave ingenious veils of euphemism to conceal the ugly fact of violence. At times he has talked too sonorously of "authority," "justice," and "law," as though these honorific expressions alone could transform coercion into simple restraint. True, the psychological impact of power is softened and depersonalized if it is made to appear the agent of an objective good. True, too, there are numerous and subtle forms of coercion that shade off from the extreme of violence. That the application of violence is regarded as abnormal represents a significant achievement of the Western political tradition, yet if it is accepted too casually it may lead to neglect of the primordial fact that the hard core of power is violence and to exercise power is often to bring violence to bear on someone else's person or possessions. Writers before Machiavelli cannot be accused of having ignored power. The classical and mediaeval theorists had spoken long and eloquently of its brutalizing and corrupting effects on those who were called to exercise it. They rarely faced up, however, to the problem of the cumulative effect on society of the consistent application of coercion and the not infrequent use of violence. This evasion had come about largely because attention to power had arisen primarily in connection with the establishment or reform of a political system. It had been assumed that once affairs were set in motion along the prescribed paths, once proper education, the spread of knowledge or of faith, the improvement of social morality, and all of the other pressures flowing from a rightly ordered environment had begun to operate, there would be progressively less need for the systematic application of force. Nor is it easy to see in what ways the modern political theorist has illumined the problem by the focal concepts of "decision-making," "the political process," and "who gets what, when, and how." All that can be said with confidence is that euphemisms for power and violence have not been disspelled by positivism.

With Machiavelli the euphemisms were cast aside and the state was directly confronted as an aggregate of power. Its profile was that of violence. Machiavelli believed that the vitalities of politics could not be controlled and directed without the application of force and the threat at least of violence. This conclusion was sustained partly by a certain scepticism about what Yeats once called "the profane perfection of mankind." It was also the outcome of a conviction about the inherent instability of the political world which could be combated, and then only partially, by resolute action. Equally important, however, in making power and violence urgent matters was the nature of the context in which power was exerted: the tightly-packed condition of political space which mocked any merely verbal attempt at translating power into simple direction or supervision of the affairs of society. Inevitably the role of the political actor was to dispense violence. This was most sharply defined in the case of the ruler who, after seizing power, was compelled "to organize everything in that state afresh." [88] "The new prince, above all other princes, cannot possibly avoid the name of cruel." [89] Even when the political actor was not faced with the task of creating a *tabula rasa,* he could not avoid inflicting injuries on some one. He must act while hemmed in by vested interests and expectations, privileges and rights, ambitions and hopes, all demanding preferential access to a limited number of goods.

If this were the nature of political action, what has been called an obsession with power on Machiavelli's part might be better described as his conviction that the "new way" could make no greater contribution than to create an economy of violence, a science of the controlled application of force. The task of such a science would be to preserve the distinguishing line between political creativity and destruction. "For it is the man who uses violence to spoil things, not the man who uses it to mend them, that is blameworthy." [90] The control of violence was dependent upon the new science's being able to administer the precise dosage appropriate to specific situations. In corrupt societies, for example, violence represented the only means of arresting decadence, a brief but severe shock treatment to restore the civic consciousness of the citizenry.[91] In other situations there might well be a diminishing need for extreme actions; men could be managed by playing on their fears, by using the threat rather than the actuality of coercion. But every application had to be considered judiciously, because the indiscriminate exercise of force and the constant revival of fear could provoke the greatest of all dangers for any government, the kind of widespread apprehension and hatred which drove men to desperation. The true test of whether violence had been rightly used was whether cruelties increased or decreased over time.[92]

This preoccupation with economy was manifest also in Machiavelli's discussion of the external forms of violence — war, imperialism, and colonialism. One of the basic aims of the *Art of War* was to demonstrate that, while military action remained an unavoidable fact of the political condition, its costliness could be reduced by proper attention to strategy, discipline, and organization. *The Prince* and *The Discourses* followed the same theme of economy with counsels like these: a prince ought carefully to consider his resources, because, while a war may be started out of whim, it could not be as easily stopped; an unreliable army was an inefficient instrument of violence because it multiplied devastation without any of the compensations of victory; to avoid a necessary war was costly, but to prolong it was equally prodigal; a prince who found his position weakened by a victory had overestimated his power resources.[93]

In the matter of imperialism Machiavelli adverted to the example of Rome for the significant reason that Roman imperial policy had sought to preserve the wealth of the subject populations and their native institutions, thereby limiting the cost in devastation for both conqueror and conquered. If imperialism were handled efficiently the destructive consequences could be minimized, and the whole transaction reduced to a mere change in power.[94] In contrast to Rome's controlled use of violence were those destructive wars which had been compelled by necessities, such as hunger, plague, or overpopulation.[95] Necessity was the enemy of calculated violence.

While Machiavelli's economy of violence subsumed both domestic and external actions, it never seriously entertained the proposition that the incidence of force could be appreciably lessened in international politics. The effects of violence might be controlled, but the resort to it would not diminish. He saw quite clearly that the absence of arbitrating arrangements, such as law and institutional procedure, left the international field more exposed than the domestic to conflicts of interest and the drives of ambition.[96] On the other hand, he believed that the internal politics of society could be structured by a variety of methods aimed at minimizing the need for extreme acts of repression. The importance of law, political institutions, and habits of civility was that in regularizing human behavior they helped to reduce the number of instances in which force and fear had to be applied.

Machiavelli's most important insight into the problem of internal power politics came when he began to explore the implications of a political system based on the active support of its members. He grasped the fact that popular consent represented a form of social power which, if properly exploited, reduced the amount of violence directed at society as a whole. One reason for the superiority of the republican system consisted in its being maintained by the force of the populace, rather than by force over the populace.[97] The economy of force which resulted from the people's feeling a sense of common involvement with the political order made it in the interests of the prince to cultivate their support. Lacking this, he would have to draw on his own fund of violence and the eventual result would be "abnormal measures" of repression. "The greater his cruelty, the weaker does his regime become." [98] Far from limiting his initiative, popular approval could be utilized to depreciate the great cost in violence of radical reforms. In a revolution by consent (*commune consenso*), only the few had to be harmed.[99]

In evaluating Machiavelli's economy of violence it is easy to criticize it as being the product of a technician's admiration for efficient means. A century like ours, which has witnessed the unparalleled efficiency displayed by totalitarian regimes in the use of terror and coercion, experiences difficulty in being tolerant on the subject. Yet to see Machiavelli as the philosopher of Himmlerism would be quite misleading; and the basic reason is not alone that Machiavelli regarded the science of violence as the means for reducing the amount of suffering in the political condition, but that he was clearly aware of the dangers of entrusting its use to the morally obtuse. What he hoped to further by his economy of violence was the "pure" use of power, undefiled by pride, ambition, or motives of petty revenge.[100] A more meaningful contrast to Machiavelli would be the great modern theoretician of violence, Georges Sorel. Here is a true example of the irresponsible political intellectual, fired by romantic notions of heroism, preaching the use of violence for ends which are deliberately and proudly clothed in the vague outline of the irrational "myth," contemptuous of the cost, blinded by a vision of virile proletarian barbarians who would revitalize the decadent West.[101] In contrast, there was no hint of child-like delight when Machiavelli contemplated the barbarous and savage destructiveness of the new prince, sweeping away the settled arrangements of society and "leaving nothing intact." There was, however, the laconic remark that it was better to be a private citizen than to embark on a career which involved the ruin of men.[102] This suggests that the theorist like Machiavelli, who was aware of the limited efficacy of force and who devoted himself to showing how its technique could be used more efficiently, was far more sensitive to the moral dilemmas of politics and far more committed to the preservation of man than those theorists who, saturated with

moral indignation and eager for heroic regeneration, preach purification by
the holy flame of violence.

V I Ethics: political and private. In most commentaries, Machiavelli's
prince has emerged as the heoric ego incarnate, exhilarated by the
challenges of political combat, unencumbered by moral scruples, and utterly
devoid of any tragic sense of the impermanence of his own mission. In the
preceding pages we have deliberately used the term "political actor" instead
of "prince" or "ruler" to suggest that if the prince is looked upon as a kind
of actor, playing many roles and wearing many masks, we may then better
see that Machiavelli has given us something more than a single-dimensional
portrait of a power-hungry figure. What we have is a portrait of modern
political man drawn with dramatic intensity: if there was heroism, there was
also anguish; if there was creativity, there was also loneliness and uncertainty.

These overtones were part of the new setting in which political action
occurred. Machiavelli's actor was, to borrow a phrase from Merleau-Ponty,
"l'expression d'un monde disloqué." [103] He performed in a universe hushed
in moral stillness: there were no prefigured meanings, no implicit teleology
— "it looks as if the world were become effeminate and as if heaven were
powerless" [104] — and no comforting backdrop of a political cosmos, ruled
by a divine monarch and offering a pattern for earthly rulers. Yet by his
vocation, political man was compelled to act, to affirm his existence as a
thoroughly politicized creature. To be committed to political action meant
surrendering the multiple dimensions of life, and concentrating exclusively
on the single dimension of politics.

By the nature of his situation political man must be an actor, for he ad-
dresses himself not to a single political condition, but to a variety of political
conditions. Circumstances change, the conjunction of political factors follows
a shifting pattern, hence the successful political actor cannot afford a consistent and uniform character. He must constantly rediscover his identity in
the role cast for him by the changing times. [105] The mercurial quality of Machiavelli's political actor stands in sharp contrast to the classical and mediaeval
conception of the character of the good ruler. The older writers had viewed
political knowledge as enabling men to establish stable situations, points of
fixity within which ethical behavior became possible. Towards this end, they
emphasized the importance of training men's characters so that virtue, for
example, would be an habitual disposition towards the good. [106] For this
reason classical and mediaeval writers tended to be suspicious of "prudence"

and rarely ranked it among the supreme virtues.[107] Prudence implied a character which reacted too glibly to changing conditions.

Machiavelli's criticism of traditional moral theory was not, as has often been supposed, founded on cynicism or amorality. Nor is the more valid contention, that he was intent on divorcing the norms of political conduct from those governing private relationships, fully correct. Instead his concern was, first, to indicate the situations where political action ought to conform to the standards commonly applied to private conduct. Thus when a government operated within a stable, secure environment it ought to follow the accepted virtues such as compassion, good faith, honesty, humaneness and religion. Under these circumstances public and private ethics were identical.[108] But Machiavelli's second concern was to point out that, because most political situations were unstable and subject to flux, "a commonwealth and a people is governed in a different way from a private individual." [109] To adopt the rules of accepted morality was to bind one's behavior by a set of consistent habits. But rigidities in behavior were not suited to the vagaries of an inconsistent world. Moreover, to act uniformly merely armed one's opponents with a foreknowledge of your probable reactions to a given situation.[110] There was the further difficulty that one must act in a world where the other actors did not follow the same code.[111] To be sure, a similar issue arose in private relationships when other men did not honor the same moral usages, yet the cases were different because the responsibilities were different: in the one the individual suffered for being a moral man in an immoral society, while in the other a whole society might be injured because of the moral scruples of the ruler.[112]

But if politics posed issues for which common morality was inadequate, it did not follow that there was no connection between political action and traditional moral dictates. In the first place, it was difficult to govern a society and gain support if all of the ruler's actions violated the moral usages cherished by society. As a political actor, the ruler must be a "skilful pretender and dissembler," he must "seem" to have the virtues of good faith, charity, humanity, and religion. This was part of his mastery in the art of illusions. "Men are so simple and so subject to present needs that he who deceives in this way will always find those who will let themselves be deceived." [113]

The basic question, however, was whether Machiavelli believed morality to be nothing more than a useful factor in political manipulation. Did morality constitute a set of restraints or merely a datum for successful action? Machiavelli's own words are so crucial that they deserve to be quoted at length:

I will even venture to say that [the virtues] damage a prince who *possesses them and always observes them,* but if he seems to have them they are useful. I mean that he should seem compassionate, trustworthy, humane, honest, and religious, and *actually be so;* but yet he should have his mind so trained that, when it is necessary not to practice these virtues, he can change to the opposite and do it skilfully. It is to be understood that a prince, especially a new prince, cannot observe all the things because of which men are considered good, because he is often obliged, if he wishes to maintain his government, to act contrary to faith, contrary to charity, contrary to humanity, contrary to religion. It is therefore necessary that he have a mind capable of turning in whatever direction the winds of Fortune and the variations of affairs require, and . . . that *he should not depart from what is morally right, if he can observe it,* but should know how to adopt what is bad, when he is obliged to.[114]

This passage suggests that instead of belaboring Machiavelli for pointing out the limitations of private ethics, attention ought to be directed instead at the dual role which is thus created for the political actor. He is made to perform in an atmosphere of tensions where accepted moral values limit his behavior in normal circumstances, while a distinctively political ethic, accompanied by the new knowledge, comes into play when circumstances of necessity appear. By itself each form of ethic is inadequate. The normally bad acts justified by the political ethic would, if unrestrained by the inhibiting pressure of common morality, encourage unlimited ambition and all of its destructive consequences. On the other hand, if common morality were to be extended to situations for which it had not been designed, the consequences would be destructive of the order and power which made private morality possible. It was the anguishing situation of the political actor that he must decide which form of ethic should govern, but while the new science could facilitate his choice it could not compensate for the fact that he must partially dwell outside the realm of what is usually considered goodness. This means, in effect, that Machiavelli broke with classical theory which had approached the problems of political action with the question of how men could develop their moral potentialities through a life devoted to political office. But for Machiavelli the problem became more acute, for the issue no longer involved the statesman's quest for a moral perfection which, by its very moral quality, would benefit the community; it involved instead the political actor who was driven to break the moral law in order to preserve his society.

There was still another reason why politics could not satisfy the aspiration towards moral fulfillment. Traditional ethical notions operated on the assumption that the result of ethical conduct would be the creation of a desirable or more desirable state of affairs; that, for example, to act honestly or in good faith would produce situations which would be characterized by honesty and good faith. But Machiavelli rejected this notion of the literal translation of ethical acts into ethical situations and substituted instead a notion of the irony of the political condition. "Some things seem to be virtuous, but if they are put into practice will be ruinous . . . other things seem to be vices, yet if put into practice will bring the prince security and well-being." [115] Thus there was a kind of alchemy in the political condition whereby good was transmuted into evil, and evil into good.[116] Take, for example, the classical virtue of liberality which prescribed that acts of generosity should be done in a restrained manner. For Machiavelli's political actor such advice would be absurd; he was not a private donor, but a public figure whose actions, to be significant, needed a well-publicized flourish, even a vulgar display. But even with this amendment, it was doubtful that liberality qualified as a political virtue at all. The political actor usually expended not his private resources but public revenues. In a political setting liberality was translated into taxes, and these, in turn, were certain to breed popular resentments. Hence the vice of niggardliness became a political virtue; it was transformed, in fact, into liberality because it gave the subject a greater share of his own property.[117] Again, take the case of the trusting ruler who refused to believe that most men were vicious and ready to deceive at every turn. If a ruler of this type were to govern according to the virtue of clemency, he would soon be driven to adopt increasingly more severe and cruel measures in order to retain power. On the other hand, the contradictions of politics were such that a ruler who applied rational cruelty at the proper time would be more truly humane. Cruelty, when used economically, was more merciful than clemency, for where the first injured only the few and the rest were restrained by apprehension, the second bred disorders which injured the *una universalità intera*. Nevertheless, the justification of cruel measures was not meant to imply that any method of retaining power was equal in moral worth to any other method. Cruelty might be useful in attaining certain ends, such as security, but it could not bring true glory.[118]

Machiavelli's concern with the shortcomings of traditional ethics and his quest for a suitable political ethic stemmed from a profound belief in the discontinuities of human existence. This was expressed in his view of history. History was conceived not as a smoothly flowing continuum, but as a process which irrupted in destructive frenzy, obliterating the achievements and memory of the past and condemning man to a perpetual labor of recovery.[119] Equally important, there were discontinuities between the forms of existence at a particular time. Religion, art, economic activity, private life and public seemed to be carried on according to special logics of their own, unconnected by any overarching heteronomous principle.[120] Thus man dwelt in a fragmentized universe and his special anguish came from being condemned to live in several alien worlds at once. If political existence was to be lived in a world of its own, it was imperative that there be relevant criteria for ordering existence. Relevancy, in turn, was conceived by Machiavelli in terms of the conditions to which the criteria appertained; that is, to the particular world of politics. This was expressed in his frequent use of the word *necessità* in describing political situations. By *necessità* he did not mean a form of determinism, but rather a set of factors challenging man's political creativity, manageable only if man treated them as strictly political, excluding all else from his span of attention.[121]

In terms of ethics this did not mean that politics was to be conducted without ethical criteria, but that the criteria could not be imported from the "outside." The failure to appreciate this has led many modern critics of Machiavelli into false dilemmas. It does not follow, as one modern writer would have it, that because politics demands an ethic different from private life that "moral imperatives do not have absolute value." [122] This is to put the issue badly, for the real questions are, what morals? what is meant by "absolute"? The whole point of Machiavelli's argument was to urge that precisely because of the unescapably autonomous nature of politics, it was all the more compelling that criteria for action be established and that appropriate means be fashioned for their implementation. In brief, the denial of heteronomy need not entail a denial of morality in politics, any more than the impossibility of ethical criteria follows from the denial of ethical absolutes.

VII The discovery of the mass. The notion of the political actor was developed primarily in *The Prince*, because in this work Machiavelli was intent on describing how national regeneration could be accomplished by a single individual of superior talents. The whole work was dominated by a conception of personal politics with the result that the heroic figure of the prince overshadowed any suggestion that politics could be conducted through impersonal institutions. It is well known that in *The Discourses* Machiavelli's viewpoint was that of a convinced republican. It is also generally agreed that the same conception of political action and the same

kinds of advice were consistently adhered to in both works. In evaluating the difference between the two, most students have taken the position that the monarchical absolutism recommended in *The Prince* had been intended solely as a desperate remedy for a badly corrupted political condition.[123]

While undoubtedly there is much to be said for this interpretation, I believe that a great deal more can be learned by a somewhat different approach. If in *The Discourses* the political hero largely disappears, Machiavelli must have reasoned that the types of action which the prince alone could accomplish were now either unnecessary or could be entrusted to the people. Similarly, if in the earlier work Machiavelli looked to the prince's desire for personal glory and *virtù* to supply the dynamics of political action, then he must have believed that under a popular government there was no call for this *élan* or else that certain substitutes could be cultivated. To uncover the implications in these two propositions we must first examine their common referent, the people. In doing this we hope to show that, to an important degree, the difference between *The Prince* and *The Discourses* consists in a greater appreciation on Machiavelli's part of the political capabilities of the masses and correspondingly greater doubts about the utility of political heroes. It will also be suggested that in the course of this development Machiavelli showed a greater insight into the nature of the political mass than any other thinker before the nineteenth century.

In *The Prince* it was apparent that Machiavelli had begun to sense the growing significance of the masses. "Now it is more necessary to princes, except the Turk and the Sultan, to satisfy the people rather than the soldiers, for the people are more powerful." [124] While this was important evidence that Machiavelli had grasped that the basis of politics was being broadened and that the factor of the people would have to be taken into account in future reckonings, the notion which dominated *The Prince* was that of the mass as malleable matter ready to respond to the shaping hand of the hero-artist: *"ed in Italia non manca materia da introdurvi ogni forma."* [125] Moreover, the gullibility of *la moltitudine* was the necessary precondition for the art of illusions practiced by the political actor: "the crowd is always caught by appearance and by the outcome of events, and the crowd is all there is in the world; there is no place for the few when the many have room enough." [126]

Machiavelli's insight into the manageability of the masses takes on added significance if we recall his advice that the prince ought "to satisfy" the desires of the people. The juxtaposition of the political hero and the masses, which was the central theme of *The Prince,* represented, at bottom, a juxtaposition of compatible desires or passions. The hero could achieve glory and realize his *virtù* in the exercise of an absolute mastery which, in creating order and rooting out corruption, would satisfy the desire of the masses for security.[127] To understand why it was that Machiavelli believed the masses to be not only pliant but also suitable material for the political art of the prince, we must turn to the ninth chapter of *The Prince* where the problem of a monarchy based on consent was treated. Of all the forms of monarchy this was the one most preferred by Machiavelli, primarily because power could be retained without "the wickedness or other intolerable violence" so necessary to the political adventurer.[128] A system of this kind, it was pointed out, could be reared on one of two foundations, the people or the aristocracy, but, due to the mutual antagonisms between them, it could not find support in both groups.[129] Machiavelli's advice to the prince was to seek the favor of the people, to establish a *principato civile*. This choice was dictated by the belief that the people represented more suitable matter, not in the sense of being more virtuous, but of being more governable. The ruling passion of the aristocrats was an insatiable ambition for dominating other groups, hence no arrangement could ever contain them for long. On the other hand, the people were "easily" (*facile*) ruled, as "they demand no more than not to be oppressed." [130] Because the people primarily desired security for their wives and property, the problem of political space could be handled rather easily. The more heroic ambitions of the nobility, however, could not be fulfilled without disrupting political space, or in Machiavelli's words, "without injury to others." [131] Thus the best political matter was to be found in those who have possessions and want to retain them, not in those who want to acquire more.[132] It was because the demands of the masses were minimal ones which could be satisfied without endangering the ruler's power, and because, as "have's," they were plagued by fears and insecurities and hence were easy to manipulate, that Machiavelli found them to be the most reliable basis of power. They responded best to the prescriptions of the new science, to controlled doses of fear and violence, to the alternating caress of love and hope, thus making brutality and cruelty unnecessary.[133]

The compatibility between the new science and the political qualities of the masses was of crucial significance, because it was a sign of a certain restiveness on Machiavelli's part with the political hero. In *The Prince* and in *The Discourses* he held consistently to the position that in a badly corrupted society a single ruler must be the chosen instrument of regeneration, "enforcing obedience until such time as the material has become good." [134] But the "civic principality," mentioned above, was not intended for a corrupt condition, hence it would seem logically to follow that the order of heroic talents demanded in a corrupt state would not be required. In Machiavelli's words, the ruler of a civic principality need not possess "pure ability or pure fortune" (*o tutta virtù o tutta fortuna*), but only a "fortunate astuteness" (*un 'astuzia fortunata*).[135] This emphasis on "astuteness" was a sign that Machiavelli had come to see that while the demonic energies of the hero could be creative, they could also be politically destructive. If this were true, then he would be a dubious instrument of the new science, less reliable than the people.

The choice between the political hero and the masses was posed squarely in *The Discourses* when Machiavelli confronted the commonplace assertion that no durable political system could be erected on as unstable a foundation as the people.[136] Machiavelli's rebuttal began with an interesting evasion: we cannot decide between the relative merits of a prince or people if both are considered in a condition outside the law. But, of course, the notion of a prince *legibus solutus* had been the main hope of *The Prince;* in *The Discourses,* however, Machiavelli was most impressed by the nihilistic urges of the prince, hence he contended that there was no choice between an unbridled prince and a legally uncontrolled people; both were equally destructive. The true test, therefore, was to compare the two when they were under the law. The verdict was in favor of the people, yet the grounds were the significant point. A people accustomed to living under the law soon exhibit the political virtues impressed upon them: they become stable, prudent, grateful, and reverential to the authority of the law. But while the people's virtue came from submitting to the law, the *virtù* of the prince necessarily took the form of creative destruction of laws and institutions. Hence at the stage where a republican system was feasible, heroic *virtù* was anachronistic.[137]

The transition to a new type of *virtù* involved a redefinition of princely *virtù*: the true prince would be one who, in the act of realizing his *virtù,* would render himself superfluous. The criteria for judging his actions would be these: did the state survive the founder's death and was it capable of generating its own momentum? As Machiavelli wrote, "The security of a republic or of a kingdom, therefore, does not depend upon its ruler governing it prudently during his lifetime, but upon his so ordering it that, after his death, it may maintain itself in being." [138] This was put even more succinctly in Machiavelli's advice to Pope Leo X on the reform of the government of Florence: it should be so organized "that it will administer itself." [139]

If princely *virtù* were to be superseded, what was now needed was a form of *virtù* which would support rather than create institutions. And if heroic politics were to give way to a mass-oriented politics, then the problem was to attract the masses to support the political order by meeting the material needs of the people, protecting their possessions, and eliminating dangerous inequalities in the society. But how could this be done? Wasn't it true that the same dilemmas of limited goods, unlimited ambitions, and crowded political space would reappear to plague a political system based on the satisfaction of interests? In trying to resolve these issues Machiavelli was led to examine more closely than any of his predecessors the nature and dynamics of interest politics and to advance further than any writer since Aristotle the superiority of the politics of resolution as over against the politics of imposition. The truly novel element in Machiavelli's approach was that it not only converted the problem of interest into the central problem of political theory, but that he sought to accompany this with a theory which indicated both the salutary effects of socio-economic conflicts and the techniques by which they might be resolved. By moving in this direction Machiavelli helped launch the redefinition of the political association, a redefinition which, by starting with the legitimacy of conflicts of interest, would end by doubting that such an association could afford to pursue final solutions in the handling of conflicts. A republic, as Machiavelli noted, presupposed divisions, and hence could not be kept to a perfect unity of purpose.[140]

To the contemporary student of politics one of the most interesting aspects of Machiavelli's analysis was its recognition of the complexity of interests. While the basic conflicts arose between people and nobility,[141] and while the existence of the lower class created further difficulties, these three classes contained divisions within themselves. There were cleavages between the new nobility and the old. Artisans and merchants, as well, formed separate interests which were further fragmented into organized guilds and companies.[142] These various interests took on special political significance once they joined energies to form parties or factions. The quest for preferential treatment by organized interests or coalitions of interests was distinguished from the natural and inevitable divisions in a society. "When accompanied by factions and parties, [divisions] are injurious; but when maintained without them they contribute to the prosperity of republics." [143] Nevertheless, Machiavelli contended, factions ought not to be eliminated but regulated. The friction generated by factional struggles was evidence of vitality in a system. The great example of salutary frictions was provided by the Roman constitutional system where the contests between the patricians and the plebs had resulted in better laws and greater liberties. In other words, the relatively unrestrained flow of political forces had issued in arrangements which were better because they were more comprehensive and inclusive of the basic interests of the society.[144] Moreover, the Roman example also demonstrated that the occasional instabilities of factional strife need not destroy the power of the system, for when Rome faced external threats, the opposing interests immediately laid aside their private quarrels to rally to the defense of the *patria*.[145] The upshot of Machiavelli's argument was to recast the notion of political unity in accordance with the new picture of political society as a diagram of interest-propelled forces. For if the nature of political society was such that its unity presupposed rather than excluded the jarring effects of interest groups, then unity was the resultant of the satisfaction of conflicting interests. But at this point a further dilemma issued from the coexistence of two contradictory principles: Machiavelli held that the political order must insure the equality of treatment of its members, and at the same time he asserted that a political system could not survive unless the dominant interests were satisfied. Yet in a political condition of limited and relative goods, it is apparent that appeasement of powerful groups cuts across the principle of equality — a dilemma which has never been solved within the interest theory of politics. For the natural response of those entrusted with making political decisions is to draw a table of priorities in conformity to the relative power and influence of the contending forces. Priority, however, is not equality.

A political system can accommodate the idea of equality with that of the free play of interests, and the unequal aggregates of power and influence resulting from the competitive struggle for advantage, only by searching for some substitute source of emotional loyalty. A system professing equality is in great need of an obscuring "myth," an enveloping loyalty to cover the fact that economic, social and political equality have, at best, a very limited practical meaning. Without systematically treating the problem, Machiavelli, nevertheless, did touch upon what has perhaps become the most effective substitute for equality, the substitute of national feeling. In terms of manipulative politics, the utility of national sentiment lies not only in the intensity of emotion which it engenders, but in its surface resemblance to the principle of equality: all men, regardless of wealth, station, and pedigree, share the common quality of a distinctive national identity and no one can claim or prove that he has more of it than anyone else. National identity represents an inexhaustible category of good. The foregoing can be summarized by saying that if unity presupposed conflicts of interest, then the admission of conflict, in turn, demanded a common national loyalty which could be evoked to set limits to disputes or to exact sacrifices from those less favored

by the table of public priorities. It might be paradoxical, but it is not accidental, that the first truly modern political theory should unite the "realism"
of interest politics with the "idealism" of nationalism.

There was, however, a far more ominous implication in the vitalities of
conflict. Earlier we have noted Machiavelli's insistence that external expansion was essential to the life of the body politic. Under an absolute monarchy the prince's desire for glory and the maintenance of his power
could be depended upon to supply the necessary driving force towards expansion. In a republic the dynamics of imperialism were closely linked to
the interest struggles arising out of class ambitions and desires. The impetus
to imperialism was now to come from the extension of domestic power
drives. Again Rome furnished the model:

> . . . Had the government of Rome been such as to bring greater tranquillity,
> there would have ensued this inconvenience, that it would have been weaker,
> owing to its having cut off the source of supply [i.e., factional conflicts] which
> enabled it to acquire the greatness at which it arrived, so that, in seeking to
> remove the causes of tumults, Rome would have also removed the causes
> of expansion.[146]

All that remained in order to demonstrate the superiority of popular imperialism over monarchical imperialism was to connect the imperialist dynamics of popular government with the politics of interest. What had to be
shown was that a popular government could generate greater power than a
monarchy because it used the benefits of conquest for the interests of a
greater number.

> . . . Experience shows that cities have never increased either in dominion or
> wealth, unless they have been independent. . . . The reason [why Athens
> and Rome attained greatness after expelling their kings] is easy to under-
> stand; for it is not the well-being of individuals that makes cities great, but
> the well-being of the community . . . It is only in republics that the common
> good is looked to properly . . . and, however much this or that private
> person may be the loser on this account, there are so many who benefit
> thereby that the common good can be realized in spite of those few who
> suffer in consequence.
>
> The opposite happens where there is a prince; for what he does in his
> own interests usually harms the city, and what is done in the interests of the
> city harms him. Consequently, as soon as tyranny replaces self-government
> the least of the evils . . . are that it ceases to make progress and to grow
> in power and wealth: more often than not, nay always, what happens is that

it declines. And should fate decree the rise of an efficient tyrant, so ener-
getic and proficient in warfare that he enlarges his dominions, no advantage
will accrue to the commonwealth . . .[147]

It is apparent from these passages how far Machiavelli has travelled from
classical and mediaeval thought. Where Aquinas, for example, had declared
that the common good was qualitatively different in nature from that of the
individual, Machiavelli took the notion to represent a preponderance of interests and forces within the community.[148] Where Aristotle had warned that
the acquisition of empire would undermine the common good of the community,[149] Machiavelli converted imperialism into a natural extension of
that good. Above all, he had shown that the mass was not only pliant matter,
but also dynamic energy; and that energy, when attracted by interest, was
convertible into a power greater than that of any other system. It became a
principle which the English republicans of the next century eagerly embraced.
As Harrington warned in his peroration on the republic of Oceana: "Oceana
is as the Rose of Sharon, and the Lily of the Valley . . . She is as comely as
the Tents of Kedar, and terrible as an Army with Banners." [150]

VIII Politics and souls. There were two devices on which Machiavelli relied to curb the excesses of factional conflict. The first,
consisting of institutional arrangements, was symptomatic of Machiavelli's
assumption that the activities of factions were similar in nature to the thrust
of forces in physics. The delicate task, however, was to establish institutional
arrangements which, while permitting the expression of diverse ambitions
and interests, as well as venting the "changeful humors" of society, would
also create countervailing forces.[151] For example, the force of ambition could
be turned to the benefit of a republic if the political arrangements contained
established avenues for the pursuit of power: the open play of ambition not
only obviated the dangers of hidden conspiracies, but by encouraging the
ambitious to court public favor, a subtle force was created which helped
to divert political actions towards public rather than private ends. In short,
the influence of the constituency would be institutionalized.[152] So impressed
was Machiavelli by the possibilities of popular institutions for attracting,
and yet domesticating, great talents, that he came to believe that a system of
free elections could overcome the mortality of individual greatness by insuring a continual supply of fresh talents: virtue could thus be extended
to infinity.[153]

The discovery of institutional substitutes for the prince was the logical complement to the importance which Machiavelli attached to the satisfaction of interests. It was this which makes Machiavelli one of the forerunners and founders of the great tradition of interest politics, a tradition which was continued by Harrington, Locke, Hume, and Bentham, and received its classic expression in James Madison's Letter Ten of the *Federalist Papers*. But, as we noted earlier, a significant redistribution of emphasis in political theory implies omission. What had been excluded by the theory of interest? In order to make the point clear we can recall a passage from Plato's *Republic* which symbolized both the classical and mediaeval attitudes to the exercise of power. The passage was one where Adeimantus set forward the considerations which a theory of justice must meet:

> You must not be content with proving that justice is superior to injustice; you must make clear what good or what harm each of them does to its possessor . . . So I want you, in commending justice, to consider only how justice, in itself, benefits a man who has it *in him,* and how injustice harms him, leaving *rewards and reputation out of account.* I might put up with others dwelling on those outward effects . . . but [not] from you . . . You must not be content merely to prove that justice is superior to injustice, but explain how one is good, the other evil, in virtue of the *intrinsic effect each has on its possessor, whether gods or men see it or not.*[154]

The significant part of the passage lies in the contrasting approaches to political action: "rewards and reputation" and "outward effects" on the one side, "intrinsic effects" on the other. When these distinctions are applied to Machiavelli's thought, it becomes obvious that politics has become external to its participants. This, in turn, fits nicely with his emphasis on the protection of material interests. The belief that politics was concerned with externals and that the promotion of man's interior life did not belong to the province of the political provided an interesting parallel with Luther's doctrine of "Christian liberty" and the general Protestant notion of "conscience," both of which supported the belief that politics had nothing to do with man's internal state.

The growing alienation between the *bona interiora* and the kinds of goods at which political action aimed can also be traced if we turn to Machiavelli's second device for controlling the effects of factions. This centered around the attempt to create a civic virtue which would serve to discipline and curb the desires and ambitions of the masses. The means for this would be the laws, institutions, education, and religious system. In this connection the greatest emphasis was placed on military organization which came to assume a role analogous to that of education in Plato's system. "The security of all states is based on good military discipline, and where it does not exist, there can neither be good laws or anything else that is good." [155] If all citizens were exposed to the rigors of military life, as the Romans had been, and if their virtue were then put to the test, "it will be found that always and in all circumstances they will be of the same mind and will maintain their dignity in the same way." [156] The value of military experience lay in the contrasts which it presented to the legitimized scramble for place and preference in civil society. An army, at its best, was akin to a tightly unified community, fostering a warm intimacy among its members which allowed them to act as one and to accept the self-sacrifice which was otherwise absurd.[157] Military institutions, while they might thus be analogous to Plato's system of education, had however a fundamentally different objective, not the illumination of the soul but the disciplining of those very passions which the dexterous political actor presupposed and which it was his business to encourage.

While these methods varied, there was one common quality which they shared: each was intended solely to influence the external conduct of the citizens. This was most evident in Machiavelli's treatment of religion. Like Hobbes later on, he contended that original Christianity had been completely acceptable as a civic religion. Now, however, it taught the wrong virtues of self-abnegation, humility, and other-worldliness; it taught, in short, those virtues connected with the interior goods of the soul. A true civic religion ought to encourage a proper fear and respect for authority and help inculcate military valor.[158]

Machiavelli's conception of civic virtue marked an important stage in the development of modern political thought and practice, for it symbolized an end to the old alliance between statecraft and soul-craft. Henceforth it would be increasingly taken for granted that while the cultivation of souls and personalities might be a proper end of man, it did not provide the focus of political action. This can be stated more strongly by saying that the new science was not conceived as the means to human perfectibility. This pessimistic strain, which grew out of the realization that the new knowledge must be conversant with evil and that its major concern was to avoid hell, confirms that it was a post-Christian science rather than one inspired directly by classical models. The assertion that "all men are wicked and that they will always give vent to the malignity that is in their minds when opportunity offers" was one which Greek political science never entertained and Christian doctrine never doubted.[159] But if Machiavelli's sense of evil and, if one likes, sin, sets him apart from the Greeks, it also denies him any relationship to the liberal and collectivist schools of social science of the late eighteenth and nineteenth centuries. The tradition begun by Machiavelli was carried on by Hobbes, Locke, and Hume; it was a tradition singularly devoid of illusions about man's political condition. It was reserved for men like Rousseau, Saint-Simon, and Comte to endow political theory with the notion of innocence.

◦§ EIGHT §◦

Hobbes:

Political Society as a System of Rules

Philosophy will clip an Angel's wings,
Conquer all mysteries by rule and line,
Empty the haunted air . . .

KEATS

The Chinese . . . are reported to have a way of writing the word "crisis"
by two characters, one of which signifies "danger," the other "oppor-
tunity."

LOUIS WIRTH

I The revival of political creativity. Machiavelli's political theory had been oriented towards the order of problems created by the human energies and vitalities which had burst through the mediaeval system of restraints. He had tried to reshape the concepts of political theory so that they might better grasp the reality of individuals, groups, and states jostling for advantage within a determinate space. One result of Machiavelli's reformulation of political theory was to draw attention to the dynamic element of the uninhibited pursuit of interest and to establish interest as the departure point for most subsequent theorizing. Although he had succeeded in uncovering this new dimension of political life — "new" not by reason of discovery but by way of emphasis — Machiavelli failed to furnish an adequate analysis of the

239

necessary presuppositions of interest politics. What did the pursuit of interest assume in the way of social and political arrangements? of rules which would control the inevitable struggle between rival groups and individuals? It was not enough to assert with Machiavelli that the problem of politics was to satisfy interests, or that where they could not be satisfied the parties must accept a compromise, or that when compromise proved unavailing coercion must be introduced. Machiavelli's prescriptions were woefully lacking in one vital element: some comprehensive principle, some notion of a unifying consensus for coping with the interest-ridden nature of the new politics. For if interests were the expression of what is particular to an individual or group, the pursuit of different interests was latent with conflict and, ultimately, anarchy. Moreover, if the identity of individuals, groups and classes derived from their different interests, how was it possible to establish a set of restraints which it would be in the interest of each to observe? In other words, didn't the pursuit of interests presuppose what was most difficult of attainment in a society of particulars, the sense of a common life? It was this sense of a common life which was most glaringly absent in Machiavelli's political theory. Machiavelli's political actors take decisions, conflict rages between group and group, there is thrust and riposte between princes, but no reflection of an ordered set of relationships among men of the same social grouping, no sense of shared loyalties, no feel for the continuity of a collectivity extending over time. For all of his insight into conflict Machiavelli never managed to explain how civic *virtù* alone could develop a sufficient consciousness of commonalty to support the disorder and destructiveness inherent in factional politics.

The crisis in community, far from being a peculiarity of the molecular state of Italian politics, can be documented in the religious theories of the late sixteenth and early seventeenth centuries. The pressing problem confronting Luther, Zwingli, and Calvin was to bring Protestant man back to a consciousness of community after having first encouraged his individualism. The most vivid expression of these difficulties was to be found among the various sects cast up during the revolutionary travails of seventeenth-century England. Groups such as the Brownists, Seekers, Baptists, and Separatists held to the belief that a church was in the nature of a voluntary association. This notion was popularly expressed in the covenant idea which rested church authority on the free consent of the individual members. By placing the religious association on a foundation of individualism, the sectarians found themselves faced with the problem that even a church had to accommodate different kinds of interests. As one influential writer put it:

In that polity or government by which Christ would have his churches ordered, the right disposal of the power therein . . . may lie in a due and proportioned allotment and dispersion (though not in the same measure and degree) into diverse hands, according unto the several concernments and interests that each rank in his Church may have, rather than in an entire and sole trust committed to any one man . . .[1]

The admission of different interests inevitably dissolved the older conception of the church as the tightest possible corporate group.

Consider that we may be one in one Christ though we think diversely, and we may be friends though not brethren, and let us attain to *union though not to unity*.[2]

As this last remark indicates, the fundamental issue being raised was, on what terms could religion be carried on once the church had ceased to be a tightly knit unity? Translated into political terms, the issue read: on what basis could the practice of government be conducted once the society was no longer a community? Must political societies, as Milton protested, remain content with "the forced and outward union of cold, and neutral, and inwardly divided minds"?[3] That this had become the central question was implicit in Hobbes's demonstration of the natural starting point for political inquiry. A science, he remarked, was not like a circle that allowed us to begin at any point. The subject matter of political science could be brought "into the clearest light" if the idea of justice were first examined. The quest for justice, however, was not directed towards finding some general ethical principle which would unite the members of society, but rather an inquiry into the rational grounds for private interest or particularity; that is, why "any man should call anything rather his own, than another man's." In the same way that church organization had been forced to cope with the individualism of tender consciences, political society had now to create a form of association for governing men who "from their very birth, and naturally, scramble for everything they covet, and would have all the world, if they could, to fear and obey them."[4]

The mere fact that questions of this nature were cropping up in both political and religious thought provides impressive evidence that men no longer felt that the community represented a natural unity. This, in turn, provoked the great challenge which preoccupied the political thought of the seventeenth and eighteenth centuries: if a community was not the product of nature, could it be constructed through human art? Hobbes's assertion, that "by art is created that great Leviathan," was but a terse way of saying what others had said and acted upon for almost a century. The notion of political creativity, which had lain dormant almost since the classical period, took on fresh life under the combined stimulus of ideas of church-building and state-building following upon the political and religious upheavals of the sixteenth century. The civil wars and revolution which brought anarchy to seventeenth-century England aroused a sense of opportunity in Hobbes similar to that expressed by the men of the sixteenth century as they surveyed the chaotic flux of their own times. For more than a hundred years, enormous pressures had been building inside English society, and only the genius of the Tudors had managed to keep the lid on. After the uneasy interlude of James I, demands for political, social, religious and economic change converged to disrupt the old order. Seventeenth-century England became a kind of laboratory for political experiment, as king, parliament, and army fought for supremacy. It was an age of bold schemes and disturbing visions. Before the deluge came, Laud had struggled to reform the established church into a stronger agency of belief and a surer support for the throne. Strafford worked tirelessly to cut away the encrusting vestiges of the past and transform the monarchy into an efficient instrument of governance. During the 1640's the visions became wilder and more apocalyptic as the suppressed excitement of the sectarians burst forth. "The present state of the world is running up like parchment in the fire and wearing away." [5] In some quarters men were caught up in the belief that England and the world stood on the edge of regeneration: "Nations shall become the nations of Christ, and the government shall be in the hands of the Saints." To still others Christ's return would usher in an era where men would "work in righteousness and lay the foundation of making the earth a common treasure for all." [6] In Hobbes the excitement of the age was cloaked in the language of science and mathematics, but this did not prevent him from expressing a vision of the possible estate of man which soared beyond that of the sixteenth-century writers. There was no capricious *fortuna* to devil human progress, no inscrutable God to remind man of his being a favored alien in a world he had not fashioned. This was to be political philosophy in an age of intellectual, as well as political and religious, revolution. Where Machiavelli's thought had contained only some striking anticipations of the coming modes of scientific thought and could therefore combine modernity with a cult of antiquity, and where Luther and Calvin might skirt the Middle Ages to recapture the wisdom of Augustine and the simplicity of the apostolic teachings, Hobbes wrote from the midst of a scientific revolution which seemed to snap the continuity between the present and the past, exposing the wisdom of the ancients as convenient targets for sarcasm. The claims of science, that the mysterious phenomena of the universe were open and accessible to the methods of mathematics, appeared so undeniable to a mind like Hobbes that he boldly prepared to apply the same assumption to the political world. There was a potential congruence between the phenomena of politics and the concepts of the human mind, provided that these concepts were founded on the right method. When armed with the right method, and further armed with opportunity, man could construct a political order as timeless as a Euclidean theorem.

Thus Machiavelli, Luther, and Calvin might pray to different gods, and Hobbes pray to none at all, yet all four were at one in their response to chaos: chaos was the material of creativity, not a cause for resignation. They were all Platonists in the spirit of their assumption about the plasticity of human arrangements and the efficacy of the human will, and this despite (or perhaps even because of) the dark view each had of human nature. It was reserved to Tom Paine, in company with the Utopian Socialists and Comte, to wed creativity to a theory of man's innocence. The activism so characteristic of Machiavelli, Luther, Calvin, and Hobbes was accompanied also by a certain impatience towards the traditional modes of knowledge and the accepted practices of their respective fields. Times of crisis are notoriously uncongenial to the mellower wisdom of Aristotle, to a fondness for gradual becoming and modest tinkering, to the respect tendered to customary practice and common opinion. While the passing of the mediaeval world might sadden some men, like Sir Thomas More, and lead others, like Montaigne, to ironical detachment, for Machiavelli, the Protestant Reformers, and Hobbes, the human condition presented latent but exciting possibilities which summoned men to mastery. Whether disorder took a political or religious form, it aroused the impulse to build societies.

Yet there was another side to the dream of creativity: fear. Fear had been a natural reaction to the conditions of the sixteenth century. Religious ferment had combined with the travail of national centralization to make disorder a constant possibility and stability a tenuous achievement. Society was continually being threatened by a reversion to "political nature." It was not surprising that men as diverse as Luther and Bodin had voiced the same warning that only a powerful coercive authority spelled the difference between anarchy and order. In the ontology of political thought, order has been the equivalent of being, anarchy the political synonym for non-being. Hobbes's England had experienced political revolution and religious conflict of such intensity as to draw a whole society to the edge of nothingness. So dramatic had been the suddenness with which England had been plunged into war and revolution, so great had been the devastation, and so bitter had been the enmities that for the next three centuries and more English politics was conducted on the unwritten premise that history ought not be allowed to repeat itself.

This experience with the political void inspired one of the most important conceptions of the political thought of the seventeenth and eighteenth centuries, that of "the state of nature," the condition of political nothingness. While for later critics this notion provided a convenient way of winning cheap philosophical victories over writers like Hobbes and Locke, to the men of the seventeenth century the state of nature conveyed a vivid and far from fictitious meaning. It was the dramatic contrast to their deep belief in the possibilities of political construction; it was the source of the anxiety which shaded their hopes and caused their dogmas to trail off into questions.

II **Political philosophy and the revolution in science.** In earlier pages we have pointed out that the concept of "political nature" had been most sharply delineated during periods of great change and upheaval. The need to establish a field of intelligible meanings among political phenomena becomes acute when traditional social and political arrangements appear to be breaking down into a kind of primal condition. This had been the case with Plato in the Greek world of the fifth century, with Augustine and the backdrop of the sack of Rome and the crisis in classical thought, with Luther and Calvin and the events of the Reformation, and, finally, with Machiavelli and the political disorganization of Renaissance Italy. These periods of crisis have appeared as so many possibilities for resettling the shaken foundations of action and the accepted modes of thought and feeling. Crisis had meant opportunity, the chance for thought to abandon the postures of selective criticism or wholesale acceptance dictated by normal times, and to assume, instead, the bolder stance of prescribing the patterns of wholesale reconstruction. This belief that the ordering function of political theory is best realized when human existence has been reduced to a *tabula rasa* had been implicit in Plato's notion of a "new colony" and in his search for the impressionable young tyrant. These were but the imagery of political opportunity, as were the "new prince" and the "new principality" of Machiavelli.

The Hobbesian concept of the state of nature exhibited this same pattern of crisis and opportunity. It reflected an age of political and religious turmoil wherein the constitutional and ecclesiastical settlement of the Tudors was dissolving and men were bitterly at odds over the shape of the new order. Like Plato, Augustine, Machiavelli, and Calvin before him, Hobbes believed that the irregularities prevailing in political phenomena could be brought to order only through action informed by knowledge. In an age where men called "not only for peace, but also for truth," Hobbes believed that for the first time political philosophy was genuinely in a position to bring both truth and peace. The benefits of valid political knowledge were now accessible because of the revolutionary advances in the sciences. Political nature, therefore, was to be restored to order by a political philosophy purged of Aristotelian and scholastic influences and reshaped according to the models of mathematical and scientific thinking.

By placing his hopes in an alliance with science, Hobbes helped to magnify an anxiety which had entered political philosophy for the first time with Machiavelli and has persisted into modern political science. It was an anxiety growing out of a concern at the "backward" state of political philosophy. "If the moral philosophers had as happily discharged their duty, I know not what could have been added by human industry to the completion of that happiness, which is consistent with human life." [7] The belief that the value of political philosophy could be measured by the achievements in science and mathematics has come to be the peculiar burden of modern political thought. It is to be seen in the way that the contemporary political scientist expends much of his energy anxiously wondering if his methods are scientific and if the scientist will grant him the seal of respectability. The natural course for those dazzled by modern science is to inquire into the reasons for its spectacular advance. This was the course followed by Hobbes and it had some fateful consequences for political philosophy.

"Science" — to use Hobbes's comprehensive term — had progressed so rapidly because scientists had been bold enough to break with traditional modes of thought and inquiry. They had refused to follow the path of building slowly on past achievements, of zealously preserving the main corpus and modifying only where necessary. The unprecedented development of "science" was pictured by Hobbes as an intellectual drama of creative destruction. Men had taken a radically new look at the universe, shedding their preconceptions and purging from their categories the vestiges of Greek teleology and Christian cosmology. By intellect alone, without appeal to superhuman authority and without relying upon non-rational and non-sensory faculties, man had created a rationally intelligible cosmos without mystery and occult qualities.

Deeply impressed by the dramatic potentialities of this procedure, whereby man created intelligibility among the phenomena of nature, Hobbes then turned to convert it to the uses of philosophy, to make creative destruction the starting point for philosophical method. True philosophizing commenced with what Hobbes designated "privation"; that is, an imaginative act of destruction, a "feigning the world to be annihilated." [8] In wishing away the world, Hobbesian man announced his independence of pre-existent meanings and proclaimed his own right to recreate meaning. From the resources of his own remembrances and from the "phantasms" deposited by sensory experience he could construct a new "reality."

What was breathtaking about the enterprise was that it rested upon a conception of truth not as a faithful report of external "reality" but as an "arbitrary" construction of the human mind. By the rational ordering of names the universe took on intelligible meaning and man became the maker of his own rationality: to know a "truth," such as the sum $2 + 3$, was "nothing else but to acknowledge that it is made by ourselves." [9] A valid proposition or a logical demonstration consisted of a certain ordering of words; however, the meaning attached to words was not inherent but derived from an act of human will:

> . . . The first truths were arbitrarily made by those that first of all imposed names upon things, or received them from the imposition of others. For it is true (for example) that *man is a living creature,* but it is for this reason, that it pleased men to impose those names on the same thing.[10]

Thus meaning was rooted in an act of "arbitrary" imposition, and even the seemingly objective character of reason could not escape its dependence upon the origins of words. Reason consisted in *"reckoning,* that is adding and subtracting, of the consequences of general names agreed upon for the *marking* and *signifying* of our thoughts." [11] The crucial point, however, was that for Hobbes the "arbitrary" and the creative were synonymous. Hobbesian man emerged as the Great Artificer, the creator of science, mathematics, and philosophy, the architect of time and space, values, and truth itself. Even religion depended on man's ingenuity, inasmuch as the "signs" by which God was honored were in fact meaningful signs of honor because men considered them such. "That is a true sign which by the consent of men becomes a sign." [12]

The hopes for the advancement of human knowledge, which Hobbes had equated with logical demonstration and the unambiguous use of names, were intensified in the case of political philosophy. The knowledge attainable by a true political philosophy was comparable in certainty to the truths of geometry and, *pari passu,* superior to the contingent truths of physics:

> Geometry, therefore is demonstrable, for the lines and figures from which we reason, are drawn and described by ourselves; and civil philosophy is demonstrable because we make the commonwealth ourselves. But because of natural bodies we know not the construction, but seek it from effects, there lies no demonstration of what the causes be we seek for, but only of what they may be.[13]

This pointed to the interesting implication that the "nature" confronting the political philosopher differed in crucial respects from the "nature" of the physicist: the universe of science was one which man did not create; he only created language about it. It was a universe not only antecedent to language, thought, and man himself, but one which he seemingly could not alter. In the last analysis, therefore, the words employed by the physicist ought to be governed by phenomena, not phenomena by the words. As Hobbes noted in his discussion of "physics":

> The principles . . . upon which the following discourse depends, are not such as we ourselves make and pronounce in general terms, as definitions; but such, as being placed in the things themselves by the Author of Nature, are by us observed in them . . .[14]

The case of politics was quite different, for, as Hobbes repeatedly insisted, political knowledge was a form of knowledge which consciously aimed at overcoming "political nature," of creating situations unknown to nature — as when men were made to act peacefully after having previously been at each other's throats.

The "nature" of politics, then, permitted a freer hand in imposing names and assigning meanings. And what converted the model of science and mathematics into an exciting possibility were the tumultuous conditions of seventeenth-century England. They seemed to provide the heaven-sent opportunity which political philosophers often desired but rarely encountered. While philosophy was confined to an imaginative act of "privation," the act of annihilation with which political philosophy began had, in an age of civil war and revolution, an implicit foundation in reality:

> For as in a watch, or some such small engine, the matter, figure, and motion of the wheels cannot well be known, except it be taken in sunder, and viewed in parts; so to make a more curious search into the rights of states, and duties of subjects, it is necessary (I say not to take them in sunder, but yet that) they be so considered, as if they were dissolved . . .[15]

The potentialities of political knowledge were to be unfolded in the construction of that "greatest of human powers," an artificial Leviathan "compounded of the powers of most men" arranged in such a way that "the use of all their powers" would depend on a single sovereign will. Here the political philosophy of Hobbes had caught up the classical notion of political creativity and wedded it to a secularized version of the Augustian God. The abolition of the state of nature would be a godlike act, a "creation out of nothing by human wit."

> . . . The *pacts* and *covenants,* by which the parts of this body politic were at first made, set together, and united, resemble that *fiat,* or the *let us make man,* pronounced by God in the creation.[16]

When the social covenant is understood as the highest expression of political creativity, we can more easily appreciate the tremendous hold which it had for the writers of the seventeenth and eighteenth centuries. Too often the element of voluntary agreement has been taken as the whole meaning of the covenant. If we remember that the covenant was made possible by a preliminary act of imaginative emancipation which abolished both present and past, then we can better recapture the excitement it aroused. In this respect Paine and Jefferson in America and the revolutionary writers of France were the faithful echoes of Hobbes in insisting that every generation could reckon as its birthright the right to recreate society as it saw fit. This was but to follow Hobbes's claim that man could become the creator of meanings for the political universe.

III **The promise of political philosophy.** Like his patron Bacon, Hobbes did not consider science or philosophy justifiable for their own sake, or for the sheer "inward glory and triumph of mind" that comes from mastering "some difficult and doubtful matter." The "end of knowledge is power" and "the scope of all speculation is the performance of some action" which would advance "the commodity of human life." [17] In terms of these criteria philosophy had served mankind well; not philosophy as practiced by Aristotle and the Scholastics, but philosophy as redefined to include mathematics and science:

> But what the *utility* of philosophy is, especially of natural philosophy and geometry, will be best understood by reckoning up the chief commodities of which mankind is capable . . . Now, the greatest commodities of mankind are the arts; namely, of measuring matter and motion; of moving

ponderous bodies; of architecture; of navigation; of making instruments for all uses; of calculating the celestial motions, the aspects of the stars, and the parts of time; of geography, etc. . . . .

After pointing out that these arts were unknown in many parts of the world, Hobbes concluded:

What, then, makes this difference, except philosophy? Philosophy, therefore, is the cause of all these benefits.[18]

Similarly, Hobbes seemed to promise that a rightly grounded political philosophy could bring benefits hitherto unknown:

Though nothing can be immortal, which mortals make; yet, if men had the use of reason they pretend to, their commonwealths might be secured, at least from perishing by internal diseases.[19]

This had the authentic ring of the earlier tradition of philosophizing which attributes to the political theorist an "esemplastic" power of remoulding a whole society and a time medium just this side of eternity. But the basic question is whether political philosophy, as defined by Hobbes, could fulfill its promises. Could it really assist men in solving the range of issues usually considered "political" or was it, by virtue of the structure Hobbes gave it, capable only of solving certain limited problems? What we shall try to show in the following pages is that there was an important anticlimax in Hobbes's thought, that what appeared as a grandiose promise of certain benefits, such as an "eternal" constitution, turned out in the end to be considerably less. This disparity between promise and performance issued from some confusions which Hobbes made between philosophy and science, and between geometry and science. Their net effect was to whittle away at the architectonic pretensions of political theory and to leave it with the task of dealing with the primary foundations or initial premises of political order.

The explanation for this oddity lies in two interrelated aspects of his system: the definition of philosophy and the analysis of experience. In his *Elements of Philosophy* Hobbes defined philosophy as

such knowledge of effects or appearances, as we acquired by true ratiocination from the knowledge we have first of their causes or generation: And again, of such causes or generations as may be from knowing first their effects.[20]

He then carefully added that, although "Sense and Memory of things" could be considered as knowledge, "they are not philosophy" because they were "not gotten by ratiocination." Philosophy, then, was not concerned with sense perception or with experience, excepting the experience "men have of the proper use of names in language." [21] This definition of philosophy or "science" was summed up in the *Leviathan* in these terms:

> . . . When the discourse is put into speech, and begins with the definitions of words, and proceeds by connexion of the same into general affirmations, and of these again into syllogisms; the end or last sum is called the conclusion; and the thought of the mind by it signified, is that conditional knowledge, or knowledge of the consequence of words, which is commonly called SCIENCE.[22]

Thus Hobbes gives us a strikingly modern conception of philosophy as concerned with linguistic "truth"; that is, with the status of logical propositions. Put in its simplest terms, this meant that philosophy was to concentrate on the requirements of clear thinking, on the rules of discourse, and not on furnishing us with reports about the true nature of "reality." Obviously this definition of philosophy held more modest possibilities for advancing the welfare and happiness of mankind, yet we must try to understand why Hobbes was so excited on this score and why he believed the concentration on language to be common to philosophy, geometry, and science.

The first step in clarifying these problems is to note Hobbes's explanation for the advance of mathematics. "In geometry," Hobbes declared, "which is the only science that it hath pleased God hitherto to bestow on mankind, men begin at settling the significations of their words, which settling of significations they call definitions, and place them in the beginning of their reckoning." [23] This emphasis on definitions and linguistic clarity was repeatedly introduced by Hobbes as the explanation for the success of the mathematician and the scientist, and it was the solid bedrock to his hopes for mankind generally: "the light of human minds is perspicuous words, but by exact definitions first snuffed and purged from ambiguity; *reason* is the *pace*; increase of *science*, the *way*; and the benefit of mankind, the *end*." [24] This raised the question, however, of the nature of the "truth" accessible to a philosophy based upon rational demonstration and unambiguous definition. Hobbes carefully avoided identifying philosophy with the systematic ordering of sense impressions or experience; instead, he concluded that the type of "truth" sought by philosophy consisted in truths about langauge. "True and false are attributes of speech, not of things." [25] Thus truth was to be considered as a property attaching to linguistic entities, or, in Hobbes's succinct statement, "truth and a true proposition is all one." [26] It followed that the task of philosophical reasoning was not to disclose the true "nature of things" but to give us conclusions "about the name of things." [27]

The first reaction of a modern reader to Hobbes's argument would be to point out that it rests upon a serious confusion of the methods of science with those of mathematics. Scientific method we regard as not being first and foremost a matter of logic and definition in the way that a Euclidean theorem is. Except for the elementary importance of clear thinking in any systematic enterprise, science is primarily concerned with a method of experimentation which seeks empirical verification for its hypotheses. Geometry, which served as the model for Hobbes, does not purport to test its propositions by an appeal to experience, but rather on the consistent use of fixed definitions. No amount of empirical observation, therefore, can prove or disprove a proposition in geometry. This distinction between geometry and science, between a logic of discourse and a logic of discovery, is important because philosophy has come to be far closer in method to geometry than to science. In the words of a contemporary, the philosopher "must not attempt to formulate speculative truths, or to look for first principles, or to make a priori judgments about the validity of our empirical beliefs. He must, in fact, confine himself to works of clarification and analysis . . ." [28] While this may represent a somewhat extreme position and while Hobbes would certainly have denied much of the first sentence, there can be no question that he was far closer to accepting the idea that the concern of philosophy was with linguistic rather than empirical truths. But he came to this position largely on the basis of the mistaken notion that the methods of geometry and science were akin. It is true that in certain passages he allotted a larger place to knowledge based on experience and even inferred the important distinction between the methods of science and those of philosophic logic.[29] Yet while Hobbes might proclaim that "forasmuch as all knowledge beginneth from experience, therefore also new experience is the beginning of new knowledge, and the increase of experience the beginning of the increase of knowledge," [30] he never looked upon this kind of knowledge as supplying a certain basis for the improvement of man's condition.

In his conception of political philosophy we find again that geometry is the model:

> The skill of making, and maintaining commonwealths, consisteth in certain rules, as doth arithmetic and geometry; not, as tennis-play, on practice only: which rules, neither poor men have the leisure, nor men that have had the leisure, have hitherto had the curiosity, or the method to find out.[31]

This assertion rested on the assumption that it was not only possible to reduce the political art to certain infallible rules, but that it was also desirable. To achieve this Hobbes had to dispose of rival claims to political knowledge. More specifically, he had to combat the position represented by Machiavelli that adequate generalizations could be constructed from experience and that political action would be more certain of success if it imitated the methods of ancient heroes. Machiavelli had come perilously close to saying that politics was in fact not a theoretical study at all, but a subject for common sense wedded to experience and versed in the lessons of history.

Hobbes's refutation was significant in that he made no attempt to demonstrate that the nature of politics was such as to demand exact knowledge rather than prudence. Instead he relied on the limitations of experience in scientific matters to demonstrate the insufficiency of prudence in politics. In science, he explained, experience could supply a kind of knowledge concerning "the effects of things that work upon us from without," but such knowledge lacked the conclusiveness of demonstrative knowledge based on analytically true propositions. By its nature, "experience concludeth nothing universally." The same logical limitations held for political prudence, because prudence was "nothing else but conjecture from experience." Its conclusions were based on past occurrences of "what is likely to come to pass, or to have passed already," hence prudence could never rise above being knowledge of only a presumptive kind.[32] And just as "demonstration" stood as the highest form of scientific knowledge, so "sapience or wisdom" represented the most certain form of knowledge in political philosophy. Wisdom did not derive from experience but from "industry"; that is, from the skill in attaching names to phenomena and in the use of "a good and orderly method." Wisdom was a knowledge not of facts but of the consequences of facts, which was another way of saying it represented a knowledge of causes which gave men power to reproduce the desired effects. This, in turn, entailed a sharp distinction between political philosophy and history. History consisted of a "register of knowledge of fact," capable of furnishing men with prudence, but political philosophy was the product of reason, and "nothing is produced by reasoning aright, but general, eternal and immutable truth."[33]

But after distinguishing the "immutable" truths of political philosophy from the presumptive knowledge of prudence, and after promising that the former could teach men the secret of "immortal peace" and an "everlasting" constitution, the whole argument seems to end not in a bang but a sputter. The great end of political philosophy was apparently confined to certain negative benefits:

. . . The utility of moral and civil philosophy is to be estimated, not so much by the commodities we have by knowing these sciences, as by the calamities we receive from not knowing them.[34]

Thus political philosophy could not furnish men with "the greatest commodities"; its value was in providing instruction about the basic principles of order which sustained all of the other and greater aspects of civilization. "*Leisure* is the mother of *philosophy*; and *Commonwealth* the mother of *peace* and *leisure*." [35]

The anticlimax to Hobbes's political philosophy has laid him open to some hard charges by later critics. He has been accused of having lowered the sights of political philosophy from a concern with man's highest good to an ignoble preoccupation with mere survival values; or of having "built his whole moral and political doctrine on observations regarding the extreme case" of civil war and anarchy.[36] We would submit, however, that the circumscribed role of political thought was the outcome of limitations inherent in the Hobbesian conception of philosophy. Philosophical knowledge had been identified with linguistic truth and was to be sought through clarity of definitions and meanings. In its political version, philosophy aimed at peace rather than at scientific advance. Peace was considered a condition where men followed rules; that is, definitions of conduct that were clear, unambiguous and authoritative. In the same way that the activities of a mathematician qua mathematician were governed by the usages accepted in mathematics, the activities of the citizen qua citizen were subject to the rules governing civil life. The subject-matter of political philosophy, then, was political rules and the language and definitions appropriate to them. The importance of language and rules was written into the very substance of the Hobbesian political philosophy, coloring his conception of the state of nature, the form taken by the covenant, the position of sovereign and subject, the status of law and morals, and the role of reason in politics.

As a starting point for discovering how the shape of political philosophy was moulded by philosophy's concern with linguistic truths we turn to two key passages from Hobbes's writings:

. . . Knowledge is the remembrance of the name or appellation of things, and how everything is called, which is, in matters of common conversation, a remembrance of pacts and covenants of men made amongst themselves, concerning how to be understood of one another . . . But when men remember not how things are named, by general agreement, but either mistake and misname things, or name them aright by chance, they are not said to have science but opinion.[37]

> The cause . . . of civil war is that men know not the causes neither of war nor peace, there being but few in the world that have learned those duties which unite and keep men in peace, that is to say, that have learned the rules of civil life sufficiently . . . Seeing, therefore, from the not knowing of civil duties, that is, from the want of moral science, proceed civil wars, and the greatest calamities of mankind, we may very well attribute to such science the production of the contrary commodities.[38]

Political philosophy, then, was not to be envisaged as a body of cumulative knowledge aimed at helping men cope with the issues arising from a constantly changing world. Its logic was not the logic of discovery, of searching always for new principles and comprehensive generalizations. It dealt, instead, with the logic of political discourse; that is, with the language arising out of the set of agreements which defined society in political terms. Society presupposed a common set of meanings, but the inconstancy of meaning and the proclivity of man for interpreting meanings according to his own interests made it imperative that certain definitions be stipulated for the whole society. Just as there were basic rules or conventions governing the usages of geometers, there were rules or propositions distinctive to political life and necessary for its survival. Unless "line" were defined by each and every geometer in the same way, no universe of discourse would be possible among geometers, and hence no science of geometry. Similarly, unless a political "right," for example, carried the same meaning for each citizen — or at least each citizen behaved as though he were conforming to the same definition — there could be no communication among the members of the same society, no reasonable expectations, and hence there would soon be no society. And just as geometry employed certain fictions or "as if's" about the nature of straight lines, circles, and triangles in order to create a closed system of lines and figures, self-consistent and self-contained, the political system, too, represented an artificial construction, a set of fictional "as if's" of a purely logical kind. "For a body politic, as it is a fictitious body, so are the faculties and will thereof fictitious also." [39]

If the role of definitions in political philosophy was to supply the fundamental rules underpinning society, these definitions must be based upon a form of knowledge as certain and immutable as the truths of geometry. "Where men build on false grounds, the more they build, the greater is the ruin." [40] This ruled out experience, not only because of its tentative nature, but more importantly because experience was ultimately an individual matter and, as such, too subjective to furnish the fundamental assumptions of society. Reason alone could establish the infallibility necessary in these matters. But — and here Hobbes approached the crux of the problem — whose reason was to be used in politics? That this should have been a basic query for Hobbes was indicative of a troubling uncertainty that had come to surround the status of reason. Aristotle and Aquinas would never have dreamed of asking such a question, for to them the issue did not concern X's reason as against Y's, but reason as against non-reason. In contrast, Hobbes, as a good nominalist, rejected an hypostasized reason on the same grounds as he had rejected an hypostasized experience: there existed only individual reason and individual experience. And, consistent to the last, Hobbes distrusted individual reason as he had individual experience:

> This common measure, some say, is right reason: with whom I should consent, if there were any such thing to be found or known in *rerum natura*. But commonly they that call for right reason . . . do mean their own . . . But no one man's reason, nor the reason of any one number of men, makes the certainty; no more than an account is therefore well cast up, because a great many men have unanimously approved it.[41]

This led to a paradox which had an important bearing on many aspects of Hobbes's political thought: the reasoning of the geometer had produced infallible truths, but the reasoning of private men issued only in disagreement. Why, Hobbes asked, was reason more "objective" in the one case? If the meanings assigned words were the results of human actions, then, as Hobbes repeatedly pointed out, words inevitably would be changed, either consciously or through carelessness, and their meaning distorted. This raised two distinct but related questions: first, if one accepts Hobbes's charge that the language of politics was riddled with meaningless or ill-defined words, one must also accept the implied assumption that a desirable standard existed for political words, or else the notion of distortion was itself meaningless. From where, then, was such a standard of purity to be derived and, once established, how was it to be preserved? The second question relates to the success which science and mathematics had achieved in avoiding the pitfalls of ambiguity and obscurity of usage. Hobbes tried to explain the greater precision of the language of mathematics by an argument drawn from history. The "perfect pattern of logic" established by the ancient geometers and the later triumphs of Copernicus, Galileo, and Harvey had been possible because, unlike political philosophers, the former had managed to avoid the crippling influence of "Aristotelity" and mediaeval scholasticism with their semantic nonsense about "essences" and "spirits." But as Hobbes recognized, this was but a partial explanation at best, for it did not account for the fact that, once mathematics and its allies had pointed the way to successful methods, political philosophy stubbornly refused to follow.

The first difficulty he perceived was one arising from the broader constituency of political discourse. The language of politics was more widely used, as the remarkable debates at Putney and the flood of pamphlet literature proved, because politics was a more pervasive activity than, say, geometry.[42] The market-place character of politics resulted in a language that was at once less determinate and precise in its meaning. Men "take for principles those opinions which are already vulgarly received, whether true or false." The language of politics, as it now existed, was akin to "common conversation," deriving its meanings from "vulgar use." [43] In contrast, the language of science and mathematics was restricted to a smaller circle of participants, and hence faulty usage was less likely to occur, and when it did it could be more easily detected. A more serious distinction between these two realms of discourse lay in the consequences flowing from bad usage. In the case of mathematics there would be retarded progress, but a confused political vocabulary was far more serious:

> In those things which every man ought to meditate for the steerage of his life, it necessarily happens that not only from errors, but even from ignorance itself, there arise offences, contentions, nay, even slaughter itself.[44]

The likelihood of distortion in political words was enhanced by another peculiarity of political discourse. Words tended to become charged with human interests and passions; as a modern philosopher might say, they become "emotive" and are used not to signify factual statements but personal preferences.[45] This problem did not crop up in mathematics and science, because interests did not enter into technical controversies.

> . . . The doctrine of right and wrong is perpetually disputed, both by the pen and the sword: whereas the doctrine of lines, and figures, is not so; because men care not, in that subject, what be truth, as a thing that crosses no man's ambition, profit or lust.[46]

This aspect reappeared in another form, namely, the persistence of bad usage because it served the power ends of an institution. Hobbes's favorite example here was the Catholic Church: by a deliberate policy the Church sought to preserve its position through enforcing a scheme of words and concepts designed to still men's doubts and to evoke obedience to those guarding the mysteries. The moral of it all, and one not lost on Hobbes, was that words, even when wrongly employed, could be instruments of power when their meanings were enforced by authority.[47]

In the light of these considerations, what implications for political language were to be drawn? If "names have their constitution, not from the species of things, but from the will and consent of men," [48] then the political question comes down to whose consent? which men? While in science the answer was readily forthcoming, in politics, as we have seen, words were subject to a variety of distorting factors and lacked the inner check of a professional group intent on semantic order. In moral and political philosophy "every man thinks that in this subject he knoweth as much as any other." Was it possible, then, to institute a political version of objective reason, an agency for the formulating of public truth? To discover how Hobbes attempted to answer these questions we must turn to his famous concept of the state of nature. This concept has been treated by most commentators in terms of the origins of sovereign power. But it is equally significant for the light it throws on Hobbes's approach to the problem of political knowledge. The state of nature symbolized not only an extreme disorder in human relations, causing men to consent to the creation of an irresistible power; it was also a condition distraught by an anarchy of meanings. In nature each man could freely use his reason to seek his own ends: each was the final judge of what constituted rationality. The problem posed involved more than the moral issues arising from man's vanity or his desire for pre-eminence. It was a genuinely philosophical one involving the status of knowledge. For when vanity and egotism are translated from the language of morals to the language pertinent to knowledge they are summed up in one word, subjectivity; they raise issues of correct belief as well as of right conduct. The state of nature formed the classical case of subjectivism, and in trying to resolve the attendant problems, Hobbes explored a whole range of significantly new topics: the function of political language, the meaning of objectivity and truth in a political context, and the place of political philosophy in an intellectual world dominated by the model of science and mathematics.

IV   The language of politics: the problem of constituency.

. . . Good and evil are names given to things to signify the inclination or aversion of them by whom they were given. But the inclinations of men are diverse, according to their diverse constitutions, customs, opinions; as we may see in those things we apprehend by sense . . . but much more in those

which pertain to the common actions of life, where what this man commends
. . . the other undervalues . . . Whilst thus they do, necessary it is there
should be discord and strife. They are therefore so long in the state of war,
as by reason of the diversity of the present appetites, they mete good and
evil by diverse measures.[49]

To describe the state of nature as a state of subjectivity rather than as
simply the absence of a sovereign power points to Hobbes's belief that the
dissolution of sovereignty was more an effect than a cause of social collapse.
It formed the climax to a steady increase in disagreement concerning common
and fundamental meanings and, as such, it permits us to see how precarious
for Hobbes was the distinction between the state of nature and civil society
and how deep was the imprint of contemporary conditions on his thought.
The multitude of bickering sects spawned during the age, ranging from
Presbyterian sobriety to millennarian ecstasy, had all been nurtured on Reformation doctrines of private judgment, private conscience, and the priesthood of all believers. All England seemed ablaze with inner lights. To
Hobbes, however, these diverse opinions had shattered the outward unity
of belief so necessary to political peace. By encouraging strife and fanaticism
the sects had in effect created a state of nature in religious affairs which was
but preliminary to a total state of nature pervading the whole society. These
same tendencies had taken a political turn in groups like the Levellers, Diggers, and Fifth Monarchy men. Whatever their intramural rivalries might
be, they seemed to Hobbes to share the common vice of proclaiming as truth
what was only "private knowledge of good and evil, which cannot be granted
without the ruin of all government." [50]

A more strictly political form of subjectivity was typified by the parlia-
mentarian's criticism of his sovereign's action, or by the protest of the village
Hampden that no national emergency existed to justify the king levying
an unprecedented tax. In each instance the claim elevated private reason and
experience above the settled judgments of society's spokesmen. To Hobbes,
all of these tendencies, in both their political and religious expression, had
come down to this: In a world where reason was being used as a destructive
instrument to attack established institutions and beliefs, how was it possible
to settle on a clear and unambiguous meaning of reason? All of the competing claims to reason, which were so abundant at the time, were, in Hobbes's
view, mere appeals to "private reason," to reason swayed by each man's desire to seek "that which is good for him." Private reason, therefore, could not
be tolerated because it bred a confusion of meanings which destroyed the
body politic as a communicating whole.

This attack on private judgment was prompted by one of Hobbes's most original yet least noted contributions to political theory. This was the recognition that a political order involved more than power, authority, law, and institutions: it was a sensitive system of communication dependent upon a system of verbal signs, actions, and gestures bearing generally accepted meaning. Hence one of the most important factors in establishing and maintaining the identity of a political society was a common political language. For all of its importance, however, a political language represented a precarious achievement. Like all words, those of the vocabulary of politics possessed no intrinsic significance. "Right," "justice," "liberty," "property," etc., conveyed a meaning which had been assigned them: they were human creations. While these characteristics held for all words, the language of politics differed in the crucial respect that the commonness of meanings depended on a ruling power capable of enforcing them; that is, of declaring, for example, the precise meaning of a right and punishing those who refused to accept the assertion. When this authority was prevented from enforcing definitions, society was reduced to a condition where each member was at liberty to assign to words whatever meanings he chose.

Within this context, the act of covenanting, whereby each man surrendered his natural right to the sovereign, represented more than a method for establishing peace. It was the agency for creating a political universe of unequivocal meaning. The transformation of the state of nature into a civil society marked the change from a condition where the "peculiar and true ratiocination of every man" was replaced by the "reason of the supreme." [51] At the same time, the conventionalist argument, that words come to mean what they do by a kind of *consensus mundi,* reappeared in the covenant which signified men's intentions to establish a civil society and to relinquish their natural powers to the sovereign.

> That is a true sign which by the consent of men becomes a sign . . . that is honorable which by the consent of men, that is to say, by the command of the city, becomes a sign of honor.[52]

But the element of popular consent in the making of meanings was, in its political translation, confined to authorizing some agent to act on behalf of the people. In consenting to the covenant the several individuals agreed to accept the public definitions of the sovereign in exactly the same way as they had agreed to allow the sovereign to represent their consent on all other matters. Meanings, then, became "public" by virtue of the representative and consensual basis of the political organ authorized to pronounce the definitions or rules. By reason of this function, the sovereign stood as the public agent committed to ending the "inconstant significations" of words arising out of the varying "nature, disposition, and interest" of men.[53] Through the act of submission men had exchanged the uncertainty of nature's code for a set of "common rules for all men." In endowing the sovereign with an absolute legislative power they had erected a Great Definer, a sovereign dispenser of common meanings, a "publique reason." Through the medium of the rules set forth in the civil law, the sovereign would settle the meaning of rights and duties, the distinctions between "mine" and "thine," and would, in short, establish an "objective" moral world in politics.

> [Since] all violence proceedeth from controversies . . . concerning *meum* and *tuum,* right and wrong, good and bad, and the like, which men use every one to measure by their own judgments; it belongeth also to the judgment of the same sovereign power, to set forth and make known the common measure by which every man is to know what is his, and what another's; what is good and what bad; and what he ought to do, and what not . . .[54]

Instead of the hopeless confusion of private standards, all actions could now "be esteemed good or bad by their causes and usefulness in reference to the commonwealth."[55] This was Hobbes's answer to the question of what was the standard of rationality in politics: the rational, the objective was what was general, common, and enforceable by virtue of its issuing from a publicly recognized authority. Political truth was not an intrinsic quality, but a function of the requirements of peace and order.

In the foregoing it is easy to see how the redefinition of political reason had come to associate reason, not with truth, or intrinsic validity, but with certainty. Since there was no guarantee that the judgment of the sovereign might not be capricious, ill-advised, and badly informed, this meant sacrificing all of the traditional marks of reason and inserting instead the criteria of definiteness and enforcement. From this perspective, man's achievement in subduing political nature had issued in a realm of political meanings whose sole guarantee of coherence was an act of power. At bottom, then, a deep irrationalism pervaded Hobbesian society, for the sovereign could assign any content he wished to public meanings.

This brings us to the final aspect of Hobbes's concern with words. While the creation of a sovereign power might insure certainty of meaning in the political world, and while he might symbolize men's consent to certain determinate usages, it did not follow that he would institute a language and a set of definitions conforming to the methods of political philosophy. Did this mean that there were really two kinds of political language, one being a second-best type actually operative in practice, the other the language of systematic political philosophy? The issue was between linguistic purity on the one hand, and, on the other, language as a form of communication which would serve the end of social cohesion. As Locke later noted, an important distinction ought to be observed between "civil" and "philosophical" or scientific communication. The wider audience presupposed by the former entailed a certain sacrifice of precision and consistency in the interests of common acceptance. The aim of "civil" language comprised social unity as well as the promotion of understanding: language was "the great instrument and common tie of society." [56] This dilemma faced by Hobbes was partly owing to a failure to realize what other apostles of "scientific" politics have not yet seen, that one of the basic reasons for the unsurpassed progress of science was that scientific discourse, unlike political discourse, had rejected not only the common vocabulary of everyday life, but also the modes of thought familiar to the common understanding. The crucial issue then became whether the elevation of politics to a science meant that political philosophy too would have to outdistance the common understanding and abandon much of the common vocabulary. As Hobbes noted, "to govern well a family and a kingdom are not different degrees of prudence, but different sorts of business; no more than to draw a picture in little, or as great, or greater than the life, are different degrees of art." [57] In his last important political publication this distinction between political knowledge and everyday experience was sharpened. Writing retrospectively about the civil wars, he concluded that the actions taken by Parliament had demonstrated that "diligence and natural wit" might well be sufficient for managing private estates, but in politics men should have acted on the basis of "infallible rules and the true science of equity and justice." [58] But if common experience were not enough, and if in comparison to geometry "politics is the harder study of the two," what warrant could there be for expecting a sovereign to measure up to the demands of the new science? Hobbes himself confessed:

> Considering how different this doctrine is, from the practice of the greatest part of the world . . . and how much depth of moral philosophy is required, in them that have the administration of the sovereign power; I am at the point of believing this my labor, as useless, as the commonwealth of Plato.[59]

Mirrored in Hobbes's despair was the full pathos inherent in the quest for a science of politics: fired by the belief that the desperate situation of political man could be ameliorated only through knowledge, yet trapped by the realization that as knowledge was rendered more precise and scientific it surrendered the hope of easy acceptance in the workaday world of the average person. To the extent that knowledge became scientific it also became more esoteric, hence the only way that political knowledge could be translated into a shared public philosophy was through imposition by authority and acquiescence by the citizenry. Although Hobbes stubbornly clung to the belief that he had so clarified the principles of politics as to make them readily comprehensible, the last hope of this rigid determinist and firm opponent of *fortuna* was that events would cast up some kind of political miracle, some new Dionysius:

> I recover some hope, that at one time or other, this writing of mine may fall into the hands of a sovereign, who will consider it himself (for it is short, and I think clear,) without the help of any interested, or envious interpreter; and by the exercise of entire sovereignty, in protecting the public teaching of it, convert this truth of speculation, into the utility of practice.[60]

V Political entropy: the state of nature. The concept of the state of nature has long been recognized as strategic to Hobbes's argument for despotism: absolute sovereignty was the logical complement to riotous anarchy. Rather than retrace familiar ground, we shall turn to some neglected aspects of the idea. As a starting point, it is suggested that Hobbes's portrayal of the state of nature was colored by irony and absurdity and that these were the mark, not of a dispassionate man of science patiently cataloguing the frantic movements of the human animal caught in a maze of its own devising, but of a sardonic moralist.

There was a double absurdity to the state of nature: logical and moral. It was a condition of the absolute maximization of rights, a perfect state of freedom. Men have a right to do and say what they want. In this sense, the state of nature represented the extreme "idealization" of the claims for religious and political freedom being pressed in seventeenth-century England. The state of nature also combined opposing economic ideas of the time: all property was in common in the sense that no one possessed a lawful title to private property — this for the advocates of primitive communism, like the Diggers. At the same time, the acquisitive impulse was unrestrained by any legal limits. But the ironical result was that in having an unlimited right men could enjoy nothing. Enjoyment presupposed security, yet security was incompatible with absolute liberty. The absurdity of this situation was twofold. It was logically absurd because the right of everyone to everything contradicted the right of anyone to anything; an absolute right was at war with itself.[61] The situation was also morally absurd: under perfect freedom, man the freedom-loving animal becomes *homini lupus*. There was even a kind of "biologic" absurdity, for where might makes right there was always the possibility of the puniest man employing his cunning to kill the strongest.

The solution of a sovereign power which abolished the state of nature had its share of irony and absurdity also. The absolute right to all things which had been the source of chaos was, nevertheless, a part of man's nature, but one which threatened to annihilate his existence. Hence while the establishment of civil society not only contradicted man's right, and therefore his nature, it stood as the only condition which did not contradict his existence. Similarly, there was irony, too, in the creation of the awful Leviathan. While an absolute sovereign might end the intolerable condition of nature, it did not carry the promise of absolute security, perfect peace, or plenty for all. The price of peace, as Hobbes stressed, was the erection of a power which might oppress individuals, demand the fruits of their labor, and even require the sacrifice of their lives. The greatest of all human achievements could not transcend the moral ambiguities of the human condition.[62]

The final and ineradicable irony was man himself. He alone of all the animals possessed speech and was capable of science, yet he alone could turn speech into deception, ideas into sedition, learning into mystification. It was this irony which alienated man from his own nature: animals, living without science and speech and therefore ignorant of the arts of falsification, dwelt together sociably, while man, the unrivaled creator of science, language, and thought was by nature apolitical.[63] He must labor to construct societies, to adopt the guise of civility, carrying always the guilty knowledge that he alone could undo his own achievements. The political order, for all its greatness, did not represent the fulfillment of man's natural impulse towards life in an ordered society, as the classics had taught, but a calculated triumph of man over himself:

> The final cause, end, or design of men, who naturally love liberty, and dominion over others, in the introduction of that restraint upon themselves, in which we see them live in commonwealths, is the foresight of their own preservation, and of a more contented life thereby; that is to say, of getting themselves out from that miserable condition of war, which is necessarily consequent . . . to the natural passions of men . . .[64]

These ironical overtones rule out interpreting the state of nature as belonging to the remote past, or as a strictly logical device designed to demonstrate the logical necessity of absolute sovereignty. Instead, it represented an imaginative reconstruction of a recurrent human possibility, a reconstruction intended to illumine the meaning of human events and to point out the desirable path of human actions. The state of nature stood as a timeless model built on the causes and consequences of political breakdown. Its meaning remained eternally contemporary and urgent. Its absurdity lies in man's failure to take to heart its lessons, while its irony gains force from the paradox that to understand the state of nature men must first understand civil society; they must first realize that they have been able to live in peace in order to appreciate the ungovernable pride and passion which have led them back to war; that, in short, the political order was not a condition without precedent, but a prior condition once enjoyed, but then lost, and must now be recaptured. Hobbes had made it clear that the state of nature was a distillation of experience, a conceptual shorthand for describing "what manner of life there would be, where there were no common power to fear." The content of the state of nature could be filled in by consulting "the manner of life which men that have formerly lived under a peaceful government, use to generate into, in a civil war." [65]

As the symbol of the dissolution of the political order into the "chaos of violence," the state of nature had an ambivalent relationship with the time-dimension of history. In one sense it was connected to history by its function of symbolizing any political situation characterized by the absence of an effective sovereign power. In this sense, the concept did not belong solely to the past or even to the present. Its status was that of an ever-present possibility inherent in any organized political society, a ubiquitous threat which, like some macabre companion, accompanied society in every stage of its journey. It was present each night, as men sealed themselves in their homes and succeeded only in locking in fear. And even when wise policy had secured the internal life of a commonwealth, there remained the state of nature in international politics, constantly pressing in on societies and threatening to undo the permanent peace promised by philosophy.[66] Thus, far from marking the literal origins of political society, the state of nature denoted a relapse, a reversal of time. It was a kind of political version of *Genesis,* without sacral overtones and without sin, but a fall, nevertheless, from the highest level of human achievement, life in a civilized society.

In another sense, however, the state of nature stood outside history, and it is this ahistorical aspect that has led to the frequent charge that Hobbes lacked a sense of history. This argument falls, because it misunderstands the problem. It was not that Hobbes lacked a feel for continuities, but that the condition depicted was essentially ahistorical. This did not mean that the state of nature was unconnected to historically operative causes, for, as we have noted, it was synonymous with civil war and the destruction of sovereign institutions. But by the same token of its destructiveness, the state of nature was severed from history. A civil war was in the nature of a "break" in social existence, a suspended moment which threatened to initiate a reversal of time. The links between past, present, and future had been snapped, and men were left alone in an awful stillness where the past was silent and the future unbeckoning:

> In such condition, there is no place for industry; because the fruit thereof is uncertain; and consequently no culture of the earth; no navigation; nor use of the commodities that may be imported by sea; no commodious building; no instruments of moving, and removing . . . no knowledge of the face of the earth; no account of time; no arts; no letters; no society.[67]

When contrasted with this condition, political society symbolized humanity's triumph over nature, and, since nature had no history in the human sense, society also marked man's creation of history, or more precisely, his recovery of it. The re-establishment of order changed man's relationship to time. The human animal alone was conscious of living amidst a succession of fleeting moments, and because of the fears and anxieties aroused by life in the state of nature he became a time-haunted creature — viewing the future with "a perpetual solicitude of the time to come." [68] Conversely, the creating of the political order, which made possible a "commodious" life and all of the arts of civilization, meant that man could face the future without "perpetual solicitude." For Hobbes, as for Marx later on, the "future" became meaningful by means of an act essentially political in nature.

VI The sovereign definer.

> The only way to erect such a common power . . . is [for men] to confer all their power and strength upon one man, or upon one assembly of men, that may reduce all their wills, by plurality of voices, unto one will . . .[69]

It is one of the oddities of Western political thought that the critics' image of the Hobbesian theory of sovereignty should have been anticipated in the famous frontispiece adorning the 1651 edition of the *Leviathan*. The drawing shows the sovereign as a huge figure towering above his surroundings like some regal Gulliver, brandishing in one hand the military sword, in the other the sceptre of justice. Nestled in the valley below lies a tiny, thriving city, its geometrical tidiness clearly symbolizing the peace and order made possible by the giant looming in the background. Thus the picture seems a perfect summary of Hobbes's thought: the blessings of peace are assured only when society is in total subjection to an absolute authority. This impression of the awesome power of the sovereign seems further confirmed by the vivid language with which Hobbes described his Leviathan: "mortal god," "the greatest of human powers," "the greatest dominion that can be granted . . . limited only by the strength and forces of the city itself, and by nothing else in the world."

Yet there is another feature of the frontispiece worth noting. The sov ereign's powerful body is, so to speak, not his own; its outline is completely filled in by the miniature figures of his subjects. He exists, in other words, only through them. Equally important, each subject is clearly discernible in the body of the sovereign. The citizens are not swallowed up in an anony-mous mass, nor sacramentally merged into a mystical body. Each remains a discrete individual and each retains his identity in an absolute way. What is suggested here is that the substance of power assigned the sovereign was less impressive than the rhetoric surrounding it. This is not to say that Hobbes sought consciously to mislead his audience, for in a very special sense his awesome language was quite justified. Within the confines of the Hobbesian view that political philosophy dealt with the construction of a non-empirical, logically consistent system of propositions, the Hobbesian sovereign occupied a truly awesome position. He was the unchallengeable master of the system of rules or stipulative definitions fundamental to po-litical peace. The importance of rules and the accompanying image of political society as an association articulated through rules tends to give the Hobbesian order the appearance of a *Rechtsstaat:*

> The safety of the people, requireth further, from him, or them that have the sovereign power, that justice be equally administered to all degrees of people; that is, that as well the rich and mighty, as poor and obscure persons, may be righted of the injuries done them; so as the great, may have no greater hope of impunity, when they do violence, dishonour, or any injury to the meaner sort, than when one of these, does the like to one of them: for in this consisteth equity; to which, as being a precept of the law of nature, a sover-eign is as much subject, as any of the meanest of his people.[70]

But the truly novel element lay in the attempt to understand political society as one would any kind of association governed by rules. Laws and agreements operated in political society in much the same way as the criteria governing the activities of mathematicians or participants in a game:

> *Civil law,* is to every subject, those rules, which the commonwealth hath commanded him, by word, writing, or other sufficient sign of the will, to make use of, for the distinction of right and wrong; that is to say, of what is contrary, and what is not contrary to the rule.[71]

If these analogies are pursued, many of the seemingly disparate strands of Hobbes's philosophy fall into an intelligible pattern. If rules were a central feature of society, then questions of clarity of language fully deserved the extensive treatment accorded them by Hobbes. Again, every system of rules, whether it be those governing the behavior of stock-traders or of tennis-players, requires a body to interpret the rules, lay down new regulations, and punish infractions. The position of the Hobbesian sovereign, as the grand master of the rules and ultimate dispenser of definitions, was analogous to the Board of the Stock Exchange or the United States Lawn Tennis Association. Moreover, logical consistency in the ordering of names and meanings, which had been strongly emphasized in Hobbes's philosophy, is obviously essential: one rule ought not to contradict another. In a system of rules, rationality had none of the transcendent quality of "right reason." Instead, rationality was equivalent to consistency or non-contradiction.

The Hobbesian laws of nature were drawn up to guide the member in his role as a rule-observer: they constituted a kind of digest of the rules or "axioms" of conduct appropriate to those who were members of a system of agreements. The first and "fundamental" law of nature dictated that men should seek peace, since peace formed the end of the system of rules. Other laws of nature prescribed the types of "civil manners" which would promote peaceful behavior. For example, men must not only fulfill their promises to abide by the rules, but each "ought to strive to accommodate himself to the rest" and not seek revenge or engage in actions which might provoke others into breaking the rules.[72] The code of civility, with its attendant virtues of equity, justice, temperance, and prudence, was not essentially bourgeois or even anti-aristocratic, as has sometimes been claimed. It was a code of virtues in a narrowly political sense. Its aim was to fashion governable men, men whose goodness was politically relevant only insofar as it affected their role as rule-observers. As Hobbes recognized, a system of rules is non-regenerative. A player does not obey the rules in the expectation that this will make him a good man or even a good player. Observance of the rules thus becomes a kind of tautology in behavior. To want to play tennis, for example, means that we want to engage in a form of activity defined by the rules of tennis. This is comparable to being a member of Hobbesian society, for in both cases one agrees to abide by a system of rules.[73] But the rules were not designed to make Hobbesian men moral in any sense except in a tautologically political one. The nature of rules, in this respect, formed a striking parallel to Hobbes's theory of truth as a linguistic property. Rules, too, were not intended to disclose the "nature of things" or the substance of morality, but only to prescribe how men ought to act within a system of rules. Consistent with the limited end of the system, enforcement of the rules was aimed at educating not the whole man but only a facet. Punishment sought only to instill a greater sense of rule-consciousness in the members, that is, it aimed to insure that a proscribed type of behavior would not be repeated and that in the future the offender would be more inclined to follow the official regulations.[74]

A system of rules, as Hobbes recognized, was self-contained: an infraction, for example, is not to be judged by standards drawn from other types of activity. This is what Hobbes meant when he identified "good" and "bad" with the definitions of the legal rules. Admittedly this introduced some confusion and much alarm, and he would have been on safer ground had he followed consistently the terminology of "observance," i.e., obedience, and "non-observance," i.e., disobedience. For it is obvious that the observance of rules did not hinge on the goodness defined by the rules, but rather on the status of the participants.

At the same time that a body of rules represented a closed system, its scope was not coextensive with the whole range of possible human activities. The rules of a card game are operative only on those who choose to play the game; and when they are not playing they cease to be bound by them. Similarly, the laws and agreements of Hobbesian society were meant to cover only a certain selected range of activity and to leave substantial areas open to individual discretion. "In all kinds of actions by the laws pretermitted, men have the liberty, of doing what their reasons shall suggest, for the most profitable to themselves." [75] It is easy to see here much that foreshadows the early nineteenth-century liberal theory of the free society. The relationship between Hobbes and the early liberals can be traced by examining the way in which he attempted to use the idea of a system of rules to reconcile two of the major postulates of liberalism, the interest-motivated individual and the idea of equality. If "every man by nature seeketh his own benefit and promotion," and if, at the same time, "men that think themselves equal will not enter into conditions of peace, but upon equal terms," how was it possible to accommodate these two seemingly conflicting demands?

Hobbes's solution was both ingenious and far-reaching in its implications. As noted earlier, when each individual consented to becoming a member of a system of rules, he was guaranteed a basic equality with every other member. This idea was embodied in Hobbes's second law of nature which prescribed that each man ought to "be contented with so much liberty against other men, as he would allow other men against himself." [76] This meant that one man could not possess any more rights than another, and it also entailed that each was to be treated equally by the system of rules to which each was equally subject. This was similar to the rules of a game: one player may perform a different role from another within the game, but each has the same rights in relation to the rules. In this vein Hobbes warned the sovereign that in such matters as dispensing justice and levying taxes there must be equality of treatment; men come to believe justice is "but a vain word" when they see

> how in all places, and in all ages, unjust actions have been authorized by the force, and victories of those who have committed them; and that potent men, breaking through the cob-web laws of their country, the weaker sort, and those who have failed in their enterprises, have been esteemed the only criminals . . .[77]

But this does not exhaust the complications of equality, for it still had to be reconciled with the inequalities produced by the relatively unhampered pursuit of interest. Hobbes recognized that the inequalities of wealth, social status, education and the like had often led to protests of social injustice. In other words, social inequality in the past had been criticized on the grounds of justice, not equality. What Hobbes did was to eliminate this possibility by proceeding to absorb the notion of justice into that of equality: ". . . justice is a certain equality, as consisting in this only; that since we are all equal by nature, one should not arrogate more right to himself, than he grants to another, unless he have fairly gotten it by compact." [78] In addition to associating justice with equality of rights, the two ideas were fused in still another sense. Justice also meant keeping one's promises, especially the promise contained in the original covenant.[79] In Hobbes's interpretation, the person who conciously sought to avoid performing his promises did so in the hope of gaining an advantage over those who considered themselves bound to the agreements; that is, he sought an unequal status.[80]

As an operative principle within a system of rules, justice thus had come to mean equality of rights and equality of treatment. In other words, justice was equated with "fairness." But this raised the question of how egotists could be expected to act fairly towards each other. Hobbes's answer was that the cardinal principle to be observed by the members was "do not that to others, you would not have done to yourself." Fairness, then, did not demand that the individual forsake egotism but only that he imaginatively substitute others for himself. A more difficult question arose in connection with the behavior of those who had been officially authorized to arbitrate disputes. If a judge, for example, were to adhere to the principle of fairness binding on private members he would necessarily favor one party over the other; that is, he would treat one party as he would himself. Hobbes perceived the difficulty and sought to overcome it by establishing criteria of neutrality: the judge's personal interest ought not to be involved in the decision in any way; and he ought not to bear favoritism or malice towards any of the parties. A just or fair decision could not be judged by any objective standard of reason or justice, but was instead merely a decision lacking in bias.[81]

Obviously these criteria do not advance much of a solution, for even assuming they are fulfilled, the fact remains that a judge, or any public official in a comparable position, cannot avoid rendering a decision which will favor one interest over another. Hobbes's difficulty originated in an overly simple view of adjudication as involving questions of ownership or of infraction of a rule. In actuality, the most difficult cases occur when a tribunal has the responsibility for interpreting public policies. The question of a "fair" railroad rate is not of the same order as a question of breach of contract or theft. Nevertheless, it is difficult to see how the modern solution of making a tribunal representative of the interests involved is superior. A tribunal composed of a representative of the trade unions, of business management, and of some group called the "public" surrenders the Hobbesian criteria of neutrality and replaces it by the notion that a fair decision is one to which the interested parties have agreed. The special difficulties of this solution are that it is apt to produce decisions which merely register the effective power of the interests involved, or which reflect the limits of society's tolerance; that is, how much an interest can get without provoking a hostile reaction.

The idea that justice is identical with fairness and equality has become part of the ideology of liberalism, and we see it reflected in such phrases as "equal opportunity," "fair trade," and "fair trial." Their substance had been summarized in Hobbes's remark that freedom was "nothing but the honour of equality of favour with the other subjects." [82] Thus what Hobbes had established and what liberalism had accepted was a strictly political definition of equality: it was, significantly, a socialist party which called for "fair shares" of economic goods. The equality of the Hobbesian citizen pertained only to his status as member; that is, to the relationship he had with the system of public rules. This meant that the range of inequalities arising from sources other than the rules was not relevant to the "political" status of the member. And given the fact that Hobbes believed that many types of human activity were politically irrelevant, it is difficult to depict him as a forerunner of totalitarianism.

There were, however, some far-reaching political implications in the notion that fairness consisted of treating different individuals in the same way. It takes the sting out of equality and makes it a welcome requirement of administration. It is always far simpler to govern by uniform rules. In viewing political society as a system of rules, Hobbes had come upon the point that Colbert was soon to convert into a guiding principle of administration and de Tocqueville later made famous in his study of pre-revolutionary France: namely, that the task of a centralized, bureaucratic state is facilitated if it can deal in uniformities rather than in individual differences. For when men are treated with uniform fairness, the problem of what is an unjust act becomes admirably simple: it is a discriminatory act which provokes "indignation in the multitude." [83]

At the same time, the logical corollary to equal rights and equal treatment was equal subjection and dependence. "In every commonwealth where particular men are deprived of their right to protect themselves, there resideth an absolute sovereignty." [84] The citizen had thus become synonymous with the subject, and when this was combined with an animus against the rich and the noble, we have the first clear expression of the idea of a classless *political* society.[85] This was tersely put in one of the marginal summaries to the eighteenth chapter of *Leviathan*: "The power and honour of subjects vanisheth in the presence of the power sovereign." [86]

This emphasis upon "complaisance" — "that every man strive to accommodate himself to the rest" — should give pause to those who have interpreted Hobbesian society in exaggerated atomistic terms. When society has become a loose collection of discrete individuals, each enjoying a public status of equality, the end result is not an extreme individualism but conformity. Men "become at last weary of irregular jostling, and hewing one another, and desire with all their hearts, to conform themselves into one firm and lasting edifice." Once "the rude and cumbersome points of their present greatness" have been "taken off," the common denominator of social uniformity is ready for exploitation.[87]

. . . We may consider that there is in men's aptness to society, a diversity of nature, rising from the diversity of affections; not unlike to that we see in stones brought together for building of an edifice. For as that stone which by the asperity, and irregularity of figure, takes more room for others, than itself fills; and for the hardness, cannot easily be made plain, and thereby hindereth the building, is by the builders cast away as unprofitable, and troublesome; so also, a man that by asperity of nature, will strive to retain those things which to himself are superfluous, and to others necessary; and for the stubbornness of his passions, cannot be corrected, is to be left, or cast out of society, as cumbersome thereunto.[88]

Visible in the mirror of Hobbesian society is the faint profile of de Tocqueville's America.

VII Power without community.
For all of its fruitfulness, the conception of political society as a system of rules was inadequate. It rested upon the fallacy of believing that the essential problems of politics could be reduced to ones involving the interpretation of rules, the determination of infractions, and finality of judgment. As we have noted earlier, political decision-making is rendered difficult because of its having to deal with conflicting yet legitimate claims. The complexities are further compounded by the scarcity of goods which are to be distributed and by the relative value which they bear. Given the nature of politics, political action is a much subtler process than Hobbes allowed. It was all very well to talk of the sovereign as *non est potestas super terram quae comparetur ei*, but the issue which must be examined is whether his terrifying power was confined within the domain of an artificial, linguistically determined system of signs and definitions. If it is granted that the nature of politics is not exhausted by the conception of a system of rules, the pertinent query is whether the power of the sovereign would be effective in dealing with the kinds of issues insoluble by the logic of rules. Confessedly the master inside his realm of logic, what is the sovereign's power outside, where the writ of consistency and non-contradiction is irrelevant?

Hobbes was driven to rest his sovereign's power on the narrow foundation of logic because of certain basic assumptions incorporated into his theory as a whole, and it was these which served also to undercut the political, as distinguished from the logical, power of the sovereign. The first assumption had to do with Hobbes's conception of man as an apolitical being who "is made fit for society not by nature, but by education." [89] Although man might undergo a continual schooling in the rudiments of civility, this in no way transformed him into a social animal. Even as a member of society, he retained his particularity, because society itself was the product of an explicit agreement between individuals whose commonalty resided solely in each having made the same choice. An isolated instance of agreement, however, could not fuse them into a common identity or corporate unity, because political alienation had been perpetuated into society. The "mutual and common fear" infecting man's relationships in the state of nature, and destroying any sense of fellowship, was retained. Now, however, the object of fear was institutionalized in the sovereign.[90] Society did not mark the abolition of fear, but the displacement of a generally diffused fear by a determinate one.

The whole point of social arrangements was to demand as little as possible in the way of a qualitative transformation of man. As Hobbes insisted, "the fault is not in men, as they are the *matter*; but as they are the *makers* and orderers" of commonwealths.[91] Where the Christian tradition had insisted that because the "matter" had been faulty from the start, the "makers" would be imperfect, Hobbes accepted man's nature, but contended that an "infallible" political knowledge would improve man as a maker — but without improving man. The political order, for all of its compelling necessity, remained an alien presence, limited to playing upon the "outside" of man. For man himself was a "public" bit of matter in motion, a being whose "inside" was no different from the universe "outside." Political power operated externally to man, because man was all externality.

As we have already noted in the case of Machiavelli, the "political" had come to be associated with the exterior, "public" side of man, and here again Hobbes deepened the revolution in thought. This is borne out in Hobbes's treatment of religion. Machiavelli, for all of his scepticism and anti-clericalism, had still believed that the primitive vitality of Christianity could be recaptured and converted to a source of political strength. But Hobbes, writing from the bitter experience of sectarian controversy, could see religion only as a potential source of political disunity, an area to be controlled rather than exploited. Superficially, the religious role allotted the Hobbesian sovereign seemed despotic in the extreme. He was the "supreme pastor" and "sovereign prophet" with full power over doctrine, ritual, and ecclesiastical personnel. Moreover, his subjects had surrendered their claims to private judgment and private conscience, hence he became the embodiment of the "public conscience." [92] Yet the political potentialities inherent in this role went untapped. Earlier writers had nearly all agreed that religion might contribute to political unity, only if it were internalized as a basic determinant of human thought and action. This was lost on Hobbes because he was incapable of appreciating religion on any other plane than the political: "seeing a commonwealth is but one person, it ought also to exhibit to God but one worship." [93] The result was to convert religion from a substantive principle, invading the deepest intimacies of human life, to a formal principle of external conformity, affecting only public behavior and penetrating not at all into the inner preserve of the mind:

> . . . By the captivity of our understanding [in religious matters] is not meant the submission of the intellectual faculty to the opinion of any other man; but of the will to obedience, where obedience is due. For sense, memory, understanding, reason and opinion are not in our power to change.[94]

A sovereign, then, might awe men to obedience but "belief and unbelief never follow men's commands." [95] Thus Hobbes arrived at a position similar to the Lutheran notion of "Christian liberty" that coercion could not affect internal belief. Yet this was at the cost of surrendering a powerful support for the political order. In religion, as in other aspects of his politics, Hobbes's guiding assumption was that a political order required no more than an outward set of "civil manners": it did not exact a conformity of souls.

All of these considerations point to the fact that the Hobbesian political order was not regenerative. It did not seek to fashion a "new man" nor did it demand that men purge their old natures. It sought, instead, to exploit man as he was and to promise him the assured satisfaction of his desires if he would agree to accepting certain limits on them. Hobbesian society had been charged not with overcoming particularity but with guaranteeing it. The individual's natural desires were not evil, as the Christians had held, nor did they need the discipline of reason, as the classical writers had declared. The trouble with natural desires was that they were self-defeating, because "many men at the same time have an appetite to the same thing." [96] L'enfer c'est d'autrui. The function of the political order was to satisfy particular claims by protecting each man in his acquisitions. This was but to drive alienation deeper by formalizing into a system the definition of happiness which already divided each man from his fellows: ". . . this race we must suppose to have no other goal, nor other garland, but being foremost." [97]

Calculating, egotistic, and alone even in society, Hobbesian man was poor political matter from which to generate the dynamics of power. He lacked the basic element which writers from Plato to Machiavelli had never neglected and Rousseau was to rediscover: that the stuff of power was not to be found in the passively acquiescent subject but in the "engaged" citizen, the citizen with a capacity for public involvement and an ability to identify himself with his governors through active support. When viewed in the perspective of political thought, the startling aspect in Hobbes's theory of sovereignty was its belief that from a society of disconnected singulars effective political power could be generated. This assumption grew out of a view of power as the product of a system of dependencies established when men agreed to surrender their right to self-protection in exchange for the protection enforced by the sovereign. "A *body politic* or civil society . . . may be defined to be a multitude of men, united as one person by a common power, for their common peace, defence, and benefit." [98] Thus a political "union" had been effected because power was now concentrated instead of diffused among several centers. By identifying "union" with the dependency of isolated individuals and with the existence of a single, determinate will, Hobbes convinced himself that he had created a power so mighty that, in its absence, society had no existence. "The sovereignty is the soul of the commonwealth; which once departed from the body, the members do no more receive their motion from it." [99] Although this language was strongly reminiscent of ancient and mediaeval ideas of rulership as a life-giving force, an *élan vital,* which sustained the body politic, there was also one crucial difference: the Hobbesian sovereign stood outside his society, an Archimedes without any real leverage except that supplied by fear. His power lacked the sustaining support of society, because society itself was but a loose collection of discrete individuals.

It was this picture of an isolated sovereign, ruling a society which lacked the attributes of community, that Hobbes defended against the papal writer, Cardinal Bellarmine. Bellarmine's error, Hobbes argued, "is that he says the members of every commonwealth, as of a natural body, depend one of another." Hobbes clearly sensed the drift of the mediaeval analogy. An organic body implied a close-knit interdependence among the members, an integrated structure of different but connected powers. Hence while a distinct power of direction was assigned the ruler, his effectiveness depended on the ability to elicit other forms of power to support his own. Hobbes countered this by his own analogy which pictured the body politic as a purely mechanical contraption with its springs and gears visible to an embarrassing degree.[100] The contrived nature of society excluded any natural dependency among the members. A political machine, by definition, was devoid of any subtle connective tissue of needs and affections which blended the parts into an organic whole. "It is true," he concluded against Bellarmine, that men "cohere together; but they depend only on the sovereign, which is the soul of the commonwealth; which failing, the commonwealth is dissolved into a civil war, no one man so much as cohering to another for want of a common dependence on a known sovereign; just as the members of the natural body dissolve into the earth, for want of a soul to hold them together." [101]

Some measure of what had been lost by this approach can be understood by comparing it with the idea of power as illustrated by an extract from a statute of Henry VIII where a claim to absolutism, fully as extensive as that of any Hobbesian sovereign, was couched in the language of corporate solidarity:

> Where by divers sundry old authentic histories and chronicles, it is manifestly declared and expressed, that this realm of England is an empire . . . governed by one supreme head and king, having the dignity and the estate of the imperial crown of the same, unto whom a body politic, compact of all sorts and degrees of people, divided in terms, and by names of spirituality and temporality, be bounden and ought to bear, next to God, a natural and humble obedience: he being also institute and furnished . . . with plenary, whole, and entire power, pre-eminence, authority, prerogative and jurisdiction, to render and yield justice to all manner of folk, residents, or subjects within his realm, in all causes, matters, debates, and contentions . . .[102]

The difference between the Hobbesian and Tudor conceptions of the relationship between sovereign power and the community might be compared to Coleridge's distinction between the imagination which merely joins and the imagination which truly fuses; that is, between a sovereign who presides over a society whose unity was no more deeply etched than billiard balls within a triangular frame and, on the other hand, a ruler governing a society so engrained with a continuing cohesion that, as Hooker had said, "we were then alive in our predecessors, and they in their successors do live still." [103]

There were some signs that Hobbes realized his undifferentiated community was a feeble prop for power, and his desperate attempt to bring a closer intimacy between subject and sovereign was visible in the oddly sacramental tones coloring some of his language. Thus he spoke of the sovereign will as one "whereof is included and involved the will of every one in particular"; and that the sovereign will "contains" the will of all citizens so that his power was compounded "of the forces of all the citizens together." In another place he described the creation of political society as a process by which men "have grown together into a civil person." [104] Yet this strangely unnominalistic language could not overcome the artificial quality of an agreement among individuals unable to surrender the hard nucleus of their particularity: a contract may establish relationships, but it is not a source of unity nor the expression of commonalty. This was why the Hobbesian sovereign had to be "authorized" to act: he could not "represent" a community for there was none to represent except at the most elemental level of fear and insecurity. And because the Hobbesian community had surrendered its unity, unity must now be located with the unified will of the sovereign. Western political theory had to await Rousseau who undertook to join what Hobbes had carefully separated: Rousseau revived the older notion of a community as a corporate fellowship and then endowed it with the unity of will associated with the Hobbesian sovereign; community and public will were one.

VIII

Interests and representation. The second broad principle decisively influencing the nature of sovereign power was the concept of "interests." It was this element, Hobbes believed, which united the members of any human association.[105] By placing interest at the center of the political association Hobbes continued the theme begun earlier by Machiavelli. To elevate interest was to single out what was essentially private and least capable of representation at a public level. And to insist on the "rationality" of individual interest was to redefine reason so that its public, general character was lost. Reason was then easily transformed into an agency of personal subjectivism: "For the thoughts are to the desires, as scouts, and spies, to range abroad, and find the way to the things desired."[106] However, it was not the rational status of interests alone that set the basic problem, but rather their radically individual, unceasingly dynamic, and fundamentally unsharable nature. These attributes of interest were rooted in the psychology of Hobbesian man. While the nature of passion and thought remained the same for all men, the objects at which they aimed were different due to variations in the "constitution" and education of each individual. The result was wide disagreement among men, because their preferences were dictated by passions for different objects or by different valuations of the same object. "Good" and "bad," therefore, lacked any universal status, being merely the adjectival expression of the desires of an individual in relation to a particular object.[107] At the same time, interest introduced an essentially competitive element. It "consisteth in comparison. For if all things were equal in all men, nothing would be prized."[108] The condition of relative scarcity presupposed by the doctrine of interest bred a perpetual dynamic — "life itself is but motion" — which took the form of "a perpetual

and restless desire of power after power, that ceaseth only in death." [109] All
of these considerations culminated in Hobbes's doctrine of "felicity," which
was the definition of happiness in an age of interest:

> . . . The felicity of this life consisteth not in the repose of a mind satisfied.
> For there is no such *finis ultimus* . . . nor *summum bonum* . . . Felicity is
> the continual progress of the desire, from one object to another, the attaining
> of the former, being still but the way to the latter. The cause whereof is,
> that the object of man's desire, is not to enjoy once only, and for one instant
> of time; but to assure, the way of his future desire . . . he cannot assure the
> power and means to live well, which he hath present, without the acquisition
> of more . . .[110]

The formula of power, then, had to be adapted to an age where man was
alienated from the ways of society and where man's aspirations were defined in terms of a good that was insatiable, forever unattainable, and divisive
in its nature. Power now had to be exercised in a society where the possibility
of a sharable good had been denied, where, in other words, the older idea
of a "fused" community — produced by love, or emotion, or knowledge —
was no longer entertained. Power had shed the older legitimizing idea of a
common good, for in a political universe of disconnected particulars a "common" good had no meaning. Nor could Hobbes fall back on the traditional
notion that authority might be made the embodiment of reason; as we have
seen, reason had ceased to mean a comprehensive principle whereby particulars could be integrated and harmonized, and, instead, had itself been yoked
to particularity. The formula of legitimacy which Hobbes finally developed
was embodied in the idea of a "sovereign representative." [111]

In modern democratic theories representation has come to have a variety
of meanings. Sometimes it refers to the nature of the group empowered to
take decisions: hence we might speak of "a representative committee" or legislature. Or representation, in a very loose sense, may be associated with a
method of choosing officials: thus we might say "a wide variety of opinions
was represented at the polls." Finally, the representative element might be
located not in a process but in the substance of the decision itself, meaning
that more than one point of view or interest has been incorporated into the
decision. The common factor in all of these definitions, however, is the notion that political arrangements ought to reflect the variety of interests present
in society. It was this idea of representation which Hobbes explicitly rejected
on the grounds that a variety of interests could be represented only in the
form of a variety of wills. Several wills aiming at different and often con-

flicting ends could not issue in a political act, because the essence of public action lay in its single and unequivocal character:[112]

> A multitude of men, are made *one* person, when they are by one man, or one person represented; so that it be done with the consent of every one of that multitude in particular. For it is the *unity* of the representer, not the *unity* of the represented, that maketh the person *one* . . .[113]

In this definition the essence of representation was a procedure of authorization which reflected the radical doctrine of interests in Hobbes's theory. The covenant signified an agreement of "every one with every one" to obey a "common" authority. The sovereign, however, did not denote a medium for representing the interests of the parties to the agreement; this was patently impossible because of the divisive nature of all interests excepting that of peace. Instead, the sovereign's representativeness consisted entirely of a fiction: he was authorized to act in the name of the society because each had agreed to "own and be reputed author" of all the sovereign's decisions. But it was a fiction cut to fit the specifications of Hobbesian man. The only possible way that authority could be legitimized in a society of egotists was for each citizen to accept the commands of the sovereign "as if" they were his own: "every particular man is author of all the sovereign doth." It was this that makes the sovereign "their common representer." [114]

But what guarantee was there that the sovereign would be truly representative and seek the interests of his subjects? While in several passages Hobbes had insisted that the sovereign had a "duty" to promote the advantage of the members, this could only mean that he had an interest in doing so. The Hobbesian theory excluded any other definition of duty.[115] This led Hobbes to conclude that there could be no genuine conflict between the interests of sovereign and subject, because it was in the interest of the sovereign to have prosperous, contented, and "lusty" citizens.[116] Like his subjects, the sovereign sought his own good; that is, his actions too were essentially private acts aimed at a particular end, but by the alchemy of his position they were transmuted into public and general acts, redounding to the good of his subjects and, *ipso facto,* himself. This was the same theory of representation adopted by the early Utilitarians, the only change being the substitution of the middle-classes for the sovereign.[117] Both Hobbes and the Utilitarians shared the naïve assumption that, in a society of egotists, all that was needed to erase the conflict between public and private ends was the creation of a public, institutionalized ego.

The transformation of authority into a public ego, of society into a loose collection of individuals equal in rights, secured in their possessions, and officially encouraged to seek their particular interests, marked a revolutionary change in the conception of politics. It was not merely that politics was conceived as an activity instrumental to the attainment of interests; this had always been an important element in Western political thought. Rather the crucial change lay in the view that politics was significant only insofar as it impinged upon men's interests. To the extent that politics did not appear vitally linked to interest, it held no compelling attraction. What is our grievance, Hobbes querulously demanded, if most of the citizens in a monarchy were denied "a hand in public business"?

> I will tell you: to see his opinion, whom we scorn, preferred before ours; to have our wisdom undervalued before our own faces; by an uncertain trial of a little vain glory, to undergo most certain enmities . . . to hate and to be hated . . . to lay open our secret councils and advices to all, to no purpose, and without any benefit; to neglect the affairs of our own family: these, I say are grievances.[118]

In the Hobbesian aversion to politics and the apathy towards political participation there was something of the mentality of Fallada's *kleiner Mann*: the little man who rejoiced when the proud and mighty were humbled; who applauded when the power of the wealthy was curbed; who seriously argued the superiority of monarchy over other forms of government because it was less expensive; who watched without complaint the growing distance between subject and sovereign, resentful only when the sovereign failed to maintain the equality between citizens; and who soothed his own political impotency with the thought that:

> Whosoever therefore in a monarchy will lead a retired life, let him be what he will that reigns, he is out of danger. For the ambitious only suffer; the rest are protected from the injuries of the more potent.[119]

What we have mirrored here was the emergence of economic interest in full competition with political participation. But once interest had achieved a supreme position, politics fell into decline. On its side, interest presented a compellingly immediate and intimate quality, a tangible projection of the self — "something that is his own" — which was later given classic expression in Locke's theory of property. Politics, on the other hand, seemed remote and abstract, incapable of evoking a feeling of personal involvement. Adam Smith assured his readers that "we may often fulfil all the rules of justice by sitting still and doing nothing."[120] The effect of this line of argument was to destroy the distinctive identity of the "political," by merging it with interest. The reduction of politics to interest has cast a powerful shadow on modern politics:

one need only pick up a newspaper and read of this or that politician, administrator, or judge removing himself from a particular controversy because of a "conflict of interests." It fell to modern liberalism to give the fullest, and perhaps the crudest expression of this line of thought: "the principle on which public institutions ought to be formed," Bentham declared, is that an office-holder can be expected to subordinate office to personal advantage. Yet this presents no cause for alarm, at least not to the innocent, because when the principle "is applied to all men universally, it is injurious to none." What is significant is the implicit assumption that a political office is itself an "interest" exactly on the same level as any other kind of interest. "It is only by the magnitude of the scale that public trusts differ from private trusts." [121] Apparently the suggestion is no longer seriously entertained that there is a peculiar dignity or status to public office which exacts an obligation transcending the personal interest of the occupant. The epitaph to the majesty of the political was supplied by Bentham:

> It is to the interest of the public that the portion of respect which, along with the salary, is habitually attached to any office should be as small as possible.[122]

The declining significance of the political contains a clue to the political apathy of the middle-classes. It was epitomized in the nineteenth-century French liberal, Benjamin Constant. In the essay, *De la liberté des anciens comparée à celle des modernes,* he argued that, unlike the citizen of the ancient *polis,* the modern citizen could no longer find any enjoyment in "the active and constant participation in collective power." In the classical city "the will of each had a real influence" which gave rise to a "lively and continuous pleasure" in participation. For the modern citizen, however, political activity was in the nature of an "abstract supposition." "Lost in the multitude, the individual rarely perceives the influence that he exercises," and hence is content with "the peaceful enjoyment of private independence," asking only that he be protected by legal rights from physical injury, that his privacy be respected, and his property safe. The epitaph of the political community was that "individual existence has little embodiment in political existence." [123]

IX Politics as a field of forces. The eclipse of the notion of community was expressed by Hobbes in a form of political imagery inspired by the categories of geometry and physics. This imagery is well worth examining in some detail, not only because it reveals how deeply scientific modes of thought had permeated his political philosophy,[124] but, more important, because the Hobbesian model of society was implicitly adopted by the liberalism of the next two centuries as its own and accepted by conservatives, such as Burke, de Maistre, and Hegel, as the target of their attacks. The imagery was inspired by a picture of man as a bundle of potential energy or "power." As body, man was "power nutritive, power motive, and power generative"; as mind he possessed "power conceptive" and "power motive." [125] These powers were manifested through two forms of "motion": "vital" motion, which referred to the continuous, involuntary motions of the body needed to sustain life, and the other "animal" or "voluntary" motion which covered those acts "first fancied in our minds." [126] It was this latter class of "animal motions" which most concerned Hobbes. Drawing on Galileo's principles he argued that men were set in motion only by some external force or push:

> That, whereto nothing is added, and from which nothing is taken, remains in the same state it was. That which is no way touch'd by another, hath nothing added to nor taken from it.[127]

The response of a body to external stimuli took the form either of "attraction" or "repulsion," or in words more appropriate to man, "appetite" and "aversion." Appetite represented motion towards some object, aversion motion away from some object. These two basic responses were not only descriptive of human behavior, but also the source of human values: "whatsoever is the object of any man's appetite or desire, that is it which he for his part calleth *good*: and the object of his hate and aversion *evil*; and of his contempt, *vile* and *inconsiderable*." [128] Due to the press of his desires, man was always in motion, striving for honor, pre-eminence, and "felicity": "while we live, we have desires and desire presupposeth a farther end . . . there can be no contentment but in proceeding . . ." [129]

What was odd in this picture of man was that desire was almost completely severed from the conditioning of class or social status. Consequently, each individual appeared as an atom, somewhat different in composition but having the same general appearance, hurtling across a flat social plane; that is, a landscape without any visible contours of social distinctions to bar his path or predetermine his line of motion. Yet the "power" of an individual's motion, his rate of acceleration so to speak, obviously presupposed various types of social distinctions or what Hobbes called "instrumental" powers, such as wealth, reputation, influential friends, knowledge, and, with very brief mention by Hobbes, aristocratic privileges.[130] In this "field" of forces in motion the lines of action pursued by individuals frequently collided; "equal powers opposed, destroy one another; and such their opposition is called contention." But these intersecting motions also pointed to the location of true power in society: "And because the power of one man resisteth and hindereth the effects of the power of another: power is simply no more, but the excess of the power of one above that of another." [131] The problem that then must be faced was this: in a context where human motions whirled across a social plane, what kind of power did the Hobbesian sovereign possess? what was implied when the sovereign undertook political action?

Once again Hobbes seemed to leave no doubt that his sovereign was intended to have an impressive concentration of power at his disposal:

> The greatest of human powers, is that which is compounded of the power of most men, united by consent, in one person . . . that has the use of all their powers depending on his will . . .[132]

But what did Hobbes mean here by "compounded"? He admitted that, strictly speaking, "it is impossible for any man really to transfer his own strength to another, or for that other to receive it." [133] Rejecting the view that power was formed from little parcels of individual power deposited with the sovereign, Hobbes turned once more to the image of society as a "field" of forces. Political power was construed as a form of public motion and, like all forms of motion, its effectiveness depended upon the absence of impediments. The exercise of power required nothing more than the clearing of a path among the private motions infesting political space. The purpose of the covenant, therefore, was to elicit from the members an acknowledgment of the sovereign's right of way. By the terms of the agreement, the individuals agreed to will *not* to act, thereby clearing the way for the will of one "artificial person." In the terminology of the covenant, they "renounce" or "transfer" to the sovereign their absolute natural right to protect themselves, and in so doing they abdicate the "field" of action by withdrawing their wills. The extraordinarily negative character of power was underlined in Hobbes's definition of what is meant by a person "laying down" his right:

> [It] is to *divest* himself of the *liberty*, of hindering another of the benefit of his own right to the same. For he that renounceth, or passeth away his right, giveth not to any other man a right which he had not before, because there is nothing to which every man had not right by nature: but only standeth out of his way that he may enjoy his own original right, without hindrance from him . . .[134]

Thus despite the proud boast that Leviathan would be the "greatest of human powers," it was apparent that sovereign power did not signify creation *ex nihilo* but the enjoyment of an old condition; the sovereign retained the original right enjoyed by all men in the state of nature, and whereas his subjects had surrendered this right in order to escape the state of nature *vis-à-vis* each other, the sovereign remained in that condition in his relations with them. The universality of a right to all things was thus perpetuated, but now particularized in one sovereign person or group:

> For the subject did not give the sovereign that right; but only in laying down theirs, strenghtened him to use his own, as he should think fit, for the preservation of them all: so that it was not given, but left to him . . . as entire as in the condition of mere nature . . .[135]

In this definition political action was the capacity to act without being resisted, and its success was contingent upon the subject's promise not to act. When this is cast into the language of appetite and aversion, the actions occurring on the plane of political space take on a certain rhythm. The sovereign represented the movement of the "public appetite and will" towards some objective, but his appetite, in turn, aroused fear or aversion among the subjects, causing them to withdraw so that his appetite might become effective. But the rhythm of movement towards and movement away did not affect the whole of political space, because, as we have seen, there were many areas in which Hobbes believed that men might best be left to their own resources. Hence it was only where the sovereign felt it necessary to pre-empt a specific domain that the rhythm would be reasserted. And the rhythm would be sustained as long as the sovereign did not touch the raw nerve of self-preservation and force the subject to lash back to protect himself.

These same categories of space and motion reappeared in the relationships between subjects. The ever-present possibility of conflicts between private lines of motion was to be solved through the sovereign power to enact laws.

> The use of laws, which are but rules authorized, is not to bind the people from all voluntary actions; but to direct and keep them in such a motion, as not to hurt themselves by their own impetuous desires, rashness or indiscretion; as hedges are set, not to stop travellers, but to keep them in their way.[136]

The function of legal regulations was to prescribe the legitimate lanes of action in political space which private persons could pre-empt. "Every man hath more or less liberty, as he hath more or less space in which he employs himself." [137] In the case of a subject who possessed a legal right this was equivalent to granting him access to some object. This constituted freedom which Hobbes defined as "the absence of opposition" or of "external impediments to motion." At the same time, the right of one subject automatically barred the path of another to the same object; that is, hindered his motion or freedom.[138] Thus the appetite of one subject becomes realizable because the sanction of the law has inspired aversion or withdrawal on the part of the other individuals.

In the last analysis, the Hobbesian conception of political power was a grossly oversimplified, even hollow, one. The power to act required only the elimination of hindrances rather than the active enlistment of the private power and support of the citizens. The citizens had simply to stand aside and not interfere. If sovereign power were effective because it induced withdrawal, how could the soverign ever hope to join his subjects' wills to his in the pursuit of a common endeavor? Hobbes tried to meet this objection by arguing that when the subject transferred his right to the sovereign he simultaneously transferred "the means of enjoying it, as far as lieth in his power."[139] This empowered the sovereign to "use all the power and faculties of each particular person to the maintenance of peace, and for common defence."[140] Yet when we search for examples of what is meant by transferring the means of enjoyment, we are presented only with negative instances. Thus the man who transferred his land-title to another was obligated to leave "whatsoever grows upon it"; the person who sells his right to a mill must not seek to divert the stream which drives it; and, finally, the householder who sells his title must not bar occupancy.[141] In the light of these examples, the assertion that the sovereign "hath the use of so much power and strength conferred on him, that by terror thereof, he is enabled to form the wills of them all" seems almost a *non sequitur*. It was his contemporary, James Harrington, who most acutely sensed the weakness of the Hobbesian sovereign and pointed out the fatal contradiction. On the one side, Hobbes had allowed that property constituted a form of power and that, therefore, aggregates of private property were consolidations of private power. On the other hand, he stubbornly insisted that "it is men, and arms, not words, and promises, that make the force and power of the laws."[142] But, as Harrington pointed out, this ignored the fact that the effective force of the sovereign was crucially dependent on the support of private power. Therefore, as long as power was dispersed in private hands, the covenant remained but "words and breath," a "toy." A sovereign who sought to overawe the wealthy by waving the sword conjured up the picture, not of mighty Leviathan, but of a "mere spitfrog."[143]

NINE

Liberalism

and the Decline of Political Philosophy

. . . The rich have feelings, if I can put it this way, in every part of their possessions . . .

ROUSSEAU

Much is won if we succeed in transforming hysterical misery into common unhappiness.

FREUD

I **The political and the social.** If we were to imagine two intelligent readers of Hobbes, each equally distant from him in time, the first representing the middle of the fifteenth century, the other the middle of the nineteenth, we would naturally expect each to make radically different criticisms on some points, but we might be less prepared to find them agreeing on others. Our fifteenth-century reader would be shocked by Hobbe's sardonic treatment of religion and the ruthless way he divested political philosophy of all traces of religious thought and feeling. The nineteenth-century man, surveying Hobbes from the vantage point of Marx and the classical economists, would pronounce him utterly lacking in any understanding of the influence of economic factors upon politics.[1] Both criticisms would add up to the conclusion that Hobbes had achieved a "pure" political theory by sloughing off religious elements while remaining innocent of economics.

Nevertheless, this does not constitute the full significance of what Hobbes had done, nor exhaust the criticisms of our two imaginary readers. Despite the gap of several centuries, and the different idioms of expression, they would have agreed that Hobbes had failed to grasp the interconnections between social and political factors and, consequently, his postulate of a distinct political order contained a presence as ghostly as any concocted by his theologically-minded contemporaries. From the one side, the representative of the age of de Tocqueville, Comte, and Spencer would charge that Hobbes had ignored the extent to which political practices were shaped by social relationships, and hence had mistaken superstructure for foundation. In a different idiom, the spokesman of the earlier age would register the like complaint. He might say that had Hobbes been able to restrain his impulse to win debating points over the scholastics, he could have appropriated some valuable insights about the interrelations of government and society. The use of the organic metaphor by mediaeval writers had been, for all its seeming absurdity, indicative of a keen perception of social interdependencies and the functional relationship between political and economic factors. A mediaeval writer would never have allowed himself to be caught in the Hobbesian error of treating the institution of property as a simple set of juristic relations between subject and sovereign with no attention paid to the social influence of property rights.

At first glance these criticisms appear just, for Hobbes had no genuine theory of society in the same sense as either earlier or later writers. But instead of pursuing this point we might pause to ask the question it begs: why do these criticisms appear just as well as obvious? One answer is that we are so accustomed to having political problems reduced to economic causes, or the influence of class structure, social relations, or cultural conditioning, that we turn impatiently from a writer who fails to follow form. What is interesting about this sort of response is its connection with the theoretical outlook which dominates much contemporary thinking in the social sciences. The case usually advanced for the superiority of the social sciences over traditional political philosophy rests on much the same assumption as the case made against Hobbes: that political phenomena are best explained as the resultant of social factors, and hence political institutions and beliefs are best understood by a method which gets "behind" them to the "underlying" social processes which dictate the shape of things political.

Stated in these terms, the controversy between political philosophy and social science is ostensibly a methodological one involving a question which experience alone can answer. Unfortunately, many political philosophers, especially those who insist upon a close connection between politics and ethics, would reject this statement of the problem on the grounds that it commits political philosophy to a preoccupation with method at the expense of moral concerns. It might be suggested, however, that both the proponents of social science and the ethically-minded political philosopher advocate an approach which misses the same point. The issue is not solely methodological, nor even primarily ethical in character, but substantive; that is, it concerns the status of politics and the political. When modern social science asserts that political phenomena are to be explained by resolving them into socio-logical, psychological, or economic components, it is saying that there are no distinctively political phenomena and hence no special set of problems. On its face, this assertion appears to be a purely descriptive statement, devoid of evaluative overtones and therefore innocent. Actually, it is nothing of the sort. It rests upon an evaluation which remains concealed because its his-torical origins are not well understood. It is possible to view politics as a derivative form of activity, one that is to be understood in terms of more "fundamental" factors, if it is believed that the political possesses no distinc-tive significance, pertains to no unique function, and occupies no loftier plane than, say, that of any large-scale organization.

This suggests that modern social science appears plausible and useful for the same reason that modern political philosophy appears anachronistic and sterile: each is symptomatic of a condition where the sense of the political has been lost. While the one flourishes, the other flounders in uncertainty of what, if anything, constitutes its subject-matter. These developments may seem rather unimportant, involving perhaps the resettlement of a few displaced academics. It may not be far-fetched, however, to suspect a com-mon root to the philosopher's lack of any coherent notion of what is truly political and the groping failure of Western societies to sustain a belief in the importance of political activity except by appealing to a confused mix-ture of diluted religious ideas spiced with a dash of market-place virtues.

These considerations help to place Hobbes's contribution in a clearer light. Whatever his shortcomings, he shows us what we have lost in the way of a sense of the political. For Hobbes, the political in a society comprised three elements: the authority whose unique office it was to superintend the whole and to exert directive control over other forms of activity; the obligations which rested on those who accepted membership; and the system of com-mon rules governing publicly significant behavior. In a similarly unequivocal way Hobbes stated the basic task of political philosophy: to identify and define what was truly political. In this view, the function of theory was to help identify a specific type of authority and its province of activity. To identify and to define is to abstract certain characteristic roles and activities in order to subsume them under a classifying scheme. Every clasification entails limits which allow us to distinguish the subject from others. Thus in identifying that which was political, Hobbes was simultaneously delimiting its scope. This meant, for example, that political action was restricted to the kind of goods attainable through political means; other goods might exist and might even be superior, yet if they were impossible to attain through political methods, or if attainable, too costly, or too trivial, they lay outside the political province. Similarly, while political duties were of crucial concern to political philosophy and to political authority, they by no means exhausted the totality of human relationships nor rated as man's highest role. Many important areas of human activity were therefore without direct political relevance; they became the subject of political notice when their consequences threatened to disrupt the settled relationships constituting society.

But the rigorous manner in which Hobbes outlined the character of the political concealed the fragile presupposition on which the whole case rested. The identity of the political was in large measure a product of beliefs, almost an act of faith. It existed by a process of self-authentication; that is, because men believed it existed and governed their actions accordingly. This is what Hobbes meant by the "artificial" character of the political order and why he insisted that in every political system, regardless of type, the people really ruled. As Hume later said, "it is . . . on opinion only that government is founded." [2]

In calling attention to the element of belief as part of the complex of political things we are not arguing a naïve Berkeleian view that the political is purely a creature of belief having no more of reality than we choose to grant. Whether we acknowledge them or not, facts such as political power do exist; whether we entertain a conception of political membership or not, none of us can easily escape assuming certain relationships with public authorities, nor can we evade the burdens and sacrifices entailed by living in a politically organized society. Nevertheless, it remains true that however crude or sophisticated our notions on these matters, our beliefs exert an appreciable effect on the way we perceive political happenings and how we react in political settings, and these in turn are bound to affect the course of events. Given the connection subsisting between thoughts (or attitudes) and events, a markedly different alteration in perspectives on politics and the political is bound to influence the practices associated with a particular tradition. To grasp the direction of these changes may contribute in some small way to undertsanding our present predicaments. Few would contest the proposition that today Western societies exhibit little in the way of a widespread political consciousness among its members and fewer still would doubt that political things are mostly held in disrepute by the members of these societies. In concrete form, the effects of the declining status of the political can be found in the frenzied realization that political loyalty has become a problem; that a generation of soldiers, scientists, and public officials has grown up without the rudiments of an education in civility; and that we can all too easily imagine ourselves having committed the same acts of disloyalty had we been similarly situated.

These developments have been in the making for over a century and a half. The main trends in political thought, irrespective of national or ideological variations, have worked towards the same end: the erosion of the distinctively political. That which rests upon the shifting basis of belief can, by the same token, be undermined by belief. The subversion of belief is accomplished most effectively when an established notion is challenged by an idea common to a wide variety of outlooks. The basic concept which was pitted against the political was "society." It was a fundamental notion common to such contrasting ideologies as liberalism and conservatism, socialism and reaction, anarchism and managerialism. Today it serves as the focus of the social sciences, especially in sociology and anthropology, and this perhaps justifies designating social science as the legatee of an earlier controversy in which "society" displaced the political.

The rediscovery of society, which quickly became a dominant concern of post-Hobbesian thought, occurred by two somewhat different routes. One was followed by an oddly assorted group which included Montesquieu, Burke, de Maistre, Comte, and de Tocqueville. Despite many sharp disagreements they shared the viewpoint that the authority of political institutions was founded upon a myriad of social authorities and nourished by a variety of private loyalties. These elements furnished the necessary cohesives which held society together; should they be weakened, as occurred towards the end of the *ancien régime,* the political order would topple of its own weight. The focal point of inquiry, therefore, was to be directed at the system of social gradations; at the complex of non-rational "prejudices" which disposed men towards obedience and subordination; at the ties spun by local community, parish, and manor into a web of association stronger than any that conscious thought could conceive.

The second route to society, the one which will be discussed in this chapter, was followed by Locke, the classical economists, the French liberals, and the English Utilitarians. We shall try to show how the concept of society emerged in Locke's writings; how gradually society came to be conceived simultaneously as an entity distinct from political arrangements and as the shorthand symbol of all worthwhile human endeavor; and how these developments left little scope and less prestige for the political. The political became identified with a narrow set of institutions labelled "government," the harsh symbol of the coercion necessary to sustain orderly social transactions. The choice lay, as Bastiat put it, between *"société libre, gouvernement simple"* or *"société contrainte, gouvernement compliqué."* [3]

The classical economists of the eighteenth century wove these themes into an elegant and convincing system. There is no grosser caricature of these writers than the one which implies that their analyses were founded on a few simple propositions about "economic man" and that, like good metaphysicians, they always managed to "save the appearances" by falling back on the workings of an amiably conspiratorial "unseen hand." In reality their writings exhibited an abiding interest in the ways that regularized economic behavior created order in human relationships, relating them in time and space and integrating them into a rhythmic pattern without relying upon compulsion. It was this last quality, the relative absence of coercion in economic transactions, that tinted the economists' model of society with antipolitical tones and ultimately made it an alternative to the older conception of a politically directed system. This is nicely illustrated by one of their favorite notions, the division of labor. This principle, Adam Smith explained, stemmed from man's natural "propensity to truck, barter, and exchange one thing for another." By inducement rather than coercion, without invoking a general superintending authority, the division of labor drew men together in interdependency, encouraging each to develop his talents in the most socially beneficial way. The principle operated to delineate the social topography, etching in a series of functionally differentiated roles, adjusting activities one to the other, and developing routines of cooperative endeavor. Through this and similar notions the economists worked towards the elaboration of a theory of a social system; that is, an integrated series of functions whose cumulative effect seemed close to alchemy: by organizing human activity, the puny power of individuals was compounded into a huge, disciplined social power. "The social mechanism is very ingenious and very powerful . . . Each man . . . has more enjoyment in one day than he himself could produce in many ages." [4]

The offspring of this kind of theorizing was a non-political model of a society which, by virtue of being a closed system of interacting forces, seemed able to sustain its own existence without the aid of an "outside" political agency. As Adam Smith put it, no political prime mover was needed because each individual "has a principle of motion of its own." The full implications of the social system for the status of the political were stated by Smith's contemporary, David Hume: while government is useful, even necessary, "it is not necessary in all circumstances; nor is it impossible for men to preserve society for some time without having recourse to such an invention." [5]

The decline of political categories and the ascendancy of social ones are the distinguishing marks of our contemporary situation where political philosophy has been eclipsed by other forms of knowledge. In the present age we naturally turn to the sociologist or economist to supply prescriptions for society's ills. We assume that they, rather than the political theorist, possess the relevant kind of knowledge. Comte may have been premature in crowning sociology queen of the sciences — at that stage she might very well have been queen since she was hardly a subject — but today the title is less disputed. Today we have accepted as an operating assumption the claim of nineteenth-century sociology that knowledge of the social order "can scarcely fail to affect our judgments as to what is progressive and what retrograde — what is desirable, what is practicable, what is utopian." [6] When the late Karl Mannheim nominated the sociologist for the role of the new intellectual elite we may have felt uneasy but not surprised. Or when a prominent anthropologist announced that the time had come for the anthropologist to play a determining role in public policies because, compared to the political and social scientist, he could at least commit better mistakes, [7] we may be intrigued by the naïve form of the argument, but its substance we take seriously.

This state of affairs, in which political theory has become an aimless activity whose traditional role has been absorbed by cognate disciplines, is not to be explained by pointing an accusing finger at the encroachments of other disciplines, nor even in terms of some disorder internal to political theory itself, such as a failure to attain a settled methodology. We can gain a firmer purchase on the problem if we recognize that this impoverishment is common also to the wider enterprise of which political theory is a part, namely philosophy. Philosophers, too, have suffered deprivation as other forms of knowledge have, by a kind of squatter's sovereignty, come to contest and pre-empt their domain. This raises the provocative question of whether some interconnection exists between the state of philosophy and political theory on the one hand, and the character of the liberal tradition on the other. The clue to the answer lies with the pivotal figure of John Locke, for insofar as modern philosophy is oriented towards empiricism and the analysis of language, Locke is admittedly one of its founders. And to the extent that modern liberalism can be said to be inspired by any one writer, Locke is undoubtedly the leading candidate. We shall take up this suggestion shortly and try to indicate the connections between Locke's philosophy and liberalism and their resulting influence on the status and subject-matter of political theory.

In examining what the early liberals themselves had written I found myself compelled to abandon a whole set of preconceptions derived from recent commentaries. At the end I concluded that our present age has for a variety of reasons lost touch with the original temper and outlook of liberalism and hence is willing to accept at face value the vulgar caricature of liberalism offered by Marxists, romantic conservatives, "realists," and neo-orthodox theologians.[8] Liberalism has been repeatedly characterized as "optimistic" to the point of naïveté; arrogant in its conviction that human reason ought to stand as the sole authority for knowledge and action; bewitched by a vision of history as an escalator endlessly moving upwards towards greater progress; and blasphemous in endowing the human mind and will with a godlike power of refashioning man and society in entirety.

For the most part these criticisms have little or no support in the writings of the liberals. They seem plausible only because the critics have lumped together two distinct traditions of political thought: democratic radicalism and liberalism.[9] Although the former drew inspiration from Locke, its outlook was largely moulded by eighteenth-century rationalism and the experience of the French Revolution. Liberalism, on the other hand, had its roots in the period before the French Enlightenment. It, too, leaned heavily on the political principles of Locke, yet most important to its development are the later stages in which it was filtered through classical economics and exposed to the philosophies of David Hume and Adam Smith, two thinkers distinguished by a profound respect for the limits of reason and the pervasiveness of irrational factors in man and society. One of our tasks in the following pages is to disentangle this second tradition from the first and to show that liberalism was a philosophy of sobriety, born in fear, nourished by disenchantment, and prone to believe that the human condition was and was likely to remain one of pain and anxiety.

II **Liberalism and the sobrieties of philosophy.** It was remarked earlier that periods of crisis tend to awaken in political philosophers an impulse towards mastery, a belief that mind can furnish the formula for controlling the dynamics of change, and that, guided by this knowledge, political power can transform society into a community tinged by truth. But crisis can induce timidity as well, and it is this response which colored the whole development of English liberalism long before the French Revolution. We have become so accustomed to picturing liberalism as a fighting creed, outfitted for storming the ramparts of privilege, that we find it difficult to entertain the hypothesis that Lockian liberalism was fully as much a defense against radical democracy as an attack on traditionalism. In France and the United States as well, liberalism emerged as a post-revolutionary reaction. Voltaire's boast, *"Je suis grand démolisseur,"* [10] was as alien to the temperament of nineteenth-century French liberals as Rousseau's theory of popular sovereignty. In the early years of the American republic, liberal writers sought a substitute object for the patriotic and political impulses fostered by the ideas and events of the revolutionary war. The Constitution served their purpose, and they succeeded in surrounding it with a wealth of legend and symbol so that in the end the "myth" of 1789 overcame that of 1776.[11]

In the memory of Locke's generation the period of the Commonwealth and Protectorate came to symbolize the temporary triumph of radicalism — religious, social, and political. The traditional symbols of authority, as epitomized in the monarchy, the established Church, and the House of Lords, had been abolished. Repeated efforts had been made to transform the House of Commons, and a brief, though abortive, experiment was launched to govern England by a written constitution. These sweeping reforms had been the practical translation of the sense of opportunity which had infected the political theories of the period. The reading public had been bombarded with prescriptions for the wholesale renovation of society, ranging from Winstanley's communist utopia to Harrington's blueprint for republicanism.

This age of continual crisis and rampant political imagination furnished the background to Locke's biography.[12] His father had fought in the parliamentary army, and his own education at Oxford came at a time when Puritan suspicions about the home of lost causes ran high. As a youth he had witnessed the attempt to turn England into a holy commonwealth. With others he had welcomed the restoration of the monarchy in 1660, but in the feverish months which preceded the accession of James II, Locke was deprived of his university position and felt compelled to flee the country; along with other political émigrés he returned with William II to the tense atmosphere of the revolutionary settlement. In his lifetime he had seen England torn by religious dissensions, disturbed by economic change, and, as the confidant of Shaftesbury, he had been close to the center of what proved to be the beginnings of English party politics.

Locke summed up his reactions to "the dizzy whirlpool of events" in words that were strangely suggestive of Plato's *Seventh Letter*: "I had no sooner perceived myself in the world, but I found myself in a storm, which has lasted almost hitherto." [13] The parallel with Plato, however, ends as abruptly as it began, for nowhere in Locke's writings was there the faintest trace of that architectonic impulse which stirs at the first whiff of opportunity and seeks creative release in drawing plans for the ordering of a disordered world. Through his studies and friendships with many of the eminent intellectual and scientific leaders of the day Locke kept well informed of the exciting currents in science and philosophy. Yet his imagination was never stirred by the thought of joining the rapidly growing knowledge of science to the discipline of philosophy and bringing both to bear on the opportunities presented by a disturbed and directionless political society. At the very start of the *Essay Concerning Human Understanding* he juxtaposed the possibilities of science and philosophy. On the one side the scientist, represented by such "master builders" as Boyle and "the incomparable Mr. Newton"; on the other, the philosopher whose modest ambition it was to be "employed as an under-labourer in clearing the ground a little, and removing some of the rubbish that lies in the way to knowledge . . ." [14] This was an odd note in a century where political philosophers were promising men an immortal commonwealth secured by an infallible political science; where Spinoza had declared that "it is the nature of reason to perceive things under a certain form of eternity"; and where scientists were imparting a new depth and order to the universe. Nevertheless, the persistent theme that binds the *Essay* was of philosophy's limitations. The book, he explained, had originated from a discussion group which had set for itself the task of examining "what objects our understandings were or were not fitted to deal with." And as the *Essay* took form it became an inquiry not into the outermost possibilities of man's mind but into the limits of the "little world of his own understanding." [15]

Man, according to Locke's famous description, enters the world with a mind "void of all characters, without any ideas." Through sensation and reflection, ideas come to be scribbled upon the "white paper" of the mind, forming a circumscribed world from which there was no escape, at least not by natural means. Man had no choice but to labor with the materials presented by the senses.[16] He may artfully contrive them into new combinations, survey them from this angle and that, and laboriously analyze the internal processes of the mind, but he could never break out of a world bounded by "sounds, tastes, smells, visible and tangible qualities":

> But it is not in the power of the most exalted wit, or enlarged understanding, by any quickness or variety of thought, to *invent* or *frame* one new simple idea in the mind, not taken in by the ways before mentioned . . . The dominion of man, in this little world of his own understanding being much what the same as it is in the great world of visible things; wherein his power, however managed by art and skill, reaches no farther than to compound and divide the materials that are made to his hand; but can do nothing towards the making the least particle of new matter, or destroying an atom of what is already in being . . . [17]

And almost two hundred years later substantially the same position was reaffirmed by the leading liberal of the age, John Stuart Mill:

> In these and all other artificial operations [i.e., the application of human art to nature] the office of man is . . . a very limited one; it consists in moving things into certain places. We move objects, and by doing this, bring some things into contact which were separate, or separate others which were in contact: and by this simple change of place, natural forces previously dormant are called into action, and produce the desired effect. Even the volition which designs, the intelligence which contrives, and the muscular force which executes these movements, are themselves powers of nature.[18]

The cramped quarters assigned philosophy by liberals was but the specific application of a general estimate about the human condition which had first been described by Locke and then accepted into the main stream of later liberalism. Where Plato had set as the target of human aspiration "the completest possible assimilation to god" and Aristotle had exhorted men "to put off mortality as far as possible," [19] Locke had confined man to a middling sort of condition, incapable of omniscience or perfection, "a state of mediocrity, which is not capable of extremes . . ." The philosophy best suited to man's limited possibilities was one which concentrated on "the twilight of probability" between "sceptical despair" and proud presumption.[20] This subdued and sober temper had a decisive influence on the way that Locke and his followers viewed the problems of political theory and practice.

Taking first of all the problem of political action, its range of possibilities and the kind of knowledge it presupposes, we can say that although no *logically* necessary connection obtains between a theory of knowledge and a theory of political action, and that a writer may believe in the possibility of arriving at absolutely valid truths and yet counsel a very cautious line of action, there tend, nevertheless, to be strong psychological bonds connecting thought and action. Men feel more confident when assured that their activity is based upon intellectual certainty; they are more apt to engage in sweeping plans when convinced they possess truth in the round. In this sense we can say that the roots of the divergence between the liberal and the radical democratic traditions lie in their contrasting faiths concerning the ability of the human mind to fathom reality and to translate the results into practical actions. The first tradition was symbolized in Locke's remark that "our minds are not made as large as truth nor suited to the whole extent of things," the second by Holbach's definition of truth as "the conformity of our ideas with the nature of things." [21] Holbach's confident assertion symbolized the philosophical temper behind the grandiose schemes of social reconstruction projected during the French Revolution,[22] while Locke's warning against confounding the truths accessible to men with the totality of possible truths was accepted into the main stream of English liberal thought. There it worked to erode confidence in the possibility of political philosophy's providing the knowledge for dramatic advance. This occurred not by way of any explicit denial of the possibilities of genuine political knowledge, nor by any scepticism about the effectiveness of political action. Instead the shift in outlook leading to a reduction in the status and prestige of political theory and practice was gradual and indirect. In these and other respects it forms a remarkable parallel to what happened to Calvinism during roughly the same period. Weber and Tawney have shown that in the seventeenth and eighteenth centuries Calvinist groups underwent a significant change in outlook and behavior amounting to a re-evaluation of norms and a re-direction of activity. Instead of the preoccupation with salvation, action was directed at getting ahead in the world. The driving force which had originally been enlisted in the service of religious ends was now transferred to economic and social concerns. This same activist itch was, as we shall see, a salient trait in the Lockian liberal image of man. If we remember that Locke and many of his most influential followers were either Nonconformists or rebels against Anglicanism — and we need only mention Adam Smith, Bentham, and the Mills — it suggests that the change in Protestantism analyzed by Weber constituted something more than a parallel to certain developments in liberalism: it raises the possibility that liberalism showed some of the same patterns of development as Protestantism.

Thus Locke had argued that philosophy — and by this he certainly meant a "philosophy" oriented and informed by Christian values — should surrender its traditional concern with man's inner state and ultimate destiny, and turn instead to examining the kind of knowledge which would enable men to exploit the natural world.

> We are not born in heaven but in this world, where our being is to be preserved with meat, drink, and clothing, and other necessaries that are not born with us, but must be got and kept with forecast, care and labour, and therefore we cannot be all devotion, all praises and hallelujahs, and perpetually in the vision of things above . . .[23]

And the same point later was made more laconically by Adam Smith when he remarked that the "sublime contemplation" of God's wisdom ought not to be "the great business and occupation of our lives." [24] Philosophy, according to Locke's directive, ought to promote the "advantages and conveniences of human life"; its concern ought to be with the everyday world and its ambitions satisfied by the modest improvements possible there. The increase of wealth and conveniences provided "a large field for knowledge; proper for the use and advantage of man in this world . . . Why should we bemoan our want of knowledge in the particular apartments of the universe, when our portion here only lies in the little spot of earth where we and all our concernments are shut up?" [25] Practicality and action — these became the watchwords of philosophy, so much that in the end philosophy came to doubt the serious importance of its own enterprise: "The most sublime speculations of the contemplative philosopher can scarce compensate the neglect of the smallest active duty." [26]

The effect of turning philosophy outwards was to accept existing society as a datum, susceptible to minor modifications but always within the frame of reference supplied by the *status quo*. This, in turn, implied a form of political knowledge in which precision and certainty were neither necessary nor desirable. Consequently to the liberal writers there existed a clear distinction between the certain truths resulting from the manipulation of human abstractions, as in mathematics, and the highly tentative probabilities possible in those matters wherein man lacked a free hand. And what remained all-important was that liberals identified the area of political knowledge with the latter, radicals with the former. Political knowledge, Locke pointed out, is similar to prudence in being undemonstrable. It depends upon "various and unknown interests, humours, and capacity of men, and not upon any settled ideas of things." Men must rely, therefore, on "the history of matter of fact, and a sagacity in inquiring into probable causes, and finding out an analogy in their operations and effects."[27] A similar outlook reappeared in the writings of Adam Smith. In *The Theory of Moral Sentiments* he drew a sharp contrast between "the public spirited man" and "the man of system." The former "will respect the established powers and privileges even of individuals, and still more those of the great orders and societies into which the state is divided." The man of system, however, combines arrogance with an aesthetic vision, and overrides any deviation from or opposition to the total realization of his "ideal plan":

He seems to imagine that he can arrange the different members of a great society with as much ease as the hand arranges the different pieces upon a chess board; he does not consider that the pieces upon the chess board have no other principle of motion besides that which the hand impresses upon them; but that, in the great chess board of human society, every single piece had a principle of motion of its own altogether different from that which the legislature might choose to impress upon it.[28]

III **The political claims of economic theory.** In its mature form liberalism expressed the same misgivings as conservatism about taking political theory seriously. Even Bentham, the theoretician incarnate, argued that "the propensity to push theory too far is acknowledged to be almost universal."[29] And in a passage full of ancient political analogies he pointed out that political theory must repress the aesthetic impulse with its form-and-matter implications. The science of law "is to the art of legislation what the science of anatomy is to the art of medicine: with this difference, that the subject of it is what the artist has to work *with,* instead of being what he has to operate *upon*."[30] What determined the liberals' attitude was not merely a belief that the complexity of social interrelationships posed insurmountable difficulties to rational or purposive action, but the feeling that political activity had lost its charm and excitement. Writers of such contrasting temperaments as Matthew Arnold and Frédéric Bastiat * expressed the same aesthetic reaction against politics as a mildly depraving activity. Arnold, troubled by "all this political operating," counseled young liberals "to think less of [organizational] machinery, to stand more aloof from the area of politics at present, and rather to try to promote . . . an inward working." Bastiat warned that even the slightest extension of government action beyond the absolute minimum led to *"une prépondérance exagerée"* of the political.[31] But Arnold's introspective mood was not widely shared, and most liberals followed the view that man affirmed his existence through economic activity. What seemed important was the way that men went about the business of creating wealth; what concerned the individual was the strategy of social advance. Thus to the liberals action meant first and foremost economic action.

The primacy of economic action, as well as the tendency on the part of liberals to treat economic phenomena as identical and coextensive with social phenomena, was greatly encouraged by the methods and assumptions employed by the classical economists of the eighteenth century. In tracing out the endless ramifications of such notions as the division of labor, the relationship between class structure and the organization of production and distribution, the causal connections between the variables of wealth and population and their effects on progress; and in exposing the motivations which drove men to adopt one form of economic behavior rather than another, the economists were fashioning a body of knowledge coeval with the whole of organized social life. The next step was natural and almost inevitable. If economics was the knowledge of society, nothing save humility could prevent the economist from assuming that society's relationships and multifarious activities, in short, society's life, could be summarized through various economic categories. The economist could, for example, formulate a concept like the annual product and treat it as a shorthand symbol for the activities of society's members during a given year. Similarly, if asked what were the constituent elements of society, the economist responded that society was divided into definite "parts," such as laborer, landowner, and entrepreneur, and these, as the younger Mill expressed it, "are considered in

---

* Frédéric Bastiat (1801-1850) was a highly popular French publicist who did much to spread the orthodox classical economic doctrines of liberalism. His chief targets were socialism and economic protectionism. His thinking was greatly influenced by Benjamin Franklin, Adam Smith, and the nineteenth-century American economist, Henry Carey.

political economy as making up the whole community." Again, the economist assumed that his studies displayed the answer to what kind of psychological motivations set men in motion and largely determined their social behavior: it was the desire to better their social status, a desire which "comes with us from the womb, and never leaves us until we go into the grave," a desire which found its natural outlet in economic action.[32]

In reducing social life to economic terms, the economists turned to a theory of action which had vast implications for politics and political theory. The unique aspect of their theory was the contention that purposive activity could be undertaken successfully without reference to any supporting or authorizing principle excepting that of "nature." "Man," Adam Smith wrote, "is generally considered by statesmen and projectors as the materials of a sort of political mechanics. Projectors disturb nature . . . it requires no more than to let her alone." [33] The teachings, as well as the control-mechanisms, associated with the traditional authorities of church, class, and political order were held to be unnatural. Hence what was truly radical in liberalism was its conception of society as a network of activities carried on by actors who knew no principle of authority. Society represented not only a spontaneous and self-adjusting order, but a condition untroubled by the presence of authority.

These qualities of social action — absence of authority, spontaneousness, and the tendency towards self-adjustment — were taken to mean that social action lacked the characteristic element of political action, the necessity to resort to power. Industry, Spencer declared, is a "spontaneous" form of activity operating on the principle of "voluntary cooperation"; men "work together by consent." [34]

The age-old function of distributing goods according to some standard of justice was transferred from the political sphere and assigned to the impersonal judgment of the market mechanism.[35] What little survived of the concept of justice consisted of a Hobbesian principle of fairness or, more popularly, of the identification of justice with security: small wonder that by the middle of the nineteenth century liberals came to doubt that political justice existed at all. As Bastiat declared, "the end of law is not, rigorously speaking, to cause justice to prevail," but "to prevent injustice from reigning. In fact, it is not justice which has a real existence, but injustice. The one results from the absence of the other." [36] For the liberals, what little remained of purposive politics was, interestingly enough, largely identified with the function of Locke's philosopher. The political counterpart to rubbish-removal consisted in the repeal of all inherited policies and laws which, nourished on the illusion that politics was to some degree a creative enterprise, obstructed social and economic action:

> . . . As matters stand, almost the whole consists in undoing what has been done, and in obviating the inconveniences that would result from the carrying on this process of undoing in an abrupt and inconsiderate manner.[37]

The older themes of political theory as a saving form of knowledge and political action as a means of regeneration were not lost to the Western tradition. What liberalism dropped was picked up by eighteenth-century radicalism and restored by nineteenth-century revolutionary socialism. "Nothing is impossible for a legislator," wrote Mably, "for he holds, so to speak, our heart and spirit in his hands; he can fashion new men." And at the heart of Marxism was the claim that society could be transformed by political action informed by the knowledge of historical laws. Political action, to be meaningful, must be revolutionary in character, for it was only by an act of creative destruction that man "finally cuts himself off from the animal world . . . and enters conditions which are really human." [38]

Among liberals, however, the lack of interest in political action, the conviction that economics formed the proper study of mankind and economic activity the proper end, hastened the decline of political theory. For these beliefs encouraged the imposition of economic categories onto political thought with the result that the role and status of political theory came to be usurped by economic theory. Liberals came to assert not only that economics was the most useful form of knowledge for the individual in his pursuit of happiness, but that it also provided the necessary prescriptions for handling the common affairs of society. To find the intellectual source of these developments we must return to Locke and, specifically, to his statement concerning the purposes of the political order. Government, he declared, existed "for the procuring, preserving, and advancing" of men's "civil interests." These interests, in turn, comprised "life, liberty, health, and indolency of body, and the possession of outward things." The political could therefore be said to reside in the sum of protective arrangements which left men to "acquire what they farther want." [39] Obviously, however, the kind of knowledge dealing with the protection of possessions was, once it had been translated into practical guarantees, something to be taken for granted in much the same way that the fence-maker's knowledge is taken for granted by a homeowner concerned only to keep his fence in good repair. On the other hand, the form of knowledge which enabled men to acquire what they wanted had an immediate and continuing attraction.

At first writers like Smith were content to advance the limited claim that economics formed a subsidiary branch of statesmanship, concerned primarily with the way a society gained its subsistence and accumulated sufficient revenue for the public services.[40] By the early nineteenth century, however, a larger province was being claimed, one that indicated that the new science was eager and able to take over the territory originally held by political philosophy: that of possessing the sovereign knowledge pertaining to the welfare of the community as a whole. Politcial economy, McCulloch* declared, was the study of the best interests of society. Since it was a subject concerned with how "to obtain the greatest possible amount of wealth with the least possible difficulty," it was a science which, by definition, promoted the interests of all classess.[41] Moreover, there existed a direct relation between wealth and civilization — "a poor people are never refined, nor a rich people ever barbarous" — hence the science which studied wealth qualified as the master science. "The establishment of a wise system of public economy can compensate for every other deficiency." "Wealth is independent of the nature of government." [42]

And thus it was that by the first part of the nineteenth century economic theory had begun to demand for itself the mantle of political theory and to shoulder the burden of pronouncing on the good of the whole society. This was brought home in the imaginary dialogue written by James Mill, a dialogue remarkable for its deliberate adoption of the tone and style of the first great political philosopher — as though to make more emphatic the displacement of political by economic theory:

B. "We may . . . lay it down, with your consent, as a general proposition, that wherever a great many agents and operations are combined for the production of a certain result, or set of results, a commanding view of the whole is absolutely necessary for effecting that combination in the most perfect manner."

A. "I agree."

B. "But a commanding view of a whole subject, in all its parts, and the connexion of these parts, is it anything but another name for the theory, or science of the subject? Theory (*theoria*) is literally view; and science is *scientia*, KNOWLEDGE; meaning view or knowledge, not solely of this and that part but, like that of the general with his army, of the *whole.*"

---

* John Ramsay McCulloch (1789-1864), a Scot, was a prolific writer. In addition to several economic and statistical studies he edited Smith's *Wealth of Nations* and Ricardo's works. He was a loyal follower of classical economic ideas rather than an original thinker.

A. ". . . you mean to say that the theory or science of political economy is a commanding view of the vast combination of agents or operations engaged in the producing for the use of man, the whole of the things which he enjoys and consumes . . . the things which he denominates the matter of wealth — the great object to which almost all the toils and cares of human beings are directed."

B. "You have anticipated me correctly."

A. "You would farther proceed to ask me . . . whether the innumerable operations . . . may not take place in more ways than one; in short, in a worse way, or a better way? Whether it is not of importance that they should take place in the best way? And whether the difference between the best way and the worst way is not likely to be very great . . . And to all these questions I should answer in the affirmative." [43]

In the exercise of their sovereign position economists gradually began to extend their specialized concepts and techniques of analysis to political phenomena. Thinking that the results would be instructive if the institutions of government were subjected to the same type of analysis that had proven so effective in handling other types of activity, the economists asked the innocent question: since all forms of activity naturally fell into one of two classes, "productive" or "unproductive," where was the activity of governing to be placed? Although it could not be said to be productive in the sense that farming or manufacturing were, and notwithstanding that it lived parasitically off the productive labor of other groups, government was not wholly useless in the way that some non-productive activities were. Why not, therefore, subsume it under the principle of the division of labor? This solution allowed government to be treated as a form of activity which, while not itself productive, contributed to maintaining conditions which permitted society to go about the basic task of producing. Someone, after all, had to be responsible for preserving law and order, seeing to it that roads were in good repair and national defense in proper shape.

As a result of this and similar types of reasoning, many traditional political concepts receded in importance or vanished altogether. "As society becomes settled and organized," Spencer wrote, "its welfare and progress become more and more independent of anyone." Social harmony, instead of being the responsibility of a governing authority, was the design of no one; it was the resultant flowing from the spontaneous equilibrium of economic forces. The status of citizen was absorbed into that of producer, and political participation, despite the heroic efforts of liberal reformers to extend the franchise, appeared to be more in the nature of a defensive measure than a self-fulfilling activity: "each is the only safe guardian of his own rights and interests" and hence justice demanded an equal suffrage where every single individual should count "for as much as any other single individual in the community." To be able to vote was to be in a better position to defend one's interests.[44]

IV

The eclipse of political authority: the discovery of society. From the previous discussion it is manifest that as the liberal cluster of assumptions and propositions took shape it revealed an implicitly anti-political quality. This can be understood more fully by examining briefly the relationship between Locke, the originator of the liberal tradition, and Hobbes. One of the characteristic features of the Hobbesian system was its vigorous assertion of the distinctiveness of the political. The most vivid expression of this was the contrast Hobbes drew between the state of nature and the political order, between unrestrained naturalism and the artificial restraints imposed by political authority in support of civilization. The political order, society, and civilization formed a trinity in which society and civilization were dependent upon the political order and all three had in common an artificial and anti-naturalistic character. At the same time, Hobbes took special pains to insist that what was political possessed an identity of its own, that, for example, political authority was not to be confused with or usurped by some religious or social authority. Locke not only rejected these antitheses, he confounded them. He accomplished this by reading back into the state of nature a benign *political* condition having all of the idealized marks of a political society and none of its drawbacks.

> Every offence that can be committed in the state of nature may in the state of nature be also punished equally, and as far forth as it may in a commonwealth . . . [the law of nature is] as intelligible and plain to a rational creature and a studier of that law as the positive laws of commonwealths, nay, possibly plainer . . . Much better it is in the state of nature [than in an absolute monarchy] wherein men are not bound to submit to the unjust will of another.[45]

The effect of treating as political what Hobbes had considered to be not only pre-political but anti-political was to obscure the identity and depreciate the status of the political. The state of nature was asserted to be a condition of "perfect freedom," unmarred by "any superior power on earth" or "the legislative authority of man." It was also a state of perfect equality "wherein all the power and jurisdiction is reciprocal, no one having more than another"; where all were free to act and to order their possessions as they saw fit, subject only to the eternal moral dictates of the law of nature. Political power was present, but being dispersed among all of the members, each of whom stood under a rational obligation to assist the others in enforcing the law of nature, it lacked determinate, institutionalized form.[46] Finally, the state of nature was pre-eminently a social condition where men dwelt in "one community of Nature," hence for Lockian man the political order could never be an invention, only a rediscovery of the natural; never the vital pre-condition of a community, only its superstructure. Denied its contrast with nature, the political order lost its quality of dramatic achievement. It was offered by Locke as a modest, common-sense remedy to the "inconveniences" of the natural state, something like a better set of accommodations for those who already were home-owners, rather than a shelter erected in desperation by the shelterless.

The social and political norms embodied in this *ideal state of nature* were given a sharper outline through contrast with another model condition, the state of war.[47] The identifying marks here were a "declared design of force" aimed at reducing someone to the "absolute" power of another, and the absence of a "common superior on earth to appeal to for relief." While the state of nature was confined to a purely pre-civil stage, the state of war represented an aberration potentially present in both the ideal state of nature and civil society, an aberration in the sense that it destroyed the distinctive element of community common to both: the agreement to live by a common law, the law of nature in the one case, the positive law of the state in the other.

The next step in Locke's argument has always presented puzzling problems in interpretation. Did Locke conceive of political society as originating in the state of nature or in the state of war? If the first explanation is adopted, the individual's decision to enter political society appears either inexplicable or superfluous. For if political society is an improvement over nature what are we to make of Locke's description of the state of nature as idyllic? If the natural condition were generally harmonious, peaceful, and rational, why leave it? If it is marred only by "inconveniences," is this sufficient cause for choosing another mode of life? On the other hand, if political society is to be deduced from the state of war, how is it possible to resist the logic of Hobbes and its conclusion that political society necessarily involves a structure of power and authority sufficient to overcome anarchy and its recurrent possibility? Since most interpretations have assumed that Locke derived political society from one or the other of these conditions, they have concluded that his liberal state was achieved despite the careless reasoning of its author — which is to rank Locke as a philosopher less by grace than for his good works. More recently it has been fashionable to argue, especially among those who find Lockian political society originating in the state of war, that Locke is really Hobbes in liberal clothing — which is a sort of political version of the Bacon-Shakespeare controversy.[48]

These interpretations appear to me faulty because they fail to pay sufficiently close attention to Locke's language. What Locke did was to interject a third condition, one distinct from what he called the "perfect state of nature" and the state of war. For purposes of clarity we shall designate it the *fallen state of nature* because it has certain suggestive similarities to Troeltsch's distinction between the Christian conception of the natural law prevailing before the fall from grace and the "fallen" natural law regnant over the sinful state which followed.

> . . . Were it not for the corruption and viciousness of degenerate men, there would be no need of any other [society], no necessity that men should separate from this great and natural community and by positive agreements combine into smaller and divided associations.[49]

That Locke meant to convey the impression of a different situation from that in the ideal state of nature, and yet one not to be confounded with the state of war, is indicated by the ominous language which he employed in preparing a plausible context for the contract. The natural condition, he tells us, is "full of fears and continual dangers," and "the greater part" of its inhabitants, far from being rational interpreters of the law of nature, as we had been led to suppose, are described as "no strict observers of equity and justice."[50] Men are impelled towards civil society because they are anxiety-ridden, "uncertain" about their rights, "full of fears." But since they are fleeing the fallen state of nature — for the ideal state by definition has no "inconveniences" — their search for a better arrangement will of necessity be guided by knowledge of the ideal condition; that is, by the norms which allow them to recognize the "deficiencies" of the fallen state. In short, the "defects" that rendered the fallen state intolerable were cognizable only in the light of the norms embodied in the ideal state. This becomes apparent in the "remedies" (a significant bit of usage implying restoration rather than innovation) for the fallen condition. These are: a common law, a method for impartial judgment, and an enforcing power: and all three hark back to arrangements which had been in force in the ideal state.[51]

The upshot of Locke's argument was to obscure the political character of civil society. Its political qualities did not appear *ab nihilo;* they had been anticipated by the political form given the ideal state of nature. What can be said to be genuinely new political elements in civil society were introduced via the explicit agreement whereby men accepted a common body of rules and promised to obey the decisions of the majority. But more important was the minimal character of the political order. By this is meant not that the powers and jurisdiction of government were closely restricted, for Locke's language allowed generous scope for government action, but rather that Locke initiated a way of thinking in which society, rather than the political order, was the predominant influence. Instead of asking the traditional question: what type of political order is required if society is to be maintained? Locke turned the question around to read, what social arrangements will insure the continuity of government?

Locke launched his attack against the traditional model of society, wherein ordered social relationships and institutions were sustained by the direction imparted from a political center, by substituting a conception of society as a self-activating unity capable of generating a common will. In the next century Rousseau was to state in more systematic fashion this idea of society as a volitional entity, but already in Locke we can discern its first vague outline and hence the beginnings of a movement in thought which ultimately broke the monopoly of the political order as the sole public will. A close look at the language which Locke used to describe the fundamental contract gives some indication of this trend. The act of agreement called for the resignation by "every one of the members" of his natural powers into "the hands of the *community.*" This implied that a "community" existed before civil society was invented. ". . . Men give up all their natural power to the *society* which they enter into, and the *community put* the legislative power into such hands as they think fit with this trust . . ." [52] The collective power of society receives even more explicit recognition in Locke's description of what occurs when government puts itself in a state of war with its citizens. In the event that a government violated its trust, power reverted to "society." Society, in turn, possessed sufficient unity of will to "act as supreme and continue the legislative . . . or erect a new form, or under the old form place it in new hands . . ." [53] It has been frequently said in criticism of Locke that he provided no defined procedures which the citizenry could invoke when it felt justified in revolting against government. This point misses the mark, because what is important in Locke's theory is that when an arbitrary government provokes revolution it does not find itself faced by a disorganized mass of individuals, but by a "society"; that is, by a coherent group.

Locke's conception of revolution as a social act marked a significant departure from the previous tradition. In sixteenth-century writings, such as the *Vindiciae contra tyrannos,* or in the brief remarks of Calvin concerning the role of the *ephori,* and again in the political theory of Althusius, there had been a conscious effort to contain the right of resistance by identifying its exercise with specific institutions, such as a church, local assemblies, or specified magistrates.[54] Locke, however, located the right with "society," or, more specifically, with the majority.[55] In designating the majority as the instrument through which society acts, Locke dealt still another blow to the distinctive role of the political order. He conceived the majority independently of political processes and institutions; a force that supplied dynamic direction to society but one that originated outside political processes and institutions. ". . . It being necessary to that which is one body to move one way, it is necessary the body should move whither the greater force carries it, which is the consent of the majority." Locke however was not content to argue the role of the majority merely on the basis of its superior power. Might had to be clothed in right; that is, the majority had to be given authority. This was achieved through the basic contract: each "puts himself under an obligation to every one of that society to submit to the determination of the majority, and to be concluded by it . . ."[56] In this way ultimate authority was identified with society. This had a significant effect upon the status of the political order, for the "socialization" of authority was accomplished by stripping authority from political institutions and leaving the latter dependent on society. A good example of this was Locke's treatment of the institution of monarchy which traditionally had been viewed as the supreme embodiment of political authority. Locke transformed kingship into mere executive office, without independent status, the mere agent of society. Its role was that of "image, phantom, or representative of the commonwealth, acted by the will of the society, declared in its laws . . . He has no will, no power, but that of the law."[57]

V **Society and government: spontaneity versus coercion.** Earlier it was briefly suggested that Locke had reversed the traditional priorities to establish society as the support of the political order rather than the reverse. This point can be made more precise by turning to Locke's concept of private property. The connection between property and the supportive role of society lies in Locke's identification of property with society rather than with the political order. The social character of property, and its resulting significance, have been overlooked by most commentators who have been intent to emphasize instead the contrast between the Hobbesian and Lockian views of property and to demonstrate how one logically led to despotism and the other to limited government and individual rights. It is usually pointed out that Hobbes had held that, by strict logic, there could be no property rights prior to civil society because no effective power existed to enforce recognition of the right. Thus, by making property rights derivative from the will of the sovereign, Hobbes added one more element of power to Leviathan. In contrast, Locke asserted that private property had existed prior to the founding of civil society and this, so it is argued in most interpretations, affected his theory of governmental power and individual rights. If property were a pre-political right which men brought with them into civil society and one which they did not surrender, political power was faced with an imposing limitation. This interpretation, however, suffers from a misplaced emphasis. Far from advocating the immunity of property rights to political control, Locke made it abundantly clear that in the act of joining political society men submitted their possessions to its control. Security of possession did not, to his mind, mean the absence of political regulation, but only that such regulation ought not to be "arbitrary"; that is, incapable of being defended as in the common interest.[58] A more important weakness in the interpretation mentioned above is its failure to see that Locke was as fully intent on converting property into a bulwark of the political order as he was on providing for the preservation of this right.

To realize the significance of this we must go back to the pre-political origins of property. Now Locke's assertion that property preceded government made sense only if he simultaneously assumed the existence of society. What allows the act of appropriation to issue in "private" possession is that others will recognize the validity of the act. In other words, appropriation is individual in character, but the recognition which converts it into an effective right is social. In this sense, property can be said to be a social institution, identified with society rather than with the political order, The next stage is to show that the political order depended in large measure upon the social institution of property, or more precisely, that the promise of the members to obey political commands was registered through the social institution of property rather than through the "political" contract. What we are suggesting here is a revision of the common interpretation of Locke's theory of consent.

The usual interpretation is that the consensual basis of Locke's political society is contained in the "express" contract, as Locke called it, whereby each member signified his willingness to obey. Assuming this view to be correct, it is possible to conclude that Locke construed the problem of obligation in terms of a purely "political" act, occurring at a single moment, and that he optimistically believed that the stability and continuance of government were assured even though they depended on nothing more than the single promise of each member to keep his word. Against this view we would suggest that the express contract occupied a subordinate role in maintaining the loyalty of the members over any stretch of time; that its significance was confined to two unique occasions, the founding of political society and the overthrow of government when there was appeal to the original agreement; and that the major device for securing the continuing consent of the members was the institution of private property. Support for these propositions is to be found in Locke's doctrine of "tacit" consent. This form of agreement was introduced by Locke to overcome the objection that the original or express compact could not explain why later members, who might not have been parties to the original agreement, were nevertheless obliged to accept the commands of political authorities. The question, then, was whether an individual, in the absence of any explicit promise on his part, could be said to have consented to obey a government. Locke's answer was that an element of consent was indicated by such seemingly disparate acts as the exercise of property rights, travelling on the highways, or taking lodgings "only for a week." Obviously a net cast as widely as this would capture more individuals than any single express act of covenanting. Above all, it could be applied to later generations in a way that the express covenant could not. This becomes clearer as Locke's argument unfolds. He dropped the extreme and dubious claim that brief residence or use of the highways constituted true marks of political obligation and concentrated instead on the consensual significance of property rights. Any person who enjoyed property rights, *ipso facto,* was placed on the same footing with the original covenanters. His property and person became subject to the jurisdiction of the political society and he was obligated to obey its commands. The only distinction between the two forms of consent lay in the proviso that if an individual who had entered society by the tacit method surrendered his property rights, he was at liberty to leave, whereas the others were "perpetually and indispensably obliged." [59]

The final touch to the argument was to employ the institution of property inheritance to undercut the favorite notion of radicalism that each generation was free to reconstitute political society.[60] According to Locke, when an individual accepted a property bequest his act signified a "voluntary submission" to political society, because the enjoyment of his legacy depended upon the protections afforded by the law.[61] In this way the transmission of property supplied a recurrent affirmation of the explicit contract. The continuity of political society was assured by being linked to the perpetuation of economic possessions. At the same time, the seeming unity of a "generation" was dissolved by the act of inheritance that necessarily occurred in a series of disconnected, individual instances.[62] In summary we can say that Locke succeeded in converting property into an ingenious instrument for silently coercing men to political obedience. Surely the coercions were not less for saying that men were free to reject inherited wealth or to leave society without one's property. Hence what Locke remarked of the power that property gave to fathers over their children could with equal justice be said of the power it gave society over the members: "This is no small tie" on their obedience.

Locke's candid recognition of the coercive element in ownership is revealing of the emerging liberal attitude towards coercion. Liberals proved to be unconcerned about the compulsions arising from a system of property because the pressures seemed to be impersonal and lacking in physical duress. On the other hand, liberals could become agitated over political power because it combined both a personal and a physical element. Locke defined political power as "a right of making laws with penalties of death and, consequently, all less penalties for the regulating and preserving of property, and of employing the force of the community in the execution of such laws, and in the defense of the commonwealth from foreign injury, and all this only for the public good." [63] This tough-minded view of power is interesting for the way it identifies power with physical coercion and for its implication that this was the only kind of power at the disposal of government. The identification of government with coercion became part of the liberal outlook and was tersely summarized by Bastiat, the nineteenth-century French political economist: "It is of the essence of government that it acts on the citizens by way of constraint." [64]

In many ways the political thought of the two centuries after Locke constituted one long commentary on the three themes just discussed: the equating of government with physical compulsion, the emergence of society as a self-subsistent entity, and the willingness to accept compulsion from an impersonal source. As we shall see later, liberalism itself admitted that in a society organized for the pursuit of desires, some modicum of constraint was necessary and hence government was necessary. Yet liberals also insisted that "society," in the words of Herbert Spencer, "goes on without any ministerial overseeing . . ." In recent years this same cluster of ideas reappeared when classically-minded liberals attacked the popular notion of "planning." Once again the same pejorative contrast was drawn between "the spontaneous forces of society" and the "coercion" employed by political direction. Once again the same suspicions of power exercised by a determinate, identifiable authority were coupled with an explicit preference for "the impersonal and anonymous mechanism of the market." Since the market represented merely the registered response of the consumers, i.e., "society," the resulting compulsion and inequalities had the advantage of being not only an impersonal, collective judgment but also a "democratic" one:

> Under an unhampered market economy the appraisal of each individual's effort is detached from any personal considerations and can therefore be free both from bias and dislike . . . Salaries and wages do not depend on arbitrary decisions . . . Labor is, under capitalism, a commodity and is bought and sold as a commodity. [This] makes the wage earner free from any personal dependency . . . Consumers' choices do not concern the persons engaged in production; they concern things and not men.[65]

Liberals, however, were not the sole beneficiaries of the Lockian heritage. Radicals, such as Tom Paine and William Godwin, showed that a shift in emphasis combined with doctrinaire reasoning could produce a conception of society markedly different from that advocated by Locke but not without strong suggestion of his influence. Paine and Godwin accepted Locke's identification of the political with the coercive power of government, yet they denied that this factual assertion ought to provide the basis for the proper model of a political system. The new form for the political had to be sought elsewhere. Accordingly, they looked to society, with its characteristics of spontaneous cooperation, the peaceful satisfaction of needs, and the absence of central control, as the paradigm for the political order. In Paine's description, government should be "a national association acting on the principles of society." [66] The same argument was extended by Godwin to justify anarchism. If government were converted into a mere executive agent of society, as both Paine and the more orthodox liberals argued it should, the next stage of human advance would be one where society was capable of acting for itself.[67]

To model the political order after society, to re-create the spontaneity, naturalism, and peaceful relationships of society in a political setting was but to hanker after a non-political condition. The hostility towards politics gained further momentum in the nineteenth century and again it was the Lockian notion of society as a self-subsistent entity which supplied the inspiration for a wide variety of theories each sharing in this animus. One form which this took was the attempt to substitute administration for politics as the central method for handling social problems. In the bizarre theories of the Utopian Socialists, such as Fourier and Owen; in the managerial or technocratic society depicted by Saint-Simon; and, finally, in the Marxist-Leninist conception of the "withering away of the state," there was common agreement that society, given certain reforms, would spontaneously generate its own life. Politics and the political order, on the other hand, existed only because of the social cleavages stemming from outmoded forms of economic organization. Once these had been set right, conflict would cease and with it the *raison d'être* of the political order. The political art, like handicrafts, would be an historical curiosity. It would be replaced by the "administration of things"; that is, by a series of operations so highly routinized as to call for no greater knowledge or ability than that possessed by a competent bookkeeper.

Modern pluralism, which we shall discuss at greater length in the next chapter, represents still another offshoot of the same tradition. Like the anarchist and the Utopian Socialist, the pluralists too preferred "society," but for a somewhat different reason. Society was the repository of groups and associations which, to the pluralists, constituted the primary social realities.[68] The pre-eminence of the political order was viewed as the consequence of the mistaken belief that society required a supreme or sovereign authority. Most socially necessary functions were in fact being performed by voluntary groups, while the fulfillment of individual personality found its natural setting in group life rather than in the exercise of political citizenship. In the end the pluralists were driven to a position strangely similar to that of the managerialists, communists, and Lockian liberals. The shadow of the political order was preserved because, in a society of autonomous groups, some kind of coordinating power was needed — which is to say the political order is justified more out of weariness than design. But whether the modern political theorist is willing to concede a bookkeeping function to the political order, or whether he describes its task as "coordination," are largely irrelevant. For both are symptomatic of the penchant of modern political thought for converting political problems into administrative ones.[69] It has been a long road from the philosophers of Plato to the expert commissions of Herbert Hoover.

VI   **Liberalism and anxiety.** Liberalism has usually been regarded as an activist philosophy *par excellence,* identified with the demand for "natural liberty" and for the removal of those clogging restraints which prevented man from pursuing his interests, expressing his thoughts, or im-proving his social position. When we read the following from a modern exponent of classical economic liberalism we assume it faithfully repro-duces the bourgeois ideal: the mark of "the great businessman" is "his indefatigable inventiveness and fondness for innovations . . . He embodies in his person the restless dynamism and progressivism inherent in capital-ism . . ."; again, in speaking of the hopeful young man embarking on his career of acquisition: "as he grows older and realizes that many of his plans have been frustrated, he has no cause for despair. His children will start the race again . . . Life is worth living because it is full of promise." [70] Thus it is accepted as axiomatic both by opponents and defenders that liberalism drew its strength from a robust confidence in man's creative abil-ities and a simple conviction that the natural world was so benevolently arranged that rational action and "strenuous effort" automatically produced happiness. The question we shall explore is whether liberalism was orig-inally quite as naïve and confident, or quite as innocent of despair, as is so often assumed. If the question is put: what, according to the classical liberal theorists, moved man to action and, once in motion, what provided un-ceasing stimulus to his continuous activity, a far different profile appears, one deeply shaded by anxiety.

To appreciate this, it is necessary to go back to Locke's *Essay* which forms a kind of textbook for the psychology of liberal man. According to Locke, the springs of human action were not to be found in any simple desire to enjoy pleasure and avoid pain, much less in any lofty motive to advance the "greater good." "That which *immediately* determines the will" issued from a feeling of "uneasiness," a desire for "some absent good . . . Whatever we feel of uneasiness, so much it is certain we want of happi-ness . . ." [71] Far from being a condition of simple frustration, it had been shrewdly designed by a benevolent deity to insure the survival of the species. "The chief, if not only spur to human industry and action is uneasiness." [72] Yet the notion that nature promoted happiness by the circuitous route of human anxieties contained the first traces of a growing sense of man's alienation from nature and hence lent a kind of frantic quality to his ac-tivity. The "deception" practiced by nature, Smith wrote, "rouses and keeps in continual motion the industry of mankind." [73] The overtones of a funda-mental hostility between man and nature became more pronounced as the liberals recognized that two of the fundamental principles of their philos-ophy, the institution of private property and the act of labor which created property, were both directed against nature in order to force her favors.

This view of labor and private property as part of an organized assault upon nature, as well as the uneasiness which it bred, had been implicit in Locke's description of the origins of private property. In the Lockian state of nature "all the fruits [the earth] naturally produces and beasts it feeds belong to mankind in common, as they are produced by the spontaneous hand of nature." But nature's bounty was insufficient in itself to support human advance, or, as Locke phrased it in the *Essays on the Law of Nature,* nature's goods are not "increasing in proportion with what men need or covet." In order to exist, therefore, man is compelled to "subdue" nature, exploit her riches and draw out her secrets.[74]

The relationship between man as producer and nature as the exploitable stuff of production remained a continuing source of anxiety for liberal writers. As the nineteenth century wore on, liberalism increasingly manifested what can only be called a guilt complex about nature. For on the basis of the proposition central to political economy, that labor and production were the fundamental processes whereby a society maintained its existence, that, as McCulloch put it, "nature spontaneously furnishes the matter of which commodities are made, but, until labour has been expended in appropriating matter, or in adapting it to our use, it is wholly destitute of value," [75] it followed that that society which erected production into a way of life could be fairly described as an organized assault on nature. In the words of the American economist H. C. Carey,* "wealth consists in the power to command the always gratuitous service of nature, whether rendered by the brain of man, or by the matter by which he is surrounded, and upon which it is required to operate." [76] By the middle of the nineteenth century, however, the exploitation of nature had ceased to be viewed as a game of wits in which nature surrendered to those who had solved her secrets. The spirit of gamesmanship was shattered on the realization that the activity directed at nature, far from being played by the measured tempo of gambit and ploy, was more an insane ritual, performed to the jagged rhythm of creation and destruction, and leaving exposed a deep sense of guilt among the participants:

Everything which is produced perishes, and most things very quickly . . . Capital is kept in existence from age to age not by preservation, but by per-

---

* Henry C. Carey (1793-1879) was an influential American economist whose basic work, *The Principles of Social Science* (1858-1859), was widely read on the Continent as well as in America. Most historians of economic doctrines have classified Carey as an "optimist" for his attempts to revise the gloomy implications of the "law of diminishing returns." Originally a free trader, he later became an advocate of protectionism.

petual reproduction: every part of it is used and destroyed generally very soon after it is produced, but those who consume it are employed meanwhile in producing more.[77]

The final touch to the encounter between man and nature was supplied by the Malthusian theory which, in retrospect, seems in equal parts an account of nature's revenge and of man's expiation. In Malthus' description, the "laws of nature" were grim decrees relentlessly exacting retribution from societies for years of wilful violation. The assault on nature had been waged under the foolish belief that nature was a bottomless cornucopia, but the impending crisis in the means of subsistence was nature's reply to man's presumption. More cunning still was the punishment which nature had devised. Compliance with nature's laws demanded sexual abstinence as one of the means for easing population pressures. This meant, however, that the human condition could be eased only by setting man at war with his own nature. Nature implants in man an instinctual desire to produce offspring, but this drive is thwarted by nature's own warning that each offspring merely increases the numbers pressing on the limited supply of necessities. Yet if man tries to restrain his natural appetites, he is driven to find outlets in vice. Thus what nature implants in man in the way of sex drives she frustrates by way of a niggardly subsistence: after years of exploitation she has turned on her tormentor.[78] It is small wonder that to the younger Mill nature had become a kind of horror:

> . . . Her powers are often towards man in the position of enemies, from whom he must wrest, by force and ingenuity, what little he can for his own use . . . Nature impales men, breaks them as if on the wheel, casts them to be devoured by wild beasts, burns them to death . . . and has hundreds of other hideous deaths in reserve, such as the ingenious cruelty of a Nabis or a Domitian never surpassed.[79]

During the nineteenth century nature's hostility received further confirmation by the Darwinian theory of the endless struggle of the species to maintain itself in an ever-threatening environment. It is significant that one of the most influential schools of liberalism deriving from "social Darwinism," namely that of the late John Dewey, should have emphasized the need of man's readjustment to nature rather than his triumph over it.[80]

At the same time that liberal man was growing steadily alienated from nature he was also becoming painfully conscious that the price exacted for civilized society was the repression of his own nature. In our own day Freud has argued that civilization consists of a set of necessary but repressive arrangements evolved to control, thwart, and divert man's drive for the gratification of his natural instincts. The irony of progress lay in the fact that it could be achieved only at the expense of man's natural desires and hence of his happiness.[81] Substantially the same analysis had been made by John Stuart Mill more than a half century earlier. "Civilization," he had written, "in every one of its aspects is a struggle against the animal instincts. . . . It has artificialized large portions of mankind to such an extent that of many of their most natural inclinations they have scarcely a vestige or a remembrance left." [82] Mill differed from Freud not only by clinging to a greater optimism about the durability of civilized restraints, but, above all, by urging an all-out war against instinct. Since "nearly every respectable attribute of humanity is the result not of instinct, but of a victory over instinct," the aim of education should be "not simply to regulate [the undesirable instincts] but to extirpate, or rather . . . to starve them by disuse." [83] How well Mill and the liberals succeeded in their campaign of repression can be measured perhaps by the phenomenal success of psychiatry: psychoanalysis is the science necessitated by the liberal ethos.

The anxieties besetting liberalism were further intensified through the alliance which quickly developed between liberal political theory and classical economics. Locke had earlier pointed out that "whenever either the desire or the need of property increases among men, there is no extension, then and there, of the world's limits . . . It is impossible for anyone to grow rich except at the expense of someone else." [84] Nevertheless, scarcity did not constitute a basic presupposition of liberalism until the alliance with economics was secured. One of the peculiarities of economics as a body of knowledge was its insistence on the primary importance of the scarcity of goods and wealth. Consequently the early economists accepted as their special concern the job of examining the processes whereby nature's scanty resources were allocated among the various classes of society and the operation of the various factors which set limits to wealth and productivity. The concepts employed in early economic analysis invariably denoted rigid or inelastic quantities, such as land, labor, capital, or wage fund. The consequence of these ideas was to strengthen the implication that we have already noted in Locke's conception of the role of philosophy; namely, that human action was confined within rather narrow limits and that the existence of an imposing number of fixed conditions eliminated the opportunities for large-scale action of a truly creative kind. As the younger Mill expressed it,

howsoever we may succeed in making for ourselves more space within the limits set by the constitution of things, we know that there must be limits

. . . There are ultimate laws, which we did not make, which we cannot alter, and to which we can only conform.[85]

The stark estimate of the English economists respecting the potentialities of production stood in sharp contrast to the expansive sentiments represented by the French Physiocrat, Mercier de la Rivière, who declared that man could create an organization "which would necessarily produce all the happiness that can be enjoyed on earth."[86] The difficulty, as the English writers pointed out, was that production depended on investment, and hence the decision as to where and how capital ought to be invested was always governed by the fixed amount of capital available. As Bentham put it, "just so much capital as is employed in [one] way, is prevented from being employed in any other." Bentham went on to point out in the *Manual of Political Economy* that the fundamental principle or "groundwork of the whole" was "the limitation of industry by the limitation of capital."[87] It was this proposition that dictated the classical attack on all forms of government interference. Bounties, monopolies, preferential taxation, etc., were all based on the fallacy that new wealth could be produced by government regulation. In reality, political action could only divert existing capital into channels which it would not otherwise follow: "what they had transferred, they thought they had created." Moreover, as Smith asserted, "every derangement of the natural distribution of stock is necessarily hurtful" and, in the last analysis, unjust, because it benefits one group or class at the expense of another.[88] These ideas were carried over into the problem of distribution and serve to explain the sense of helplessness among the economists when they confronted the condition of the working classes. The new science of economy had posited the existence of a fixed fund for wages in any given year; hence no amount of agitation on the part of the workers for a greater share could soften this harsh fact.[89]

It is within this context of scarcity that the liberal concept of work is to be understood. Later interpretations have strongly suggested that work was something the bourgeoisie undertook with gusto: motivated by the endless possibilities of acquisition they hurled themselves into economic activity and converted hard work into a joyous dedication. Although the interpretation forwarded by Weber and Tawney, which emphasizes the assimilation of work to a type of religious calling, is far closer to the truth, it fails to bring out the parallel between the insecurities besetting the Calvinist believer and the anxieties accompanying economic action, just as it neglects the joyless attitude common to both the search for salvation and economic security. Work, as the liberal writers never tired of insisting, was not a free choice but a grim necessity. From the beginning of human history, Locke declared, "the law man was under" made him an "appropriating" animal. "God commanded, and [man's] wants, forced him to labor." [90] The nature of labor was made more explicit by Adam Smith but with an element of irony added. Work was elevated into being the primary source of economic value, but it was also an act of deprivation. To labor meant to suffer, to lose ease, liberty, and happiness. "Although man abhors pain and suffering," wrote one of Smith's French disciples, "he is condemned by nature to suffering and privation unless he undergoes the pain of work." [91] Far from being the spontaneous expression of personality drives, labor was depicted by the classical economists, such as McCulloch, as an Old Testament punishment: "the eternal law of Providence has decreed that wealth can only be secured by industry — that man must earn his bread by the sweat of his brow." [92]

These injunctions took on further poignancy with the development of the law of diminishing returns, a notion which the younger Mill reckoned "the most important proposition in political economy." According to Senior's* succinct formulation, "with every increase of the labor bestowed, the aggregate is increased, [but] the increase of the return is not in proportion to the increase of the labour." [93] After it was realized that the continued expenditure of energy and wealth was self-defeating, only the addition of the Malthusian thesis was required for the fears of the liberals to verge towards hysteria. If, as Malthus maintained, population advanced at a steady geometric ratio while the food supply lagged at an arithmetic pace, the issue no longer concerned the distribution of fairly constant quantities but coping with a growing scarcity of basic necessities.

What was involved here was nothing less than a crisis in the whole liberal outlook on history. Again this has been obscured by a blanket of misinterpretations. Radicals like Condorcet might assert that the "perfectibility of man is indefinite," and human intelligence would reach a stage where error would be "almost impossible." Militants like Priestley might prophesy that the end of the world "will be glorious and paradisiacal, beyond what our imaginations might now conceive," [94] but the liberal tradition which drew

* Nassau Senior (1790-1864) was at one time Professor of Political Economy at Oxford and served on several royal commissions. He was author of the report on which the Poor Law of 1834 was based. He subscribed to the basic principles of classical economics and developed them with great clarity and precision. Among his most impressive writings were those which tried to define rigorously the bounds and limits of economic science.

from Adam Smith differed from both these by virtue of its more sober estimate of the human condition and by its selection of a different set of questions for investigation. There was only a sceptical doubt about limitless progress, and little taste for futurist speculation. What interested Smith was the slow transition from barbarism to civilization, and what caught his curiosity was the role of non-rational forces and the unintended consequences of actions. Progress was not the product of conscious purpose, but of a concatenation of factors which included many actions undertaken for ends quite different from the results that actually occurred.[95] Instead of attending to history as a relentless progression from one plateau of achievement to another and still higher one, the liberal tradition was haunted by the specter of a "static society" or, as it was often called, "the stationary state." Following Montesquieu's conception of the "spirit" of a social system, Smith argued that every society had a potential limit of wealth determined by its complex of laws, institutions, climate, and natural resources; beyond this limit it could not go. When society had exhausted its economic energy, it would be unable to muster a wage fund sufficient to meet the needs of a growing working population.[96] By the time Malthus wrote his *Essay on Population* (1798), this notion of the natural limits of economic expansion had moved to the center of attention. The stage was now prepared for a direct challenge to the sanguine views of Godwin and Condorcet that there were no fixed boundaries to human advance. Malthus proceeded to show that the lag between food supply and population growth operated as an unbreakable "natural law" which predetermined the limits of progress at any given stage of history. Inevitably the triumphal march towards progress would slowly slacken and gradually assume the cadence of a wake. Instead of the Enlightenment notion that the unfolding of historical time was synonymous with advance, time was now viewed as the carrier of unhappiness, possibly even retrogression.[97]

With the publication of John Stuart Mill's *Principles of Political Economy* (1848) the "stationary state" was accepted as inevitable by the most influential liberal writer of the century. Mill tried to make the best of it by arguing that when the plateau of productivity and wealth had been reached, men would no longer be obsessed by the pursuit of wealth and hence the possibility was open for a richer spirituality and a gentler ethic.[98] Yet the argument itself marked the inversion of one of the basic liberal postulates concerning history: instead of the belief that moral and intellectual progress depended upon unceasing material advance, true progress was identified with the stage when material growth had ceased.

Liberal doubts about the possibility of continued progress were but part of a troubled outlook on society. In the seventeenth century, liberalism had been characterized by a confident belief in the capaciousness of society, in the existence of sufficient social space to accommodate the driving energies unleashed by Protestantism and capitalism. Locke had based the primitive right of property on the fact that, before the invention of money, there had been sufficient land for all. Even when money had been introduced by consent and had ushered in an era where many men were without land, i.e., without a social plot they could call their own, Locke stoutly maintained that the large unused areas in the world still afforded enough social mobility to forestall a crisis.[99] In the eighteenth century the liberal conception of social space was given more precise form by the classical economists. They utilized the Lockian premise of spaciousness to attack mercantilist restrictions, guild controls, monopolies, and conspiracies. Every arrangement which impeded movement, or established the monopolistic right of some group to dominate a particular sector of society, should be removed.[100] If human action were thus left free to respond to the dictates of natural incentives and the laws of the market, there would be little danger of these lines of action colliding. There existed opportunity and room for all.

Substantially the same argument was employed when liberal political theory turned to the problem of group rivalries or "factions." In the *Federalist Papers* Madison argued brilliantly that group conflict could not be extirpated in a free society and hence the only hope was to dissipate its intensities over a wide area. The solution was a federal republic extending over a broad geographical area, "a greater sphere of country." And it was precisely because of the almost illimitable space at its disposal, Madison contended, that the American republic could succeed where smaller republics had failed.

But in the early nineteenth century doubts began to be expressed about the adequacy of space at man's disposal. In France Benjamin Constant wondered whether the task of government consisted merely in removing hindrances (which would be sufficient were there ample room for human action), or whether it ought not to try "to preserve each individual in the plot (*partie*) he had come to occupy" (which would be a policy more consonant with a crowded condition).[101] These faint symptoms of social claustrophobia became pronounced when the full meaning of Malthus' theories had been accepted. "Man is necessarily confined in room," Malthus declared, because nature had been "comparatively sparing in the room and the nourishment" necessary to sustain a growing population. From this crowded condition stemmed a vast number of social evils: vice, overcrowded and filthy cities, the depressed condition of the working classes, general restlessness in society, and a readiness on the part of the masses to seek quick and radical remedies to their distress.[102] ". . . It is some hardship," the younger Mill pointed out, "to be born into the world and to find all nature's gifts previously engrossed, and no place left for the new-comer." Appalled at the ethic of a crowded, industrialized society, with its "trampling" and "elbowing," and dismayed at the ugliness of urbanized civilization, Mill sought comfort in solitude and communion with nature:

> It is not good for man to be kept perforce at all times in the presence of his species. A world from which solitude is extirpated is a very poor ideal. . . . Nor is there much satisfaction in contemplating the world with nothing left to the spontaneous activity of nature; with every rood of land brought into cultivation . . . every flowery waste or natural pasture ploughed up, all quadrupeds or birds which are not domesticated for man's use exterminated as his rivals for food . . .[103]

In view of the emerging picture of society, as one where the avenues of movement were steadily being jammed, the older model of social space could not be maintained. This was made more evident once the problem of scarcity was introduced into a setting where individuals and groups could not avoid rubbing up against each other. In other words, the end product of crowdedness and shortage was not just social friction but class war. In confronting the problems issuing from an economy of scarcity, the liberals were driven to do what practically every political theory must; namely, to justify a system inherently unequal in its distributive principle. In economic terms this called for an explanation of why the wealth annually produced by society had to be divided unequally among the various classes. As a consequence, the liberals were led to formulate a theory of class struggle which anticipated one of the basic principles of later socialism. Locke had called attention to the "pulling and contest" between the main economic interest groups, and later Bentham saw in all of history "a universal scramble" among ruling groups for money, power, and prestige.[104] The obvious conclusion to be drawn from a situation of scarcity and conflict was stated by James Mill:

> The results are exceedingly different, when nature produces the objects of desire not in sufficient abundance for all. The source of dispute is then exhaustless; and every man has the means of acquiring authority over others, in proportion to the quantity of those objects which he is able to possess.[105]

The liberals were not so naïve as to believe that rational explanation alone could dissipate the dangerous discontents which would naturally arise among those who felt slighted after the cake had been sliced. They recognized that sooner or later the aggrieved groups would locate the source of their misery in private property and then a general assault on the system could be expected. This was the chain of reasoning which led to the liberal theory of the state. The state existed not only to preserve property, but to provide a generalized feeling of security in a society where "the idle and improvident are always desirous of seizing the earnings of the laborious and frugal." [106] The liberal conception of the state was rooted in psychological anxieties rather than acquisitiveness:

> It is only under the shelter of the civil magistrate that the owner of that valuable property, which is acquired by the labour of many years, or perhaps of many successive generations, can sleep a single night in security. He is at all times surrounded by unknown enemies, whom, though he never provoked, he can never appease, and from whose injustice he can be protected only by the powerful arm of the civil magistrate continually held up to chastise it.[107]

Against this backdrop of economic scarcity, contending classes, crowded space, and the limited possibilities of ameliorative action, anxious man emerges as the creation of liberalism. Nineteenth-century existentialism and twentieth-century neo-orthodox theology have elevated to moral and philosophical status what liberalism had experienced as fact. It was anxiety which drove liberal man to unrelenting activity — anxiety from struggling to eke out existence in the face of a hostile nature, anxiety from the precarious state of possessions in a society where the masses were often desperately hungry, and, equally strong, anxiety stemming from the appetites instilled by society. Locke had noted that socially acquired habits infected men with an "itch after honour, power, and riches" — a craving which bred a "fantastical uneasiness." [108] "Fear and anxiety," Smith declared, "are the great tormentors of the human breast" — an outlook which made his dictum that "man was made for action" appear less the confident counsel of a brisk headmaster than a physician's sedative for neurosis. It remained for Bentham to point out "the great advantages attendant on a busy life" by advising his readers to have "projects" always in mind; it was these which gave men an assurance of a "future." Busyness as a way of life had more to recommend than the "painful probe" of one's inner life. Self-knowledge, far from being the liberating pursuit that the classical writers had claimed, was something most men found painful and repellent. "Self-study" meant stripping off the "slight tincture" of socially altruistic motives, and exposing self-interest in all of its primal rawness.[109]

To interpret the liberal phrenesis as the sign of an inner confidence, or as the ideology of a bustling, acquisitive class in the ascendancy, is to miss the pathos of action cultivated as an escape from gnawing doubts. It is this pathos which gave a grim overtone to liberal man's "pursuit of happiness," the phrase used by Locke and later immortalized by Jefferson. Happiness could be described as a "pursuit" precisely because it was unstable and elusive.[110] And as happiness became increasingly identified with money, that is with a relative and highly insecure good, it would seem that the dedication of liberal man to the pursuit of happiness was a form of masochism, and that for society to enshrine this pursuit as a sacred right was to give legal status to anxiety.

To quell any possible doubts about whether this kind of happiness was worth having, economists thought it necessary to exhort men to be acquisitive, as though doubts could be drowned in further activity. To the liberal economists acquisitiveness was not the natural, spontaneous instinct that their critics have thought, but a type of motivation to be acquired, or, better yet, instilled. In advocating, as political economists did, a general system of education to promote the stimulation of desires, political economy wrote a prescription which intensified the insecurity and futility that its own theories had revealed. Thus, in a striking anticipation of the theory of endless titillation now practiced by modern commercial advertising, McCulloch wrote:

> The first and grand object ought always to be to excite a taste for superfluities; for, when once this taste has been excited, it is consequently easy to give it any particular bias or direction; and until it has been excited, society can make no progress.[111]

Small wonder that by the middle of the nineteenth century John Stuart Mill was led to a passionate protest against "the all-engrossing torment" of industrialism and to counsel Englishmen and Americans "to moderate the ardor of their devotion to the pursuit of wealth." [112]

VII **Beyond the pleasure principle: the problem of pain.** The picture of liberal man as anxiety-ridden might seem at odds not only with the usual portrait drawn by conservative critics but also with what the liberals themselves said about the primary importance of the pursuit of happiness or pleasure. Bentham's assertion, that "every man's necessary impulse is towards the economy of happiness," is usually taken to represent the liberal tradition's view of man as a creature who naturally desires happiness and who bases his conduct on a course of action which will attain this end.[113] Yet the phrase employed by Bentham, "the economy of happiness," hinted at the belief of liberals that happiness had to be pursued with cunning and tracked down methodically precisely because of the scarce nature of the objects with which it was identified. Moreover, given "the scanty materials of happiness," as James Mill phrased it, and given the reduction of the human condition to one where men experienced either pain *or* pleasure, it would seem to follow that the possibilities for pain exceeded the opportunities for pleasure.[114] This suggests that the liberal's desperate insistence on the primacy of the pleasure-principle as the dominant motivation was meant to compensate for the real source of his worries: the predominance of pain in the world. What John Stuart Mill wrote about his father could be easily extended to the liberal tradition as a whole: "he had . . . scarcely any belief in pleasure . . . He deemed very few of them worth the price which, at least in the present state of society, must be paid for them." [115] What these expressions imply is that liberalism, perhaps to a greater degree than any other political theory, first revealed how exposed were the nerve ends of modern man, how heightened his sensitivity to pain. "Never has it happened to me," Bentham confessed, "to witness suffering on the part of any creature, without experiencing, in some degree or other, a sensation of the like nature in my own nerves." [116]

Our thesis is, in short, that the anxieties besetting liberal man were rooted in his belief in the ever-present possibility of pain and that this belief, in turn, shaped in an important way his attitudes towards the role of government, the possibilities of political action, the nature of justice, and the function of law and legal penalties. "The whole of government," Bentham was to write, "is but a connected series of . . . sacrifices." [117]

In exploring this problem we must recognize that we are dealing with a notion that underwent important changes, that, in other words, liberalism manifested a developing sensitivity to pain to the point that Malthus could speak of "misery and the fear of misery" [118] as the "law of necessity" reigning over the human condition. The first major writer, relevant to the tradition we are dealing with, to emphasize the significance of pain had been Hobbes. He had singled out "aversion" as one of the basic forms of human motion which, when translated into the driving fear of violent death, became the creative force provoking men to the rational decision of forming a commonwealth.[119] Yet it was precisely this latter aspect of fear as a creative force, to be manipulated for positive ends, that separated the Hobbesian from the later liberal conception of fear. Hobbes had transferred fear between men, which had been the essence of the state of nature, to fear of men towards their sovereign. In short, Hobbesian society was sustained by the institutionalization and perpetuation of fear.

Although Locke agreed that the natural condition was "full of fears and continual dangers," he thought that the establishment of civil society would diminish these evils and the pains associated with them.[120] On the whole, Locke accorded pain a position of parity with pleasure. "Nature . . . has put into man a desire of happiness and an aversion to misery," and both of these sensations were expressions of the divine arrangement. Pleasure functioned to spur men into activity, and without it "we should neither stir our bodies nor employ our minds." Pain, on the other hand, served only to warn men away from harmful lines of action.[121]

In the early eighteenth century a shift in emphasis began to appear, one which reshuffled the Lockian elements into a new combination wherein pain loomed as the dominant factor in the divine arrangement. The best expression of this is to be found in a brief essay written by Benjamin Franklin in 1725 entitled *A Dissertation on Liberty and Necessity, Pleasure and Pain*. What Franklin did was to alter the notational principle of Locke's theory, first, by placing pain at the center, and, secondly, by identifying man's anxiety or "uneasiness" with a desire to escape from pain rather than with the pursuit of a fugitive happiness. "How necessary a Thing in the Order and Design of the Universe this *Pain* or *Uneasiness* is, and how beautiful in its Place!" Uneasiness, Franklin argued, was "the first Spring and Cause of all Action" and man's conduct was shaped by the fundamental end of gaining freedom from uneasiness. Pleasure was not eliminated as a goal of human striving, but it was radically redefined. It no longer stood as an alternative distinct from pain. Pleasure was in fact rooted in pain in that the escape from pain was the attainment of pleasure: "*Pleasure* is wholly caus'd by *Pain* . . . The *highest Pleasure* is only Consciousness of Freedom from the *deepest Pain* . . ."[122]

The primacy of pain was accepted into classical economics as well. Smith flatly declared that pain "is in almost all cases a more pungent sensation than the opposite and correspondent pleasure."[123] The fullest recognition came with Bentham, however. "The real question" concerning all living beings, animal or human, was not "Can they *reason*? nor, Can they *talk*? but, Can they *suffer*?"[124]

Given the centrality of pain for liberal man, Bentham's preoccupation with penal reform becomes clearly understandable. His concern to define punishment as precisely as possible, to establish a definite ratio between the degree of punishment and the magnitude of the crime, emanated from the hope of confining pain as narrowly as possible by making it more objective.[125]

The ubiquity of pain, its elevation to a psychological status equal and sometimes superior to that of pleasure, occupied a central place in the classical theory of economic behavior. Exchange relationships, for example, were discussed in terms of the pleasures to be gained by the transaction as balanced against the pains involved in surrendering an object which had itself been produced by an act of suffering, that is, labor. Similarly the act of production was rooted in pain: in the exertions of the laborer and the denial of indulgence which had allowed the entrepreneur to accumulate capital.[126]

The reality of pain in the liberal scheme of things makes it necessary to reconsider the widespread belief that the "economic man" of liberalism was dominated almost exclusively by the motive of acquisitiveness. In reality, the *homo economicus* of liberal theory was a creature not so much obsessed by the quest for gain as one frightened by the ever-present prospect of loss. "Bankruptcy is perhaps the greatest and most humiliating calamity that can befall an innocent man." To suffer a loss in the competitive struggle for advantage was to experience a far deeper sensation than that accompanying a highly profitable transaction. The pains of deprivation were greater than the pleasures of acquisition: "by the nature and constitution of the human frame, sum for sum, enjoyment from *gain* is never equal to suffering from loss." [127]

Thus liberal man emerges as a being supremely sensitive to the specific form of pain produced by the loss of wealth or status. The preservation of the self, therefore, becomes a more formidable task for the liberal than it had been for Hobbes. According to Hobbes the desire for self-preservation was basic in the sense of being a response to the threat of violent death. Self-preservation was thus closely bound to man's physical integrity and not to his worldly goods or position. Admittedly Hobbesian man did not take kindly to the loss of his goods or status, yet deprivation did not shake the very fibers of his being. The personality of liberal man, however, was sensitively attuned to the world of wealth and status. Self-preservation was broadened to include not merely "life" but "the means of it"; that is, liberty and property.[128] As Locke had shown, man's personality had been extended into external objects and when those objects were taken away, the resulting shock profoundly affected human sensibilities. This meant that there were now several possible threats to the self over and above the physical kind; it meant further that the intensity of pain suffered in the loss of wealth or status was equal to the pain of physical hurt. This was recognized by Bentham when he accorded the desire for profits a status of equality with the desire for self-preservation. By this reasoning Bentham was led to argue that the fear aroused by the loss of profits was equal in intensity to the fear of violent death, and hence the pain consequent upon economic loss was comparable to that of physical injury.[129] Liberal man moved in a world where pain and deprivation threatened him from all sides. His fears were compressed into a single demand: social and political arrangements must ease his anxieties by securing property and status against all threats excepting those posed by the competitive chase itself.[130] His aversion to pain defined that demand even more closely: to be secure was to be able to "count on things," to be able to act with the comforting knowledge that one's property would not be snatched away, a contract would not go unperformed, a debt would be honored. Everything hinged on having secure expectations. The fundamental institution of private property was itself "only a foundation of expectation." [131] So crucial to liberal man was the sense of secure expectations that ultimately the satisfaction of expectations was identified with justice. In Bentham's jurisprudence justice was defined as the "disappointment-preventing principle" and the whole system of civil law was dedicated to "the exclusion of disappointment." [132]

Expectations were deemed fundamental by the liberals not only because it allowed men "to form a general plan of conduct," but because it endowed the individual with an historical identity. Stated somewhat differently, expectation formed the liberal counterpart to the conservative principle of the continuity between generations:

> . . . It is by means of [expectations] that the successive moments which form the duration of life are not like insulated and independent parts but become parts of a continuous whole. Expectation is a chain which unites our present and our future existence and passes beyond us to the generations which follow.[133]

From the argument concerning expectations and the fears expressed about loss or deprivation, it becomes apparent that it was not economic loss in a pure sense which created apprehension, but rather the decline in social status attendant upon economic loss.[134] As Smith recognized, once the basic necessities had been satisfied, the main stimulus to further acquisition lay in the desire for social prestige and approval. "The desire of becoming the proper objects of this respect, of deserving and obtaining this credit and rank among our equals is, perhaps, the strongest of all our desires." But the importance attached to status made the possibility of loss of status appear "worse than death." Man's suffering was more intense, Smith declared, "when we fall from a better to a worse situation than we ever enjoy when we rise from a worse to a better." [135] The fears and anxieties connected with preserving status in an intensely competitive world were heightened by the sentence which society pronounced on the poor man. It was not his economic misery that made him an object of horror, but his bitter social isolation: his poverty "places him out of the sight of mankind," and other men have "scarce any fellow-feeling with the misery and distress which he suffers . . . To feel that we are taken no notice of necessarily damps the most agreeable hope and disappoints the most ardent desire of human nature." [136]

The ethical response of liberalism to the uncertainties of social status took shape in the doctrine of prudence.[137] As far back as Locke there had been two distinct but related aspects of prudence which had been singled out for attention. First, prudence emerged as the natural accompaniment of man's middling status in the universe, the corollary to his shedding the illusion of heroic abilities. Second, as a style of behavior, prudence was the direct expression of an ethic of timidity rather than daring. These two aspects were summarized in Locke's remark:

> The next thing to happiness in the other world is a quiet and prosperous passage through this, which requires a discreet conduct and management of ourselves in the several occurrences of our lives. The study of prudence then seems to me to deserve the second place in our thoughts and studies.[138]

These two themes, prudence as a middle-range virtue and as part of an ethic of timidity, were continued by Adam Smith, but with a significant addition. He identified the "middling" quality of prudence not only with man's cosmic rank but with his social status as well. Prudence, in other words, expressed the moral style of bourgeois man. The nature of "men in the inferior and middling stations of life" was shaped by two specific social imperatives: they are overawed by the rules of justice, and hence their conduct is directed by a desire to avoid legal infractions; and their social success "almost always depends upon the favour and good opinion of their neighbours and equals." Thus prudence represented a neat convergence of three elements: a "middling" social status, a modest and unheroic conduct appropriate to that status, and a middle-range set of objectives — "such fortune . . . as men in such stations can reasonably expect to acquire." [139] The classical formulation of the doctrine is to be found in Smith's portrait of the "prudent man." Here prudence was conceived as the type of knowledge suited to a character that was "cautious rather than enterprising." It was virtue cut not for the restless, aggressive buccaneering entrepreneur — the "robber-baron" type of late nineteenth-century America — but for those who wished to retain status by avoiding "any sort of hazard." These uncertainties were nicely expressed in the declamation of a nineteenth-century American orator: "Be bold! And everywhere, BE BOLD! BE NOT TOO BOLD!" [140] According to Smith's characterization, the prudent man was one who was careful to live within his income, and to be satisfied with "small accumulations," hesitant to go "in quest of new enterprises and adventures," and, like apolitical Hobbesian man, reluctant to engage in political activity except from "self-defense." His virtues of frugality and thrift were not practiced from a carefully calculated scheme to accumulate capital so as to slowly extend his economic power, but rather were "defensive" virtues aimed at cutting his losses and preserving his social position.[141]

The same liberal psychology of fear and anxiety which had elevated status-preservation to the place occupied by self-preservation in the Hobbesian scheme led directly to installing security as the main end of human activity and social policy.[142] The problem was formulated concisely and candidly by Bentham in connection with his discussion of the ends of legislation. There were, he decided, four main objectives at which the law-maker should aim: subsistence, economic abundance, equality, and security. The first two items, subsistence and abundance, could be best achieved by inaction on the part of government; that is, by leaving individuals free to pursue the best economic opportunities. The crux of the difficulty was presented by equality, for if a deliberate policy were adopted to equalize fortunes, the resulting fears on the part of the wealthy classes concerning their property would paralyze initiative. It followed that equality must give place to security of possession, because the psychological malaise attendant upon social leveling would be felt more deeply, that is, produce more pain, than the pleasures experienced by those whose lot would be somewhat improved.[143] As Smith had put it earlier, "a very considerable degree of inequality is not near so great an evil as a very small degree of uncertainty." [144]

VIII Liberalism and moral judgments: the substitution of interest for conscience.

In the minds of later political writers, liberalism has come to be identified with the view that man is essentially rational in nature and that his conduct is in fact governed by reason. Once again, however, this widespread notion about liberalism is quite mistaken. We shall try to show in the following pages that, in terms of dominant emphasis, the liberal tradition contained very strong reservations about the controlling function of reason in human behavior. In addition, it will be suggested that while the liberals often proclaimed the need for rational political policies and objective public judgments, they actually produced a theory which made objective social and political judgments impossible. In order to understand why liberals failed on this score it is necessary to fix their starting point. This was the problem left unsolved by the Protestant Reformers and Hobbes: the problem of subjectivism implicit in both the Protestant belief in the primacy of individual judgment and the Hobbesian insistence that human judgments were inevitably tainted by personal bias or by interest. As the political philosophy which accepted the Protestant heritage of the right of individual judgment and went beyond Hobbes in converting the fact of individual bias into a norm, liberalism shouldered a burden it could not carry.

As a starting point it is necessary to rid our thinking of the caricature of liberal man as a reasoning machine. Rather, liberal writers beginning with Locke and extending through Smith, Hume, and the Utilitarians emphasized repeatedly that man was a creature of strong passions. Locke himself had alluded to "the lawless exorbitancy of unconfined man" and had remarked that "passion" and "interest" had, in the state of nature, caused men to misapply the laws of nature; civil society, from this point of view, formed the remedy to man's passions.[145] Accordingly, Locke denied that "each person is at liberty to do what he himself, according to circumstances, judges to be of advantage to him." [146] But after liberalism was crossed with classical economics, this was precisely what liberals could not deny. They could not because, unlike Locke, they had ceased to believe that judgments about right conduct were rational or objective. Passion and desire, with all of their bewildering personal variations, were the stuff of moral judgments. The lesson liberals learned from Hume and Smith was that reason was not the source of moral judgments nor the main spring of human conduct. Morals were the products of human feelings. They originated in desires and needs and were approved by the passions. Reason was delegated the role of determining the most efficient means to achieving the ends proposed by feeling. "It is by hopes and fears," wrote Bentham, "that the *ends* of action are determined; all that reason does is to find and determine the means." [147]

In the classical conception of economic behavior passion was not only enthroned in a directive role, but it performed the same function in economic conduct as it did in moral conduct. Just as Hume had argued that the rational element in moral conduct was confined to discovering the means for gratifying the ends dictated by the passions, so the economists looked upon rational calculation as instrumental to fulfilling the objects of desire.[148] Hence the textbook picture of liberal man as born in foresight, baptized in shrewdness, and confirmed in calculation is about as distorted as possible: acquisitiveness was founded on desire.

If this is appreciated we are in a position to see how liberalism transformed the older notion of the common good from an object posited by reason to one rooted in desire. Again there was an exact parallel between moral theory and economic theory which was best exemplified in the writings of Adam Smith. Because unaided reason was an inadequate means to guide behavior along morally desirable paths, "nature" generously makes good the deficit by endowing men with the necessary passions or "appetites" for the ends of self-preservation and the propagation of the species. Moreover, she implants in man an "instinctive" sense of what to approve and disapprove and thereby creates the moral norms of society. Thus what is designated the common good of society is the product of passion or appetite, not reason. Similarly, the economic well-being of society occurs by way of man's attempt to satisfy his own selfish desires. Smith's famous "unseen hand," which so many commentators have interpreted as a symbol of the convergence of rational plans, individually conceived, into a rational good for the whole society, was exactly the same as Smith's theory of individual moral behavior: both the moral good of society and its material well-being had their origins in instinct, desire, and passion; and neither was the result of action intended to advance the good of society as a whole.[149]

When liberals of the late eighteenth and early nineteenth centuries did finally assert that the passions ought to be brought more strictly under the control of reason, the effects on the psychological condition of liberal man were disastrous. Taking its cues from the teachings of the economists, liberal moral theory became a body of teachings dedicated to the proposition that the essence of rational conduct consisted in the sacrifice of present pleasures for future ones. This was but to appropriate for the purposes of moral theory the fundamental psychological principle underlying the economists' concept of capital accumulation. According to the economists, capital was formed because individuals were able to postpone their gratifications to the future. Capital was defined by Senior as "abstinence." And since abstinence was recognized as self-inflicted pain, one might say that capitalist society was defined in terms of voluntary self-mutilation.[150] In Bentham's famous tract,

Defense of Usury, the usurer emerges as the symbol of self-denial: "Those who have the resolution to sacrifice the present to future are natural objects of envy to those who have sacrificed future to the present." [151] The usurer, however, is identical with the liberal definition of a moral agent, [152] and hence it is not extreme to characterize liberal moral theory as the catechizing of repression.

At this point it is necessary to retrace the argument in order to extend it in other directions. We have noted that liberal theory had located moral judgments in the passions. It is fair to say, however, that this inquiry had been largely concerned with the nature of individual moral judgments rather than with the sort of common moral beliefs or consensus that society presupposes. Throughout almost all of his major writings, Locke had shown a lively interest in the problem of consensus, yet he remained dissatisfied with the results of his thinking. The difficulty, as he conceived it, arose from the fact that consensus could be achieved only if a sufficiently widespread agreement on moral issues existed. This, in turn, meant agreement among individuals who differed greatly in their capacities for understanding. This naturally led to the query of what kind of knowledge was suitable for maintaining consensus. Was it to come from philosophy? If not from that source, might it come from religion?

In his early *Essays on the Law of Nature* Locke took the position that the vital political knowledge was contained in the dictates of the law of nature which Locke viewed as a divine decree sustaining the whole universe, as well as the society of men. It contained a perfect list of the moral obligations without which society "would fall to the ground." [153] ". . . If you abolish the law of nature . . . you banish from among mankind at the same time the whole body politic, all authority, order, and fellowship among them." [154] At this point, however, the difficulties began to emerge, with the result that Locke's notion of the law of nature became less a solution than an index to his perplexities about the moral basis of the community. Having avowed that faith, trust, and the performance of contracts were essential to the continuance of civilized living, and that the law of nature contained the rationally discoverable teachings on these subjects, it would seem to follow that the continuance of society was assured to the extent that the members were capable of grasping the meaning of natural law. Yet almost all of Locke's writings reveal a growing scepticism about the ability of the great majority of men to arrive at an understanding of natural law. True notions of moral obligation could be ascertained only by methods far beyond the competence of the average mentality. For traditional or inherited morality could not be identified with the law of nature, nor was the law an innate teaching inscribed in each conscience, much less the set of teachings accepted by men everywhere, regardless of time, place, or degree of civilization.[155] To know the law of nature in the true sense, and not merely to have a "belief" or "opinion" about it, constituted an exacting intellectual inquiry of a kind which few men could follow out.

This conclusion was patently ill-suited to the theory of society elaborated by Locke in the *Treatises:* a society based on the consent of each of the members implied that each was a moral agent fully capable of understanding the moral postulates on which society rested. But how could this be squared with Locke's belief, which he subscribed to as late as 1681, that "I cannot but think morality as well as Mathematics [is] capable of demonstration"? [156] The one position assumed easy access to moral judgments, the other that such judgments were open only to an expertly trained intellect. Most students of Locke have proceeded on the belief that the problem was solved in the *Treatises* by Locke's notion of natural law, but the fact is that Locke left the problem exactly where it had been in his previous writings. The law of nature was viewed as a body of essential political truths discoverable by reason, yet there was the difficulty that, for the vast majority, human reason had been corrupted.[157]

The failure of commentators to appreciate the significance of this issue has prevented them from locating the place where Locke attempted to resolve it; namely, in his essay on *The Reasonableness of Christianity* (1695). Here was his answer to the question of where to find a body of moral teachings appropriate to the modest and often vulgar understanding of the common run of men composing the political community. The substitute for the exacting knowledge of natural law and a mathematicized morality was to be found in the Christian ethic. While the Christian ethic was not less rational than the philosophic, it had the immense advantage of being better suited to the understanding of the "vulgar." In the classical world, according to Locke, the knowledge of true virtue had been restricted to the few. The masses of men had been kept in ignorance by the "priests," save for a few crude teachings tossed out to preserve a minimum civic morality.[158] Moreover, the classical writers had not only left some ethical problems unsolved, they had failed to systematize their teachings into a coherent whole and, above all, they had neglected to provide a form of "authority" sufficiently compelling to make men observe moral teachings. These deficiencies had been overcome by the teaching summarized in the Sermon on the Mount: it brought a morality suited to the common understanding, one surrounded by the awesome miracle of revelation, and accompanied by a notion of a Deity who employed future rewards and punishments to enforce observance of His moral commands. In sending these teachings to mankind, Locke wrote:

> God seems herein to have consulted the poor of this world, and the bulk of mankind. These are articles that the laboring and illiterate man may comprehend. This is a religion suited to vulgar capacities . . . The greatest part of mankind have not leisure for learning and logic, and superfine distinctions of the schools. Where the hand is used to the plough and the spade, the head is seldom elevated to sublime notions, or exercised in mysterious reasoning. It is well if men of that rank (to say nothing of the other sex) can comprehend plain propositions, and a short reasoning about things familiar to their minds, and nearly allied to their daily experience. Go beyond this, and you amaze the greatest part of mankind; and may as well talk Arabic to a poor day-labourer, as the notions and language that the books and disputes or religion are filled with; and as soon you will be understood. . . . Had God intended that none but the learned scribe, the disputer, or wise of this world, should be Christians, or be saved, thus religion should have been prepared for them, filled with speculations and niceties, obscure terms and abstract notions . . . If the poor had the gospel preached to them, it was, without doubt, such a gospel as the poor could understand; plain and intelligible . . .[159]

These remarks on Christianity also serve to explain why it was that Locke never embarked on the project, which he mentions frequently, of reducing ethics to a series of mathematical propositions.[160] To be sure, he occasionally expressed doubts about the feasibility of the enterprise, but it is more probable that he was deterred by the limited social utility of the idea. The bulk of mankind would not have been able to comprehend the work. Above all, he had discovered that Christianity, by "democratizing" the teachings of the law of nature, had rendered the whole scheme superfluous.

> [Even had philosophy] gone further, as we see it did not, and from undeniable principles given us ethics in a science like mathematics, in every part demonstrable; this would not have been so effectual to man in this imperfect state, nor proper for the cure. The greatest part of mankind want leisure or capacity for demonstration . . . And you may as soon hope to have all the day-labourers and tradesmen, the spinsters and dairy-maids, perfect mathematicians, as to have them perfect in ethics this way. Hearing plain commands is the sure and only course to bring them to obedience and practice. The greatest part cannot know, and therefore they must believe.[161]

It is apparent from the foregoing considerations that Locke, having despaired of a rational ethic accessible to the majority of men, had taken refuge in Christianity, but only at the cost of converting the latter into a species of "ideology"; that is, a set of simplified beliefs suited to the vulgar understanding. This is not to imply that Locke looked upon religion either in the crude way that Hobbes had, as a convenient aid to enlisting obedience, or in the cynical way that Gibbon was to characterize the religions of Rome, "considered by the people as equally true; by the philosopher as equally false; and by the magistrate as equally useful." Quite the contrary, Locke was a devout if somewhat unorthodox Christian, and, what is more important, he rested his political and moral theories on the assumption that Christianity was still a viable force in Western societies.

This, however, makes it all the more significant that Locke, a believer, should have unwittingly joined forces with Machiavelli and Hobbes to undermine further the political significance of the Christian heritage. Despite the inroads of secularism and scepticism the Western political tradition had for several centuries taken for granted the viability of what may be called a "common Christian conscience." Both in theory and in practice the tradition had assumed the continuing presence of a common outlook and moral response among the members of society. In addition, that men shared a common element of conscience meant that they could "know" and understand each other and communicate by accepted moral signs. In contrast to these notions of conscience as a common, unifying force, Locke, while upholding the value of conscience, pictured it as a divisive force. In the *Essay Concerning Human Understanding* he explicitly ruled out conscience as a reliable source of common moral rules. It was "nothing else but our own opinion or judgment of the moral rectitude or pravity of our own actions." [162] The resulting variations among individual consciences rendered it almost useless for creating the measure of agreement necessary to society.

As a consequence Locke was led to deny any presumption in favor of conscience in political matters. This point was driven home in the *Second Treatise* where it was emphasized that the "private judgment" exercisable in the state of nature was surrendered to the "legislative" and that each individual was obligated to assist in a positive manner the judgments of the legislative because they were "his own judgments." [163] As Locke declared in another connection:

. . . We do deny that each person is at liberty to do what he himself, according to circumstances, judges to be of advantage to him. You have certainly no reason for holding that each person's own interest is the standard of what is just and right, unless you let every single man judge in his own case . . .[164]

Nor was this conclusion significantly qualified by Locke's discussion of the so-called "right of revolution." Although at one point he allowed that "every man is judge for himself" when the ruler had betrayed his trust, Locke immediately revised this by saying that the "proper umpire" in such cases was "the body of the people." [165] When stated in this form, conscience surrendered what had been its most striking aspect, its individual quality; it became, instead, a social or collective form of judgment.

As Locke's argument reveals, the growing distrust of conscience stimulated the search for a new kind of conscience, social rather than individual, one that would be an internalized expression of external rules rather than the externalized expression of internal convictions. In later pages we shall try to show in greater detail how the idea of the social conscience developed, but here our concern is, so to speak, with the residual elements of conscience, with the aspects of individual conscience which were not collectivized but transformed. The idea of the individual conscience had been put forward mainly by religious non-conformists to combat both hostile communities and organized religions. Thus individual conscience, unlike the later notion of the social conscience, was intended as a defense against the group rather than a method for inducing individual conformity to the group. With the decline of religious feeling and the growth of toleration, an important change took place in the idea of conscience. No longer needed to protect deviant opinions from religious persecution, conscience and its attributes could be detached from the inner life and used to protect what a growingly secular society most treasured; namely, wealth and status, or more briefly, "interests." Under the auspices of liberalism, the great transformation was effected whereby "individual interest" was substituted for individual conscience. Interest gradually came to play the same role in political and social thought that conscience had played in religion. It was invested with many of the same sanctities and immunities, for, like conscience, it symbolized what was most valued by the individual and what was to be defended against the group or society.

These developments throw further light on the anxiety-complex of liberalism. Although interest might usurp the place of conscience and succeed to many of its characteristics, one vital difference was ineradicable and a source of considerable uneasiness for the liberals. Protestantism had always claimed

that the strength of conscience lay in its wholly internal character and, therefore, whatever took place in the external world, such as the loss of material
goods or physical injury, was powerless to affect conscience. In contrast,
interest was closely involved with wealth and status, with the sort of objects
which depended on outside occurrences. Hence, as liberals discovered to
their sorrow, consciences might become "tender" in a hostile environment,
but interests became insecure.

By way of preliminaries, we need not stress the fact that interest was
accorded a central place in liberal theory. Of all the principles of action,
Bentham had declared, "personal interest" is the "most powerful, most constant, most uniform, most lasting, and most general among mankind." As
liberalism understood it, interest was distinguished by an intensely personal
quality. To cite Bentham once more, "there is no one who knows what is
for your interest so well as yourself . . ." [166] Moreover, the exclusive nature
of interest rendered it impossible that anyone could really advance the interest of another: impossible not merely because each individual acted primarily from motives of self-interest, but also because an interest existed in
the closest possible intimacy to the individual holding it. No outsider, not
even one prompted by altruistic motives, could ever know enough to act
benevolently.[167] Nor was it a crushing rejoinder to protest that the individual might still be mistaken about where his "true" interests or happiness
lay. What was important was not any supposed "objective" status of interest
but what each individual believed to be his interest. As John Stuart Mill later
pointed out, the test of what is desirable is whether in fact men do desire
it,[168] and hence it would be inherently self-defeating to impose a "truer"
interest on men who stubbornly refused to recognize it as such.

Now these attributes of interest — its individualistic character, the subjectivity of a judgment about it, and the impossibility of forcibly imposing
it — were a faithful reproduction of those attributes assigned to conscience
by Locke in his classic *Letter Concerning Toleration*. It is too often forgotten that Locke's case for toleration marked a decisive shift in the notion
of conscience. The "Puritan conscience" had been conceived by its defenders
as a disciplined mode of judgment, one controlled by the "objective" standard of Scripture and steeped in religious instruction. One of the main reasons that the sects of the seventeenth century championed toleration was the
possibility that a dissenting conscience might in fact be testifying to what
was true. In contrast, what was controlling in Locke's argument was that
conscience stood for a form of conviction rather than a way of knowing.
Thus conscience meant the subjective *beliefs* held by an individual, and from

this definition flowed the same characteristics which were later attached to interest. Like individual interest "the care of every man's soul belongs unto himself, and is to be left unto himself." Similarly, in matters of conscience each has "the supreme and absolute authority of judging for himself," because "nobody else is concerned in it." [169] Nor was it any more availing to impose true belief than to dictate the proper interests of individuals: "no religion which I believe not to be true can be either true or profitable unto me." [170]

That interest and conscience had coalesced was not lost upon the men of the eighteenth century; freedom to pursue one's interests was interchangeable with the freedom to worship as one saw fit. The new era, wrote Morellet, is one of "freedom of conscience in trade"; or, as Lord Shelburne put it, "the era of Protestantism in trade." [171] In retrospect, there was substance in Sidney Webb's gibe at Utilitarianism for being "the Protestantism of Sociology." [172]

That there should have been parallels between Locke's doctrine of conscience and later liberal notions of interest is not at all surprising. Locke himself had drawn the parallel by basing his plea for toleration, at least in part, upon the example of economic activity: The proper policy towards religious non-conformists should be the same as in "private domestic affairs" and "the management of estates . . . Every man may consider what suits his own convenience, and follow what course he likes best." And in the same way that "no man complains" or thinks it any of his concern when his neighbor commits a financial blunder, so no man should feel exercised at his neighbor's bizarre notions about religious salvation. It follows that the individual cannot be compelled by state action to become a true believer, any more than a man "can be forced to be rich." [173]

The decline of individual conscience in liberal theory ushered in a new social world where men, no longer able to communicate on the basis of a common interior life, were reduced to knowing each other solely from the outside; that is, on the basis of socially acquired responses and values. To know men only from the "outside" implied that man had become estranged from man, which corresponds exactly with Locke's terse description of the human condition where individual consciences are strangers to each other: "no particular man can know the existence of any other being, but only when, by actual operating upon him, it makes itself perceived by him." [174] Man becomes conscious of his fellows only when he and they collide; conflict and friction are thus the sources of man's awareness of man. It was this realization which later caused Bentham to declare that it was futile "to dive into the unfathomable regions of motives, which cannot be known." All that men could know for certain was the consequences of an individual's actions, never his reasons for doing them.

These same doubts underlay the liberal argument against government intervention into economic activities. The basic assertion, that each was the best judge of his own interests and hence no outside agency could properly dictate his happiness, rested squarely on the belief that no individual could truly understand another.[175] It followed that no governing groups could legitimately act for the best interests of the members of society, because the judgment of such a group lacked any secure basis. No common link existed connecting the separate valuations which individuals placed on things. No one could say for certain what things another held dear or with what intensity his inner being was attached to them.

The interior life of the individual remained a deep mystery precisely because the common conscience of Christianity had evaporated and man, only as a series of external acts, could be understood in a sure way. [176] The epitaph for conscience was stated by Bentham in his usual bald way when he said it was "a thing of fictitious existence." And Bentham also made it abundantly clear that men no longer had any real incentive to that self-knowledge which leads to the examination of the inner life.

> But by interest he is at the same time diverted from any close examination into the springs by which his own conduct is determined. From such knowledge he has not, in any ordinary shape, any thing to gain, — he finds not in it any source of enjoyment.[177]

At the same time, since every act of will and of the intellect was reducible to interest, there remained nothing to examine internally: man's soul had been factored out.[178]

Having reduced man to mere externality and stripped him of conscience, it was easy for the liberal economists to treat him as a material object — a style of analysis which later provoked the bitter denunciation of Marx. This development in liberalism is best illustrated in the way that the Lockian idea of property was transformed. Locke had conceived property as beginning when individual men cultivated the common land of the state of nature. The act of labor consisted not only in the physical alteration of external objects but in the projection of individual personality into the objects. In this way the individual came to possess a "peculiar right," a distinctive identity gained through an act of private appropriation.[179] The psychic affinity between the individual and his property postulated by Locke was retained by the later liberal economists, but they identified it with the property of the capitalist rather than the laborer. The capitalist's personality alone suffered when his property was threatened: the laboring classes were denied the privilege of neurosis. This, of course, was almost unavoidable, given the fact that the act of labor, as organized by industrialism, no longer could be said to create objects which the laborer could claim. The next step was to assimilate the skills and energies of the laborer into a "factor of production," an impersonal element without psychic overtones:

> A labourer is himself a portion of the national capital; and is to be considered, in all investigations of this sort, merely as a machine which it has required a certain quantity of labour to construct . . .[180]

Gradually the emphasis on labor as a source of right, which had been the main theme in Locke, shifted to labor as a source of power. The contrast between capitalist society and Locke's great natural society — "sharing all in one community of nature" — could not have been more sharply expressed than by the way economists reduced the great majority of men to exploitable units of power, "labor-power" as Marx called it. The "command of labour," wrote Senior, is "the principal instrument of production" and "can be employed at will in the creation of whatever is most wanted . . . Estimated indeed in one class of objects, and it is the class most coveted by man, we mean power and pre-eminence, the value of the command of labour is almost invariable." [181] In the graphic summary of Bentham, the new power urge was given blunt expression, and in the collision between the exploiters and the exploited the full alienation implicit in the act of labor is revealed: men have become so estranged that only a situation of conflict could evoke a consciousness of each other:

> The preparation in the human bosom for antipathy towards other men is, under all circumstances, most unhappily copious and active. The boundless range of human desires, and the very limited number of objects . . . unavoidably leads a man to consider those with whom he is obliged to share such objects, as inconvenient rivals who narrow his own extent of enjoyment. Besides, human beings are the most powerful instruments of production, and therefore everyone becomes anxious to employ the services of his fellows in multiplying his own comforts. Hence the intense and universal thirst for power; the equally prevalent hatred of subjection. Each man therefore meets with an obstinate resistance to his own will, and is obliged to make an equally constant opposition to that of others, and this naturally engenders antipathy towards the beings who thus baffle and contravene his wishes.[182]

IX **Liberalism and conformity: the socialized conscience.** Liberalism has always been accused of seeking to dissolve the solidarities of social ties and relationships and to replace them by the unfettered, independent individual, the masterless man. In reality, the charge is almost without foundation and completely misses the liberal addiction towards social conformity. In one sense, of course, every political society has prescribed certain basic norms of social behavior for its members, and every form of political theory, with the exception of anarchism, has acknowledged this. But the notion of social conformity carries more serious implications beyond the obvious fact that society cannot exist for long if its members do not observe common ways of behavior. It implies, first, that the individual "adjust" his tastes, actions, and style of life to a social denominator. Social conformity is at war with what Baudelaire called "dandyism," the "best element in human pride," the need "to combat and destroy triviality." [183] Secondly, social conformity not only assumes that individual adaptation will contribute to social cohesion and order, but that a happy and successful life for the individual can be attained only by observing society's standards; that is, the generalized expression of the wants, values, and expectations held by most of the members. Thirdly, and most crucially, the individual is invited to do more than "accept" social norms; their external quality must be overcome so that they can be appropriated into the inner life of the individual. In short, social norms should be internalized and, as such, operate as the individual's conscience. Conscience thus becomes social rather than individual.

The route from individual to social conscience begins with Locke's discovery of the significance of non-legal, privately enforced norms. He pointed out that although men had, on entering society, agreed not to employ force "any further than the law of the country directs," they retained a considerable social force outside the law. Locke called this the "law of opinion or reputation." He based it on the observation that men exercised "the power of thinking well or ill, approving or disapproving of the actions of those whom they live amongst." These judgments tend to become "the common *measure* of virtue and vice" and, in many ways, to punish violators more effectively than positive law. No man, Locke noted, can endure being at odds with his "club" and no man can live conscious that he is disliked by all. "This is a burden too heavy for human sufferance." [184]

Although Locke did not follow out the rich suggestions in his own analysis, he had touched on two basic themes which became central in later liberal theories. In the first place, he clearly indicated that social norms could be understood as a species of control distinct from political power or legal authority. Secondly, Locke posed for the individual conscience the problem of social definitions of ethical values: if society should insist that its norms were in the nature of moral goods, and not merely convenient rules on the same level as, say, traffic regulations; if, in other words, the individual were compelled to confront society's norms as equal in status to ethical choices of any type, the consequences of non-conformity would be more serious. For the heavy sanctions which society could bring to bear — economic, social, and psychological — rendered an act of defiance far more consequential to the individual than any action of a private variety.

Contrary to what modern interpretations of liberalism have led us to suppose, we find later liberals devoting a surprising amount of emphasis to justifiying the necessity and desirability of social conformity. The fullest expression of this is to be found in Smith's *Theory of Moral Sentiments* which was basically an inquiry into the nature and source of the moral judgments man makes about himself and his fellows.[185] The urgency of the inquiry itself was prompted by the character imputed to man by the liberals: motivated by self-interest and dominated by passion, liberal man did not inspire much confidence that he could make choices according to some impersonal, rational standard. Nature's remedy, Smith argued, was to implant an "impartial spectator" within the human breast, an unbiased tribunal to which moral judgments could be referred. If, for example, I am about to undertake an action and wish to be assured of its rightness, or if I have already acted and wish to be confirmed in my choice, I must consult an imaginary outsider. This can be achieved if I place myself in someone else's position and assume his motives and passions: fairness and impartiality of judgment are attainable primarily in the "judgment of others." [186]

But what was the source of the judgments rendered by the spectator? Smith's answer was that they came from the opinions of society. Our moral judgments, then, were in the nature of mirrored reflections; they relayed social values to the individual conscience. What distinguished social man from isolated man was that the former possessed a conscience sensitive to social influences, a "mirror" of "the countenance and behavior of those he lives with."

But if the impartial spectator represented an internalized set of social norms, Smith did not claim that when an individual judges an act he is engaging in a rational action. When the individual appeals to the spectator he is not seeking an accord between two rational judgments, his own and the spectator's, but a "concord of affections." The actor "longs" for the spectator to have the same passionate intensity about the act. This, Smith held, was impossible, for no outsider could experience the same emotional involvement as the parties to the action. Hence there was no recourse but for the actor to flatten the high pitch of his passions, tone it down so that the spectator could enter. Although the individual "naturally prefers himself to mankind," he must be made to feel that, in the eyes of society, "he is but one of the multitude, in no respect better than any other in it." Each, therefore, must "humble the arrogance of his self-love and bring it down to something which other men can go along with." [187] Thus our passions had to be restricted to a "certain mediocrity," because, in the last analysis, the spectator was not judging the act itself but the reactions or passions of the actor involved.[188] Smith went on to point out that, "of all things," the individual has the "greatest desire" to conform. Experience has warned him of the terrible vengeance exacted of those who flaunt socially prescribed norms: almost as one, the members of society turn on the violator, shaming him, and throwing their support to those he had injured. Guilt-ridden and terrified by what he has done, "rejected and thrown out from the affections of all mankind," he undergoes the suffering torments of isolation in a world where "everything seems hostile." In panic he attempts to flee, only to discover that "solitude is still more dreadful than society." The "horror" of loneliness "drives" him back to society, "loaded with shame and distracted with fear," prepared to render expiation. So deeply have social norms become riveted into the human psyche that expiation could only be described by Smith in terms of the religious experience which social conscience has obviously displaced. The offender has become a penitent desperately seeking forgiveness from the deities he has wronged:

> Man is . . . taught to reverence the happiness of his brethren, to tremble lest he should, even unknowingly, do anything that can hurt them, and to dread that animal resentment which he feels is ready to burst out against him . . . As, in the ancient heathen religion, that holy ground which had been consecrated to some god was not to be trod upon . . . and the man who had even ignorantly violated it became piacular from that moment . . . until proper atonement should be made, so, by the wisdom of nature, the happiness of every innocent man is in the same manner rendered holy, consecrated, and hedged round . . . not to be wantonly trod upon . . . without requiring some expiation, some atonement, in proportion to the greatness of such undesigned violation.[189]

With the emergence of Utilitarianism in the last quarter of the eighteenth century the conformity principle assumed a wider meaning. Social norms are not only to be accepted but exploited and manipulated. Since, according to Bentham, "society" was nothing but a convenient fiction for an aggregate of individuals, the recipe for success consisted of knowing how to manage "others." "A man must keep well with public opinion." In his *Deontology* Bentham assumed the role of the Dale Carnegie of Utilitarianism, detailing the techniques whereby the individual could ingratiate himself with others, warning against the kind of behavior which others found offensive, with all of these counsels dedicated to the end of inducing others to assist in one's campaign for wealth and social prestige. "It is every man's *interest* to stand well in the affections of other men" so as to amass a "good-will fund" rather than an "ill-will fund." The "compound interest" thus accumulated "is happily limitless." [190] The revealing aspect of this advice on how to win friends and influence people is that it contained not the slightest hint that the individual was merely playing a public role, giving lip-service to social conventions which he secretly despised. So successfully had liberal men internalized social norms and so completely had they come to take the place of conscience that the distinction between "outer" and "inner," between convention and conscience, had been all but erased.

At first glance, the odd thing about this development is that it should have been welcomed and encouraged by liberals. After all, there is no denying that early liberalism announced itself as a philosophy dedicated to defending the sanctity and independence of the individual. If, however, we ask: against whom was the individual to be defended? we shall be better able to explain how liberalism so fatally misunderstood the crushing power of social conformity. It is usually asserted that, from the beginning, liberalism had urged the liberation of men from all kinds of authority, religious, political, social and intellectual: *ecrasez l'infâme de l'autorité!* This, however, is only partially correct and, in the case of society's authority, quite misleading. An examination of the liberal case against political authority discloses an indictment, not of political authority in general, but of authority personified and personalized. When it was directed against monarchy the charge was that the monarch had exercised his authority in an "arbitrary" or "capricious" way; that is, according to personal whim rather than by the "objective" requirements of law or rational policy. Arbitrariness, in this definition, formed the political equivalent of the Protestant charge that the pope had transformed institutional authority into personal power. This parallel has further significance because, like Protestantism, liberalism then faced the same unpleasant dilemma of having expelled one form of subjectivism only to replace it by another: was subjectivism overcome by substituting citizens for kings any more than by substituting a congregation for the pope? Whether they would acknowledge it or not, liberals had gone to school with Hobbes and learned that the synonym for private judgment was anarchy.[191] True, liberals were enthusiastic about encouraging private judgment in religious and economic matters, and Locke's *Letters on Toleration* explicitly advocated the one and implicitly, the other. The basis of the argument was that in these areas the individual alone was affected by his exercise of private judgment. But political decisions, though they might be taken by an individual in authority, were general in impact, affecting the totality of the members. Thus the problem for the liberal was how to fashion the arrangements which would overcome private judgment in political matters yet support a state of nature in economic and religious affairs.

Before it could devise a formula for defending the individual against personal political authority, liberalism, like Protestantism, had to reckon with the principle of equality. The solution was offered at the outset by Locke. Although "all men by nature are equal," this did not mean for Locke any more than it had for Luther's priesthood of believers, "all sorts of equality." Liberals were not only prepared to accept differences of birth, status, and wealth as natural facts, but to welcome these inequalities as socially useful. By equality the liberals understood a relationship to political authority rather than a sociological fact. Accordingly equality was defined by Locke as "that equal right that every man hath to his natural freedom, without being subjected to the will or authority of any other man." [192] From these two considerations, the fear of subjectivism and the value of equality, the liberal formula for authority was derived. Subjectivism was to be overcome by ridding authority of its personal elements. The political society is formed by an act of consent in which each man resigns his natural power "into the hands of the community"; that is, to an impersonal authority. The community, in turn, acts through a system of laws designed to treat individuals indifferently: "the community comes to be umpire by settled standing rules, indifferent and the same to all parties." [193] Thus authority comes to be identified with the community, while the individuals who are actually entrusted to act on behalf of the community do so only because they are "authorized" to act. Authority, in other words, is subtly transformed from the natural fact it had been for centuries into the weak fiction that the agent's act was legitimate because it had been authorized by the society: his act is our act.

From this point on, the peculiarity of the liberal tradition was its distrust of determinate, personal authority, authority whose power was visible and traceable to a specific person, such as a pope or monarch. As Spencer later summarized the case, man "must have a master; but the master may be Nature or may be a fellow man. When he is under the impersonal coercion of Nature, we say that he is free; and when he is under the personal coercion of some one above him, we call him . . . a slave, a serf, or a vassal." [194] As these sentiments imply, the liberal was eager to surrender to impersonal power, power which seemingly belonged to no specific individual. The entity which satisfied these longings was society. Its power was impersonal and was directed against all of the members indifferently. Society was no single individual: it was none of us, yet it was all of us.

Bentham supplies the perfect example of this line of development. Of all the quirks of his genius, the least endearing was his famous Panopticon project for prison reform. He proposed a circular type of prison structure which would permit a single warden to survey from the center all the inmates at any time. Knowing they were under constant scrutiny, the prisoners would behave in the required way. Obviously this was too illiberal a notion to apply unaltered to normal existence, but with a slight change, say, substitute society for the warden, would not the social non-conformist feel the same pressure for compliance as the prisoners, but with the added advantage of having no identifiable overseer? Should it be objected that this merely substitutes a new tryanny for the old, we have only to bear in mind, according to Bentham's comforting argument, that society operates only through public opinion and each of us is a member of the public. If public opinion compels us to conform we are really coercing ourselves — which is a neat way of translating Rousseau's general will into the language of liberalism.[195] The "tribunals of public opinion" take over where the sanctions of the law cease, coercing self-regarding men to a consciousness of the interests of others. Bentham saw future progress in terms of a slowly shrinking area of penal law and a steadily widening influence of the "moral law" enforced by public opinion: it was the ideal of a new economy of power without violence. He prophesied that when the moral science of utility had become accepted, the future would be one, not of complete individualism, but where "the dependence of every man upon the good opinion of all besides will be increased, and the moral sanction grow stronger and stronger." And here is Bentham's peroration on the shape of the future society:

A whole kingdom, the great globe itself, will become a gymnasium, in which every man exercises himself before the eyes of every other man. Every gesture, every turn of limb or feature, in those whose motions have a visible influence on the general happiness, will be noticed and marked down.[196]

Blindness to social coercions persisted in the thought of nineteenth-century liberal writers and accounts in no small measure for the failure of liberalism to comprehend the phenomena of "mass societies." The true measure of this is to be found in the political ideas of John Stuart Mill. Today Mill's fame derives from his impassioned plea for individual freedom and his acute analysis of the social pressures working to destroy variety and spontaneity in human character. As he explained in his *Autobiography,* the essay *On Liberty* was an indictment of the "oppressive yoke of uniformity in opinion and practice." And true enough the essay contained many noble passages defending the right of the individual to go his own way despite the offense it might give to the opinions of society. ". . . The sole end for which mankind are warranted, individually or collectively, in interfering with the liberty of action of any of their number, is self-protection . . . His own good . . . is not a sufficient warrant." [197] Yet there remained a hopelessly unreal quality about Mill's principles of liberty, one which has the effect of reducing them to mere preaching, even if of a highly commendable kind. For when it is asked, how are these principles to be enforced? Mill could give no answer because his own argument had compromised the integrity of the only means possible, namely government. If society is the enemy of individuality and if, at the same time, the dangerous development of modern democracy is that it makes government the agent of society, it is hardly to be expected that society's agent could intervene to protect the individual from society. Even more perplexing was the contradictory tendency of Mill to fall back on the very power of society which he had sought to expel in *Liberty.* The same Mill who had accused Comte of aiming at "a despotism of society over the individual," who had welcomed de Tocqueville's profound analysis of social conformity, nevertheless proposed that the tyranny of opinion be invoked in order to promote some of his own pet causes. First, his personal *bête-noire,* the old problem of overpopulation, could be alleviated, Mill argued, if there were sufficiently intense social disapproval of large families. "Any one who supposes that this state of opinion would not have a great effect on conduct, must be profoundly ignorant of human nature." Secondly, Mill's argument in *Representative Government* for an "open" rather than a secret ballot was founded on the proposition that voting was a public trust and hence "should be performed under the eye and criticism of the public . . ." It is less dangerous, Mill concluded, for the individual to be influenced by "others" than by "the sinister interests and discreditable feelings which belong to himself, either individually or as a member of a class." Finally, Mill's sympathies with moderate socialism were derived in part from a belief that a society based on communal ownership had superior methods at its disposal for compelling the lazy members to produce. Under capitalism, incentives of self-interest had failed to eliminate parasitism, for the parasites had been only too willing to follow their self-interest in concocting ingenious ways to avoid work. But under socialism the bulk of the members would have a common interest in the productive output of the society, hence the malingerer would face the solidified resentment of the community. Where the private employer could only dismiss a worker, socialist society could stigmatize him by public opinion, "the most universal and one of the strongest" methods of control.[198]

If a thinker as sensitive as Mill failed to understand fully the threat of social conformity, it is idle to expect greater insight from writers of lesser stature. Thus, Bastiat, guileless as ever, insisted that "full and complete liberty" was naturally conjoined to "the surveillance of social authority"; this without the slightest inkling that he had married incompatibles.[199] If anything, liberals became more stubborn on the subject. As late as the end of the nineteenth century, Herbert Spencer saw no incongruity in lumping together freedom, industrialism, and social pressures into one pattern, "industrial society," which was declared to be completely antithetical to the rigors of a controlled "military society" — as though industrialism contained no coercive sanctions of its own and social conformity no distaste for spontaneity:

> That form of Society towards which we are progressing, I hold to be one in which government will be reduced to the smallest amount possible, and freedom increased to the greatest amount possible — one in which human nature will have become so moulded by social discipline into fitness for the social state, that it will need little external restraint, but will be self-restrained . . . one in which the spontaneous cooperation which has developed our industrial system . . . will produce agencies for the discharge of nearly all social functions, and will leave the primary governmental agency nothing beyond the function of maintaining those conditions to free action, which make such spontaneous cooperation possible. . .[200]

In retrospect the long journey from private judgment to social conformity appears as the desperate effort of liberals to fashion a substitute for the sense of community that had been lost. For what liberalism had thought it had solved, it had only exposed as a problem. Smith had been content with the thought that only a modest degree of unity was possible in a society of disconnected particulars, a mere "correspondence" in feelings "sufficient for the harmony of society." "Though they will never be unisons, they may be concords, and this is all that is wanted or required." [201] Yet Smith's whole theory of moral judgments disclosed how alienated men had become, for only by a highly self-conscious act of sympathetic imagination could one man enter into the feelings of another.

The precarious base upon which liberals rested society testified to their having misunderstood the fundamental problem. They conceived the issue as one of reconciling freedom and authority, and they solved it by destroying authority in the name of liberty and replacing it by society, but only at the cost of exposing freedom to society's controls. To the nineteenth and twentieth centuries fell the task of stating the problem more correctly: not freedom versus authority, or Man against the State, but authority *and* community.

✑ TEN ✑

The Age of Organization
and the Sublimation of Politics

. . . The isolated individual is sick.

G. C. HOMANS

. . . Social man . . . is the masterpiece of existence.

EMILE DURKHEIM

It is as a member of a group that the individual is most pliable.

KURT LEWIN

I **The age of organization.** To describe adequately recent and contemporary conceptions of what is political is a risky undertaking, full of the pitfalls that come from standing so close to events and interpretations of events. Accepting the risks, nevertheless, let us begin with some obvious remarks and then try to see what their implications hold.

Most of us would agree, I suppose, that during the last hundred and fifty years there has been an unprecedented democratization of political life. Democratic political systems have spread thoughout the Western world; political rights have been extended to all classes of society; governments are generally expected to be accountable and responsive to popular electorates; politically oriented interest groups of a voluntary kind flourish in most West-

352

ern societies; and mass political parties are equally familiar. At the same time, a tremendous amount of political activity is everywhere apparent. Vast sums of money are expended for political purposes. Political parties have steadily developed their organizational powers to the point where the electorate is manageable. Political issues are often agitated the length and breadth of societies.

This picture might have to be modified, however, by considerations of a contrasting sort. There is substantial evidence that participation in public affairs is regarded with indifference by vast numbers of members. The average citizen seems to find the exercise of political rights burdensome, boring, and often lacking in significance. To be a citizen does not appear an important role nor political participation an intrinsic good. This is confirmed in some degree by the topics which have preoccupied political scientists over the past half century: the apathy of the voters; a "phantom public" unable to express a coherent opinion; and the low estate of politics as a vocation. Thus, despite the appearance of vitality, politics possesses little prestige and popular interest in political matters remains sporadic. By reducing citizenship to a cheap commodity, democracy has seemingly contributed to the dilution of politics.

Is it, then, the decline of the political element that is most characteristic of our age, and is this what preoccupies recent political theories? Before replying to the first question, we must introduce another consideration. One of the oddities of the times is that while there has been a noticeable decline in political interest in non-totalitarian societies, social scientists have been busy discovering political elements outside the traditional political structures. No longer do legislatures, prime ministers, courts, and political parties occupy the spotlight of attention in the way they did fifty years ago. Now it is the "politics" of corporations, trade unions, and even universities that is being scrutinized. This preoccupation suggests that the political has been transferred to another plane, to one that formerly was designated "private" but which now is believed to have overshadowed the old political system. We seem to be in an era where the individual increasingly seeks his political satisfactions outside the traditional area of politics. This points to the possibility that what is significant in our time is the diffusion of the political. If this should be the case, the problem is not one of apathy, or of the decline of the political, but the absorption of the political into non-political institutions and activities. This, in turn, implies that there still exists in the West an impressive capacity for political participation and interest which is not, however, being diverted towards the traditional forms of political life.

The plausibility of these ideas might be supported by briefly noting certain aspects of modern totalitarianism. One of the most striking is the radically political character of these systems. It is illustrated by the attempt of totalitarian governments to render the political factor all-pervasive and the ultimate referent of existence. By deliberate policy, they have extended political control into every significant human relationship and organized every important group in terms of the goals of the regime. No effort has been spared to arouse among the citizens a strong sense of involvement and identification with the political order. Time and again they have puzzled critics by the ability to muster widespread popular support. This suggests that totalitarian systems have been able to tap successfully the potential for participation which non-totalitarian societies have only diverted. This does not mean that totalitarian practices represent a model, but only that they have demonstrated, perversely perhaps, that the political animal is not extinct.

By this line of reasoning, we are led to ask: what has happened in the conditions of existence to cause this transference of the political? Why is it that political citizenship has been crowded out by other, more satisfying forms of membership? To raise questions such as these is to ask: what kind of a social environment does modern man inhabit? While several answers are possible, it is difficult to imagine one that would be persuasive and yet neglect the obvious fact that today the individual moves in a world dominated by large and complex organizations. The citizen faces "big government"; the laborer, a large trade union; the white-collar worker, a giant corporation; the student, an impersonal university. Everywhere there is organization, everywhere bureaucratization; like the world of feudalism, the modern world is broken up into areas dominated by castles, but not the castles of *les chansons de geste*, but the castles of Kafka. General Motors Corporation is a triumph of organization; so is the Pentagon; and so is totalitarianism. If any one writer can be said to have charted the organizational world, it was Max Weber. This is what he had to say about the world of bureaucracy and administration:

> The whole pattern of everyday life is cut to fit this framework. For bureaucratic administration is . . . always from a formal, technical point of view the most rational type. For the needs of mass administration today, it is completely indispensable. The choice is only that between bureaucracy and dilettantism in the field of administration.[1]

This is a world which Hobbes might have enjoyed: one created by human wit, where rational action has become a matter of routine, and magic banished. It is also a world which has severely modified the postulates of politics. Take, for example, the problem of social classes. From the seventeenth through the nineteenth centuries most political theorists had regarded it as part of their role to advance proposals for harmonizing the admittedly divergent interests and aims of the several socio-economic groups within society. Today, however, the issue no longer seems as urgent, at least not in the industrially advanced countries, such as the United States, Great Britain, Germany, and the Soviet Union. The concept of "social class" now lives the peaceful existence of any sociological category, and de Tocqueville has proved a better prophet than Marx. Equality has exchanged position with social inequality and has become the more pervasive phenomenon. The classical conception of capitalism, as entertained by Adam Smith or Marx, no longer corresponds with the realities of either the worker's condition or the role of the entrepreneur. In this connection Saint-Simon, rather than Marx, had the truer appreciation of the future. The typical unit of today's economy is the business corporation. Its effectiveness depends, as Saint-Simon had foreseen, on the close collaboration of the administrator and the scientist-technician. It is directed by the sort of elite that Saint-Simon had predicted: engineers, managers, and bankers. Gradually this charmed circle is being widened to admit Saint-Simon's favorite group, the scientist. The complexity and magnitude of corporate operations have largely nullified the claims of inherited wealth and privilege, and these have been replaced by the criterion which Saint-Simon tirelessly advocated: the criterion of functional skills; that is, skills defined in terms of the operating needs of the enterprise. Except for the exclusion of the creative "artist," the outlines of Saint-Simon's *industriels* have been faithfully reproduced in modern managerial society. Moreover, Saint-Simon's warning, that the single most pressing issue confronting the society of the future would be to raise the material and moral lot of the workers, has been heeded. Under the combined stimulus of the new gospel of "enlightened management" and the pressures exerted by a highly organized trade union movement, the workers are now cared for with a solicitude that would have gratified Saint-Simon and astounded the Manchester economists.

While these changes have not ushered in an age of industrial peace, the conflicts which arise between workers and management are by no means peculiar to capitalism. That they have plagued the Soviet system as well suggests they are peculiar only to a bureaucratized economy.[2] Similarly, the proper role of trade unions in an interdependent, acutely sensitive economy seems to raise the same order of problems under British socialism, American capitalism, and Russian communism. It was a late and influential teacher at the Harvard Business School who remarked that whether a society is democratic, fascist or communist is irrelevant, for "the industrial problem is otherwise the same for all." [3]

These changes are part of a larger picture in which private ownership of the means of production and private property in general have ceased to be crucial political topics. It would take considerable effort to unearth a contemporary textbook writer who argues that the modern corporation is truly "privately" owned in the sense that the owners are perfectly justified in doing whatever they wish with their "property." A number of years ago Lord Keynes noted a "tendency of big enterprise to socialize itself" and today it is not unusual to find writers using phrases like "collective capitalism" to characterize the new system.[4] Contemporary socialist movements are one casualty of a situation where ownership is no longer an explosive political issue. The British Labour Party has lost its enthusiasm for further nationalization of industry,[5] while the West German trade union movement, traditionally a pillar of orthodox Marxism, embraces "co-determination" in industry, an arrangement which leaves existing rights of ownership undisturbed.[6] On the other side, acquisitiveness is no longer preached with the same confidence by the representatives of the owning classes. Young business executives are exhorted to acquire instead a sense of "social responsibility." [7] Thus even the bourgeoisie no longer seem to care. For, as Schumpeter pointed out, the old system of private property has evaporated and has been replaced by a society of corporations which no *one* person owns, apartment houses in which occupants merely dwell, electrical appliances which belong to the finance company rather than the user.[8]

It is not surprising, therefore, that styles have changed in politics as well. Today politics is rarely occupied with attacks on the "system" of an existing society. Everyone accepts it. Today systems are not attacked but "subverted."

What we are witnessing is a wholesale reaction against the old-style politics of "interest" which had centered around the system of private property. In the world of organizational politics men are no longer exercised by the ancient battle cries of inequality. Organizations require interdependent functions, and each functionary is just as necessary as — and hence in a sense equal to — every other. Proudhon pointed this out about a century ago:

> Differences of aptitude or of skill in the worker, of quality or quantity, disappear in social work, when all the members have performed according to their capabilities; then they have done their duty . . . The discrepancy between individual capabilities is neutralized by the general effort.[9]

The widespread hostility towards economic motives as well as the relative lack of interest in the issue of equality are both bound up with one of the dominant themes of modern thought, the revival of social solidarity.[10] The rapid technological changes and high social mobility of industrial societies have left in their trail uprooted populations with a deep sense of loneliness and bewilderment. The symptoms of personal demoralization have preoccupied the psychologist, as the symptoms of social disorganization have the sociologist. These sciences have agreed that modern man is desperately in need of "integration." His need to "belong" and to experience satisfying relations with others can be fulfilled if he is able to "identify" himself with an adequate group, one which will provide him with membership; that is, a defined role and assured expectations. When these themes are joined to those briefly alluded to earlier we have the central focus of our present chapter: the political in an organizational age which longs for community.

II Identifying a tradition of discourse. These are some of the important features of the modern temper. To describe how they have developed raises a preliminary question of method: to what writers over the past century and a half shall we turn in order to observe the emergence of our own patterns of thought? The customary procedure is to assign recent writers, as one would recruits, to various ideological camps — socialism, reaction, liberalism, and so on — and once the armies are evenly matched, draw the lines, sound the bugle, and let the hostilities begin, with the sure knowledge that the groupings established accurately reflect the development of political thought during the past century. This procedure seems to me to be quite wrong. As was suggested earlier, despite the ideological differences between various societies, the contemporary Western world confronts a common order of problems. This is not to minimize ideological divergencies, nor to assert that the United States is the "same" as the Soviet Union or Nazi Germany. A common order of problems does not necessitate a uniform response. Nevertheless, the hard truth is that the differences in ideology and practices are not always as sharp as one would perhaps like. A common order of problems *does* set limits to the range of possible choice.

These remarks are in the nature of a fair warning of the unorthodox procedure followed in the present chapter. Among the writers discussed some have been labelled reactionaries and some utopians; other have been designated socialists or communists and still others have been categorized as managerialists, or stigmatized as apologists for contemporary capitalism; and, if it does not appear anticlimactic, some have been singled out because they are the founders of modern social science. This procedure of collecting under a single roof thinkers as diverse as de Maistre, Saint-Simon, Hegel, Marx, Durkheim, Lenin, and the spokesmen of managerialism may seem an affront to the niceties of interpretation. If so, it is intentional. The present chapter is intended as an argument against the fetish of ideological interpretation which compels us to look at past theories through constrictive peepholes. My premise is that the ideas which have significantly influenced our political and social world, and shaped the way that we interpret it, represent a blend of the theories of a highly diverse group of writers. In the way that we understand the world we are partly the debtors of Marx, but also of de Maistre, partly of Lenin, but also of managerialism. There can, however, be no adequate understanding either of ourselves or our world unless we first overthrow the tyranny exercised by ideological categories and return to the notion of a tradition of discourse. The nineteenth-century writers and their successors have been engaged in a continuous discussion in which there has been considerable agreement on the nature of the problems to be faced, the procedures and concepts of analysis, the values to be sought and the evils to be eliminated. This community of preoccupations constitutes a tradition of discourse.

The community of discourse among social and political writers of the nineteenth and twentieth centuries was facilitated by the widely shared methodological assumptions associated with positivism. Although there were some important exceptions to the reign of positivism, and Hegel would be one, its influence extended to Saint-Simon, Fourier, Proudhon, Comte, Marx, the English Fabians, and the founders of modern social science, such as Durkheim, Freud, and Weber. All were, in varying degrees, animated by the conviction that the study of society could be advanced if its practitioners succeeded in assimilating the spirit and general methods employed in the more "exact" sciences. By means of observation, classification of data, and testing, social phenomena could be made to yield "laws" predicting the future course of events.

It would be superfluous to document positivist tendencies in our age, but what does require amplification is the connection between acknowledged positivists, like Marx or a modern sociologist, and the reactionary theocrats. To do this it is first necessary to dispel the prejudice that the "science of society" was an idea unique to radical writers of the nineteenth century. It is too readily assumed that Marx and Comte, for example, were the direct heirs of an older scientific outlook, extending back to Bacon, Hobbes, and Harrington, in which science had largely been conceived as the sworn enemy of the traditional authorities of manor, throne, and altar. In the eighteenth century, however, the belief that science necessarily carried radical social implications began to be questioned, and in Montesquieu's *Esprit des lois* an attempt was made to dissociate the idea of a science of society from the idea of radical reform: "I write not to censure anything established in any country whatsoever . . . I should regard myself the happiest of mortals if I were successful in advancing reasons why every man ought to love his prince, his country, his laws . . ." [11] Writing in an age of censorship Montesquieu may have been quite guilty of an understandable desire to placate authority, yet there existed a strongly conservative tendency in his method of analysis. He dwelt repeatedly on the complex and ingenious interrelations of social facts; the interdependence of political authority, social status, manners, morals, and laws; the ingenuity of arrangements which conscious action could never duplicate; the need to adjust to "givens" and to modify only within very narrow limits. "Facts" and "relations" and "social laws" — these became the conceptual weapons for combatting the rationalistic and reformist tendencies of modern political thought.

The transformation of the idea of a social science into a bulwark of order was accelerated by the efforts of two writers, de Maistre* and de Bonald,** who are often treated as champions of irrationality, freakish throwbacks to a pre-scientific age. But they appear to be pre-scientific only when judged by the abstract, highly rationalistic image of science treasured by the seventeenth and eighteenth centuries. The idea of science began to change, however, and by the nineteenth century the hard core of science was believed to consist of facts and observations. This conception of science formed the basis of the widespread effort of the nineteenth century to found a science of society. It also smoothed the way for an alliance between science and reaction. Reac-

---

* Joseph de Maistre (1753-1821) was born of a distinguished family in Savoy. Driven into exile when the French revolutionary armies overran Savoy, he joined the court of the King of Sardinia and was appointed ambassador to Russia (1803-1817). Cultured and highly intelligent, he provided the opponents of the French Revolution with a wonderfully literate and distinctive philosophy. His later influence extended in several directions and can be found in Comte, Saint-Simon, and Durkheim. He has been highly praised in our century by writers like Maurras and Claudel.

** Louis de Bonald (1753-1840) was exiled by the French Revolution, but later became Minister of Instruction (1808) and a deputy (1815). Like de Maistre, he was enormously learned, but he lacked the grace and brilliance of the former. His style was crabbed and pedantic, yet he deserves to be ranked with de Maistre as one of the great philosophers of the reaction.

tionary, Catholic, and theocratic though they may have been, both de Maistre and de Bonald were "progressive" and "advanced" in their tough-minded appreciation of facts. "Facts are everything in questions of policy and government." [12] Both writers fought as stubbornly as any positivist or modern social scientist against the notion that the true nature of society could be fathomed by abstract and rationalistic methods. *"Le premier . . . maître en politique,"* declared de Maistre, is the concrete facts of history. History was "experimental politics." [13] Both writers rejected the contention that the study of nature and of political society required wholly different procedures — a contention de Maistre contemptuously dismissed as a *"bizarrerie,"* while de Bonald flatly asserted that the time had come to analyze society through "the same approach" utilized in "the exact sciences." The latter further claimed that his own *Théorie du Pouvoir* followed the premise that "algebra has been applied to geometry; now it should be applied to politics." [14] Neither of these writers would have quarrelled with the later assertion of Durkheim that ethics "is a system of realized facts," for both of them would have agreed with his conclusion that the reduction of ethics to a science of facts necessarily imparted "a conservative attitude." [15] They would also have joined in Durkheim's lament that, while in the other sciences men unhesitatingly submit to the facts, in social matters men persist in the arrogant illusion of omnipotence.[16] As de Bonald had contended, "if laws are the necessary relationships deriving from the nature of things" — a phrase that re-echoes in Saint-Simon, Proudhon, Comte, and others — "these relationships establish themselves necessarily; then man, although free, cannot retard their development." [17] In this respect the reactionaries were no different from Marx or sociologists like Durkheim: all of them utilized "necessity" as a bridge for smuggling facts into the territory of norms. By declaring certain relationships to be reflective of "the nature of things," the compulsion resident in the facts themselves was discreetly obscured. This was typified in a famous passage of Durkheim where he distinguished "normal" from "pathological" conditions and declared the former to be "founded in the nature of things." One was justified, he concluded, in "erecting this normality of fact into a normality of right." [18]

The belief that there existed discoverable "laws" governing social phenomena; that the operation of these laws was "necessary" in the sense that to resist them was to invite social calamities; and that consequently, these laws carried prescriptive injunctions to which men ought to conform — all these added up to a view of society which left no room either for politics and the practice of the political art, or for a distinctively political theory. "In the old system," Saint-Simon declared, "society is governed essentially by men; in the new it will no longer be governed except by principles." [19] Similarly, Proudhon: "It is always the government of man, the rule of will and caprice . . . It ought to be the expression of fact." He, too, looked forward to a time when politics would be reduced to an impersonal body of principles and men would be governed by scientific truths: "Politics is a science, not a stratagem; demonstrated truth is man's true chief and his king." [20] The century was nearly unanimous in its contempt for politics: the Utopian Socialists* banished it from their ideal communities; Marx predicted the withering away of the state and its replacement by an administration of "things" based on the necessary laws of society. Durkheim summed matters up: "political questions have lost their interest"; they affect only "a small part of society," never its "vital knot." We must look "under this superficial covering" to find "how the great social interests exist and act." [21]

Instead of the older theme of politics, or even the more recent one of economics, the century turned to "society" which became the symbol of its intellectual preoccupations, the source of a new *mystique,* the *Magna Mater* of an age that wanted desperately to commune. Here is what Proudhon, one of the great individualists, who made a vocation of hating authority, said:

> I look upon society, the human group, as being *sui generis,* constituted by the fluid relationships and economic solidarity of all individuals, either of the nation, or of the locality or corporation, or of the entire species . . . a being which has its own functions, foreign to our individuality; its ideas which it communicates to us; its judgments which resemble ours not at all; its will which is in diametric opposition to our instincts; its life which is not that of the animals or of the plant, even though there are some apt analogies . . .[22]

---

* Utopian Socialism was a phrase coined by Engels to describe the type of socialism represented by writers like Fourier, Saint- Simon, and Owen. Engels' characterization was intended to emphasize the "pre-scientific" quality of their socialism; that is, they believed that a socialist society could be created by an act of will, either in the form of experimental communities, or by means of education. In contrast, the Marxian position was declared to be "scientific" because it had demonstrated that socialism was not a matter of choice but of historical necessity. Although the label "Utopian Socialist" has passed into general usage, it has sometimes been employed rather loosely to cover writers, such as Proudhon, who do not properly belong alongside Fourier or Owen. Moreover, Engels erred in lumping Saint-Simon with the Utopians. Strictly speaking, Saint-Simon was not a socialist, for he did not propose the abolition of private property or social inequality. At the same time, like the Marxists, he believed that the operation of certain historical laws made the new society inevitable. In this chapter I shall use "Utopian Socialism" to refer to Fourier and Owen and to distinguish them from Saint-Simon and Proudhon.

The century endowed society with a status as distinctive as that previously accorded the political order, surrounding it with the affectionate metaphors that another age had reserved for the church,[23] personifying it as the life-force ultimately shaping politics, economic life, and culture. The century had adopted the article of faith that no creation, no object, no thought, no act could be rightfully called "mine." Everything was society's creation. Even the highest flights of human aspiration and creativity — art, literature, religion, and philosophy — were stripped of mystery and exposed as "expressions" of society.[24] All shades of opinion unanimously agreed that economic production must be analyzed as a social process in which it was impossible to single out the contributions of specific individuals. Although it fell to the socialists to exploit this particular line of thought into a justification for the abolition of private ownership, property was merely the most spectacular casualty among privacies of all kinds.

For an age that was dubious about whether God existed, and for a science, like sociology, that no more needed *that* hypothesis than did the mathematician Laplace, there was a surprising eagerness to attribute to society the transcendence denied God. God is "only society transfigured and symbolically expressed." "Insofar as he belongs to society, the individual transcends himself, both when he thinks and when he acts." [25] Society is God, or more precisely, through society man plays God — this was the passionate belief of the century. All men, Saint-Simon had declared, were afflicted with a power urge; all are struggling to replace "the fantastic being who rules all of nature." [26] For the present, the century decided to allow God to retain control of the heavens — this would be challenged later — and to turn its energies to playing God in the universe of society. In the social world man is master: he "raises himself above things and makes laws for them, thus depriving them of their fortuitous, absurd, amoral character; that is, insofar as he becomes a social being. For he can escape nature only by creating another world where he dominates nature. That world is society." [27] With the advent of industrialism the century realized that a great instrument was ready at hand for shaping nature to man's design. Marx systematized the thinking of the age when he theorized that industrial society formed a unified social environment, a "social nature," which exerted a control over the social character of man as complete as that of Darwanian nature over the physical life of organisms. The industrial system selects some human capabilities, rejects others, adapts some, destroys others; it encourages some of man's potential, stunts the rest, and leaves man "a crippled monstrosity"; it establishes a hierarchy between and within classes; it imperiously commands that the natural tempo of human life be adjusted to the rhythms of the machine — "a continuity, uniformity, regularity, order, and even intensity of labor . . ."[28] Under capitalism disharmony and alienation prevailed between man and "nature." Industrialized "nature" stood as "an alien force existing outside" man, "growing out of our control, thwarting our expectations, bringing to naught our calculations." In the society of the future, however, the "violence of things" over persons would give way to "the control and conscious mastery of these powers"[29] and modern man would be as securely entrenched in the governance of his world as the mediaeval God had been in His.

In contemporary thought the drama of man as God appears to have played out to its climax: nature is no longer distinct from society, but, by the powers of organization, it has been taken from God and absorbed into society:

> With the gradual integration of unplanned events into a planned society an important stage in the technical control of nature is reached. The newly controlled provinces of nature lose their original character and become functional parts of the social process.[30]

The glorification of society was presaged by the discovery of nineteenth-century writers that man was, in Proudhon's words, *un animal vivant en société,* a being whose nature was shaped by social groups and whose natural destiny it was to serve as a palimpsest registering the crisscross of social interrelationships. De Bonald, reactionary, theocrat and royalist, donated the watchword for the age: "everything tends to create aggregates in the social world . . ."[31] Or, in the formulation of another writer, "Society means the sum total of relationships; in a word, system."[32] The words were those of Proudhon, self-proclaimed anarchist and individualist; they might just as easily have come from any number of sociologists, reactionaries, communists, and spokesmen for the modern corporation.

III **Organization and community.** The preoccupation with "society" gave rise to two closely interrelated problems which troubled almost every major nineteenth-century writer and continues to perplex the present. They are the problems of community and of organization. Stated in very broad language the thesis of the following pages is this: the political and social thought of the nineteenth and twentieth centuries largely centered on the attempt to restate the value of community, that is, of the need for human beings to dwell in more intimate relationships with each other, to enjoy more affective ties, to experience some closer solidarity than the nature of urbanized and industrialized society seemed willing to grant. In terms of theorizing, this quest led to the elaboration of what Proudhon called the *"métaphysique du groupe."* At the same time, the thought of the period followed another direction, one which presented a serious threat to the communitarian development. In the words of an older historian, the nineteenth century was "a period saturated with the idea of organization." [33] Just as Aristotle's dictum that man is a political animal had reflected the ethos of a highly political age, so Saint-Simon accurately reported on the guiding belief of the organizational age: The superiority of men over other animals "results directly from a superiority of organization." [34]

The writers who ranked organization foremost among social phenomena inevitably emphasized considerations far different from those preoccupying the theorists of community. The organizationists looked upon society as an order of functions, a utilitarian construct of integrated activity, a means for focusing human energies in a combined effort. Where the symbol of community was fraternity, the symbol of organization was power.

Among nineteenth-century writers the idea of organization was partly associated with economic or technological considerations, but in its mature form, such as we know it today, it has meant far more. Organization also signifies a method of social control, a means for imparting order, structure, and regularity to society. In this respect the idea of organization owes far more than is often realized to the counter-revolutionaries, de Maistre and de Bonald, who discovered in organization the antidote to the disorders afflicting post-revolutionary France. What made this discovery of general significance, and led to the absorption of reactionary elements into later social and political theory, was that disorder or *anomie* appeared a constant threat long after the Reign of Terror and Jacobinism had been forgotten. The "lack of organization characterizing our economic condition," Durkheim declared, existed in all departments of social life; men had come to accept as normal the abnormality of disorder.[35] And, in the words of a contemporary student of industrial practices, "politically and socially . . . we have no industrial civilization, no industrial community life, no industrial order or organization." [36] When the spokesman for managerial society echoes the lament of Saint-Simon — "A real solution will only come when society is integrated around its major activity, business" [37] — he is paying unconscious tribute to de Maistre as well; his faith is that business can provide a principle of order as well as a method of production.

It was not conservatives alone who held a deep faith in the saving powers of organization. The fundamental contribution of Lenin to Marxist theory was along similar lines. He "completed" Marxism by adding a theory of action based on the proposition that the creation of a compact revolutionary organization was the precondition for the successful overthrow of capitalism. If organization could conquer nature for the capitalist, it could surely conquer society for the proletariat. Similarly, recent advocates of economic "planning" have relied on the talisman of organization as the means of deliverance from the social chaos of uncontrolled capitalism. Mannheim's writings are particularly instructive in this connection because of their neat synthesis of Saint-Simonian and Leninist ideas. His diagnosis was pure Saint-Simonism: "every country alike is groping for a new way of organizing industrial society." Like Saint-Simon before him, Mannheim announced that "the technical and structural foundations of modern society have been completely transformed," and from this he drew an identical warning: the "successful organization of society cannot be left to chance." [38] But when Mannheim turned to consider the modes of action suitable to modern society, Saint-Simon is exchanged for Lenin. According to the Leninist theory of revolution, the progressive bureaucratization and centralization of society had greatly simplified the task of the revolutionaries. Under modern conditions the revolutionaries needed only to seize certain strategic control-points and the whole of society would fall under their direction. Mannheim adopted a similar assumption with one qualification. In an organizational age, where only levers had to be pressed, revolutionary action could be dismissed as an unnecessary and costly atavism. Capitalism had perfected the organization of society and thereby had made it possible for a "planning elite" to gain "control of the whole" by capturing a few "key" positions. Just as the strategy of the Leninists was aimed at controlling the few nerve-centers of society, "planning is the reconstruction of an historically developed society into a unity which is regulated more and more perfectly by mankind from certain central positions." [39] Planning, like revolution, is a form of strategy which seeks to bring power to bear at crucial, sensitive points and always in the right proportion. [40]

Whatever differences there were in diagnosis and prescription, most of the major writers were agreed on the general formula — organization: organization of a socialist commonwealth where competition and private ownership of the instruments of production were abolished and work was administered along more rational lines; organization of society into a vast hierarchy of authority where, as de Maistre would have it, king and pope, assisted by a public-spirited aristocracy, would reinstitute stability and peace (or, substitute Comte's hierarchy of savant-priests, and the point is the same); organization of society on the basis of professional and producing groups, as Durkheim suggested; or, as many recent writers have urged, organization of society under the control of managerial elites who alone possessed the requisite knowledge for maintaining social equilibrium in an age of successive technological revolutions. The primacy assumed by the idea of organization was not the achievement of any one school but of many. Each of us, as members of societies dominated by organized units, is part socialist, part reactionary, part managerialist, part sociologist. Organizational man is a composite.

The idea of community and the idea of organization did not develop as two separate and parallel strands during the nineteenth and twentieth centuries. What is interesting, and at times poignant, is the way that they converge. The nostalgia for the vanished warmth of the simple community and the obsession with the possibilities of large-scale organization are frequently piled on top of each other. As the century wore on and men were sobered by the impracticality of recapturing the shared warmth of a close communion, they stubbornly refused to surrender the hope of community. Instead, they insisted on imputing its values to the stark and forbidding structures of giant organizations. ". . . The organization of a well-ordered system requires that the parts be strongly bound to the whole and dependent on it." [41] The overtones of this remark were communal; the theme was organizational.

The idea of organization as both power and community figures prominently in contemporary theories. The existence of organization, declares one sociologist, not only creates "newly deployable energy" but "a unity of persons rather than of technicians." [42] The tenor of these remarks is strongly expressive of the modern writer's continuing search for a synthesis of power and community similar to the one achieved by the mediaeval church. Beginning with de Maistre and de Bonald a succession of social and political theorists have voiced their admiration for the subtle blend of power, belief, and solidarity of mediaeval society. The decisive point in this development occurred when radicalism, in the person of Saint-Simon, agreed with the reactionaries that mediaeval Catholicism was an eternal reminder both of the fundamental importance of authority in the preservation of society and of the necessity of some form of religion which would provide a minimum ethic and a bond of fraternity. Religion had the charm of a novel discovery for the nineteenth-century precursors of social science; some of them, like Saint-Simon and Comte, thought so highly of religion that they enthusiastically undertook to invent new ones. The oddities of these "religions" need not detain us, but what was important was that radicalism had appropriated for its own purposes the insights of the reactionaries. Saint-Simon invented a religion because of a conviction that the cold workings of a scientific society could not be supported without a foundation of common belief and that human appetites aroused by the promise of a material millennium could not be contained unless a religious ethic existed.

This style of argument had been established early in the nineteenth century by de Bonald. Without questioning the sincerity of de Bonald's religious convictions, one can detect a fundamental incongruity between the highly rationalistic, almost geometrical cast of his thought, the tough insistence on the need for an absolutely sovereign power, his contempt for any form of individuality and, on the other hand, his appeal to a religion founded on the saving doctrine of love and humility. Yet there was no incongruity, because de Bonald, for all his protestations of belief, had lost touch with the older meaning of religion. For de Bonald, as for many later social scientists, religion had been swallowed by sociology:

> Others have defended the religion of man; I defend the religion of society. . . . in the future [religion] will be considered from a broader point of view, one relative to the society, whose laws it ought to rule and regulate by endowing it with what it could not otherwise secure, a rationale for the power of commanding, and a motive for the duty of obeying.[43]

In more recent times the social utility of religion has been expressed in a nostalgia for the values of the Middle Ages. Durkheim, as well as many of the proponents of "guildism" in England, have drawn inspiration from the mediaeval system of corporations and guilds and pointed approvingly at the moral solidarity and the restraints on acquisitiveness that prevailed.[44] The late Elton Mayo hoped that the human relationships which might be developed in the factory system would provide a substitute for "the simple religious feeling of mediaeval times" [45] — a rather startling variation on *laborare, orare*. Erich Fromm, one of the most influential of the neo-Freudian revisionists, has written with approval of the condition of mediaeval man: although not free, "neither was he alone and isolated . . . Man was rooted in a structuralized whole, and thus life had a meaning which left no place, and no need, for doubt." [46] To complete the thread of connections, the late Karl Mannheim argued that the sociologist had none of the rationalistic liberal's suspicions of religious values and institutions and hence could better appreciate the social function of mediaeval Catholicism:

> Today, of course, we have greater understanding than ever of the achievement of a mediaeval basic theology and even of the need for an organized spiritual power.[47]

The sociological appreciation of religion has had a discernible effect upon recent theories of organization. The problem that many recent theorists have posed is the one that had perplexed Saint-Simon earlier: if large-scale organizations are the central units around which contemporary life is mainly organized, how can they exchange their old identities, as structures of authority and power, for a new one which combines authority with a feeling of community among the members? The mission of the organization is not only to supply goods and services, but fellowship as well. The confidence of the modern writer in the power of organization stems from a larger faith that organization is man's rejoinder to his own mortality. Accordingly, the contemporary writer, in describing great organizations like the business corporation, tends to fall back on the language of religion. A good example of this, and one drawn from a sober-minded writer, is A. A. Berle's *The Twentieth Century Capitalist Revolution*. The United States, he writes, has committed itself to a society dominated by the large corporate enterprise; these units have become the "collective soul" and "conscience-carrier of twentieth century American society." The corporation represents the means whereby "we are plotting the course by which the twentieth century in America is expected to produce an evolving economic Utopia, and, apparently, the potential actually exists, bringing that dangerous and thrilling adventure within human reach for the first time in recorded history." Appropriately the last chapter of this book is entitled "Corporate Capitalism and the 'City of God.' " [48]

These intellectual tendencies are closely related to the main concern of our previous chapters, the search for the political. In community and in organization modern man has fashioned substitute love-objects for the political. The quest for community has sought refuge from the notion of man as a political animal; the adoration of organization has been partially inspired by the hope of finding a new form of civility. To clarify these notions it is proposed that we analyze two "ideal" theories of community and organization: our theorist of community will be Jean-Jacques Rousseau, citizen of Geneva, and our theorist of organization, Henri Comte de Saint-Simon, the self-proclaimed "Founder of the Industrial Doctrine."

IV **Rousseau: the idea of community.** Few men have been more deeply at odds with society than Rousseau; fewer still have spoken as powerfully of the need for community. Yet this was not one more paradox in the most paradoxical of thinkers. Because Rousseau felt his own alienation so deeply, he was prepared to sacrifice more for society, as well as to demand more from it. The alienation expressed in his writings was total, extending to all levels of existence. "We no longer live in our own place, we live outside it . . . Man is now beginning to be at war with himself." [49] Man has turned his own mind against himself: "a state of reflection is a state contrary to nature, and a thinking man is a depraved animal." [50] Society, with its inducements to rivalry and ambition, had trapped man into adopting a social self which stifled the authentic or natural self. "Then it is that man finds himself outside nature and at strife with himself." [51] Society, instead of helping man in developing his capacities, stunts what it has not stifled and leaves behind a caricature of human potentialities. "Our wisdom is slavish prudence; our customs consist in control, constraint, compulsion. Civilized man is born and dies a slave. The infant is bound up in swaddling clothes, the corpse is nailed down in his coffin. All his life long man is imprisoned by our institutions." [52] Political life reflects the same estrangement between man and his surroundings. Political arrangements are shrewdly designed by the rich and powerful and foisted upon the poor and weak to keep them in subjection: "all ran headlong to their chains . . . they had just enough wit to perceive the advantages of political institutions, without experience enough to see the dangers." [53]

What gave pathos to human alienation was that man could never regain his natural self, a point that Rousseau's critics have tended to ignore when charging him with favoring a return to the primeval slime. The anguish of the human condition was that man could never go back to the warm, dark womb of nature. "Savage man and politicized man are so fundamentally different in heart and by inclinations that what gives happiness to the one reduces the other to despair." [54]

The gulf that separated Rousseau from his century was nowhere more deeply marked than in his rejection of the uncritical worship of "society." Hume, the classical economists, and later Paine and Godwin, had rated social life the highest form of human achievement and the vital condition for the development of morality and rationality. The interdependence of each on all, which was the marvelous secret of society, furnished a basis for the complex structure of cooperation and the division of labor which had enlarged man's productive power and extended his mastery over nature. Rousseau did not doubt that interdependence and cooperation had enhanced man's power and that the process of socialization had endowed man with conscience and rationality. Instead, he questioned whether reason, conscience, morality, and productive power — in short, all that the century meant by society and civilization — were unmixed benefits. If the course of social evolution had "improved the human understanding while depraving the species, and made man wicked while making him sociable," there must be a radical ambiguity accompanying each benefit and pervading society as a whole. What was it, then, that society did to man? what moral wound did it inflict on his nature to cause him to employ reason in the service of deception and make conscience accessory to his crimes? why was man "depraved" and "perverted" by society? [55]

No satisfactory answer could be had, Rousseau believed, without first understanding man's nature in the most radical sense of that term: not man's nature as it had been shaped by society, but as it existed in the state of nature, man stripped of all socially acquired habits, desires, and morality, in short, man as raw self, as *Id*. In the state of nature man had been at peace with himself, because life had been reduced to the essentials of survival. Man's passions and instincts had been fully sublimated in the attempt to satisfy his immediate wants, and hence a kind of equilibrium had been established: what he needed he desired, and what he desired he needed. Civilized man, in contrast, had fabricated endless complications to existence. As a creature whom society had rendered rational and endowed with imagination, he uses what he has acquired to make his condition miserable. He is cursed by the ability to imagine new needs, to extend without limit the horizon of his possibilities, to turn reason into cunning and place it at the service of desire. He has destroyed the balance between needs and desires: what he needs he does not desire, what he desires he does not need. Living in close proximity to others multiplies his wants; he is forced into making comparisons between what he has and what others have. Existence is turned into a running sore of discontent.[56] Now man must compete with others for the objects of desire; he must adopt stratagems of dissimulation, hypocrisy, and insincerity. "To be and to seem become two totally different things." [57] Soon he is led to the fatal discovery that other men can be used to satisfy his own wants, and other men, in turn, discover that he is equally useful to them. Thus begins the web of interdependence, woven from desire, that the philosopher gilds with soothing phrases like "cooperation," "interdependence," and "division of labor." For Rousseau these were all euphemisms concealing the fundamental moral problems posed by an interdependent society. Interdependence necessarily presupposes dependence and inequality:

> From the moment one man began to stand in need of the help of another . . . equality disappeared, property was introduced, work became indispensable, and vast forests became smiling fields, which man had to water with the sweat of his brow, and where slavery and misery were soon to germinate and grow up with the crops.[58]

Thus human needs, instead of uniting men, divide them: the state of war is to be found in society, not nature. "Take away our fatal progress, take away our faults and vices, take away man's handiwork, and all is well." [59]

Rousseau's solution for the ills of society was not to beckon men to the woods, nor to advocate the destruction of all social interdependencies. He proposed, instead, a paradox: let us create a society which causes men to grow closer to one another, to become so strongly solidary that each member will be made dependent on the whole society and, by that very fact, be released from *personal* dependencies. Rousseau's solution was one which belonged to the tradition of close communion, with the solutions of other writers who have been appalled at the consequences of large-scale, impersonal aggregates, who prefer the pulsating life of the small group to the cold, exterior unity of massive institutions. Like D. H. Lawrence, Rousseau believed that "men are free when they belong to a living, organic, *believing* community . . ." [60] Yet, in one sense, Rousseau pitched his demands higher than the primitive Christian or modern sectarian, far higher than later theorists of socialist utopias. He demanded of society something that had never been voiced before, but has been repeated since, something more than the conditions for a moral life, more than the opportunity for self-development, more than material necessities. The community must be designed to satisfy man's feelings, to fulfill his emotional needs. The Rousseau for whom "to exist is to feel," for whom authentic experience came from what was vivid and immediate — "How many men between God and me!" —, for whom "sincerity" and "simplicity of heart" were primary virtues, a temper such as this could only be appeased by human relationships that were direct, personal, and intense. "My dear fellow citizens, or rather my brothers . . ." [61] What Luther aspired to in man's relationship with God, Rousseau transferred to man's relationships with his fellows:

Every man is virtuous when his particular will is in all things conformable to the general will, and we voluntarily will what is willed by those whom we love . . . [If men were aware] of their own existence merely as a part of that State, they might at length come to identify themselves in some degree with this greater whole, to feel themselves members of their country, and to love it with that exquisite feeling which no isolated person has save for himself . . .[62]

The quest for personal identity was to be fulfilled by the creation of a corporate community, a *moi commun,* where each simultaneously discovered himself in the closest possible solidarity with others: *"Nous recevons en corps chaque membre comme partie indivisible du tout."* [63]

Here in Rousseau's conception of community were the elements of what Fourier later called *le groupisme*. In one form or another it reappeared whenever there was demand for the revival of social solidarity: in Utopian Socialism, in Hegel's philosophy, in the pluralist thought of Figgis and Cole, and in contemporary writers who seek in the factory a substitute for community. The purest restatement of Rousseau, however, is to be found in one of the founders of modern sociology, Emile Durkheim.[64] The affinities between the two are worth exploring because Durkheim's interest in the problems of group solidarity, social disorganization, and social cohesion has been perpetuated in the concerns of contemporary sociology. Durkheim has been the medium, so to speak, by which Rousseau has left his mark on modern social science.

The *mystique* which Rousseau had woven about the group was accepted by Durkheim and made the basis of his analysis of group life: "A group is not only a moral authority which dominates the life of its members; it is also a source of life *sui generis*. From it comes a warmth which animates its members, making them intensely human, destroying their egotisms." [65] For Durkheim the revitalization of group life seemed the only remedy to restoring the blunted moral sense of the age. The malaise afflicting industrial society was traced to the individual's being released from primary group attachments and allowed to move in a society without moral guideposts.[66] Morality, Durkheim insisted, was the reflection of a solidary way of life, an amalgam of many minds and a thousand practices. It was embodied in what Durkheim dubbed "collective representations." [67] These forms, Durkheim contended, while they represented a synthesis of individual consciousnesses, were remarkably similar to Platonic ideas; they attained an independent existence where they obeyed "laws all their own." They were internalized within individuals, yet they simultaneously remained outside, imposing their directives on him, supplying the fundamental categories of ethics, perception, and action. They were "the highest form of the psychic life." As in Rousseau's community, no tension existed between self and society; there was only the *moi commun* of perfect identification. "To desire a morality other than that implied by society is to deny the latter and, consequently, one's self." [68]

There was one other continuity between the thought of Rousseau and of Durkheim, which further illuminates some preoccupations and underlying assumptions of modern social science. Durkheim's theory of "collective representations" or, in his alternative phrase, "the collective conscience," was formulated to meet the same order of problems, and hence contained many of the same prejudices, as Rousseau's general will. There were two attributes of

Rousseau's general will which are apposite here: one concerned the source of the general will, the other its quality. The general will was to issue from the community acting in unison; as a collective judgment the general will would be more likely to approximate an impersonal rule. The collective character of the general will also assured the individual of his freedom, for to the extent that he submitted to a communal judgment he avoided dependence on another individual. Moreover, the general will was superior in quality to an individual judgment, and its normative status furnished the justification for applying compulsion to the individual: in being coerced into complying with the command of the general will, the individual was made to do what he would want to do if he were capable of modifying his own egotism.

These same considerations dominated Durkheim's "collective conscience": like Rousseau's community, the group was designated "a moral person," one capable of "containing individual egos" and "of maintaining a spirited sentiment of common solidarity." The collective conscience was "the work of the community," and coercion employed on its behalf was legitimate because it was coercion at the service of morality, not of wealth or strength.[69] Finally, in the same way that the general will was the supreme expression of Rousseau's community, the collective conscience was "the highest form of the psychic life"; in obeying it the individual was elevated from his simple egotism, or what Rousseau had called his "particular will."[70] In its highest form this "combination of all the individual forces" reflected a community as solidary as any Rousseau would have wanted, *"une vie commune"* where "all the individual consciences [were] in unison and combination." The collective conscience embodied "something other than the totality of individuals that compose it."[71]

V Freedom and impersonal dependence. There was an additional element in Rousseau's conception of community, one which contrasted sharply with the intimate, face-to-face existence described earlier. It originated in Rousseau's conviction that if the community were to approximate in some degree the independence, equality, and freedom of the natural condition, political relationships would have to be highly impersonal. The community was to be ordered in such a way that, in place of the prevailing dependence on *persons,* the individual would be dependent on impersonal entities or "things." Rousseau's argument is worth exploring because it foreshadowed one of modernity's basic articles of faith: that to be dependent on some impersonal force — call it "history," "necessity," "World-Spirit," "laws of nature," or "society" — is to commune with reality and to experience "true" freedom.

Rousseau's argument was developed upon the basis of certain conjectures about existence in the state of nature. In the state of nature men had lived in relative isolation from each other, untroubled by imaginative possibilities, ignorant of social distinctions, of family life, and even of speech. Each went his separate way, unmindful of others because he did not need them. "Those barbarous ages were the golden age, not because men were united, but because they were isolated." [72] To be independent of others meant to be free from any *personal* authority or power. In the natural condition, authority and power resided solely in impersonal nature.[73] The physical forces of the environment were felt by all, but in a manner that was equal and indiscriminate. The sun shone on the good and bad alike. Thus the natural condition was one where the individual was subject to the general laws of nature, but independent of his fellows:

> There are two kinds of dependence: dependence on things, which is the work of nature; and dependence on men, which is the work of society. Dependence on things, being non-moral, does no injury to liberty and begets no vices; dependence on men, being out of order, gives rise to every kind of vice, and through this master and slave become mutually depraved.[74]

Here, in outline, was the prescription for society: to approximate the impersonal equality of nature by creating a close community, to locate independence in mutual dependence. One could not hope for a restoration of man's primitive independence, for men now counted heavily on the amenities which only civilized cooperation could provide. Yet if independence were impossible, there might still be freedom from personal servitude. This could be accomplished by founding a political society wherein each prescribed rules for himself.[75] Similarly, if men could not return to a condition where all were equally subject to nature's law, they could form a society where each was equally subordinate to the whole. "The total alienation of each associate, with all his rights, to the entire community" established "the condition equal for all." [76] And if he had lost forever subjection to the impersonal power of nature, he might substitute a system in which only the impersonal authority of the law held sway. In submitting to the law, *"personne ne commande,"* and men *"n'aient point de maître."* The law establishes in civil society "the natural equality between men." [77]

The social contract symbolized the arrangement designed to protect each member "from all personal dependence." Instead of the dependence on nature, and instead of the dependence on individuals or classes, as in perverted societies, each would be dependent on the whole. "Each, in giving himself to all, gives himself to no one." [78] The precondition of perfect dependence required the voluntary and total surrender by each individual of all his rights and powers. Each ought to be "perfectly independent" of the others as individuals, but each should be bound by *"une excessive dépendance"* on the community.[79] These considerations also appear in the famous conception of the general will, the sovereign authority and supreme expression of the political community. Rousseau emphasized once more the attribute of generality in order to bring out the analogy with nature. The general will, like the forces of nature, disdained to deal with particular objects, but, with a majestic impersonality, confined itself to generalized ends common to all. The more general an object, the less its particularity, the less its selection reflected a subjective, personal judgment. Hence to the extent that the general will aimed at general interests, the more faithfully it emulated nature's reign. "Private interest tends always to preferences, the public interest to equality." [80] This reasoning led to Rousseau's celebrated dictum that the general will could force men to be free. What he meant by this ominous phrase was that compulsion might be employed in order to force men into dependence on the whole community, thereby freeing them from dependence on particular individuals.[81]

It is often said that Rousseau's political ideas were archaic from the outset because they were meant to apply to the political life of a small society. This criticism has not, however, prevented Rousseau's communitarian ideal from playing a highly influential role in nineteenth and twentieth century theories. Perhaps it was because Rousseau had rekindled some widespread and deeply felt need for a close community that we find succeeding writers returning time and again to the main elements of Rousseau's conception and stressing once more the high value of social solidarity, the necessary subordination of the individual to the group, the importance of impersonal dependence, the redemptive vocation of membership, and the benefits accruing from a close identification between individual and aggregate. The quest for community undertaken by so many writers, who have reflected so many different political persuasions, suggests that Rousseau's conception of community has turned into a specter haunting the age of organization, a continuing critic of the sort of life lived within large-scale, depersonalized units, a reminder that human needs demanded more than rational relationships and efficient routines. In the writings of Proudhon, Durkheim, the English pluralists, or, more recently, Erich Fromm, the communitarian ideal has been preserved and revitalized to the point where it forms a distinct tradition. Yet it has never succeeded in disabusing our age of the enchantments of organizational power and splendor. Where the communitarians have succeeded is in making the champions of organization conscious of the deficiencies of organizational life. The result has been, as we shall note later, that the organizationists have tried to engraft elements of community onto the main stem of organization, hoping thereby to lessen the contrast between the two. In their dialectical tension community and organization present certain parallels with the older religious dualism of church and sect. The modern communitarians follow the sect-tradition, elevating the spontaneous life of the group above the institutionalized order of the organization, while the organizationists belong to the church-tradition of revering a structure of authority and distrusting the spontaneous expression of the membership. The communitarians are "Lutherans," the organizationists "Catholics."

V I Saint-Simon: the idea of organization. Some political writers are read for the nobility of their thought; others because of their precision and tough-mindedness; still others are much like old shoes, comfortable and familiar; and, finally, there are those who provoke and disturb. Some writers, however, are neither noble, profound, consistent, familiar, nor provocative, but they are read, nevertheless, because somehow they have sensed the future drift of things and charted it with a naïve clarity. Saint-Simon was such a writer. Almost all of his commentators have agreed on two points: that he was able to perceive the future in an almost uncanny way and that he was mentally unstable and at times quite mad. What no one seems to have pointed out is that, given the sort of future he predicted, his madness may well have been a necessary precondition for his foresight. In Saint-Simon the age of organization found its philosopher and, in his writings, its manifesto: "The philosophy of the eighteenth century was critical and revolutionary; that of the nineteenth will be inventive and organizational." [82] The foundations of organization theory were set down by Saint-Simon with the conscious intent of establishing a defense against political instability and social disorder. More precisely, organization theory was born in response to the troubled aftermath of the French Revolution; it carried many of the birthmarks of the traditional search of political theorists for order. "The general upheaval experienced by the people of France" had led to a situation where "all the existing relations between the members of a nation become precarious, and anarchy, the greatest of all scourges, rages unchecked, until the misery in which it plunges the nation . . . stimulates a desire for the restoration of order even in the most ignorant of its members." [83] Unknown to the men of the eighteenth century, new intellectual and social forces had slowly been gathering strength for centuries until they had burst through the anachronistic system with a "frightful explosion." The two elemental forces were science and industry; they contained a "logic" which ought to govern the shape of existing arrangements. "The necessary and organic social bond" was to be found in "the idea of industry . . . Only there shall we find our safety and the end of the revolution . . . The sole aim of our thoughts and our exertions must be the kind of organization most favorable to industry." [84]

In Saint-Simon's vocabulary "organization" connoted far more than a simple condition of social harmony and political stability. Organization promised the creation of a new structure of power, a functioning whole superior to the sum of the tiny physical, intellectual, and moral contributions of the parts. "Men shall henceforth do consciously, and with better directed and more useful effort, what they have hitherto done unconsciously, slowly, indecisively, and too ineffectively." [85] As a system of power, organization would enable men to exploit nature in a systematic fashion and thereby bring society to an unprecedented plateau of material prosperity. This required the rational arrangement of the functioning parts, the subordination of some tasks to others, the direction of work by those who possessed the relevant knowledge of industrial processes. Industrial organization required a new social hierarchy for the present "society is a world that is upside down." The new social pyramid would represent an ascending scale of contributions, from the workers at the bottom to the industrialists, scientists, and artists at the top. The principle of function, defined in terms of the needs of an industrial order, became the new principle of legitimation. The *industriels,* as Saint-Simon dubbed the scientists, artists, and industrialists, symbolized the essential skills needed to maintain an industrial civilization. The identification thus established between the talents of special groups and the general welfare of society made it easy for Saint-Simon to adopt for his own purposes the argument of the classical economists for the freedom of the businessman. Just as the public interest was inevitably furthered by the businessman's unhampered pursuit of private gain, so Saint-Simonian society was to benefit from allowing the *industriels* to develop their special skills to the fullest and to pursue their own ends without restriction: their "particular interests are perfectly in accord with the common interest." [86] How influential this plea was to become may be judged by recalling that it has taken the threat of oblivion before the unlimited freedom of the scientist could be questioned.

Among the most significant of Saint-Simon's contributions to organization theory was his recognition that the logic of organization was at loggerheads with the claims of equality popularized by eighteenth-century revolutionary theories. Organization and equality were antithetical ideas in that the former demanded hierarchy, subordination, and authority, while the latter denied all three. Saint-Simon also understood, however, that it was possible, even necessary, for industrial society to strike a bargain with equality: necessary because no order could be maintained except on a mass basis; possible because the material needs of the masses could be satisfied by the application of science to production. The masses desired neither liberty nor literal equality, only the alleviation of their material lot. If this were accomplished, they would give unstinting loyalty to the system and, as an extra dividend, produce more efficiently.[87] The industrial order, by providing a new structure for society, a new principle of authority, a new form of integration, was to be the counter-revolutionary antidote to the agitation of the masses, the de-revolutionizing remedy for "the present social agony."

Saint-Simon had created a theory of organization which, on its surface, bore certain affinities with Rousseau's ideas. The rationale which Rousseau had introduced to justify the general will in forcing men to be free was refurbished by Saint-Simon and introduced as an imperative of social science. The "principles" of organization, he contended, were "necessary" and hence "true." In compelling men to conform to the dictates of organization, the new elite would not be imitating the ways of the political despot. The commands of a political ruler could not avoid being coercive because they were based on subjective judgments. But the new order would be governed not by men, but by scientific "principles" based on the "nature of things" and therefore "absolutely independent of human will."[88] In this way organizational society promised the rule of scientific laws rather than men and the eventual disappearance of the political element entirely. Government would be "reduced to nothing, or almost nothing." Political action "will be reduced to what is necessary for establishing a hierarchy of functions in the general action of man on nature" and to clearing away obstacles to "useful work."[89] The direction of society was to take the form of administration; that is, the control over things rather than men. Human energies would be redirected, away from the attempt to dominate each other, to the goal of dominating nature. Energies no longer sapped by class struggle could be combined and magnified by organization in order to take up once more the struggle abandoned by liberalism in its mood of despair:

The development of action against nature has changed the direction of this sentiment [of domination] by leveling it against objects. The desire to command men has slowly transformed itself into the desire to make and remake nature in accordance with our will.

From this time on, the desire to dominate, which is innate in all men, has ceased to be pernicious, or at least we can foresee an epoch when it will not be harmful any longer, but will become useful.[90]

Organization as power over things — this was the lesson taught by Saint-Simon. It was a lesson taken to heart by socialists and capitalists alike. In this respect Marx, for example, was not the spokesman of radicalism but the representative of an age. Although *Das Kapital* contained a biting indictment of capitalism for its dehumanization of the worker, it also expressed unabashed admiration for the new leviathan of productive power created by capitalists. Marx compared it to a military unit in which the striking force of the group was greater than the sum of the individual powers taken separately.

Not only have we here an increase in the productive power of the individual, by means of cooperation, but the creation of a new power, namely, the collective power of masses . . . In modern industry man succeeded for the first time in making the product of his past labor work on a large scale gratuitously, like the forces of nature.[91]

The century soon discovered that what Marx and others had attributed to industrialism applied with equal force to all types of large-scale organization — governmental, educational, and social. Any organization involved an arrangement dovetailing human actions into desired consequences; simplifying a variety of complex operations; mustering vast resources so that they flowed into the structure to emerge transformed; pooling diverse human talents — some highly skilled, some rudimentary, but all specialized — into a common cooperative effort. "The more numerous and varied the elements and relationships concurring in the formation of a group, the more centralized becomes power, and the more clearly does existence partake of reality." [92] In this contrived blend of energy, skill, and resources, the century believed it had hit upon a discovery of power as breath-taking as any boasted by the sciences, *"la science du mécanisme sociétaire"* Fourier called it.[93]

In the twentieth century the fascination with organization reached new heights. Organization was conceived to be the means whereby twentieth-century man transcended his individual limitations. Wealth, power, plenty, and knowledge were all to be had through a kind of social alchemy. But more important, these achievements apparently did not require, as religious transcendence did, a "new man." Man could accomplish great things without himself becoming great, without developing uncommon skills or moral excellence. The secret of organization was that it compensated for human shortcomings; it served, in Lord Beveridge's phrase, to "make common men do uncommon things." What man could not accomplish individually, he could by collective organization; puny alone, mighty in aggregate. "The primary step in cooperation is to envisage biological characteristics of individuals as limitations which can be overcome by cooperation." [94] When cooperation is multiplied, interconnected, and further diversified, the resulting organization constitutes a world that far exceeds the rational comprehension of the individual participant. The shortcomings of man, however, are not of sufficient consequence to deter the organization from accomplishing its ends. The organization, in its infinite cunning, accepts as given "the limits of humans as mechanisms for computation and choice," [95] and proceeds on the assumption followed long ago by de Maistre that a structured arrangement can overcome human failings:

> It is only because individual human beings are limited in knowledge, foresight, skill, and time that organizations are useful instruments for the achievement of human purpose; and it is only because organized groups of human beings are limited in ability to agree on goals, to communicate, and to cooperate that organizing becomes for them a "problem." [96]

According to contemporary writers, organization does more than increase man's power or compensate for his shortcomings; it is the grand device for transforming human irrationalities into rational behavior. Planning, which is organization in the socialist idiom, is described by Mannheim as the "rational mastery of the irrational." "The greater the degree of technical and institutional control in a given society, the greater the radius of both action and foresight." [97] The most systematic exposition of this encounter between irrational man and rational organization has been given by Herbert Simon, one of the most brilliant and original writers in the field of administrative theory. He starts from two antitheses: the non-organizational man who lacks the knowledge to make informed choices, who is bewildered by the whirl of events with its numerous alternatives and is highly uncertain of the consequences of his choices. "It is impossible for the behavior of a single, isolated individual to reach any high degree of rationality." [98] In contrast, the potency of the organization is such that it accepts human limitations but arranges them in such a way that a rational decision or organizational action results — in much the same manner that hamburger might be reground into sirloin steak.[99] Organizations are "the most rationally contrived units of human association," and hence when men are shaped to its demands their behavior becomes rational, more so than in "any other sector of human behavior . . . Rational choice can hardly exist without a theory of organization." [100]

Organizations employ a variety of devices designed to imbue behavior with rationality. The organization specifies the individual's duties and functions; it assigns authority within the structure so that the member will know where to look for commands; it establishes limits to his choices; shapes his attitudes so that the individual comes to feel a sense of identity with the whole; directs stimuli at the individual and thereby induces orderly behavior. By these arrangements an environment is established where a "correct" choice by the individual is possible; that is, a choice adapted "to the organization objectives." [101]

> Since these institutions largely determine the mental sets of the participants, they set the conditions for the exercise of docility, and hence [sic] of rationality in human society. Human rationality, then, gets its higher goals and integrations from the institutional setting in which it operates and by which it is moulded . . . The rational individual is, and must be, an organized and institutionalized individual.[102]

This kind of reasoning naturally provokes the question of whether the proposition, that organization endows man's behavior with rationality, is not a tautology. If organizational behavior is defined as *the* standard of rational behavior, and if "progress in the technique of organization is nothing but the application of technical conceptions to the forms of human cooperation," [103] the individuals who conform to its norms are, *ipso facto,* rational. Yet the proposition, while tautological, is hardly empty of significance. For by representing the organization as the epitome of rationality, as being that which man is not, organization theory has succeeded in creating a standard of non-human excellence. The organizationists have obligingly admitted this:

> The idea that organizations should be built up round and adjusted to individual idiosyncrasies, rather than that individuals should be adapted to the requirements of sound principles of organization, is as foolish as attempting to design an engine to accord with the whimsies of one's maiden aunt rather than with the laws of mechanical science.[104]

Thus to the ancient question that Socrates directed at Protagoras, in what ways does a man become better if he follows the prescriptions of another, the contemporary reply is: as a man he doesn't become better at all, but as an organizational function he does.

Administrative theory is peculiarly the theory of intended and bounded
rationality — of the theory of the behavior of human beings who *satisfice*
because they have not the wits to *maximize* . . . [To satisfice is to adopt]
a course of action that is satisfactory or "good enough." [105]

VII Organization theory and methodology: some parallels. To round out our sketch of the recent and contemporary fascina-

tion with organization, we should like to suggest something of the depths of
the attitudes involved. One way of doing this is to draw attention to some
significant parallels between theories of organization and theories of methodology. There is no need to emphasize the popularity of contemporary discussions of method, particularly among the highly self-conscious social scientists.
What I am suggesting here involves more than parallel obsessions. To the
theorist of organization, the patterns of such structures supply a "logic" to
human behavior comparable to the way that methodological procedures guide
intellectual inquiry. Some hint of these parallels is contained in a remark of
one of the leading organizational theorists: "What is important here, however, is the superlative degree to which logical processes must and can characterize organization action as contrasted with individual behavior . . ." [106]
What organization is supposed to accomplish for human behavior and society,
method supplies for inquiries into society and behavior.

The connections between organization theory and methodology had been
foreshadowed in the thought of Saint-Simon. Disturbed by the seemingly
aimless and chaotic state of the intellectual disciplines he had reasoned that
if all forms of disorder had their origins in faulty organization, the confusions of the intellect, like those of society, could be dispelled by the same
remedy. The condition of present-day knowledge, he told the scientists, was
one of "disjointed ideas because they are not related to any general concept,
and your society [of scientists] is not organized systematically." [107] The kind
of method which would restore order was explained in the following terms:
"Select an idea to which all other ideas can be related, and from which all
principles can be deduced." Once the right method had been established it
could be applied to all fields of inquiry, and results as spectacular as those
achieved in the sciences would become universal.

The parallel established by Saint-Simon can be stated simply: a method is
a form of organization, an organization is a form of method. In its social form
organization is a method of establishing a set of relationships among persons, ordering their activities towards some definite purpose, and arranging

their tasks in ascending scales of complexity. Similarly, Saint-Simon made it clear in his proposal for a new encyclopaedia that intellectual affairs were to have their table of organization:

A good encyclopaedia would be a complete collection of human knowledge arranged in such order that the reader would descend, by equally spaced stages, from the most general scientific conception down to the most particular ones.[108]

A similar point of view was expressed by Proudhon later in the century. He contended that intellectual operations of a high order followed a "law of series" which could be adapted to social organization where it would bring enormous benefits:

In the scientific order, methods; in industry, technical procedures; in education, discipline; everywhere divisions and series — this is what will progressively raise the basis of societies to a level of the most sublime intelligence . . .[109]

In the recent literature of organization or administration these tendencies have usually taken the form of arguing that, just as scientific procedures and "laws" are true regardless of social setting, so the "laws" or "principles" of organization have the same universal validity and necessity. Organization, like method, is a timeless logic; its principles "can be studied as a technical question, irrespective of the purpose of the enterprise, the personnel composing it, or any constitutional, political or social theory underlying its creation."[110]

Pervading much of the recent theorizing on method is the promise that right method will enhance and extend man's power over nature and society: method provides us with the power to predict the course of phenomena, and hence to put them under our control. More striking still, method, like organization, is the salvation of puny men, the compensatory device for individual foibles, the gadget which allows mediocrity to transcend its limitations. On the one side organization, by simplifying and routinizing procedures, eliminates the need for surpassing talent. It is predicated on "average human beings."[111] The organizational hero would be a contradiction in terms; an order of talents, if not subversive, at least embarrassing.

At first glance, the emphasis on "bounded rationality," "common men," would seem to be at the furthest remove from the qualities we associate with scientific method. Our normal mental image is of the scientist as hero: a Galileo, a Newton, or an Einstein. We must, however, avoid confusing what it means to invent or *discover* a method with what it means to *use* one that has already been discovered, to distinguish between, say, a Euclid and the schoolboy who learns to manipulate geometrical propositions. This difference can be underscored by viewing method as a leveling device: the average college student in mathematics can employ a particular formula to produce results as accurate as those of the genius who discovered it. Long ago Descartes had written that "The child who has been instructed . . . in the elements of Arithmetic, and has made a particular addition, according to rule, may be assured that he has found, with respect to the sum of the numbers before him, all that in this instance is within the reach of human genius." [112] Similarly, Bacon reported with pride, "my way of discovering sciences goes far to level men's wits, and leaves but little to individual excellence; because it performs everything by the surest rules and demonstrations." [113] Two centuries later Proudhon pointed out that, while it demanded genius to discover laws, and hence there was no explaining the mysterious creativity of a "Plato, Aristole, Spinoza, Kant, Fourier," once the secret had been revealed, as in Proudhon's own "serial theory," we can, "children that we were yesterday, follow in the footsteps of giants, and, by a sudden illumination, we find ourselves to be their equals."

> The task of learning in science being incomparably easier than that of discovery . . . the march of ordinary minds is more rapid by its continuity than the always more troubled soaring of the intellectual elite . . . the series strengthens the weak and imposes limits on genius . . . Now truth reveals itself to all; today to Newton and Pascal, tomorrow to the herdsman in the valley and the journeyman in the shop.[114]

The parallel was extended further by Proudhon into a favorite area. If there was one consistent theme in all of his writings it was his hatred of personal authority. The social solution to the problem of authority was to be found in submitting to the true principles of social organization. Similarly, in adhering to the rules of scientific method, Proudhon's sage bowed before authority, but authority of an impersonal kind:

> Genius is nothing more than anticipation of the method, an expression which designates man's vivid presentiment of the rule, and of the need for submitting one's self to it. The height of genius consists in the keen perception of the law.[115]

More ominously, just as organization theorists had warned that an organization could not be adjusted to individual idiosyncrasies, social scientists, like Max Weber, for example, found the imperious demands of method in-

tolerant of what he contemptuously called the "cult of the personality." [116]
Thus method, like organization, tends to depersonalize, to restrict to a minimum the distinguishing traits of the individual, whether he follows the rules
of method or obeys the rules of the organization. Methodological destructiveness has come a long way since Hobbes amused himself by "feigning" the
annihilation of the world. Now method has been turned on man in order
to root out the personal peculiarities which disqualify him both from being a
competent methodologist as well as a proper subject for scientific generalizations. This has been brought out in a most illuminating way by Mannheim.
He began by contrasting older forms of self-observation with modern techniques. In the case of the mediaeval saints, for example, self-observation was
rooted in "a kind of egotism"; "they were concerned with themselves, and
themselves alone"; that is, they sought "self"-perfection. The spirit of the
modern observer is quite different. He "approaches himself experimentally,
just as he approaches the objective facts of the world." He is concerned with
self, but only to the end that he can "use his knowledge of the origins of his
psychological defects as a universal remedy for society as a whole."

> In the same tradition, the modern sociologically oriented psychologist or
> psychoanalyst, having once traced certain of his own psychological troubles
> . . . does not rest content until he has produced a theory which enables him
> to combat similar psychological difficulties in other men. This form of self-
> analysis has a levelling tendency and disregards individual differences be-
> cause it is concerned with the general aspects of the human personality and its
> capacity for transformation.[117]

There is a further and still more fundamental sense in which modern theories of method converge with theories of society. A method dictates a principle of selection; it groups relevant data and ignores others; some phenomena are admitted, others excluded. When these ideas are transferred to social
theory, they tend to support the aggregate and to denigrate the individual.
The aggregate or the collective is to social theory what relevant facts are to
method; *pari passu,* the antisocial or unintegrated individual falls under the
same suspicion as an irrelevant fact. Appropriately, sociology, the most meth-
odologically self-conscious of the social studies, was launched as a science
of the aggregate. According to Comte, the science of man could only deal
with collective phenomena; it was compelled to exclude the individual from
its purview. "Society" was the focus of inquiry and it "exists only where a
general and collective action is exercised." [118]
It might not appear at all odd that writers intent on analyzing and ex-

plaining social organization should insist that the facts relevant to such inquiries should be social in nature rather than individual. Logically, the study
of society should center on interacting phenomena; doubtless no "laws" or
general statements could be constructed from isolated or unique phenomena,
unless one were intent upon a science of the bizarre. Viewed from another
angle, however, the emphasis on "social facts," which Durkheim treated as
central to the procedure of sociology, conceals some interesting attitudes
characteristic of modern thought. First of all, it suggests the same suspicion
of the individual that has been so prominent in Western thought ever since
Burke and the French reactionaries had joined issue with the French Revolution. Thus de Bonald had accused the *philosophes* of preaching a philosophy
which exalted human pride, a *"science du moi."* They "have made the philosophy of man *individual,* of *me.* I have wanted to make the philosophy of
man *social,* the philosophy of *us . . ."* [119] Like the non-conforming person,
the individual fact is wayward, eccentric, unclassifiable — and to be unclassifiable is to come perilously close to being insignificant. "Everything existing
is grouped" — and this from Proudhon, one of the century's arch-individual-
ists. "Outside of the group there are only some abstractions and phantoms." [120]
Secondly, a "social fact" by definition is public, external, more easily observ-
able than the facts of private conscience, or inward disposition. In keeping
with this, Durkheim specifically denied that sociology could be based on the
study of individual psychology: "every time a social phenomenon has been
explained directly by a psychic phenomenon, it is certain that the explanation
is false." [121] Now, as far back as Hobbes, as we have already noted, man had
been viewed as a public bit of matter, presenting only an "outside" surface. In
Durkheim's statement of the "rules" for studying social facts this viewpoint
was converted into a formal system. The characteristics of social facts (including "moral facts") are such that they can be studied as "things"; that is,
from the outside, external to the observer.[122] It is not at all surprising that
this procedure should have been anticipated by the arch-reactionary de Bonald, who devoted his intellectual life to combatting the individualism of the
eighteenth century. To obtain a "fixed point of departure," he wrote, we must
turn to "a perceivable and external fact," one "located in the moral order of
things." It "is not to be found in *l'homme intérieur"* but in *"l'homme ex-
térieur ou social"*; that is, "in society." [123]

These tendencies were given further force by the growing appreciation
among social theorists of the crucial role played by social functions in maintaining the "system" of society. "Functionalism" provided a nice opportunity
for the social theorist to inject his preferences in defining those functions

which were necessary to the effective operation and continued progress of the social system and those which were not. "Functionalism" implied a principle of exclusion comparable to the methodological notion of "relevance": to be "functional" was good, to be "dis-functional" bad, or at least socially superfluous. Saint-Simon had been one of the first to state this idea and he did it with his customary flourish. What would happen to France, he asked, if she were suddenly to lose three thousand of her leading scientists, bankers, industrialists, artists and artisans? The answer: "The nation would become a lifeless corpse." On the other hand, what consequences would result if France were to lose thirty thousand of her nobility, bureaucrats, ecclesiastics, and rich land-owners? The answer: None.[124] The reason? Functionalism: the first group was performing socially useful tasks, the latter was not.

The notion that the proper role of the individual was equivalent to the performance of a social function was later taken up by Durkheim and developed with surprising overtones of hostility towards individualism. He accused those who, with a Proustian delicacy, practiced the fine art of developing the total personality, of engaging in "a loose and flabby discipline":

> To fight against nature we need more vigorous faculties and more productive strength . . . we rather see perfection in the man seeking, not to be complete, but to produce . . . In one of its aspects, the categorical imperative of the moral conscience is assuming the following form: Make yourself usefully fulfill a determinate function.[125]

Our proper role, Durkheim argued, was to be "an organ of society"; and to discharge it we must subordinate the individual conscience to the "collective conscience," for "there is no [private] conscience that is not in some ways immoral." In performing our roles we follow a life of action, and action is "altruistic" because "it is centrifugal and disperses existence beyond its own limitations." The *vita contemplativa,* on the other hand, "has about it something personal and egoistic . . . To think . . . is to abstain from action . . . to abstain from living.[126]

The belief that individuals could be classified as "functional" and "dis-functional" continued throughout the nineteenth and into the twentieth century and steadily assumed more ominous tones. Certain groups and classes were selected for extinction or harsh social sanctions. In the writings of the Utopian Socialists, Marx, Proudhon, communists, and managerialists, there is the same Olympian ruthlessness as, first, aristocracy, then peasantry, then capitalists, then kulaks, and then intellectuals were abstracted, formed into a group, found wanting in some crucial respect, and discarded. Mayo wrote scornfully of those who "dwell apart from humanity in certain cities of the mind — remote, intellectual, preoccupied with highly articulate thinking." [127] Mannheim blithely designated as "irrational" any class which was hostile to "the modern process of production." This included not only "the lower middle class," but an even more delicately defined classification, "the new middle class" which

> attempts to rescue itself by using all the political techniques at its command in order to reverse the process of industrial development, to restrict the extension of rationalized industry, and to prevent the development of the modern rational type of man with all his humane ideals.[128]

What is important in these tendencies is not the particular group that is singled out, for it is quite beside the point that Mayo should have for intellectuals the same contempt Mannheim had for the "new middle class." Rather what is important is the passionate condemnation of large classes of human beings on professedly objective grounds, namely social science. Could it be that this is a kind of "theoretical genocide," the intellectual's reflected phantasy of the most hateful talent of our time, the "liquidation" of large groups on the grounds of their social inutility and/or danger? There is something disheartening about the way that those who have protested the horrors of totalitarianism should have been so oblivious to their own urges.

VIII Organization, method, and constitutional theory. We shall conclude our discussion of the community of assumptions which unites modern theories of organization and method by pointing out how many of these assumptions have reappeared in the modern theory of constitutionalism. The same hopes, the same fears, which inspired theorists of organization and method have been at work in constitutionalist thinking as well.

When we designate a political system as "constitutional" we usually have the following elements in mind: first, legal procedures for vesting authority among the various office-holders; second, effective restraints upon the exercise of power; third, institutionalized procedures for insuring the responsibility and accountability of public officials; and, fourth, a system of legal guarantees for enforcing the rights of citizens.

Our concern here is not with the merits of such a system, considerable though these may be. Rather we want to inquire into the reasoning which has been used to justify constitutional practices and arrangements. The following would, I think, pass as an acceptable statement of the gist of the modern theory of constitutionalism: The main aim of a constitutional form of government is to limit the exercise of political power to prevent its being abused. These purposes, it is believed, can be achieved without sacrificing the ends of peace or order which are essential to any type of political system. Constitutionalism requires both a certain organization of public offices and a strictly prescribed method of handling business.

The underlying assumptions, the fundamental suspicions, and the basic outlook of constitutionalism had been vividly set out by the great philosopher, Immanuel Kant. There is a special force to what Kant had to say, because, in his writings on moral philosophy, he had strongly condemned the notion of "interest" as a criterion of goodness, yet in his political philosophy he installed it at the very center. In response to the criticism that a republican constitution presupposed "a state of angels," Kant declared:

> But now nature comes to the aid of this revered, but practically ineffectual general will which is founded in reason. It does this by the selfish propensities themselves, so that it is only necessary to organize the state well (which is indeed within the ability of man), and to direct these forces against each other in such wise that one balances the other in its devastating effect, or even suspends it. Consequently the result for reason is as if both selfish forces were nonexistent. Thus man, although not a morally good man, is compelled to be a good citizen. The problem of establishing a state is soluble even for a people of devils, if only they have intelligence, though this may sound harsh.[129]

The same general direction had been followed earlier in the American *Federalist Papers*. The Federalists had accepted as axiomatic that the shape of constitutional government was dictated by the selfish nature of man and his restless pursuit of interest. The question, in other words, was how to constitutionalize a Hobbesian society. The answer, moreover, was true to the spirit of Hobbes: "But what is government itself but the greatest of all reflections on human nature? If men were angels, no government would be necessary." [130] The aim of a political organization was not to educate men, but to deploy them; not to alter their moral character, but to arrange institutions in such a manner that human drives would cancel each other or, without conscious intent, be deflected towards the common good. As Hume expressed it: "A republican and free government would be an obvious absurdity if the particular checks and controls provided by the constitution had really no influence and made it not the interest even of bad men, to act for the public good." [131]

For the Federalists, the problem of establishing a constitutional balance could be solved if "the interests of the man [were connected] with the constitutional rights of the place . . . Ambition must be made to counteract ambition." [132] To check the aggrandizements of interest groups several devices were to be installed: by extending the "orbit" of the political society, and thereby multiplying "the number of interests and sects," additional barriers to majority rule would exist.[133] To make certain that the lawmakers did not pass harmful legislation, there would be provisions that "they can make no law which will not have its full operation on themselves and their friends . . ." [134] Throughout the whole system there would be a maze of checks designed to prevent the abuse of power by controlling the discretionary action of those in authority: not only would power be divided between separate departments, but between the federal government and the various states; checks and balances would be introduced so that each department could protect itself against encroachments by rival departments; all elected officials would have stated terms of office; various "filtering" devices, such as the indirect election of the Senate and the President, were to be installed to drain off the effects of popular passions at election times. But always the main hope lay in pitting power against power, not to achieve but to prevent.[135]

What is significant about these tendencies in modern constitutional theory lies not merely in what was said but in what was omitted. We look in vain for any theory of political education,[136] of political leadership, or, until recently, of social consensus. As in theories of organization and method, constitutionalism relied on rules and procedures to the virtual exclusion of the art of politics. For, according to Harrington, the politician's role is to accept the dynamics of society; the politician "adds nothing but the Banks." [137] The theory that emerges is not so much one that eliminates politics but trivializes it. As Hume testified, "a constitution is only so far good as it provides a remedy against maladministration." [138] It follows that whatever virtue or excellence there would be properly belonged more to the system than to its operators. In the classical formulation of Harrington: "And as a *Commonwealth* is a government of *Lawes* and not Men; so is this the *Principality* of the Virtue, and not of the *Man* . . ." Only a "demagogue" would contend that the basic concern of a political system should be to secure good men. The true maxim read, "Give us good orders, and they will make us good men." For "as Man is sinful, but yet the world is perfect, so may the Citizen bee sinful, and yet the Commonwealth bee perfect." [139]

Thus in the constitutionalist argument we can detect the same leveling tendencies present in the idea of correct method. For substantiation we will cite again from Descartes' *Discourse on Method* where the leveling effect is underscored and the suspicion of surpassing excellence hinted at:

> Good sense is, of all things among men, the most equally distributed . . . the diversity of our opinions . . . does not arise from some being endowed with a larger share of Reason than others, but solely from this, that we conduct our thoughts along different ways, and do not fix our attention on the same objects. For to be possessed of a vigorous mind is not enough; the prime requisite is rightly to apply it. The greatest minds, as they are capable of the highest excellencies, are open likewise to the greatest aberrations; and those who travel very slowly may yet make far greater progress, *provided they keep to the straight road*, than those who, while they run, forsake it.[140]

The same suspicion of greatness was reproduced in constitutional theory and Lord Bryce may well have asked in *The American Commonwealth* why "great men" rarely were elected president, just as, more recently, General de Gaulle has cavilled against *le système*. For the "system" had been consciously designed to eliminate the need for greatness:

> In the smallest court or office, the stated forms and methods by which business must be conducted are found to be a considerable check on the natural depravity of mankind . . . And so little dependence has this affair on the humours and education of particular men that one part of the same republic may be wisely conducted and another weakly by the very same men, merely on account of the differences of the forms and institutions by which these parts are regulated.[141]

Similarly, the claim of the methodologist that scientific method helps to reduce the "personal factor" to a minimum is reproduced in the effort of constitutionalists to depersonalize politics, to confine the "human factor" to a minimum, to enthrone a "government of laws, and not of men." In the words of Royer-Collard,* one of the prominent French constitutional theoreticians of the early nineteenth century:

> The difference between the sovereignty of the people and the sovereignty constituted in free governments is that in the former there are only *persons* and *wills;* in the latter there are only rights and interests, the individualities disappearing; everything is elevated from the particular to the general.[142]

---

* Pierre Royer-Collard (1763-1845) was an influential writer and politician. He served as President of the Chamber in 1828 and as deputy from 1830-1842. In his speeches and writings he consistently defended the Charter of 1814, a mildly liberal constitution promulgated by Louis XVIII. As the intellectual leader of the "Doctrinaires" he advocated a conservative and legalistic form of liberalism which feared power and distrusted the extension of the suffrage.

These depersonalizing tendencies have been supported by the belief that if a prescribed procedure is closely adhered to, the desired result will follow of strict necessity. That correct method cannot err has been the common faith of organizationists, methodologists, and constitutionalists. The organizationist avers that a rationally organized structure will weld unexceptional talents into a powerful apparatus for producing both decisions and products; the methodologist is likewise convinced that the right technique will yield identical results for genius and mediocrity alike; the constitutionalist, for his part, contends that his system of government is an equally ingenious contrivance for producing answers yet lays demands on its practitioners no heavier than those imposed by the organizationist or methodologist. As Harrington wrote, the problem of political organization is to "frame such a Government as can go upon no other than the public Interest." [143]

These similarities are neither coincidental nor to be explained by some vague reference to a common temper. Constitutional theory is both a variant of organizational theory and a political methodology. The existence of these affinities is confirmed in the strong fascination constitutionalists have had for the idea of applying scientific methods to the study of politics. Three of the most prominent modern writers associated with the quest for a science of politics — Harrington, Montesquieu, and Hume — were all constitutionalists. This, of course, is not to imply that the exponents of a science of politics have invariably been constitutionalists. My point is that constitutionalists have been especially susceptible to the lures of scientific method because of an assumption that a constitutional system provides a field of phenomena, so to speak, which is uniquely receptive to scientific methods. This assumption has been nourished by certain characteristics in the operation of a constitutional system. It is a system that lays down explicit procedures for developing regularities and uniformities in human behavior. The several roles of legislator, administrator, executive and judge are all carefully prescribed by law and practice. Over time it is expected that these prescriptions will become internalized in those who perform the roles mentioned above. In this way the desired prohibitions and permissions are built into the ways of behavior. By means of these practices the system posits a common denominator of political decorum, one which cancels out both knavery and excellence and treats them as deviant behavior. Thus a constitutional government is a system for directing stimuli which will control human actions and outlooks and, by so doing, make them predictable.

From here it is but a short step to a science of politics. Political theorists were quick to realize that if a scientific "law" is a generalization made possible by the uniformities, and never the idiosyncrasies, of phenomena, a constitutional system furnished ready-made regularities. A political science, wrote Hume, seeks "the general truths which are invariable by the humour or education whether of subject or sovereign." Truths of this type were possible because constitutional arrangements eliminated the significance of individual peculiarities either of knowledge or virtue:

> So great is the force of laws and of particular forms of government, and so little dependence have they on the humours and tempers of men, that consequences almost as general and certain may sometimes be deduced from them as any which the mathematical sciences afford us.[144]

IX **Communal values in organization.** It is now time to return to the basic theme of social organization. Saint-Simon's discovery of organizational power had dazzled the age with the promise of satisfying human desires to the fullest. Not the abolition of poverty, but the creation of plenty was the beckoning goal. The clamor accompanying the full mobilization of society for an attack on nature only temporarily drowned certain doubts. Perhaps the tumult and the shouting were diversions which merely distracted attention from the fact that the assault on nature was a form of escapism. Societies might enjoy power and plenty and yet be poor in the vital element of community, and perhaps in industrial cooperation men were only seeking an artificial substitute for fraternity. Saint-Simonian society had promised great benefits, yet the cost was high: it had demanded subordination, but had withheld fellowship:

> As a result [of the progress of the division of labor], men necessarily depend less on each other individually but each one of them depends more on the mass . . . Now the vague and metaphysical idea of liberty as it is current today . . . would tend significantly to impede the action of the mass on individuals. From this point of view it would be contrary to the development of civilization and the organization of a well-ordered system, which requires that the parts should be strongly bound to the whole.[145]

Saint-Simon himself had sensed that some element was lacking. At an early stage he had believed that "the spirit of the age" demanded an ethic founded on "palpable, certain and present interests . . . Egoism is essential to the security of organisms." Later, however, he was aghast at the effects of egoism upon social solidarity. "Society is today in a state of extreme moral disorder; egoism is making terrible progress, everything tends towards isolation." [146]

To remedy the situation Saint-Simon proposed an *ersatz* religion, one tailored simultaneously to the needs of industrialism and social unity. The details of the *New Christianity* need not detain us, for, in a fundamental sense, they are irrelevant to Saint-Simon's basic claims. At bottom Saint-Simon's society, like that of other organizationists, staked its claims on the promise to give what Rousseau had denied society could give, namely happiness. Rousseau had allowed that civilized man might attain virtue but never true happiness. Virtue demanded control of the passions, while happiness involved the gratification of the passions and thus necessarily led to misery and conflict with others. "Happiness shatters itself and perishes under the shock of the human passions." [147] Rousseau concluded that the quest for community and the pursuit of happiness were mutually exclusive. The basis of solidarity had to be sought elsewhere. "We become attached to our fellows less because we respond to their pleasure than because we respond to their pains." Men can unite because they are capable of sharing their common condition of pain; to communicate is to commiserate. "If our common needs unite us by interest, our common miseries unite us by affection." [148] Pity becomes the all-important virtue, for it alone expresses our common humanity, our communion in pain.[149] Rousseau's "sorrowful picture of suffering humanity" was intended as a warning that man could never escape his finitude, nor find surcease to his pains:

> All men are born poor and naked, all are liable to the sorrows of life, its ills, its needs, its sufferings of every kind; and all are condemned at length to die. This is what it really means to be a man, this is what no mortal can escape.[150]

For Saint-Simon, however, finitude was a source of frustration. Every type of man, he wrote, is driven by the urge to power. The soldier, the geometer, the scientist, and the philosopher struggle "to scale the plateau on whose height stands the fantastic being who rules all of nature and whom every man who has a strong constitution tries to replace." [151] To struggle, to act, to satisfy desires, these were the techniques for confining pain to a small place in the human economy.[152] A whole society, organized and united, employing the latest knowledge from science, could conquer happiness by satisfying desires.

Hobbes had earlier taught the lesson that power and desire are bred by the scramble for scarcities, that as the offsprings of alienated men they set the problem of community, not the solution. Writers of the first half of the nineteenth century chose to believe otherwise and in theories, such as those of the

Utopian Socialists, they have left behind an instructive record of the pathetic attempt to unite the incompatibles of power, desire, and community. They wrote under the passionate conviction that the millennium could be ushered in if only the secret of productivity were unraveled. They found their thread of Ariadne in human desires and followed it relentlessly. The secret was simple: it called for cunning methods of arousing human desires and then enlisting the released energies for the task of production. They called their societies by such names as "New Harmony," but Plato had described their outlines long ago in his "first city," the *civitas cupiditatis.*

The most sustained effort at combining productive power, desire, and community was made by Charles Fourier (1772-1837). The language of community was sprinkled throughout his writings: *"harmonisme," "régime harmonien," "harmonie sociale,"* [153] but if we cut through these amiable sentiments expecting to find a life of common involvement, we shall find instead an artful arrangement of egos. Fourier aimed at community but ended by achieving merely the organization of desires.

The creation of an association, Fourier wrote, presupposed "the art of forming and mechanizing" the human passions. The revolution that was to be effected in society consisted of converting work from a source of pain to one of pleasure.[154] Work was to be rendered "attractive," that is, something to which men would be naturally drawn by virtue of desire or self-interest. Instead of adjusting man's personality to the demands of work, the new society would reverse this to modify work in accordance with human desires and wants. The members of the association would be free to move from task to task as their passions might prompt. Working groups were to be organized along lines set by the separate passions; even the most minute passions were given their due. All the rose-lovers, for example, would be grouped as a whole and then divided according to those who preferred white rather than red roses.[155]

Thus would be created a true community, richly structured according to the diversity of passions, spontaneous in its patterns of work, closely differentiated in its class structure — "the poor must enjoy a graduated ease in order that the rich may be happy" — and highly productive in its output: "The new order will acquire greater vigor and wealth, because there will be more passions." [156] There would be a constant stimulation from the competition and rivalry among the members of the same "passional series" and between the series themselves, for they were arranged so as to be *"contrasté, rivalisé, engrené"* — a foreshadowing of "socialist emulation" and Stakhanovism.

But was it a community, or had the communitarian idea been sidetracked

by the fascinating play of the organized passions "of about 2000 persons, socially united, upon a mass"? Ultimately, the productive potential of the arrangement assumed central importance: "The passional series aim always at
the end of utility, the increase of riches, and the perfection of industry." [157]

There were two basic flaws in Fourier's conception of community, one being a principle of organization which undermined the solidarity of each with
all, the other a belief about human nature which destroyed the possibility
of each becoming integrated with himself. After having traced the ills of
liberal society to unlimited acquisitiveness, Fourier naïvely proceeded to
systematize the disease. "True happiness consists in enjoying great riches
and an infinite variety of pleasures"; true happiness, thus, lay in the satisfaction of desires. The task was therefore to organize the community for this
purpose and to control the effects of egoism by satiation. Without organization "the passions are but unchained tigers, incomprehensible enigmas. The
passions cannot be repressed . . . but their course can be altered." [158] The
task of "social science" was to develop a *mathématique des passions*" for
shaping and regularizing the passions so that they could be directed along
proper channels. Quite unconsciously Fourier had incorporated the Hobbesian notion of desire — a passion was defined by Fourier as a desire which
carries "our activity towards a determined end" — and then had tried to
construct a society with the fewest possible impediments to the 810 passions
attributed to man's nature. The "mortal enemy" of desire was the prevailing
system of morals. "Morality teaches man to be at war with himself, to resist
his passions, repress them, scorn them . . . ," [159] but the new order promised
to satisfy them to the hilt.

Fourier admitted that a society based on egoism was reduced to relying
on ignoble inducements, but he argued that "in a century wholly obsessed
with commerce and stock-jobbing" no other vehicles except interest and *les
bénéfices pécuniaires* were available. It was necessary for the social order to
assure "to each a graduated opulence" which was "the object of all desires." [160]
What was never explained was how interest generated the affective ties of
community. As Proudhon sarcastically remarked apropos of Fourier's organization of society around 810 distinct passions: "Society does not live; it
is on the dissecting table." [161] In the same way that the human personality
had been minutely divided into innumerable parts, each of them seeking its
separate satisfaction, the fundamental activity of work had been fragmented
to permit each individual to float from task to task: fragmentation was the
answer to boredom, and society must be organized on the assumption that
man was no longer a whole. [162]

There is no need here to describe in any detail the scheme of Robert Owen, Fourier's near contemporary. Again "the great object of society" was asserted to be "to obtain wealth and to enjoy it." Once more there was the fascination with "an invention which will at once multiply the physical and mental powers of the whole society to an incalculable extent . . ." There was the same reliance upon self-interest, as when Owen appealed to the businessmen for support, promising a huge increase in profits if only they would give as much thought and care to their "living machines." [163]

But power over things meant directing power "outside" society and towards nature. It implied, as in fact Saint-Simon had asserted, that power over society would no longer be needed, and that, as Proudhon said, work would organize itself. But if social demoralization should continue despite industrial progress, if the organized pursuit of material betterment should prove as disturbing to social life as the old-style economy, the new theory would have solved little.

Doubts such as these began to emerge during the nineteenth century as writers began to sense that the theory of industrialism merely masked a collective egoism and hence could not satisfy the human need for solidarity and belonging. What was needed, so the century reasoned, was not only organized power over nature, but organized power over society and, ultimately, over man. In this way the century returned to another tradition, one that had emerged contemporaneously with Saint-Simonism: this was the tradition of de Maistre and de Bonald. In the ideas of the reactionary theocrats the century found a pre-industrial outlook which, when incorporated with Saint-Simon's ideas, served to enrich and to shade the harsh angularities of the industrial idea. The reactionaries supplied a sociological strain, including a deeper insight into the irrationalities of man and society, a more catholic appreciation of the role played by diverse groups in the social system, and a greater understanding of the function of authority. In an age of dynamic change and crumbling social structures there was a desperate need for a body of knowledge dealing in the conserving function of social institutions; a body of knowledge built on the categories of the conservative reaction to the French Revolution; a body of knowledge that was "reactionary" without being regressive. As Comte so conveniently put it, we need "equally the inheritance of de Maistre and that of Condorcet . . . a doctrine equally progressive and hierarchic." [164]

For the reactionaries, order was synonymous with a society etched by systems of authority at every level: the family, corporations of artisans and merchants, professional societies, local communities, provincial authorities, a clear system of social classes headed by the nobility, powerful ecclesiastical institutions, strongly held religious beliefs, and, finally, a ruling authority, preferably a monarch, who would "personify the society." [165] Order, then, presupposed a set of clearly defined functions whereby the major tasks of the society were performed. These tasks, in turn, were prescribed by the requirements of order; hence the question became, what kind of social authorities were most likely to attract the obedience and deference of the members, the unthinking loyalty and emotional support so necessary in controlling passionate, egoistic, and sinful men? The question was not, as it had been for Saint-Simon, who, or what group, possessed the requisite technical skills. It is sufficient here to recall that for de Maistre the nature of the social order was best symbolized, not by the scientist or industrialist, but by the hangman, the man authorized to apply the highest punishment in the name of the whole society.[166] The hangman proceeds with his job, the monarch with his, because each was supported by a *mystique* which evoked awe and obedience. But there could be neither awe, authority, function, nor social structure as long as the idea of equality was taken seriously. Order demanded subordination, inequality, social differentiation. These were, in de Bonald's phrase, "necessary relationships."

Now if disorder had been merely a problem stemming from the French Revolution there would not have developed, in all probability, a close continuity between the theorizing of the reactionaries and that of a later age. A continuity did develop, however, and the preoccupation with social disorganization persisted because industrialism, which was quickly recognized to be a revolution, came to play the same disturbing social role that 1789 had for an earlier generation. Relationships between classes were altered, new patterns of social and political power developed, masses of men exchanged rural modes of life for the urbanized environment created by industrialism, the old codes of morals and behavior were disturbed, and conflict between social classes seemed more intense than it had been in the past. With the exception of Marxists, the response of most theorists was remarkably similar in emphasis to the analysis of the French Revolution provided by the reactionary theocrats, de Maistre and de Bonald.

Instead of a malediction against the "satanic" revolution, the modern writer complains of the rapidity with which technological change has outdistanced older modes of control, and along with the diagnosis of industrial disorder has come a renewed appreciation of the insight of the reactionaries into the conditions of stability: "orderly society," writes a contemporary industrial sociologist, "is based upon routine, custom, and habitual association

. . . The practical problem is to investigate the type of social structure which can maintain itself while adapting its form to the ceaseless advance of material invention." [167]

These continuities become more striking when we remember that it was a sociologist, Durkheim, who coined the concept which best expressed the anxieties of the age: *anomie*, or social disintegration, the condition where society lacked a guiding sense of direction. The economy of the modern society, he wrote, lay in a chronic state of *anomie*; its essentially orderless character was infecting all areas of social life; religious, familial, and moral restraints had all declined in effectiveness; human passions raged uncontrolled by curbs or bounds.[168] Durkheim was also a great critic of human pride and presumption, and in this he recalls his countryman, de Maistre, who had inveighed against the eighteenth century for undermining all forms of authority and thereby leaving human passions without control: man "does not know what he wants; he wills what he does not want; he wants what he does not will; he wills to will." [169] Although Durkheim might have been writing as a sociologist, the language was as authentically mediaeval and moralistic as any used by de Maistre:

It is not true, then, that human activity can be released from all restraint. Nothing in the world can enjoy such a privilege. All existence being a part of the universe is relative to the remainder; its nature and method of manifestation accordingly depend not only on itself but on other beings, who consequently restrain and regulate it . . . Man's characteristic privilege is that the bond he accepts is not physical but moral; that is, social . . . Because the greater part of his existence transcends the body, he escapes the body's yoke, but is subject to that of society.[170]

In his description of a society ridden by *anomie* Durkheim provided his age with an up-to-date version of the Hobbesian state of nature: it was the same authorityless condition; without effective moral or legal controls; the same riot of egoism. The difference was an ironic one: where Hobbesian men killed each other in the state of nature and finally formed civil society to halt the slaughter, Durkheim's man finds life in society intolerable and is driven to kill himself.

The obsession with *anomie* was rooted in the yearning for solidarity, and nineteenth-century sociology conceived its task to be of redefining the conditions of social cohesion. Solidarity, Durkheim wrote, was a "social fact"; that is, it could be studied as an object. The study of solidarity "grows out of sociology." [171] By placing it at the center of their concerns, the sociologists forged another connecting link with the reactionaries. The latter had been the theorists par excellence of social cohesion. Their theories, and *mutatis mutandis,* those of later sociologists, were founded in fundamental opposition to the liberal view of society as an artificial arrangement arising from a conscious act of agreement. According to the reactionaries, man needed not just society, but society ordered, structured, and integrated. A truly solidary society could never be produced by agreement, because it would lack the natural prerequisites of cohesion, namely power and authority. This was the big assumption that sociology accepted: power and authority were natural because they were necessary to social solidarity. Power, de Bonald had declared, was the creation neither of force nor agreement; it was "necessary"; that is, "conforming to the nature of beings in society; and the causes and the origin of it were wholly natural . . . Society cannot exist without general power, nor man without society." [172] In the echo of Durkheim: "Every society is despotic . . . Still, I would not say that there is anything in this despotism: it is natural because it is necessary . . . Societies cannot endure without it." Constraint, he continued, "issues from the very entrails of reality." [173] The following words from a widely used contemporary textbook might well have been written by de Maistre: "Political order is dependent on the stability of authority . . . Too little legitimacy is a major source of political instability." [174]

The supremacy of society and the need for authority formed a refrain that was endlessly repeated throughout the century — and by a very mixed chorus. Perhaps a better word than refrain would be chant, for there was a mediaeval quality about the way that the century amended the ancient text to read: *nulla salus extra societatem,* or, in de Bonald's version, "outside of political and religious unity, there is neither truth for man, nor salvation for society." [175] Without a stable society, an unquestioned authority, the tight bonds of family, community, vocational group, and religious order, the individual feels lost, beset by an overwhelming sense of loneliness and personal futility. The modern breviary runs heavily to the virtues of "integration" and "self-identification." A people without structure, de Bonald declared, was "only some individuals, isolated from each other, with neither ties nor cohesion among them." [176] Even so staunch a champion of individualism as Proudhon dwelt on the "superior individuality of collective man," "the reality of collective man," and proclaimed that "outside the group there are only some abstractions or phantoms." [177] "Excessive individualism," warned Durkheim, signifies that the individual has been detached from social ties; it breeds a predisposition towards "egoistic" suicide.[178] And the modern student of industrialism concerned over the correlation between low productivity and low morale among the workers concludes that, in a period of incessant technological change and uprooted populations, "the individual inevitably experiences a sense of void, of emptiness, where his fathers knew the joys of comradeship and security." The "feeling of security and certainty derives always from assured membership." [179] And if these sentiments smack too much of capitalist ideology, we need only turn to Marx: "When the laborer cooperates systematically with others, he strips off the fetters of his individuality and develops the capabilities of the species." [180]

The pervasiveness of these ideas was such that they penetrated the most diverse types of minds and created a community of outlook among thinkers who, on the surface, seemed to have very little in common. Take, for example, the philosophical idealist, F. H. Bradley, and the Fabian Socialist, Sidney Webb — a most incongruous pair at first glance. But, in fact, were they?

Like so many of the thinkers already mentioned, Bradley's social theory took shape as an attack on liberalism, or, more specifically, on the Utilitarian version of it. He denied that the individual — isolated, autonomous, unique — could provide either the starting point of social or moral theory, or the criterion for judging the adequacy of social arrangements. [181] The value of the human person was acquired through the educative influence of society; the "real" was to be located in "wholes," while the subjective and capricious were properties of individual uniqueness. Goethe's counsel, "strive to be a whole; and if you cannot, then join a whole," was amended by Bradley to read: "you cannot be a whole *unless* you join a whole." The individual's task was to exchange "his private self" for the role of a "function in a moral organism," to learn to identify his will with that of the whole — a formulation that Rousseau could not have bettered. [182] The whole embodied an objective morality, one that no individual had created; here was where the individual discovered his "true self," [183] where his mind and will became interfused with the minds and wills of others in a manner reminiscent of Durkheim's collective conscience. [184]

This was the argument of Bradley, recluse, philosophical idealist, the classical example of the conservative closet-philosopher. But in Sidney Webb, the intellectual-turned-activist, the tough-minded practical theorist and architect of Fabian Socialism, we find the argument for the superiority of the collective couched in language identical with that of Bradley, Durkheim, and, ultimately, Rousseau:

A society is something more than an aggregate of so many individual units . . . it possesses existence distinguishable from those of any of its components . . . its life transcends that of any of its members . . . the individual is now created by the social organism of which he forms a part. [185]

In Durkheim's theory the role and duties of the individual were viewed as defined by the division of labor existing in society, and for Bradley it was the social "station" which endowed the individual with morality and significance:

> What I have to do I have not to force on a recalcitrant world: I have to fulfill my place — the place that waits for me to fill it . . . I realize myself morally, so that not only what ought to be in the world is, but I am what I ought to be, and find so my contentment and satisfaction.[186]

And for Webb it was the "social organism" which set the "function" of the individual:

> If we desire to hand on to the afterworld our direct influence, and not merely the memory of our excellence, we must take even more care to improve the social organism of which we form part, than to perfect our own individual developments . . . The perfect and fitting development of each individual is not necessarily the utmost and highest cultivation of his own personality, but the filling, in the best possible way, of his humble function in the great social machine.[187]

X   **The attack on economic rationalism.** Integration, belonging, solidarity — all of these notions testified that the century had come to believe that the human condition could not be adequately understood nor solidarity achieved by means of economic categories. Industrialism was a fact which the century was quite willing to accept, but it refused to accept the proposition that industrialism was fundamentally an economic phenomenon. Instead it initiated a new line of thought, one which attempted to "sociologize" the economic system by treating economic arrangements from the standpoint of their impact upon social order and integration:

> The economic services [rendered by the division of labor] are picayune compared to the moral effect that it produces, and its true function is to create in two or more persons a feeling of solidarity.[188]

Instead of dealing with the economics of production, ownership, and labor, sociologists like Durkheim and Weber sought to analyze the social implications of economic behavior and institutions. The result of these inquiries was far-reaching: economic criteria gradually began to be displaced and social ones substituted; acquisitiveness and the pursuit of interest were attacked for their social destructiveness. In short, the whole ethos of classical liberalism was being challenged.

The attack on economic rationalism in the name of social solidarity acquires importance because it was so universal. Had it emanated solely from the socialists or communists its significance would not have been as great. But in fact the defenders of capitalism quickly came to accept the case against liberal economics. Unless this is appreciated it is otherwise quite puzzling why, for example, a highly influential educational institution, such as the Harvard Business School, has for the past few decades consistently lectured present and future business executives on the urgency of revising the naïve belief that a corporation or a business is to be administered solely by the standards of profit and productivity. The basic tenet of the new business creed is: "The manager is neither managing men nor managing work . . . he is administering a social system." [189] Yet the same gospel is also being preached to the workers. The British worker is told that while it may have been legitimate to resort to strikes and stoppages in order to coerce the old hard-faced employers, it is wrong to obstruct the policies of the boards governing the nationalized industries. A nationalized industry is owned by the "community" and hence the worker, as a member of the community, is really working for the social whole. In other words, social values are more important than rational acquisitiveness.

The main lines of the attack had been set in the early nineteenth-century writings of the reactionaries. The individualism, acquisitiveness, and rational self-interest of liberal societies had been blasted as destructive of social solidarity. "Commerce," wrote de Bonald, "has become the only concern of their governments, the only religion of their people, the only subject of their quarrels. The egoism, the factitious and immoderate desires, the extreme inequality of wealth, like a devouring cancer, have attacked the conservative principles of societies." [190] A similar point of view was expressed by Hegel when he diagnosed the ills of "civil society" as "particularity"; that is, anarchic egoism. Civil society for Hegel represented an "ideal type" of society modelled on the principles of Adam Smith: a society where the individuals pursued their own selfish ends; only their interdependence prevented the system from shattering. Fortunately the state intervened to impose limits (*Grenzen*) and barriers (*Schranken*) which, resented at first, were later internalized in the individual consciousness where they served to restrain the riotous welter of egos.[191] The attack on acquisitiveness was repeated in the writings of Carlyle, the Utopian Socialists, and by Nietzsche, Sorel, Lenin, and the ideologists of Fascism. By the twentieth century, bourgeois morality had become a riddled corpse.

The most interesting example of this development was provided by Marx.

It is not often realized that one of the fundamental tendencies of Marx's thought was anti-economic. His writings were not only devoted to discrediting liberal economics but to picturing a society in which economic categories had been transcended. In a basic sense he was protesting against the same developments as the reactionaries: the tendency of liberal rationalism to dissolve social ties, reducing society to a mass of isolated individuals, and the individual to a condition bereft of all illusions save self-interest. All "natural relationships," Marx declared, had been dissolved "into money relationships." The concept of "alienation," which had loomed large in the early writings of Marx, stood as a protest against the desocialization of man. "The individual," he emphasized, "is a *social being*"; for in the most human of all activities, production, men "enter into definite connections and relations with one another." But private ownership in the means of production has perverted the social character of these relations. All joy has been taken from work and the products of man's labor have assumed the shape of "an alien and hostile force," one which has enslaved the worker and reduced him to a brutalized condition. Man has been "ousted from society." [192] The historical mission of the proletariat was to re-assert man's social nature by shattering the existing arrangements, wherein man was treated as an economic and political animal. Man would then be reunited directly with the productive process; he would attain "self-activity." "Only in community with others has each individual the means of cultivating his gifts in all directions." [193]

When we turn to later writers, to Durkheim, and the students of industrial sociology and business management, the same hostility to liberalism is manifest. Modern social science supplies a critique of liberal capitalism and private property as devastating as any emanating from the extreme left, and evinces a hostility towards the liberal view of man and society as deep as any expressed by the counter-revolutionary right. Durkheim was the central figure in this connection, for he grasped clearly that the liberal theory of interest, as formulated by Hobbes and perpetuated by Locke and the Utilitarians, was the main enemy. "Individualism," he wrote sardonically, "is of course not necessarily egoism, but it comes close to it." The text of his attack was a faithful rendition of what de Bonald had said earlier: "Interest has come to be the god of mankind, and this god has demanded all the virtues as a sacrifice." The task of the sociologist, for Durkheim, was the study of "how the unleashing of economic interests has been accompanied by a debasing of public morality." [194]

According to Durkheim, the elevation of the pursuit of interest denied the fundamental essence of morality: morality was the crystallization of restraints on egoism and desire. "Nothing remains but individual appetites, and since they are by nature boundless and insatiable, if there is nothing to control them they will not be able to control themselves." Liberal man looked upon these restraints as "obstacles," but by destroying them he turned life into a "torment," a chase without rule, restraint, or limit. Liberal society, therefore, was not mildly sick; it was deformed, abnormal — as the high rate of suicide, crime, and divorce indicated. To return to a "healthy" society we must recognize that health resides in moderation, in disavowing "overweening ambition," "increased desires," and "the futility of endless pursuit."[195] This meant the extirpation of the Hobbesian urge for "felicity" which motivated bourgeois society, of that "longing for the infinite" which left only a trail of social demoralization and personal futility. "Those who have only empty space above them are almost inevitably lost in it . . ."[196]

As befitted a society based on Hobbesian man, its characteristic phenomena was violent death, although self-inflicted. "Anomic suicide" was the peculiar expression of an acquisitive society, while "egoistic suicide" was equally symptomatic of a society vitiated by "excessive individualism."[197] These forms of suicide, Durkheim held, were both the expression and the resultant of the deficit in social solidarity which was the malaise of modern life: "Purely economic relations leave men external to one another . . . There is nothing less constant than interest."[198] The pursuit of interest gave rise to only the most casual contacts, "an external link" which left the parties "outside each other." Beneath the fabled harmony of interests lay "a latent or deferred conflict," a "state of war." Unless human society were to submit to moral restraints, to place itself under a "moral personality above particular personalities," and to revivify group life, *anomie* would run its bitter course.[199] The lesson for industrial society was clear: "If, then, industry can be productive only by disturbing [the] peace and unleasing warfare, it is not worth the cost." What is fundamental "is not the state of our economy, but rather the state of our morality."[200]

The hostility towards the liberal theory of interest was such that even within the radical camp interest was hunted down and scotched. Although Lenin would never admit to having revised Marx's ideas, the fact remains that he successfully demolished one of the postulates which Marx had derived from the liberal theory of interest. Marx had warned that at a stage just prior to the revolution, the proletariat might be misled into favoring bourgeois objectives and values. Marx referred to this phenomenon as "false consciousness"; its characteristic being that the proletariat would be deceived into believing that its "true" interests were compatible with those of the now dominant class. For example, if the proletariat were gullible enough to believe that its standard of living would steadily improve with the continual expansion of capitalism, and that, therefore, the basic motive for revolution ceased to exist, the proletariat could be said to have fallen victim to a false picture of social reality. Under no conditions could capitalism ever guarantee the worker the full fruits of his labor without destroying the essential premises of capitalism. Therefore if the worker were truly conscious of where his interests lay, he would pledge himself to the overthrow of capitalism. Now, insofar as the Marxian concept of "true consciousness" signified a correct estimate of economic advantage, it merely represented a modified restatement of the old liberal belief that genuinely rational behavior was synonymous with understanding and acting upon one's true material interests. Lenin, however, recognized that if rationality were identified with material interest the proletariat might be satisfied with agitation aimed at achieving the usual objectives of orthodox trade unionism; that is, higher wages, better working conditions, and shorter hours of labor.[201] Should capitalism prove capable of satisfying these material aims, the proletarian movement might well stagnate at the stage of "trade-union consciousness" and never attain a revolutionary temper. "Spontaneity" therefore came to be a term of abuse, a protest against the temptations of "materialism" on the part of a proudly materialistic philosophy. Economic rationality, trade union consciousness, and spontaneity were all conceived as aspects of the syndrome of liberal rationalism, and all were equally opposed to "revolutionary consciousness." For true or revolutionary consciousness could only be induced or imposed from the "outside"; it could not be developed "naturally" or "spontaneously" by the proletariat in the course of its historical development. To meet this need became the task of the revolutionary elite.[202]

Had Lenin's analysis been strictly a quirk of revolutionary theory it would not be particularly relevant to our study; but it happened, instead, to be symptomatic of a broad tendency in twentieth-century thought. The literature of capitalist apologetics has assigned to a managerial elite the function of defining the "true consciousness" of the workers. As one writer has advised, when the workers present "logico-economic arguments" the manager should view these as "rationalizations"; a perceptive manager will inquire if "this logic is not cloaking something more."[203] At the same time that the worker's economic grievances are being sublimated by social therapy, the ancient ethic of the business manager is being similarly diverted from such purely economic goals as profit and production. Thus all along the line there is the call to transcend despicable material interests for the preservation of the social group: what the worker really wants is *camaraderie*; what the managerial elite must give is social integration.[204]

XI **Organization theory: rationalism versus organicism.** So intense has been the reaction against economic motivations that the sophisticated defenders of capitalism have joined in as well. They have acknowledged that cut-throat competition and what Fourier had called the *frénésie de production* had aroused widespread fears and contributed greatly to social divisiveness. The issue, as one of the great theorists of modern managerialism has put it, "is not that of the sickness of an acquisitive society; it is that of the acquisitiveness of a sick society."[205] No longer are the defenders of corporate capitalism occupied with justifying private ownership; instead they see the basic problem as one of restoring communal solidarity in the industrial age. It is even admitted that Marxism and Communism, while in some respects reactionary, are at least groping "to recapture something of the lost sense of human solidarity." Just as Burkean society had offered man his "little platoon" of fellowship, modern industrial society has its reasonable facsimile in "the facts of spontaneous social organization at the working bench."[206] No longer must the factory or even the large corporate organization be modeled on the cold image of the assembly line: It is "a social system," a community of producers "differentiated, ordered, and integrated."

The elevation of social values above economic values calls for a change in the function of management from "administration" to "social integration." The logic of efficiency, symbolized by that arch-rationalist, the production engineer, is superseded by the art of governing, symbolized by the manager, by one who is indoctrinated with Freudian psychology and the other modern teachings which emphasize that a social system, even that of a rationally organized factory or bureaucracy, is pervaded by non-logical conduct. The error of modern management is that it

> tends to subsume the problems of group collaboration under the technical problems of production and efficiency. As a result, collaboration is conceived of as a logical contrivance for getting people to work together by appealing primarily to their individual economic interests.[207]

Perceived as a social system, a factory is as nicely niched and graduated as the *ordo* of Augustine or the society of de Maistre. "Each job has its own social values and its rank in the social scale."[208] A working group is revealed as something precious, not to be disbanded or discarded on the harsh grounds of competitive efficiency. Yet value is not the monopoly of the small unit alone. Imperceptibly the values of the small group are extended to large organizations and the latter, too, stand revealed as the transvaluation of the old business values: they "symbolize the community's aspirations, its sense of identity," and, as symbolic representations, they have "some claim on the community to avoid liquidation or transformation on purely technical or economic grounds." [209]

It follows, too, that the liberal fetish of progress must be severely modified, for the danger to social groups and organizations in an age of industrialism lies not in stagnation, but in the disruptive effects of technological innovation. The modern manager, therefore, must, in defense of "human values," stand ready to resist the changes proposed by the "logicians" of industrial engineering who are just as eager to subordinate social values to the mathematics of production schedules as the French revolutionaries were ready to lop away regional loyalties and sentiments in order to tidy up the boundary of an *arrondissement*.[210] The "social system" of the factory organization "is bound together by sentiments which change slowly and resist change, because rapid change is destructive of routines and rituals, of habits, and of conditioned behavior. Such a change is painful even to a dog." [211] The same warning, in almost the same words, that Burke hurled at those who would rip the tissues of the body politic in order to make the whole more consonant with philosophical abstractions now is voiced by the managerialist:

> The social codes which define a worker's relation to his work and to his fellows are not capable of rapid change. They are developed slowly and over long periods of time. They are not the product of logic, but of actual human association; they are based on deep-rooted human sentiments.[212]

If it is asked what image of society is it that inspires many of these writers, the answer is that it is one surprisingly nostalgic for the simplicities of primitive societies. The flip remark, "we have the goods, but the natives have the morale," conceals a certain nostalgia.[213] In the highly unified character displayed by primitive society, in the way that the individual is subordinated to and integrated with the group, in the method by which society furnishes a comprehensive code and set of cues for the behavior of each of its members, in short, in all of the techniques of social control, primitive societies have naturally acquired what modern society so desperately needs. Although great care is taken to warn that contemporary societies ought not to turn backwards, there is, nevertheless, no mistaking the didactic purpose of these primitive models:

In these primitive communities there is room for an individual to develop skill, but there is no latitude for the development of radical or intelligent opinions . . . The unit is, in a sense, the group or commune, and not the separate individuals; the development of anything in the nature of personal capacity must be subordinate to the whole. With us it is quite otherwise; the intent of education in a complex society is to develop intelligence and independence of judgment in the individual . . . Over almost the entire area of a man's life the [primitive] society thinks for him; and he learns only the social responses he must produce in reply to given signals. This is a very restricted method of living, but it is highly integrate and "functional" . . . It is very comfortable for the individual who does not need to "wrestle with a solitary problem." [214]

What is it that the modern is seeking through the fetish of primitivism? Certainly he does not seriously want a return to custom-bound, tabu-ridden society. A clue to this puzzle is to be found in the "naturalness" which the managerialists and some sociologists ascribe to these societies. Despite their meticulous and rigid codes of social behavior, it is said that these peoples display a wonderful "spontaneity" in cooperating for common ends. Now these words, "natural" and "spontaneous," are interesting words that have evoked complex and varied responses over the past few centuries. The way in which they have been used by the Mayo school of managerial theory is better understood in relation to the history of political theory than to the anthropology of Malinowski. For when it is asked against what group are the criticisms of the sociologically oriented managerialists being directed, it becomes clear that the issue that is being fought out today in the literature of organization theory is remarkably similar to the one debated by Burke and the French revolutionary theorists. It is the issue of "political sociology" versus "political rationalism." When the contemporary sociologist of organization exalts the values of "spontaneity," "naturalness," and "traditional ways of behavior," he is using the authentic idiom of Burke; when he protests against the rational-mathematical logic of the efficiency engineer on the grounds that an organization is a living thing, he is echoing Burke's argument that the subtle allegiances and non-rational loyalties binding society together ought never to be judged by a hard Cartesian logic nor made to accord with the symmetrical vision of some social geometer.

Today there are two distinct schools of thought concerning the nature of organizational life. There are those who, like Burke, picture an organization as a social organism which has evolved over time. An organization, whether it is a business corporation or a governmental bureaucracy, represents a complex response to a particular historical environment, an institution which constantly adjusts to the needs, sentiments, and emotions of its members, and the members to it. The primary function of these organizations is not to produce profits in the most rational manner possible, nor to delight the production engineer by virtue of its efficiency. Instead, it is to promote the values of social stability, cohesion, and integration. We shall call this group the "organicists."

The second group, in contrast, views organizations as rationally arranged structures designed for specific purposes, such as making goods or "making" decisions. For this group of writers, efficiency is primary. They will have none of the Burkean bias against rational, self-conscious planning. We shall call them the "rationalists."

The representatives of rationalism, including writers like Herbert Simon and Chester Barnard, speak a matter-of-fact language; Simon, in particular, has a fondness for the spare metaphors of mechanics. Thus an organization is "a system in equilibrium, which receives contributions in the form of money or effort, and offers inducements in return for these contributions." [215] In the thinking of this group there is no trace of romanticism, no fondness for modes of natural growth, only a world of hard rationalism: "Organizations are the least 'natural,' most rationally contrived units of human association." [216] "Formal organization is that kind of cooperation that is conscious, deliberate, purposeful." [217] The rationalists are most impressed by the capabilities of an organization for focusing human energy and pooling human talents; they see its primary values in efficiency of operation and the ability to survive rather than in communal solidarity. For Simon, the "principle that is implied in all rational behavior" is "the criterion of efficiency." Efficiency, however, carries broader implications than the coordination of different operations for a prescribed end. Its aim is to create a special environment which will induce the individual to make the best decision — and "best," in this context, means a decision most helpful to the needs and ends of the organization.[218] It involves setting limits to individual actions and attitudes, exposing behavior to a "well-conceived plan" initiated by a "controlling group."

Highly revealing of the rationalists' outlook is the way they have handled the problem of authority. Their theory can rightly be called Hobbesian. In Simon's writings, for example, the discussion of authority centers on the ability to command subordinates; no concessions are made to eliciting consensus or agreement among the members. There is a no-nonsense quality about authority: its presence is felt whenever a subordinate accepts the decision of a superior and "holds in abeyance his own critical faculties." The superior does not try to convince his underling but only "obtain his acquiescence." Authority, in brief, is "the power to make the decisions which will guide the actions of another." [219] There is no sentimentalizing over the need to create a sense of participation or belonging. To be sure, loyalties are desirable, but mainly in the form of "organizational loyalties," which smooth the way for the decision of authority. The ideal member is one who has been conditioned to permit "the communicated decision of another to guide his own choices . . . without deliberation on his part on the expediency of those premises" — which is to define "choice" in a curious way, as action without deliberation.[220] The organization emerges as a triumph of collective rationality which extends rationality to each member insofar as he responds to its stimuli:

> Since these institutions largely determine the mental sets of the participants, they set the conditions for the exercise of docility, and hence of rationality in human society.[221]

The theory of the rationality of organizational behavior presented by this school has some further resemblances to Hobbes. The "final test" of any organization, Barnard declares, is "survival." [222] But more important, the organization is regarded as a contrived world, one as "artificial" as the Hobbesian universe, resting on nothing more than man's affirmation that it shall exist. It is also rational and can be understood rationally because men have made it. Like Leviathan, it is the response to chaos. These points are illustrated in Simon's remarkable contrast between "economic man" and "administrative man":

> Economic man deals with the "real world" in all its complexity. Administrative man recognizes that the world he perceives is a drastically simplified model of the buzzing, blooming confusion that constitutes the real world. He is content with the gross simplification because he believes that the real world is mostly empty — that most of the facts of the real world have no great relevance to any particular situation he is facing, and that most significant chains of causes and consequences are short and simple.[223]

In reaction to the rationalist position there has emerged in recent years a protest against the austerely efficient approach to organization. One example of this is the pioneering writings of Elton Mayo. The bulk of his work centered on the relationship between productivity and worker morale, and he concluded that morale was largely a function of the health of the small social group organized around specific jobs. In one sense Mayo's ideas fall in the tradition of small community theorizing, and they recall at many points the concerns of Fourier and Owen.

More significant, however, is the recent attempt to discover communal values in the large corporation and administrative organization. The ideas of Burke and the philosophy of organicism are pressed into service to explain the world of giant bureaucracies. The major theorist of this development is Philip Selznick. The starting point is one which denies that "formal" organization theory can ever fully capture the subtleties and rich social life of a living structure. Just as Burke had ridiculed the notion that a rationalistic and abstract theory of a political constitution could ever provide a faithful abridgement of the life of a nation, Selznick takes issue with the contemporary heirs of Sieyès and Paine: formal organizations "never succeed in conquering the non-rational dimensions of organizational behavior . . . No abstract plan or pattern can — or may, if it is to be useful — exhaustively describe an empirical reality." The members of an organization "have a propensity to resist de-personalization, to spill over the boundaries of their segmentary roles, to participate as *wholes*." [224] Admittedly an organization can be viewed as a rational, formal structure, an "economy" governed by the criteria of "efficiency and effectiveness," but from another perspective it appears as an "adaptive social structure" with certain "needs" radically different from the narrow ones of an "economy." These "needs" are ones which Burke would have applauded, for they are couched in the delicate language of organic growth: like any organism, an organization requires "security" in its environment, "stability" in its lines of authority, subtle patterns of informal relationships, modes of communication, "continuity" in its policies, and "homogeneity" in its outlook.[225]

In Selznick's later writings, the organic aspects of an organization are separated even more sharply from the strictly rational ones. The word "organization" is reserved for what is a "technical instrument" useful in directing human energies towards a fixed goal; it is a tool, rationally designed for specific technical ends, and, like any tool, expendable. The social aspects of the organization are then sorted out and designated an "institution": an institution "is more nearly a natural product of social needs and pressures, a responsive adaptive organism." Its adaptations are identical with Burke's evolutionary view of society; they are "natural and largely unplanned." "As an organization acquires a self, a distinctive identity, it becomes an institution." [226] To understand an "institution" requires a mode of cognition different from the logic of the engineer. "We must draw upon what we know about natural communities," for we are dealing with precious, living aggregates.

To the degree that organizations evolve into "natural communities" they become valued for their own sakes, for "to institutionalize" is "to *infuse with value* beyond the technical requirements of the task at hand." [227]

Thus far the pure language of Burke: spontaneity, natural processes, adaptative organisms, and non-rational behavior. But, it must be remembered that Selznick is describing not a rural and pre-industrial society, a world of squires, manor houses, and faithful retainers, but the world of General Motors, the Pentagon, and the large public university. To liken a corporation to a natural community evokes the question: what does it mean to be a member of such a community? where is the natural aristocracy of Burke and where is the natural relationship, evolving slowly and unconsciously over time, between the members and the governing elite? The answers that Selznick gives are cast, not in the language of Burke, but in that of Saint-Simon. Words like "spontaneous" are used to describe the relationship between member and the controlling group, but they have been divested of all unpremeditation and serve only as the shell to manipulation.

"Maintenance of social values," Selznick writes, "depends on the autonomy of elites," and hence participation is "prescribed" for the members "only when there is a problem of cohesion." Despite Selznick's avowal that one of the felt needs of the members was not to feel "manipulated," and that the loyalties of the members were vital ingredients infusing the bare structure of an organization with a human warmth, he discovers that these "commitments" and "identifications" cause difficulties; they limit "the freedom of the leadership to deploy its resources." [228] The tension is neatly resolved by arranging for a conjunction between the aims and requirements of leadership and the sentiments of those led. By some alchemy, "spontaneity" and "manipulation" are rendered compatible:

> When we say that policy is built into the social structure of an organization, we mean that official aims and methods are *spontaneously protected* or *advanced*. The aspirations of individuals are so stimulated and controlled, and so ordered in their mutual relations, as to produce the desired balance of forces. [229]

Now Selznick's conclusion is in no significant sense different from that reached by the "rationalist" Simon. "Human behavior . . . gets its higher goals and integrations from the institutional setting in which it operates and by which it is molded." Once the proper "attachment or loyalty to the organization" has been bred in the member, it is "automatically" guaranteed that "his decisions will be consistent with the organization objectives"; that is, he will have an "organization personality." [230] The convergence of the two theories at the point of manipulation faithfully mirrors one of the fundamental points of agreement between nearly all writers of recent times: the belief that the world created by organizational bureaucracies is and should be run by elites. And at this point the challenge to the political becomes explicit, and now we turn to how it has been posed.

XII The attack on the political. In the nineteenth century the anti-political impulses nurtured by classical liberalism took on a depth and pervasiveness unmatched in previous centuries. "The irksome situation" of today, Proudhon declared, was due to *une certaine maladie de l'opinion . . . qu'Aristote . . . a nommé* POLITIQUE." [231] The abolition of the political was proclaimed by almost every important thinker, and most projects for a future society excluded political activity from the routine of daily life. For, as Marx put it, "only *political superstition* believes at the present time that civil life must be held together by the State, when in reality the State is held together by civil life." [232] Nor was this anti-political complex the private possession of any particular school. It was manifest in Saint-Simon, the Utopians, Proudhon, Comte, Durkheim, the Fabians, and the managerialists.

Now, as we have noted in previous chapters, the anti-political impulse was an old one, with roots deep in the very beginnings of political speculation. Consequently, our concern is not to re-emphasize old animosities but to isolate the peculiar manifestations of anti-politicism in the recent age and, more particularly, to indicate the unique substitutes that have been offered. Our inquiry, in short, is directed at the sublimation rather than at the elimination of the political.

The starting point of the nineteenth century was one which had been prepared by classical liberalism, the antagonism between "state" and "society," between institutions, authorities, and relationships that men believed to be political and the relationships of a social, economic, and cultural sort that men believed to be "private" or "outside" politics. In Proudhon's words:

> We must understand that outside the sphere of parliamentarism, as sterile as it is absorbing, there is another field incomparably vaster, in which our destiny is worked out; that beyond these political phantoms, whose forms capture our imagination, there are the phenomena of social economy, which, by their harmony or discord, produce all the good and ill of society. [233]

As the writers of the century reflected on the past, they gradually concluded that the eighteenth century, or, more accurately, 1789, marked the turning point to a future rid of the suffocating atmosphere of politics. The great revolution came to symbolize the time when the political order had mustered its failing forces for a last-ditch attempt to assert its general responsibility for the well-being of society. Proudhon claimed that the unintended result of the French Revolution had been to sharpen the identity of two incompatible entities, society and government. The latter, he asserted, was "a factitious order," out of harmony with the principles of "a natural order conceived in accordance with science and labor." The task allotted to the nineteenth-century revolution was to reverse and destroy the political tendencies nourished by 1789, but to do so with the *caveat* that "no question of touching society itself" should be entertained. Society was sacrosanct, "a superior being, endowed with independent life, and in consequence remote from any idea on our part to reconstruct it arbitrarily." "From the political order," Proudhon pleaded, "let us pass to the economic order." [234]

By mid-century, however, the tone alters somewhat: political intervention into the affairs of society was not really dangerous, as Saint-Simon and the Utopian Socialists had believed, but merely trivial in its effects. Reality was socio-economic in nature; political action could not appreciably modify the fundamental character of reality, nor could political theory truly understand it. As Marx declared:

> *Political* thought is really *political* thought in the sense that the thinking takes place within the framework of politics. The clearer and more vigorous political thought is, the *less* it is able to grasp the nature of social evils.[235]

Among later and less revolutionary writers than Marx there was the same belief in the ultimate futility of politics. At its very worst, they held, political action might pervert human affairs; at its best, it could only register social reality, but in no sense could political action supply a creative direction. Governments may crush an individual, Durkheim asserted, "but against the social condition (*état*) itself, against the structure of society, they are relatively powerless." Political action, he continued, operates from a point far too remote to penetrate the souls of the citizens and employs methods far too crude to be able to impose uniform regulations "against the nature of things." [236]

To the writers of the late nineteenth century, as well as to their more recent successors, society presented a bafflingly complex structure held together by the cooperative efforts of millions of anonymous persons. This was the theme of Durkheim's famous concept of the division of labor, of Proudhon's idea of social solidarity, of Marx's vision of the future society. The common belief of all of these writers was that social cooperation stood as the complete antithesis to politics. Proudhon spoke for the age when he wrote that *"le dernier mot"* of politics is *"la* FORCE." [237] The modern managerialist is equally emphatic: ". . . the political sphere deals with power. And power is only a tool and in itself ethically neutral. It is not a social purpose and not an ethical principle." [238] Any political system, even democracy, declares another writer in the same tradition, is but an "artificial substitute for human cooperation," and one that "has brought all kinds of ills and abnormalities in its train." Politics has conflict as its *raison d'être,* and the politician feeds on these ills, exploits them by Machiavellian techniques, and traffics in popular passions and illusory grievances. "Political nostrums" supply no solution, because "the real problem is how to set each individual function to do its best for society." [239]

In these criticisms the century articulated its ultimate longing: to commune with the underlying reality of society. What was truly human was the social condition. For Durkheim, for the English pluralists, such as Figgis and Cole, and for the American managerialists, as well as for psychoanalysts like Erich Fromm, the values of society were epitomized in small group relationships — just as they had been for Proudhon and the Utopian Socialists. Only private groups and occupational associations possess the power, Durkheim wrote, to "drag" isolated individuals "into the general torrent of social life." Locked deep in society was the life force for which the century searched.[240]

At bottom the century desperately longed to transcend the political. The most powerful, and in many ways the most representative, expression of this point of view was to be found in Marx's writings. In previous ages, he wrote, political relationships had been supreme; they had pervaded all aspects of life and had overlaid the social and economic nature of groups with a political veneer. The emergence of the modern, centralized state constituted a "political revolution" which had shattered "the *political character of civil society*." What Marx meant by this paradox was that the State, on the one hand, had established a monopoly of power and authority, "a real State," by destroying the autonomy of corporations, guilds, and the feudal class structure; and, on the other hand, had drained "political" loyalties from these lesser associations and transferred them to the political order itself. In this way the political order became "a matter of general concern." But the effects of this development on society were momentous. Society was dissolved into a welter of isolated individuals, while the individual was deprived of contact with the rich life of community and association and left imprisoned in his own naked egotism. In the future the harmful effects of this "political" change would be repaired. The political dimension would be transcended; the concept of the citizen would be exchanged for that of the human person; the individual would be released from his artificially created status as a political animal and restored to his natural status of a social animal:

> The social life from which the worker is *shut out* is a social life very different in kind and extent from that of the *political* sphere. The social life . . . is *life* itself, physical and cultural life, human morality, human activity, human enjoyment, real *human* existence. Human life is the *true social life* of man. As the irremediable exclusion from this life is much more complete, more unbearable, dreadful and contradictory, than the exclusion from political life, so is the ending of this exclusion . . . more fundamental, as *man* is more fundamental than the *citizen, human life* more than *political life*.[241]

Marx's attack on the state expressed a widespread conviction of the century that unless some drastic measures were taken to halt the progressive isolation of individuals, the growing power of the state would crush what was best and most promising in the human condition. While the nineteenth-century liberals had sought to diminish the threat by installing a variety of constitutional gadgets, other writers turned towards society to find havens of refuge for the individual. The Utopians found their solution to *étatisme* in the small self-sufficient community; de Tocqueville believed that democratic societies could avoid over-centralization only if they maintained a viable system of local self-government and encouraged the growth of voluntary associations; Durkheim and the English pluralists looked to a society of nearly autonomous vocational groups to offset the thrusts of state power. Thus there was widespread agreement that social isolation was the root-cause of *étatisme* and that if it could be overcome the power of the state would dry up at its source.

It would be ungenerous to doubt the genuineness of these anxieties or to imply that the century was following a spurious lead. Our concern, however, is with the consequences of the diagnosis and the remedy. To reject the state meant denying the central referent of the political, abandoning a whole range of notions and the practices to which they pointed — citizenship, obligation, general authority — without pausing to consider that the strategy of withdrawal might further enhance state power. Moreover, to exchange society or groups for the state might turn out to be a doubtful bargain if society should, like the state, prove unable to resist the tide of bureaucratization. Both of these possibilities have been realized. Suspicion of the state has reduced the codes of civility to the appearance of rituals which we follow half in shame and half in embarrassment. At the same time, the discovery that precious little in human life is immune to bureaucratization has disspelled some of the magic of the group. These developments provide the contemporary setting for the re-enactment of political roles and the recital of political ideas: with the discrediting of the political order and the retreat to society which itself manifests growing symptoms of bureaucratization, the political has re-emerged, but disguised in the trappings of organizational life. What has been denied to the political order has been assimilated to the organizational order. This transferral has not been difficult, for, as Proudhon pointed out a century ago, the identity and the legitimacy of the political consists only in "certain signs or ornaments, and in the performance of certain ceremonies";[242] hence if modern man refuses to believe in the importance of these symbols and rituals, he is free to shift his support to other objects. And how easy the transition is: "the Rights of Man can be made just as safe in corporate hands as they were in individual hands." [243]

The political life of organizations began with the discovery that a private organization, like the modern business corporation, displayed most of the distinguishing marks of a political order:

> The corporation is now, essentially, a monostatist political institution, and its directors are in the same boat with public officeholders.[244]

It was argued that a huge aggregate, such as General Motors, a cartel like I. G. Farben, a monopoly like Standard Oil, all wield power equal to that of many governmental bodies. They command enormous resources, human as well as natural; their wealth often exceeds that of many governmental jurisdictions; their actions affect the lives and welfare of countless individuals; their influence extends beyond the merely economic sphere, penetrating legislatures, governmental agencies, and political parties. It follows that, if these entities seem to act like political societies, they can be studied through the categories of political science.[245] For example, if the corporation is a political form, it must possess "authority" over its members. According to one popular writer, the "authority" of the governing group of a corporation is obtained by a process identical with that depicted by the great contract writers of political theory:

> The modern corporation is thus a *political* institution; its purpose is the creation of legitimate power in the industrial sphere . . . The political purpose of the corporation is the creation of a legitimate social government on the basis of the original power of the individual property rights of its shareholders. The corporation is the *Contrat social* in its purest form.[246]

In keeping with this discovery of the "political" in organizations, the concepts and notions associated with the discredited political order are salvaged for use in describing its successor. Terms like "government," "kitchen-cabinet," "final judicial function," "Supreme Court," "representative institution," "order," "trustees for the community," and "just consent of the governed" are scattered about the literature of organization.[247]

The culmination of this trend is most clearly revealed by Selznick's recent work, *Leadership in Administration.* The social world of today, he declares, is organized around "largely self-governing" organizations of huge size. Because of the enormous resources which they command, they have an inescapable responsibility, or rather their leaders do, for the "well-being of numerous constituents." These institutions are *"public* in nature," because they are "attached to such interests" and deal "with such problems as affect the welfare of the entire community." [248] As befits entities which have assumed the mantle of the political, the modern business executive "becomes a statesman" and, to a large degree, his organization sheds its technical or administrative character for the higher dignity of an "institution"; that is, "a responsive, adaptive organism" well-deserving of the time-honored name of "polity." The claim to a political status resides in the fact that the modern organization is confronted by the same type of problems familiar to the life of the political order. "There is the same basic constitutional problem" of accommodating "fragmentary group interests" to "the aims of the whole"; of elaborating statesman-like policies which will "define the ends of group existence"; of ordering internal conflicts by establishing "consent" and maintaining a "balance of power." [249] As the profile of leadership takes full shape, we find that we have run the full cycle and are back once more with the first of political philosophers —

> creative men . . . who know how to transform a neutral body of men into a committed polity. These men are called leaders; their profession is politics.[250]

XIII Elite and mass: action in the age of organization. Selznick's argument, which is a highly sophisticated and literate example of what can be found among many writers, is not concerned solely to establish the political character of business organizations. Rather the more general aim is to demonstrate that the politicalness of a corporation does not come from the fact that the corporation is a business enterprise, but from the fact that it is a large and powerful organization. In other words, the organization is the dominant and ubiquitous phenomenon of society, and whether it carries the

adjective "business," "government," "military," or "educational" is largely
irrelevant. All organizations are inevitably "political" in character, or, conversely, what is most politically significant in the modern world is contained
in organizational life.

This being the case, the question naturally arises, how do these theorists
view politics? A partial answer is that they perceive political problems from
an elitist position. In Selznick's words, elites are "objectively necessary" for
the maintenance and development of social institutions and culture.[251] The
form of elitism expressed in this literature has certain superficial affinities
with, say, Platonism: it believes that those few who have the qualifications for
exercising the highest social functions should be in the positions of highest
authority. Fundamentally, however, contemporary elitism is indebted to a far
different and more recent conception; namely, that an elite is a group whose
superiority rests on its excellence in manipulation. The *locus classicus* of this
formulation was in the writings of Pareto, but it has become commonplace
in a wide variety of twentieth-century theorists: in Lenin's theory of the party
elites; in Nazi and Fascist ideologies; in the various theorists of managerialism; and in Mannheim's conception of the role of social scientists in the
planned society.[252] Now the crucial theme in all of these writings, and
the one which supplies the dialectical counterpoint to the elitist strain, is the
emergence of the "masses." The concept of the masses haunts modern political and social theory: to disenchanted liberals like Ortega y Gasset, it
represented the dreaded enemy of culture; to others, like Lenin and, more
particularly, Fascist and Nazi writers, the masses represented the pliable
stuff of revolutionary opportunity. Although there are a wide variety of definitions of the "masses," Selznick has given one which describes fairly well
what most writers have in mind: "When the normal inhibitions enforced by
tradition and social structure are loosened . . . the undifferentiated mass
emerges." [253] This kind of definition sets the stage for the dramatic confrontation between the "elite" and the "mass": the elite is a sharply defined group,
possessing clear qualifications and performing a vitally useful role in the
social system. The concept of the elite fits naturally with a tradition of political and social theory in which hierarchy, order, and differentiation are
fundamental ideas: a tradition as old as political thought itself and as recent
as modern sociology. The mass, in contrast, is undifferentiated, amorphous,
banal in its tastes, lacking in a defined role and conscious purpose, the unat-
tractive deposit of an age of rapid social change, the lost social battalion without ties of communication, affection, and loyalty. "Mass connotes a 'glob of
humanity,' as against the intricately related, institutionally bound groupings

that form a healthy social organism." The "disease" of contemporary society is "mass behavior." [254]

The juxtaposition of "mass" and "elite" is highly informative of the present condition of theorizing, for it discloses that contemporary theory is, in a special sense, post-Marxian, and, in terms of mood, disenchanted. History has not only been unkind, it has been positively malicious. Instead of the highly self-conscious proletariat, the proud bearers of man's historical destiny, history has given us the vulgar mass; instead of Adonis, Quasimodo. Marx had depicted the working class as disciplined, purposeful, the symbolic representative of humanity's future triumph — "philosophy can only be realized by the abolition of the proletariat, and the proletariat can only be abolished by the realization of philosophy" — as well as the symbol of humanity's past. The proletariat had suffered on the cross of history for all humanity; "its sufferings are universal"; its present misery was "not a *particular wrong* but *wrong in general*"; its future emancipation promised to be "a *total redemption of humanity*."

Now if, instead of the proletariat, history has disgorged a "glob of humanity," it is not Marx who is teacher to the new age of mass society but Lenin; it is not the prophet of proletarian victory who speaks to the contemporary condition, but the strategist who perfects the instrument of action, the elite. If it is to be the elite, rather than the proletariat, who actually lead the way, the strategy is not to smash the pseudo-proletariat or masses, but to manipulate it. It is "our duty," Lenin wrote, "to go down *lower* and *deeper*, to the real masses." [255]

What makes Lenin a central figure for our study is that he glimpsed sooner than most writers the possibilities of organization as the action medium best suited to a mass age. Organization was to mass in Lenin's theory what idea had been to matter in Plato's: that which imparted form to the formless. Lenin was the first to seize the implications of transferring politics, political theory, political action — all that we have subsumed under the "political" — to the plane of organization. He taught that politics and the political had meaning only within an organizational setting. Industrialism and large-scale organization did not necessarily render political things unnecessary, nor did "administration" provide a complete substitute, as Saint-Simon and others had supposed. The trick was not to destroy the political, but to absorb it into organization, to create a new compound. The measure of Lenin's success is that his lessons have become the common property of the age; the irony is that his prescription for revolution has also been used to preserve giant capitalism.

The central point of Lenin's argument was the refutation of an assumption common to classical liberalism, early socialism, and Marx as well: the primordial importance of economic phenomena. While other writers, professing to follow Marx, had also expressed anxieties about the continued and stubborn vitality of capitalism, Lenin not only rendered this problem irrelevant by turning the focus of revolutionary theory upon pre-capitalist societies, but, above all, he taught that the greatest danger to the revolutionary movement lay in allowing the workers to become preoccupied with economic issues. If the proletariat went whoring after material class interests, its tough revolutionary temper would surely soften and victory would be lost. Self-interest was self-interest, and it no more encouraged proletarian than capitalist heroics.[256]

Lenin proceeded to discard the eighteenth and nineteenth century notion that significant action meant economic action. Political action was rescued from limbo and restored to a new primacy, new because revolution was proclaimed the quintessential form of political action. "The fact that economic interests are a decisive factor *does not in the least imply* that the economic [i.e., trade union] struggle must be the main factor, for the essential and 'decisive' interests in classes can be satisfied *only* by the radical *political* changes in general." [257] For Lenin the "political" dealt with the comprehensive, with what transcended class horizons and interests; hence the workers had to rise above economic consciousness and acquire an "all-sided political consciousness" responsive to *"all cases* of tyranny, oppression, violence, and abuse, no matter *what class* is affected." [258] He insisted that "political activity had its logic quite apart" from either terrorism or economic struggle, and he accused his opponents of committing "the fundamental error" of believing it possible "to develop the class political consciousness of the workers *from within* the economic struggle." [259] "True" consciousness was political rather than economic, because revolutionary overthrow constituted a basically political act with a basically political objective.[260] The workers, therefore, had to be educated to a political consciousness, which meant, in a very ancient notion, gaining a synthetic view of the whole:

> The consciousness of the masses of the workers cannot be genuine class consciousness, unless the workers learn to observe from concrete, and above all from topical, political facts and events, *every* other social class and all the manifestations of the intellectual, ethical and political life of these classes; unless they learn to apply practically the materialist analysis and the materialist estimate of *all* aspects of the life and activity of *all* classes, strata, and groups of the population.[261]

Having asserted the primacy of political action, Lenin then turned to the question of how best to pursue it. His answer, as we have already stated, was organization, and it was a choice which symbolized a crucial turning point in the Western tradition. When we look back on the late nineteenth and early twentieth century from the vantage point of what we know about Lenin's thought, it is possible to see in a clearer light what the protests of writers like Nietzsche, Kierkegaard, and Sorel had meant. Kierkegaard's lonely, desperate "leap" to God, Nietzsche's solitary superman struggling against the toils of a mediocre, bourgeois world, Sorel's "myth" of the spontaneous general strike by a proletariat welded to unity only by an heroic impulse — these were all last-ditch efforts to secure some place for unorganized individual action. They were last gasps of a romanticism doomed to expire before the age of streamlined organizations and rationally efficient bureaucracies. Nor was this a protest confined to deformed theologians and syphilitic philosophers, for nowhere was the anguishing tension between the world of organization and the creative individual more clearly revealed than in the thought of Max Weber, perhaps the greatest of sociologists.

No one saw more clearly than he that bureaucracy and large-scale organization were the fundamental phenomena of modern political, social, and economic life. No one was more unstinting in admiration for the routinized rationality, the impersonal fairness, the high level of expertise exhibited by these structures.[262] Yet there was a strong note of ambiguity and soft whispers of pathos: "the fate of our times" is that man must dwell in the "disenchantment of the world." Mystery has been banished and "the bearing of man has been disenchanted and denuded of its mystical but inwardly genuine plasticity." [263] Yet in his famous essay, *Politics as a Vocation*, along with its clear-eyed recognition of the way bureaucracy has invaded all political realms — party, government, and legislature — Weber plaintively pleaded for a conception of political leadership cut to truly classical proportions. Weber's leader is a political hero, rising to heights of moral passion and grandeur, harried by a deep sense of responsibility. But, at bottom, he is a figure as futile and pathetic as his classical counterpart. The fate of the classical hero was that he could never overcome contingency or *fortuna*; the special irony of the modern hero is that he struggles in a world where contingency has been routed by bureaucratized procedures and nothing remains for the hero to contend against. Webers' political leader is rendered superfluous by the very bureaucratic world that Weber discovered: even charisma has been bureaucratized. We are left with the ambiguity of the political man fired by deep passion — "to be passionate, *ira et studium*, is . . . the element of the political *leader*'

— but facing the impersonal world of bureaucracy which lives by the passionless principle that Weber frequently cited, *sine ira et studio,* "without scorn or bias." [264]

For Weber there remained one sanctuary of personal action, one province where man could affirm himself in a world otherwise dominated by rationalized and highly intellectualized processes. The area of choice or fundamental values was one which, by nature, stubbornly resists scientific method and other techniques of objectivity; it was the last preserve of passion.[265] This casts a quite different light on Weber's endlessly labored and refined distinction between the scientifically knowable realm of "facts" and the subjective, nonscientific realm of "values." The wall between the two was not erected, as Weber's interpreters have sometimes implied, simply to shield the objective sphere of science from contamination by arbitrary values and personal idiosyncrasies. It was equally the result of a desperate effort on Weber's part to secure some sphere where affirmation was possible and, most important, where bureaucratic and scientific rationality were impossible. Yet the matter did not rest there, for Weber left a final irony for personal action to contemplate: each individual bore the awful responsibility for choice at this ultimate level but each was denied anything like the scientist's sense of certainty: "the ultimately possible attitudes towards life are irreconcilable, and hence their struggle can never be brought to a final conclusion." [266]

Nostalgias such as these had no place in Lenin's thought. The latter was mesmerized by the potentialities of organization. One does not have to supply a gloss to say that Lenin looked upon organization as the Archimedean lever for overthrowing a whole society. He himself used the metaphor.[267] "If we begin with the solid foundation of a strong organization of revolutionaries, we can guarantee the stability of the movement as a whole." Revolution, far from being the "spontaneous" uprising of an oppressed and exasperated mass, was an "art" requiring delicate timing; spontaneity rendered organization "more necessary." [268] Only through organizational intelligence could the revolutionaries assess "the general political situation," develop "the ability to select the proper moment for the uprising," and enforce discipline among the local organizations so that the latter would "respond simultaneously to the same political questions." [269] Thus organization provided preconceived direction and form to the bubbling ferment of "spontaneous" revolutionary forces; it maintained "a systematic plan of activity" over time and preserved "the energy, the stability and continuity of the political struggle." Through organization the revolutionaries could "concentrate all these drops and streamlets of popular excitement" into "a *single* gigantic flood." [270] Above all, the "all-sided and all-embracing political agitation" undertaken by organization helped to rivet the elite to the mass; organization brings the elite *"into closer proximity to, and merges* the elemental destructive force of the crowd with the conscious destructive force of the organization of revolutionaries." [271]

As Lenin spelled out the details of revolutionary organization, a different, almost aesthetic note, crept into his writing. He began to look upon the "apparatus" with the jealous pride of the artist, heaping scorn on those who would "degrade" the organization by turning it towards tawdry economic objectives and "immediate goals," bemoaning the "primitiveness" of the existing organization which had "lowered the prestige of revolutionaries in Russia." The task of the organization was to raise the workers "to the level of revolutionaries," not to degrade the organization to the level of "the average worker." Above all, when the revolutionary situation ripened, special care must be taken to avert the danger of the party organization being "overwhelmed" by the revolutionary wave. For its own protection, the organization must be powerful enough to master the "spontaneity" of the masses.[272]

Lenin's emphasis on the "small compact core" of professional revolutionaries as the vital cog of the organization led him to the question of what kind of democracy, and how much, could be permitted. His answer established a framework of argument that was to be duplicated by later writers concerned with the same broad question. It was the procedure adopted by Michels in his famous study of the oligarchical and bureaucratic tendencies in professedly democratic parties; by Chester Barnard in his analysis of the contradictions between the requirements of administrative leadership and democratic practices; by students of organization concerned at the way mass society, with its penchant for "radical leveling," "prevents the emergence of an effective social leadership." [273] What is important here is the way that the question is posed: how much democracy can organization endure? — never the reverse. Lenin's answer was a model of candor:

> Bureaucracy *versus* democracy is the same thing as centralism *versus* [local] autonomism, it is the same organizational principle of revolutionary political democracy as opposed to the organizational principle of the opportunists of Social Democracy. The latter want to proceed from the bottom upwards . . . The former proceed from the top, and advocate the extension of the rights and powers of the centre in respect of the parts . . . My idea . . . is "bureaucratic" in the sense that the Party is built from the top downwards . . .[274]

Democracy, therefore, had to be redefined in a way more consonant with the imperatives of organization and elitism. Membership had to be severely restricted so as not to compromise the highly professional quality of the leadership. At the same time, a type of bureaucratic democracy would encourage talented workers to rise to positions of leardership: as in the modern corporation, there was to be room at the top.[275] The "real" guarantee of democratic responsibility to the membership lay in the close-knit solidarity of the elite, the "complete, comradely, mutual confidence among revolutionaries." [276]

When Lenin came to consider the task of building the new order, he relied once more on the same prescription: construction, as well as destruction, required systematic organization and a compact leadership group. Like Calvin contending with the sectarians who believed that "enthusiasm" alone could sustain the church, Lenin had to dispose of the anarchist argument that, with the destruction of the old order, men could proceed directly to a condition where power was unnecessary. "The proletariat," Lenin asserted, "needs state power, the centralized organization of force, the organization of violence . . ." [277] To be sure, the old-style politics would be abolished, for, thanks to the advances of capitalism, most governmental tasks had been so greatly simplified that they could be discharged by the simple routines followed in post offices. Gradually society would evolve towards the "non-political state," which, while not the final phase, would be a definite advance over the past.[278]

Lenin provided an illuminating glimpse into the workings of the organizational mentality when he turned to consider what was to be abolished of the political and what was to be retained. Politics, as represented by party rivalries, legislative maneuvers, the frictions generated between governmental units, and the struggle for group advantage, was to be suppressed: organization excluded politics. But those aspects of the political congenial or necessary to organization were to be retained. Thus the proletarian state was said to need "a certain amount of subordination" and "some authority or power." Above all, bureaucracy itself would be perpetuated: "to destroy officialdom immediately, everywhere, completely — this cannot be thought of." It was a mere "anarchist dream" to hold that "all administration" and "all subordination" could be disposed of.[279]

The affection which Lenin had lavished on the revolutionary organization was now transferred to the governmental machinery. He asserted that revolutionary society would not only exploit the advanced techniques of capitalist administration, but would perfect and purify them. No longer would public positions be degraded into being mere springboards for obtaining more lucrative posts in private industry; no longer would the careless, gentlemanly tradition of the civil service prevail. This was to be a pure organization, undisfigured by parasites. "Our problem here is only to *lop away* that which *capitalistically disfigures* this otherwise excellent apparatus . . ." [280]

In the light of his admiration for the beauties of organization and his faith in its creative power, there is small wonder that Lenin was eager to put it to the test. Like later theorists of organization, he was undismayed by the lack of resources available, the low level of skills and literacy, the appalling distance between reality and aspiration. To those faint-hearted followers who pleaded that the revolution should be postponed until human nature could be educated to the demands of the new age, Lenin replied with what was a classic statement of the faith of the new age of organization: "No, we want the Socialist revolution with human nature as it is now, with human nature that cannot do without subordination, control, and 'managers.'" [281]

One final problem remained: how was organization to be squared with Marx's prophecy of a future society where the state would "wither away" and coercion would lose its rationale? For Lenin this was no problem. He agreed that ultimately there would be true or "primitive" democracy, but he conceived it to be democracy within the premises of organization, or, more accurately, he thought that the perfection of organization would be identical with true democracy. The progressive simplification of work would obviate the need for expert talents and place all functions within the reach "of every single individual." Since "democracy means equality," the development of organization could satisfy this criterion by breaking down complex jobs into simple operations. "The whole of society will have become one office and one factory, with equal work and equal pay." [282] In short, true organization *is* equality.

The prescience of Lenin's theories is confirmed by their reappearance in the conservatively-oriented literature of organization theory.[283] What Marx did to Hegel, writers like Selznick have done to Lenin; that is, turned him upside down. The new formula is not pure Leninism, but Leninism clothed in the language of Burke. The fondness for large scale organization displayed by contemporary writers largely stems from anxieties provoked by the emergence of the mass. They see organizations as mediating institutions, shaping disoriented individuals to socially useful behavior and endowing them with a desperately needed sense of values. These large entities supply the stabilizing centers, which not only integrate and structure the amorphous masses, but control them as well.[284] The role which Selznick assigns the elite seems more indebted to Burke than to Lenin. The ruling group, he warns, is not in a position analogous to the sculptor, free "to mould the organization according to his heart's desire . . ." Instead, its posture is "essentially conservative." [285] To preserve the life of the group was a task which could not be reduced to a question of balance sheets, any more than Burkean society could be treated as "a partnership agreement in a trade of pepper and coffee," or the Leninist revolutionary movement as a mere instrument to advance trade-union interests. The administrator is responsible for the life-processes of a "polity." [286] To accomplish his ends effectively it is necessary that he win the "consent" of the members. But "consent" in the age of organization does not connote self-government, much less the idea of participation as practiced in the ancient "polity." It means, instead, "commitment," which is something far different. "Commitment" is the special prescription for a mass age where men are isolated and their lives depersonalized and bleak. Their wants are psychic and hence to be satisfied by "integration" rather than made more anxious by the demands of participation.[287] The aim of the elite, therefore, is to convert "neutral men" into a "committed polity."

Now it is also true that Selznick sometimes uses commitment as a synonym for "loyalty" and "loyalty" is said to involve "rational, free-willed consent." [288] While this might appear to be either a bit of careless usage or a deceptive strategy to exploit some "hurrah-words," it is also squarely in the manipulative tradition. Selznick's notions of "commitment," "loyalty," and "rational, free-willed consent" have as much of choice and spontaneity about them as Lenin's theory of "democratic centralism" has of democracy:

> By long habituation, sometimes also as a result of aggressive indoctrination, the individual absorbs a way of perceiving and evaluating his experience. This reduces his anxiety by lending the world of fact a familiar cast; and it helps assure an easy conformity with established practice.[289]

As Selznick makes clear, "participation" is "prescribed . . . only when there is a problem of cohesion." Moreover, there is the cautionary reminder that the member must not be allowed to over-commit himself, for this builds up rigidities which limit "the freedom of the leadership to deploy its resources." [290]

Other "political" aspects of the organizational "polity" are similarly transformed into ready counters of manipulation by the leadership. The rules or "laws" of the organization, the "pluralism" of its structure are all useful devices for facilitating the task of governing. The beliefs of the members are described as "ideologies," and they are the objects of a "technique" for manipulating "socially integrating myths." [291] Although at one point "administrative ideologies" are said to emerge "in spontaneous and unplanned ways," our previous discussion has prepared us for the legerdemain which transforms "spontaneity" into direction. "A well-formulated doctrine," quite unsurprisingly, is discovered to be "remarkably handy for boosting internal morale, communicating the bases for decisions, and rebuffing outside claims and criticisms."

When we say that policy is built into the social structure of an organization, we mean that official aims and methods are *spontaneously protected or advanced*. The aspirations of individuals and groups are so stimulated and controlled . . . as to produce the desired balance of forces.[292]

XIV   **Concluding remarks.** These last few chapters have singled out those themes that seemed to be among the more important for understanding the dominant direction being followed by recent political thought. It would be foolish, however, to maintain that justice has been done either to the richness and variety of recent speculation, or to its perversities. Consequently it would be crudely dogmatic to conclude with a pronouncement about *the* problem of contemporary political and social speculation. What follows is merely a brief summary of some of the difficulties that recent theory has gotten into and some highly tentative pointers about a possible way out.

From an examination of recent theorizing, it is fairly clear that a reaction against some of the major categories of political thought has occurred. It is important, however, not to misunderstand its nature. As we have seen in the last chapter, it is not the animus against politics and the political that is characteristic of our time; on the contrary, recent thought has been highly ingenious in discovering political phenomena in almost every important human activity. We shall return to this point in a moment, but here we need only re-emphasize that it is not anti-politicism as such that is peculiar to the present, but rather the sublimation of the political into forms of association which earlier thought had believed to be non-political.

The reaction we are witnessing requires a more complex explanation. Expressed in a somewhat awkward way, it is a reaction against the *general* nature of traditional political theory and, along with this, against the claims of the political to a scope as wide as society itself. Perhaps this can be made clearer by indicating briefly what I mean by the *general* quality of the political.

Throughout the long development of the Western tradition of political thought, there has been a recurrent tendency to identify what is political with what is general to a society. The inclusiveness of political society, for example, has always been contrasted with the parochialisms of family, class, local community, and sect. Again, the general responsibility for the welfare of the whole society has been consistently regarded as the special function of the political order. To take another instance, the status of citizen has been conceived in terms of a role which defined the individual's duties and expectations in matters of general concern. Finally, political authority has been defined as the authority representing the generality of society and speaking in its name. These tendencies, in turn, have been registered in the claims of political theory itself to be a body of knowledge and wisdom concerned with society's attempt to articulate what is common or general to its life.

In contrast, recent social and political theory has had a more restricted focus. Its values have been more local, being concerned with smaller groupings and associations. This has been true not only of those writers like the Utopian Socialists, Proudhon, Durkheim, and the pluralists, but also of those who adhere to the so-called "group theory of politics." In the words of one of the most influential of the group theorists, "When the groups are adequately stated, everything is stated." [293] Localism, in short, is the earmark not simply of those who are concerned to prescribe new forms of social and political organization, but equally of those who profess to be interested solely in explanation and description. The contemporary social scientist tends to adopt modes of understanding and analysis that are dissective, even scholastic; he is constantly seeking intellectual classifications more manageable than the broadly political one. He is inclined to analyze men in terms of class-orientations, group-orientations, or occupational orientations. But man as member of a general political society is scarcely considered a proper subject for theoretical inquiry, because it is assumed that "local citizenship" — man as trade-unionist, bureaucrat, Rotarian, occupant of a certain income-tax bracket — is the primary or determinant influence on how man will behave as a political citizen. The same procedure is followed in dealing with beliefs. The individual is viewed as a shopper carrying several distinct parcels, one containing his "vocational" ideology, another his "class" ideology, a third his "minority" attitudes, and, perhaps, a fourth and more discreet one holds his "religious ideology." The metaphor, however, is much too euphemistic, for the final impression left by this kind of analysis is that each of us is imprisoned consecutively, so to speak, within a series of disconnected beliefs. None of us is credited with a general set of notions, for we are analytically meaningful only when lodged within certain classifications.

The chopping-up of political man is but part of a broader process which has been at work in political and social theory. During the past two centuries the vision of political theory has been a disintegrating one, consistently working to destroy the idea that society ought properly to be considered as a whole and that its general life was best expressed through political forms. One result of this kind of theorizing has been to flatten the traditional *majestas* of the political order. This has been achieved by reducing the political association to the level of other associations at the same time that the latter have been elevated to the level of the political order and endowed with many of its characteristics and values. In recent years the impetus towards this development has come from two sources. First there have been the champions of groupism — and in this category I would include the advocates of small communities, the pluralists, Durkheim, those who laud the values of the factory as a social system, and the contemporary defenders of corporate organization — all of whom agree that man's personality and needs can be satisfied in some grouping smaller than and different from traditional political entities. At the same time, they are unwilling to grant either that there are any general human needs which are uniquely fulfilled in political life, excepting possibly the need for peace and defense, or that there is any need, individual or social, which requires integrating forms of activity.[294] The assumption prevailing among most groupists has been that the perpetuation of society requires the performance of a certain number of functions. These functions, in turn, are the complement to a determinate number of human needs. The next step in this chain of reasoning calls for listing the number of these functions that are being satisfactorily discharged by non-political associations or groups, such as trade unions, churches, corporations, and other private or voluntary groupings. The *sum* of group functions is then subtracted from the totality of socially necessary functions, and the precious little that remains is allowed to be the province of the political order. And more often than not the remainder turns out to involve mainly administrative functions. In this way the political order comes to occupy the status of residuary legatee, shouldering those tasks which other groups or organizations are unwilling or unable to perform. But always there is the hope of steadily reducing the number of political functions and always the attempt to add one more political function to the groups.

A second line of argument has also contributed to the depreciation of the politicalness of the political order. This has consisted of politicizing the character of non-political groups. Business leaders are designated "statesmen" who are responsible for the governance of their polity-corporations; conflicting elements within a trade union are likened to political parties;[295] membership and participation in groups and corporations are viewed as raising the same order of problems as political citizenship.

Both of these tendencies have converged to produce a picture of society as a series of tight little islands, each evolving towards political self-sufficiency, each striving to absorb the individual members, each without any natural affiliations with a more comprehensive unity. A typical example of this thinking was the comment of the former Dean of the Harvard Business School. After praising the "accomplishment" whereby the factory had become "the stabilizing force around which [the workers] developed satisfying lives," he went on to point out that this had been achieved "in spite of technological changes within the plant and social chaos in the community outside." [296] What is significant in this remark is the implicit belief that group life cannot only be perfected in the face of a chaotic "outside," but that by steadily increasing the number of healthy groups there will no longer be any "outside" to worry about. Equally implicit, the political order is assumed to be part of this "outside," "too remote morally and spatially to possess anything of the living reality of active collaboration for individuals." [297] Thus the contemporary vision of the social universe is one where political society, in its *general* sense, has disappeared. Selznick offers us a society dotted by large bureaucracies, each an autarchic polity with no organic connections between them, only an arena of diplomacy and negotiation for the new organizational statesmen. Berle, the ex-New Dealer, is fully satisfied by the way that the modern corporation has developed into a planning institution and looks forward to the time when "the state is not to be the dominant factor." [298]

Notions such as these are typical of the contemporary flight from that general dimension which, in the past, has served as the basis for viable theories of political life. It is not surprising, therefore, that recent theory has failed to produce a body of political ideas dealing with a general order; that is, an order whose function it would be to integrate the discontinuities of group and organizational life into a common society. Moreover, the divorce between what is political and what is general has repeatedly led recent writers into paths of futility. I mean by this that they have tried to pose political problems in what are essentially non-political settings; the result has been a series of dead ends. An instructive example of this is the problem of the responsibility of corporate management. Writers like Berle and Drucker have been acutely worried by the growing autonomy of management at a time when the corporate form is dominating much of social life. Berle, for instance, has pointed out that the modern corporation is becoming less and less dependent upon the capital supplied by individual stockholders. His whole analysis of the problem, beginning with the classic *The Modern Corporation and Private Property,* has consisted in large part of treating the corporation as though it were a political entity and hence susceptible to political kinds of questions. My point, however, is that an approach of this kind leads to confusions because the concept of political responsibility is out of place in this context. Political responsibility has traditionally connoted a form of responsibility owed to a general constituency and it has been a problem precisely because society contains a multiplicity of groups. Other writers have attempted a solution to the same problem posed by Berle by arguing that management is responsible to a variety of constituencies, such as the stockholders, workers, other busines corporations, and the vague group called the "public." But this line has been equally fruitless because it seeks to solve the problem by diffusing responsibility; that is, it too ignores the consideration that what makes responsibility political is its general quality deriving from what is common to the constituents.

The error in these theories comes from trying to assimilate political conceptions to non-political situations. Whether corporate management or trade-union leadership can be held responsible; whether membership in churches, benevolent societies, or other voluntary associations provides a satisfying experience for the individuals involved — all of these and similar questions are undeniably legitimate, but they do not belong to the species of political problems, and if we assume that they do, we obscure genuine political problems in a confusion of contexts. Even supposing that a coherent and satisfying theory of managerial responsibility is produced, the responsibility in question should not be designated political because of the restricted nature of the constituency. "Political" responsibility has meaning only in terms of a general constituency, and no multiplication of fragmentary constituencies will provide a substitute. Similarly, to contend that individual participation can be satisfied in a political way within the confines of non-political groups is to deprive citizenship of its meaning and to render political loyalty impossible.[299] When used in a political sense, citizenship and loyalty have meaning only in reference to a general order. Long ago Aristotle had insisted that the political association, by virtue of its superior comprehensiveness and purpose, had a stronger claim on men's loyalties than any lesser association and that political membership was therefore superior to other forms of membership. In terms of function and purpose, a lesser association, such as the family or the religious group, served a limited good and hence could justifiably extract only a partial loyalty. A political association, however, was conceived by him as promoting a more comprehensive good — that of the whole community — and hence was deserving of a fuller obedience.

In rebuttal to this argument it may be replied that the fragmentation of the political and its assignment to other associations and organizations are the necessary price for achieving some measure of individual self-determination, freedom, and participation in the modern world. The alternative of reviving the political dimension of existence seems an invitation to totalitarian-ism. There can be no denying that totalitarian systems have re-asserted the political with a vengeance. They have destroyed the autonomy of groups and replaced it with a highly coordinated general policy; they have oriented every major human activity towards political goals; through propaganda and controlled education they have instilled among the citizens a strong sense of the political order and a firm belief in the exalted status of political mem-bership; through plebiscites and mass elections they have mobilized a gen-eral form of support and approval.

Recognizing the cogency of this reply, the question still remains, does the re-assertion of the general political dimension and of the function of general integration necessarily demand such an extreme solution? Is it rather that the contemporary challenge is to recognize that totalitarianism has shown that societies react sharply to the disintegration wrought by the fetish of groupism; that they will resort to even the most extreme methods to re-assert the political in an age of fragmentation? If this should be the case, the task of non-totalitarian societies is to temper the excesses of pluralism. This means recognizing that the specialized roles assigned the individual, or adopted by him, are not a full substitute for citizenship because citizenship provides what the other roles cannot, namely an integrative experience which brings to-gether the multiple role-activities of the contemporary person and demands that the separate roles be surveyed from a more general point of view. It means further that efforts be made to restore the political art as that art which strives for an integrative form of direction, one that is broader than that supplied by any group or organization. It means, finally, that political theory must once again be viewed as that form of knowledge which deals with what is general and integrative to men, a life of common involvements. The urgency of these tasks is obvious, for human existence is not going to be decided at the lesser level of small associations: it is the political order that is making fateful decisions about man's survival in an age haunted by the possibility of unlimited destruction.

◄§ NOTES ঽ►

Chapter One

PAGE

2   [1] To be sure, there is Plato's lament that certain truths are uncommunicable. Whatever may be said about such truths, they cannot be said to have any philosophic value. The same holds for the so-called secret doctrines imputed to the ancient philosophers. Esoteric doctrines may be accepted as a form of religious instruction, but not of philosophical teaching.

5   [2] George Orwell, *England, Your England* (London: Secker & Warburg, 1954) p. 17. Aquinas, *Summa Theologiae* Ia, IIae, Q. 21, art. 4, ad 3 um.

7   [3] It is important to guard against the idea that institutions represent some higher, impersonal agency. An institution is a determinate group of people performing certain functions within an organizational pattern.

7   [4] Suzanne Langer, *Philosophy in a New Key* (New York: Mentor, 1952) pp. 58-59.

10   [5] *Protagoras,* 321-325 (Jowett translation). The question concerning whether the myth of Protagoras represents Plato's own thoughts is treated by Ronald B. Levinson, *In Defense of Plato* (Cambridge: Harvard University Press, 1953) pp. 293-294; W. K. C. Guthrie, *In the Beginning* (London: Methuen, 1957) pp. 84 ff.

14   [6] R. Carnap, *The Logical Foundations of Probability* (Chicago: University of Chicago Press, 1950) Ch. I; and the discussion of C. G. Hempel, "Fundamentals of Concept Formation in Empirical Science," *International Encyclopedia of Unified Science,* Vol. II, no. 7 (1952) pp. 6 ff.

15   [7] Hesiod, *Works and Days,* pp. 263-265, 275-285. See also Sir John Myres, *The Political Ideas of the Greeks* (New York: Abingdon Press, 1927) pp. 167 ff.; and the two excellent studies by Gregory Vlastos, "Solonian Justice," *Classical Philology,* Vol. XLI (1946) pp. 65-83, and "Equality and Justice in Early Greek Cosmology," *Ibid.,* Vol. XLII (1947) pp. 156-178.

16   [8] The phrase "political metaphysic" is used for the first time in a sense similar to that of mine by Pierre S. Ballanche, *Essai sur les institutions sociales dans leur rapports avec les idées nouvelles* (Paris, 1818) p. 12.

17   [9] *Leviathan,* II, xxi (p. 137) in the Oakeshott edition (Oxford: Blackwell).

17   [10] *Second Treatise of Civil Government,* 57. The same argument, including the metaphor of boundaries, is followed in A. D. Lindsay's influential book, *The Modern Democratic State* (London: Oxford University Press, 1943) p. 208. See

the reflection of the problem of the political structuring of space in a speech by the seventeenth-century parliamentary lawyer, Oliver St. John: without its "Polity and Government," England was "but a piece of Earth, wherein so many men have their Commorancy and abode, without ranks or distinction of men, without property in anything than Possession." Cited in Margaret Judson, *The Crisis of the Constitution* (New Brunswick, New Jersey: Rutgers University Press, 1949) p. 354. For a sixteenth-century example, see Edward Dudley: "This root of concord is none other thing but a good agreement and conformytie amongest the people or the inhibitauntes of a realme, citie, towne or fellowship, and every man is content to do his dewtie in the office, rome or condicion that he is sett in, And not to maling or disdaine any other." *The Tree of Commonwealth,* D. M. Brodie, ed. (Cambridge: Cambridge University Press, 1948) p. 40.

17   [11] Bentham, as cited in Lionel Robbins, *The Theory of Economic Policy in English Classical Political Economy* (London: Macmillan and Company, Ltd., and St. Martin's Press, Inc., 1952) p. 12.

17   [12] *Dr. Faustus,* trans. H. T. Lowe-Porter (London: Secker and Warburg, 1949) p. 301.

18   [13] This imaginative element is not the same as utopianism in that it is less an attempt to soar above present realities than an attempt to view existing realities as transformed possibilities. This is evident, for example, in Bodin, who disclaimed any utopian objectives, yet his own work cannot be said to be a description of sixteenth-century France. It was, instead, an attempt to project present tendencies into the future:

> "We aim higher in our attempt to attain, or at least approximate, to the true image of a rightly ordered government. Not that we intend to describe a purely ideal and unrealizable commonwealth, such as that imagined by Plato, or Thomas More the Chancellor of England. We intend to confine ourselves as far as possible to those political forms that are practicable." [Jean Bodin, *Six Books of the Commonwealth,* M. J. Tooley, ed. (Blackwell: Oxford, n. d.) p. 2.]

One of the most fruitful analyses in this matter is to be found in Sorel's attempt to distinguish his "myth" from utopian thinking, *Réflexions sur la violence,* 10th ed. (Paris: Rivière, 1946) pp. 46 ff.

18   [14] *Biographia Litteraria* (Everyman) Ch. IV (p. 42), XII (p. 139), XIV (pp. 151-152). See also the discussion in Basil Willey, *Nineteenth Century Studies* (London: Chatto and Windus, 1949) pp. 10-26.

19   [15] *Laws,* 706 (Jowett translation).

20   [16] *Henri Comte de Saint-Simon, Selected Writings,* ed. and trans. F. M. H. Markham (New York: Macmillan, 1952) p. 70.

21   [17] A modern view, such as that expressed by Heisenberg, places science closer to political theory in this respect:

> "The dangers threatening modern science cannot be averted by more and more experimenting, for our complicated experiments have no longer anything to do with nature in her own right, but with nature changed and transformed by our own cognitive activity." [Cited in Erich Heller, *The Disinherited Mind* (New York: Meridian, 1959) p. 33.]

22   [18] Alfred N. Whitehead, *Adventures in Ideas* (New York: Macmillan, 1933) p. 54.

22   [19] There is an interesting protest by Renan, the nineteenth-century historian, concerning the difficulties of expressing certain new ideas in the French language:

> "The French language is adapted only to the expression of clear ideas; yet those laws that are most important, those that govern the transformations of life, are not clear, they appear to us in a half-light. Thus, though the French were the earliest to perceive the principles of what is now known as Darwinism, they turned out to be the last to accept it. They saw all that perfectly well; but it lay outside the usual habits of their language and the mold of the well-made phrase. The French have thus disregarded precious truths, not because they haven't been aware of them, but because they simply cast them aside, as useless or as impossible to express." [Edmund Wilson, *To the Finland Station* (New York: Anchor, 1953) p. 38.]

23   [20] Letter to Vettori, December 10, 1513, *The Prince and Other Works,* ed. Allan H. Gilbert (New York: Hendricks House, 1941) p. 242.

24   [21] *Process and Reality* (New York: Macmillan, 1929) p. 31.

26   [22] W. K. C. Guthrie, *The Greeks and Their Gods* (Boston: Beacon Press, 1955) p. 28.

26   [23] Thucydides, *The Peloponnesian War,* I, 140; Polybius, *Histories,* xxxvii, 4; xxxviii, 18, 8; Sallust, *Bellum Catilinae,* viii. 1. The classical conception of *fortuna* is discussed by David Grene, *Man in His Pride, A Study in the Political Philosophy of Thucydides and Plato* (Chicago: University of Chicago Press, 1950) pp. 56 ff.; Charles N. Cochrane, *Christianity and Classical Culture,* rev. ed. (London: Oxford University Press, 1944) pp. 456 ff.; W. Warde Fowler, "Polybius' Conception of *Tyché,*" *Classical Review,* XVII, pp. 445-459.

27   [24] Augustine, *De Civitate Dei,* IV, 18; VI, 1; VII, 3; and see Cochrane, *op. cit.,* pp. 474 ff.

27   [25] Calvin, *Institutes of the Christian Religion,* I, v, 11.

27   [26] T. S. Eliot, *Four Quartets* ("Burnt Norton," I, II) in *The Complete Poems and Plays* (New York: Harcourt, Brace, 1952) pp. 117, 119.

Chapter Two

PAGE

29   [1] There are useful discussions of prescientific modes of thought in H. A. Frankfort and others, *Before Philosophy* (London: Pelican, 1951) pp. 11-36, 237-262; F. M. Cornford, *From Religion to Philosophy* (London: Arnold, 1912); Hans Kelsen, *Society and Nature* (Chicago: University of Chicago Press, 1943) pp. 24 ff., 233 ff.

29   [2] F. M. Cornford, *Before and After Socrates* (Cambridge: Cambridge University Press, 1920) pp. 8 ff.; Werner Jaeger, *Paideia,* trans. Gilbert Highet, 2nd ed., 3 vols. (New York: Oxford University Press, 1945) Vol. I, pp. 150 ff.

29 [3] The relevant fragments have been translated by Kathleen Freeman, *Ancilla to the Pre-Socratic Philosophers* (Oxford: Blackwell, 1952) frag. 17 (p. 53); frag. 26 (pp. 55-56); frag. 35 (pp. 56-57); and by John Burnet, *Early Greek Philosophy*, 4th ed. (London: Black, 1948) pp. 197-250. See also the remarks of F. M. Cornford, *The Laws of Motion in Ancient Thought* (Cambridge: Cambridge University Press, 1931) pp. 31-32.

29 [4] Burnet, *op. cit.*, p. 143.

29 [5] *Ibid.*, frag. 43 (p. 136).

29 [6] Freeman, *op. cit.*, frag. 2 (p. 24), frag. 14 (p. 32).

29 [7] "But the relationship of the social element in Greek thought to the cosmological was always a reciprocal one: as the universe was understood in terms of political ideas, such as *diké, nomos, moira, kosmos,* equality, so the political structure was derived from the eternal order of the cosmos." Werner Jaeger, *The Theology of the Early Greek Philosophers* (New York: Oxford University Press, 1947) p. 140. There are also relevant remarks in Burnet, *op. cit.*, p. 151.

30 [8] *Phaedo*, 96-97; Cornford, *Before and After Socrates*, pp. 3-8.

30 [9] *Phaedo*, 98-99.

31 [10] The translation has been taken from Sir Ernest Barker, *Greek Political Theory, Plato and His Predecessors* (London: Methuen, 1918) pp. 83 ff.; and there is also a version in Freeman, *op. cit.*, frag. 44 (pp. 147-149). Further discussion and references can be found in T. A. Sinclair, *A History of Greek Political Thought* (London: Routledge, 1951) pp. 70-73; and a sympathetic account by E. A. Havelock, *The Liberal Temper in Greek Politics* (London: Cape, 1957) pp. 255 ff.

32 [11] *Statesman,* 258 c. I have used the translation by J. B. Skemp published by the Yale University Press, New Haven, 1952. All translations from the *Statesman* will be from this edition. There is an earlier attempt to define the statesman in *Gorgias,* 452-453.

32 [12] *Statesman,* 276 b; *Republic* IV, 427.

33 [13] *Statesman,* 305 e.

34 [14] *Gorgias,* 508 (Jowett translation).

34 [15] *Statesman,* 271 d.

34 [16] *Ibid.,* 269 C.

34 [17] *Ibid.,* 272 A.

34 [18] *Laws,* 712 A (Jowett translation).

34 [19] *Statesman* 292 d.

34 [20] *Ibid.,* 297 b.

35 [21] *Epistle VII,* in L. A. Post, *Thirteen Epistles of Plato* (Oxford: Clarendon Press, 1925) 326 a-b.

35 [22] *Three Philosophical Poets* (Cambridge: Harvard University Press, 1944) p. 139. See also the remarks of Sorel along these same lines in *Réflexions sur la violence,* pp. 208-212. Compare Plato, *Sophist,* 235 C.

35 [23] *The Laws of Plato,* trans. A. E. Taylor (London: Dent, 1934) V, 746; *Republic,* VI, 503.

36 24 *The Republic of Plato,* trans. Francis Macdonald Cornford (London: Oxford University Press, 1945) VI, 484 (all translations from the *Republic* will be from this edition); *Laws,* XII, 962.

36 25 *Laws,* I, 644 E-645.

36 26 *Euthydemus,* 292 B-C (Jowett translation); *Laws,* VI, 771. The serious nature of political philosophy has been well brought out by Leo Strauss, *Natural Right and History* (Chicago: University of Chicago Press, 1953) pp. 120 ff.

36 27 *Statesman,* 297 b; *Laws,* I, 650.

36 28 *Republic,* VI, 491-496; *Laws,* VI, 780 A; VII, 788 A, 790 A; X, 902-904; XI, 923.

37 29 *Republic,* VI, 496 D.

38 30 *Euthydemus* 305 B-306 D.

38 31 *Statesman,* 295 a-b; 293 a.

38 32 This aspect of Plato's thought was grasped by Nietzsche. See the remark cited in H .J. Blackham, *Six Existentialist Thinkers* (London: Routledge, 1952) p. 24. For Plato's view that philosophy was a totally ordering science, see *Republic* 531 D, 534 E; *Sophist* 227 B.

38 33 *Gorgias,* 466-470.

39 34 *Plato's Cosmology; the Timaeus of Plato,* trans. F. M. Cornford (New York: The Library of Liberal Arts, No. 101, 1957) 28 a-b. Reprinted by permission of the publishers.

39 35 See in general the discussion in F. M. Cornford, *Plato's Theory of Knowledge* (New York: Humanities Press, 1951); Sir David Ross, *Plato's Theory of Ideas,* 2nd ed. (Oxford: Clarendon Press, 1951) which stresses the changes in Plato's thinking on this subject. For a critical analysis, K. R. Popper, *The Open Society and Its Enemies,* 2 vols. (London, Routledge, 1945) Vol. I, especially Chs. 3-4; and for a response to Popper see Ronald B. Levinson, *In Defense of Plato* (Cambridge: Harvard University Press, 1953) pp. 18, 454, 522, 595-596, 627-629).

39 36 *Statesman,* 269 d; *Theaetetus,* 181 B-183 C; *Philebus,* 61 E.

39 37 *Laws,* VII, 797; also VI, 772; VIII, 846.

39 38 *Laws,* IV, 706 (Jowett translation).

40 39 *Republic,* V, 461.

40 40 On the Sophists, see W. Jaeger, *Paideia,* Vol. 1, 286-331; Mario Untersteiner, *The Sophists,* trans. Kathleen Freeman (Oxford: Blackwell, 1954).

40 41 *Laws,* IV, 715 (Taylor translation).

41 42 *Epistle,* VII, 325 e.

41 43 *Philebus,* 63 e-64 a.

41 44 *Republic,* IV, 421; V, 465; *Laws,* IV, 715; X, 902-904; XI, 923. These passages should be compared with Plato's discussion of the nature of the forms in *Philebus,* 65 A; Gorgias, 474; *Timaeus,* 31 C.

41 45 *Republic,* VI, 500.

41 46 *Ibid.,* VII, 540.

42   47 *Ibid.,* VII, 521.

42   48 *Ibid.,* VII, 520.

44   49 *Gorgias,* 506 (Jowett translation).

45   50 *Ibid.,* 513; *Republic,* IV, 426.

45   51 *Gorgias,* 517. In this connection, there is an implicit similarity between Plato's conception of the poet and his strictures against politicians. Like the latter, the poet does not possess true knowledge; hence, he can only reproduce what pleases the multitude. *Republic,* X, 602 A.

46   52 *Republic,* VI, 500.

46   53 *Republic,* I, 342.

46   54 See Nietzsche's famous discussion of the Apollonian and Dionysian spirits in *The Birth of Tragedy;* Guthrie, *The Greeks and Their Gods,* pp. 183 ff.; Jane Harrison, *Prolegomena to the Study of Greek Religion,* 3rd ed. (New York: Meridian, 1955) p. 439.

46   55 For Plato's conception of analogy, see the *Statesman,* 277 a-279 a. The weaver analogy dominates the *Statesman;* the artistic examples are especially prominent in the *Republic;* the medical recurs in both dialogues and in the *Laws.* On medicine, see Jaeger, *Paideia,* Vol. III, pp. 3-45, 215-216, and on the arts generally, see Rupert C. Lodge, *Plato's Theory of Art* (London: Routledge, 1953). The limitations inherent in Plato's use of analogy are discussed by Renford Bambrough, "Plato's Political Analogies," *Philosophy, Politics, and Society,* ed. Peter Laslett (Oxford: Blackwell, 1956) pp. 98-115. See also on this topic the brilliant study by Richard Robinson, *Plato's Earlier Dialectic,* 2nd ed. (Oxford: Clarendon Press, 1953) pp. 202 ff.

47   56 *Statesman,* 311 c.

47   57 *Republic,* III, 399; IV, 410 A; VIII, 564, 568; *Statesman,* 293 d, 309 a; *Laws,* V, 735.

47   58 *Statesman,* 310 a.

47   59 *Ibid.,* 309 a.

48   60 *Republic,* VII, 540.

48   61 *Ibid.,* VI, 500.

48   62 *Laws,* IV, 708. See controls over immigration in *Ibid.,* V, 736.

48   63 *Laws,* III, 684; V, 736.

48   64 *Ibid.,* IV, 709-712. Plato's relationship to Dionysius is discussed in Ludwig Marcuse, *Plato and Dionysius; A Double Biography,* trans. Joel Ames (New York: Knopf, 1947); and Jaeger, *Paideia,* III, p. 240.

49   65 *Republic,* V, 463-464.

49   66 *Philebus,* 51; *Republic,* VII, 527. There are discussions of the relationship between mathematics and politics in Robert S. Brumbaugh, *Plato's Mathematical Imagination* (Bloomington: Indiana University Press, 1954) pp. 47 ff.; Maurice Vanhoutte, *La Philosophie politique de Platon dans les "Lois"* (Louvain, 1953) p. 44.

49 67 *Laws,* V, 747.

50 68 *Ibid.,* II, 664 E. In his effort to prove that Plato was obsessed with stemming the flux of human affairs, Popper has overlooked completely Plato's concern to provide for "movement" as well. See his discussion, *op. cit.,* Vol. I, Chs. 3-4.

50 69 *Protagoras,* 326 B; *Republic,* III, 401.

50 70 *Laws,* V, 738, 744-745; VI, 757-758; VI, 773, 775; VIII, 816, 828; *Republic,* III, 396-397, 400, 414. Note also Plato's remarks on how an interruption of the rhythm of the reproductive process contributes to social disintegration, *Ibid.,* VIII, 546. Compare the following from a modern sociologist:

> "There can be no society which does not feel the need of upholding and re-affirming at regular intervals the collective sentiments and the collective ideas which make its unity and its personality. Now this moral remaking cannot be achieved except by the means of reunions, assemblies and meetings where the individuals, being closely united to one another, reaffirm in common their common sentiments; hence come ceremonies which do not differ from regular religious ceremonies, either in their object, the results which they produce, or the processes employed to attain these results." [Emile Durkheim, *The Elementary Forms of the Religious Life,* trans. J. W. Swain (London: Allen and Unwin, 1915) p. 427. Reprinted by permission of the Free Press, Glencoe, Ill.]

50 71 *Laws,* VII, 809, trans. A. E. Taylor (London: Dent, 1934).

51 72 *Republic,* IV, 420-421, 427; V, 465.

52 73 It ought to be noted, however, that the outlines of a theory of political action, closer to that put forward here, were latent in Plato's discussion of the "second-type of measurement" in *Statesman,* 284 e. Unfortunately, the discussion remained imperfect because of Plato's tendency to consider the problem of action solely through the categories of "excess," "deficiency," and the "mean."

52 74 *Statesman,* 293 a-c; 296 a-e.

52 75 *Crito,* 50-53 (Jowett translation).

53 76 *Republic,* I, 342, 345-346; IX, 591.

54 77 Cited in Erwin R. Goodenough, "The Political Philosophy of Hellenistic Kingship," *Yale Classical Studies,* Vol. I, pp. 55-102 (1928) at p. 86.

54 78 Eusebius, *De Laudibus Constantini,* I, 6; III, 4-5; V, 1; and the references in George H. Williams, "Christology and Church-State Relations in the Fourth Century," *Church History,* Vol. 20 (1951) pp. 3-33.

54 79 *The Commonwealth of Oceana,* ed. Henry Morley (London, 1887) pp. 71, 173.

54 80 *Social Contract,* II, vii.

55 81 Compare Goodenough's discussion (*op. cit.,* pp. 90-91) of the Hellenistic notions of the relationship between the ruler and his subjects with Lenin's famous remarks about "trade union consciousness" in "What is to be Done?" *Selected Works,* 12 vols. (London: Lawrence and Wishart) Vol. 2, pp. 62-66, 98-107, 151-158.

55 82 For some of Plato's attitudes towards power, see the following: *Gorgias,* 470, 510, 526; *Laws,* III, 691, 693, 696; IV, 713-714; IX, 875.

55 [83] On this point, see the discussion of Michael B. Foster, *The Political Philosophies of Plato and Hegel* (Oxford: Clarendon Press, 1935) pp. 18 ff. For some critical remarks on Foster's approach, see H. W. B. Joseph, *Essays in Ancient and Modern Philosophy* (Oxford: Clarendon Press, 1935) pp. 114 ff.

55 [84] *Republic,* VII, 521.

56 [85] *Ibid.* For the apolitical character of the philosopher, see *Theaetetus,* 173 A-E.

57 [86] The problem of knowledge and *eros* is discussed by F. M. Cornford, *The Unwritten Philosophy,* ed. W. K. C. Guthrie (Cambridge: Cambridge University Press, 1950) pp. 68-80; Jaeger, *Paideia.,* II, pp. 186 ff.; Levinson, *op. cit.,* pp. 81 ff.

58 [87] See Anders Nygren, *Agape and Eros,* trans. Philip S. Watson (Philadelphia: Westminster Press, 1953) especially pp. 166 ff.; and from a Thomist position, M. C. D'Arcy, *The Mind and Heart of Love* (New York: Meridian, 1956) pp. 62-96.

57 [88] *Republic,* IX, 590.

57 [89] *Politics,* III, ii, 15, 1276 a; III, iii, 7, 1276 b.

57 [90] *Politics,* III, xi, 1281 b 6-9; III, xiii, 1283 a 1-4; III, xiii, 1283 b 9-12. This is not to deny that Aristotle thought some claims were superior to others and that a man of pre-eminent virtue ought to be given full power. But it is also significant that the last conclusion comes only after a long argument which raises doubts as to whether such a person was likely to appear frequently enough to raise a real problem. The question of the value of some claims over others is perhaps not to be resolved satisfactorily on a theory of contribution, as Aristotle held, yet it is difficult to see the superiority of modern democratic theories which begin from the premise of equal claims. The problem inherent in the democratic approach is that the distributive role thrust on the political order militates against the equal treatment of competing claims.

58 [91] *Ethics,* I, vii, 1097 b 11-12.

59 [92] *Ibid.,* I, iii, 1094 b 12-29; I, vii, 1098 a 20-34 (trans. W. D. Ross) in *The Basic Works of Aristotle,* ed. Richard McKeon (New York: Oxford University Press, 1941).

59 [93] *Physics,* II, 1. 193 b 15-16 (trans. R. P. Hardie and R. K. Gaye in the McKeon edition).

59 [94] See the discussion in W. L. Newman, *The Politics of Aristotle* (Oxford: Clarendon Press, 1887) Vol. I, pp. 21-24.

59 [95] *Politics,* III, xiv, 1286 a-1286 b. The argument here opposed Plato's contention that a good ruler, like a true physician, ought not to be hampered by the law. Aristotle took the common sense view that the ruler, like any expert, may be affected by his own passions. Plato's reply, that such a ruler does not qualify for his position, was rebutted as frivolous logic by Aristotle: What practical good is it to a community to discover that the ruler has betrayed his art? Aristotle goes on to reject the analogy to the arts at *Politics,* III, xvi 1287 a 18-1287 b 8.

61 [96] *Politics,* II, ii, 1261 a 18-39; VII, xiii, 1332 a 15.

62 [97] *Ethics,* V, v, 130 b 30.

62 [98] The materials of American constitutional law cases are relevant here. The

Supreme Court has long wrestled with the problem of "rational" legislative classifications, and the entire series of cases dealing with the segregation issue of "separate but equal" facilities for the two races is very much to the point.

62 [99] Strauss, *op. cit.,* p. 11.

63 [100] *Politics,* III, xiii, 1283 a 21-1283 b.

63 [101] *Politics,* II, v, 1263 b.

64 [102] *Politics,* I, ii, 1253 a.

64 [103] *Statesman,* 310 a; 310 e.

66 [104] A. T. Quiller-Couch, ed., *The Poems of Matthew Arnold, 1840-1867* (London: Oxford University Press, 1930) p. 272.

67 [105] *Republic,* I, 348 ff.

67 [106] *Laws,* III, 691 (Jowett translation).

68 [107] *Statesman,* 298 a-300 d.

68 [108] *Republic,* VIII, 546.

Chapter Three

PAGE

70 [1] *Politics,* III, 1276 a 5.

72 [2] *Annals,* III, 54 in M. Hadas, ed., *The Complete Works of Tacitus* (New York: Random House, 1942). All quotations from Tacitus will be from this edition.

73 [3] The space-consciousness of the Greeks is emphasized in Julius Kaerst, *Geschichte des Hellenismus,* 2 vols., 3rd ed. (Leipzig: Teubner, 1927) Vol. I, pp. 10-11, 28 ff.; Victor Ehrenberg, *Aspects of the Ancient World* (Oxford: Blackwell, 1946) pp. 40-45.

73 [4] *Republic,* V, 469 B-470; *Politics,* 1265 a, 1324 a 19 b 34, 1333 b.

73 [5] The best recent discussion of this experience is to be found in J. A. O. Larsen, *Representative Government in Greek and Roman History* (Berkeley: University of California Press, 1955); see also the readings in Sir Ernest Barker, *From Alexander to Constantine* (Oxford: Clarendon Press, 1946) pp. 65-82.

74 [6] It should be added, however, that Aristotle is believed to have written two treatises, one on kingship and the other on colonies, but these have unfortunately been lost. See also Hans Kelsen's argument that Aristotle consciously rejected Alexander's policy of reconciling diverse peoples and of treating them more or less equally: "Aristotle and Hellenic-Macedonian Policy," *International Journal of Ethics,* Vol. XLVIII (1937-1938) pp. 1-64; and see also the remarks in Werner Jaeger, *Aristotle,* trans. Richard Robinson (Oxford: Clarendon Press, 1934) pp. 117-123.

74 [7] See the discussion in Jaeger, *Paideia,* Vol. III, pp. 71-83, 263-289; Victor Ehrenberg, *Alexander and the Greeks,* trans. Ruth Fraenkel von Velsen (Oxford: Blackwell, 1938) pp. 61-102 ("Aristotle and Alexander's Empire"); Kaerst, *op. cit.,* Vol. I, pp. 138-153.

75 [8] *Panegyricus*, 16. On Isocrates generally, see Ernest Barker, *Greek Political Theory, Plato and his Predecessors* (London: Methuen, 1918) pp. 100-105; T. A. Sinclair, *A History of Greek Political Thought* (London: Routledge, 1952) pp. 133-139; and for more detailed treatment, Jaeger, *Paideia*, Vol. III, pp. 46-155; G. Mathieu, *Les idées politiques d'Isocrate* (Paris, 1925).

75 [9] *Panegyricus*, 173-174.

75 [10] *To Philip*, 127 in *Isocrates*, trans. G. Norlin and L. Van Hook, 3 vols. (Cambridge: Harvard University Press, 1928-1945).

76 [11] Sir William W. Tarn, *Alexander the Great*, 2 vols. (Cambridge: Cambridge University Press, 1948), especially Vol. 2, Appendices 22, 24, 25. W. W. Tarn and G. T. Griffith, *Hellenistic Civilization*, 3rd ed. rev. (London: Arnold, 1952) Ch. II. Tarn's thesis, that Alexander was not influenced by Stoic ideas, has been criticized by M. H. Fisch, "Alexander and the Stoics," *American Journal of Philology*, Vol. 58, pp. 59-82, 129-151 (1937). The rejoinder can be found in the same journal: "Alexander, Cynics and Stoics," Vol. 60, pp. 41-70 (1939). Ulrich Wilcken, *Alexander the Great*, trans. G. C. Richards (New York: MacVeagh, 1932) p. 221, is also hostile to Tarn. See also A. D. Nock, "Notes on ruler-cult," I-IV, *Journal of Hellenic Studies*, Vol. 48, pp. 21-42 (1928). E. R. Goodenough, "The Political Philosophy of Hellenistic Kingship," *Yale Classical Studies*, Vol. 1 (1928), pp. 55 ff. There is an important revision of Goodenough's position in Louis Delatte, "Les Traités de la Royauté d'Ecphante, Diotogène et Sthénidas," *Bibliothèque de la Faculté de Philosophie et Lettres de l'Université de Liège*, Vol. 97 (1942). See also on this general period Barker, *From Alexander to Constantine*, Part I.

76 [12] For a general introduction, see Michael Grant, *Roman Imperial Money* (London: Nelson, 1954) p. 8 and *passim*.

77 [13] Goodenough, *op. cit.*, pp. 91 ff.

77 [14] Tacitus, *History*, IV, 74.

78 [15] Epictetus, *Discourses*, III, 3, trans. E. P. Matheson in *The Stoic and Epicurean Philosophers*, ed. W. J. Oates (New York: Random House, 1940).

78 [16] See generally the following: T. A. Sinclair, *A History of Greek Political Thought*, Chs. XII-XIV; M. M. Patrick, *The Greek Sceptics* (New York: Columbia University Press, 1929), especially pp. 137 ff.; A. J. Festugière, *Epicurus and his Gods*, trans. C. W. Chilton (Oxford: Blackwell, 1956); N. W. DeWitt, *Epicurus and his Philosophy* (Minneapolis: University of Minnesota Press, 1954), especially Chs. X, XIV; D. R. Dudley, *A History of Cynicism* (London: Methuen, 1937); Tarn and Griffith, *Hellenistic Civilization*, pp. 325 ff.; Barker, *From Alexander to Constantine*, Pts. III-IV; E. Bevan, "Hellenistic Popular Philosophy" in *The Hellenistic Age* (Cambridge: Cambridge University Press, 1923) pp. 79-107; J. Kaerst, *op. cit.*, Vol. I, pp. 471 ff.

78 [17] Cited in Festugière, *Epicurus and his Gods*, p. 28.

78 [18] Epictetus, *Discourses*, III, 13.

78 [19] Authorized Doctrine 31. See De Witt, *op. cit.*, p. 295.

79 [20] The following contain useful discussions of Stoicism: E. V. Arnold, *Roman Stoicism* (Cambridge: Cambridge University Press, 1911), is still valuable, although outdated in many respects; M. Pohlenz, *Die Stoa*, 2 vols. (Göttingen: Vandenhoeck and Ruprecht, 1948-1949); Barker, *From Alexander to Constantine*, pp.

19 ff.; G. H. Sabine and S. B. Smith, eds., *Cicero on the Commonwealth* (Columbus: Ohio State University Press, 1929), contains a sympathetic account of Stoic doctrines.

79 21 Cleanthes, *Hymn to Zeus*, cited from Arnold, *op. cit.*, p. 85.

80 22 Seneca, *Epistulae morales*, XCV, 52.

80 23 Epictetus, *Discourses*, I, ix, trans. P. E. Matheson.

80 24 *Meditations*, IV, 4.

81 25 See the remarks in Émile Bréhier, *Chrysippe et l'ancien stoicisme* (Paris: Presses Universitaires, 1951) pp. 209 ff., 261 ff.

81 26 E. Gilson, *Les Métamorphoses de la Cité de Dieu* (Louvain: Publications Universitaires de Louvain, 1952) pp. 6-7.

81 27 *Meditations*, IV, 23.

82 28 There are brief, general discussions of Roman virtues in R. H. Barrow, *The Romans* (Pelican, 1949) pp. 22 ff.; W. Warde Fowler and M. P. Charlesworth, *Rome* (London: Oxford University Press, 1947) pp. 37 ff.; M. L. Clarke, *The Roman Mind* (London: Cohen and West, 1956) pp. 89-102, 135 ff.; more detailed discussions can be found in Sir Samuel Dill, *Roman Society from Nero to Marcus Aurelius* (New York: Meridian, 1956) pp. 291 ff., 411 ff.; Michael Grant, *op. cit.*, pp. 166 ff., discusses the representation of the virtues in the coinage of the imperial period.

82 29 H. H. Scullard, *Roman Politics, 220-150* B.C. (Oxford: Clarendon Press, 1951) p. 223. See also the remarks of Tacitus, *Agricola*, 4, where Agricola said that as a youth he had nearly developed a love of philosophy greater than became "a Roman and a senator."

83 30 *De Legibus*, trans. C. W. Keyes (Cambridge: Harvard University Press, 1928) III, xix, 45.

85 31 *De re publica*, trans. C. W. Keyes (Cambridge: Harvard University Press, 1928) II, 1, 2.

85 32 *The Histories*, trans. W. R. Paton (Cambridge: Harvard University Press, 1923) VI, 10. See also Polybius's rather contemptuous dismissal of Plato's ideal state at VI, 47.

85 33 *Laws*, trans. R. G. Bury (Cambridge: Harvard University Press, 1926) III, 702 E.

85 34 *The Histories*, VI, 2 (Paton translation).

85 35 In addition to the more tolerant position of Aristotle, see also the remarks of Isocrates, *Panegyricus*, 79-80, where the activity of political clubs is accepted.

86 36 Scullard, *op. cit.*, pp. 8-30; Lily Ross Taylor, *Party Politics in the Age of Caesar* (Berkeley: University of California Press, 1949) pp. 62 ff.

86 37 In addition to Scullard, *op. cit.*, there is the brilliant and provocative analysis by Ronald Syme, *The Roman Revolution*, 2nd ed. (Oxford: Clarendon Press, 1952). See also Lily Ross Taylor, *op. cit.*; M. Gelzer, *Caesar, der Politiker und Staatsmann*, 3rd ed. (Munich: Callwey, 1941). Mommsen's *History of Rome*, for all of its tendency to project mid-nineteenth-century German politics into the politics of the late Roman republic, is still worth reading for its strong sense of the political.

86   [38] Cited in Taylor, *op. cit.*, p. 7; cited in Syme, *op. cit.*, p. 12.

86   [39] *De officiis*, I, xvi.

86   [40] *Ibid.*, II, viii-ix.

87   [41] *Ibid.*, II, xxi.

87   [42] *De re publica*, I, II; *De officiis*, I, xliii.

87   [43] *De re publica*, I, xxxii, 49 (Keyes translation).

88   [44] *Bellum Catilinae*, trans. J. C. Rolfe (Cambridge: Harvard University Press, 1921) LIII, 5-6.

88   [45] ". . . A commonwealth is the property of a people. But a people is not any collection of human beings brought together in any sort of way, but an assemblage of people in large numbers associated in an agreement with respect to justice and a partnership for the common good." *De re publica*, I, xxv, 39-xxvi, 41.

89   [46] *Pro Sestio*, 97-99. See also Hermann Strasburger, *Concordia Ordinum* (Leipzig: Noske, 1931); C. N. Cochrane, *Christianity and Classical Culture*, pp. 58 ff.; and the critical comments of Syme, *op. cit.*, pp. 15-16, 81, 153-154.

89   [47] *De officiis*, II, xxi.

89   [48] *Annals*, III, 66.

89   [49] *De legibus*, I, xxv, 39; xxxii, 49.

90   [50] Sallust, *Bellum Catilinae*, LII, 11.

90   [51] *Bellum Catilinae*, XXXVIII, 3-4 (Rolfe translation). See also the remarks in Syme, *op. cit.*, pp. 153 ff., and C. Wirszubski, *Libertas as a Political Idea at Rome During the Late Republic and Early Principate* (Cambridge: Cambridge University Press, 1950) pp. 31 ff.

90   [52] *Pharsalia*, I, 670.

91   [53] *The Histories*, VI, 2, trans. W. R. Paton. An excellent discussion of the relationship between Polybius's ideas and the circumstances of his time can be found in Kurt von Fritz, *The Theory of the Mixed Constitution in Antiquity* (New York: Columbia University Press, 1954).

91   [54] *De Domo Sua*, 33.

91   [55] See Wirszubski, *op. cit.*, pp. 9-15, and the references cited there.

92   [56] Tacitus, *Annals*, III, 26; Seneca, *Epistulae morales*, XC, 4 ff.

92   [57] Compare Tacitus, *Annals*, II, 33, with III, 54.

92   [58] *Aeneid*, I, 286 ff.; *Georgics*, I, 500 ff. It is not surprising that in the acclaim rendered Augustus there should have been traces of the old forms and languages used to worship Alexander. See Syme, *op. cit.*, p. 305, and references cited there.

93   [59] *De Clementia*, trans. J. W. Basore (Cambridge: Harvard University Press, 1928) I, i, 2-3.

93   [60] *De Clementia*, I, iv, 1. The extent to which the emperor had come to tower over political society can be seen in the opening words of Diocletian's edict on price-fixing (303 A.D.): "It is fitting therefore that we, who are the parents of the human race, should look to the future in order to grant, by the remedies of our

foresight, a relief that human kind had long hoped for but could not itself provide." Quoted in M. P. Charlesworth, "The Virtues of a Roman Emperor," *Proceedings of the British Academy,* Vol. 23, pp. 105-133 (1937) p. 111.

93   61 *Ibid.,* p. 121. The intermixture of political and religious themes is discussed at length in the following: M. P. Nilsson, *Greek Piety,* trans. H. J. Rose (Oxford: Clarendon Press, 1948) pp. 85, 118-124; E. Peterson, "Der Monotheismus als politisches Problem," in *Theologische Traktate* (Munich: Hochland-Bucherei, 1951) pp. 52 ff.; Barker, *From Alexander to Constantine,* Pt. III, Ch. 3; Goodenough, *passim;* Delatte, *passim;* M. P. Charlesworth has emphasized the Greek preparations for the later Roman ruler-cults in "Some Observations on Ruler-Cult especially in Rome," *Harvard Theological Review,* Vol. 28, pp. 5-44 (1935); and also of interest by the same author, "Providentia and Aeternitas," *ibid.,* Vol. 29, pp. 107-132 (1936). The treatises, *On Monarchy* by Dio Chrysostom and the *Panegyric on Trajan* by Pliny the Younger, are full of relevant passages.

93   62 Quoted in Charlesworth, "The Virtues of a Roman Emperor," *op. cit.,* p. 121.

94   63 *Politics,* 1327 b.

Chapter Four

Hebrews I:10; XI:15-16; *Didache* 9-10 (an early manual of instruction for Christian converts and probably dates from the second century).

98   [7] *Romans* xiii.

98   [8] *Colossians* 1:16; and the commentary by Cullmann, *op. cit.,* pp. 50 ff. Cf. also G. B. Caird, *Principalities and Powers. A Study in Pauline Theology* (Oxford: Clarendon Press, 1956).

98   [9] *Romans* 13:1-5.

98   [10] Cullmann, *op. cit.,* pp. 50 ff.

99   [11] *Romans* 12:2.

99   [12] I *Peter* 2:9.

100 [13] *Apologeticus,* 39; *De Corona,* 13.

100 [14] *De Idololatria,* 18, 19.

100 [15] *Epistle to Diognetus* in Henry Bettenson, ed., *The Early Christian Fathers* (London: Oxford University Press, 1956) p. 74. (Hereafter this collection will be cited simply as Bettenson, *Fathers.*) The date and authorship of the *Epistle* are uncertain, although the work is usually placed in the second or third centuries.

101 [16] *Contra Celsum,* III, 28, as translated in Bettenson, *Fathers,* p. 312. There is an excellent scholarly edition of this work by Henry Chadwick (Cambridge: Cambridge University Press, 1953). See also Jean Danielou, *Origen,* trans. W. Mitchell (New York: Sheed and Ward, 1955) especially pp. 40 ff.

101 [17] I *Corinthians* 12:12.

101 [18] The Eucharist in the early church is discussed in Lietzmann, *op. cit.,* Vol. I, p. 238.

101 [19] See Lietzmann, *op. cit.,* Vol. I, pp. 63, 124, 150 ff.; Vol. II, pp. 124 ff.

101 [20] Following the rendering of *Colossians* 1:24 by C. H. Dodd, *The Meaning of Paul for Today* (New York: Meridian, 1957) p. 74.

101 [21] I *John* 3:14.

103 [22] Virgil, *Eclogue* IV; *Aeneid,* I, 286 ff., VI, 852 ff.; Horace, *Odes,* I, 12; Tacitus, *History,* IV, 74; Seneca, *De Clementia,* I, 3. See also the decrees collected in Barker, *From Alexander to Constantine,* pp. 210-214.

103 [23] Horace, *Odes,* I, 35 (W. S. Marris translation) in C. J. Kraemer, Jr., ed., *The Complete Works of Horace* (New York: Random House, 1936) p. 177.

103 [24] *Apologeticus,* 39. Compare *De Idololatria,* 18, 19.

104 [25] *Apologeticus,* 31.

104 [26] See, for example, Commodian, *Carmen apologeticum,* 889-890, 921-923 with its gloating joy that Rome, which had afflicted the world for so long, "Rome rejoiced while the rest of the world groaned," will at last be destroyed.

104 [27] Jerome, *Epistle* lx and cxxiii.

105 [28] See the discussion and references in Walter Ullmann, *The Growth of Papal Government in the Middle Ages* (London: Methuen, 1955) pp. 101-108. There is a great deal of relevant material in the several articles by Franklin L. Baumer:

"The Conception of Christendom in Renaissance England," *Journal of the History of Ideas*, Vol. VI (1945), pp. 131-156; "The Church of England and the Common Corps of Christendom," *Journal of Modern History*, Vol. XVI (1944), pp. 1-21; "England, the Turk, and the Common Corps of Christendom," *American Historical Review*, Vol. L (1944), pp. 26-48. For a brief, concise summary see Denys Hay, *Europe. The Emergence of an Idea* (Edinburgh: Edinburgh University Press, 1957).

105   [29] *Two Letters Addressed to a Member of the Present Parliament on the Proposals for Peace* in E. J. Payne, *Burke, Select Works* (Oxford: Clarendon Press, 1904) p. 70.

105   [30] See, for example, Barbara Ward, *The West at Bay* (New York: Norton, 1948); Arnold Toynbee, *The World and the West* (London: Oxford University Press, 1953); Christopher Dawson, *The Revolt of Asia* (London: 1957).

106   [31] And see I *Timothy* 2:1-2.

106   [32] *Epistle to the Hebrews* 12:28.

106   [33] *Romans* 13:4.

106   [34] Cited in G. F. Reilly, *Imperium and Sacerdotium according to St. Basil the Great* (Washington: Catholic University Press, 1945) p. 45.

106   [35] The volume by Adolf Harnack, *The Constitution and Law of the Church in the First Two Centuries*, trans. F. L. Pogson and ed. H. D. A. Major (New York: Putnam, 1910) reflects an interesting recognition on the part of the great historian of the political aspects of the young church. It was written largely in response to Rudolf Sohm's pioneering work, *Kirchenrecht*, 2 vols. (Munich & Leipzig: Duncker and Humblot, 1892, 1923) which analyzes the early developments through concepts dominantly juristic and political.

107   [36] *Contra Celsum*, iii, 30, as adapted from Barker's translation in *From Alexander to Constantine*, pp. 440-441.

107   [37] See, for example, Irenaeus, *Adversus Haereses*, III, xxiv, 1.

107   [38] Ignatius, *To the Ephesians*, xiii; *To the Magnesians*, vii. Both of these translations are from Bettenson, *The Early Christian Fathers*, pp. 55, 58.

107   [39] *To the Ephesians*, vi; *To the Smyrnaeans*, viii (Bettenson, *op. cit.*, pp. 54-55, 67).

108   [40] *De Catholicae ecclesiae unitate*, 5; *Epistle*, lxvi, 7.

108   [41] Cyprian, *Epistle*, xxxiii, 1 (Bettenson, *Fathers*, p. 367); also Irenaeus, *Adversus Haereses*, III, ii-iii (*Ibid.*, pp. 123-126). The principle of apostolic succession is discussed in its historical aspects by C. H. Turner, "Apostolic Succession," in H. B. Swete, ed., *Essays on the Early History of the Church and Ministry*, 2nd ed. (London: Macmillan, 1921) pp. 93-214.

109   [42] On these matters the following contain useful discussions: Lietzmann, *op. cit.*, Vol. II, Chs. 8-12; S. L. Greenslade, *Schism in the Early Church* (New York: Harper, 1953); W. H. C. Frend, *The Donatist Church* (Oxford: Clarendon Press, 1952); G. G. Willis, *Saint Augustine and the Donatist Controversy* (London: SPCK, 1950); L. Duchesne, *Early History of the Christian Church*, 4th ed., 2 vols. (London: Longmans, 1912) Vol. II, Ch. 3.

110   [43] *De Monogamia*, 7.

110 **44** From a speech by Caecilius of Bilta as contained in *The Writings of Cyprian,* ed. Alexander Roberts 10 Vols. (Edinburgh: Ante-Nicene Library, 1886-1907) Vol. II, pp. 200-201.

110 **45** *De Exhortatione,* 7.

110 **46** The discussion by Monsignor R. A. Knox, *Enthusiasm* (New York: Oxford University Press, 1950), while witty and lively, is marred by a complete inability to grant that there might have been good and compelling reasons for schismatics and heretics to protest against institutionalism. Compare the wiser judgment (writing from an Anglican viewpoint) by Greenslade, *op. cit.,* pp. 204 ff., which concedes benefits from these controversies on much the same grounds as the present study argues the utility of political conflict.

111 **47** See Tertullian, *De Pudicitia,* 21 (in Bettenson, *Fathers,* pp. 183-184).

111 **48** Cited in Greenslade, *op. cit.,* p. 172 and n. 12.

111 **49** Cyprian, *Epistle,* lix, 5, as contained in Bettenson, *Fathers,* p. 370.

112 **50** On these points, see G. G. Willis, *op. cit.,* especially Chs. III-IV; Frederick W. Dillistone, "The anti-Donatist Writings," in Roy W. Battenhouse, ed., *A Companion to the Study of St. Augustine* (New York: Oxford University Press, 1955) Ch. VII; Hugh Pope, *Saint Augustine of Hippo* (London: Sands, 1937) Chs. VII-VIII.

112 **51** Gregory Dix, *Jew and Greek, A Study in the Primitive Church* (London: Dacre Press, 1953) pp. 21 ff.; Lietzmann, *op. cit.,* Vol. II, p. 105, and sources cited there. Also of interest in this connection is how the translation of the Old Testament into the Septuagint introduced the politically charged overtones inevitable in Greek. For examples, see G. B. Caird, *Principalities and Powers,* pp. 11-12. Caird remarks (p. 15), "It is interesting to note that a hellenistic Jew, reading the Scriptures in the Septuagint version, took the title 'Lord of the powers' to mean that God's providence functions for the most part through a system of powers, including those which are responsible for government."

112 **52** *Epistle to the Hebrews* 1:8; 11:15-16, 33-34; 12:22-23, 28; 13:14.

112 **53** *Philippians* 3:20; and see Barker, *From Alexander to Constantine,* pp. 398-399 from which I have borrowed this example. Lietzmann, *op. cit.,* Vol. II, p. 52 has rendered the scriptural passage as "our home, in which we have citizen rights, is in heaven." See also the note in Dodd, *op. cit.,* p. 17, n. 7. Tertullian's use of this passage is also suggestive in *Adversus Marcionem,* III, 24.

112 **54** *Epistle,* ccxxvii.

113 **55** *Contra Celsum,* IV, 5. Lactantius, *Divinae Institutiones,* I, iii.

113 **56** Origen, *De Principiis,* III, v, 6 (Bettenson, *Fathers,* pp. 292-293); Tertullian, *Adversus Praxean,* 3; Athanasius, *Contra Gentes,* 43; *De Incarnatione,* 17; *Expositio Fidei,* 1. For discussions of the political aspects of Christian ideas and concepts, see the following: K. M. Setton, *Christian Attitude towards the Emperor in the Fourth Century* (New York: Columbia University Press, 1941) pp. 18-19 and *passim;* G. H. Williams, "Christology and Church-State Relations in the Fourth Century," *Church History,* Vol. 20, No. 3, pp. 3-33 and No. 4, pp. 3-26 (1951), which is a masterly article; E. H. Kantorowicz, *Laudes Regiae* in *University of California Publications in History,* Vol. 33 (1946).

113   [57] *Apologeticus*, 38, 3; *De Idololatria*, 19.

114   [58] Taken from Greenslade, *op. cit.*, p. 37.

115   [59] Cyprian, *Epistle*, lv, lxxi, 1, and lxxiv, 4-5. See Bettenson, *Fathers*, p. 374.

116   [60] Cited from Greenslade, *op. cit.*, p. 19.

117   [61] Although the discussion in Greenslade, *op. cit.*, pp. 56-57, 124, does not consciously compare these religious problems to political ones, it is all the more striking that with the substitution of a few phrases his remarks would easily apply to political matters. Basic in this matter is Augustine's *De Baptismo*.

117   [62] The remark from St. Basil is contained in Reilly, *op. cit.*, p. 42. The reference to mad dogs comes from Ignatius, *To the Ephesians*, vii.

117   [63] *Romans* 13:3-4.

118   [64] *Adversus Haereses*, V, 24.

118   [65] *De Cultu Feminarum*, ii, 2.

118   [66] Cyprian, *Epistle*, IV, LXIX; *De Unitate*, xxiii, 21.

118   [67] *Epistle* 93 in *St. Augustine, Letters*, trans. Sister Wilfrid Parsons (New York, 1953) Vol. 10, p. 59, in the series *The Fathers of the Church*. Some of the most important statements by Augustine on the question of persecution are to be found among the following *Epistles*: 87, 97, 185. Also relevant is *Contra Epistulam Parmeniani*, I, vii-xiii. The following contain useful commentaries on these matters: J. N. Figgis, *Political Aspects of St. Augustine's "City of God"* (London: Longmans, 1921) Lectures III, IV; J. E. C. Welldon, ed., *St. Augustine's "De Civitate Dei,"* 2 vols. (London, 1924) Vol. 2, pp. 647-651; Willis, *op. cit.*, pp. 127-143; Gustave Bardy, *Saint Augustin*, 7th ed. (Paris, 1948) pp. 325 ff.; Gustave Combès, *La doctrine politique de Saint Augustin* (Paris, 1927) pp. 330 ff.

118   [68] *Epistle*, 185.

118   [69] Augustine's "realistic" appreciation of power has proved attractive to a latter-day Christian who shares many Augustinian views on man's nature: see Reinhold Niebuhr's essay, "Augustine's Political Realism," in *Christian Realism and Political Problems* (New York: Scribner's, 1953) pp. 119-146.

118   [70] *Epistle* 93 in *St. Augustine, Letters*, Vol. 10, pp. 74-75.

121   [71] *Vita Constantini*, III, I; *De Laudibus Constantini*, XIV; see also *Praeparatio Evangelica*, I, 4. There is an excellent discussion of Eusebius in F. D. Cranz, "Kingdom and Polity in Eusebius," *Harvard Theological Review*, Vol. 45, pp. 47-66 (1952); and see Peterson, *op. cit.*, pp. 88 ff.; N. H. Baynes, "Eusebius and the Christian Empire" in *Byzantine Studies and Other Essays* (London: Athlone Press, 1955) pp. 168 ff.

122   [72] *De Civ. Dei*, XIV, 28 (Dods translation).

123   [73] *De Civ. Dei*, XII, 21; XV, 4; XIX, 13, 26. G. Combès, *op. cit.*, pp. 76-77; Sir E. Barker, "St. Augustine's Theory of Society" in *Essays on Government* (Oxford: Clarendon Press, 1946) pp. 243-269. F. E. Cranz, "St. Augustine and Nicholas of Cusa in the Tradition of Western Christian Thought," *Speculum*, Vol. XXVIII, pp. 297-316 (1953) has tended to minimize Augustine's appreciation of existing society. There is an excellent study of Augustine's earlier ideas by the same author, "The Development of Augustine's Ideas on Society before the Donatist Contro-

versy," *Harvard Theological Review,* Vol. 46, pp. 255-316 (1954). Much relevant material is also to be found in C. Dawson, "St. Augustine and His Age" in *A Monument to Saint Augustine* (London: Sheed and Ward, 1930); this volume contains several useful articles, including one on Augustine's philosophy by Father D'Arcy.

123 [74] Three useful analyses of Augustine's language are: R. H. Barrow, *Introduction to St. Augustine, The City of God* (London: Faber, 1950) pp. 20 ff.; R. T. Marshall, *Studies in the Political and Socio-Religious Terminology of the De Civitate Dei* (Washington, 1952); H. D. Friberg, *Love and Justice in Political Theory. A Study of Saint Augustine's Definition of the Commonwealth* (Chicago, 1944).

123 [75] *De Civ. Dei,* XIX, 13. There are good discussions of the principle of *ordo* in the following: Gilson, *op. cit.,* pp. 154-155; Barker, "St. Augustine's Theory of Society," pp. 237 ff.; Barrow, *op. cit.,* pp. 220 ff.

123 [76] *De Civ. Dei,* XI, 18, 22; XII, 2, 4. The relationship between *ordo* and love has received careful analysis in a number of works: Gilson, *op. cit.,* pp. 217-218; John Burnaby, *Amor Dei* (London: Hodder and Stoughton, 1938), especially pp. 113 ff.; T. J. Bigham and A. T. Mollegen, "The Christian Ethic" in R. W. Battenhouse, ed., *A Companion to the Study of St. Augustine,* pp. 371 ff.; Anders Nygren, *Agape and Eros,* trans. P. S. Watson, 1 vol. ed. (Philadelphia: Westminster, 1953) pp. 449 ff.

123 [77] *De Civ. Dei,* XIX, 13.

123 [78] There is a vast amount of literature covering the Augustinian conception of time. The following are useful: Gilson, *op. cit.,* pp. 246 ff.; Jules Chaix-Ruy, *Saint Augustin, Temps et Histoire* (Paris, 1956); H. I. Marrou, *L'Ambivalence du temps de l'histoire chez Saint Augustin* (Montreal and Paris, 1950) is especially useful for its emphasis on the social bearing of time; J. F. Callahan, *Four Views of Time in Ancient Philosophy* (Cambridge: Harvard University Press, 1948), Chapter IV is a more formal treatment of the problem. There are some surprisingly appreciative remarks in B. Russell, *A History of Western Philosophy* (New York: Simon & Schuster, 1945) pp. 352-355. There are relevant passages in Augustine's *Confessions,* Bk. XI, and *Ep.* 137, which should also be considered.

124 [79] Cicero, *De Divinatione,* I, 27.

124 [80] *De Civ. Dei,* XI, 6; *Ep.* 137 *passim.*

124 [81] In his book *Christ and Time,* Professor Oscar Cullmann has described how the early Christians looked on the coming of Christ as marking the center of the time-line. In Him the past had been fulfilled and all that was to follow had been decided. See also the discussion of Karl Löwith, *Meaning in History* (Chicago: University of Chicago Press, 1949) pp. 182 ff., which largely follows Cullmann; and in general, R. L. P. Milburn, *Early Christian Interpretations of History* (London: Black, 1954); two articles by A. H. Chroust, "The Metaphysics of Time and History in Early Christian Thought," *New Scholasticism,* Vol. 19, pp. 322-352 (1945); "The Meaning of Time in the Ancient World," *Ibid.,* Vol. 21, pp. 1-70 (1947).

124 [82] *Gelasians* I:26; *Epistle to the Hebrews* 11:1; *Romans* 8:24; *De Civ. Dei,* XII, 13-14; XIX, 4; *De Doctrina Christiana,* II, 43-44; see also the discussion in R. E. Cushman, "Greek and Christian Views of Time," *Journal of Religion,* Vol. 33, pp. 254-265 (1953). H. Scholz, *Glaube und Unglaube in der Weltgeschichte* (Leip-

zig, 1911) pp. 137 ff. The problem of "progress" in Augustine's philosophy of history has been carefully examined by T. Mommsen, "St. Augustine and the Christian Idea of Progress, the Background of the City of God," *Journal of the History of Ideas*, Vol. 12, pp. 346-374 (1951). Augustine's earlier views are discussed by Cranz, "The Development of Augustine's Ideas on Society before the Donatist Controversy," *op. cit.*, pp. 273 ff. Additional material may be found in Löwith, *op. cit.*, Ch. IX; J. Pieper, *The End of Time*, trans. M. Bullock (New York: Pantheon, 1954) *passim*. Augustine's approach to history, with its combination of an over-all synthesis and sensitivity to the varied nature of historical phenomena, is an interesting example of the case that cannot be subsumed under Isaiah Berlin's suggestive categories: *The Hedgehog and the Fox* (New York: Simon and Schuster, 1953) and *Historical Inevitability* (London: Oxford University Press, 1954). The problem of the extent to which Augustine can be properly said to have held a philosophy of history is discussed by H. Scholz, *op. cit.*, *Vorrede*, where it is maintained that Augustine did not elaborate such a philosophy. See also Gilson, *Les Métamorphoses de la Cité de Dieu*, pp. 37 ff.; Cochrane, *op. cit.*, Ch. XII.

125   [83] *De Civ. Dei*, XIX, 17.

126   [84] *De Civ. Dei*, I, 29.

126   [85] *De Civ. Dei*, XIX, 21. Augustine's discussion of Cicero's definition has been the subject of a continuing controversy: R. W. and A. J. Carlyle, *op. cit.*, Vol. I, pp. 165 ff., held that Augustine removed the concept of justice from his definition of the state. This was denied by J. N. Figgis, *op. cit.*, Ch. III. There is a judicious summary of the matter in C. H. McIlwain, *The Growth of Political Thought in the West* (New York: Macmillan, 1932) pp. 154-160. Gilson has admitted that Augustine "forced" the text from Cicero: *Les Métamorphoses de la Cité de Dieu*, pp. 38-39, fn. 1.

126   [86] *De Civ. Dei*, XIX, 21.

127   [87] *De Civ. Dei*, XIX, 24.

127   [88] *De Civ. Dei*, XIX, 24.

127   [89] Cicero, *Ad. Fam.*, V, 12; Caesar, *De bello civili*, III, 68, 1.

128   [90] *De Civ. Dei*, V, 24; *De Doctrina Christiana*, I, 23. See also Augustine's remarks on sin and human pride and their effect in perverting the use of power: *De Musica*, VI, 13-15, 40-41, 48, 53; *De Libero arbitrio*, I, 6, 14. Barrow, *op. cit.*, p. 230, also has some useful remarks.

128   [91] Figgis, *op cit.*, pp. 78, 84 ff., inclined towards viewing Augustine as a forerunner of the later sacerdotalism of the Middle Ages; H. Reuter, *Augustinische Studien* (Gotha, 1887) pointed out the implications of predestination theory for the power of the Church; Harnack, *History of Dogma*, 7 vols., translated from the third German edition by J. Millar (London: Williams and Norgate, 1896-1899) Vol. 5, pp. 140-168, also pointed out the weakening effect of predestinarianism but concluded that Augustine strengthened the theoretical position of the Church.

128   [92] Battenhouse, *op. cit.*, pp. 184-185; Willis, *op. cit.*, pp. 113 ff. Relevant passages from Augustine are: *De Baptismo*, I, 10, 15-16; IV.1; III.23; III.4.

129   [93] S. J. Grabowski, "Saint Augustine and the Primacy of the Roman Bishop," *Traditio*, Vol. 4, pp. 89-113 (1946), concludes that Augustine held consistently to

the doctrine of ecclesiastical supremacy. See also E. Troeltsch, *Augustin, die christliche Antike und das Mittelalter* (Munich and Berlin, 1915) pp. 26 ff.

129   [94] *De Doctrina Christiana,* I, 23; *De Civ. Dei,* V, 17; XIX, 15.

130   [95] *De Civ. Dei,* VI, 26; XII, 1, 9; XIV, 9, 28; XVI, 3, 4; XVII, 14; XIX, 5, 10, 23.

130   [96] *De Civ. Dei,* XII, 1.

130   [97] *De Regimine Principum,* Lib. I, cap. I.

130   [98] *Rights of Man,* Pt. II, Ch. 1.

131   [99] *Principles of Social and Political Theory* (Oxford: Clarendon Press, 1951) pp. 2-4.

131   [100] Friedrich Engels, *Origins of the Family, Private Property, and the State* (Moscow, 1948) pp. 241-242. It should be mentioned that modern sociologists have continued the distinction on somewhat different grounds. See, for example, Ferdinand Tönnies' polar concepts of *Gemeinschaft* and *Gesellschaft* in *Fundamental Concepts of Sociology,* trans. Charles P. Loomis (New York: American Book Company, 1940); Emile Durkheim's contrast between *solidarité méchanique* and *solidarité organique* in *The Division of Labor in Society,* trans. George Simpson (Glencoe: Free Press, 1947) Book I, Chs. 2-3; and Robert M. MacIver's concept of "Community" in *The Modern State* (Oxford: Clarendon Press, 1926) pp. 451 ff.

131   [101] *De moribus ecclesiae,* XXX, 63.

131   [102] The blend of nationalist and religious sentiments appears clearly in Rousseau's proposed constitution for Corsica. Each citizen was to swear the following oath:

> "In the name of God Almighty and on the holy Gospels I herewith, by a sacred and irrevocable oath, bind myself with my body, my property, my will and all my might to the Corsican nation to belong to it in complete ownership with all my dependents." [C. E. Vaughan, *The Political Writings of Jean-Jacques Rousseau,* 2 vols. (Cambridge: Cambridge University Press, 1915) Vol. II, p. 350.]

132   [103] The basic work here is H. de Lubac, *Corpus Mysticum,* 2nd ed. (Paris, 1949). I have also drawn on the excellent study by E. H. Kantorowicz, "Pro Patria Mori in Mediaeval Political Thought," *American Historical Review,* Vol. 56, pp. 472-492 (1951), and *The King's Two Bodies* (Princeton: Princeton University Press, 1957) Ch. V. Further material can be found in: A. H. Chroust, "The Corporate Idea and the Body Politic in the Middle Ages," *Review of Politics,* Vol. 9, pp. 423-452 (1947); G. B. Ladner, "Mediaeval Thought on Church and Politics," *Ibid.,* pp. 403-422.

132   [104] *Summa Theologiae* II, III, Q. 69, art. 5. I have used the translation by the English Dominican Fathers, *The "Summa Theologiae" of Saint Thomas Aquinas,* 22 vols. (New York: Benziger Brothers, Inc., 1913-1927) Vol. XVII, p. 175.

133   [105] Sir John Fortescue, *De Laudibus Legum Anglie,* ed. and trans. S. B. Chrimes (Cambridge: Cambridge University Press, 1949) Ch. XIII; Kantorowicz, "Pro Patria Mori in Mediaeval Political Thought," *op. cit.,* pp. 486 ff.; E. Voegelin, *The New Science of Politics* (Chicago: University of Chicago Press, 1952) pp. 42-46.

133   [106] *The Political Writings of Jean Jacques Rousseau,* Vol. II, p. 437.

133   107 Rousseau, *The Social Contract,* G. D. H. Cole, ed. (Everyman) Book I, Ch. 8, pp. 18-19.

133   108 Joseph Mazzini, *The Duties of Man and other Essays* (Everyman) pp. 56-58.

134   109 Numerous examples of this can be found among the following works: E. Lewis, *Medieval Political Ideas,* 2 vols. (London: Routledge and Kegan Paul, 1954) Vol. 2, pp. 387, 391, 421, 425; O. von Gierke, *Political Theories of the Middle Ages,* trans. F. W. Maitland (Cambridge: Cambridge University Press, 1900) pp. 30 ff.; W. Ullmann, *Medieval Papalism* (London, 1949) Chs. IV-V; *The Growth of Papal Government in the Middle Ages* (London: Methuen, 1955) *passim;* B. Tierney, *Foundations of the Conciliar Theory* (Cambridge: Cambridge University Press, 1955) *passim.*

134   110 *Summa Theologiae* IIIa, Q. 75, art. 1; IIIa, Q. 73, art. 3; IIIa, Q. 8, art. 1; Q. 67, art. 2; Q. 73, art. 1, ad 3; Q. 73, art. 3-4; Q. 65, art. 3, ad 1. A good general discussion of the historical background to the Thomistic conception of the common good is to be found in I. T. Eschmann, "A Thomistic Glossary on the Principle of the Pre-eminence of the Common Good," *Mediaeval Studies,* Vol. V, 1943, pp. 123-165.

134   111 *Summa Theologiae* IIIa, Q. 65, art. 1.

134   112 *Summa Theologiae* IIIa, Q. 65, art. 3, ad 2; Q. 65, art. 4; Q. 73, art. 8, ad. 1; Q. 73, art. 11, ad 1; III (Suppl.), Q. 34, art. 3.

135   113 *Summa Theologiae* III (Suppl.), Q. 34, art. 2, ad 2.

135   114 *Summa Theologiae* III (Suppl.), Q. 34, art. 1.

135   115 *Summa Theologiae* I, Q. 108, art. 2 in A. C. Pegis, ed. *The Basic Writings of Saint Thomas Aquinas,* 2 vols. (New York: Random House, 1945). In this connection Thomas's discussion of government in general ought to be consulted: *Summa Theologiae* I, Q. 103; also III *Contra Gentes* I.

136   116 *Summa Theologiae* Ia, IIae, Q. 93, art. 3 (Pegis edition).

136   117 *Summa Theologiae* IIIa, Q. 64, arts. 5, 6, 8; Q. 65, art. 1; Q. 78, art. 1; Q. 82, arts. 5, 6.

136   118 *Summa Theologiae* Ia, IIae, Q. 93, art. 1; IIIa, Q. 78, art. 1.

136   119 *Summa Theologiae* IIIa, Q. 82, art. 6. The notion of "representation" in mediaeval political thought has been examined in Gierke, *op. cit.,* pp. 61 ff.; Voegelin, *op. cit., passim;* Tierney, *op. cit.,* pp. 34-48, 125-127, 176-186, 235-237; G. Post, "*Plena Potestas* and Consent in Medieval Assemblies," *Traditio,* Vol. I, pp. 355-408 (1943).

138   120 Cited in E. Lewis, *op. cit.,* Vol. 2, p. 578.

Chapter Five

142   1 *Defensor Pacis,* Lib. I, xii.

142   2 A certain amount of qualification is needed here. There is no doubt that the secularization of political thought in the sixteenth century had been foreshadowed

earlier by the writings of men like John of Paris, Marsilius, and Pierre Dubois, to mention only the better known examples. But since the origins of an intellectual tendency present a quite different order of problems from that of the full impact of an idea, I have felt justified in turning directly to the sixteenth century.

143   [3] *Reformation Writings of Martin Luther,* ed. Bertram Lee Woolf (London: Lutterworth, 1952) Vol. 1, p. 345. Thus far two volumes have appeared. Hereafter this will be cited as Woolf.

143   [4] Woolf, Vol. 1, p. 303.

143   [5] There is a good analysis, although directed solely at religious issues, of Luther's vocabulary in the excellent volume by Gordon Rupp, *The Righteousness of God* (New York: Philosophical Library, 1953) pp. 81 ff.

144   [6] Harold J. Grimm, "Luther's Conception of Territorial and National Loyalty," *Church History,* Vol. 17, pp. 79-94, at p. 82 (June, 1948). Substantially the same point is made by John W. Allen, *A History of Political Thought in the Sixteenth Century,* 2nd ed. (London: Methuen, 1941) p. 15; and by Preserved Smith, *Life and Letters of Martin Luther,* 2nd ed. (Boston: Houghton Mifflin, 1914) pp. 214, 228; and Mackinnon, *op. cit.,* Vol. 2, p. 229. Ernest G. Schwiebert has argued that Luther wrote essentially as a theologian, but that his political ideas derived largely from mediaeval sources. See "The Mediaeval Patterns in Luther's Views of the State," *Church History,* Vol. 12, pp. 98-117 (June, 1943).

144   [7] *Works of Martin Luther,* ed. Charles M. Jacobs, 6 vols. (Philadelphia: Muhlenberg Press, 1915-1932) Vol. 5, p. 81. Hereafter this will be cited as *Works.*

145   [8] ". . . Cuique suum arbitrium petendi utendique relinqueretur, sicut in baptismo et potentia relinquitur. At nunc cogit singulis annis unam speciem accipi eadem tyrannide . . ." *D. Martin Luther Werke* (Weimar Ausgabe, 1888-   ) Vol. 6, p. 507 (hereafter cited as *Werke*); Woolf, Vol. 1, pp. 223-224.

145   [9] Woolf, Vol. 1, pp. 127-128, 162.

146   [10] Woolf, Vol. 1, p. 224.

146   [11] Luther had read and admired Gerson, D'Ailly, and Dietrich of Niem. He does not appear to have become acquainted with the anti-papal writings of William of Occam until relatively late. For a general discussion of these matters, consult James MacKinnon, *Luther and the Reformation,* 4 vols. (London: Longmans, 1925-1930) Vol. I, pp. 20-21, 135; Vol. II, pp. 228-229; Rupp, *op. cit.,* p. 88; R. H. Fife, *The Revolt of Martin Luther* (New York: Columbia University Press, 1957) pp. 104 ff., pp. 203-244.

146   [12] Woolf, Vol. 1, pp. 224-225; *Works,* Vol. 1, p. 391; *Luther's Correspondence and Other Contemporary Letters,* ed. Preserved Smith and Charles M. Jacobs, 2 vols. (Philadelphia: Muhlenberg Press, 1918) Vol. 1, p. 156.

146   [13] Woolf, Vol. 1, p. 121.

146   [14] *Ibid.,* p. 123; *Werke,* Vol. 2, pp. 447-449.

147   [15] For a further discussion, see Roland H. Bainton, *Here I Stand; A Life of Martin Luther* (New York: Mentor, 1955) pp. 115-116; Ernest G. Schwiebert, *Luther and His Times* (St. Louis: Concordia, 1950) pp. 464 ff.; Heinrich Boehmer, *Martin Luther: Road to Reformation,* trans. J. W. Doberstein and T. G. Tappert (New York: Meridian, 1957).

147   [16] Woolf, Vol. I, pp. 122, 167.

148   [17] In this connection, Luther's letter to John, Elector of Saxony, was significant: "There is no fear of God and no discipline any longer, for the papal ban is abolished and everyone does what he will . . . But now the enforced rule of the Pope and the clergy is at an end in your Grace's dominions, and all the monasteries and foundations fall into your Grace's hands as the ruler, the duty and difficulty of setting these things in order comes with them." Smith and Jacobs, *op. cit.,* Vol. 2, p. 383. On several occasions, Luther was to lament the release of the rulers from papal controls. See *Works,* Vol. 4, pp. 287-289.

149   [18] *Freiheit eines Christenmenschen, 23 (Werke,* Vol. VII).

149   [19] Luther's long apprenticeship in scholasticism is discussed in Mackinnon, *op. cit.,* Vol. I, pp. 10-27, 50 ff.

149   [20] Woolf, Vol. 1, pp. 225, 227-229; Smith and Jacobs, *op. cit.,* Vol. 1, pp. 60, 64, 78, 150, 169-170, 359.

149   [21] Luther's distinction between Scripture and the Word of God is analyzed by Rupert E. Davies, *The Problem of Authority in the Continental Reformers* (London: Epworth Press, 1946) pp. 31 ff.; and by Ernst Troeltsch, *The Social Teaching of the Christian Churches,* trans. O. Wyon, 2 vols. (London: Allen and Unwin, 1931) Vol. 2, p. 486. In connection with Luther's quest for the "original" meaning of Scripture, it might be added that he was aided by contemporary humanist scholars, such as Reuchlin and Erasmus, who were seeking to recapture the true meaning of Scripture by means of philological researches.

150   [22] Thomas's argument that the sacrament represented more than a sign is to be found in *Summa Theologiae* III, Q. 60, art. 1-3. The necessary connection between the sacraments and salvation is developed in *S. T.* III, Q. 61, art. 1. The role of the sacraments as a power which causes or infuses grace is described in *S. T.* III, Q. 62, art. 1, 4. This aspect is extended in *S. T.* III, Q. 63, art. 3, and Q. 65, art. 3, ad 2, where Thomas emphasizes the way in which the sacrament imprints a "character" on the soul. The relationship between the ministration of the sacraments and ecclesiastical offices is defined in *S. T.* III, Q. 65, art. 3, ad 2; Q. 67, art. 2, ad 1-2; Q. 72, art. 8, ad 1. Finally, it is significant that the doctrines of ecclesiastical supremacy and the Pope's *plenitudo potestatis* are inserted in the discussions of the sacraments: *S. T.* III, Q. 62, art. 11.

150   [23] Cited in J. S. Whale, *The Protestant Tradition* (Cambridge: Cambridge University Press, 1955) p. 58. I am indebted to this excellent work for its discussion of the contrasting forms of sacramental usage.

151   [24] *Works,* Vol. III, pp. 234-237; Vol. IV, p. 265. See the recent survey by F. E. Cranz, "An Essay on the Development of Luther's Thought on Justice, Law, and Society," *Harvard Theological Studies,* Vol. XIX (1959).

151   [25] *Works,* Vol. III, pp. 238-240, 426.

151   [26] *Works,* III, pp. 252, 261-262.

151   [27] *Works,* III, p. 252.

152   [28] Woolf, Vol. 1, pp. 114, 318.

152   [29] *Ibid.,* p. 113.

152   [30] *Works,* Vol. 2, p. 262.

153   [31] *Ibid.,* Vol. 1, p. 349.

153   [32] *Werke,* Vol. XIV, p. 714.

153   [33] *Works,* Vol. III, p. 252.

154   [34] *Ibid.,* p. 262.

154   [35] *Works,* Vol. 3, 262.

154   [36] Woolf, Vol. 1, pp. 115, 247, 249, 318, 367; *Works,* Vol. III, pp. 326-328.

154   [37] Woolf, Vol. 1, pp. 115, 117, 181; *Works,* Vol. IV, pp. 79, 82.

154   [38] Woolf, Vol. 1, p. 120; *Works,* Vol. IV, pp. 76-77.

155   [39] Woolf, Vol. 1, pp. 119-120.

155   [40] Woolf, Vol. 1, pp. 227-229. These sentiments were underlined in Luther's *Letter to the Christian Reader* (1522): ". . . When I compare scholastic with sacred theology, that is with Holy Scripture, it seems full of impiety and vanity and dangerous in all ways to be put before Christian monks not forearmed with the armor of God." Luther then turned admiringly to Tauler and the *Theologia Germanica* and voiced the hope that under the influence of the mystics "there will not be left in our earth a Thomist or an Albertist, a Scotist or an Occamist, but only simple sons of God and their Christian brothers. Only let not those who batten on literary dainties revolt against the rustic diction, nor despise the coarse coverings and cheap garments of our tabernacle, for within is all the glory of the king's daughter. Certainly if we cannot get learned and eloquent piety, let us at least prefer an unlearned and infantile piety to an impiety which is both eloquent and infantile." Smith and Jacobs, *op. cit.,* Vol. 2, pp. 135-136. Compare Augustine, *Epistle* 138, 4-5.

155   [41] Although the Conciliarist theory had stressed the notion of a religious community which judges, the conception was weakened not only by the practical fact that nationality was undermining the ideas of a universal society of Christians, but also by the inability or unwillingness of the Conciliarists themselves to surrender the hierarchical and monarchical categories of thought. See the discussion in Lewis, *Medieval Political Ideas,* Vol. II, pp. 369-377.

155   [42] *Works,* Vol. I, pp. 349-357.

155   [43] Compare *Works,* Vol. I, p. 361; Vol. 4, p. 75; Vol. 5, pp. 27-87; Vol. 6, p. 148. Luther's theory of the Church has been discussed by Karl Holl, "Luther," *Gesammelte Aufsätze zur Kirchengeschichte* (Tubingen, 1923) Vol. 1, pp. 288 ff.; Troeltsch, *op. cit.,* Vol. 1, pp. 477-494; William A. Mueller, *Church and State in Luther and Calvin* (Nashville: Broadman Press, 1954) pp. 5-35; Wilhelm Pauck, "The Idea of the Church in Christian History," *Church History,* Vol. 21, pp. 191-213, at pp. 208-210 (Sept., 1952) and by the same author, *The Heritage of the Reformation* (Glencoe: Free Press, 1950) pp. 24-54; Lewis W. Spitz, "Luther's Ecclesiology and His Concept of the Prince as *Notbischof*," *Church History,* Vol. 22, pp. 113-141 (June, 1953); John T. McNeill, "The Church in Sixteenth Century Reformed Theology," *Journal of Religion,* Vol. 22, pp. 251-269 (July, 1942); Whale, *op. cit.,* Ch. VII.

156   [44] This aspect of Augustine is brilliantly described in Cochrane, *Christianity and Classical Culture,* pp. 359 ff. There are some relevant remarks also in E. Voegelin, *The New Science of Politics,* pp. 81-84.

156   ⁴⁵ *De Civitate Dei*, XX. And see Scholz, *Glaube und Unglaube in der Welt-geschichte*, pp. 109 ff.

157   ⁴⁶ *Works*, Vol. VI, p. 186.

157   ⁴⁷ *Works*, Vol. V, pp. 81-82.

158   ⁴⁸ *Ibid.*, Vol. IV, p. 23. On this same point, see: Vol. III, pp. 231-233; Vol. IV, pp. 28, 248-253, 266-269, 299 ff.; Vol. V, p. 38; Vol. VI, p. 460.

158   ⁴⁹ Woolf, Vol. 1, p. 117; Pierre Mesnard, *L'Essor de la philosophie politique au XVIe siècle* (Paris: Vrin, 1951) pp. 204-217.

158   ⁵⁰ There is a recent discussion of this problem in Spitz, *op. cit.*, pp. 118 ff.; and see the references cited there. In addition there are some interesting remarks in Friedrich Meinecke, "Luther über christliches Gemeinwesen und christlichen Staat," *Historische Zeitschrift*, Vol. 121, pp. 1-22 (1920).

158   ⁵¹ Woolf, Vol. I, p. 114.

158   ⁵² *Ibid.*, pp. 114-115, 129-130, 141, 147, 226-227, 232, 275.

158   ⁵³ *Ibid.*, p. 167.

159   ⁵⁴ *Works*, Vol. III, p. 235; Vol. IV, pp. 289-291.

159   ⁵⁵ Woolf, Vol. I, p. 298. It is true that Luther occasionally praised customary law, but a close examination of the context of the argument shows that he was contending that customary laws were better adapted to local conditions than imperial laws, and not that customary laws were salutary restraints. McNeill, "Natural Law in the Thought of Luther," *loc. cit.*, has underlined the role of natural law and reason in Luther's writings, but again the context was one where Luther was asserting that natural law and reason or equity allowed the ruler to override existing law or customs. Natural law, in other words, played a liberating as well as a restraining role in Luther's thought. See Woolf, Vol. I, p. 187; *Works*, Vol. 6, pp. 272-273. One of the few occasions wherein Luther cited Aquinas for support involved an argument in favor of an unlimited secular power in times of emergency. See *Works*, Vol. 3, p. 263.

160   ⁵⁶ *Works*, Vol. III, p. 234.

160   ⁵⁷ *Ibid.*, pp. 235-236.

160   ⁵⁸ Woolf, Vol. I, pp. 357-358; *Works*, Vol. III, p. 235; Vol. IV, pp. 240-241; *Werke* (Weimar Ausgabe), Vol. I, pp. 640-643.

161   ⁵⁹ *Works*, Vol. III, p. 239-242, 248; Vol. VI, pp. 447 ff.; Woolf, Vol. I, pp. 234, 357, 368-370, 378-379.

161   ⁶⁰ *Works*, Vol. IV, p. 220; Smith and Jacobs, *op. cit.*, Vol. II, p. 320.

161   ⁶¹ *Works*, Vol. VI, p. 460; Vol. III, pp. 231-232; Vol. IV, pp. 23, 28; Smith and Jacobs, *op. cit.*, Vol. II, p. 492.

161   ⁶² *Works*, Vol. I, p. 271; Vol. III, pp. 255-256.

162   ⁶³ *Ibid.*, Vol. I, pp. 262-264; Vol. III, pp. 211-212; Vol. IV, pp. 226-228. Some commentators have made a great deal of the joint declaration of 1531, wherein Luther sanctioned resistance to the Emperor. But when this is measured against the main body of his writings, its evidential value is small. Moreover, it would seem that the declaration was largely the work of Melanchthon. Luther affixed his own sig-

nature only after a great deal of agony and self-searching. A year previously he had warned against resisting the Emperor. See MacKinnon, *op. cit.,* Vol. IV, pp. 25-27.

162   ⁶⁴ J. N. Figgis, *Studies of Political Thought from Gerson to Grotius, 1414-1625,* 2nd ed. (Cambridge: Cambridge University Press, 1931) pp. 55-61.

162   ⁶⁵ *Werke,* Vol. XVIII, p. 389.

163   ⁶⁶ *De Regimine Principum,* Lib. I, cap. XII.

164   ⁶⁷ *Works,* Vol. IV, pp. 16-22. On this topic, see the discussion by Benjamin N. Nelson, *The Idea of Usury* (Princeton: Princeton University Press, 1949) pp. 29 ff.

164   ⁶⁸ *Ibid.,* pp. 240, 308; Vol. V, pp. 43 ff.

Chapter Six

166   ¹ *Works of Martin Luther,* ed. Charles M. Jacobs, 6 vols. (Philadelphia, 1915-1932) Vol. 2, pp. 10, 29-30. Hereafter this edition will be cited as *Works.* In connection with Luther's conception of society, see Charles Trinkhaus, "The Religious Foundations of Luther's Social Views" in *Essays in Medieval Life and Thought* ed. J. H. Mundy, R. W. Emery, and B. N. Nelson (New York, 1955) pp. 71-87.

166   ² See F. H. Littell, *The Anabaptist View of the Church,* 2nd ed. (Boston: Starr King Press, 1958) esp. Chs. I (B), II, III.

167   ³ The phrase "holy violence" occurs in the writings of a seventeenth-century Puritan writer, Richard Sibbes, and is cited by Jerald C. Brauer, "Reflections on the Nature of English Puritanism," *Church History,* Vol. 22, pp. 99-108 (1954), p. 102. For the general characteristics of Anabaptist thinking, see Robert Friedman, "Conception of the Anabaptists," *Church History,* Vol. 9, pp. 335-340 (1940); Harold S. Bender, "The Anabaptist Vision," *Ibid.,* Vol. 13, pp. 3-24 (1944); Roland H. Bainton, *The Reformation of the Sixteenth Century* (Boston, 1952) pp. 95 ff.; J. S. Whale, *The Protestant Tradition* (Cambridge, 1955) pp. 175 ff. The close relationship between "peaceful" and "violent" forms of Anabaptism is discussed in Lowell H. Zuck, "Anabaptism: Abortive Counter-Revolt Within the Reformation," *Church History,* Vol. 26, pp. 211-216 (1957).

167   ⁴ *Works,* Vol. 5, p. 81.

168   ⁵ P. Imbart de la Tour, *Les origines de la Réformation,* 4 vols. (Paris, 1905-1935) Vol. 4, p. 53.

168   ⁶ "Letter from Calvin to Sadolet," *Tracts Relating to the Reformation,* trans. Henry Beveridge, 3 vols. (Edinburgh, 1844) Vol. 1, p. 37.

169   ⁷ *The Institutes of the Christian Religion,* trans. John Allen, 2 vols. (Philadelphia: Westminster Press, n.d.) Vol. 2, pp. 281-283 (IV, i, 8-10). Hereafter this will be cited as *Inst.,* and all translations, except where indicated, will be from it.

169   ⁸ "For unless we are united with all the other members under Christ our Head, we can have no hope of the future inheritance. . . . But all the elect of God are so connected with each other in Christ, that as they depend upon one head, so

they grow up together as into one body, compacted together like members of the same body; being made truly one, as living by one faith, hope, and charity, through the same Divine Spirit, being called not only to the same inheritance of eternal life, but also to a participation of one God and Christ . . . the saints are united in the fellowship of Christ on this condition, that whatever benefits God confers upon them, they should mutually communicate to each other." *Ibid.,* Vol. 2, pp. 271-272 (IV, i, 2-3).

169   ⁹ *Commentaries on the Epistle of Paul the Apostle to the Romans,* trans. John Owen (Edinburgh, 1849) p. 458. Hereafter this will be cited as *Commentaries on Romans.* On this same point, see Josef Bohatec, *Calvins Lehre vom Staat und Kirche* (Breslau, 1937) p. 271.

169   ¹⁰ ". . . such care as we take of our own body, we ought to exercise the same care of our brethren, who are members of our body; that as no part of our body can be in any pain without every other part feeling corresponding sensations, so we ought not to suffer our brother to be afflicted with any calamity without our sympathizing to the same." *Inst.,* Vol. 2, pp. 696-697 (IV, xvii, 38). A supplementary bond was also provided by the sacrament of baptism which initiated the member into the "society of the church." *Inst.,* Vol. 2, pp. 583, 611 (IV, xv, 1; xvi, 9).

170   ¹¹ *Commentaries on Romans,* pp. 458-459.

170   ¹² *Works,* Vol. 4, pp. 234-237; and see the Augsburg Confession (1530), Pt. II, art. VII, in Philip Schiff, ed., *The Creeds of Christendom,* 3 vols. (New York, 1877) Vol. 3, pp. 58 ff.

171   ¹³ *D. Martin Luthers Werke* (Weimar Ausgabe, 1888-   ) Vol. 30, Part II, pp. 435, 462.

171   ¹⁴ *Works,* Vol. 2, pp. 37-38, 52.

171   ¹⁵ Note the analogies drawn by Calvin between religious and political institutions. *Inst.,* Vol. 2, pp. 483 ff. (IV, xi).

171   ¹⁶ *Inst.,* Vol. 2, pp. 477-483 (IV, x, 27-29; IV, xi, 1).

171   ¹⁷ *Inst.,* Vol. 1, pp. 52, 218, 220, 232 (I, ii, 1; xvi, 1-3; xvii, 1). The substance of these passages is that God is not "idle and almost asleep" but "engaged in continual action."

172   ¹⁸ *Inst.,* Vol. 2, pp. 89-90, 770-771 (III, xix, 14; IV, xx, 1).

172   ¹⁹ *Calvani Opera,* ed. G. Baum, E. Cunitz, and E. Reuss, 59 vols. (Braunschweig, 1863-1900) Vol. 2, pp. 622-623; Vol. 4, p. 358 (*Inst.,* III, xix, 15). These volumes form part of the *Corpus Reformatorum,* and hereafter they will be cited as *Opera.*

173   ²⁰ *Inst.,* Vol. 2, p. 90 (III, xix, 15).

173   ²¹ *Inst.,* Vol. 2, pp. 422-423 (IV, viii, 8).

173   ²² *Inst.,* Vol. 1, p. 74 (I, v, 11).

173   ²³ *Inst.,* Vol. 2, pp. 452-453 (IV, x, 5).

174   ²⁴ *Inst.,* IV, x, 27. Here I have followed the translation of Henry Beveridge in his edition, 2 vols. (Grand Rapids, Mich.: Eerdmans, 1953) Vol. 2, p. 434.

174   ²⁵ *Inst.,* Vol. 2, p. 439 (IV, xi, 1) (Beveridge translation). Calvin consciously sought to widen the power of jurisdiction by tracing it back to the Jewish Sanhedrin and thereby capitalizing on the extensive authority of that body.

174 **26** *Inst.,* Vol. 2, pp. 503-504 (IV, xii, 1).

174 **27** See the discussion of Pierre Mesnard, *L'Essor de la philosophie politique au XVIe siècle,* 2nd ed. (Paris, 1952) pp. 283 ff.

175 **28** *Inst.,* Vol. 2, pp. 273-274 (IV, i, 4). It is important to note that the ultimate power of excommunication was placed specifically in the hands of the higher officers of the church; that is, the pastors and the Council of Elders. The power was specifically excluded from the province of the magistrates and the congregation.

175 **29** *De Civitate Dei,* Lib. XVIII, cap. 51.

176 **30** *Inst.,* Vol. 1, pp. 35-36 (Ded. Epist.), 86-87 (I, vii, 1-2); Vol. 2, pp. 417-419 (IV, viii, 2-4); "Letter to Sadolet," *Tracts,* Vol. 1, p. 50.

177 **31** Herbert D. Foster, "Calvin's Program for a Puritan State in Geneva," *Collected Papers of Herbert D. Foster* (privately printed, 1929) p. 64; Emile Doumergue, *Jean Calvin. Les hommes et les choses de son temps,* 7 vols. (Lausanne, 1899-1928) Vol. 5, pp. 188 ff.; Mesnard, *op. cit.,* pp. 301 ff.; E. Choisy, *L'état chrétien calviniste à Genève au temps de Theodore de Beze* (Geneva, 1902); and for a recent discussion of the Genevan experience, as well as a sympathetic general survey of Calvinism, see John T. McNeill, *The History and Character of Calvinism* (New York, 1954) Chs. ix-xii.

177 **32** In Doumergue's magisterial work on Calvin, there is a spirited defense of the thesis that Calvin's theory of the church embodies a strong "representative" element. Yet Doumergue's argument is weakened by his failure to ask: what and whom do the officers of the church represent? He is content, instead, to indicate the several passages where Calvin provided for congregational approval of certain church officers. The difficulty here is that election is not the same as representation, especially when it is not accompanied by a power of recall. Hence even though Calvin declared that the ministers constituted a *corpus ecclesiae repraesentans* (*Opera,* Vol. 14, p. 681), his meaning was that the ministers represented the purposes of the church as defined by Scripture. He did not mean that the ministers represented the wills or separate interests of the members of the congregation, hence Doumergue's attempt to relate the Calvinist theory of the church to modern representative government is not convincing. See his discussion, Vol. 5, pp. 158-162.

177 **33** *Inst.,* Vol. 2, pp. 318-319 (IV, iii, 2); see also p. 317 (IV, iii, 1).

178 **34** *Inst.,* Vol. 2, p. 424 (IV, viii, 9). I have slightly altered the translation.

178 **35** *Inst.,* Vol. 2, p. 417 (IV, viii, 2).

178 **36** The authority and dignity of the pastoral office, according to Calvin, belonged not "to the persons themselves, but to the ministry over which they were appointed, or to speak more correctly, to the Word, the ministration of which was committed to them." *Inst.,* Vol. 2, p. 424 (IV, viii, 9). American constitutional lawyers will recognize in this a forerunner of the role the Supreme Court in the nineteenth century claimed for itself when interpreting the Constitution in the exercise of its power of judicial review.

180 **37** *Inst.,* Vol. 1, p. 223 (I, xvi, 4).

181 **38** *Inst.,* Vol. 1, p. 233 (I, xvii, 1).

181 **39** *Inst.,* Vol. 2, p. 771 (IV, xx, 2).

181 **40** *Inst.,* Vol. 2, p. 90 (III, xix, 25).

181 41 "Had we remained in the state of natural integrity such as God first created, the order of justice would not have been necessary. For each would then have carried the law in his own heart, so that no constraint would have been needed to keep us in check. Each would be his own rule and with one mind we would do what is good. Hence justice is a remedy of this human corruption. And whenever one speaks of human justice let us recognize that in it we have the mirror of our perversity, since it is by force we are led to follow equity and reason." *Opera,* Vol. 27, p. 409. See also *Opera,* Vol. 7, p. 84; Vol. 49, p. 249; Vol. 52, p. 267; and the discussion in Chenevière, *La pensée politique de Calvin* (Paris, 1937) pp. 93-94.

181 42 *Inst.,* Vol. 1, p. 294 (II, ii, 13).

181 43 *Inst.,* Vol. 2, p. 774 (IV, xx, 4).

181 44 *Inst.,* Vol. 2, p. 90 (III, xix, 15); Vol. 2, p. 771 (IV, xx, 2).

181 45 *Inst.,* Vol. 2, p. 90 (III, xix, 15); Vol. 2, pp. 772-773 (IV, xx, 3).

182 46 *Inst.,* Vol. 2, p. 772 (IV, xx, 2).

182 47 *Inst.,* Vol. 2, p. 772 (IV, xx, 2). I have slightly changed the translation; see the text in *Opera,* Vol. 2, p. 1094. In connection with this point, it is interesting to note how Calvin reversed the usual argument and asserted that obedience to human superiors helped to habituate men to obedience to God, *Inst.,* Vol. 2, p. 433 (II, viii, 35).

182 48 Cited in Doumergue, *op. cit.,* Vol. 5, p. 45.

182 49 Compare Calvin's use of the *corpus mysticum* to that of the fifteenth-century writer Sir John Fortescue, *De Laudibus Legum Anglie,* ed. and trans. S. B. Chrimes (Cambridge, 1949) cap. xiii. The whole problem of the influence of the Eucharist on political ideas remains to be explored. Some suggestive points are to be found in two articles by Ernst H. Kantorowicz, "Pro Patria Mori" in Medieval Political Thought," *American Historical Review,* Vol. 56, pp. 472-492 (April, 1951), and "Mysteries of State: An Absolutist Concept and Its Late Mediaeval Origins," *Harvard Theological Review,* Vol. 48, pp. 65-91 (Jan., 1955). Fundamental for this problem is Henri de Lubac, *Corpus Mysticum,* 2nd ed. (Paris, 1949).

183 50 *Inst.,* Vol. 1, pp. 790-791 (III, x, 6).

183 51 *Inst.,* Vol. 1, p. 757 (III, vii, 5).

184 52 *Inst.,* Vol. 1, p. 294 (II, ii, 13).

184 53 *Inst.,* Vol. 1, pp. 295-296 (II, ii, 14-15); pp. 298-299 (II, ii, 17-18); pp. 366 (II, v, 19).

184 54 *Inst.,* Vol. 1, p. 295 (II, ii, 13).

184 55 *Inst.,* Vol. 1, p. 296 (II, ii, 15).

185 56 *Inst.,* Vol. 1, p. 296 (II, ii, 13). The translation has been slightly changed; see the text in *Opera,* Vol. 2, p. 197.

185 57 *Inst.,* Vol. 1, p. 397 (II, viii, 1).

185 58 *Inst.,* Vol. 2, p. 789 (IV, xx, 16).

186 59 *Inst.,* Vol. 2, p. 787 (IV, xx, 14). The phrase is derived from Cicero, *De Legibus,*

III, 1.2, and is related to the classical tradition of the ruler as *lex animata;* see Erwin R. Goodenough, "The Political Philosophy of Hellenistic Kingship," *Yale Classical Studies,* Vol. 1 (1928) pp. 55 ff.

186 [60] See Mesnard, *op. cit.,* pp. 285-289; Chenevière, *op cit.,* p. 298.

186 [61] *Opera,* Vol. 52, p. 267.

186 [62] *Commentaries on Romans,* p. 481.

186 [63] *Ibid.,* p. 480.

187 [64] *Commentary on the Book of Psalms,* trans. James Anderson, 5 vols. (Edinburgh, 1845-1849) Vol. 3, p. 106; *Inst.,* Vol. 2, pp. 801-802 (IV, xx, 27).

187 [65] Given the lofty ends served by allegiance — "God has not intended men to live *pêle-mêle*" (*Opera,* Vol. 51, p. 800) — it is not surprising to find Calvin hostile to contract theory. This was not owing to any desire on his part to release rulers from their obligations, but rather to his belief that social duties ought not to be the subject of a crude bartering arrangement. *Inst.,* Vol. 2, pp. 801-802 (IV, xx, 27).

187 [66] *Inst.,* Vol. 2, p. 805 (IV, xx, 32).

187 [67] *Inst.,* Vol. 2, p. 790 (IV, xx, 16); p. 798 (IV, xx, 24).

187 [68] "Catechism of 1537," *Opera,* Vol. 22, p. 74.

188 [69] *Inst.,* Vol. 2, p. 805 (IV, xx, 32).

188 [70] *Inst.,* Vol. 2, p. 804 (IV, xx, 31); *Opera,* Vol. 4, p. 1160.

188 [71] *Opera,* Vol. 29, pp. 557, 636-637; Chenevière, *op. cit.,* pp. 346-347.

188 [72] *Works,* Vol. 5, pp. 51-52.

189 [73] *Inst.,* Vol. 2, pp. 773, 787 (IV, xx, 3, 14).

191 [74] *Opera,* Vol. 43, p. 374; and the discussion of John T. McNeill, "The Democratic Element in Calvin's Thought," *Church History,* Vol. 18, pp. 153-171 (Sept., 1949).

191 [75] A. S. P. Woodhouse, ed., *Puritanism and Liberty* (Chicago: University of Chicago Press, 1938) p. 53.

192 [76] *Commentaries on Romans,* p. 459.

192 [77] *Inst.,* Vol. 2, p. 272 (IV, i, 3).

Chapter Seven

196 [1] *Of the Laws of Ecclesiastical Polity,* III, i (14); VIII, i (5).

197 [2] *De Republica Anglorum,* ed. L. Alston (Cambridge: Cambridge University Press, 1906) Book I, Chapter 2 (p. 10).

197 [3] See the suggestive remarks on this problem as it appears in literature: R. P. Blackmur, *Form and Value in Modern Poetry* (New York: Anchor, 1957) pp. 35-36.

197 [4] "What other control can be found for greed, for secret and unpunished misdeeds than the idea of an eternal master who sees us and judges even our most intimate thoughts. We do not know who first taught this doctrine to man. If I knew

him and was certain that he would not abuse it . . . I myself would build him an altar." Voltaire, *Oeuvres complètes,* 52 vols. (Paris: Moland, 1883-1885) Vol. 28, pp. 132-133.

198   ⁵ See generally Hans Baron, *The Crisis of the Early Italian Renaissance,* 2 vols. (Princeton: Princeton University Press, 1955); *Humanistic and Political Literature in Florence and Venice at the Beginning of the Quattrocento,* 2 vols. (Cambridge, Mass.: Harvard University Press, 1955); "Das Erwachen des historischen Denkens im Humanismus des Quattrocento," *Historische Zeitschrift,* Vol. 147, pp. 5-20 (1932). Also relevant for the background of Machiavelli's thought is Allan H. Gilbert, *Machiavelli's "Prince" and Its Forerunners* (Durham: University of North Carolina Press, 1938); Lester K. Born, *The Education of a Christian Prince* (New York: Columbia University Press, 1936), Introduction.

198   ⁶ *The Prince,* XV (1). Unless otherwise indicated, I have used the translation by Allan H. Gilbert, *"The Prince" and Other Works* (New York: Hendricks House, 1946). The number in parenthesis above refers to the paragraph of the chapter in this edition.

In the passages cited above there is a great deal of controversy about whether the "predecessors" referred to were classical or mediaeval writers, like Dante, or to more recent publicists of the 15th century. For various points of view on this problem see the following: L. Arthur Burd, ed., *Il Principe* (Oxford: Clarendon Press, 1891) p. 282; Felix Gilbert, "The Humanist Concept of the Prince and *The Prince* of Machiavelli," *Journal of Modern History,* Vol. XI, pp. 449-483 (1939) p. 450, n. 3.

199   ⁷ *Prince,* XI (1). In his discussion of this chapter in *Machiavelli's "Prince" and Its Forerunners,* pp. 60-61, Gilbert omits any analysis of this passage. This oversight leads him to argue erroneously that Machiavelli is as willing to advise a politically minded pope as any other prince, perhaps thinking it possible that the liberation of Italy might come from a prince of the Church.

199   ⁸ Machiavelli's contempt for papal government should not, of course, be taken to infer a disregard for the importance of the papacy in Italian and foreign diplomacy.

200   ⁹ *Prince,* II (2); III (1); *The Discourses on the First Ten Books of Titus Livius,* trans. Leslie J. Walker, 2 vols. (New Haven: Yale University Press, 1950) Book I, ii (9-10), ix (3). The number in parenthesis refers to Walker's paragraphs.

200   ¹⁰ *Prince,* I, *passim.* See also XIX (18) where Machiavelli disdains to call a particular government new because it retained so much of the old.

200   ¹¹ *Ibid.,* VI (2).

200   ¹² *Ibid.,* XXIV (3).

200   ¹³ *Ibid.,* XXIV (1).

201   ¹⁴ *Ibid.*

201   ¹⁵ *Ibid.,* VI (2). See the analysis of Severtus (XIX, *passim*) and the remarks on Francesco Sforza's sons (XIV (2)).

201   ¹⁶ *Ibid.,* XIV (1).

201   ¹⁷ *Discourses,* II, Preface (7).

201   ¹⁸ *Ibid.,* I, xl (10); III, xi (1).

202 ^{19} *The History of Florence* (London: Bohn, 1854) III, iii (p. 125); *Discourses*, II, Preface (6-7).

202 ^{20} *Ibid.*, I, lv (6-8, 9).

202 ^{21} I have used the word "mass" here and throughout in order to convey the sense of a body of matter whose elements are largely undifferentiated and controllable as a whole. Needless to say, the word is not intended to suggest "a mass society" in the sense that this phrase carries in contemporary sociology and political science. A good example of the meaning for this essay is to be found in *The History of Florence* where Machiavelli describes the people as slow to generate motion, but when they are once aroused, a trifle will set them off. [VI, v (285)].

203 ^{22} *History*, II, viii (92-93); III, iii (128-129); IV, iii (172-173); VI, iv (278-281).

203 ^{23} See the famous analysis of the errors committed by Louis XII in his invasion of Italy: *Prince*, III (9).

203 ^{24} The best study of Machiavelli from this position is Leonard Olschki, *Machiavelli the Scientist* (Berkeley: privately printed, 1945). Also useful are Herbert Butterfield, *The Statecraft of Machiavelli* (London: Bell, 1940) p. 59 ff.; Ernst Cassirer, *The Myth of the State* (New Haven: Yale University Press, 1946) Chapters X-XII; James Burnham, *The Machiavellians* (New York: Day, 1943) Part II; Augustin Renaudet, *Machiavel*, 6^e ed. (Paris: Gallimard, 1956) pp. 12-13, 119 ff., for an interpretation of Machiavelli as a "positivist." For a corrective to these views see J. H. Whitfield, *Machiavelli* (Oxford: Blackwell, 1947) especially Chapter I. An extensive and critical estimate of Whitfield's volume has been made by Mario M. Rossi, *Modern Language Review*, Vol. XLIV (1949) pp. 417-424. There is a review of current interpretations by Wolfgang Preiser, "Das Machiavelli-Bild der Gegenwart," *Zeitschrift für die gesamte Staatswissenschaft*, Band 108, s. 1-38 (1952).

203 ^{25} *Il Principe*, XV, p. 283 (line 5) in L. Arthur Burd's edition, *op. cit.* Hereafter this will be cited as *Il Principe*.

204 ^{26} As a sample of the literature on this problem see the following: Friedrich Meinecke, *Niccolò Machiavelli, Der Fürst und kleinere Schriften* (Berlin, 1923) s. 7-47; Cassirer, *op. cit.*, pp. 142-143; Burd, *op. cit.*, p. 365, note 19; Felix Gilbert, "The Humanist Concept of the Prince and *The Prince* of Machiavelli," *The Journal of Modern History*, Vol. XI, pp. 449-483 (1939), p. 481 ff.; and by the same author, "The Concept of Nationalism in Machiavelli's Prince," *Studies in the Renaissance*, Vol. I, pp. 38-48 (1954). For a general discussion of Machiavelli's linguistic usages see Fredi Chiappelli, *Studi sul linguaggio del Machiavelli* (Florence, 1952).

204 ^{27} *Prince*, XXVI, p. 95 of the translation by Luigi Ricci and E. R. P. Vincent in the Modern Library edition (New York: Random House, n.d.).

204 ^{28} *Ibid.*, XXVI (2). I have slightly altered the translation. See also the discussion of Kenneth Burke, *A Rhetoric of Motives* (New York: Prentice-Hall, 1950) pp. 158-166.

205 ^{29} *Prince*, XXVI (6).

205 ^{30} *Discourses*, III, i (1-3).

205 ^{31} *Ibid.*, III, i (3-5).

205 [32] Note Harrington's language in the following: "Formation of Government is the creation of a Political Creature after the Image of a Philosophical Creature; or it is an infusion of the Soul or Facultys of a Man into the body of a Multitude . . . The Soul of Government . . . is every whit as necessarily religious as rational." *A System of Politics in The Oceana and Other Works of James Harrington,* edited by John Toland (London, 1737) pp. 499-500. Comparable remarks can be found in Algernon Sidney, *Works* (London, 1772) pp. 124, 160, 406, 419. In Zera S. Fink, *The Classical Republicans* (Evanston: Northwestern University Press, 1945), there is a good discussion of the relationship between Machiavelli and these seventeenth-century writers.

205 [33] The recent study by John W. Gough, *Fundamental Law in English Constitutional History* (Oxford: Clarendon Press, 1955) is, as its title implies, largely a study of legal thought in a narrow sense. But see the quotations on pp. 100, 121-122 for ideas similar to the sort of thing discussed above. The huge pamphlet literature of the period before and during the Civil War contains many illustrations of the above thesis. Both the parliamentarians and royalists imbued the notion of fundamental law with religious overtones. For examples see Margaret A. Judson, *The Crisis of the Constitution* (New Brunswick, New Jersey: Rutgers University Press, 1949) pp. 53-54, 62-63, 193-194, 338, 360; Francis D. Wormuth, *The Royal Prerogative, 1603-1649* (Ithaca: Cornell University Press, 1939) pp. 6, 8. In the political thought of the American Revolution the fundamental principle was identified frequently with the people. James Wilson, for example, mentions the "one great principle, the *vital* principle I may well call it, which diffuses animation and vigor through all the others. The principle I mean is this, that the supreme or sovereign power of the society resides in the citizens at large . . ." Randolph G. Adams, *Selected Political Essays of James Wilson* (New York: Copyright, 1930, F. S. Crofts and Co., Inc.) p. 196.

206 [34] Harold D. Lasswell and Abraham Kaplan, *Power and Society, A Framework for Political Inquiry* (New Haven: Yale University Press, 1950) pp. xiii-xiv.

207 [35] Letter to Vettori, April 9, 1513 in Gilbert, *The Prince,* p. 228 (2).

207 [36] *Discourses,* II, Preface (5); II, xviii (9); III, xxvii (4); *History,* IV, iv, p. 179.

207 [37] Letter to Vettori, April 16, 1527 in Gilbert, *The Prince,* p. 270 (2).

208 [38] *Prince,* XVIII (5). It is in this context of dilemmas that Machiavelli's famous doctrine of *raison d'état* ought to be interpreted.

> "This counsel merits the attention of, and ought to be observed by, every citizen who has to give advice to his country. For when on the decision to be taken wholly depends the safety of one's country, no attention should be paid either to justice or injustice, to kindness or cruelty, or to its being praiseworthy or ignominious. On the contrary, every other consideration being set aside, that alternative should be wholeheartedly adopted which will save the life and preserve the freedom of one's country." [*Discourses,* III, xli (2)].

The proper emphasis is not that moral prescriptions must be ignored when one is confronted with the task of saving one's country, but that politics is such a condition that the country cannot be saved except by violating ethical injunctions. The classic discussion here is that of Friedrick Meinecke, *Machiavellism,* trans. D. Scott (London: Routledge, 1959). For a criticism of Meinecke, see C. J. Friedrich, *Constitutional Reason of State* (Providence: Brown University Press, 1959).

208 [39] *Discourses,* I, xviii (6).

208 [40] Cited in Gilbert, *The Prince,* p. 44.

208 [41] *Il Principe,* XV, p. 285 (line 3).

208 [42] *Discourses,* III, xxxvii (3).

209 [43] Letter to Guicciardini, May 17, 1521, in *Lettere di Niccolò Machiavelli* (Milan: Bompiani, n.d.) p. 144.

209 [44] *Prince,* XV-XVIII *passim.*

209 [45] Burnham, *op. cit.,* p. 40 ff.; Butterfield, *op. cit.,* p. 69 ff.; and the criticism of the latter by Walker in his edition of the *Discourses,* Vol. I, pp. 92-93.

209 [46] Augustine, *De Civitate Dei,* III, 6, 14-15, Machiavelli's position is in *The Prince,* VI and *Discourses,* I, ix.

210 [47] Quoted from Felix Gilbert, "Machiavelli: The Renaissance of the Art of War," in Edward M. Earle, ed., *Makers of Modern Strategy* (Princeton: Princeton University Press, 1944) pp. 8-9).

211 [48] *Prince,* XXVI (2); *Discourses,* I, lvi *passim;* II, xxxii (6); *History,* VI, vii (pp. 299-301); VIII, vii (pp. 401-402). For Guicciardini *Opere,* ed. V. de Capariis (Milan, 1953) p. 431.

211 [49] *Discourses,* I, lvi (3). In Joseph Kraft, "Truth and Poetry in Machiavelli," *Journal of Modern History,* Vol. XXIII, pp. 109-121 (1951), p. 110, there is an appreciation of the non-rational elements. The notion of Fortune and its historical background is discussed by V. Cioffari, "The Function of Fortune in Dante, Boccaccio and Machiavelli," *Italica,* Vol. XXIV, No. 1 (March, 1947) pp. 1-13. In Machiavelli Fortune ceases to be an instrument of the Divine Will as it had been in Dante. For him it symbolized uncontrollable factors.

211 [50] For an example see the excellent study of Machiavelli in Pierre Mesnard, *L'essor de la philosophie politique au XVIe siècle,* pp. 17-85.

212 [51] *Discourses,* I, vi (9). Note also Galileo's classic statement of this principle:

"I cannot without great astonishment — I might say without great insult to my intelligence — hear it attributed as a prime perfection and nobility of the natural and integral bodies of the universe that they are invariant, immutable, inalterable, etc., while on the other hand it is called a great imperfection to be alterable, generable, mutable, etc. For my part I consider the earth very noble and admirable precisely because of the diverse alterations, changes, generations, etc., that occur in it incessantly." [*Dialogue Concerning the Two Chief World Systems — Ptolemaic and Copernican,* trans. by Stillman Drake (Berkeley: University of California Press, 1953) p. 58.]

212 [52] *Discourses,* II, xxiii (5); III, xxxi (1); "Frequently the desire for victory so blinds men that they see nothing but what seems favorable to their aim," III, xlviii (my translation). See also the interesting remarks on the kind of illusions to which émigrés are especially susceptible: II, xxxi (1). On the illusions created from the hope that a short-run situation will be permanent: *History,* II, iv (pp. 178-180); V, iv (231-232); *Prince,* XV (1); *Discourses,* II, xxvii.

212 [53] *Il Principe,* XVIII, p. 306 (lines 9-11); *Discourses,* I, xxiv (1); II, xxii (1).

212 [54] *History,* IV, ii (p. 164).

213 [55] *Discourses,* II, xxiv; *Prince,* XX.

213 [56] *Discourses,* III, xxxi (4).

213 [57] *Ibid.,* II, xxiii, xxvii (1); II, x-xi; xxx; III, xxv; *History,* IV, iv (*passim*).

213 [58] *Ibid.,* VI, iv (282); VIII, i (p. 308); VIII, ii (p. 320).

213 [59] *Discourses,* I, xlvi (2); II, xiv (2); *History,* III, vii (p. 149); V, iv (p. 226).

214 [60] *Discourses,* I, ii (13); III, xvii (2).

214 [61] *History,* V, i (pp. 202-203). This principle was also reflected in Machiavelli's belief that every form of government was defective, hence the traditional six-fold classification of types of government was less significant to the political scientist than the ease with which one type passed into its opposite. *Discourses,* I, ii (4).

214 [62] *Ibid.,* I, vi (9).

214 [63] *Ibid.,* II, i (50); II, iv (5); *History,* V, ii (pp. 213-214). On this point see Gilbert, *Machiavelli's "Prince" and Its Forerunners,* p. 27 ff.

214 [64] *Discourses,* I, xliv; I, lvii; *History,* VI, vii (304).

214 [65] *Discourses,* III, i.

215 [66] *History,* V, i (p. 202). I have changed the translation slightly.

215 [67] *Discourses,* II, Preface.

216 [68] *Ibid.,* I, Preface (3).

216 [69] ". . . a prudent man ought always to follow the footsteps of great men, and to imitate those who have been especially excellent, in order that his prowess, if it does not equal theirs, at least may give some odor of it." *Prince,* VI (1).

216 [70] *Discourses,* I, vi (6); *Prince,* XXI (7).

216 [71] See Butterfield, *op. cit.,* p. 19; Walker, *op. cit.,* Vol. I, p. 108 ff.

217 [72] *Prince,* III (7-8); *Discourses,* I, xxiii (1-3, 6); I, xxxiii (2-3, 6).

217 [73] The classical passages are to be found in *The Life of Castruccio of Lucca.* It has been translated in Gilbert's edition of *The Prince.* Useful in this connection is J. H. Whitfield, "Machiavelli and Castruccio," *Italian Studies,* Vol. 8 (1953) pp. 1-28.

217 [74] *Prince,* XXI (7).

217 [75] *Discourses,* II, Preface (7).

218 [76] *Ibid.,* I, xxxvii (1).

218 [77] *Prince,* II, *passim;* VI, (4).

218 [78] *Discourses,* I, vi (7, 9).

218 [79] *Prince,* VI (4).

218 [80] *Ibid.,* III (4-7); *Discourses,* III, xvi (3).

219 [81] *Ibid.,* III, xvi.

219 [82] *Prince,* XXI (8); *History,* II, i (pp. 46-47).

219 [83] *Discourses,* II, v (4).

219 [84] *Prince,* II; *Discourses,* I, vi (7).

219 [85] *Ibid.*, I, vi (9). At one point Machiavelli used the metaphor of a tree which needs a trunk large enough to support several branches [*Discourses*, II, iii (3)]. Relevant also was his criticism of Sparta for its failure to adjust itself to the demands of imperialism [*Ibid.*, II, iii (2-3)]. The methods of expansion for a republic were examined in *Ibid.*, II, iv.

220 [86] *Discourses*, I, ii (13).

220 [87] *Discourses*, I, i (8); *History*, II, ii (52-53).

221 [88] *Discourses*, I, xxvi (1).

221 [89] *Prince*, XVII (1).

221 [90] *Discourses*, I, ix (2).

221 [91] *Ibid.*, III, xxii (4). Yet there were also societies which had become so corrupt as to be beyond redemption. Here power was unavailing. *Discourses*, I, xvi (2).

222 [92] *Prince*, VIII (7); *Discourses*, I, xlv (3-4); III, vi (3-4). In *Prince*, XIX there was a significant contrast drawn between the degree and kind of violence needed to establish a new state, as exemplified by Severtus, with that needed to maintain a state, as in the case of Marcus. Only the latter is called truly glorious by Machiavelli.

222 [93] *Discourses*, II, x; III, xxxii; *History*, VI, i.

222 [94] *Discourses*, II, vi, xxi, xxxii.

222 [95] *Ibid.*, II, vii.

222 [96] See the working-paper of Machiavelli reproduced in *Machiavel, Toutes les lettres,* ed. E. Barincou, 2 vols. 6th ed. (Paris: Gallimard, 1955) Vol. I, p. 311.

223 [97] *Discourses*, I, ix (3).

223 [98] *Ibid.*, I, xvi (5).

223 [99] *Ibid.*, III, vii (2).

223 [100] *Ibid.*, II, xx (4); III, viii (2). This concern appeared most clearly in the remarkable passage where he described the fate awaiting those who have profaned the means of violence. The good prince, we are told, who used power to restore the health of the community was assured of eternal renown; those who had destroyed or mutilated their principalities were condemned to eternal infamy. [*Ibid.*, I, x (9-10)]. A special damnation awaited the inept ruler who, having succeeded to a secure and free state, proceeded to squander it foolishly. [*Ibid.*, I, x (1, 2, 6); III, v (2)]. Moreover, like religion, politics has its hagiology, its gradation of saints composed of those who had used power creatively. The first rank belonged to the founders of religions; next, those who have established kingdoms or republics; then in order of excellence were the generals, men of letters, and lastly, those who have excelled in any of the arts. But there was also a parallel list of the nihilists, enemies of promise who had destroyed religions, kingdoms, republics, letters and virtue itself.

While Machiavelli's attempt at a politico-theological myth may not seem very convincing, and while we may question his seriousness in expecting the political actor to be swayed out of fear for the judgments of history, these considerations do testify to the moral seriousness of the new science.

223 [101] *Réflexions sur la violence*, 10th ed. (Paris, 1946) pp. 120-122, 168, 173-174, 202, 273.

223 [102] *Discourses*, I, xxvi (3).

224 [103] Maurice Merleau-Ponty, *Humanisme et terreur*, 8th ed. (Paris: Gallimard, 1947) p. 205. It might be added that Merleau-Ponty has contributed a very suggestive analysis of Machiavelli from an existentialist viewpoint: "Machiavélisme et humanisme," in *Umanesimo e scienza politica* (Milan, 1951) pp. 297-308. For a recent statement of the traditional view that Machiavelli was a "teacher of evil" and profoundly anti-Christian, see Leo Strauss, *Thoughts on Machiavelli* (Glencoe, Ill.: Free Press, 1958).

224 [104] *Discourses*, II, ii (7).

224 [105] *Prince*, XV (2); XVIII (5); *Discourses*, III, ix; Letter to Soderini (1513?), *Toutes les lettres*, Vol. II, 327.

224 [106] Aristotle, *Politics*, 1332 b; 1337 a 11; see Aquinas: "Justice is a habit (*habitus*), whereby a man renders to each one his due with constant and perpetual will." *Summa Theologiae*, II, II, Q. 58, art. 1.

225 [107] An important exception is the recognition by Aquinas of a distinctively political form of prudence: "*et ideo regi ad quem pertinet regere civitatem regnum, prudentia competit secundum specialem et perfectissimam sui rationem. Et propter hoc 'regnativa' ponitur species prudentiae.*" (*Ibid.*, II, II ae, Q. 58, art. 1.)

225 [108] *Prince*, XV (2); XVIII (5).

225 [109] Cited in *Il Principe* by Burd, p. 290 fn.

225 [110] *Prince*, XV (1).

225 [111] *Ibid.*, XVIII (3).

225 [112] *Discourses*, II, xii (1).

225 [113] *Prince*, XVIII (3).

226 [114] *Ibid.* (5).

227 [115] *Ibid.*, XV (3).

227 [116] *Ibid.*, XV; *History*, V, i (202-203).

227 [117] *Prince*, XV-XVI. Aristotle (*Ethics* 1120 a 10-12) distinguished between liberality and magnificence, the latter being a political virtue. In his discussion he contrasted magnificence with niggardliness, defining the latter not as stinginess but vulgar display.

227 [118] *Prince*, VIII (3).

228 [119] *Discourses*, II, v.

228 [120] *Ibid.*, II, Preface (3); II, v.

228 [121] *Ibid.*, I, i (7-9); iii (3); xxviii (3); II, xii (6); III, xii (1).

228 [122] Wilhelm Nestle, "Politik und Moral im Altertum," *Neue Jahrbücher für das Klassische Altertum, Geschichte und deutsche Litteratur und für Pädagogik,* (1918) s. 225.

229 [123] George H. Sabine, *A History of Political Theory*, rev. ed. (New York: Holt,

1950) pp. 337-338, 347; John W. Allen, *A History of Political Thought in the Sixteenth Century*, p. 465; Mesnard, *op. cit.*, pp. 35 ff.

229   [124] *Prince*, XIX (18).

229   [125] *Il Principe*, XXVI, p. 369 (lines 5-6). Many commentators have attributed to Machiavelli the view that the state was a work of art and the role of the prince that of a political artist. This approach was first suggested by Jacob Burckhardt's great work, *The Civilization of the Renaissance in Italy*, trans. S. G. C. Middlemore (Vienna: Phaidon Press) Pt. I. For a more recent expression of the same point of view see Friedrich, *op. cit.*, pp. 16-19. The whole problem presented by Burckhardt's analysis is given thorough discussion by Wallace K. Ferguson, *The Renaissance in Historical Thought* (Boston: Houghton Mifflin, 1948) pp. 188 ff. In view of Machiavelli's emphasis upon "necessity" and his devaluation of the role of the prince in the *Discorsi*, Burckhardt's thesis needs to be revised.

229   [126] *Prince*, XVIII (6), IX (2); *Discourses*, I, xii (8).

230   [127] *Prince*, XXVI; *Discourses*, I, xvi.

230   [128] *Prince*, IX (1).

230   [129] *Discourses*, I, xvi; *History*, III, i (p. 108).

230   [130] *Prince*, IX (4); XVII (4).

230   [131] *Ibid.*, IX (2).

230   [132] *Discourses*, I, v (6-7); IX (3).

230   [133] *Ibid.*, I, v (3); I, lvii (2).

230   [134] *Ibid.*, I, xvii (4).

231   [135] *Il Principe*, IX, p. 237 (line 20) and p. 238 (line 1).

231   [136] *Discourses*, I, lviii.

231   [137] *Ibid.*, (5, 8); *History*, IV, i (p. 157). In this respect the prince reappears in a kind of sublimated way in the institution of the temporary dictatorship which Machiavelli borrowed from the Roman republic. On this point see *Discourses*, I, xxxiii (6), xxxiv.

231   [138] *Discourses*, I, xi (6). See the critical remarks on Cosimo di Medici based on the decline of Florence after his death: *History*, VII, i (p. 315); VII, ii (p. 318).

231   [139] *Discourse on Reforming the Government of Florence* in Gilbert's edition of *The Prince*, p. 92 (par. 31).

232   [140] *History*, VII, i (p. 306); *Discourses*, I, v; I, xlvi.

232   [141] *Discourses*, I, lv (9); II, xxv (1); *Reforming the Government of Florence* p. 79 (par. 1).

232   [142] *Reforming the Government of Florence*, pp. 85-86 (par. 16, 19); *History*, II, iii (pp. 60-61); III, iii (pp. 127-128); III, iv (p. 133); III, vi (p. 144); IV, vi (p. 190).

232   [143] *Ibid.*, VII, i (p. 306).

233   [144] *Reforming the Government of Florence*, p. 80 (par. 3), pp. 89-90 (pars. 26-27); *Discourses*, I, ii (18); I, iv (2, 6); I, vi; I, vii (1); I, viii; *History*, VI, i (pp. 306-307).

233 [145] *Discourses,* II, xxv (1).

234 [146] *Discourses,* I, vi (5). Mediaeval writers, like Egidius Romanus, had identified factional politics as an important element of the tyrant's power. See Gilbert, *Machiavelli's "Prince" and Its Forerunners,* pp. 163-164. What Machiavelli did was to rid the dynamics of factions of their associations with tyranny and align them with republicanism.

235 [147] *Discourses,* II, ii (2-3).

235 [148] *Ibid.,* II, ii (2).

235 [149] *Politics,* VII, 133 b-134 a.

235 [150] Cited in Fink, *op. cit.,* p. 52.

235 [151] *Discourses,* I, vii (1).

235 [152] *Ibid.,* III, xxviii; I, lii.

235 [153] *Ibid.,* I, xx (2).

236 [154] *Republic,* II, 366-367 (Cornford translation). See the stimulating discussion by Charles S. Singleton, "The Perspective of Art," *The Kenyon Review,* Vol. XV, pp. 169-189 (1953). This article is essentially concerned with Machiavelli's political theory and I am deeply indebted to it.

237 [155] *Discourses,* III, xxxi (5).

237 [156] *Ibid.,* III, xxxi (7).

237 [157] *Ibid.,* III, xxxv-xxxvii. For a modern expression of the communal qualities of military existence see Sartre's document of the French Resistance, "La république du silence," *Les Lettres Françaises,* IV (Paris, September 9, 1944) p. 1.

237 [158] *Discourses,* II, ii (6-7).

237 [159] *Ibid.,* I, iii (1).

Chapter Eight

PAGE

241 [1] From Thomas Goodwin and Philip Nye's Introduction to John Cotton's *The Keys of the Kingdom of Heaven* (1644) as contained in A. S. P. Woodhouse, ed. *Puritanism and Liberty,* p. 294. While this view of the church did not go uncontested it was significant that its critics did recognize that the central argument was from interest. As an example of these protests, see *Ibid.,* pp. 304-305.

241 [2] John Saltmarsh, *Smoke in the Temple* (1646) as contained in *Ibid.,* p. 182. The italics have been added.

241 [3] *Aeropagitica* in *Milton's Prose,* ed. M. W. Wallace (London: Oxford University Press, 1925) p. 312.

241 [4] *The English Works of Thomas Hobbes,* ed. Sir William Molesworth, 11 vols. (London, 1839) Vol. VII, p. 73; *De Cive or the Citizen,* ed. Sterling P. Lamprecht (New York: Appleton-Century-Crofts, 1949) Ep. Ded. (pp. 4-5). Hereafter the Molesworth edition will be cited simply as *E.W.* Similarly, the Lamprecht edition will be referred to as *Cive.*

242   [5] Woodhouse, *op. cit.*, p. 379.

242   [6] *Ibid.*, pp. 234, 380-381, 390.

245   [7] *Cive*, Ep. Ded., p. 3; see also *Leviathan*, ed. Michael Oakeshott, xxx (p. 220); *The Elements of Law*, ed. Ferdinand Tönnies (Cambridge: Cambridge University Press, 1928) I, xiii, 3-4 (hereafter referred to as *Law*); *E.W.*, Vol. 1, pp. 7-9.

246   [8] *E.W.*, Vol. I, p. 91.

246   [9] *Cive*, xviii, 4.

246   [10] *E.W.*, Vol. I, p. 36.

246   [11] *Leviathan*, v (pp. 25-26).

246   [12] *Cive*, xv, 16-17.

247   [13] *E.W.*, Vol. VII, p. 184; Vol. I, pp. 387-389.

247   [14] *Ibid.*, Vol. I, p. 388.

247   [15] *Cive*, Preface to the Reader, pp. 10-11.

248   [16] *Leviathan*, Introduction (p. 5); x (p. 56); *Law*, II, i, 1.

248   [17] *E.W.*, Vol. I, p. 7.

249   [18] *Ibid.*, Vol. I, p. 8.

249   [19] *Leviathan*, xxix (p. 209).

249   [20] *E.W.*, Vol. I, p. 3.

250   [21] *Law*, I, vi, 1.

250   [22] *Leviathan*, vii (p. 40).

250   [23] *Ibid.*, iv (p. 21).

250   [24] *Ibid.*, v (pp. 29-30).

250   [25] *Ibid.*, iv (p. 21).

250   [26] *Law*, I, v, 10.

251   [27] *Opera Latina*, ed. Sir William Molesworth, 5 vols. (London, 1845) Vol. V, p. 257.

251   [28] A. J. Ayer, *Language, Truth and Logic*, 2nd ed. (New York: Dover, 1946) p. 51. Reprinted by permission of Dover Publications, Inc.

251   [29] Excellent discussions of these problems are to be found in Dorothea Krook, "Thomas Hobbes's Doctrine of Meaning and Truth," *Philosophy*, Vol. XXXI, (1956), pp. 3-22; Richard Peters, *Hobbes* (Middlesex: Penguin, 1956) Ch. II. I have borrowed freely from both on certain matters. Also useful in this connection is the critical discussion of Oakeshott's interpretation by J. M. Brown, "A Note on Professor Oakeshott's Introduction to the *Leviathan*," *Political Studies*, Vol. I (1953) pp. 53-64.

251   [30] *Law*, I, ix, 18.

251   [31] *Leviathan*, xx (p. 136).

252   [32] *Law*, I, iv, 10-11; *Leviathan*, iii (pp. 15-16).

252   [33] *Law*, I, vi, 1; *Leviathan*, v (p. 29), xlvi (pp. 435-436).

253 [34] *E.W.,* Vol. I, p. 8.

253 [35] *Leviathan,* xlvi (p. 436).

253 [36] Leo Strauss, *Natural Right and History,* pp. 191, 196.

253 [37] *Law,* II, viii, 13.

254 [38] *E.W.,* Vol. I, pp. 8-10; Vol. VI, pp. 362-363; *Cive,* Preface, *passim.*

254 [39] *Law,* II, ii, 4.

254 [40] *Leviathan,* xx (p. 136), XXVI (p. 176).

255 [41] *Law,* II, x, 8; *Leviathan,* v (p. 26). See also: *Law,* II, vi, 12-13; *Cive,* xiv, 17; xv, 15-18; *Leviathan,* xxvi (pp. 176-177); xxxvi (p. 291); *E.W.,* Vol. VI, pp. 22, 121-122.

256 [42] *Cive,* Preface (pp. 7-8).

256 [43] *Law,* I, xiii, 3; *Leviathan,* xxxiv (pp. 255-256).

256 [44] *Cive,* Preface (p. 8).

256 [45] Hobbes's insight into the relationship between interest and ideas makes him one of the early forerunners in the study of "ideology." The best example of this is to be found in his discussion of the Catholic church and mediaeval scholasticism; *Leviathan,* v (pp. 24-25), xlvii (p. 451 ff.).

256 [46] *Ibid.,* xi (pp. 67-68). "For I doubt not, but if it had been a thing contrary to any man's right of dominion, or to the interest of men that have dominion, *that the three angles of a triangle, should be equal to two angles of a square;* that doctrine should have been, if not disputed, yet by the burning of all books of geometry, suppressed, as far as he whom it concerned was able."

257 [47] *Ibid.,* xlvi (p. 442). Hobbes, of course, did not examine the possible implication that in a system of conscious deception the deceivers must know the true norm.

257 [48] *E.W.,* Vol. I, p. 56; *Law,* II, viii, 13.

258 [49] *Cive,* iii, 31.

258 [50] *Ibid.,* xii, 6.

259 [51] *Ibid.,* ii, 1.

259 [52] *Ibid.,* xv, 17.

260 [53] *Leviathan,* iv (pp. 24-25); *Cive,* iii, 31.

260 [54] *Leviathan,* v (p. 26); xxvi (pp. 172-173); *Law,* II, i, 10; II, ix, 7; *Cive,* vi, 16. On Hobbes's scepticism and nominalism see Oakeshott's introduction to his edition of *Leviathan* and also Krook, *op. cit.*

260 [55] *E.W.,* Vol. VI, p. 220.

261 [56] *Essay Concerning Human Understanding,* III, i, 1.

261 [57] *Leviathan,* viii (p. 45).

261 [58] *E.W.,* Vol. VI, p. 251.

261 [59] *Leviathan,* xxxi (p. 241).

262 [60] *Ibid.*

263 [61] *Law,* I, xiv, 10.

263   [62] *Leviathan*, xviii (p. 120), xix (p. 124); *Cive*, Preface (p. 15).

263   [63] *Cive*, v, 4-5; *Leviathan*, xvii (pp. 111-112).

263   [64] *Ibid.*, xvii (p. 109).

264   [65] *Ibid.*, xiii (p. 83), xiv (pp. 92-93); xviii (p. 120); xxxvi (p. 285); *Law*, I, xiv, 12; II, ii, 13. This is confirmed from another direction by what Hobbes called the "cognitive or imaginative or conceptive" power of the mind. See his remarks in *Law*, I, i (8).

264   [66] *Leviathan*, xiii (pp. 82-83). If the argument is correct that the state of nature was not intended by Hobbes as simply a chronologically prior condition to civil society, but an interlude between order and restoration, it would also explain Hobbes's much-criticized theory of the laws of nature. With the exception of the law of self-preservation, all of the Hobbesian laws of nature obviously dealt with matters concerning which men had had some previous knowledge.

265   [67] *Ibid.*, xiii (p. 82).

265   [68] *Ibid.*, xii (p. 70).

265   [69] *Ibid.*, xvii (p. 112).

266   [70] *Ibid.*, xxx (p. 225).

267   [71] *Ibid.*, xxvi (p. 173).

267   [72] *Ibid.*, xiv-xv *passim*.

268   [73] The rule-character of Hobbesian society is clearly reflected in the discussion of ignorance and excuses and their relation to rules. *Ibid.*, xxvii (p. 190 ff.).

268   [74] "A Punishment is an end inflicted by public authority, on him that hath done, or omitted that which is judged by the same authority to be a transgression of the law; to the end that the will of men may thereby the better be disposed to obedience" [*Ibid.*, xxviii (p. 202)].

268   [75] *Ibid.*, xxi (p. 138).

269   [76] *Ibid.*, xiv (p. 85).

269   [77] *Ibid.*, xxvii (pp. 192-193), xxx (pp. 225-226); *Cive*, xiii, 10-11.

269   [78] *Ibid.*, iii, 6; *Law*, I, xvi, 5.

269   [79] *Leviathan*, xv (p. 93 ff.).

269   [80] *Ibid.*, xv (pp. 95-96); *Law*, I, xvi, 1-6; I, xvii, 10.

270   [81] *Cive*, iii, 26; *Law*, I, xvi; xviii, 10; *Leviathan*, v (p. 26); xxvi (p. 27).

270   [82] *Law*, II, iv, 9.

271   [83] *Leviathan*, xxx (p. 228). In *Law*, I, xvii, 7, Hobbes declared that two parties do not take their case before a judge in the hope of a "just" sentence, because "that were to make the parties judges of the sentence." Instead, they seek "equality" of treatment, that is, a decision not based on "hatred" or "favour" by the judge towards one of the parties.

See, on centralization and uniformity, *Testament politique du Cardinal de Richelieu*, ed. Louis André, 7th ed. (Paris: Laffont, 1947) p. 321 ff.; A. de Tocqueville, *L'Ancien régime*, ed. G. W. Headlam (Oxford: Clarendon, 1949) pp. 31-68; and for a continuation of these themes, Bertrand de Jouvenal, *On Power, Its Nature and the History of its Growth* (New York: Viking, 1949) Chs. 6-7, 9-10.

271   [84] *Law,* II, i, 19.

271   [85] *Leviathan,* xxx (pp. 229-232).

271   [86] *Ibid.,* xviii (p. 119). "The inequality of subjects, proceedeth from the acts of sovereign power; and therefore has no more place in the sovereign, that is to say, in a court of justice, than the inequality between kings and their subjects, in the presence of the King of Kings" [*Ibid.,* xxx (p. 226)]. One argument advanced in support of monarchy was that it introduced less inequality inasmuch as there was only one superior (*Cive,* x, 4). Note also the summary: "a city is defined to be one person made out of many men whose will by their own contracts is to be esteemed *as the wills of them all,* insomuch as he may use the *strength and faculties of each single person* for the public peace and safety" [*Ibid.,* x, 5 (Italics added)].

271   [87] *Leviathan,* xxix (p. 210).

272   [88] *Ibid.,* xv (p. 99).

272   [89] *Cive,* i, 2 (footnote).

273   [90] *Leviathan,* xiv (pp. 89-90); *Law,* I, xix, 6; II, i, 6.

273   [91] *Leviathan,* xxix (p. 210).

273   [92] *Ibid.,* xlii (pp. 355-356).

274   [93] *Ibid.,* xxxi (p. 240).

274   [94] *Ibid.,* xxxii (p. 243); xl (pp. 307-308).

274   [95] *Ibid.,* xlii (p. 237). And note Hobbes's attack on the Inquisition, *Ibid.,* xlvi (p. 448).

274   [96] *Cive,* i, 6; *Leviathan,* xiii (pp. 80-81); *Law,* I, xiv, 5.

274   [97] *Ibid.,* I, ix, 21.

275   [98] *Ibid.,* I, xix, 8.

275   [99] *Leviathan,* xxi (p. 144).

275   [100] *Ibid.,* Introduction (p. 5).

276   [101] *Ibid.,* xlii (p. 379).

276   [102] Act in Restraint of Appeals, 24 Henry VIII c. 12 (1533), as contained in G. B. Adams and H. M. Stephens, *Select Documents of English Constitutional History* (New York: Macmillan, 1935) p. 229.

276   [103] *Laws of Ecclesiastical Polity,* I, x, 8.

276   [104] *Law,* II, ii, 11; *Cive,* v, 12; vi, 14, 18.

277   [105] *Leviathan,* xxii (p. 146). "By *systems,* I understand any number of men joined in one interest or business."

277   [106] *Ibid.,* viii (p. 46). "From desire, ariseth the thought of some means we have seen produce the like of that which we aim at . . ." [*Leviathan,* iii (p. 14)]. These notions closely anticipate Hume's famous dictum that "reason is and ought to be the slave of the passions." Hume's intellectual kinship with Hobbes lies in

their common notions about interest and the relation of reason to interest. These affinities with Hobbes helped to distinguish Hume's conservatism from that of Burke. See my discussion, "Hume and Conservatism," *The American Political Science Review*, Vol. XLVIII, No. 4 (December, 1954), pp. 999-1016.

277   [107] *Leviathan*, Introduction (p. 6), vi (p. 32).

277   [108] *Ibid.*, viii (p. 42). "And because the constitution of a man's body is in continual mutation, it is impossible that all the same things should always cause in him the same appetites, and aversions: much less can all men consent, in the desire of almost any one and the same object" [*Leviathan*, vi (p. 32)].

278   [109] *Ibid.*, xi (p. 64).

278   [110] *Ibid.*, xi (pp. 63-64).

278   [111] Until very recently there had been no close study of Hobbes's theory of representation; neither Oakeshott nor Strauss have given it serious attention. The most important attempt at filling this gap is Raymond Polin, *Politique et philosophie chez Thomas Hobbes* (Paris: Presses Universitaires, 1953) p. 221 ff. In many ways this is the best general discussion of Hobbes that exists.

279   [112] This idea has several affinities with mediaeval thought and points to the need for a close study of the Aristotleian and mediaeval influences perpetuated into the Hobbesian theory of sovereignty; for example, compare the above with Aquinas, *De Regimine Principum*, Lib. I, i-ii.

279   [113] *Leviathan*, xvi (p. 107).

279   [114] *Ibid.*, xvi, xviii (pp. 105-108, 113-115).

279   [115] *Law*, II, ix, 1.

279   [116] *Law*, II, v, 1; II, ix, 1; *Cive*, x, 2, 18; *Leviathan*, xxx (pp. 227-228); *E.W.*, Vol. VI, p. 34.

279   [117] See James Mill, *Essay on Government* (Cambridge: Cambridge University Press, 1937) p. 71.

280   [118] *Cive*, x, 9.

280   [119] *Leviathan*, xxviii (p. 209); xviii (p. 112-113); *Cive*, x, 6-7.

280   [120] Adam Smith, *Theory of Moral Sentiments*, in *Works* (London, 1812) Vol. I, p. 138.

281   [121] Jeremy Bentham, *Bentham's Handbook of Political Fallacies*, ed. H. A. Larrabee (Baltimore: Johns Hopkins Press, 1952) pp. 82, 106.

281   [122] *Ibid.*, p. 110.

281   [123] *Oeuvres politiques de Benjamin Constant*, ed. C. Louandre (Paris, 1874) pp. 260-269, 281.

282   [124] The close connection between Hobbes's political philosophy and his view of science has been denied in Strauss's brilliant but overly ingenious book, *The Political Philosophy of Hobbes*. Strauss has argued that the main lines of Hobbes's political thought had been foreshadowed in his "pre-scientific" phase, when, as a "humanist," he translated Thucydides and wrote long commentaries on Aristotle's *Rhetoric*. What is troublesome about this interpretation is not only that there were precious few political comments in these writings to justify the elaborate edifice

constructed by Strauss, but that it also involves a cavalier dismissal of *A Short Tract on First Principles* which belonged to the same "humanist" period.

The *Tract* contains several of the main principles of Hobbes's scientific philosophy and, as one recent commentator has said, "the *Tract* is fairly bursting with consequences which are drawn out in Hobbes's subsequent political writings." (J. W. N. Watkins, "Philosophy and Politics in Hobbes," *The Philosophical Quarterly*, Vol. 5 (1955), pp. 125-146, at p. 128). Moreover, the *Elements of Law*, which is regarded as the earliest and least mature of Hobbes's systematic political writings, was replete with many of the scientific statements posited in the *Tract*. Finally, but of great importance, Professor Strauss' preoccupation with the "humanist" phase, and his projection of it into the later writings, has distorted Hobbes by treating his theories almost entirely as "moral" problems. Yet, as we have tried to show above, the "moral" issues were only part of the story, and not always the most important. Hobbes himself was deeply concerned with the status of knowledge and surely he was just as much intent on answering the question, "what are valid grounds for accepting one political idea rather than another?" as he was with moral evaluations. The great contribution made by Oakeshott has been to insist that Hobbes was a philosopher concerned with a whole range of genuinely philosophical problems.

282   [125] *Law*, I, i, 4-8.

282   [126] *Leviathan*, vi (p. 31).

282   [127] *A Short Tract on First Principles*, printed in Tönnies edition of *The Elements of Law* as Appendix I, p. 152.

282   [128] *Leviathan*, vi (pp. 31-32); *Law*, I, vii; *A Short Tract on First Principles*. pp. 161, 165-166.

282   [129] *Law*, I, vii, 6-7; I, ix, 1, 3, 5; *Leviathan*, xi (pp. 63-64).

282   [130] *Ibid.*, x (pp. 56-57).

283   [131] *Law*, I, viii, 4.

283   [132] *Leviathan*, x (p. 56).

283   [133] *Law*, I, xix, 10; *Cive*, v, 11.

283   [134] *Leviathan*, xiv (pp. 85-86); *Cive*, v, 11; *Law*, II, i, 7; II, i, 18-19.

284   [135] *Leviathan*, xxviii (p. 203).

284   [136] *Ibid.*, xxx (p. 227).

284   [137] *Cive*, ix, 9.

285   [138] *Leviathan*, xxi (pp. 136-137). The notion of liberty as the absence of impediments was perpetuated in the literature of classical economics where it took the form of a plea for the abolition of restraints on economic "motions." The same idea is apparent in the definition of value by the 19th century American economist, Henry Carey: value "is simply our estimate of the resistance to be overcome, before we can enter upon the possession of the thing desired." *Principles of Social Science*, 3 vols. (Philadelphia, 1858) Vol. I, p. 148. In the same tradition is the following by a contemporary social scientist: "Whatever else it may mean, freedom means that you have the power to do what you want to do, when you want to do it, and how you want to do it. And in American society the power to do what you want, when you want, how you want, requires money. Money provides power and

power provides freedom." C. W. Mills, *The Power Elite* (New York: Oxford University Press, 1957) p. 162.

285 139 *Ibid.,* xiv (p. 90); *Law,* II, i, 8, 18-19; *Cive,* v, 7.

285 140 *Ibid.,* v, 9; x, 5; *Law,* II, i, 14.

285 141 *Leviathan,* xiv (p. 90).

285 142 *Ibid.,* xlvi (p. 447).

285 143 "The hand which holds the sword is the militia of a nation; and the militia of a nation is either an army in the field or ready for the field upon occasion: wherefore this will come to what pastures you have, and what pastures you have will come to the balance of property, without which the public word is but a name or mere spitfrog" [*The Oceana and Other Works of James Harrington,* ed. John Toland (London, 1737) p. 41].

Chapter Nine

286 1 The nineteenth-century critic would have to admit that Chapter XXIV of *Leviathan* contained a typical mercantilist analysis. Nevertheless, the criticism remains valid that Hobbes did not conceive an integral relation between economic factors and political phenomena. In this he was inferior both to his predecessor, Jean Bodin, and his contemporary critic, James Harrington.

289 2 "Of the First Principles of Government" in *Essays, Moral, Political, and Literary,* ed. T. H. Green and T. H. Grose, 2 vols. (London: Longmans, 1898) Vol. I, pp. 109-110; Adam Smith, *An Inquiry into the Nature and Causes of the Wealth of Nations,* ed. E. Cannan, Modern Library (New York: Random House, 1937) Bk. V, ch. i (p. 670) (hereafter cited as *Wealth*). For a shrewd perception into this problem see the remarks of Proudhon, *Oeuvres complètes* (Paris, 1868) Vol. III, p. 43 (par. 91).

291 3 *Oeuvres complètes,* 7 vols. (Paris, 1862-1878) Vol. I, p. 427 (hereafter cited as Bastiat, *Oeuvres*).

292 4 Bastiat, *Oeuvres,* Vol. VII, pp. 27, 57-60. For the same notion in Adam Smith see *Wealth,* I, i-ii (pp. 4-9, 13 ff.). Spencer viewed the division of labor as "part of a still more general process pervading creation, inorganic as well as organic . . . [It] had neither been specially created, nor enacted by a king, but had grown up without forethought of anyone." *Essays, Scientific, Political, and Speculative,* 3 vols. (New York: Appleton, 1910) Vol. III, p. 323 (hereafter cited as *Essays*); *The Study of Sociology* (New York: Appleton, 1899) p. 65.

The sociological bearing of the classical economists has been described by A. Small, *Adam Smith and Modern Sociology* (Chicago: University of Chicago Press, 1907); G. Bryson, *Man and Society: the Scottish Inquiry of the Eighteenth Century* (Princeton: Princeton University Press, 1945). A good survey of Smith's ideas is to be found in J. Viner, "Adam Smith and Laissez Faire," *The Long View and the Short, Studies in Economic Theory and Policy* (Glencoe, Ill.: Free Press, 1958) pp. 213-245. See also the recent work by J. Cropsey, *Polity and Economy; an Interpretation of the Principles of Adam Smith* (The Hague: Nijhoff, 1957).

292 [5] *A Treatise of Human Nature*, Bk. III, ii, 8. There is an extended treatment of this theme in Elie Halévy, *Growth of Philosophic Radicalism*, tr. M. Morris (London: Faber and Faber, 1928) pp. 199-200.

292 [6] Spencer, *The Study of Sociology*, p. 64.

292 [7] K. Mannheim, *Essays on the Sociology of Culture* (London: Routledge, 1956) pp. 91-170; S. F. Nadel, *Foundations of Social Anthropology* (London: Cohen and West, 1951) p. 55. ("The blunders of the anthropologist will be 'better' blunders.")

293 [8] Typical of what may be called the "vulgar conception of liberalism" are the following: R. Kirk, *The Conservative Mind* (Chicago: Regnery, 1953) pp. 21, 24, 108; P. Viereck, *Conservatism Revisited* (London: Lehmann, 1950) pp. xi-xii; K. Mannheim, *Ideology and Utopia* (New York, 1936) pp. 199-202; R. Niebuhr, *The Nature and Destiny of Man*, 1 vol. ed. (New York: Scribner's, 1947) Vol. I, pp. 102-107; Vol. II, p. 240; *Christianity and Power Politics* (New York: Scribner's, 1940) pp. 84, 92-93, 102-103; W. Röpke, *The Social Crisis of Our Time* (Chicago: University of Chicago Press, 1950) pp. 48-53; J. H. Hallowell, *Main Currents in Modern Political Thought* (New York: Holt, 1950) pp. 110-115, 620-624, 669-674; E. H. Carr, *The Twenty Years' Crisis 1919-1939* (London: Macmillan, 1951) Chs. 3, 4; H. Morgenthau, *Scientific Man and Power Politics* (Chicago: University of Chicago Press, 1946) Chs. 2, 8.

293 [9] On this distinction see G. H. Sabine, "The Two Democratic Traditions," *Philosophical Review*, Vol. LXI (1952) pp. 451-474 and, more generally, J. L. Talmon, *The Rise of Totalitarian Democracy* (Boston: Beacon, 1952) pp. 1-13, 249-255.

294 [10] Cited in B. Groethuysen, *Philosophie de la Révolution française précédé de Montesquieu*, 4th ed. (Paris: Gallimard, 1956) p. 157.

294 [11] Frank I. Schechter, "The Early History of the Tradition of the Constitution," *American Political Science Review*, Vol. IX (1915) pp. 707-734; Edward S. Corwin, "The Constitution as Instrument and Symbol," *American Political Science Review*, Vol. XXX (1936) pp. 1071-1085; Max Lerner, "Constitution and Court as Symbols," *Yale Law Review*, Vol. XLVI (1937), p. 1290.

294 [12] The best biography is the most recent: Maurice Cranston, *John Locke* (London: Longmans, 1957).

295 [13] Cited in A. C. Fraser, ed., *John Locke, An Essay Concerning Human Understanding*, 2 vols. (Oxford: Clarendon Press, 1894) Vol. I, p. xviii.

295 [14] *Essay Concerning Human Understanding*, Epistle to the Reader, Vol. I, p. 14 of Fraser's edition. All subsequent quotations from the *Essay* will be from this edition and it will be cited as *ECHU*.

296 [15] *ECHU*, Epistle to the Reader, Vol. I, p. 9; II, ii, 2.

296 [16] *ECHU*, II, i, 2-4; III, xi, 23.

296 [17] *ECHU*, II, ii, 2; II, i, 24.

296 [18] J. S. Mill, *Three Essays on Religion*, 3rd ed. (London: Longmans, 1885) p. 8.

296 [19] *Theaetetus* 176b; *Nichomachean Ethics*, x, 1117b, 33.

297 [20] Lord King, *The Life of John Locke, with Extracts from His Correspondence, Journals and Common Place Books*, 2 vols., 2nd ed. (London, 1830) Vol. I, p. 210; *ECHU*, Introduction, vi; IV, xiv, 1-2.

297   ²¹ King, *op. cit.*, Vol. I, p. 161; *ECHU*, Introduction, 7; IV, iii, 24; and the discussion in R. I. Aaron, *John Locke*, 2nd ed. (Oxford: Clarendon, 1955) p. 238; Holbach as cited in Talmon, *op. cit.*, p. 273.

297   ²² "Government, morals, habits everything has to be rebuilt. What a magnificent site for the architects! What a grand opportunity of making use of all the fine and excellent ideas that had remained speculative, of employing so many materials that could not be used before, of rejecting so many others that had been obstructions for centuries and which one had been forced to use." Cited in F. A. Hayek, *The Counter-Revolution of Science* (Glencoe, Ill.: Free Press, 1952) p. 109.

298   ²³ Cited in H. R. Fox-Bourne, *The Life of John Locke*, 2 vols. (New York: King, 1876) Vol. I, p. 396.

298   ²⁴ Adam Smith, *Theory of Moral Sentiments*, in *Works* (London, 1812) Vol. I, p. 516. I have used the sixth edition of *The Theory of Moral Sentiments* and hereafter it will be cited as *TMS*.

298   ²⁵ Fox-Bourne, *op. cit.*, Vol. I, pp. 224-226; Lord King, *op. cit.*, Vol. I, pp. 162-165; *ECHU*, IV, xi, 8.

298   ²⁶ *TMS*, p. 417.

299   ²⁷ Cited in Fraser, *op. cit.*, Vol. I, pp. xxxi-xxxii.

299   ²⁸ *TMS*, pp. 407-411. See also Benjamin Constant, *Oeuvres politiques*, ed. C. Louandre (Paris, 1874) p. 402; and Bentham, "Anarchical Fallacies," *Works*, ed. J. Bowring, 11 vols. (Edinburgh, 1838-1843) Vol. II, p. 498.

Smith's attack on the aesthetic impulse in political thought and action was in reality part of his attempt to redefine the nature of political aesthetics, and in so doing, to reduce the legislative role of political philosophy. He insisted that government could be properly an object of beauty, that "we take pleasure in beholding the perfection of so grand and beautiful a system, and we are uneasy until we remove any obstruction that can in the least disturb or encumber the regularity of its motions." Beauty, however, was not associated with the end of an activity but with the means. In short, an object or an activity could be designated as beautiful insofar as it was functionally useful; that is, "fitted either to promote or to disturb the happiness both of the individual and of the society." Although in political matters beauty came to be almost synonymous with efficiency, it was never identified as the main end. An aesthetic motive might cause men to seek out the "obstructions" preventing the "several wheels of the machine of government" from moving with "more harmony and smoothness, without grating upon one another," but an aesthetic objective ought not to be pursued in disregard of the suffering of men. (*TMS*, pp. 309-323.) Bastiat, too, warned against those theorists who viewed humanity as *"une matière inerte recevant du pouvoir la vie, l'organisation, la moralité et la richesse . . ."* (*Oeuvres*, Vol. IV, pp. 366-367.)

The denial of architectonics in theory and practice was also a part of Burke's conservatism. What is perhaps less understood is that this denial passed into modern sociology. This can be seen by examining Durkheim's appreciation of these elements in Montesquieu's thought. See his essay *Montesquieu et Rousseau, Précurseurs de la Sociologie* (Paris: Rivière, 1953) pp. 84-85, 96. This tendency has not been universally accepted, for in the writings of the late Karl Mannheim, for example, there is clearly expressed the belief that to sociology falls the task of supplying a comprehensive program for the reform of society and that political action can and must operate on a grand scale. See especially his *Man and Society in an Age of Reconstruction* (London: Routledge, 1951).

299   [29] *Bentham's Handbook of Political Fallacies,* ed. H. A. Larrabee, p. 195.

299   [30] *An Introduction to the Principles of Morals and Legislation* (New York: Hafner, 1948) Preface, p. xxxi (italics in the original) (hereafter cited as *Morals and Legislation*). See also Bastiat, *Oeuvres,* 4th ed. (Paris, 1878) Vol. IV, pp. 364-366.

300   [31] Arnold, *Culture and Anarchy,* ed. J. D. Wilson (Cambridge: Cambridge University Press, 1932) pp. 19, 36; Bastiat, *Oeuvres,* Vol. IV, p. 350. See also Guizot's essay, *Democracy in France* (New York, 1849) p. 81.

301   [32] Smith, *Wealth,* I, vi, xi (pp. 52, 248); II, i-ii, iii (pp. 265-279, 324-325); IV, vii (p. 566); and note how society is epitomized in terms of capital (*ibid.,* I, iii, pp. 320-321); IV, iii (p. 464). See also J. R. McCulloch, *The Principles of Political Economy* (Edinburgh, 1825) pp. 244-246 (hereafter cited as *PPE*); Nassau Senior, *Political Economy* (London, 1850) p. 81 (hereafter cited as *PE*); J. S. Mill, *Principles of Political Economy,* ed. Sir W. J. Ashley (London: Longmans, 1920) II, iii, 1 (p. 23) (hereafter cited as *PPE*).

301   [33] From a paper of Smith's cited by Dugald Stewart, *Essays on Philosophical Subjects* (London, 1795) p. lxxxi. See also the study of W. Cropsey, *Polity and Economy, op. cit.*

301   [34] Spencer, *Essays,* Vol. III, pp. 450-451; *Jeremy Bentham's Economic Writings,* ed. W. Stark, 3 vols. (London: Allen and Unwin, 1952-1954) Vol. III, p. 333 (hereafter cited as *Econ. Wr.*).

301   [35] Smith, *Wealth,* I, vii-viii; IV, ii.

301   [36] Bastiat, *Oeuvres,* Vol. IV, pp. 360-361.

302   [37] Bentham, *Econ. Wr.,* Vol. I, p. 223.

302   [38] Mably, *De la Législation,* 2 vols. (Lausanne, 1777) Vol. II, p. 31; and see the biography by E. A. Whitfield, *Gabriel Bonnot de Mably* (London: Routledge, 1930); also the discussion by Talmon, *op. cit.,* p. 54 ff.; Friedrich Engels, *Herr Eugen Dühring's Revolution in Science,* Marxist Library (New York: International Publishers, n.d.) p. 318. Bastiat (*Oeuvres,* Vol. IV, p. 367 ff.) collected a mass of quotations to illustrate the same sort of dangers in radical thought that Talmon has recently pointed out.

302   [39] *The Works of John Locke,* 9 vols., 12th ed. (London, 1824) Vol. X, pp. 10, 42.

303   [40] Smith, *Wealth,* IV, Introduction (p. 397).

303   [41] McCulloch, *PPE,* pp. 7-9.

303   [42] McCulloch, *PPE,* p. 23; J. B. Say, *A Treatise on Political Economy,* translated from the fourth edition by C. R. Prinsep and C. Biddle (Philadelphia: Lippincott, 1857) p. xv; *Traité d'économie politique,* 2 vols. (Paris, 1803) Vol. I, p. ii.

304   [43] Cited in Lionel Robbins, *The Theory of Economic Policy in English Classical Political Economy* (London: Macmillan, 1952) pp. 175-176. See also Bastiat, *Oeuvres,* Vol. IV, p. 388.

305   [44] For the documentation of these points see the following: Smith, *Wealth,* II, iii (pp. 315-326); IV, ii (p. 424); *TMS,* p. 405; *Lectures on Justice, Police, Revenue,*

and Arms, ed. E. Cannan (Oxford: Clarendon Press, 1896) pp. 1-4; T. R. Malthus, *An Essay on Population,* 2 vols. (London: Dent, 1914) Vol. II, pp. 87, 192-193; Senior, *PE,* pp. 76, 81; J. S. Mill, *Considerations on Representative Government* (London: Oxford University Press, 1912) Ch. III (p. 187), VII (p. 249); Spencer, *Essays,* Vol. III, p. 313. The unproductive nature of government became a favorite theme with Saint-Simon; see the famous passage as translated in *Henri Comte de Saint-Simon, Selected Writings,* ed. F. M. H. Markham (New York: Macmillan, 1952) pp. 72-73, and compare to Bentham, *Morals and Legislation,* p. 5 (fn.). An important clue showing the spread of economic categories was in Smith's appropriation of the old idea of the organic body politic for economic purposes, *Wealth,* IV, vii, ix (pp. 571-572, 638).

305   [45] *Two Treatises of Government,* II, 12, 13. Hereafter all references to this will be cited either as *First* or *Second Treatise.*

306   [46] *Second Treatise,* 4, 22.

306   [47] The two conditions were, Locke noted, "as far distant as a state of peace, goodwill, mutual assistance, and preservation, and a state of enmity, malice, violence, and mutual destruction are one from another." *Second Treatise,* 19.

307   [48] See, for example, J. Mabbott, *The State and the Citizen* (London: Hutchinson, 1948) pp. 20-21; L. Strauss, *Natural Right and History,* pp. 221-222, 227-233. A sharply critical, and generally correct, attack on the Strauss interpretation has been made by J. W. Yolton, "Locke on the Law of Nature," *Philosophical Review,* Vol. LXVII (1958), pp. 477-498.

307   [49] *Second Treatise,* 128; *Works,* Vol. V, pp. 224, 248. For Troeltsch's distinction, *The Social Teachings of the Christian Churches,* tr. O. Wyon, 2 vols. (London: Allen and Unwin, 1931) Vol. I, pp. 152-161, 343 ff.

307   [50] *Second Treatise,* 123-124, 136; Fox-Bourne, *op. cit.,* Vol. I, p. 174.

307   [51] *Second Treatise,* 4.

308   [52] *Second Treatise,* 87, 136 (emphasis added).

308   [53] *Second Treatise,* 243. Locke is admittedly inconsistent here. Earlier he had argued that through the legislative power the members "are united and combined into one coherent living body" and that "this is the soul that gives form, life, and unity to the commonwealth." (*Second Treatise,* 212.) Later, however, he argues that when the legislative is dissolved society can still act.

309   [54] *A Defense of Liberty Against Tyrants* (*Vindiciae contra Tyrannos*), ed. H. J. Laski (New York: Harcourt, Brace, n.d.) pp. 93, 97-100, 102-106, 109-111, 126-136; Calvin, *Institutes,* IV, xx, 31; *Opera,* Vol. XXIX, pp. 557, 636-637; C. J. Friedrich, ed., *Politica Methodice Digesta of Johannes Althusius* (Cambridge, Mass.: Harvard University Press, 1932) xix, 7; xx, 20-21. See the discussion in P. Mesnard, *L'Essor de la philosophie politique au XVIᵉ siècle,* pp. 340 ff., 593 ff.

309   [55] *Second Treatise,* 96-97, 209, 230. Locke's doctrine of majority rule is discussed at length, and in extreme fashion by W. Kendall, *John Locke and the Doctrine of Majority Rule* (Urbana, Ill.: University of Illinois Press, 1941). Kendall's interpretation has been criticized, but unsatisfactorily, by J. W. Gough, *John Locke's Political Philosophy* (Oxford: Clarendon Press, 1950) p. 24 ff.

309   [56] *Second Treatise,* 96-97.

309   [57] *Second Treatise*, 151.

310   [58] *Second Treatise*, 120-121, 131.

311   [59] *Second Treatise*, 119-122. It ought to be added that Locke's argument concerning the obligation of those who resided for only a brief time or who used the roads was probably intended to cover the landless members of society also. His failure to devote any sustained attention to the obligations of this group affords a striking confirmation of our thesis that he conceived political power to depend on social arrangements; that is, on the social power of the propertied.

311   [60] This was a favorite argument with eighteenth-century radicals like Rousseau, Paine and Jefferson. See Rousseau's *Social Contract*, Bk. I, ch. ii, iv and the letters of Jefferson in A. Koch and W. Peden, eds., *The Life and Selected Writings of Thomas Jefferson* (New York: Random House, 1944) pp. 448, 675.

312   [61] *Second Treatise*, 73.

312   [62] "Did one generation of men go off the stage at once, and another succeed, as is the case with silk worms and butterflies, the new race . . . might voluntarily . . . establish their own form of civil polity without regard to the laws or precedents which prevailed among their ancestors." Hume, *Essays*, Vol. I, p. 452.

312   [63] *Second Treatise*, 3.

312   [64] Cited in Robbins, *op. cit.*, p. 36.

313   [65] Spencer, *Essays*, Vol. III, p. 414; L. von Mises, *Bureaucracy* (New Haven: Yale University Press, 1944) pp. 34, 36-38, 53; F. A. Hayek, *The Road to Serfdom* (Sydney: Macmillan, 1944) pp. 27, 40, 44-45, 52.

313   [66] *Rights of Man*, Pt. II, ch. i.

313   [67] See the excellent discussion in Halévy, *op. cit.*, p. 199 ff. A good recent analysis of Godwin is contained in D. H. Monro, *Godwin's Moral Philosophy* (London: Oxford University Press, 1953).

314   [68] H. J. Laski, *A Grammar of Politics*, 4th ed. (London: Allen and Unwin, 1938) pp. 27-29, 35-37; *Authority in the Modern State* (New Haven: Yale University Press, 1927) pp. 65, 92.

314   [69] J. N. Figgis, *Churches in the Modern State* (London: Longmans, 1913) pp. 41-42; G. D. H. Cole, *Social Theory*, 2nd ed. (London: Methuen, 1921) pp. 128-143. There is a general discussion of these thinkers and Laski in H. M. Magid, *English Political Pluralism* (New York: Columbia University Press, 1941).

315   [70] von Mises, *Bureaucracy*, pp. 13, 93.

315   [71] *ECHU*, II, xxi, 31, 33, 40.

315   [72] *ECHU*, II, xx, 6; II, xxi, 34.

315   [73] *TMS*, p. 317.

316   [74] *Second Treatise*, 26 and especially 35; *Essays on the Law of Nature*, ed. W. von Leyden (Oxford: Clarendon Press, 1954) p. 211; Lord King, *op. cit.*, Vol. I, p. 162. Von Leyden's edition has been ably discussed by J. W. Lenz in *Philosophy and Phenomenological Research*, Vol. XVI (1955-1956) pp. 105-114.

316   [75] McCullogh, *PPE*, pp. 61-62.

316   [76] *Principles of Social Science*, 3 vols. (Philadelphia, 1858-1859) Vol. I, p. 186.

317   [77] J. S. Mill, *PPE*, I, v, 6 (p. 74). *"Comment se fait-il qu'après avoir échangé leurs services, sans contrainte, sans spoliation, sur le pied de* l'équivalence, *chaque homme puisse se dire avec vérité: Je détruis en un jour plus que je ne pourrais créer en un siècle."* Bastiat, *Oeuvres*, Vol. VI, p. 353.

317   [78] *Essay on Population*, Vol. I, pp. 6, 12, 153, 173; Vol. II, pp. 3-12, 151-157. There is a striking vignette of Malthus by J. M. Keynes, *Essays and Sketches in Biography* (New York: Meridian, 1956) p. 11 ff.

317   [79] J. S. Mill, *Three Essays on Religion*, pp. 20-21, 29. Arnold's lines are also appropriate here:

> "Nature is cruel, man is sick of blood . . .
> Nature and man can never be fast friends . . ."

The Poems of Matthew Arnold, 1840-1867, p. 60.

317   [80] John Dewey, *The Influence of Darwinism on Philosophy, and Other Essays* (New York: Holt, 1910) pp. 68, 72-73.

318   [81] S. Freud, *Civilization and Its Discontents*, tr. Joan Riviere (London: Hogarth, 1949) pp. 45-50, 63, 72-74, 76, 92-93.

318   [82] J. S. Mill, *PPE*, II, xiii, 1 (pp. 373-374).

318   [83] J. S. Mill, *Three Essays on Religion*, pp. 46, 56.

318   [84] Locke, *Essays on the Law of Nature*, p. 211.

319   [85] J. S. Mill, *PPE*, II, i, 1 (pp. 199-200). The last sentence of the quotation is from the first edition of *PPE;* see p. 200, fn. 1, of the Ashley volume. The persistence of the belief that economics deals with fixed and scarce quantities is to be found in the following remarks of an eminent contemporary economist:

> "We [i.e., mankind] have been turned out of Paradise. We have neither eternal life nor unlimited means of gratification. Everywhere we turn, if we choose one thing we must relinquish others, in different circumstances, we would wish not to have relinquished. Scarcity of means to satisfy given ends is an almost ubiquitous condition of human behaviour.
> "Here, then, is the unity of subject of Economic Science, the forms assumed by human behaviour in disposing of scarce means." Lionel Robbins, *The Nature and Significance of Economic Science* (London: Macmillan and Company, Ltd. and St. Martin's Press, Inc., 1932) p. 15.

319   [86] *L'ordre naturel et essentiel des sociétés politiques* (Paris: Geuthner, 1910), Discours préliminaire, pp. v-vi.

319   [87] Bentham, *Econ. Wr.*, Vol. I, pp. 213, 225.

319   [88] Smith, *Wealth*, IV, vii (pp. 592-597); Bentham, *Econ. Wr.*, Vol. I, pp. 228-229, 234 ff., 246 ff.; III, p. 324; Constant, *Oeuvres politiques*, p. 240 ff.

319   [89] Smith, *Wealth*, I, viii (pp. 69-73); Senior, *PE*, p 153.

320   [90] Locke, *Second Treatise*, 35.

320   [91] Bastiat, *Oeuvres*, Vol. IV, p. 331; VI, pp. 266-267.

320   [92] McCulloch, *PPE*, p. 7; Smith, *Wealth*, I, v (p. 33); Senior, *PE*, p. 152; Bentham, *Econ. Wr.*, Vol. I, pp. 118-119.

320   [93] Senior, *PE*, p. 26. The viewpoints of Ricardo and Malthus are discussed in C. Gide and C. Rist, *A History of Economic Doctrines*, tr. R. Richards (Boston: Heath, n.d.) pp. 120-152. J. S. Mill's ideas are in *PPE*, I, xii (p. 176 ff.).

320   [94] *Sketch for a Historical Picture of the Progress of the Human Mind*, tr. J. Barraclough (London: Weidenfeld and Nicholson, 1955) p. 199; *Essay on the First Principles of Government* (London, 1768) p. 8.

321   [95] See the perceptive article by Duncan Forbes, " 'Scientific' Whiggism: Adam Smith and John Millar," *Cambridge Journal*, Vol. VII (1954), pp. 643-670.

321   [96] Smith, *Wealth*, I, viii-ix.

321   [97] Malthus, *Essay on Population*, Vol. I, p. 5 ff.; D. Ricardo, *The Principles of Political Economy and Taxation* (London and New York: Everyman, 1911) p. 264; McCulloch, *PPE*, p. 383; J. S. Mill, *PPE*, IV, vi, 2 (p. 751).

321   [98] J. S. Mill, *PPE*, VI, iv, 4 (p. 731); IV, vi, 1-2 (pp. 746-751).

322   [99] *Second Treatise*, 27, 32-33, 35-36, 38, 45.

322   [100] *Wealth*, I, x (p. 99); IV, v (p. 497); ix (pp. 650-651).

322   [101] Constant, *Oeuvres politiques*, p. 288. There is a lively treatment of Constant's ideas from a viewpoint sympathetic to de Maistre in Dominique Bagge, *Les idées politiques en France sous la restauration* (Paris: Presses Universitaires, 1952) Pt. I, Ch. I.

323   [102] Malthus, *Essay on Population*, Vol. I, pp. 5-6, 8-9, 14, 49, 53, 60-65, 242, 308; Vol. II, pp. 18-21, 190; Bentham, *Econ. Wr.*, Vol. I, pp. 110-111; Vol. III, p. 430; Senior, *PE*, p. 41. These fears were not prominent in the United States. Jefferson, for example, employed the Malthusian thesis to contrast "the man of the old world . . . crowded within limits either small or overcharged, and steeped in the vices which that situation generates" to the man of the new world who moved easily and unconfined. A. Koch and W. Peden, ed., *op. cit.*, pp. 574, 633-634.

323   [103] *PPE*, II, ii, 6 (p. 233); IV, vi, 2 (pp. 748-750).

323   [104] Locke, *Works*, Vol. IV, p. 71; Bentham, *Handbook of Political Fallacies*, pp. 156-157; and the correspondence between the elder Mill and Ricardo, where the former remarked that "every body you meet with" agreed that "a great struggle between the two orders, the rich and the poor, is in this country commenced." *The Works and Correspondence of David Ricardo*, ed. P. Sraffa and M. Dobb, 10 vols. (Cambridge: Cambridge University Press, 1951-1955) Vol. IX, pp. 41-43. The relation of Locke's ideas to capitalism and to class conflict is ably discussed from a moderate Marxian viewpoint by C. P. Macpherson, "Locke on Capitalist Appropriation," *Western Political Quarterly*, Vol. IV (1951), pp. 550-566; "The Social Bearing of Locke's Political Theory," *Ibid.*, Vol. VII (1954), pp. 1-22.

323   [105] *An Essay on Government*, with an introduction by Sir Ernest Barker (Cambridge: Cambridge University Press, 1937) p. 3.

324   [106] McCulloch, *PPE*, p. 75.

324   [107] Smith, *Wealth*, V, i (p. 670); McCulloch, *PPE*, pp. 74-76, 82.

324   [108] *ECHU*, II, xxi, 46.

325   [109] Smith, *TMS*, pp. 7-10, 182-183; Bentham, *Deontology*, Vol. II, pp. 112, 115, and see B. Willey, *Nineteenth Century Studies* (London: Chatto and Windus, 1949)

Ch. V; *Handbook of Political Fallacies*, pp. 236-237. Bowring's remark on Bentham is appropriate in this context: "In order to stimulate him to exertion, it was necessary that something be *done* be at least the ultimate object." *Works*, Vol. I, p. ix.

325   [110] *ECHU*, II, xxi, 51-53.

325   [111] McCulloch, *PPE*, pp. 349, 401; J. S. Mill, *PPE*, I, xiii, 1 (pp. 189-190).

325   [112] J. S. Mill, *PPE*, p. 106, fn. 1; and, to the same effect, Spencer's essay, "The American," *Essays*, Vol. III, p. 471 ff.

326   [113] *Deontology*, Vol. I, p. 191 and also pp. 25, 28-29, 59, 68; *Morals and Legislation*, p. 3.

326   [114] James Mill, *Essay on Government*, p. 4.

326   [115] J. S. Mill, *Autobiography* (London: Oxford University Press, 1924) p. 40.

326   [116] Bentham, *Works*, Vol. V, p. 266.

326   [117] *Principles of Legislation*, ed. C. M. Atkinson, 2 vols. (London: Oxford University Press, 1914) Vol. I, p. 164.

326   [118] *Essay on Population*, Vol. II, p. 12.

327   [119] *Leviathan*, Ch. VI (p. 31 of Oakeshott edition).

327   [120] *Second Treatise*, 93, 123.

327   [121] *ECHU*, I, ii, 3; II, vii, 3-5; II, x, 3, 5.

327   [122] *A Dissertation on Liberty and Necessity, Pleasure and Pain*, Facsimile Text Society Edition (New York: Columbia University Press, 1930) pp. 16-20. In *Deontology* Bentham defined happiness as "the possession of pleasure with the exemption from pain." Vol. I, p. 17. And see Bastiat, *Oeuvres*, Vol. VI, pp. 622, 628-636.

327   [123] Smith, *TMS*, pp. 208-209.

327   [124] *Deontology*, Vol. I, pp. 14-17; *Econ. Wr.*, Vol. I, p. 102; Vol. III, pp. 103, 422.

328   [125] *Econ. Wr.*, Vol. III, pp. 435-437; *Morals and Legislation*, Ch. IV, XIV; *Theory of Legislation*, ed. C. K. Ogden (London: Routledge, 1931) p. 8 ff., 322 ff.

328   [126] Senior, *PE*, pp. 95-101; Spencer, *Essays*, Vol. III, pp. 449-450; Bastiat, *Oeuvres*, Vol. VI, pp. 62-64, 88, 266-267.

328   [127] *TMS*, pp. 370-371; *Wealth*, II, iii (p. 325); Bentham, *Econ. Wr.*, Vol. I, p. 239; III, p. 348; *Morals and Legislation*, Preface, p. xxv (fn.): "It is worse to lose than simply not to gain."

328   [128] *Second Treatise*, 149.

329   [129] Bentham, *Econ. Wr.*, Vol. III, p. 427.

329   [130] "The thought which have future consequences for their object are called expectations; and upon these expectations no small part of a man's happiness depends.
        "If pleasure is anticipated, and fails of being produced, a positive pain takes place of the anticipation." Bentham, *Deontology*, Vol. II, p. 107.

329   [131] *Theory of Legislation*, p. 111.

329   [132] *Deontology*, Vol. I, pp. 236-237; II, p. 108.

329   ¹³³ Cited in Robbins, *The Theory of Economic Policy in English Classical Political Economy*, p. 63.

329   ¹³⁴ Locke alluded to the insecurities of social status in a letter cautioning a friend that "mismanagement or neglect of your temporal affairs" will cause a "fall" from "your rank and station." Cited in Fox-Bourne, *op. cit.*, p. 396.

330   ¹³⁵ Smith, *TMS*, pp. 80-84.

330   ¹³⁶ Smith, *TMS*, pp. 370-371.

330   ¹³⁷ See Strauss' discussion of Locke in *Natural Right and History*, pp. 206-207.

330   ¹³⁸ King, *op. cit.*, Vol. I, p. 181.

330   ¹³⁹ Smith, *TMS*, pp. 101-102; Bentham, *Deontology*, Vol. I, pp. 189-190.

331   ¹⁴⁰ C. S. Davies as cited in J. L. Blau, ed., *Social Theories of Jacksonian Democracy, Representative Writings of the Period, 1825-1850* (New York: Hafner, 1947) p. 52.

331   ¹⁴¹ Smith, *TMS*, pp. 369-380.

331   ¹⁴² Smith, *Wealth*, IV, vi (pp. 507-509); Senior, *PE*, p. 27.

331   ¹⁴³ Bentham, *Econ. Wr.*, Vol. III, pp. 311-312, 327; *Theory of Legislation*, pp. 102-157.

331   ¹⁴⁴ *Wealth*, V, ii (p. 778).

332   ¹⁴⁵ Locke, *Works*, Vol. VI, p. 11; *Second Treatise*, 125, 128, 136; and the discussion of moral laws as "curbs and restraints" to "exorbitant desires." *ECHU*, I, ii, 13.

332   ¹⁴⁶ *Essays on the Law of Nature*, p. 207.

332   ¹⁴⁷ For evidence of these notions see the following: Smith, *TMS*, pp. 270-271, 518-519, 567-569; Hume, *An Enquiry Concerning the Principles of Morals* (LaSalle, Ill.: Open Court, 1938) I (pp. 4-5); *Treatise of Human Nature*, Everyman edition, 2 vols., III, i (Vol. II, pp. 165 ff.); Bentham, *Handbook of Political Fallacies*, p. 213.

333   ¹⁴⁸ Smith, *TMS*, p. 267; Bentham, *Econ. Wr.*, Vol. I, p. 226; Vol. III, p. 427.

333   ¹⁴⁹ Compare *TMS*, pp. 129, 146-147, with *Wealth*, IV, ii (p. 423).

333   ¹⁵⁰ Senior, *PE*, pp. 58-60, 69, 80, 89, 139-140, 152, 185; Bentham, *Deontology*, Vol. I, pp. 130-142, 160; Vol. II, pp. 14, 51-52; Smith, *TMS*, pp. 246-249, 252-254, 414-418, 464; J. S. Mill, *PPE*, II, xv, I (p. 405).

334   ¹⁵¹ *Econ. Wr.*, Vol. I, p. 154.

334   ¹⁵² Malthus, *Essay on Population*, Vol. I, p. 159.

334   ¹⁵³ *Essays on the Law of Nature*, p. 119; see also, *The Reasonableness of Christianity*, in Locke's *Works*, Vol. VI, p. 112.

334   ¹⁵⁴ *Essays on the Law of Nature*, p. 189.

335   ¹⁵⁵ *Essays on the Law of Nature*, pp. 111, 147-149, 161-165, 177, 199; and see the excellent discussion by J. W. Yolton, *John Locke and the Way of Ideas* (London: Oxford University Press, 1956).

335   ¹⁵⁶ King, *op. cit.*, Vol. I, p. 225; Fraser, *ECHU*, Introduction, Vol. I, pp. xxxi-xxxii; *ECHU*, III, xi, 16; IV, iii, 18.

335   ¹⁵⁷ *Second Treatise*, 124-125, 136.

335   ^{158} *Works,* Vol. VI, pp. 135-139; and compare Jefferson's letter to Rush, especially the summary at the end: Koch and Peden, *op. cit.,* p. 570.

336   ^{159} *Works,* Vol. VI, pp. 157-158.

336   ^{160} See the correspondence between Locke and Molyneux cited in Fraser, *ECHU,* Vol. I, p. 65 fn. 2.

336   ^{161} *Works,* Vol. VI, p. 146.

337   ^{162} *ECHU,* I, ii, 8.

337   ^{163} *Second Treatise,* 88; *Works,* Vol. V, p. 43.

338   ^{164} *Essays on the Law of Nature,* p. 207.

338   ^{165} *Second Treatise,* 241-242.

339   ^{166} *Econ. Wr.,* Vol. III, pp. 421-423, 433; and see Robbins, *op. cit.,* p. 13.

339   ^{167} Smith, *Wealth,* IV, ii (pp. 421-423); IV, v (p. 497).

339   ^{168} *Utilitarianism,* Ch. IV in *Utilitarianism, Liberty and Representative Government* (London and New York: Dent, 1910) pp. 32-33; and see the discussion by J. Plamenatz, *The English Utilitarians* (Oxford: Blackwell, 1949) pp. 135 ff. and the analysis by A. J. Ayer, "The Principle of Utility," *Philosophical Essays* (London: Macmillan, 1954) pp. 250-270.

340   ^{169} *Works,* Vol. V, pp. 26, 28, 40-42, 44.

340   ^{170} *Works,* Vol. V, p. 28.

340   ^{171} Cited in Halévy, *op. cit.,* p. 118.

340   ^{172} *Fabian Essays,* Jubilee edition (London: Allen and Unwin, 1948) p. 42.

340   ^{173} *Works,* Vol. V, pp. 22, 26. For an interesting anticipation of this argument see the selections from Roger Williams in A. S. P. Woodhouse, *Puritanism and Liberty,* pp. 267 ff.

Locke's argument was also interesting for illustrating a tendency the reverse of that implied by the famous Weber-Tawney thesis regarding the role of Protestantism in rationalizing behavioral patterns conducive to capitalism. In Locke's case it had been the other way around: economic practices were exploited to justify religious policy. We find these confusions between economics and religion nicely exhibited in Smith's *Wealth of Nations* where he seemingly breaks off economic analysis to discuss the question of whether the best religious policy was to tolerate several small sects or to favor a single national church. It quickly becomes apparent, however, that economic analysis has not been interrupted, for so strongly have economic ways of thought come to dominate Smith's outlook that he is unable to view the problem of religious policy other than in terms of the classical theory of economic competition. The choice which he finally presents is not between two types of religious organization, but between alternative economic models. In sketching his argument all we need do is to add the relevant economic notions to his discussion of religious groups and the result is two perfectly parallel lines.

The best arrangement, according to Smith, was one where every man was free "to chuse his own priest and his own religion as he thought proper" (in much the same way that the consumer is permitted a free choice among competing sellers). Admittedly the effect of this form of freedom would be to increase the number of sects (i.e., the number of sellers), yet this would lead to far fewer evils than either the situation where one sect alone was recognized (as in monopoly), or where two or three sects, "acting by concert," dominated religious life (in the manner of merchants conspiring to set prices or wages). Finally, where numerous small sects flourished in competition with each other, the religious zeal of the leaders would be moderated because "no one could be considerable enough to disturb the public tranquillity" (just as competition among small-scale producers operated to thwart the self-interest of one from becoming dominant). And in the same way that competition between entrepreneurs issued in a common good intended by none, religious rivalry unwittingly produced a religion of "good temper and moderation." *Wealth*, V, i (pp. 744-746).

340   [174] *ECHU*, IV, xi, 1.

341   [175] Bentham, *Deontology*, Vol. I, pp. 125-126; Vol. II, pp. 45-46, 136, 156.

341   [176] Bentham explicitly discussed the diminishing importance of Christian ethical sanctions in *Deontology*, Vol. I, p. 107.

341   [177] *Econ. Wr.*, Vol. III, p. 425; *Handbook of Political Fallacies*, p. 236.

341   [178] *Handbook of Political Fallacies*, pp. 235-236.

341   [179] *First Treatise*, 92; *Second Treatise*, 6, 27-41.

342   [180] McCulloch, *PPE*, pp. 115, 319.

342   [181] Senior, *PE*, p. 187.

342   [182] Bentham, *Econ. Wr.*, Vol. III, p. 430. A similar viewpoint was reflected in Bastiat's remark that the only method mankind has hit upon to avoid the pain of labor is *"de jouir du travail d'autrui."* *Oeuvres*, Vol. IV, p. 331.

343   [183] *The Essence of Laughter and Other Essays, Journals, and Letters*, ed. P. Quennell (New York: Meridian, 1956) p. 48.

343   [184] *ECHU*, II, xxviii, 7-12.

344   [185] The sub-title of the work runs: "An Essay towards an Analysis of the Principles by which Men naturally judge concerning the Conduct and Character, First of their Neighbors, and Afterwards of themselves." A useful discussion of Smith's theory of morals is Glenn H. Morrow, *The Ethical and Economic Theories of Adam Smith* (New York: Longmans, 1923).

344   [186] *TMS*, pp. 188-190.

345   [187] *TMS*, pp. 190-192.

345   [188] *TMS*, pp. 36, 127-128.

345   [189] *TMS*, pp. 142-144, 185, 203-205, 273-275.

346   [190] *Deontology*, Vol. I, pp. 32-33, 118-120; Vol. II, pp. 160-166, 263, 269, 295; Smith, *TMS*, pp. 526-527.

347   [191] Locke's contract specifically provided for the substitution of society's judgment, or that of its agents, for individual judgment: ". . . All private judgment of every particular member being excluded, the community comes to be umpire by settled standing rules . . ." *Second Treatise*, 87.

347   [192] *Second Treatise*, 54; Smith, *TMS*, pp. 382-383, 395-397; *Wealth*, V, i (pp. 670, 673); Bentham, *Econ. Wr.*, Vol. I, pp. 115-116; Vol. III, pp. 318-319, 443.

347 [193] *Second Treatise*, 87.

348 [194] Spencer, *Essays*, Vol. III, p. 450.

348 [195] *Deontology*, Vol. I, pp. 21-22.

348 [196] *Ibid.*, Vol. I, pp. 21-22, 27, 32-33, 97-98, 101, 166-168; Vol. II, pp. 37-40.

349 [197] *Autobiography*, p. 215; *Utilitarianism*, etc. *op. cit.*, pp. 72-73.

350 [198] J. S. Mill, *PPE*, II, i, 3 (pp. 205-207, 210-211); II, xii, 2-3 (pp. 364-365), xiii, 2 (377-378); *Utilitarianism*, etc., pp. 299-301. It should be noted, however, that Mill had misgivings about the potential tyranny of a socialist society. *PPE*, II, i, 3 (pp. 210-211).

350 [199] Bastiat, *Oeuvres*, Vol. I, p. 466.

350 [200] *Essays*, Vol. II, pp. 131-132.

350 [201] Smith, *TMS*, p. 27.

Chapter Ten

354 [1] Max Weber, *The Theory of Social and Economic Organization,* trans. A. M. Henderson and T. Parsons (New York: Oxford University Press, 1947) p. 337. See also the discussion by E. A. Shils, "Some Remarks on 'The Theory of Social and Economic Organization,'" *Economica* (n.s.), Vol. XV (1948), pp. 36-50.

355 [2] For management-worker conflicts in the Soviet Union see: G. Bienstock, S. M. Schwarz, and A. Yugow, *Management in Russian Industry and Agriculture* (Ithaca: Cornell University Press, 1948), pp. 32-38; B. Moore, Jr., *Soviet Politics, The Dilemma of Power* (Cambridge, Mass.: Harvard University Press, 1956) pp. 178-179, 317-331; M. Fainsod, *How Russia is Ruled* (Cambridge, Mass.: Harvard University Press, 1957) pp. 421-441.

356 [3] Elton Mayo, *The Human Problems of an Industrial Civilization* (New York: Macmillan, 1933) p. 145. (Hereafter cited as *The Human Problems.*)

356 [4] J. M. Keynes, *Essays in Persuasion* (London: Macmillan, 1931) pp. 314-315. The phrase "collective capitalism" has been coined by Gardiner C. Means, in *Collective Capitalism and Economic Theory* (a lecture at the Marshall Wythe Symposium, Williamsburg, Va., 1957).

356 [5] See the policy statement of the National Executive Committee of the British Labour Party entitled *Industry and the Nation* (London, 1957). The following is representative of the prevailing mood among some of the major theoreticians of the Party: "The basic fact is the large corporation, facing fundamentally similar problems, acts in fundamentally the same way whether publicly or privately owned." C. A. R. Crosland, *The Future of Socialism* (London: Cape, 1957) pp. 479-480.

356 [6] For a good recent survey, see Herbert Spiro, *The Politics of German Codetermination* (Cambridge, Mass.: Harvard University Press, 1958).

356 [7] "The manager is becoming a professional in the sense that like all professional men he has a responsibility to society as a whole." Editors of *Fortune* with the

collaboration of R. W. Davenport, *U. S. A.: The Permanent Revolution* (Engle-
wood Cliffs, N. J.: Prentice-Hall, 1951) p. 79.

356   [8] J. A. Schumpeter, *Capitalism, Socialism, and Democracy* (New York: Harper,
1950) pp. 141, 156, 163.

356   [9] Cited in C. Bouglé, *La Sociologie de Proudhon* (Paris, 1911) p. 18.

357   [10] "That both self-interest *and* something else are satisfied by group life is the
notion that is hardest for the hard-boiled — and half-baked — person to see." G. C.
Homans, *The Human Group* (New York: Harcourt, Brace, 1950) p. 96. "If a
number of individuals work together to achieve a common purpose, a harmony
of interests will develop among them to which individual self-interest will be
subordinated. This is a very different doctrine from the claim that individual self-
interest is the solitary human motive." E. Mayo, *The Political Problem* (Cambridge, Mass.: Harvard University Press, School of Business Administration, 1947),
p. 21.

359   [11] Montesquieu, *Esprit des lois,* preface.

360   [12] De Maistre, *Oeuvres complètes,* 14 vols. (Lyon and Paris, 1884-1886), Vol. II, p.
266. (Hereafter cited as *O. C.*)

360   [13] De Maistre, *O. C.,* Vol. I, pp. 226, 266, 426. See also the discussions in P. R.
Rohden, *Joseph de Maistre als politischer Theoretiker* (Munich, 1929) p. 40; Fran-
cis Bayle, *Les idées politiques de Joseph de Maistre* (Paris, 1945) pp. 23-28; Bagge,
Les idées politiques en France sous la Restauration, pp. 245 ff.

360   [14] De Maistre's remark is in *O. C.* Vol. I, p. 494; Louis de Bonald, *Oeuvres complètes,* ed. Migne, 3 vols. (Paris, 1859) Vol. I, p. 958 (hereafter referred to as
O. C.); Léon Brunschvicg, *Le progrès de la conscience dans la philosophie occi-
dentale,* 2nd ed., 2 vols. (Paris: Presses Universitaires, 1953) Vol. II, p. 485.

360   [15] Durkheim, *The Division of Labor in Society,* trans. G. Simpson (Glencoe, Ill.:
Free Press, 1949) p. 35.

360   [16] Durkheim, *Les règles de la méthode sociologique* (Paris: Presses Universitaires,
1947) pp. xxiii-xxiv.

360   [17] De Bonald, *O. C.,* Vol. I, pp. 127, 328, 408, 426, 467; de Maistre, *O. C.,* Vol. II, p.
253; and see Bagge, *op. cit.,* pp. 245-247, 250-251. Note, too, de Bonald on the
theory of abstract models: "An abstraction is an operation by which the intelligence separates the qualities or accidents of the subjects in order to form an ideal
being which will be susceptible to thought." *O. C.,* Vol. I, pp. 131-132. The relationship between the reactionaries and the development of sociology is discussed
in two articles by R. A. Nisbet, "De Bonald and the Concept of the Social Group,"
Journal of the History of Ideas, Vol. V (1944) pp. 315-331; "Conservatism and
Sociology," *American Journal of Sociology,* Vol. LVIII (1952) pp. 167-175.

360   [18] Durkheim, *Les règles,* pp. 57-60.

361   [19] *Oeuvres choisies de C.-H. de Saint-Simon,* 3 vols. (Brussels, 1859) Vol. II, pp.
372-374, 375-377.

361   [20] *Oeuvres complètes de P.-J. Proudhon* (Paris: Lacroix, Verboeckhoven edition,
1867) Vol. I, pp. 30, 216. (Hereafter cited as *O. C.*)

361   [21] Durkheim, *Le socialisme. La définition, ses débuts, la doctrine saint-simonienne,*

ed. M. Mauss (Paris: Alcan, 1928) p. 213. Mannheim's comments are in the same tradition: "It is possible, of course, that the age of planning will be followed by one of mere administration. It is also possible that at a later stage all that we now call history, namely, the unforeseeable, fateful dominance of uncontrolled social forces, will come to an end." *Man and Society in an Age of Reconstruction* (London: Kegan Paul, 1940) p. 193.

361 [22] Proudhon, *Philosophie du progrès* (Paris: Marpon et Flammarion, 1876) pp. 39-40.

362 [23] Note the *corpus mysticum* flavor to the following passage from Durkheim: "The only source of life at which we can morally reanimate ourselves is that formed by the society of our fellow-beings; the only moral forces with which we can sustain and increase our own are those which we get from others . . . beliefs are active only when they are partaken by many." *The Elementary Forms of the Religious Life,* trans. J. W. Swain (London: Allen and Unwin, 1915) p. 425. (Hereafter cited as *The Elementary Forms.*)

362 [24] Durkheim, *The Elementary Forms,* pp. 10, 419, 421-422. This point of view was also taken by Marx and, in our day, by Mannheim.

362 [25] Durkheim, *The Elementary Forms,* pp. 16-17, 437; *Sociology and Philosophy,* trans. D. F. Pocock (Glencoe, Ill.: Free Press, 1953) p. 52; *Les règles,* p. 4.

362 [26] Cited in F. E. Manuel, *The New World of Henri Saint-Simon* (Cambridge, Mass.: Harvard University Press, 1956) p. 305.

362 [27] Durkheim, *Division of Labor,* p. 387.

363 [28] Marx, *Capital,* trans. S. Moore and E. Aveling, rev. E. Untermann (New York: Modern Library) pp. 370-384, 396-410.

363 [29] *The German Ideology,* ed. R. Pascal (New York: International Publishers, 1947) pp. 23-24, 28, 70, 77.

363 [30] Karl Mannheim, *Man and Society,* p. 155 (fn. 1).

363 [31] The quotation from Proudhon is in *O. C.,* Vol. I, p. 176; de Bonald as cited in Brunschvicg, *op. cit.,* Vol. II, p. 489.

363 [32] Proudhon, *O. C.,* 1867, Vol. I, p. 176.

364 [33] Henry Michel, *L'idée de l'état,* Paris, 1896.

364 [34] Saint-Simon, *Oeuvres choisies,* Vol. II, p. 214.

364 [35] Durkheim, *Suicide,* trans. J. A. Spaulding and G. Simpson (Glencoe, Ill.: Free Press, 1951) p. 257.

364 [36] Peter Drucker, *The Future of Industrial Man* (New York: John Day Co., 1943) p. 13 (by permission).

364 [37] T. N. Whitehead, *Leadership in a Free Society* (Cambridge, Mass.: Harvard University Press, 1947) pp. 169, 209.

365 [38] Mannheim, *Man and Society,* pp. 6-14, 260. See also Elton Mayo, *The Social Problems of an Industrial Civilization* (London: Routledge & Kegan Paul, 1949) pp. 8, 106. (Hereafter cited as *Social Problems.*)

365 [39] Mannheim, *Man and Society,* pp. 75, 153-154, 192-193. Note, too, how Mann-

heim's distinction between the stages of "planning" and "administration" parallels Lenin's argument in *State and Revolution*.

365   [40] Mannheim, *Freedom, Power, and Democratic Planning*, ed. H. Gerth and E. K. Bramstedt (London: Routledge and Kegan Paul, 1951) pp. 108 ff.

366   [41] Saint-Simon as quoted in Durkheim, *Le socialisme*, pp. 198-199.

366   [42] Philip Selznick, *Leadership in Administration: A Sociological Interpretation* (Evanston, Ill.: Row, Peterson, 1957) pp. 8-9. (Hereafter cited as *Leadership*.)

367   [43] De Bonald, *O. C.*, Vol. I, pp. 327, 962. Bagge, *op. cit.*, p. 308. Although these elements were not completely lacking in de Maistre, his religious conceptions were a very personal mixture of Catholicism and mysticism. Both writers are sympathetically discussed by Bagge and by Brunschvicg, *op. cit.*, Vol. II, pp. 485 ff.

367   [44] Émile Durkheim, *The Division of Labor*, pp. 7 ff.; G. D. H. Cole, *Essays in Social Theory* (London: Macmillan, 1950) pp. 102-103 and *Guild Socialism Re-Stated* (London: Parsons, 1920) pp. 29, 45-51.

367   [45] Mayo, *The Political Problem*, p. 23. "The medieval ideal of the cooperation of all is the only satisfactory source of civilized procedure." *Social Problems*, p. 128.

367   [46] Erich Fromm, *Escape from Freedom* (New York: Rinehart, 1941) pp. 41 ff. It might be added that Fromm shares with the reactionaries and Comte the hostility towards the Protestant Reformation. Like these earlier writers, Fromm criticizes the Reformation for having severed men from the integrated relationship developed in the mediaeval system. Compare Fromm, *ibid.*, Ch. III with de Bonald, *O. C.*, Vol. I, pp. 106-121; de Maistre, *O. C.*, Vol. II, pp. 523 ff.; VIII, pp. 63 ff. See also Rohden, *op. cit.*, pp. 140-142.

367   [47] Mannheim, *Freedom, Power and Democratic Planning*, p. 287.

368   [48] A. A. Berle, *The Twentieth Century Capitalist Revolution* (New York: Harcourt, Brace, 1954) pp. 174-175, 182-183. See also the idea of the "soulful corporation" in Carl Kaysen, "The Social Significance of the Modern Corporation," *American Economics Association, Papers and Proceedings*, 1956, Vol. XLVII (1957) pp. 311-319 and also the critical remarks of C. E. Lindblom (*ibid.*, pp. 324 ff.), protesting against the contamination of economic theory by "theological" notions. That former New Dealers like Berle and D. E. Lilienthal, in *Big Business: A New Era* (New York, 1952), should now be busy with apologetics for managerialism testifies not only to a common order of problems among government and business, but also to an obvious decline in the distinctiveness of the political which permits an easy transfer of loyalties from "big government" to "big business." See for a wise and balanced picture of the corporate system Walton Hamilton, *The Politics of Industry* (New York: Knopf, 1957) pp. 137 ff.

369   [49] Rousseau, *Émile*, trans. B. Foxley (London and New York: Dutton, 1911) pp. 47, 64 (fn. 1).

369   [50] *A Discourse on the Origin of Inequality* in G. D. H. Cole, ed., *The Social Contract* (London and New York: Dutton, 1913) p. 237. Hereafter this essay will be cited as *Origin of Inequality* and, unless otherwise indicated, all references will be to the Cole edition.

369   [51] *Émile*, pp. 173-174, 197, 205; *Origin of Inequality*, pp. 19 (fn.), 198-199, 212-213, 232-233. See also the discussion in the excellent study by Robert Derathé, *Jean-*

Jacques Rousseau et la science politique de son temps (Paris: Presses Universitaires, 1950) pp. 139 (fn. 4), 141. (Hereafter cited as *Jean-Jacques Rousseau*.)

369   [52] *Émile*, p. 10.

369   [53] *Origin of Inequality*, pp. 220-223; *A Discourse on Political Economy* in Cole, *op. cit.*, pp. 280-281. (Hereafter cited as *Political Economy*.) *Émile*, pp. 197-198.

369   [54] C. E. Vaughan, ed., *The Political Writings of Jean-Jacques Rousseau*, 2 vols. (Cambridge: Cambridge University Press, 1915) Vol. I, p. 195. (Hereafter cited as *Political Writings*.)

370   [55] *Origin of Inequality*, pp. 205-206. ". . . Man is by nature good . . . men are depraved and perverted by society." *Émile*, p. 198. See also C. W. Hendel, ed., *Citizen of Geneva. Selections from the Letters of Jean-Jacques Rousseau* (New York: Oxford University Press, 1937) pp. 208-210.

370   [56] *Émile*, pp. 44-45, *Origin of Inequality*, pp. 186, 194. See, in general, the discussion by Robert Derathé, *Le rationalisme de J.-J. Rousseau* (Paris: Presses Universitaires, 1948). While Derathé has perhaps exaggerated Rousseau's affinities with the rationalist tradition, his analysis supplies a useful corrective to the usual interpretation of Rousseau as the arch-irrationalist.

370   [57] *Origin of Inequality*, p. 218.

370   [58] *Origin of Inequality*, pp. 214-215; *Émile*, pp. 407-409.

371   [59] *Émile*, pp. 49, 175, 245; *Origin of Inequality*, pp. 218-219, 222; Derathé, *Jean-Jacques Rousseau*, pp. 110, 146-148, 175-176.

371   [60] D. H. Lawrence, *Studies in Classic American Literature* (New York: Viking Press, 1953) p. 17.

371   [61] *Émile*, p. 261; *Origin of Inequality*, p. 161; *A Discourse on the Arts and Sciences* in Cole, *op. cit.*, p. 132.

371   [62] *Political Economy*, pp. 261, 268.

371   [63] *Du contrat social*, I, vi.

372   [64] The affinities between Durkheim and Rousseau were not accidental. Durkheim had been a close student of Rousseau's writings and contributed one of the most perceptive studies we have on Rousseau. See his *Montesquieu et Rousseau, Précurseurs de la Sociologie* (Paris: Rivière, 1953).

372   [65] Durkheim, *Division of Labor*, p. 26.

372   [66] Durkheim's analysis foreshadowed some of the basic propositions used by Erich Fromm in *Escape from Freedom* and in *The Sane Society* (New York: Rinehart, 1955) pp. 216-220.

372   [67] "Collective representations are the result of an immense cooperation which stretches out not only into space but into time as well; to make them, a multitude of minds have associated, united and combined their ideas and sentiments; for them, long generations have accumulated their experience and their knowledge." [*The Elementary Forms*, p. 16.]

Compare this to Burke's famous discussion of the "contract" and his theory of "prejudice" in *Reflections on the Revolution in France* (London and New York: Dutton, 1910) pp. 84, 93.

372   [68] Durkheim, *The Elementary Forms*, pp. 424, 440-442; *Suicide*, pp. 309-310; *Sociology and Philosophy*, pp. 38, 73.

373   [69] *Division of Labor*, p. 10; *The Elementary Forms*, pp. 443, 444; *Sociology and Philosophy*, p. 57; *Les règles*, p. 122 (fn. 1). There are further similarities between Rousseau's distinction concerning the "general will" and the "will of all" and Durkheim's "average conscience" and "collective conscience": *Suicide*, p. 318. It might also be noted that some commentators have interpreted Rousseau's general will as a theory of conscience: see G. Gurvitch, "Kant und Fichte als Rousseau-Interpreten," *Kant-Studien*, Vol. XXVII (1922) pp. 138-164, at p. 152; G. Beaulavon, ed., *Du contrat social*, 5th ed. (Paris, 1938) p. 36.

373   [70] *Division of Labor*, p. 444; *Suicide*, p. 318.

373   [71] *Suicide*, p. 319; *Sociology and Philosophy*, p. 51. A further parallel between Rousseau's general will and Durkheim's collective conscience lay in their all-embracing province which, at the same time, disqualified them from dealing with particular objects. The collective conscience dealt only in "general ideas," "categories," and "classes": *The Elementary Forms*, p. 435. There are also further comparisons to be made between Durkheim's notion of collective representations and Sorel's "myth": see *Sociology and Philosophy*, p. 29.

374   [72] Cited in Derathé, *Jean-Jacques Rousseau*, p. 146.

374   [73] *Origin of Inequality*, pp. 189, 194, 203.

374   [74] *Émile*, p. 149.

374   [75] "To find a form of association which defends and protects with the whole common force the person and goods of each associate, and in which each, in uniting himself with all, obeys only himself, and remains as free as before." *Du contrat social*, I, vi. And see *ibid.*, II, iv and I, viii ("Obedience to a law which we prescribe to ourselves is liberty").

374   [76] *Du contrat social*, I, vi.

374   [77] *Political Writings*, Vol. I, p. 245. In his *Lettre à Mirabeau*, Rousseau had declared that "the great problem of politics" is to find "a form of government which will put the law above man." *Political Writings*, Vol. I, p. 160.

375   [78] *Du contrat social*, I, vi-vii; *Political Writings*, Vol. I, p. 201; II, pp. 234-235.

375   [79] *Du contrat social*, II, xiii; *Émile*, p. 7. Independence of other individuals and dependence on the community dictated Rousseau's argument that the property of the state should be as great as possible and that of the citizen as little as possible. Wealth was suspect because it gave power over others. On these points see his *Projet pour la Corse* in *Political Writings*, Vol. II, pp. 337, 346.

375   [80] *Political Writings*, Vol. I, p. 460; *Du contrat social*, II, iv, vi.

375   [81] *Du contrat social*, I, vii.

376   [82] Cited in Manuel, *op. cit.*, p. 87.

377   [83] Saint-Simon, *Oeuvres choisies*, Vol. I, pp. 20-21.

377   [84] *Henri Comte de Saint-Simon. Selected Writings*, trans. F. M. H. Markham (New York: Macmillan, 1952) p. 69. (Hereafter cited as *Selected Writings*.)

377   [85] *Ibid.*, p. 70.

377 [86] *Ibid.,* pp. 78-80. Manuel, *op. cit.,* pp. 250, 279. For an excellent general discussion of Saint-Simon's industrialism see Élie Halévy's masterful essay "La doctrine économique saint-simonienne" in *L'Ère des tyrannies,* 2nd ed. (Paris: Gallimard, 1938) pp. 30-94. Manuel, *op. cit.,* provides the best and most recent full-dress treatment of Saint-Simon's life and thought. An older yet still valuable analysis is to be found in Michel, *op. cit.,* pp. 172-211. There are brief accounts also in such standard histories of socialist thought as A. Gray, *The Socialist Tradition* (London: Longmans, 1946), which should be used with caution when dealing with thinkers he considers serious rather than bizarre; and G. D. H. Cole, *A History of Socialist Thought,* 4 vols. (London: Macmillan, 1953-1958) Vol. I. For a recent, but extreme, view of Saint-Simon as a contributor to sociology as well as to totalitarianism, see Albert Salomon, *The Tyranny of Progress. Reflections on the Origins of Sociology* (New York: Noonday Press, 1955).

378 [87] Saint-Simon, *Selected Writings,* pp. 68, 76-78. The condition of the masses was discussed at length by Saint-Simon in *Le nouveau Christianisme.*

378 [88] Saint-Simon, *Oeuvres choisies,* Vol. II, pp. 372-374, 375-377.

378 [89] Manuel, *op. cit.,* pp. 254, 311; *Selected Writings,* pp. 70, 78-79; Durkheim, *Le socialisme,* p. 186.

379 [90] Cited in Manuel, *op. cit.,* p. 306; see also Durkheim, *Le socialisme,* p. 191.

379 [91] *Capital,* pp. 357-358, 424 (Pt. IV, xiii; IV, xv (2)). The passage cited makes an ironical contrast to Rousseau's claim that "men cannot engender new forces, but only unite and direct those already existing" (*Du contrat social,* I, vi). Yet Marx was the social scientist, Rousseau the metaphysician!

379 [92] Proudhon, *Philosophie du progrès,* p. 36.

379 [93] Charles Fourier, *Oeuvres complètes,* 3rd ed., 6 vols. (Paris, 1846) Vol. III, pp. 18-19. (Hereafter cited as *O. C.*) "The other sciences, even the noblest, like mathematics, have only petty value as long as we ignore *la science du mécanisme sociétaire* which issues in wealth, unity and happiness."

380 [94] Chester I. Barnard, *The Functions of the Executive* (Cambridge, Mass.: Harvard University Press, 1947) p. 36.

380 [95] Herbert A. Simon, *Models of Man, Social and Rational* (New York: Wiley, 1957) pp. 198, 200; Barnard, *Functions of the Executive,* p. 36.

380 [96] Simon, *Models of Man,* p. 199; James G. March and Herbert A. Simon, *Organizations* (New York: Wiley, 1958) pp. 136 ff., 203 ff.; Luther Gulick, "Notes on the Theory of Organization" in *Papers on the Science of Administration,* ed. L. Gulick and L. Urwick (New York: Institute of Public Administration, 1937) p. 4.

380 [97] Mannheim, *Man and Society,* pp. 149, 267.

380 [98] Herbert A. Simon, *Administrative Behavior,* 2nd ed. (New York: Macmillan, 1957) p. 79.

381 [99] Simon, *Models of Man,* p. 200. ". . . Organization permits the individual to approach reasonably near to objective rationality." *Administrative Behavior,* p. 80.

381 [100] Simon, *Models of Man,* p. 196.

381 [101] Simon, *Administrative Behavior,* p. 78.

381 [102] *Ibid.,* pp. 101-102. Lest this seem the "ideology" of efficiency experts in the

service of big business, we quote from Mannheim, an advocate of collectivist planning: "The growth of organization and the general interdependence of institutions make for an increase in rationality and detachment." *Man and Society,* p. 359. Most of these ideas had been implicit in Max Weber's conception of "bureaucratic rationality": *From Max Weber: Essays in Sociology,* trans. and ed. H. H. Gerth and C. W. Mills (New York: Oxford University Press, 1946) pp. 196 ff.

381   [103] Mannheim, *Man and Society,* p. 244.

381   [104] L. Urwick, "Organization as a Technical Problem" in Gulick and Urwick, *op. cit.,* p. 85.

382   [105] Simon, *Administrative Behavior,* pp. xxiv-xxv. For a more sensitive approach see Chris Argyris, *Personality and Organization* (New York, 1957) pp. 66 ff., where the question of "a basic incongruency" between personality needs and organizational requirements is explored.

382   [106] Barnard, *Functions of the Executive,* p. 186.

382   [107] Saint-Simon, *Selected Writings,* p. 25. The same points were made by Comte; note also Durkheim's warning that the sciences, like society, were in an anomic state because "they are not organized." *Division of Labor,* pp. 367-368.

383   [108] Quoted in Durkheim, *Le socialisme,* p. 131.

383   [109] Proudhon, *O. C.,* Vol. III, p. 197.

383   [110] Urwick in Gulick and Urwick, *op. cit.,* p. 49; Mayo, *Human Problems,* p. 145; see also Saint-Simon, *Selected Writings,* p. 39.

383   [111] Peter Drucker, *The Concept of the Corporation* (New York: John Day, 1946) p. 26. Drucker has modified this position in *The Practice of Management* (London: Heinemann, 1956) pp. 124-126. De Bonald's remark is relevant here: "Government . . . presupposes certain passions in man and establishes laws to control them; and these *subsist independently* of those heroic virtues which man so rarely has . . ." *O. C.,* Vol. I, p. 375. (Italics in original.)

384   [112] *Discourse on Method* in *The Method, Meditations, and Philosophy of Descartes,* trans. J. Veitch (New York: Tudor Publishing Co., n.d.) p. 163. The contrast between the Cartesian and Platonic viewpoints on this problem has been clearly brought out by Robinson, in *Plato's Earlier Dialectic,* pp. 72-73.

384   [113] *The Philosophical Works of Francis Bacon,* ed. J. M. Robertson (London: Routledge, 1905) pp. 270, 297. (Aphorisms LXI and CXII from Book I of *Novum Organum.*)

384   [114] Proudhon, *O. C.,* Vol. I, p. 14; Vol. III, pp. 196-199.

384   [115] Proudhon, *O. C.,* Vol. III, pp. 196-197.

385   [116] Max Weber, *The Methodology of the Social Sciences,* trans. and ed. E. A. Shils and H. A. Finch (Glencoe, Ill.: Free Press, 1949) pp. 2-6. Compare this to Durkheim's criticism of the "cult of personal dignity" for its bad social consequences: *Division of Labor,* pp. 172, 401-403.

385   [117] Mannheim, *Man and Society,* p. 148. Compare Hobbes: "He that is to govern a whole nation, must read in himself, not this or that particular man; but mankind . . ." *Leviathan,* Introduction. The anti-individualism which tends to accompany the quest for theoretical generalizations was brilliantly analyzed by de

Tocqueville. He also pointed out how these intellectual tendencies are associated with democratic societies whose historical bent is towards a uniformity of opinion which crushes the individual. *Democracy in America,* ed. Phillips Bradley, 2 vols. (New York: Knopf, 1945) Vol. II, Chs. i-iii.

385   [118] Cited in Brunschvicg, *op. cit.,* Vol. II, p. 518.

386   [119] De Bonald, *O. C.,* Vol. I, pp. 9, 29.

386   [120] Proudhon, *Philosophie du progrès,* p. 36. The same tendencies are apparent in more extreme form in the writings of A. E. Bentley who has supplied the basic theories for recent and contemporary group theories of politics: "The whole social life in all its phases" can be stated in terms of "groups of active men." ". . . The only reality" of ideas "is their reflection of the groups, only that and nothing more. The ideas can be stated in terms of the groups; the groups never in terms of the ideas." "The individual stated for himself, and invested with an extra-social unity of his own, is a fiction." "The society itself is nothing other than the complex of the groups that compose it." *The Process of Government* (Evanston, Ill.: Principia Press, 1949) pp. 204, 206, 215, 222. For a criticism of Bentley's tendency to eliminate the creative role of public actors see M. Fainsod, "Some Reflections on the Nature of the Regulatory Process," *Public Policy,* ed. C. J. Friedrich and E. S. Mason (Cambridge, Mass.: Harvard University Press, 1940) pp. 297-323.

386   [121] *Les règles,* p. 103; and see the discussion of Comte in Brunschvicg, *op. cit.,* Vol. II, p. 516 ff.

386   [122] Durkheim, *Les règles,* pp. 14, 15, 28.

386   [123] De Bonald, *O. C.,* Vol. III, pp. 44-45. The notion reappears in Comte in the following form: "The true path of human progress lies in . . . diminishing the vacillation, inconsistency, and discordance of our designs by furnishing external motives for those operations of our intellectual, moral, and practical powers, of which the original source was purely internal." Auguste Comte, *System of Positive Polity,* 4 vols., trans. J. H. Bridges et al. (London: Longmans, 1875-1877) Vol. I, p. 22.

387   [124] Saint-Simon, *Selected Writings,* pp. 72-73. These notions represent an extension of the famous physiocratic distinction between productive and unproductive labor which was carried forward into classical economics and, ultimately, into socialism and communism. The idea of "function" also played a prominent role in Cole's guild socialism: *Social Theory,* 2nd ed. (London: Methuen, 1921) pp. 48 ff.

387   [125] Durkheim, *Division of Labor,* pp. 42-43, 401-403.

387   [126] Durkheim, *Division of Labor,* pp. 240, 402; *Sociology and Philosophy,* pp. 40, 78; *Suicide,* pp. 278-280. There are obvious affinities here with the activism of Sorel. Durkheim's attack on the individual conscience had its parallel in F. H. Bradley's writings: "to wish to be better than the world is to be on the threshold of immortality," and "to think differently from the world on moral subjects" is "sheer self-conceit." *Ethical Studies,* 2nd ed. (Oxford: Clarendon Press, 1927) pp. 199, 200. The distrust of the intellectual was expressed in similar terms by Lenin. At one point he praised the intellectual as the revolutionary model for the worker to follow. Later he wrote that "the proletariat is trained for organization by its whole life much more radically than are many puny intellectuals." Compare "What is to be Done?" *Selected Works* (London: Lawrence and Wishart, 1944)

Vol. II, pp. 92-93 with "One Step Forward, Two Steps Back," *ibid.*, pp. 439, 442, 445-446.

388   [127] Mayo, *Social Problems,* p. 19.

388   [128] Mannheim, *Man and Society,* pp. 102-105.

389   [129] "Eternal Peace" in *The Philosophy of Kant,* ed. C. J. Friedrich (New York: Random House, 1949) pp. 452-453.

389   [130] *The Federalist,* No. 51 (p. 354). "Why has government been instituted at all? Because the passions of men will not conform to the dictates of reason and justice, without constraint. Has it been found that bodies of men act with more rectitude or greater disinterestedness than individuals?" (No. 15 (p. 102)). The page references are to the edition by E. G. Bourne (New York: Tudor Publishing Company, 1937).

389   [131] David Hume, *Essays Moral, Political, and Literary,* ed. T. H. Green and T. H. Grose, 2 vols. (London: Longmans, 1882) Vol. I, p. 99. (Hereafter cited as *Essays.*)

390   [132] *The Federalist,* No. 51 (pp. 353-354). "Such will be the relation between the House of Representatives and their constitutions. Duty, gratitude, interest, ambition itself, are the chords by which they will be bound to fidelity and sympathy with the great mass of the people. It is possible that these may all be insufficient to control the caprice and wickedness of man. But are they not all that government will admit, and that human prudence can devise?" No. 57 (p. 392).

390   [133] *The Federalist,* No. 51 (pp. 356-358); No. 10 (p. 69); No. 60 (pp. 410-412).

390   [134] *The Federalist,* No. 57 (p. 391). Cf. Locke: The estates of the subjects are less apt to be treated arbitrarily by a system where "the legislative consists, wholly or in part, in assemblies which are variable, whose members, upon the dissolution of the assembly, are subjects under the common laws of their country, equally with the rest." *Two Treatises of Government,* II, 138.

390   [135] *The Federalist,* No. 9 (p. 57); No. 28 (p. 185): "Power being almost always the rival of power . . ." See also No. 51 (p. 353) and compare Montesquieu, *Esprit des lois,* XI, 4: "Power should be a check to power."

390   [136] The *Federalists* relied primarily on "experience" to provide an education for office-holders. Compare their remarks with those of the fifteenth-century writer Sir John Fortescue, *De Laudibus Legum Anglie,* where the chancellor instructs the new prince in the intricacies of governance.

390   [137] Harrington, *The Oceana and other Works of James Harrington,* ed. J. Toland (London, 1737) p. 266.

390   [138] Hume, *Essays,* Vol. 1, p. 108; *The Federalist,* No. 68 (p. 38). Popper has subscribed to this same point of view. He argues that political theory should discard the inquiry into "Who should rule?" in favor of "How can we organize political institutions so that bad or incompetent rulers can be prevented from doing too much damage?" *The Open Society and its Enemies,* Vol. I, pp. 106-107.

390   [139] *James Harrington's Oceana,* ed. S. B. Liljegren (Heidelberg, 1924) pp. 34, 56, 185. "Good laws may beget order and moderation in the government where the manners and customs have instilled little humanity or justice into the tempers of men." Hume, *Essays,* Vol. I, p. 106.

391   140 Descartes, *op. cit.*, p. 149. (Emphasis supplied.)

391   141 Hume, *Essays*, Vol. I, p. 105.

391   142 Quoted in Bagge, *op. cit.*, p. 110. The affinities between constitutional and organizational theories is borne out in a striking way by Khrushchev's attack on the Stalinist "cult of personality." See the translation of his secret report of February 24-25, 1956 in B. D. Wolfe, *Khrushchev and Stalin's Ghost* (New York: Praeger, 1957) pp. 88-89.

392   143 Harrington, *Works*, pp. 24-41, 252.

393   144 Hume, *Essays*, Vol. I, pp. 99, 101.

393   145 Cited in Manuel, *op. cit.*, p. 413 (fn. 3).

393   146 Manuel, *op. cit.*, pp. 203, 284; Saint-Simon, *Oeuvres choisies*, Vol. I, p. 29 (fn. 1); Durkheim, *Le socialisme*, pp. 237-238.

394   147 Cited in Derathé, *Jean-Jacques Rousseau*, p. 167 (fn. 2).

394   148 Cited in *ibid.*, p. 149. Rousseau pointed out that the maxim, "do unto others as you would want them to do unto you," while more practical was less perfect than "do good but with the least possible evil to others." *Political Writings*, Vol. I, p. 163. See also the discussion in C. W. Hendel, *Jean-Jacques Rousseau Moralist*, 2 vols. (London and New York: Oxford University Press, 1934) Vol. I, pp. 48-53.

394   149 "It is not in human nature to put ourselves in the place of those who are happier than ourselves; but only in the place of those who can claim our pity." *Émile*, p. 184.

394   150 *Émile*, p. 183.

394   151 Manuel, *op. cit.*, pp. 239, 305.

394   152 See Gaston Isambert, *Les idées socialistes en France de 1815 à 1848* (Paris, 1905) pp. 126, 133.

395   153 Fourier, *O. C.*, Vol. III, p. 22; Vol. VI, pp. 3-4. See the discusson of Maxime Leroy, *Histoire des idées sociales en France de Babeuf à Tocqueville*, 4th ed. (Paris, 1950) pp. 246 ff. There is a sympathetic appreciation of the Utopian Socialists in Martin Buber, *Paths in Utopia*, trans. R. F. C. Hull (London: Routledge and Kegan Paul, 1949).

395   154 Fourier, *O. C.*, Vol. I, p. 7; III, p. 20.

395   155 Fourier, *O. C.*, Vol. I, p. 11; VI, p. 6.

395   156 Fourier, *O. C.*, Vol. III, p. 21; VI, p. 25.

396   157 Fourier, *O. C.*, Vol. I, p. 9; VI, p. xiv. Proudhon's gibe about Saint-Simon's philosophy, that it was a form of "sensual Gnosticism," applied with equal force to Fourier. See Proudhon, *O. C.*, Vol. XVII, p. 33.

396   158 Fourier, *O. C.*, Vol. I, pp. 3, 79 for the discussion of *la science sociale*. In this connection the commentaries of Leroy, *op. cit.*, p. 251 ff., and M. Lansac, *Les conceptions méthodologique et sociales de Charles Fourier* (Paris, 1926) are relevant. Isambert (*op. cit.*, pp. 129-130) correctly argued that Fourier had no genuine moral theory and hence no conception of a truly solidary community. The opposite position was maintained by E. Fournière, *Les théories socialistes au XIXe siècle de Babeuf à Proudhon* (Paris, 1904) pp. 42-43. Fourier's notion of conventional

morality as repressive suggests some crude intimations of Freud, but more suggestive are the parallels between the utopian socialists and Erich Fromm, *The Sane Society,* especially pp. 283 ff., with its plea for the small association. There are further continuities between the Utopians and contemporary city-planners which are explicitly recognized by the latter. See Percival Goodman and Paul Goodman, *Communitas. Means of Livelihood and Ways of Life* (Chicago: University of Chicago Press, 1947) pp. 2, 8.

396 [159] Fourier, *O. C.,* Vol. III, pp. 44-45, 128.

396 [160] Proudhon, *O. C.,* Vol. X, p. 77.

396 [161] Fourier, *O. C.,* Vol. VI, p. 7.

396 [162] Robert Owen, *A New View of Society and other Writings,* ed. G. D. H. Cole (London and New York: Dutton, 1927) pp. 8-9, 177, 231, 262, 284-288.

397 [163] Cited in Brunschvicg, *op. cit.,* Vol. II, pp. 514, 525 (fn. 1). And see Comte's discussion in *A System of Positive Polity,* Vol. I, pp. 49-50, 69, 83.

397 [164] De Bonald, *O. C.,* Vol. I, pp. 138, 145-155, 186, 376.

398 [165] See de Maistre's vivid description in *Les soirées de Saint-Petersbourg,* 2 vols. (Paris and Lyon: Emmanuel Vitte, 1924) Vol. I, pp. 32-34.

398 [166] Whitehead, *Leadership in a Free Society,* p. vii. The disintegrating effects of technological change on group solidarity and hierarchy is an operative assumption also in W. L. Warner and J. O. Low, *The Social System of the Modern Factory* (New Haven: Yale University Press, 1947) pp. 66-67.

399 [167] De Maistre, *Les soirées,* Vol. I, p. 67.

399 [168] Durkheim, *Suicide,* pp. 254-257; *Le socialisme,* pp. 286-287 ("Insatiability is a sign of morbidity"); *Professional Ethics and Civic Morals,* trans. C. Brookfield (Glencoe, Ill.: Free Press, 1958) pp. 11-12, 14-15, 24. The tendency to characterize unhealthy or undesirable social conditions as Hobbesian comes out most clearly in Tönnies. His *Gesellschaft* conception was explicitly modeled upon some of the salient features of Hobbes's civil society. See *Community and Association,* trans. C. P. Loomis (London: Routledge and Kegan Paul, 1955) pp. 146, 154 and also the discussion in Raymond Aron, *German Sociology,* trans. Mary and Thomas Bottomore (London: Heinemann, 1957) pp. 14-19.

399 [169] Durkheim, *Suicide,* p. 252.

399 [170] Durkheim, *Division of Labor,* p. 67.

399 [171] See the references cited in Ferdinand Tönnies, *Community and Association,* p. xxv.

400 [172] De Bonald, *O. C.,* Vol. I, pp. 47, 301.

400 [173] Durkheim, *Les règles,* p. 121; *Professional Ethics,* p. 61. De Bonald had defined liberty as consisting in "obeying perfect laws or necessary relationships derived from the nature of beings." *O. C.,* Vol. I, p. 665.

400 [174] Leonard Broom and Philip Selznick, *Sociology,* 2nd ed. (Evanston, Ill.: Row, Peterson, 1955) pp. 568, 569.

400 [175] De Bonald, *O. C.,* Vol. I, p. 967.

400 [176] De Bonald, *O. C.,* Vol. II, p. 217.

400   [177] Proudhon, *Philosophie du progrès*, pp. 36, 38, 53.

400   [178] Durkheim, *Suicide*, p. 209. One aspect of socialism welcomed by Durkheim was the effort to end the alienation of the worker from society: *Le socialisme*, pp. 33-34.

401   [179] Mayo, *Social Problems*, p. 67; *Human Problems*, p. 166. "Without fellow men to grant him social status, and unless they do grant him status, he is somewhat less than human." Richard La Pierre, *A Theory of Social Control* (New York: McGraw-Hill, 1954) p. 72.

401   [180] Marx, *Capital*, p. 361 (IV, xiii). Compare this with the following from a spokesman for the new managerialism: "The first need is to share the fortunes of an adequate group, rather than to stand alone." Whitehead, *Leadership in a Free Society*, p. 17.

401   [181] Bradley, *Ethical Studies*, pp. 163-167.

401   [182] *Ibid.*, pp. 79, 138-139, 163.

401   [183] "There is an objective morality in what has been achieved by infinite effort of the past. It comes down as a truth of my nature and is superior to my individual caprice." *Ibid.*, p. 190.

401   [184] *Ibid.*, pp. 79-80.

401   [185] "Historic" in *Fabian Essays*, Jubilee ed. (London: Allen and Unwin, 1948) p. 53 (with the permission of Burt Franklin).

402   [186] Bradley, *Ethical Studies*, pp. 180, 181.

402   [187] Webb, *Fabian Essays*, p. 54.

402   [188] Durkheim, *Division of Labor*, pp. 50, 55-56.

403   [189] Cited in C. Kerr and L. H. Fisher, "Plant Sociology: The Elite and the Aborigines" in *Common Frontiers of the Social Sciences*, ed. M. Komarovsky (Glencoe, Ill.: Free Press, 1957) pp. 281-309 at p. 304. See also E. W. Bakke, *People and Organizations* (New Haven: Yale University Press, 1951) p. 3. The article by Kerr and Fisher is an excellent critical study of the presuppositions of "factory sociology." See also R. Bendix and L. H. Fisher, "The Perspectives of Elton Mayo," *Review of Economics and Statistics*, Vol. XXXI (1949), pp. 312-321; R. Bendix, *Work and Authority in Industry* (New York and London: Wiley, 1956) pp. 308 ff.

403   [190] De Bonald, *O. C.*, Vol. I, p. 355.

403   [191] Hegel, *Philosophy of Right*, trans. T. M. Knox (Oxford: Clarendon Press, 1945) pars. 183, 185-187, 236.

404   [192] Marx, *German Ideology*, pp. 22-23, 57, 59; Karl Marx, *Selected Writings in Sociology and Social Philosophy*, ed. T. B. Bottomore and M. Rubel (London: Watts, 1956) pp. 77, 146, 170-171, 219-220. (Hereafter cited as *Sociology and Social Philosophy*.) For a discussion of these themes, see H. Marcuse, *Reason and Revolution* (New York: Oxford University Press, 1954) pp. 273 ff.; Maximilien Rubel, *Karl Marx, Essai de biographie intellectuelle* (Paris, 1957). The following from Engels expresses the Marxian attempt to transcend economic categories: "Modern economics cannot even judge the mercantile system correctly, since it is itself one-sided and as yet fenced in by that very system's premises. Only that

view which rises above the opposition of the two systems, which criticizes the premises common to both and proceeds from a purely human, universal basis, can assign to both their proper position." Engels, *Outline of a Critique of Political Economy* in Marx, *Economic and Philosophic Manuscripts of 1844,* trans. M. Milligan (Moscow: Foreign Language Publishing House, n.d.) p. 179. See also Marx, *A Contribution to the Critique of Political Economy,* trans. N. I. Stone (New York, 1904) pp. 292 ff.

404 [193] Marx, *German Ideology,* pp. 66-67, 74-75. See also Engels, *Herr Eugen Dühring's Revolution in Science,* trans. E. Burns (New York: International Publishers, n.d.) pp. 314, 318, 328-329.

404 [194] Durkheim, *Suicide,* pp. 363-364; *Professional Ethics,* p. 12. The quotation from de Bonald is in *O. C.,* Vol. I, p. 355.

405 [195] Durkheim, *Division of Labor,* pp. 13-15; *Suicide,* pp. 247-258; *Professional Ethics,* pp. 11-12. Parenthetically it might be noted that Durkheim's concept of *anomie* perpetuated the theme of Montesquieu and Rousseau that the state of war commences in civil society and not, as Hobbes would have it, in the state of nature: see *Division of Labor,* p. 15.

405 [196] Durkheim, *Suicide,* p. 257.

405 [197] Durkheim, *Suicide,* pp. 209, 258. In one sense Durkheim's argument was curious. While asserting that a greater tendency to suicide existed in highly individualistic societies, he also believed that individualism contributed a salutary tension to society. Thus the individualists tended to perform the role of a sacrificial group whose self-destructiveness was the source of its social utility.

405 [198] Durkheim, *Division of Labor,* pp. 203-204.

405 [199] Durkheim, *Division of Labor,* pp. 5-26, 119-120, 203-204; *Les règles,* pp. 112-113. See also Tönnies, *op. cit.,* pp. 74-89 where the *Gesellschaft* conception carries many of the same meanings as Durkheim's critique of interest. Relevant in this connection is Durkheim's review of Tönnies' *Gemeinschaft und Gesellschaft* in *Revue philosophique de la France et de l'étranger,* Vol. XXVII (1889) pp. 416-422.

405 [200] Durkheim, *Professional Ethics,* p. 16; *Le socialisme,* p. 297. Compare Lewin: "The realistic demands of production have to be satisfied in a way which conforms with the nature of group dynamics." *Resolving Social Conflicts* (New York: Harper, 1948) pp. 137-138.

406 [201] Karl Marx and Friedrich Engels, *Historisch-kritische Gesamtausgabe* (Frankfurt, 1927) Abt. I, Bd. 3, pp. 252-253; *German Ideology,* pp. 14-15; Engels, Letters to Schmidt and Mehring, *Karl Marx, Selected Works,* ed. V. Adoratsky, 2 vols. (New York: International Publishers, n.d.) Vol. I, pp. 383-384, 386-387, 388-389. For discussions see: Alfred Meyer, *Marxism: The Unity of Theory and Practice* (Cambridge, Mass.: Harvard University Press, 1954) pp. 14-15, 69 ff.; Rubel, *Karl Marx,* pp. 190-197; H. B. Acton, *The Illusion of the Epoch* (Boston: Beacon, 1957) pp. 125-133, 138-139; J. Hyppolite, "La structure du 'Capital' et de quelques présuppositions philosophiques dans l'oeuvre de Marx," *Bulletin de la Société Française de Philosophie,* No. 6 (1948) pp. 169-203; and also the interesting collection of texts arranged by Rubel, *Karl Marx. Pages choisies pour une éthique socialiste* (Paris, 1948) esp. pp. 34 ff.

406 [202] Lenin, *Selected Works,* Vol. II, p. 61-62.

406   [203] Whitehead, *Leadership in a Free Society,* p. 18. The classic exposition of this point of view is presented in a fascinating case study by Chester Barnard, "Riot of the Unemployed at Trenton, N. J., 1935" in *Organization and Management. Selected Papers.* (Cambridge, Mass.: Harvard University Press, 1949) pp. 51-80.

407   [204] Note Lenin's attack on those who strove "to transplant English trade unionism to their own soil and to preach to the workers that the purely trade union struggle is the struggle for themselves and for their children, and not the struggle for some kind of socialism for some future generation." *Selected Works,* Vol. II, p. 59.

407   [205] Mayo, *Human Problems,* pp. 152-153. See also William F. Whyte et al., *Money and Motivation* (New York: Harpers, 1955) pp. 2-7.

407   [206] Mayo, *Human Problems,* p. 182; L. J. Henderson, T. N. Whitehead, and E. Mayo, "The Effects of Social Environment" in Gulick and Urwick, *op. cit.,* p. 156.

407   [207] F. J. Roethlisberger, *Management and Morale* (Cambridge, Mass.: Harvard University Press, 1950) pp. 52, 62; Whitehead, *Leadership in a Free Society,* p. 82.

407   [208] Roethlisberger, *op. cit.,* p. 65; Bakke, *People and Organizations,* pp. 15 ff.

408   [209] Selznick, *Leadership in Administration,* p. 19. "One might almost say that the organization has a character, an individuality, which makes the name real. The scientist will not accept any such reification or personalizing of an organization. But participants in these organizations are subject to no such scientific scruples, and generations of men have felt and thought about the organizations they belonged to as something real in themselves." E. W. Bakke, *Bonds of Organization* (New York: Harper, 1950) pp. 152-153.

408   [210] Mayo, *Human Problems,* pp. 181-182.

408   [211] Whitehead, Henderson, and Mayo in Gulick and Urwick, *op. cit.,* p. 157; Whitehead, *Leadership in a Free Society,* pp. 91-92; Mayo, *Human Problems,* p. 165.

408   [212] Whitehead, et al., in Gulick and Urwick, *op. cit.,* p. 156.

408   [213] Roethlisberger, *op. cit.,* p. 66. ". . . My fundamental purpose in studying primitive man was to know modern man better . . ." W. L. Warner and P. S. Lunt, *The Social Life of a Modern Community* (New Haven: Yale University Press, 1941) p. 3. Note, in *ibid.,* pp. 4-5, 39, the admission that the authors ruled out the study of certain highly industrialized communities because they "seemed to be disorganized" and "highly disfunctional."

409   [214] "In such a society every tool or weapon, every ritual performance or magic and the whole kinship system is inexorably related to communal action and function." Mayo, *Human Problems,* pp. 154, 155-156.

410   [215] Simon, *Administrative Behavior,* p. 122.

410   [216] Simon, *Models of Man,* p. 199.

410   [217] Barnard, *Functions of the Executive,* p. 4.

410   [218] Simon, *Administrative Behavior,* pp. 14, 38-39, 109, 118-119.

411   [219] Simon, *Administrative Behavior,* pp. 11, 125, 126.

411   [220] *Ibid.,* p. 125.

411 [221] *Ibid.*, p. 101. See pp. 102-103 for the various ways an organization instills loyalties and creates identifications.

411 [222] Chester I. Barnard, *Dilemmas of Leadership in the Democratic Process* (Princeton: Princeton University Press, 1939) p. 7.

411 [223] Simon, *Administrative Behavior*, pp. xxv-xxvi.

412 [224] Philip Selznick, "Foundations of the Theory of Organization," *American Sociological Review*, Vol. XII, pp. 23-35 (1948), pp. 25-26 (Copyright (1948) by the University of Chicago); *Leadership in Administration*, pp. 8-9. The writings of E. W. Bakke are in the same tradition as Selznick. The members of an organization, he writes, "create a social system and a society which has a reality greater than the sum of its parts at any particular time." *Bonds of Organization*, pp. 200-201, 203. See also his notion of the "organizational charter," *ibid.*, pp. 152 ff. For the same point of view but in terms of small groups, see Kurt Lewin, *Field Theory in Social Science*, ed. D. Cartwright (New York: Harper, 1951) p. 146. The juxtaposition of empirical reality versus preconceived pattern appears also in Jacob Talmon's critique of democratic radicalism, *The Rise of Totalitarian Democracy* (Boston: Beacon, 1952); and see Talmon's explicitly Burkean theory of politics at pp. 1-6, 253-255. For a subtler presentation of this same general position, but without the admiration for bureaucracy, see the two essays by Michael Oakeshott, "Political Education," in *Philosophy, Politics and Society*, ed. Peter Laslett (Oxford: Blackwell, 1956) pp. 1-21; "Rationalism in Politics," *Cambridge Journal*, Vol. I (1947) pp. 81-108, 145-157.

412 [225] Selznick "Foundations of the Theory of Organization," *loc cit.*, p. 29.

412 [226] Selznick, *Leadership in Administration*, pp. 5, 21.

413 [227] *Ibid.*, pp. 12-13, 16-17. (Italics in the original.)

413 [228] *Ibid.*, pp. 8, 18.

413 [229] *Ibid.*, p. 100. (Italics in the original.)

414 [230] Simon, *Administrative Behavior*, pp. 101, 109; Barnard, *Functions of the Executive*, pp. 187-188. Compare also the following from a writer who belongs to the organicist group: "A society is free so far as the behavior it makes appropriate and natural for its citizens — the behavior they feel is good — is also the behavior its controls demand of them." Homans, *The Human Group*, p. 333.

414 [231] Proudhon, *O. C.*, Vol. XVII, p. 167.

414 [232] Marx, *Sociology and Social Philosophy*, p. 220.

414 [233] Proudhon, *General Idea of Revolution in the Nineteenth Century*, trans. J. B. Robinson (London: Freedom Press, 1923) pp. 45-46.

415 [234] Proudhon, *General Idea of Revolution*, pp. 74-76; *De la capacité politique des classes ouvrières* (Paris, 1868) p. 58; *O. C.*, Vol. XVII, p. 171.

415 [235] Marx, *Sociology and Social Philosophy*, p. 217. (Italics in original.)

415 [236] Proudhon, *O. C.*, Vol. III, p. 43. A "change toward democracy . . . would include, for instance, increased emphasis on human values as against superhuman values, such as the state, politics, science." Kurt Lewin, *Resolving Social Conflicts*, p. 36.

416 [237] Peter Drucker, *The Future of Industrial Man*, p. 109.

416 [238] Mayo, *Democracy and Freedom* (Melbourne: Macmillan, 1919) pp. 43, 48-50, 51-52, 65.

416 [239] Durkheim, *Suicide*, pp. 379-380; *Division of Labor*, pp. 28, 180-181, 361; *Professional Ethics*, pp. 45, 87, 90, 101-102. See also Mayo, *Human Problems*, pp. 126-127, 147, 149-150, 167; *Democracy and Freedom*, p. 6; Lewin, *Resolving Social Conflicts*, pp. 54, 57-58, 72-73, 85, 102.

416 [240] Marx, *Sociology and Social Philosophy*, pp. 233, 234-237. Compare also Tönnies, *op. cit.*, p. 29.

417 [241] Proudhon, *O. C.*, Vol. III, p. 43.

418 [242] Russell W. Davenport, as cited in Kerr and Fisher, *op. cit.*, p. 305.

418 [243] Berle, *The Twentieth Century Capitalist Revolution*, p. 60.

418 [244] *Ibid.*, p. 17; Drucker, *Concept of the Corporation*, p. 12.

418 [245] Drucker, *Future of Industrial Man*, pp. 52-53. Note, too, the argument of C. M. Arensberg and G. Tootell ("Plant Sociology: Real Discoveries and New Problems," *Common Frontiers of the Social Sciences*, pp. 314-315) that the plant manager is dealing with a political unit rather than "a cultural or emotional" one.

418 [246] Drucker, *The Practice of Management*, pp. 102-103, 139 ff.; *Concept of the Corporation*, p. 208; Berle, *The Twentieth Century Capitalist Revolution*, pp. 60, 83, 169.

419 [247] Selznick, *Leadership in Administration*, pp. 1-10.

419 [248] *Ibid.*, pp. 37, 58-59, 62-63.

419 [249] *Ibid.*, p. 61.

419 [250] Selznick, *The Organizational Weapon: A Study of Bolshevik Strategy and Tactics* (New York: McGraw-Hill, 1952) p. 278; *Leadership in Administration*, pp. 14, 121-122.

420 [251] V. Pareto, *The Mind and Society*, trans. A. Bongiorno and A. Livingstone, 4 vols. (New York: Harcourt, Brace, 1935) Vol. I, par. 246; III, pars. 2025-2057; IV, pars. 2183-2184, 2244-2267; R. Michels, *Political Parties*, trans. Eden and Cedar Paul (Glencoe, Ill.: Free Press, 1958) pp. 49-59, 80-90; G. Mosca, *The Ruling Class*, ed. A. Livingstone (New York: McGraw-Hill, 1938) pp. 65-69, 168, 171-173, 394-395, 415-427; and see the recent study by J. H. Meisel, *The Myth of the Ruling Class* (Ann Arbor: University of Michigan Press, 1958).

420 [252] Selznick, *The Organizational Weapon*, p. 283.

420 [253] *Ibid.*, pp. 284, 291.

421 [254] Marx, *Sociology and Social Philosophy*, pp. 182-183.

421 [255] Lenin, *Opportunism and Social Chauvinism*, Little Lenin Library (London: Lawrence and Wishart, 1914) Vol. XXII, p. 19. "I think that Bolsheviks remind us of Antaeus, the hero of Greek mythology. Like Antaeus, they are strong in keeping contact with their mother, the masses, who bore them, fed them and educated them. And as long as they keep contact with their mother, the people, they have every chance of remaining invincible." Joseph Stalin, *On Organization*, Little Stalin Library (London: Lawrence and Wishart, 1942) p. 21.

422 [256] The relationship between decadence and interest was one of the main themes

of Lenin's contemporary and admirer, Georges Sorel. See *Réflexions sur la vio-lence,* pp. 113-114, 115-122, 273, 315-317, 322-326 where Sorel discusses the loss of vitality on the part of the bourgeoisie and the need for an austere and heroic morality (*"la moralité de la violence"*) for the proletariat.

422   [257] Lenin, *Selected Works,* Vol. II, p. 68 (fn. 1). In this and subsequent quota-tions from Lenin all italicized words are in the original.

422   [258] *Ibid.,* p. 88.

422   [259] *Ibid.,* pp. 78, 80, 88-89, 95, 98, 101.

422   [260] "The tasks of the Social-Democrats, however, are most exhausted by political agitation in the economic field; their task is to *convert* trade union politics into the Social Democratic political struggle, to utilize the flashes of political consciousness which gleam in the minds of the workers during their economic struggles for the purpose of *raising* them to the level of Social-Democratic political consciousness . . . We must take upon ourselves the task of organizing a universal political struggle. We must train our Social-Democratic practical workers to become po-litical leaders . . ." *Ibid.,* pp. 92 (fn.), 103.

422   [261] *Ibid.,* pp. 88-89.

423   [262] Weber's discussion of bureaucracy forms an interesting comparison with Hegel's admiration for this same "universal class." Compare *From Max Weber,* pp. 196 ff. with Hegel's, *Philosophy of Right,* pars. 288 ff. and see also the discus-sion by Michael Foster, *The Political Philosophies of Plato and Hegel* (Oxford: Clarendon, 1935) pp. 160 ff.

423   [263] *From Max Weber,* pp. 139, 148, 155.

424   [264] *Ibid.,* p. 95.

424   [265] *Ibid.,* pp. 139-140, 143, 145-147, 154; *Methodology of the Social Sciences,* pp. 15-19, 54-55, 76.

424   [266] *From Max Weber,* p. 152.

424   [267] ". . . paraphrasing a well-known epigram: give us an organization or revolu-tionaries, and we shall overturn the whole of Russia." *Selected Works,* Vol. II, p. 141.

424   [268] *Ibid.,* pp. 125, 134, 138. And see the discussion in Alfred G. Meyer, *Leninism* (Cambridge, Mass.: Harvard University Press, 1957) pp. 32 ff. and Ch. 2.

424   [269] Lenin, *Selected Works,* Vol. II, p. 188.

424   [270] *Ibid.,* pp. 96, 116-117, 121, 134, 143-144; *Eve of October,* Little Lenin Library, Vol. XXIII, p. 5; *Left-Wing Communism, An Infantile Disorder,* Little Lenin Library, Vol. XVI, pp. 10-11, 75-76.

425   [271] Lenin, *Selected Works,* Vol. II, p. 184.

425   [272] *Ibid.,* pp. 122-123, 141, 145, 183-184.

425   [273] Michels, *Political Parties;* Barnard, *Dilemmas of Leadership in the Democratic Process,* pp. 10-15, 16 (fn. 7); Mayo, *Democracy and Freedom,* pp. 13, 19-20, 20-28, 33-34, 38, 42-43; Selznick, *The Organizational Weapon,* pp. 278-279.

425   [274] Lenin, *Selected Works,* Vol. II, pp. 447-448, 456 (fn. 1).

426   [275] *Ibid.,* pp. 138-139, 360-361, 373. "For revolution, it is essential, first that a ma-

jority of the workers (or at least a majority of the class-conscious thinking politically active workers) should fully understand the necessity for revolution and
be ready to sacrifice their lives for it . . ." *Left-Wing Communism*, p. 65.

426   ²⁷⁶ Lenin, *Selected Works*, Vol. II, pp. 155-156.

426   ²⁷⁷ Lenin, *State and Revolution* (New York: International Publishers, 1932) p. 23;
see also pp. 11, 17, 22.

426   ²⁷⁸ *Ibid.*, pp. 42-44, 53.

426   ²⁷⁹ *Ibid.*, pp. 42, 43, 52-53; *Opportunism and Social-Chauvinism*, pp. 26, 29. Lenin
even argued that the managerial technicians of the old system would have to be
retained in the new society. The assumption that administrative and technical skills
are universally applicable to any political or social system is a commonplace of
recent literature.

426   ²⁸⁰ Lenin, *State and Revolution*, p. 65; *Opportunism and Social-Chauvinism*, p. 26.

427   ²⁸¹ Lenin, *State and Revolution*, pp. 42-43.

427   ²⁸² *Ibid.*, pp. 82-84.

427   ²⁸³ The conservative orientation of his theory is avowed by Selznick [*The Organizational Weapon*, p. 314 (fn. 28)] in a work which not only analyzes Communist
theory of party organization, but extracts lessons from it for any theory of organization. The conservative cast to the thought of Selznick and, earlier, Mayo suggests how hopelessly anachronistic are the contemporary romantic conservative
writers. Instead of appealing to Burke, writers like Kirk and Rossiter would be
better advised to recognize their true allies.

427   ²⁸⁴ Selznick, *The Organizational Weapon*, pp. 286, 295, 313.

427   ²⁸⁵ Selznick, *Leadership in Administration*, pp. 27, 149.

428   ²⁸⁶ *Ibid.*, pp. 27-28, 37, 60, 147-148.

428   ²⁸⁷ *Ibid.*, pp. 90, 150. It is indicative of the modern notion of consent that even
a professedly "democratic" writer like Kurt Lewin, who devoted his psychological
researches to exploring the conditions conducive to a democratic group life, should
have produced a theory of "acceptance" not significantly different from the more
bureaucratic theories of Selznick. See *Resolving Social Conflicts*, pp. 116-117.

428   ²⁸⁸ The concern with "commitment" leads to a curious contrast between what
Selznick labels the "Stalinist" and the "Stalinoid": the latter is alienated, lacking
in commitment to ideals, and prone to accept expediency — "a fellow-traveler" —
while the "Stalinist" has made "the fateful leap to a new set of values" and found
a new source of spiritual support. *The Organizational Weapon*, pp. 298-307.

428   ²⁸⁹ Selznick, *Leadership in Administration*, p. 18.

428   ²⁹⁰ *Ibid.*, pp. 18, 116; *The Organizational Weapon*, p. 288.

428   ²⁹¹ Selznick, *Leadership in Administration*, pp. 96-97, 151.

429   ²⁹² *Ibid.*, pp. 14, 100.

430   ²⁹³ Bentley, *Process of Government*, pp. 208-209.

431   ²⁹⁴ See, for example, Cole, *Social Theory*, Ch. V, and pp. 132-134, and *Guild So
cialism Re-Stated*, pp. 122-124.

431   295 S. M. Lipset, "Democracy in Private Government: A Case Study of the International Typographical Union," *British Journal of Sociology,* Vol. III (1952) pp.
47-65.

432   296 W. B. Donham in his Foreword to Mayo, *Social Problems,* p. viii.

432   297 Mayo, *Human Problems,* p. 149. If management does not assume leadership
in the community, Whitehead warns, political organizations, "whose methods are
not always desirable or easy to control," will intervene. *Leadership in a Free
Society,* p. 119.

432   298 Berle, *The Twentieth Century Capitalist Revolution,* p. 175.

432   299 "It is not an easy matter to revive the sense of personal obligation to work in
a new form in which it is attached to the status of citizenship . . . That is why
many people think that the solution of our problem lies in the development of
more limited loyalties, to the local community and especially to the working
group. This latter form of industrial citizenship, devolving its obligations down
to the basic unit of production, might supply some of the vigour that citizenship
in general appears to lack." T. H. Marshall, *Citizenship and Social Class* (Cambridge: Cambridge University Press, 1950) p. 80.

⋘ INDEX ⋙

Action, political

in: early Christianity, 126-127; Cicero, 86-87; classical writers, 126; Lenin, 365, 422, 426; liberal economists, 298, 319, 331; liberalism, 297, 300, 318-319; Locke, 297, 298; Machiavelli, 200-201, 212, 216-217, 221, 224-225, 236.

in relation to: contingency, 224; crisis, 242; mass, 193-194, 229-232; political agreements, 64-66; political institutions, 83-84.

as heroic, 126.

Agape

and eros, 56.

Agreement, 64-66; see also Consensus.

Alienation, political

early Christianity, 98-99; Cynics, 78-79; Epicureans, 78-79; Hobbes, 263, 274; Machiavelli, 217, 236-237; Plato, 78; Rousseau, 368-369; Stoicism, 79, 94.

Anabaptists, 166-167, 168.

Antiphon, 30-31.

Aquinas, Thomas

idea of authority, 135-137; political elements in his theology, 134-137; sacramental ideas, 132, 134, 150.

Aristotle

citizenship, 57-58; justice, 64; knowledge, 3-4, 59; political association, 63-64; political judgments, 60-61, 62; political science, 59; unity, 63-64.

Arnold, Matthew, 300.

Augustine

action, 127; church, 124, 128-129; civitas Dei, 125-126, 129-130; compulsion, 118-119; justice, 126-127; love, 119, 123; ordo (order), 123, 157; political order, 105-